Personal financial planning

PERSONAL FINANCIAL PLANNING

PLANNING

Alternate Eighth Edition

HAROLD A. WOLF

University of Texas at Austin

ALLYN & BACON/GINN PRESS

Dedicated to the memory of my parents

Editorial production and manufacturing: Ginn Press

The first three editions of this book were authored by Maurice A. Unger and Harold A. Wolf.
The first seven editions were published under the title *Personal Finance*.

Library of Congress Cataloging-in-Publication Data

Wolf, Harold Arthur, 1923—
    Personal financial planning / Harold A. Wolf.—8th ed.
      p. cm.
    Rev. ed. of: Personal finance. 7th ed. c1984.
    Includes bibliographies and index.
    ISBN 0–205–13094–1
    1. Finance, Personal. I. Wolf, Harold Arthur, 1923–   Personal finance. II. Title.
HG179.W573 1989
332.024—dc19   88–26716
                                                         CIP

Printed in the United States of America

10 9 8 7 6 5 4 3 2 1

Contents

Preface

This book was specifically designed for students beginning their studies to become CFP™ licensees (Certified Financial Planner™). Much of its contents has been distilled and refined from my earlier books, *Personal Finance* and *Personal Financial Planning*, which have been used as college textbooks.

In recent years, financial planning has become increasingly important to more and more people. With that growth in demand, there has been a parallel growth in the financial planning profession.

Financial planning is a very complex and rapidly changing field. It is complex and rapidly changing because the underlying disciplines which make it up are complex and rapidly changing.

Financial planning encompasses the mainstream of a number of disciplines. It is a blend of finance, accounting, law, economics, actuarial science, political science or government, to name only the most obvious. Financial planning also encompasses the various specialities within these disciplines. Under finance it includes insurance and risk management, real estate, thrift and financial institutions, securities, credit and interest rates. Within the discipline of accounting, financial statements, budgeting, depreciation and taxes are involved. Law includes the specialties of taxes, government, consumer protection, retirement planning, wills, gifts, trusts and estates. Economics covers the broad field of income, savings, investment, inflation, and the political, financial and economic environment within which planning must take place.

Actuarial science deals with the logic and mathematics of interest rates and retirement planning. Political science (or government) deals with the political and social environment within which business, the consumer and the investor must function. Since there is an overlap among these various disciplines, financial planning is a blend of them all.

™CFP and Certified Financial Planner are certification marks of the International Board of Standards and Practices for Certified Financial Planners (IBCFP).

The book is organized into four parts. Part I consists of three chapters. Chapter one spells out the importance of financial planning and how it can help a person achieve his or her goals. Chapter two deals with record keeping and the personal budget, two important aspects of planning. Chapter three introduces two important tools of financial planning—the balance sheet and the cash flow statement.

Part II (Chapters 4 through 8) deals with managing income and assets. These chapters cover first the various depository institutions, consumer credit, and consumer protection laws to enable the planner's client to obtain more for his or her money. Then personal income tax planning, to legally minimize taxes, and home ownership, the largest single asset for many people, are discussed at some length.

Part III, which includes four chapters, covers all types of insurance. Chapter 9 covers risk management, and then there is a separate chapter on life insurance, health care and health insurance, followed by property and liability insurance.

Part IV introduces the various investment outlets. Chapter 13 covers investing in the various depository institutions which, generally speaking, are the safest investment, and is where the client's emergency funds are frequently put to work. Then direct investments in securities are analyzed in the next three chapters. Chapter 17, the last chapter in this section, deals with investing in securities indirectly, that is, through mutual funds. Next, other outlets for surplus funds are examined such as mortgages, rental real estate, commodities and collectibles. While many of these may not be appropriate for most of us, they may be for some investors.

Part V has a chapter on retirement planning and one on estate planning. Retirement planning is necessary to enable the person to enjoy "the good life" when the working years are over. Nearly everyone has Social Security to build on, and building on it is a necessity. The various methods of doing so are discussed. The last chapter, Retirement and Estate Planning, is designed to minimize the government's take of the deceased's assets; estate taxes are involved in this connection. It also considers final distribution of assets according to the individual's wishes.

At the end of each chapter there are a number of questions for review, some case problems, and additional suggested readings. These questions and cases serve as a summary and a review of the chapter. If the reader is able to answer them all, he or she has a good understanding of the chapter's contents. A glossary is included at the end of the book.

Acknowledgments

In the preparation of any project of this nature there are many who need to be thanked for having so graciously given of their time and encouragement.

Particular credit must be given to the hundreds of students and faculty members throughout the United States and Canada who have used my earlier college textbooks over the years, and who have provided much valuable feedback. Credit is also due to the editors and production people at Ginn Press and Allyn & Bacon. Specifically I wish to express my gratitude to Virginia Lanigan, Richard Wohl and John Gilman. Credit is also due members of the academic staff of the College for Financial Planning. Last, but not least, I must express my gratitude to my manuscript typist Mary Wingo, who did—as always—a beautiful job in preparing the material for the editors.

Harold A. Wolf
The University of Texas at Austin

1 Introduction to financial planning

Part I consists of just three chapters. Chapter one, The Importance of Financial Planning, spells out what financial planning is about, how it can help a person achieve certain goals, and to enjoy more benefits in life. It also examines the current economic and financial environment within which planning must take place. In addition, chapter one introduces inflation and the consumer price index.

Chapter two, Record Keeping and Budgeting, deals with two of the first requirements of financial planning, and the title indicates what they are. Records are essential in the financial planning process, because they are needed to set goals, determine present financial position, and plan intelligently. They are needed at the beginning of the financial planning process.

The budget is another important financial planning tool. It is like a blueprint or a road map and serves as a guide in the planning process. Without a budget the individual is like a traveler without a map—lost. A good budget helps the individual achieve financial goals by setting consumption limits and savings targets.

Chapter three examines two other items which are at the heart of financial planning: the financial statements, including the balance sheet and the cash flow statement (sometimes called the income statement). They are important because they will indicate where the individual has been financially and where he or she is now, and will help plan where he or she is going.

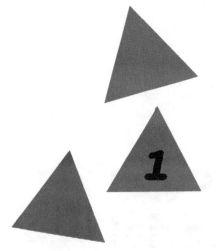

1 The importance of personal financial planning and some fundamentals

HIGHLIGHTS   In this chapter we will examine the importance and purpose of personal financial planning. In doing so we will examine the following:

1   The goals of personal finance
2   The various expenditures, consumers, business investments, and government spending
3   Specifically what financial planning consists of
4   The current economic environment in which personal finance must operate
5   Inflation and how it affects the consumer
6   How inflation is measured
7   What the rest of this book is about

INTRODUCTION

Individuals constantly make choices when disposing of their income. Even when these choices are not well thought out, it is nonetheless true that they require at least some degree of planning. Financial planning, money management, and personal financial management are all terms that are used interchangeably. In an economy such as ours, money is used to both purchase the goods and services we desire and reward us for the goods and services we provide to others. Consequently, everyone who has money at his or her disposal must necessarily do some money management. In its most basic form, financial planning has to do with the allocation of scarce resources (money income) among many alternative and competing ends. Human wants are virtually unlimited, while money income—the means to satisfy these wants—is usually quite limited. A dollar spent on clothing cannot be spent on food. Thus, choices must be made and priorities established.

Financial planning can help accomplish several things: increase income, improve the "mileage" from each dollar of expenditures, protect assets already owned, and achieve financial goals. Some individuals will plan their own finances; others will turn to professional financial planners for assistance.

THE GOALS OF FINANCIAL PLANNING

The objective of financial planning is to achieve certain goals. There are certain common goals shared by all; then there may be others which will vary from person to person, and from time to time during an individual's life cycle. They will vary as income changes, as marital status changes, and as the size and demographic factors of the person's family change.

Goals

The overall general goal is to manage all financial affairs more intelligently. A number of benefits will stem from this; income will stretch further and a person may also be able to increase his or her income. A general goal might therefore be to increase the standard of living. Planning can help a person achieve "the good life"—or at least a better one.

On the other hand, the goal might be to increase net wealth—financial planners call this "net worth"—and increasing it is frequently related to saving and investing. An increase in savings helps increase a person's net worth and, especially in the long run, a person's standard of living.

In the short run savings may require a temporary reduction in the standard of living; but since it will bear fruit over a period of time, it may serve to increase the standard of living later. It cannot be emphasized too much that virtually every budget should include an item for savings.

From time to time a person will engage in activities such as borrowing money, using credit cards, investing savings, paying taxes, buying insurance, automobiles and homes. A general goal of financial planning then is to do all of these things more intelligently.

Financial Planning involves looking ahead in order to develop a strategy that will enable a person to be where he or she wants to be, financially speaking, in five, ten, and twenty years. This should include a plan for retirement; a person should not wait until he or she is 60 or 65 years of age to do this.

Other goals or objectives of financial planning may include the following items:

(1) Acquisition and protection of property, which will be discussed in this book under investments (acquisition) and insurance (protection).

(2) Protection against financial losses relating to premature death, illness and injury, and liability. All of these can effect the income stream and assets. Use of insurance is one means of protecting against financial losses associated with these risks.

(3) Minimizing taxes both on the income stream during the earning years and on the person's estate upon death. Related to this is a plan for the transfer of assets to heirs. Tax planning, wills, gifts, and trusts are useful tools in this area.

Specific goals

In addition, there may be certain specific goals that are unique to an individual. Examples include: acquiring assets to fund a college education (this should be done as soon as possible after a child is born), starting a business, purchasing a home or a car, or planning a vacation trip around the world. The specific goals must, of course, be integrated with the general goals.

THE STEPS IN FINANCIAL PLANNING

The steps in financial planning may be summarized as including the following:

1. Setting goals. These goals must be set realistically with respect to the client's income, age, temperament, and any other pertinent factors.

2. Collecting all relevant data, as will be explained in the next chapter.

3. Identifying any barriers in achieving goals.

4. Setting a time frame within which to achieve goals.

5. Developing methods and procedures to help achieve those goals.

6. Developing a personal budget where appropriate, to aid the client in achieving his or her goals.

7. Periodically re-examining goals and monitoring the progress made in achieving them.

8. Periodically modifying goals and methods of achieving them as conditions change. For example, as the client's income, marital status, family structure, etc., change, the goal will often change.

Financial planning, then, is not a one-shot affair. Rather, it is an ongoing process. This does not mean a person must become a slave to a plan. A great deal of time is not needed; a few hours per month is frequently sufficient. Financial planning, moreover, may begin at any age; an individual is never too young or old. Moreover, he or she need not be rich to benefit from planning. Everyone will be better off with a financial plan than without one. However, the sooner in life that planning begins, the more it will help the individual to achieve his or her goals.

THE CURRENT ECONOMIC AND FINANCIAL ENVIRONMENT

The trinity of groups that make up most of the U.S. economy consists of businesses, consumer-producers and governments.[1] Each of these three groups makes decisions in attempting to achieve certain goals they have set for themselves. Each group, moreover, influences the other two, as well as the financial environment. We will briefly examine each group and the interrelationships among them.

Businesses

Most of the goods and services produced in the United States today are produced by the business sector. There are hundreds of thousands of business firms, some large like General Electric, some small like many one- or two-owner corner grocery stores. Business firms employ the majority of the labor force and are the means through which most of the income of the American people is earned. Business entities are probably the most important single factor in the economic environment. They must operate within the legal framework spelled out by the various levels of government. The business community is, however, largely a system of free enterprise and private property.

A free enterprise system is one where anyone may go into business for him- or herself. He or she need only obey the various laws that spell out the framework within which the various businesses must operate. For example, restaurants must meet minimum health and sanitation standards; no business may develop a monopoly and arbitrarily fix prices; and, of course, there are a number of consumer protection laws that businesses must adhere to. These consumer protection laws will be discussed in a later chapter.

A business system of "private property" means simply what it says. The means of production—manufacturing plants, machinery, and so on —is owned by individuals, not by the government. Most of the goods and services (output) produced in the U.S., and most of the income earned,

---

1. There are others: for example, there are churches, various nonprofit institutions, farmers, self-employed professionals, and labor unions. However, farmers and self-employed professionals are really businesses, and the members of labor unions are also part of the consumer-producers. Churches and certain nonprofit organizations, while important, account for only a small part of the total output of goods and services. There are also some people who are consumers but not producers—for example, children, the retired, and people who have been institutionalized.

is produced and earned in the private business sector. It is a very important part of the economic and financial environment.

Everyone is a consumer, and every consumer who is in the labor force is also a producer. Many consumers thus serve in a dual capacity in our economy; they buy goods and services and sell their labor services. Consumers are demanders of output and suppliers of labor to produce it. To enjoy the good life one must earn an income. In the short run individuals have to operate within a given economic environment. But as a group (for example, through unions, consumer groups, and the ballot box) individuals can also affect, to some extent, the economic environment.

Consumer-producers

The economic environment, then, consists of an interrelationship between the governments, businesses, and consumer-producers. This is illustrated in Figure 1–1, that shows consumer-producers providing labor services to business firms in exchange for money incomes. These money incomes are then used to make money payments to business firms in exchange for goods and services, which are purchased. These are consumption expenditures. The diagram shows the circular flow of money (represented by the outside arrows), which finances the flow of real goods and services (depicted by the arrows on the inside). The diagram also shows the payments of taxes by businesses and consumer-producers (in-

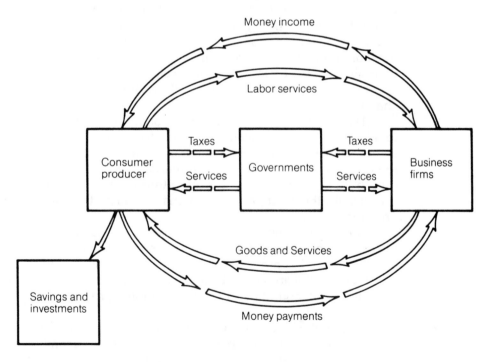

The economic environment.

Figure 1–1

dividuals) to governments in return for the services supplied by various levels of government. Also shown is a withdrawal in the form of savings from this income stream. These savings will flow back into the system when one buys bonds or stock or deposits money in a savings account. In doing this, one is making an investment expenditure or accumulating wealth in the form of earnings assets. Money, then, is the oil in the system, which is necessary for the interrelationships and permits the production and exchange of real goods and services.

Government

The three levels of government—federal, state, and local—each have specific functions to perform. Each level of government imposes taxes and provides a variety of services. The federal government major source of revenue is the personal income tax; for the states it is sales taxes and income taxes; and for local governments it is the property tax, although some local governments also have a sales and an income tax.

At one time it was believed that the government's main role was that of umpire. It was to see that the law was carried out, and it enforced contracts between individuals. In addition, it provided for the national defense. To carry out its function, the government levied taxes and made certain expenditures.

Today the role of the government has been expanded to include regulation of businesses and even individuals. More restrictions are imposed than formerly to protect the public and the environment. The philosophy is that the government is to do those things that citizens cannot do for themselves, or cannot do as well. The government has more of a welfare function now. This is sometimes called the safety net. While social security is not, strictly speaking, welfare, it is part of the safety net and is important enough that it will be discussed separately in a later chapter.

The government's actual production of services (technically referred to as "the government sector") is equal to the total wages and salaries of all government employees (federal, state, and local) including the armed forces. This is because there is no market mechanism and prices to allocate these services. We pay for them through taxes and then receive the services, for the most part, without making an additional payment via the price mechanism.

Total government employees (at all levels including the armed forces) in June 1990 was 19.7 million people. At their present wages and salaries they will earn approximately $533.1 billion during 1990. This 533.1 billion dollars is the best measure of the government's (federal, state and local) contribution to gross national product (GNP), or our well being.

Gross national product can be defined as the total economic pie produced in the United States per year. A more precise definition states "it is the total of all final *goods* and *services* produced in the U.S. per year." All goods and services are valued at their market price.

TOTAL OUTPUT, INCOME, AND SPENDING
GROSS NATIONAL PRODUCT

In the second quarter of 1990, according to revised estimates, current-dollar gross national product (GNP) rose 5.1 percent (annual rate) or $67.9 billion. Real GNP (GNP adjusted for price changes) rose 0.4 percent and the implicit price deflator rose 4.7 percent.

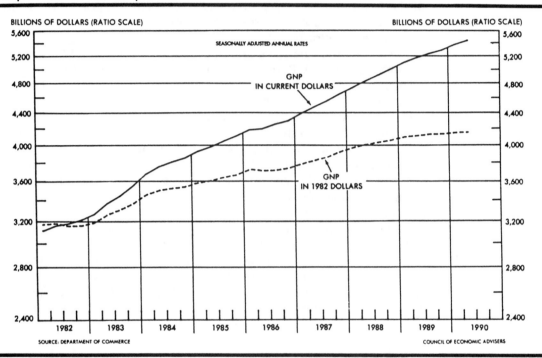

(Source: Economic Indicators, September 1990, Council of Economic Advisors, U.S. Department of Commerce, Bureau of Economic Analysis, p. 1).   Figure 1–2

Gross national product in 1990 was about $5,451.9 billion (about 5.5 trillion dollars). Consequently, the government contribution to this gross national product was about 9.8 percent, and as noted above that is the best measure of the government's direct contribution to the economy.

The business sector, on the other hand, contributed approximately $2,762.6 billion (2.8 trillion dollars) to GNP by paying producer-consumers that much in wages and salaries to produce that many goods and services. This amounted to 50.7 percent of GNP.[2] Figure 1–2 illustrates the growth in GNP since 1982.

---

2. The other approximately 39.5 percent was produced by nonsalaried (self-employed) individuals or was paid out in the form of rent, interest and profits, as well as depreciation.

The integration of the government and business sector

While the government produces only services, it does consume (buy) many goods and services from the business sector. If, for example, when the government builds a post office (it's built by a private contractor, the government merely pays for it), buys an F-16, a computer, or just some paper clips, these products are purchased from businesses. Virtually all of the goods, and many of the services, which the government buys, it buys from various businesses, and hence are included in production of the business sector noted above.

The fact that the government contributes only about 9.8 percent to the production of GNP, as noted above, does not mean that the government's impact on the economy is small. On the contrary, the government's impact is huge; but its impact is felt mainly through the business sector. Government expenditures may contribute to inflation or to higher interest rates, and in this way to reductions in business investments.

Government taxes may also contribute to declines in business investments by reducing profits. In addition, taxes may contribute to declines in consumption on the part of producer-consumers. They may also reduce the public's saving and in this way contribute to further increases in interest rates and hence business investments. Consequently, the government has a huge impact upon the economy (and hence on GNP) but, as noted, it is felt largely through the business sector.

The government, of course, also has a major impact on the private sector of the economy through the various regulatory powers noted above. The government, therefore, has a big impact on the economic and financial environment in which financial planning must take place.

Inflation

Inflation is also an important part of the economic environment. Inflation can affect the individual's standard of living because it affects how much his or her income can purchase. In this sense, inflation can be defined in two ways: a rise in the general level of prices throughout the entire economy or a decline in the value of the dollar. The amount of the decline in the dollar's value is equal to the reciprocal of the rate of inflation. On the other hand, **deflation** is an appreciation in the value of the dollar, and it comes about through a **decrease** in the overall price level. Deflation happens less freqently than inflation. During periods of inflation, those having fixed incomes find themselves with less and less buying power, while those whose incomes rise more rapidly than prices are better off.

Nominal and real income

Adjusting money, or **nominal,** income to take into account the effects of inflation provides what is known as **real income.** Real annual income is simply money income less the inflation rate for that year. If prices are rising by 5 percent per year, an individual must obtain a 5 percent annual increase in income just to stay even. Conversely, if the person's income is fixed, he or she is about 5 percent worse off every year. A person earning $40,000 today and still earning that in five years would see his or her real income fall to about $30,951.[3] If inflation continued at 5 percent annually. In 1985, the average per capita money income in the United States was about $10,905; by midyear 1990 this had grown to about $14,973. However, much of this increase was due to inflation. In real terms, average income had increased only to about $11,920. Figure 1–2 illustrates how GNP has grown in both money and real terms since 1982. In addition, Table 1–1 shows how inflation changes the value of a dollar.

After-tax money income is nominal income less taxes—federal, state and local. Taxes will, of course, vary widely from individual to individual, but even this tax adjustment will only give us after-tax nominal income. The best measure is income adjusted for both inflation and taxes; that is, after-tax real income. To obtain after-tax real income, nominal income must first be adjusted for taxes, and then further adjusted for inflation.

Taxes and after-tax real income

In addition to changing people's incomes in real terms, inflation erodes savings held in the form of fixed assets. The dollars held in bank accounts, bonds, and insurance policies will buy less and less as prices rise. Even interest earned by these investments must be adjusted for inflation. For example, if savings accounts can earn 10 percent interest but prices rise at an annual rate of 7 percent, then the real interest rate is only 3 percent per year. In some years the rate of inflation has been higher than the money interest rate, making the real return on fixed investment negative.

Other problems with inflation

Inflation also changes the debtor-creditor relationship. For example, suppose that an individual buys a home today by assuming a $100,000 mortgage. If the interest rate at the time of purchase was 10 percent, this borrower would be obligated to repay about $10,000 per year over the next thirty years. However, notice that this amount owed to the lender will always be paid in nominal dollars. Even if inflation causes prices to double over the next ten years, the homeowner is still obligated to pay only the amount originally agreed on, despite the fact that each dollar has only half the purchasing power it had in the beginning. In this case, the borrower has benefited from inflation at the expense of the creditor by being able to repay the mortgage in "cheaper" dollars.

Since inflation is part of the economic and financial environment, it is necessary to consider it when engaging in financial planning. That is, minimizing the effects of inflation is an important consideration in investment and financial planning. Therefore, it is necessary to understand

---

3. This figure is calculated using the following equation: $40,000 \, (.95)^5 = 30,951$.

Table 1−1   *Future prices*

Likely future prices on common items under inflation

	Current price	Price in 5 years		Price in 10 years	
		Inflation 5 percent	*Inflation 10 percent*	*Inflation 5 percent*	*Inflation 10 percent*
1 lb. cheese	$ 2.29	$ 2.92	$ 3.69	$ 3.73	$ 5.94
Loaf of bread	1.09	1.39	1.76	1.78	2.83
Ribeye steak (per lb.)	3.49	4.45	5.62	5.68	9.05
1 gal. milk	1.99	2.54	3.20	3.24	5.16
1 lb. hamburger meat	1.84	2.35	2.96	3.00	4.77
Dozen eggs	0.95	1.21	1.53	1.55	2.46
Men's suit	300.00	382.88	483.15	488.67	778.12
Ladies' dress	150.00	191.44	241.58	244.33	389.06
Automobile	12,000.00	15,315.38	19,326.12	19,546.74	31,124.91
Shoes	70.00	89.34	112.74	114.02	181.56

Prices may vary somewhat regionally, as well as with special sales, and some perhaps seasonally.

Income and the value of a dollar will change as shown below:

Annual salary	$25,000	$31,907	$40,263	$40,722	$64,844
Value of $1 will decline by		$0.22	$0.38	$0.39	$0.61
And will be worth		$0.78	$0.62	$0.61	$0.39

Income and the value of a dollar will change as shown above. This assumes income keeps up with inflation at either 5 or 10 percent per year for both five and ten years. See the formula below for the actual calculation.

$$\frac{\text{Base year prices}}{\text{Current year prices}} = \frac{\text{Value of money in current year}}{\text{Value of money in base year}}$$

how changes in the purchasing power of money, and hence income can affect the planning process.

Fringe benefits and psychic income

Statistics on money income often exclude fringe benefits, even though their monetary value can be calculated in many cases. Such things as free, or reduced cost, health insurance, sick leave, paid vacation, and retirement benefits often vary from job to job. Employers view these costs as legitimate costs of obtaining labor, and employees should also include them in their total income.

If a client has very generous fringe benefits, both the personal budget (chapter two) and the financial plan may reflect this. The dollar amount of savings as well as where these savings are to be invested may be affected by fringe benefits.

Psychic income, while it may be important to some people, is difficult to quantify. Some jobs are more pleasant than others, and the degree of pleasure or unpleasantness provided by any given job varies. Thus there is often an element of nonpecuniary (or psychic) income involved. Some people are willing to accept a lower money income for the prestige attached to a job. Other people may prefer to live in sunny Florida and attach some return to being able to do so. If a person wants to live in the crisp, cool air of Colorado and be within a few miles of the fine skiing slopes, he or she may have to sacrifice some money income. And, of course, money income is a main factor which must be taken into account in financial planning.

Measuring prices and inflation; the consumer price index

Since inflation is intended to describe changes in the overall level of prices, a decision has to be made as to which of the thousands of prices for available goods and services will be used in the calculation. The method most commonly used to measure inflation is a statistical device known as an ***index number.***

The Department of Labor computes and publishes what it calls the ***consumer price index (CPI),*** which serves as an estimate for the level of inflation. As just discussed, if a person's income does not keep up with the rise in this index, the individual is falling behind in what his or her income will purchase. For this reason, the CPI is also commonly called the ***cost of living index*** and is issued monthly by the Department of Labor's Bureau of Labor Statistics. To construct this index the prices of some four hundred goods and services are gathered in fifty-six cities. According to the Bureau of Labor Statistics, the index covers prices of everything people buy for living—food, clothing, automobiles, homes, house furnishings, household supplies, fuel, drugs, and recreational goods; fees to doctors, lawyers, beauty shops; rent, repair costs, transportation fares, public utility rates, etc. It deals with prices actually charged to consumers, including sales and excise taxes. It also includes real estate taxes on owned homes, but does not include income or social security taxes.[4]

The prices are weighted and averaged and then used to calculate an index number. The prices over the years 1982–1984 were combined and

---

4. U.S. Department of Labor, Bureau of Labor Statistics, *Supplement to Economic Indicators* (Rev. January 1967), Washington: U.S. Government Printing Office, 1967, p. 94.

then used as the index base and set to equal 100. Inflation is then measured from that base of 100. Since the index has risen to 129.9 by June 1990, prices have risen by 29.9 percent since the base period, or as the newspapers would say, the cost of living has risen 29.9 percent since that time.

The same dollars will now purchase 23.02 percent less than during the base period. This calculation measures the degree of inflation and the reduction in the purchasing power of the dollar.[5] Figure 1–3 shows how the cost of living has risen over the past few years. The cost of living is classified into several broad categories such as food items, nonfood items, and services such as medical services, and a composite is made up of all of these items.

WHAT THE REST OF THIS BOOK IS ABOUT

The material in this book is organized into five parts. The sequence in which they appear was chosen after a great deal of planning, experimentation, and pedagogical research. Since the book was first published over 25 years ago, hundreds of students, financial planners, college professors, and others have given us feedback, which has proven invaluable in reorganizing the material in this major revision.

The five units are:

1. Introduction to Financial Planning
2. Managing Income
3. Managing Insurance Programs
4. Managing Investments
5. Retirement and Estate Planning

Part I, "Introduction to Financial Planning," consists of three chapters designed to set the tone of things to come. The personal budget, balance sheet, and cash flow (or income) statement are presented in this part.

---

5. When prices rise, the value of the dollar falls but not by the same amount. The value of the dollar falls reciprocally. For example, if prices rise by 100 percent, say from an index of 100 to 200, obviously the value of money cannot fall 100 percent to zero. In this case the value of money fell by 50 percent. In order to calculate how much the value of money has declined with a given increase in prices, we use the following formula:

$$\frac{\text{Base year prices}}{\text{Current year priced}} = \frac{\text{Value of money in current year}}{\text{Value of money in base year}}$$

or, in the illustration,

$$\frac{100}{129.9} = \frac{X}{100} \text{ or } 129.9X = 10,000 = 76.98$$

Then $100 - 76.98 = 23.02$, the decline in the value of the dollar (money) since the average value of the years 1982–1984.

CONSUMER PRICES—ALL URBAN CONSUMERS

In August, the consumer price index for all urban consumers rose 0.8 percent, seasonally adjusted (0.9 percent not seasonally adjusted). The index was 5.6 percent above its year-earlier level.

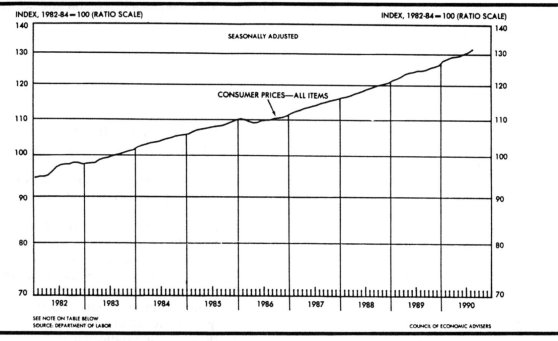

(Source: *Economic Indicators, September 1990, Council of Economic Advisors, U.S.*   Figure 1—3
Department of Labor, Bureau of Labor Statistics, p. 23).

Part II, "Managing Income," is designed to give more mileage per dollar of expenditure, including when a person should use credit or borrow money. Part II includes a chapter on taxes; legally minimizing taxes is an important goal of financial planning. Careful planning can reduce taxes, and doing so is another way of increasing spendable income. Also included here is a chapter on housing, the largest single expenditure for many people.

Part III deals with the various types of insurance frequently used by consumers—homeowners, car, life, and health. Property insurance protects assets in that if they are damaged or destroyed, they may be replaced or repaired. Health insurance helps meet expenses in the event of illness or replaces income in the event of disability. Liability insurance protects the insured from the loss of assets or income that may result if he or she is found liable for injury or death of another person or destruction of property.

Part IV deals with the investment of assets. Commonly held investment vehicles will be explored.

Part V covers retirement and estate planning. Ensuring adequate retirement income is an important goal for most people, and requires careful planning. Estate planning enables appropriate distribution of assets upon an individual's death, while reducing estate taxation and settlement expenses.

SUMMARY REVIEW QUESTIONS

These questions serve as a summary and a review of the chapter. If you are able to answer them all, you have a good understanding of the material covered by the chapter.

1. What are the goals of personal finance? How can personal finance help a person to achieve these goals?
2. What is meant by the term "consumer-producer"?
3. Explain briefly what is meant by financial planning.
4. What is the government's role in the financial and economic environment?

5. What is inflation? How would you expect inflation to affect those on fixed incomes?
6. What does it mean to state that the cost of living index has gone from 100 to 210?
7. How is the cost of living index a barometer of inflation?
8. Are an increase in prices and a decline in the value of money the same thing?
9. How do you calculate how much the value of money has declined from a given increase in prices?
10. How is inflation measured?
11. What is GNP?

CASES

1. Debra Patrick received a salary increase of $2,000 last year. Inflation was 6 percent.
   (a) What was Debra's increase in real income?
   (b) What was her increase in after-tax income?
   (c) What was her increase in after-tax real income?

2. If inflation averages 5 percent over the next ten years and a person's salary increase averages 8 percent over the next ten years, then:
   (a) What will a $10,000 car today cost then?
   (b) What will one's salary be, if it's $20,000 today?
   (c) What will the real salary be?

SUGGESTED READINGS

Brown, James and Clayton, Gary E., *Economics Principles and Practices.* Columbus, Ohio: Charles E. Merrill, 1983.

"Consumer Views." New York: CitiBank. Monthly newsletter.

"Credit Guide." Chicago: Federal Reserve Bank of Chicago.

Economic Indicators. Washington, D.C.: Council of Economic Advisers for the Joint Economic Committee. Monthly publication.

Economic Outlook U.S.A. Ann Arbor, Mich.: University of Michigan Survey Research Center. Quarterly publication.

Finance Facts Yearbook. Washington, D.C.: National Consumer Finance Association. Annual publication.

"Measuring Price Changes." Richmond, Va.: The Federal Reserve Bank of Richmond.

Personal Financial Planner. New York: Financial World Partners. Monthly publication.

"Primer on Inflation." New York: The Federal Reserve Bank of New York.

Samuelson, Paul A. *Economics: An Introductory Analysis,* 12th ed. New York: McGraw Hill, 1985.

"The Story of Inflation." New York: The Federal Reserve Bank of New York.

U.S. Census, Income of Families and Individuals in the U.S. in Current Population Reports; Consumer Income. Series P-60. Get latest series of this quarterly publication.

"Your Inflation Guide, Dollars and Sense." New York: The Advertising Council.

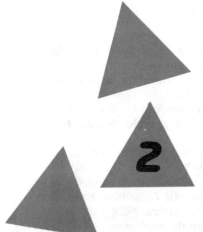

2 Record keeping and budgeting

HIGHLIGHTS   In order to plan properly, records and a budget are necessary. In this chapter we will examine the following:

1   The importance of keeping good records
2   Permanent records
3   More temporary records
4   Where records should be stored
5   Objectives and benefits of budgeting
6   Budgetary preliminaries
7   Financial goals and priorities
8   General rules of budgeting
9   The actual budgetary process
10 Suggestions for successful budgeting
11 Method of estimating income and expenditures
12 Techniques for controlling expenditures
13 Techniques for successful budgeting
14 How a computer may be used as a budgeting tool
15 How failure to budget may result in personal bankruptcy

INTRODUCTION

Most people have to live within their incomes. While this is not completely true in any one year (for example, a person may borrow to finance a large item such as a car), it is true for most people most of the time. A person who consumes more than his or her income in one year will probably be forced to consume less during the next year while repaying what was borrowed. Over a lifetime if one consumes more than one's income, one can only get out from under debts through court action—that is, through bankruptcy.

While persons have command over their money income, they have only two main alternatives as to what to do with it: consume it or save it. Most people divide their income, and while they consume most of it, they save some. Once they have committed a part of their income to consumption, they must make further decisions regarding what type of items to buy. Once a person has decided to save, say, 20 percent of his or her income, a second decision regarding where and how to invest it must be made. In this consuming and investing process, a person must constantly choose between alternatives. A limited income can never stretch over all the alternatives, so priorities must be assigned and choices made. This is more effectively carried out through financial planning. An important part of planning is organizing financial records, taking a financial inventory, and developing a budget to achieve goals. In the first part of this chapter we will discuss the records an individual should keep, how long they should be kept and when certain ones should be discarded. Then the budget will be examined. In order to do an effective job of managing money and financial affairs, it is frequently necessary to budget. As we will see, the budgeting process involves planning. A budget is really a projection of a cash flow statement. Technically speaking, a cash flow statement is a look backward at what has happened. A budget, on the other hand, is a look forward; it allocates expected future income among alternative uses. A cash flow statement (also referred to as an income statement) will indicate how an individual allocated income in the past and will help him or her budget for the future. By necessity a budget must often be an estimate of future receipts and expenditures. A **budget,** then, is a plan in the form of a projected cash flow statement that uses current and future operations to achieve certain goals that might otherwise be beyond one's reach.

RECORD KEEPING

In order to develop an appropriate financial plan for the client, the planner must be provided with adequate financial data. As the financial plan is implemented, it is important that the client maintain adequate financial records so that progress may be monitored and new strategies implemented as needed.

While the client needs to keep a lot of things, he or she need not keep everything. Moreover, some items may be discarded after a few years; others should be kept indefinitely.

20

1. Birth certificates.
2. A copy of financial statements, which will be introduced in a later chapter.
3. Insurance policies. These should be easily accessible in the event of a claim. Not only life insurance policies, but health, property, and liability, on both the home and the car, should be easily available. These may be kept in a filing cabinet in the home. Property and liability policies are generally renewed every year; and if a claim does not exist, the expired policies may be discarded. Some cautious people, however, keep these policies an extra year. Photos of household contents, especially scheduled property, should be kept also.
4. A file of the person's social security and any pension and other retirement benefits which have built up should be maintained permanently.
5. The title to the automobile and the deed to the home, together with other mortgage papers, should be neatly filed. In the case of the home, detailed records should be kept of every item. Canceled checks of mortgage payments should be kept. Also all records of improvements made on the home should be kept. If the client rents, the lease or rental agreement should be on file.
6. Marriage and divorce records are important and should be kept permanently.
7. Passports.
8. A record of all credit cards and their numbers, so that in the event of loss their use can be blocked more easily.
9. The legal documents from any court settlement in which the client was involved.
10. Securities and other investments. Corporate stock and bonds, jewelry, gold coins, and other very valuable items should probably be held in a fireproof strong box (called safety deposit box) rather than in the home. These may be rented at commercial banks and other depository institutions.
11. Wills. Most people keep their will in a safety deposit box in a bank, although a copy should be kept in the home for immediate access. Copies might also be retained by the attorney who drafted the will and by the executor.

Basic documents and permanent records

Some records need be kept only a few years and some even less.

Installment sales contracts should be kept until the item purchased is paid for. After that, the copy that the merchant or lending institution has is obtained and both copies may be destroyed. The same is true of any loans the individual may make. The paper that is signed (called a promissory note) when he or she lends someone money must be filed until the debt is paid.

Other (more temporary) records

Warranties. When an individual buys a refrigerator, television set, automobile, and so on, usually the manufacturer provides a warranty. After a few years when the warranties expire, these are of no value and may be discarded. Any service contracts should be treated the same as warranties.

Records of credit card purchases should be treated like checks. They should be held a few years and then destroyed.

Bank statements, canceled checks, and tax records should be kept for some time. Canceled checks and receipts for items that are tax deductible should be filed separately so they will be easily accessible at tax time. After the taxes have been paid, these receipts and checks as well as other checks for large amounts should be kept for at least 3 years, because that is the time the statute of limitations runs out. (The planner should note that there are some exceptions to this; in certain cases, tax returns may be audited beyond 3 years from the filing date.) Less important checks can be destroyed once a year. If items are charged on a credit card, and one check pays for many purchases, separate the charge receipts and treat them just like the checks. Records of tax-deductible items should be maintained carefully. Many people, fearful of the Internal Revenue Service, have consistently overpaid their taxes. If a person keeps adequate records, legal deductions may be taken without fear.

Keeping records, paying bills, and reconciling the monthly bank statement are things in which both members of a married couple should be involved. The same is true regarding all major financial decisions. Then in the event one of the partners is left alone in the future, he or she will not be inexperienced in these matters.

Where records should be stored

There are two possibilities for storing records: a filing cabinet in the home, and a fireproof strong box, which may be rented at a bank or other depository institution. Really valuable items such as securities, jewelry, gold coins, and the like should be stored in the strong box. Some people also store their will and life insurance policy in their safety deposit box. Others do not because in some states a court order is required to open the box of a deceased person. This takes some time, and because the insurance policy and the will may be needed almost immediately, some people keep a second copy in their home. In the case of a husband and wife, however, the safety deposit box should be rented jointly and then the above problem is solved. If the insurance policy is kept in the home, a record of the policy number should be kept in the safety deposit box.

When all important papers are stored systematically, an easily accessible retrieval system exists for any item needed.

THE PERSONAL BUDGET

Since a budget is a financial guide to spending, establishing a budget will enable one to run one's personal financial affairs better than can those persons who fail to keep a budget. By using it, one can make a real attempt to live within one's income.

A budget will also enable an individual to estimate more effectively his or her income than can a person who does not use a budget. It will force the individual into a more acute consciousness of the sums that must be set aside to meet future expenses. The individual will learn to allocate available funds among specific expenses and to estimate what may be left over for savings. Sometimes, through good habits, savings are voluntarily set aside; sometimes they are forced, as when one purchases a home or life insurance. In either case a budget makes the situation clear. Furthermore, a budget may help one identify alternative ways of spending that can lead to additional savings.

A budget will help the individual to achieve his or her financial goals. It will prevent individuals from "getting in over their head" when they borrow money and assume fixed repayment obligations. This is especially true in the case of credit cards. A budget will pinpoint credit card abuse. It may even save an individual from filing for bankruptcy. In doing all these things, a budget will enable the planner to help increase net worth and provide more financial security.

The benefits and objectives of a personal budget

Before a planner actually begins work on the budget there are some preliminary steps that should be taken in order to generate the required data, develop a set of goals and priorities, and develop a team approach to budgeting, if necessary. In many cases a client will need help in budgeting. While the client will usually be required to generate the necessary data, the professional planner will be in a position to help the client to organize it, and to set goals and priorities.

Budgetary preliminaries

After a preliminary family planning session, there should be an analysis of past expenditure patterns. If a past cash flow statement is available, this is a good place to begin. Look at current expenditures; find out where most of the money is going. To do this all family members should keep daily records of all expenditures for a few weeks. (This will give individuals a feel of their spending habits.) Total the daily expenditures each week to see how much is spent on the various categories.

Gathering the data

After several weeks of expenditures have been generated, it is time for the second family planning session. The group can now decide which, if any, expenditures seem out of line. The individual is now ready to take the next step in budgeting—setting goals and priorities.

Both short- and long-run goals should be established. One goal might be to increase savings; this may necessitate either cutting expenditures or increasing income. The decision might be made to establish a college

Setting goals

"Yes, I think I can get along on this budget for food. But how are you going to eat?" (Source: Permission Cartoon Features Syndicate; from The Wall Street Journal.)

fund for the children or to accumulate a down payment to buy a home. Plans may be made to generate a vacation fund or make the down payment on a new car. If a larger emergency liquid savings fund is needed, this could become a goal.

Longer-run goals might be to increase a person's net worth by so much over the next five or ten years, or to set up a special retirement fund. While it is difficult to convince most young people that they should start planning for retirement that early, the longer this decision is postponed, the less the dollar amount that can be accumulated for that purpose. There also may be higher-priority items for a young person than retirement planning—such as acquiring a house, emergency funds, and so on. Nevertheless, everyone including young people should be aware that they will need to plan for retirement some day.

Both long- and short-run goals should be monitored and periodically reevaluated. This will indicate what progress is being made and whether goals should be changed. For example, as income rises, one might consider raising their sights and setting new, higher goals.

Establishing priorities   After the goals have been set, they should be ranked in accordance with the priority assigned to each one. Priorities will vary from family to family—or individual to individual. A younger person will assign a lower priority to retirement planning than will an older person. A person with a large number of dependents will assign a higher priority to life insurance than otherwise. Priorities will also vary with tastes. Some people will assign a higher value to a beautiful automobile; others view a car more functionally and merely want good transportation. Moreover, as some goals are achieved (e.g., home ownership), other goals can move up on the list.

No budget will be the same for any two families or individuals, even if they both have the same income. In addition to the goals and priorities discussed above, there are some rules of thumb which are helpful.

Some rules on budgeting

1. The budget should be developed with reasonable goals in mind. For example, while a budget may permit the individual to stretch his or her income, it will not permit the person to live beyond it. If savings must be increased to provide funds for a child's education, other items must be trimmed, or income must be increased. Variations in preferences, incomes, ages, and sizes of families will result in different goals for different families.
2. The fixed items of expenditure must be provided for first; such items as rent or mortgage payments, life insurance premiums, and installment loan repayments are first priority "must" items.
3. Savings should also be a high priority. Budgeting should not be done in a manner so that savings emerge as a residual, because then they may not emerge at all. Savings must be a planned outflow in the budget to ensure meeting future goals.
4. Certain variable expenditures that are also high-necessity items—such as food, clothing, and transportation—are next.
5. Big-expense items paid less frequently than the budget period may have to be spread so that each income period bears a share of these expenses. For example, property taxes not included in monthly mortgage payments might need to be set aside monthly. The same is true of life and auto insurance where premiums are usually paid only once a year. Some people have a special "set aside" budget in which one-twelfth of each large annual payment is allocated monthly. This set-aside budget is then incorporated into the regular budget. Table 2–1 shows a set-aside budget.
6. A major expense cannot necessarily be cut just because it is large. For example, food may take a sizeable part of the budget, and that item may appear easy to cut—on paper.
7. A budget should help to develop a set of priorities on general items of expenditure, but it need not consist of a detailed set of accounts indicating where every penny is spent. While there are some rules of thumb on major items, there are also value judgments involved in choosing among different items. One person or family, because of different preferences, will spend more on clothes and less on housing than another similar family.
8. Adequate records should be kept indicating how much has been spent on each major category.

Table 2–1 Set aside budget

	Annual	Monthly
Life insurance	$ 480	$ 40
Auto insurance	420	35
Vacation fund	2,700	225
Total	3,600	300

	Jan.	Feb.	March	April	May	June	July	Aug.	Sept.	Oct.	Nov.	Dec.	Annual
Monthly set aside	$300	$300	$300	$300	$300	$300	$300	$300	$300	$300	$300	$300	$3,600

After the person has done some preliminary planning, reviewed recent past and present expenditure patterns, set some goals, and established priorities, the actual budgeting process may begin. The budget has three parts or stages which need to be completed. The three stages are (1) estimating income, (2) estimating expenditures, and (3) finalizing income and expenditures to make sure savings materialize. Do not expect savings to emerge as a residual; they must be viewed as a planned expense. This does not mean savings must appear every month, but there should be some savings in virtually all cases on an annual basis.

The budgetary process

The form of the budget is not critical, and almost any type can be used. Table 2–2 might serve as a budget. Many financial institutions have variations of similar forms and will be delighted to furnish a copy.

There is also a filled-in budget shown for a young married couple both of whom have earned income. Table 2–3 shows the estimate of income, and Table 2–4 combines income and expenditures.

The form of the budget

A budget plan

Table 2–2

Item	Amount	
Money income after taxes		$_____
Savings:		
Future goals and emergencies		$_____
Seasonal and large irregular expenses		_____
Regular monthly expenses:		
Rent or mortgage payment	$_____	
Utilities	_____	
Installment payments	_____	
Other	_____	
Total		_____
Day-to-day expenses:		
Food and beverages	$_____	
Household operation and maintenance	_____	
House furnishings and equipment	_____	
Clothing	_____	
Transportation	_____	
Medical care	_____	
Education and reading	_____	
Recreation	_____	
Personal and miscellaneous	_____	
Gifts and contributions	_____	
Total		_____
Total		$_____

Table 2-3 Cash budget, estimate of income

	Jan.	Feb.	March	Apr.	May	June	July	Aug.	Sept.	Oct.	Nov.	Dec.	Annual
Salary (take home):													
Rudy	$1,525	$1,525	$1,525	$1,525	$1,525	$1,525	$1,525	$1,525	$1,525	$1,525	$1,525	$1,525	$18,300
Sharon	1,400	1,400	1,400	1,400	1,400	1,400	1,400	1,400	1,400	1,400	1,400	1,400	16,800
Year-end bonus												1,500	1,500
Interest			50			50			50			50	200
Dividend			25			25			25			25	100
Rent													
Other													
Total income	$2,925	$2,925	$3,000	$2,925	$2,925	$3,000	$2,925	$2,925	$3,000	$2,925	$2,925	$4,500	$36,900

Table 2—4 *Monthly Cash Budget*

	Jan.	Feb.	Mar.	Apr.	May	June	July	Aug.	Sept.	Oct.	Nov.	Dec.	Annual
Income: (from Table 3–3)	$2,925	$2,925	$3,000	$2,925	$2,925	$3,000	$2,925	$2,925	$3,000	$2,925	$2,925	$4,500	$36,900
Expenditures:													
Rent	710	710	710	710	710	710	710	710	710	710	710	710	8,520
Utilities	250	280	230	200	175	150	200	220	200	210	220	250	2,585
Food	400	400	400	400	400	400	400	400	400	400	400	400	4,800
Clothing	250	250	250	250	500	250	250	250	800	250	250	250	3,800
Transportation	250	250	250	250	600	250	250	400	250	250	250	250	3,500
Insurance (set aside):													
Life											480*		900
Car												420*	
Vacation (set aside)	75	75	75	75	75	75	2,700*	75	75	75	75	75	
Medical	200	200	200	200	200	200	300	300	200	200	200	200	2,600
Recreation and entertainment	50	100	50	50	50	50	50	50	100	50	50	800	1,450
Gifts and charities	75	75	75	75	75	75	75	75	75	75	75	75	900
Taxes													
Savings	150	150	225	150	150	225	150	150	225	150	150	1,225	3,100
Household supplies	20	20	20	20	20	20	20	20	20	20	20	20	240
Set aside budget: (insurance and vacation fund)	300	300	300	300	300	300	300	300	300	300	300	300	3,600
Other (miscellaneous)	75	75	75	75	75	75	75	75	75	75	75	75	900
Total	$2,805	$2,885	$2,860	$2,755	$3,330	$2,780	$2,855	$3,025	$3,430	$2,765	$2,775	$4,630	$36,895
Surplus/(deficit)	$ 120	40	140	170	(405)	220	70	(100)	(430)	160	150	(130)	5
Cumulative surplus/(deficit)	$ 120	160	300	470	65	285	355	255	(175)	(15)	135	5	

*These items do not result in an additional cash payment because the funds needed are generated in the set aside budget lower down on the chart.

Explanation notes of Sharon and Rudy's budget:

Some expenditures vary from month to month. For example, utility bills vary usually, and expenditures on gifts are higher on birthdays and during Christmas. Expenditures on clothing and transportation too are unlikely to be uniform throughout the year.

Sharon and Rudy have a health insurance plan with their employers, but it does not provide complete coverage; consequently, they have provided for this in their budget. They have also budgeted for federal income taxes so that in the event that their withholdings are inadequate, they will have the funds with which to pay.

Savings are $1,225 in December because they have decided to save $1,000 of their bonus. They have also saved all of their interest and dividend income throughout the year, and even a bit more. Their high savings in December makes their expenditures $4,630 that month. Savings are, of course, invested (spent on acquiring earning assets).

The table shows the deficit or surplus each month and the cumulative deficit or surplus. Their budget contains a $5 surplus for the entire year.

A person can plan a budget on a weekly, monthly, or annual basis. Some experts feel it is best to plan a budget period equal to the period between income receipts—a weekly budget if one is paid weekly, and a monthly budget if one is paid monthly. Others feel this can lead to problems if the pay period (and hence the budget) is less than one month because some monthly expenses are greater than the weekly take-home pay. A person in this situation might want to budget monthly and also break the budget down by the week in order to set aside some money each week to meet large expenditures on a monthly basis. Some people, however, have a yearly and a monthly budget as well as the pay-period budget; for those whose income does not come in uniform amounts at regular intervals, the monthly or yearly budget is probably best. People who have a fluctuating income will find a budget particularly useful, since they may have a problem estimating their income accurately over whatever time period they select.

Estimating income

If the only source of income is in the form of salary or wages earned by the head of the family, there is no problem except to make a realistic estimate of the income available. Just because the head of the family is employed at $30,000 per year does not necessarily mean that income can be listed as $30,000. Instead, it might be wise to list take-home income after all deductions have been made, such as withholding taxes, Social Security, health insurance premiums that are withheld at the source, and the like. On the other hand, if an individual is self-employed, he or she might want to take the gross income and budget the taxes and Social Security payments.

If income derives from a business or profession, a more difficult problem arises. Frequently the breadwinner's annual or weekly income can be estimated, based on the volume of business the previous week, month, or year. However, some types of business might be called "feast or famine." In some months or even certain years, income is exceedingly high, and in other months or years, very low. If this is so, it is probably best to make a low estimate and have the family attempt to live within that amount.

Estimating expenditures

The reverse side of the budget coin is the expenditures. There are certain "must" items over which the individual has little control, such as rent or mortgage payments. In the long run a person can move to a cheaper apartment or sell a home and reduce these payments; in the short run these expenditures are fixed.

A person should give some immediate thought to taxes. Taxes, after all, are an expenditure, and by means of tax planning (which is part of financial planning) they can in many cases be reduced. Certain other expenditures such as food and clothing outlays can be controlled more readily. While it is difficult to reduce the food item in a budget, some reductions can be made by wiser shopping and by buying less expensive grades of food. It is also true that different families will spend different amounts for the same items. Family size differs, as noted above.

Another problem arising in budgeting concerns large annual or semiannual expenditures. If all expenditures were neatly broken down into monthly bills and if all paychecks were received monthly, one problem of budgeting would be eliminated. Unfortunately, necessary payments are frequently not so easily broken down. One might have to pay an insurance premium of $500 every September. Semiannual or annual insurance premiums are less costly than payment on a monthly basis, and consequently one might decide to take advantage of this saving. Some individuals authorize their bank to deduct one-twelfth of their annual insurance premium from their checking account and automatically put it into a special savings account. Then at the end of the year, the premium dollars are available and in the meantime a few dollars of interest will have been earned.

Inflation presents another problem in estimating expenditures. If prices are rising by, say, 5 or 6 percent per year, this must be taken into account and more money may have to be spent on food and other necessities. Inflation is a constant, ongoing process and most people receive a salary adjustment only once every year or two. Hence for a time at least, higher food prices may require lower expenditures on other items. Hopefully, after a lag, the breadwinners will receive an increase in income and recoup.

In addition to consumption expenditures, a budget should contain an item to assure that in most cases the individual (or family) will have some savings. Not all income should be consumed. In the absence of a carefully planned savings program, all too often savings will not materialize. Many people erroneously feel they can budget their expenditures and generate savings as a residual. But conscious effort is usually required to generate savings.

Savings

Many financial planners recommend saving 5–10 percent of income annually. Developing a cash flow statement will show the individual whether savings are too low. If they are and if one finds it difficult to save, arrangements can be made with the bank to have a specific amount transferred automatically from the checking to the savings account each month.

If at first expenditures (including planned savings) exceed income, then, unless the individual had planned to dip into past savings that year, he or she should go back and reanalyze expenditures. The budget should at least balance. Often on the first go around a person may be a bit extravagant. On the second analysis, items that may be cut often emerge until the budget is balanced. On the other hand, some individuals tend to underestimate consumption. Be aware of this; for the budget to work, estimates must be realistic.

Finalizing the budget

Table 2–5 shows some sample budgets developed by the Bureau of Labor Statistics for a four-person family; there is a budget for a lower, intermediate, and higher income family. Each budget applies to the urban

Sample budgets

Table 2–5   *Annual budget expenditures for a four-person family at three levels of living in the urban United States*

	Lower budget	Intermediate budget	Higher budget
Total budget	$15,323	$25,407	$38,060
Total consumption	12,069	18,240	25,008
Total food	4,545	5,843	7,366
At home	3,894	4,866	5,788
Away from home	651	977	1,578
Total housing	2,817	5,546	8,423
Shelter	2,114	4,348	5,851
House furnishings and operations	703	1,199	2,266
Transportation	1,311	2,372	3,075
Clothing	937	1,333	1,947
Personal care	379	508	719
Medical care	1,436	1,443	1,505
Other family consumption	644	1,196	1,972
Other items	621	1,021	1,718
Social Security payments	1,036	1,703	1,993
Personal income taxes	1,596	4,443	9,340

Source: Bureau of Labor Statistics. *News,* U.S. Department of Labor, "Urban Family Budgets," 1980, Latest Figures Available (Adjusted to 1987 values by applying CPI)

United States as a whole. Table 2–6 gives some budget figures developed for different cities that have different costs of living. Anchorage, Alaska, is the most expensive of all U.S. cities, according to the Bureau's figures. It should be noted that these budgets reflect a certain level of well-being, but this should not be taken as a minimum level set by the government as desirable. Note that the budgets contain only consumption items and Social Security and personal income taxes. The individual should allow for savings as an additional item in the personal budget.

Keys to successful budgeting

Successful budgeting involves first and foremost controlling expenditures and living within the budget. However, a budget also needs to be flexible and reasonably drawn in light of the individual's income. It may need to be adjusted modestly from time to time. In the long run a budget is even more dynamic and will vary over the years as circumstances change, even if income were relatively constant. In controlling expenditures it is helpful to use an expenditures log such as shown in Table 2–7, which provides an easy method of analyzing the individual accounts as well as the total budget.

Surplus and deficit budgets

The individual need not be a slave to a budget. As noted above, it is permissible to exceed budgeted expenditures in a given category in any

Annual budget for four-person family at three levels of living in various cities Table 2—6

	Lower	*Intermediate*	*Higher*
Boston	$15,402	$29,213	$44,821
New York	15,705	29,540	47,230
Philadelphia	15,116	26,567	39,560
Chicago	15,587	25,358	37,368
Cleveland	15,176	25,598	37,487
Detroit	15,107	25,208	37,721
St. Louis	15,112	24,498	35,965
Atlanta	14,419	23,273	34,623
Baltimore	15,315	25,114	38,090
Dallas	14,392	22,678	33,769
Washington, D.C.	16,702	27,352	41,137
Denver	15,093	24,820	36,979
Los Angeles	16,618	25,025	38,516
Seattle	17,124	25,881	37,396
Honolulu	20,319	31,893	50,317
Anchorage	22,939	31,840	45,119
U.S.	15,323	25,407	38,060

Source: Bureau of Labor Statistics, *News,* U.S. Department of Labor, "Urban Family Budgets," 1980, Latest Figures Available (Adjusted to 1987 values by applying CPI)

one month if there is a legitimate reason. For example, if the individual has a freezer, he or she might buy a side of beef and lay in a supply of vegetables during the growing season. In future months this should reduce the expenditures on food. Or a family may exceed its clothing expenditures in, say, September, if there are children to equip for school. To some extent these overbudgeting expenditures may be offset by reductions in other categories during the same month, but it is also possible that they will throw the entire budget into a deficit. There should, then, be some monthly budgetary surpluses later to offset them. After all, in the case of sales the individual will exceed the budgeted sums to save money in the longer run. One word of caution is in order, however. The individual should not let too many items show a deficit for too long a period of time. In addition, the total budgetary deficit for any one month should not be allowed to become too large. If a person falls into either of these traps, there is a danger that he or she will not be able to generate the necessary offsetting surplus. Over a number of months, the personal budget should be balanced with an allowance for some savings.

It was noted previously that expenditures vary somewhat from family to family because of differences in family sizes, tastes, priorities, and preferences. Expenditures also vary substantially for any given family as the years pass. To some extent, income, too, varies for any given family over

Budgetary variations over the life cycle

TABLE 2—7 Expenditures log

	January			February			March		
	Budgeted for	Spent	Surplus (+) or Deficit (−)	Budgeted for	Spent	Surplus (+) or Deficit (−)	Budgeted for	Spent	Surplus (+) or Deficit (−)
Utilities	$250	$240	$ +10	$280	$290	$ −10	$230	$225	$ + 5
Food	400	405	− 5	400	450	−50	400	375	+25
Clothing	250	260	−10	250	150	+100	250	300	−50
Transportation	250	240	+10	250	265	−15	250	225	+25
Recreation	200	220	−20	200	250	−50	200	200	—
Gifts	50	55	− 5	100	110	−10	50	60	−10
Savings	150	140	+10	150	150	—	225	210	+15
Other	75	75	—	75	70	+ 5	75	70	+ 5

While such a log does not lend itself well to controlling fixed items such as rent and insurance, it is useful in analyzing variable expenditures over which one has more control.

34

the years. These variations over the years are referred to as "life cycle variations."

When persons reach their peak earning period, income will vary with the job or profession. A person employed as an unskilled or semiskilled worker will reach the maximum within a year or two of initial employment. Unskilled or semiskilled laborers who go to work at age eighteen or twenty will have achieved their maximum income by their early twenties. This maximum (or ceiling) will rise a little bit each year as the union wins cost-of-living wage increases, as well as increases based upon additional productivity (better tools and machinery will permit workers to produce more), and workers will remain at their rising ceiling until they retire.

Skilled laborers like carpenters or electricians will reach their maximum income somewhat later in life. They have long apprenticeships to serve at a relatively low income. They will achieve their maximum income in from four to six years, sometimes even longer. (Again, this maximum ceiling rises as the years pass.) For example, pilots who bring supertankers into Houston harbor have to serve an apprenticeship of fourteen years.

Professional people like doctors, lawyers, and corporate executives generally have the longest training period of all. Doctors and lawyers are usually about thirty years old before they can practice, and then it takes additional years before they develop a clientele. Doctors and lawyers generally achieve their maximum income during their fifties. This is also generally true of corporate executives. These professional people's income often declines a bit during the last few years before they retire, especially if self-employed.

People's expenditures also follow a life cycle pattern. Young, single adults generally have no real responsibilities and usually save little. While they consume most of their income, it tends to be relatively low. Later, as they marry and start to raise families, they will begin to save as they build up an equity in houses and life insurance. However, the years between the late twenties and about forty or forty-five are also years of heavy consumption, because the family is growing up and needs to acquire durable consumer goods to fill the house it is buying. By this time incomes usually have risen substantially. After about age forty-five, consumption (certainly as a percentage of income, and perhaps absolutely) may begin to decline and savings rise. By now the children are on their own and the house is nearly paid for and is stocked with paid-for furniture and appliances. The years of heavy forced consumption are over. Individuals at this stage may begin to consume more services like travel, but they also can save more, and they will have an incentive to do so because of the approaching retirement years.

During the retirement stage of the life cycle, both income and expenditures usually decline. The standard of living does not necessarily decline. Often retired couples move to a less expensive section of the country. Also, certain payments need no longer be made. The house should be fully paid for, and life insurance no longer needed. Older people also receive a double tax exemption. On the other hand, people over sixty-five usually have higher medical expenses than younger people. Not only is their budget lower, it also contains different items. However, if they budgeted properly and were able to make substantial savings during the heavy savings years (age forty-five to sixty-five) of the life cycle, their retirement years can be pleasant.

The personal computer as a budgetary—and other—tool

More and more people are getting a personal computer, and while computer owners are still a minority they are a growing group. Using a personal computer to help manage the personal financial affairs will not only enable a person to perform this task more efficiently, but will save a great deal of time. For example, the budget may be kept on a computer or a bank statement reconciled on a computer. Income from all sources is punched in as well as major categories of expenditures such as food, clothing, housing, transportation, and the others, and the computer will do the rest. As the expenditures of the various items are punched in, the computer can give a running total on each one, and tell a person whether he or she is running behind or ahead of the budget, and which items are out of line and by how much.

The computer can do an almost unlimited number of things. It can assist in balancing and reconciling bank accounts, and can analyze and monitor security investments. The computer can also become the filing cabinet; by keeping a record of expenditures classified according to the various tax-deductible items it can speed the preparation of the tax returns, and in so doing, can make sure all legal deductions are taken. A computer can aid in tax planning. Some clients may wish to use personal computers to assist them in simplifying financial matters.

The budget and personal bankruptcies

A budget may also help to avoid bankruptcies. Most personal bankruptcies come about because people are careless in their financial planning. Often they overextend themselves by the careless use of credit. There has been a growing trend to bankruptcies over the past ten years. If an individual should ever be so unfortunate as to have to declare bankruptcy, there is a regular procedure to follow.

Bankruptcies can be classified into business and personal bankruptcies. Each in turn can be broken down into voluntary and involuntary bankruptcies; involuntary ones are forced on a person by creditors. Bankruptcy proceedings are conducted under federal law, but this law does allow for some variations from state to state. Nevertheless, a good deal of uniformity exists. The first step in filing for bankruptcy is to buy a bankruptcy kit, available for a few dollars at any store handling legal papers. This kit contains forms on which must be listed all assets, liabilities, and the creditors; the forms are then filed in federal district court. A $50 per person fee must be paid to the court upon filing. If the case appears to be complex, an attorney should be retained. After the filing, all the creditors are notified and a hearing is held before a bankruptcy referee who is acting under the jurisdiction of the federal court. While the creditors can contest the bankruptcy, it is virtually impossible to prevent a personal bankruptcy from being made effective.

A person may file for personal bankruptcy under Chapter 7 or Chapter 13 of the federal bankruptcy laws. Under Chapter 7, the person gets out from under debts by letting the creditors have those assets which they may legally seize. Under Chapter 13, the person works out a new repayment schedule over several years. Even under Chapter 13, however, debts are usually scaled down, and creditors do not receive full payment. Therefore, many people who have substantial assets choose Chapter 13.

After the bankruptcy is granted, a trustee usually is appointed to take over what assets remain and pay off those debts that can be paid. The debts are classified into an order of priorities; the administrative costs of handling the bankruptcy have first priority. They are followed by wage claims, up to a point, and then taxes. These debts are paid first and then if any assets are left, general claims receive a prorated payment.

In 1986 a new federal bankruptcy law went into effect. It significantly changed the relationship between the creditor and the debtor filing for bankruptcy. It did this by making the federal law more sympathetic toward the debtor. There are now certain assets that federal law protects from seizure to satisfy creditors' claims. The federal law also provides that if the state law is more lenient in the state where the bankruptcy is filed than is the federal law in protecting assets from seizure, the person filing bankruptcy may choose the state exemptions if he or she wishes to do so. The federally protected assets become the starting point and establish a minimum on the assets that are protected. Federally exempt assets include up to $7,500 equity in homestead property ($15,000 if one files jointly with a spouse), $1,200 in a motor vehicle, and $300 each in furniture, clothing, and other household goods. Exempt assets vary from state to state, but generally they include the homestead, a car (in some states two cars) regardless of its value, and the "tools of a trade." A house or car, however, is not protected if it has been pledged to pay off a specific debt. Therefore, a house can be seized to pay off a mortgage or a car to pay off the loan that financed the car.

There was formerly a stigma attached to personal bankruptcies, but this is less true today. Bankruptcy relieves the person of debts, and the logic behind this is that a person who has too many debts becomes economically unproductive. Relieving the individual makes him or her productive again, and hence benefits society as well as the individual. While many lenders no doubt would not lend to anyone who has ever declared bankruptcy, the person is not as bad a credit risk as one might imagine. The bankrupt person is debt-free, and the law does not permit bankruptcy to be filed again for six years. While some people have, no doubt, deliberately run up large debts and then taken the easy way out, most bankruptcies appear to be due to poor planning and poor budgeting.

SUMMARY
REVIEW
QUESTIONS

These questions serve as a summary and a review of the chapter. If you are able to answer them all, you have a good understanding of the material covered by the chapter.

1. Why is it important that the client keep good financial records?
2. Which records should be kept at home, and which should be kept in a safe deposit box?
3. Which records should be retained permanently, and which can be periodically thrown away?
4. Why is it useful to review past expenditure patterns before engaging in budgeting?
5. Discuss setting goals and establishing priorities.
6. What are the rules of budgeting?
7. How could one control expenditures?
8. Should an allowance be made in the budget for taxes if the employer withholds taxes from salary?
9. What are deficit and surplus budgets?
10. How do budgets vary over the life cycle?
11. How are a budget and personal bankruptcy related?

CASES

1. Sara McLeod has established two goals in order to buy a car and a home.
   Short-Term:
   > Down Payment on Automobile:
   > $2,000
   > Goal: to achieve in two years
   > Long-Term:
   > Down Payment on Home; $8,000
   > Goal: to achieve in eight years

   Sara believes she can earn 8 percent return on her savings.
   (a) How much will she have to save per month if she earns 8 percent?
   (b) How much if she earns 10 percent?
2. John and Helen Moonan, who are in their early thirties, have two children, a boy of five and a girl of three. John works for Exxon and earns $26,000 per year after taxes. Having recently discovered that they are saving very little, they have decided to start a budget. John would like to buy at least $50,000 more life insurance, which would cost them

$330 per year. This would amount to a total life insurance premium payment of $460 per year because John already has $20,000 of life insurance. In addition, they would like to save part of their income for the purpose of financing their children's college education and for a nest egg for themselves.

Prepare a budget to help them achieve their goal.

3. Mary Rivers has just graduated from Odessa High School in Odessa, Texas. She is going to the university next fall on a full-tuition scholarship. She will, however, have to pay her room and board, buy her own clothes and books, and meet other personal expenses. Mary has decided to live in the dormitories, where she pays a flat fee of $3,000 for room and board for the entire academic year. She can pay this sum in six equal installments, which are due on September 30, October 31, November 30, January 31,

February 28, and March 31. Mary has saved $3,400 from various summer jobs, and she will use that money to help finance her education. She would like to stretch this money as far as possible. Also, her uncle has agreed to pay one-half of her room and board fees.

Prepare a budget for Ms. Rivers that will minimize her expenses.

4. Roberta Hill has decided to clean out her file of old temporary records. What are temporary records, and how long should Roberta keep them?

SUGGESTED READINGS

Anthony, Robert, and Welsch, Glen. *Fundamentals of Financial Accounting.* Homewood, Ill: Richard Irwin, 1986.

"Bankruptcy and Alternatives." Chicago: The American Bar Association Information Services.

"Financial Pathfinder Service." New York: Merrill Lynch, Pierce, Fenner, and Smith.

Golonka, Nancy. *How to Protect What's Yours.* Washington, D.C.: Acropolis Books, 1985.

"How to Read a Financial Report." New York: Merrill Lynch, Pierce, Fenner, and Smith.

"How to Understand Financial Statements." New York: New York Stock Exchange.

Money Management. A series of pamphlets published by the Household Finance Corporation. Topics include (1) your food dollar, (2) your clothing dollar, (3) your housing dollar, (4) your home furnishing dollar, (5) your equipment dollar, (6) your shopping dollar, (7) your automobile dollar, (8) your recreation dollar, and (9) your savings and investment dollar. Contact your local Household Finance Company office for more information on these booklets.

National Consumer Finance Association. *Finance Facts Yearbook.* Washington, D.C. Annual publication.

U.S. Bureau of the Census. Income of Families and Individuals in the U.S. in Current Population Reports; Consumer Income. Series P-60. Get latest series of this quarterly publication.

U.S. Department of Agriculture. *Family Economics Review.* Washington, D.C.: Consumer and Food Economic Research Division, U.S. Department of Agriculture. Quarterly publication.

——. *A Guide to Budgeting for the Family.* Home and Garden Bulletin. Washington, D.C.: U.S. Government Printing Office.

U.S. Department of Labor, Bureau of Labor Statistics. *News.* An annual publication on budgeting.

U.S. Department of Labor, Bureau of Labor Statistics. *The Occupational Outlook Handbook,* 1989–1990 ed.

"Your Guide to Consumer Credit and Bankruptcy." Chicago: The American Bar Association.

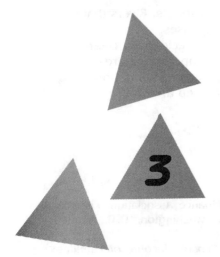

3 Financial statements; the tools of financial planning

HIGHLIGHTS

In order to plan properly, financial statements are necessary. In this chapter we will examine the following:

1   The personal balance sheet
2   The classification of assets
3   The various liabilities
4   Net worth
5   The personal cash flow (or income) statement
6   Cash inflows and outflows
7   An analysis of the balance sheet
8   The importance of net worth
9   An analysis of financial statements

INTRODUCTION; TAKING A FINANCIAL INVENTORY	After having collected all pertinent data, the next step in taking a financial inventory is to develop the personal financial statements. These will show the client's current position. These financial statements are the **balance sheet** and the **cash flow statement**, which is also sometimes called the income statement. The balance sheet shows where the client is with respect to the wealth he or she has accumulated. The cash flow statement shows a historical record of cash inflows and outflows for a given period of time.

THE PERSONAL BALANCE SHEET; STATEMENT OF FINANCIAL POSITION

A **balance sheet** is a financial statement that depicts the individual's financial position at a particular moment in time; in this respect it is like a photograph. It shows wealth as of a given point in time. Its three main components are assets, liabilities, and the difference between the two, called "net worth." The balance sheet is summarized by the following accounting equation:

$$\text{assets} - \text{liabilities} = \text{net worth.}$$

Or transposed,

$$\text{assets} = \text{liabilities} + \text{net worth.}$$

Assets

The terms "wealth" and "assets" mean the same thing; anything of value is wealth and can also be looked upon as an asset. **Assets,** then, are the tangible and intangible property an individual owns.

The things a person is buying but have not yet completely paid for are nevertheless included fully among assets at their total dollar value. The amount of money still owed is included on the other side of the balance sheet under liabilities, as we shall see below. The total value of a home, then, is an asset and the unpaid mortgage is a liability. Or in the case of a $10,000 car on which an individual still owes $6,000, the entire $10,000 is included among the assets, and the $6,000 is among the liabilities.

In order to obtain a total dollar figure for the assets, they should all be listed at their market value—that is, the price at which they could be sold (or purchased).

Classification of Assets

Assets may be divided into (1) cash and cash equivalents, (2) investment assets, and (3) use (or personal assets). Assets may also be broken down into earning and nonearning assets and financial and nonfinancial assets.

1. Cash and cash equivalents include such assets as checking accounts, savings accounts, money market funds and accounts, and the cash surrender value of life insurance policies. Some of these assets should be earmarked for the client's emergency fund.

2. Investment assets include bonds, mutual funds, stock, gold, gems and precious metals, collectibles, investment real estate, fine art, ownership interest in closely-held businesses, vested pension benefits, and similar assets.

3. The third category, use assets (sometimes also called personal assets), includes the client's residence, automobiles, boats, recreational real estate, and personal effects such as furnishings, clothes, jewelry, and similar assets.

4. Earning assets are similar to, and in part a combination of, cash and cash equivalents and investment assets described above. They are assets that yield a return. Stocks, bonds, savings accounts, and real estate that can be rented are earning assets in that they yield a return in the form of interest, dividends, or rental income. Earning assets also include the cash value of life insurance, a pension, and other retirement benefits.

5. Nonearning assets (or assets which are sometimes also referred to as personal assets) consist of personal automobiles, clothing, jewelry, household furniture, and the like. They yield no money return but they are valuable and are wealth or assets, because they provide a service to the owner. Owner-occupied homes are also considered nonearning assets; rental property, on the other hand, is included as an earning asset.

6. Financial assets include such things as stocks, bonds, bank accounts, and cash or currency.

7. Nonfinancial assets include clothes, real estate, automobiles, household furniture and appliances, and so on.

There is some overlap between certain asset classifications. For example, all financial assets except some checking accounts and idle currency are also earning assets. Most nonearning assets are also nonfinancial assets, but there are exceptions. For example, a cattle ranch or a wheat farm is an earning asset, but it is not a financial asset. It is an earning asset because the wheat or the cattle produced are valuable and may be sold; hence there is a return. However, the piece of paper (the mortgage on it) can be considered a financial asset to the lender. This is because the mortgage is a debt instrument which yields an interest income. Any piece of paper which is a legal claim to something of value is a financial asset. Therefore, a bond (a certificate of indebtedness), a stock (a certificate of ownership), or a mortgage (a specialty type of a certificate of indebtedness on real estate) are all financial assets. The largest single asset for most families is their home, and the largest single liability is the mortgage on it.

When the personal balance sheet is constructed, assets are listed on the left with a dollar value attached to them that reflects their fair market value.

Table 3–1 shows some of the major assets most commonly held by individuals. With the exception of cash-on-hand and possibly the check-

Table 3–1   *Assets*

1. Cash-on-hand	8. Home
2. Checking account	9. Automobile
3. Savings deposits	10. Boat
a. At bank	11. Motorcycle
b. At credit union	12. Personal property
4. U.S. government savings bonds	a. Household furniture
5. Corporate stock	b. Appliances
6. Corporate bonds	c. Clothing
7. Life insurance (cash value)	d. Jewelry
	e. Home computer

ing account, the assets through number 7 are earning assets. (Some checking accounts earn interest and some do not, as you will see in Chapter 4). Assets 8 through 12 are nonearning assets; or use assets. The first seven assets are also financial assets, while numbers 8 through 12 are nonfinancial assets.

Liabilities

Liabilities are the debts the individual owes to others. The amount he or she still owes on a car and the sum run up on the gasoline credit card and other charge accounts are examples. The unpaid balance (mortgage) on the family home is another example. Generally speaking, interest must be paid on the debts owed.

Liabilities may be broken down into debt that must be paid relatively soon and debt that is paid over a longer period of time. Very short-term debt is called "bills outstanding" and includes credit card charges, dental bills, utilities, rent, and so on. Many of these, especially credit card charges, are incurred for convenience; i.e., many bills can be paid with one monthly check.

Intermediate-term debt, such as an automobile installment loan, is incurred to enable a person to acquire a car earlier than otherwise would be possible. Other installment loans would include those to finance household furniture or appliances.

Long-term debt is most often acquired to buy a home; the home yields a service over a long period of time, and the debt is repaid over a long period of time. However, some long-term debt may be incurred in order to buy earning assets such as a rental house or a business. Long-term debt may also be incurred to finance a college education. When developing a personal balance sheet, only the outstanding loan balance should be shown for installment, mortgage, and other long-term loans.

Table 3–2 shows the typical set of liabilities most people will encounter during a lifetime.

Source: Drawing by Mort Gerberg © 1979 The New Yorker Magazine, Inc.

Net worth is the actual wealth of a person or family for whom the balance sheet was developed at a given point in time. It is assets minus liabilities and is usually shown by the accounting equation of

Net worth

$$\text{Total Assets} - \text{Total Liabilities} = \text{Net Worth.}$$

Liabilities

Table 3—2

1. Bills outstanding
   a. Department store charge account
   b. Bank credit card charges
   c. Gasoline credit card charges
   d. Rent due
   e. Repair bills
2. Installment loans
   a. Automobile loan (balance due)
   b. Refrigerator (balance due)
   c. College loan
3. Mortgage loans
   a. Owner-occupied
   b. Rental
4. Other loans

As such, it is the truest reflection of what the person is actually worth. If a person were to sell all of his or her assets and pay off all debts, that is what would remain. Assets are nearly always greater than liabilities, but in those relatively rare cases where they are not, the person is, technically speaking, bankrupt. Bankruptcy was examined in Chapter 2.

In order to calculate net worth it is necessary to calculate the dollar value of both liabilities and assets. The dollar amount of liabilities is easier to obtain than of assets because they are already stated in dollar terms. Assets, however, may not be. Moreover, assets may appreciate over time. Therefore, in calculating the value of assets, their market value should be used and not what was paid for them. If an organized market exists, assets can be evaluated easily. If not, estimates need to be made. In the case of securities, their market price may be published in the financial pages of the daily newspaper. In the case of a home, it is more difficult, but any realtor is able to give an accurate estimate. Similar houses that are advertised for sale may also be considered in assessing the value. The value of a car may be estimated by looking at newspaper ads of similar cars for sale. In addition, the car's blue book value will

Table 3–3   *Example of a balance sheet*

Assets		Liabilities and net worth	
Cash	$ 50	Unpaid bills	
Currency	500	Bank credit card	$150
Checking account			
Savings deposit	1,000	Other charge cards	75
Investments		Repair bill on car	125
Government bonds	1,200	Telephone bill outstanding	12
Corporate bonds	1,000	Installment loan	800
Corporate stock	1,500		
Mutual funds	1,200	Mortgage loan	
Cash value of life		Owner-occupied	50,000
insurance	1,200	Other rental	35,000
Real estate		Total liabilities	86,162
Owner-occupied	70,000		
Rental property	50,000		
Personal property			
Automobile	5,000	Net worth	$52,688
Household furniture	4,000		
Clothes	1,500		
Jewelry	200		
Other assets	500		
Total assets	$138,850		

provide a second approximation. The cash value of a life insurance policy may be obtained by calling the insurance agent who services the policy or by reviewing the annual statement.

Personal property such as household furniture, appliances, jewelry, rare coins, and clothing is more difficult to evaluate. Jewelry and rare coins may need to be appraised in order to get an accurate value. In the case of other personal property, probably the best one can do is to take its original price and adjust it downward somewhat based on its age.

Table 3–3 shows a balance sheet for a typical family. The financial assets are listed first; they go through life insurance. The other items are nonfinancial assets. Remember in the construction of any balance sheet, the assets are always to the left. The liabilities are always to the right. Below the liabilities is shown the net worth, which, together with the liabilities, is equal to total assets.

The **cash flow statement** is another important financial tool useful in planning the client's personal financial affairs. The balance sheet depicts the financial condition at a given point in time; the cash flow statement shows what has happened to the financial position over a period of time, say a year. It is an historical statement in that it indicates what has happened in the past. Nevertheless, it is a flow concept. It can be compared to a stream of water that is measured in terms of flow: so many gallons of water per minute. The personal cash flow statement measures salaries and other income as inflows and various expenditures as outflows. The statement does not consider only consumption expenditures as outflows, however. This is because each statement should have a category of savings outflows. Savings must be positively planned for and the savings that are achieved flow out and become investments, as we shall see below. Therefore the cash flow statement has three main parts: income, consumption expenditures, and savings expenditures.

THE PERSONAL CASH FLOW STATEMENT

Wages and salaries are the major source of income for most people. However, some people have interest income that they receive on savings deposits and government and corporate bonds, as well as dividends on corporate stock. Some individuals also have rental property and receive rental income. People who own small businesses receive income from those sources. Also, any of the following should be considered as income: tips; bonuses; tax rebates; gifts; inheritance; social security and other retirement benefits; and money received from the sale of securities, an automobile, or any other asset. While many people feel that money received from the sale of assets is not really income, it is part of the cash inflow; and it is the total cash inflow for the period (usually one year) that the cash flow statement is presenting and that must be taken into account.

Cash Inflows: Income and Other Cash Inflows

Table 3–4   Yearly income flow

	Jan.	Feb.	March	April	May	June	July	Aug.	Sept.	Oct.	Nov.	Dec.*	Annual
After-tax wages or salary of breadwinner	$2,000	$2,000	$2,000	$2,000	$2,000	$2,000	$2,000	$2,000	$2,000	$2,000	$2,000	$2,500	$24,500
Dividend	25			25			25			25			100
Interest income	50			50			50			50			200
Other possible income													
Total	$2,075	$2,000	$2,000	$2,075	$2,000	$2,000	$2,075	$2,000	$2,000	$2,075	$2,000	$2,500	$24,800

*Includes Christmas bonus.

Expenditures consist of all the items on which the client spends money. There should be a category for food, clothing, transportation, housing, medical care, recreation, and the like. Some of these can then be further broken down into subcomponents.

Cash outflows

Only money actually disbursed should be counted as expenditures. Bills coming due in the future are to be counted in the future. For example, automobiles purchased on the installment plan and paid for over several years must appear on the cash flow statement for several years with the dollar amount each year equal to the payments each year.

Finally, the cash flow statement should have an item for savings. This item is listed as a separate category of expenditure to emphasize the importance of saving and investing. Some financial planners list savings *before* other expenditures to emphasize that savings and investing is a planned outflow, not simply a residual of income less other expenses.

Savings

To be sure, savings are not held in the form of idle cash but are invested to become an earning asset; hence, they flow out on the cash flow statement. Nevertheless, they are different from other outflows, which are mostly consumption items. A sample of monthly income flow is shown in Table 3–4 and a sample annual cash flow statement is shown in Table 3–5.

Cash flow statement

Table 3–5

	Annual	Monthly
Income		
Wages and salaries	$24,000	$2,000.00
Interest	200	16.66
Dividends	100	8.33
Christmas bonus	500	41.67
Other	—	—
Total	$24,800	$2,066.66
Expenditures		
Food	$ 5,600	$ 466.66
Clothing	1,258	104.83
Transportation	2,100	175.00
Housing	5,200	433.33
Medical care	1,300	108.33
Recreation	1,000	83.33
Other	1,400	166.66
Taxes		
Social security	1,642	136.83
Personal income tax	4,100	341.66
Property taxes		
Savings and investments	1,200	100.00

FINANCIAL STATEMENT ANALYSIS

Both the balance sheet and the cash flow statement are analytical devices that can help in achieving the client's financial goals. Comparing these statements from year to year will show what progress is being made. As the years pass, income generally rises, as does the net worth portion of the balance sheet. Financial statements can also be used to plan ahead, especially in the purchase of big items such as automobiles, homes, and life insurance. They also can provide clues as to whether more life insurance is needed or a larger home is within the family's financial means or if it would be desirable to increase savings.

Balance sheet analysis

The assets, liabilities, and the net worth are the crucial parts of the balance sheet.

Assets

Examine assets. What are they earning? Could their yield be increased by investing them differently? Is too much money in any one asset? Should the portfolio be diversified more? Is life insurance adequate for the client? Is there too much (or too little) in highly liquid, low-earning cash or passbook savings account? These are the client's emergency funds, and an amount equal to about three to six months' income is considered adequate by most experts.

Liabilities

Examine liabilities. Is the client overextended in the use of credit? If he or she has a difficult time meeting savings objectives, this is sometimes the reason. What is the interest cost on debts? If it is relatively high and excess liquid assets are earning much less, the client should consider paying off some debts.

Net worth

It is important to look at net worth to see how it is changing from year to year. Let us return now for a moment to the accounting equation introduced earlier: Assets − Liabilities = Net Worth. If assets increase, either liabilities or net worth increase, or some combination of the two. If assets decrease, either liabilities, net worth, or both decrease. If assets increase faster than liabilities, net worth increases. If the reverse happens, net worth declines. If liabilities exceed assets, net worth becomes negative. If this happens, the individual is technically insolvent—that is, bankrupt; great care should be taken not to allow this to happen. Bankruptcy, discussed in Chapter 2, is nearly always the result of poor financial planning.

A major goal of many people is to increase net worth. If assets and liabilities are both increased by the same dollar amount, the net worth is unchanged. This could happen if someone borrows money and buys something with it. Normally, however, when an asset is purchased with borrowed funds, the buyer must make a down payment. For example, if the buyer borrows $8,000, takes $2,000 out of his or her savings account, and buys a new car for $10,000, net worth stays the same. His or her liabilities increase by $8,000 (installment debt) and so do assets; he or she has a new $10,000 car, but cash is down $2,000 and net worth is unchanged. The following changes would be reflected on his or her balance sheet. Only the changes are shown (a plus means an increase and a minus a decrease).

Assets		Liabilities and net worth	
1988 Chevrolet	+ $10,000	Installment loan	+ $8,000
Cash	− 2,000	Net worth	no change

But a person increased assets without having increased liabilities, net worth increases. The key to doing that is through savings. This brings us to the cash flow statement. If the cash flow statement has savings of $1,000 and liabilities remain unchanged, net worth will increase. The following changes are reflected on the balance sheet. As before, we show only the changes, depicted here by plusses.

Assets		Liabilities and net worth	
Savings account	+ $1,000	Liabilities	no change
		Net worth	+ $1,000

On the other hand, if a person was required to spend savings to meet expenses, both assets and net worth decline. The liquidation of assets, while not *earned* income in that year, is considered a cash inflow. The changes reflected on the balance sheet for this appear below:

Assets		Liabilities and net worth	
Savings account	− $1,000	Liabilities	no change
		Net worth	− $1,000

Paying off debt reduces liabilities, and, if it doesn't affect the individual's assets, it increases net worth. If each monthly payment reduces the $8,000 automobile loan by $200, the following changes would be reflected on the balance sheet:

Assets	Liabilities and net worth	
no change	Installment loan	− $200
	Net worth	+ $200

Thus, consumption and savings choices will affect the balance sheet. Savings will increase net worth, and liquidating savings and investments to meet expenses will reduce net worth. It should be noted that net worth is a good indicator of financial strength, and that a growing net worth indicates that the person is financially becoming stronger. Comparing balance sheets from year to year—assets, liabilities, and net worth—will show what progress the client is making.

The cash flow statement analysis

The cash flow statement should be examined to see if the client is accomplishing his or her goals. The savings portion of the cash flow statement is the key to that document. Many financial planners recommend annual savings of 5–10 percent of income; of course achievement of specific goals may require a greater (or smaller) amount of savings. A budget may be helpful in assisting clients with the achievement of savings goals, because it aids the client in consumption choices. The personal and family budget was discussed in Chapter 2.

Expenditures should also be examined to determine if any are out of line relative to income. To meet goals it is critical that consumption and savings be appropriately balanced.

SUMMARY REVIEW QUESTIONS

These questions serve as a summary and a review of the chapter. If you are able to answer them all, you have a good understanding of the material covered by the chapter.

1. What is a balance sheet? Why is it important?
2. Why is net worth measured as the difference between total assets and total liabilities?
3. Which items are included as assets? Which are included as liabilities?
4. What is the difference between a financial and nonfinancial asset? What about between an earning and a nonearning asset?
5. What is a cash flow statement? Why is it important?
6. Why are savings considered to be a key to financial planning?
7. What are the primary types of inflows and outflows listed on a cash flow statement?
8. What can be done to correct a financial situation if savings are consistently low?
9. How does the purchase of a new car partly for cash and partly financed by a loan affect net worth? Why?
10. What is the primary means of increasing net worth?
11. If in any one year an individual saves $1,000, how does this affect assets, liabilities, and net worth?

CASES

1. Linda Jann Lewis has an older car worth about $1,500. She has decided to trade it in on a new car worth $10,500 and use her old car as the down payment. She could finance the $9,000, or she could pay cash. If she paid cash,
   (a) What would happen to her assets?
   (b) What would happen to her liabilities?
   (c) What would happen to her net worth?
   (d) What would happen to all three of the above items if she financed her new car?

2. Carol Culpepper has acquired the following assets and liabilities:
   (1) Savings deposit $10,000
   (2) Life insurance (cash value) 20,000
   (3) Automobile 10,000
   (4) Installment debt on auto 5,000
   (5) Home 80,000
   (6) Mortgage debt 70,000
   (7) Household furniture 8,000
   (8) Credit card charges 300
   (9) Checking account 1,200
   Carol has an after-tax salary where she works of $28,000. Construct a balance sheet for Carol.

3. Becky Garza earns a salary of $18,000 per year "take-home pay" after all tax and other deductions. Her other income is as follows:
   (1) Interest $627
   (2) Dividends 500
   (3) Self-employed tax consulting income 3,200
   Becky rents an apartment for $500 per month. Her other expenses are as follows:

	Per month
Food	$400
Clothing	100
Utilities	60
Auto expense	200
Insurance premiums (Auto—$100; Life—$25)	125
Medical expenses	75
Contributions	50
Gifts and recreation	100
Savings	500

Prepare an income statement for Becky.

SUGGESTED READINGS

Anthony, Robert, and Welsch, Glen. *Fundamentals of Financial Accounting.* Homewood, Ill: Richard Irwin, 1986.

"Financial Pathfinder Service." New York: Merrill Lynch, Pierce, Fenner, and Smith.

Golonka, Nancy. *How to Protect What's Yours.* Washington, D.C.: Acropolis Books, 1985.

"How to Read a Financial Report." New York: Merrill Lynch, Pierce, Fenner, and Smith.

"How to Understand Financial Statements." New York: New York Stock Exchange.

National Consumer Finance Association. *Finance Facts Yearbook.* Washington, D.C. Annual publication.

U.S. Bureau of the Census. *Income of Families and Individuals in the U.S. in Current Population Reports; Consumer Income.* Series P-60. Get latest series of this quarterly publication.

II Managing income and assets

Chapters 4 through 8 deal with the expenditure of an individual's income.

Chapter 4 covers liquid assets, income, and the means of making payments. Chapter 5 discusses financing "big ticket" items, and chapter 6 outlines the federal consumer protection laws that are there to protect consumers from unscrupulous merchants and lenders.

In chapter 7 we examine Caesar's tribute—taxes. The tax bite is severe, and this chapter is designed to minimize the severity of that bite.

Chapter 8 discusses the largest single expenditure most people will ever make, purchasing a home. Buying a home requires planning and some knowledge of a specialized nature. It is our hope that the chapter will aid you in acquiring that knowledge.

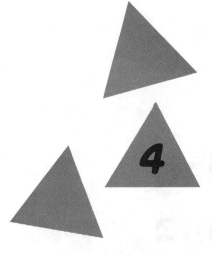

4 Depository institutions and the services they provide

HIGHLIGHTS   In order to provide an understanding of the various depository institutions and the services they provide, this chapter examines the following:

1   Checking accounts—both interest-bearing and non-interest-bearing —and how they work
2   The various depository institutions
3   How checks are cleared
4   The monthly bank statement
5   Certified and cashier's checks
6   The latest automation in depository institutions' services
7   Money orders and traveler's checks
8   Safety of deposited funds
9   Savings deposits and the various other services of depository institutions

INTRODUCTION

Financial planners are in a position to evaluate clients' expenses as well as the means of holding assets. Therefore planners should be familiar with the types of accounts and services available through depository institutions. Until recently checking accounts did not pay interest, but now a number of different kinds of checking accounts have evolved, some of which do. Four types of payment media (coins and currency, checking accounts, credit cards, and debit cards) are currently what we use to pay for day-to-day transactions. Credit and debit cards will be discussed in Chapter 5—credit cards because they involve the use of credit or borrowed money since payment is delayed, and debit cards because they are similar to credit cards but payment is immediate. Coins, currency, and checking accounts will be discussed in this chapter as will be the various depository institutions that issue checking accounts.

CASH BALANCES, LIQUIDITY, AND CHECKS

Liquidity is a relative concept indicating how close something is to money.[1] Money is the most liquid thing in the world, and an old pair of shoes that still has value is perhaps one of the least liquid things. Cash balances—or money—consist of currency, coin, and checking accounts.

The traditional checking account

A check is a written order, drawn on a depository institution by a depositor, ordering the bank to pay on demand and unconditionally a definite amount of money to bearer or to the order of a specific person or business firm named on the check. Funds in traditional checking accounts are called **demand deposits,** and they earn no interest. Checks are always payable on demand, and must be demanded within a reasonable length of time. The Uniform Commercial Code states that a check is not to be paid after six months have elapsed since it was written. For this reason checks are dated.

There are three parties to a check. The person drawing the instrument is called the **drawer;** the party requested to pay the stated amount is known as the **drawee;** and the person to whom the instrument is made payable is known as the **payee.**

There are also specialized checks referred to as **drafts.** Drafts are specialized checks written by one bank on its account in another bank. They are usually sold to a person who wishes to pay someone in a different section of the country. For example, a person in Denver might buy a draft written on a New York bank from a Denver bank and use it to pay for purchases in New York. A bank draft can be a **sight draft** (payable on demand) or a **time draft** (payable at some predetermined future time).

---

1. Some financial experts have defined liquidity as being how quickly and easily an asset can be converted to money without making a price concession.

Interest-bearing checking accounts, or **NOW Accounts** (Negotiated Order of Withdrawal), may be viewed as a specialized checking account that bears interest or a specialized savings account on which checks may be written. The NOW Account was originally authorized in 1972 but only for certain institutions in Massachusetts and New Hampshire. In March 1980, a federal law was passed that makes these accounts legal for all depository institutions throughout the United States. This specialized account is not restricted to commercial banks, but may also be issued by credit unions, mutual savings banks, and savings and loan associations. While these accounts are all NOW accounts, they are referred to by a variety of names—share drafts, save-or-spend, net worth checking, investor checking, check action, paymaster, and many others. They pay a relatively low rate of interest, and often there are substantial monthly service charges unless a minimum balance is maintained.

DEPOSITORY INSTITUTIONS AND DEPOSITS —CHECKING ACCOUNTS
Banks

Five institutions provide checking accounts as well as certain other services.[2] They are commercial banks, savings and loan associations, credit unions, mutual savings banks, and industrial banks.

The financial institutions we call banks are technically defined as commercial banks. Commercial banks have been called "the department stores of financial institutions" because under one roof they can do almost everything. Banks make loans to businesses, farmers and ranchers, individuals, and all levels of government. Banks perform the role of trustee, make available strongboxes for safekeeping valuables, and administer the nationwide credit card system that some of them have developed. Some banks also offer discount brokerage services. But the most important role of banks for the general public is to establish and service checking accounts, including clearing checks, which in turn permits our complex society to function.

Savings and loan associations

Savings and loan (S and L) associations (also called building and loan associations in some states) are evolving rapidly and are becoming more like commercial banks. At one time savings and loans performed, for the most part, only two functions, accepting savings deposits and making mortgage loans. Now S and Ls make consumer loans and commercial loans, provide trustee services, provide credit cards, and provide checking accounts. They clear checks and are now full-fledged depository institutions just like commercial banks.

---

2. Some money market mutual funds do permit check-writing privileges, but do not provide all the other services the depository institutions provide. Money market funds are discussed in a later chapter.

Mutual savings banks

Mutual savings banks (MSB) are much like savings and loan associations. MSBs, however, are all true "mutuals," they have no stockholders, and in theory the depositors are the owners. At one time they too limited their activities to accepting savings deposits and making mortgage loans, but have now expanded into other areas, and accept interest-bearing checking accounts.

Credit unions

Credit unions are voluntary cooperative associations. Members have a common bond—usually this consists of the employees of some enterprise. They still specialize in making consumer loans to their members, using these same members' savings deposits to finance the loan. In addition, credit unions may offer first and second mortgages. Credit unions do not deal with outsiders. A person must be eligible and then voluntarily join; one may not just walk in off the street and do business with a credit union. However, credit unions do offer a wide variety of deposits including the interest-bearing checking account. They clear checks and provide all the necessary checking account services for their members.

Industrial banks

Industrial banks, or "Morris Plan banks," are another type of thrift institution, they are found in about twenty states and accept both passbook savings and certificates of deposit (CDs). In some states they are also permitted to accept the interest-bearing account, the NOW account. There are not many statistics about industrial banks so most comments are only generalizations. Industrial banks are typically regulated by state banking commissions, and to a degree the regulations vary from state to state. They are specifically forbidden to act as trustees. Frequently they are required to establish reserve accounts, often as high as 15 percent of their savings deposits. In some states the law prohibits borrowing by any of the bank's officers or stockholders, and usually the state banking commissioner conducts periodic examinations of the bank. Industrial banks do not exist in many states. Most industrial banks do not provide insured deposits; they also sometimes make riskier loans. Because of this they generally pay higher interest rates than other depository institutions. Nevertheless, there are some good, well-managed industrial banks.

Service charges

Most institutions have service charges, which vary not only from institution to institution but also with the type of deposit. Service charges should be considered when selecting a checking account to minimize the cost.

Service charges are generally higher on the NOW account than on others. However, the participant earns interest on deposits, which tends to offset the service charges. If the minimum monthly balance is fairly high, the consumer will usually come out ahead with a NOW account; if it is small, a traditional account may be more appropriate.

Many institutions require a minimum monthly balance of as high as $2,000 before they waive monthly service charges on a NOW account. Credit unions, however, as a rule require much less, as do some other institutions. If service charges are assessed, they generally run from $5 to $10 per month. Some institutions also charge 10¢ or 15¢ per check.

With a regular checking account, usually no service charges are assessed if the minimum monthly balance does not fall below a certain level (usually $300, but sometimes $500). If the account falls below the minimum, a service charge is levied, usually a flat fee of $3, $4, or $5 per month. In some cases, if the minimum balance falls even lower, say below $200, this flat fee may rise a dollar or two; and if the balance falls below $100, the service charge may rise another dollar. Some institutions also add a 10¢ or 15¢ fee per check to their flat fee service charge if the balance falls below a specified minimum.

Some banks also have special noninterest-bearing (traditional) checking accounts. In such a case, usually no minimum balance is required. Rather, there is a monthly service charge of 50¢ or $1.00 and a further charge of 15¢ or 20¢ per check. Special accounts are not very popular, but they appeal to certain groups such as students who write few checks and whose balance either is low all the time or fluctuates a great deal.

Joint accounts

It is often desirable for a married couple to open a joint account. To do this both individuals must endorse the signature card. A specimen of this type of card is shown in Figure 4–1. Once the account is opened, both persons may write checks or, more precisely, draw against the account.

There are a number of advantages in opening a joint account. The bank regards it as one account; therefore, the service charges are less than they would be if the husband and wife had separate accounts. The most important advantage, however, arises in the event of the death of one of the parties. If the husband has an individual account and the wife has an individual account and the husband dies, then, until the estate of the deceased is probated, the bank will refuse to honor any checks drawn against the husband's account by the man's wife. However, when the husband and wife have a joint account, because of the nature of a joint tenancy with the right of survivorship, title to the fund usually passes immediately upon death to the survivor. The practical effect is that the wife can draw checks on the joint account after having obtained a release from the tax commission in those states having state inheritance taxes. The release can be arranged by a bank for the survivor within a few days. The major disadvantage to a joint account is that sometimes neither party knows what checks the other has drawn, and the account might be overdrawn.

Account No._____

Account Name _____

No. of Signatures
Required _____

TEXAS STATE BANK
AUSTIN, TEXAS

All the conditions on the reverse side of this card pertaining to this agreement have been read and agreed to by the undersigned. The Texas State Bank is authorized to recognize the following signatures in the payment of funds and all other transactions dealing with this account.

1._____ Soc. Sec. No. _____

2._____ Soc. Sec. No. _____

3._____ Soc. Sec. No. _____

4._____ Soc. Sec. No. _____

Res. Address	Res. Phone
City State	Zip Code
Employer	
Bus. Address	Bus. Phone
Perm. Address	City
Prev. Bank	City
Identification	
New A/C Clerk Date	Initial Deposit

Type Account   ☐ Comm   ☐ Reg   ☐ Tex   ☐ 2 + Ck
                ☐ Reg Sav   ☐ S/I Sav   ☐ 2 + Sav

Corresponding 2 + No. _____

Checks Ordered _____   Passbook Issued _____

Comments: _____

JOINT ACCOUNT BECOMING PROPERTY OF SURVIVOR UPON DEATH OF OTHER PARTY
We agree and declare that all funds now, or hereafter, deposited in this account are, and shall be, our joint property and owned by us as joint depositors with right of survivorship, and not as tenants in common; and upon the death of either of us any balance in said account shall become the absolute property of the survivor. The entire account or any part thereof may be withdrawn by, or upon the order of, either of us or the survivor and the bank shall have the right to pay the entire balance to said survivor and upon such payment shall be discharged of all liability.
NOTICE: This agreement is not effective between a husband and wife as to community funds.

_____   _____

NOTICE: Read Additional Terms and Conditions on Reverse Side

Figure 4–1   *Example of signature card.* (Source: *Texas Bank of Austin.*)

Virtually all checks in the United States are now cleared by computer, using "magnetic ink character recognition" (MICR). This is possible because each customer has an account number on his or her checks. It is printed with special ink and characters so that a computer can read it. When the customer writes a check, the bank deducts that amount from the account, and the person receiving the check has that sum added to his or her account. If two different banks are involved, then one bank has a claim on the other. Since hundreds of checks are presented for payment each day, all banks have funds flowing both in and out. Hence, in net terms, a bank will lose (or gain) very little on any given day. The clearing of checks is usually carried out by a clearinghouse association or by the Federal Reserve System. It nets the checks and then debits and credits the accounts of the proper bank.

Clearing checks

Most institutions send monthly statements to their depositors indicating the balance at that time. These statements show all deposits and withdrawals during the month, the balance at the beginning and at the end of the month, and the service charges, if any. The canceled checks are returned at the same time. Although such statements are usually sent toward the end of the month, some banks send them out over several days or even weeks to spread the work of preparing them. These monthly statements can be used by the depositors to reconcile their balances. Figure 4–2 shows an example of a monthly bank statement.

Monthly statement

Truncation is a system where canceled checks are not returned to the drawer with the monthly bank statement. Rather the statement consists of a computer printout that lists each check, its number, the dollar amount, and to whom paid. This statement would serve as proof of payment. The checks would be retained by the bank for a time and later microfilmed and the checks destroyed. Approximately 40,000 checks can be stored on a cassette tape four inches in diameter. It is estimated that stopping this avalanche of paper would save financial institutions several billion dollars per year.

Truncation

Initially, some opponents of the truncation system claimed that people would resist the concept of not being able to retain their canceled checks. To address this worry, many depository establishments that have adopted the truncation method also offer their customers a **duplicate draft** system. Duplicate drafts are nothing more than carbon copies made of each check at the time it is written. They are nonnegotiable; they simply provide the customer with a record of exactly what was written on the actual drafts. In this way the customer can feel more secure about his or her check-writing activities, while the bank, S and L, or credit union can avoid the expense of returning canceled checks through the mail. With well over fifty billion checks processed annually, the duplicate draft system should allow the public to avoid greatly increased service charges in the future.

Texas Bank
REPUBLIC OF TEXAS

AREA CODE 512 PHONE: 476-6711
P.O. BOX 1328 • AUSTIN, TEXAS 78767

Statement

ACCOUNT NUMBER
000-000-0

| 2 | 10 | 81 | DATE |

IN ACCOUNT WITH

John Doe
2205 5th Street
Austin, TX 78767

BEGINNING BALANCE	NO. OF CHECKS	TOTAL AMOUNT OF CHECKS PAID	NO. OF DEPOSITS	TOTAL AMOUNT OF DEPOSITS	OUT OF TOWN CHECKS DEP	BALANCE FOR SERVICE CHARGE	SERVICE CHARGE
891.09	36	1,531.39	2	918.22		70	5.00

DATE	CHECK	CHECK	DEPOSIT	BALANCE
7-23		BALANCE FORWARD		
7-24	20.00	40.00		891.09
7-24	171.58			
7-25	40.00	160.00		659.51
7-28	8.66	21.00		459.51
7-28	73.73			
7-29	40.00			356.12
7-31	20.00			316.12
8-1	20.00			296.12
8-4	10.11	20.00		276.12
8-4	33.00			
8-5	20.00	40.00		213.01
3-6	40.00			153.01
8-7	40.00			113.01
8-8			469.77	73.01
8-11	58.70			542.78
3-12	6.70	25.00		484.08
8-12	40.00	44.25		
8-14	40.00			368.13
8-18	8.15	13.51		328.13
8-13	50.00			
8-19	4.00	20.00		256.47
8-20	110.00			232.47
8-21	20.00		448.45	122.47
8-25	6.30	8.00		550.92
8-25	40.00	58.70		
8-25	160.00	5.00 SC		272.92

AT	AUTOMATIC PAYMENT	DM	DEBIT MEMO	LP	LOAN PAYMENT	PR	PAYMENT REVERSAL
BC	BANK CLUB	EC	ERROR CORRECTION	MD	MAIL DEPOSIT	RT	RETURNED CHECK
CR	DEPOSIT OR CREDIT	FC	FINANCE CHARGE	MP	MANUAL PAYMENT	SC	SERVICE CHARGE
DC	DEPOSIT CORRECTION	GA	GENERATED ADVANCE	OD	OVERDRAWN	TR	TRANSFER
DD	DIRECT DEPOSIT						

Figure 4-2   *A monthly bank statement. (Source: Texas Bank of Austin.)*

Contracts frequently call for payment by certified check. A ***certified check*** is one signed by the drawer and made payable to the payee in the same way any other check is drawn; however, the drawer takes the check to his or her bank and asks to have it "certified." The cashier or some other employee of the bank takes the check to the bank's bookkeeping department, and the amount of the check is subtracted from the balance of the drawer's account. The bank employee then stamps the check "certified." The bank is substituting its credit for that of the drawer, so that even if the drawer attempts subsequently to withdraw the amount from the account, he or she cannot. Furthermore, the payee of an uncertified check may have the check certified by requesting that the bank do so. Certified checks are a means of assuring the payee that the check is good in those cases where he or she lacks confidence in the drawer.

Certified checks

A cashier's check is drawn by a bank on its own order to a designated payee or to his or her order. If differs from the certified check in that it is a liability of the bank, not of an individual. A person wishing to buy a cashier's check goes to the bank and pays the face value of the check, which the bank will write on itself. There is a small fee for this service. The cashier's check serves the same purpose as the certified check. It gives the payee absolute assurance that the check can be converted into cash. However, a cashier's check can be bought from a bank by a non-depositor, whereas certified checks can be obtained only by a depositor. Some banks will sell only cashier's checks and not certified checks. Figure 4–3 shows a sample of a cashier's check.

Cashier's checks

In recent years, banks and other depository institutions have installed a fully automated twenty-four-hour-a-day teller; a machine that will accept

Automated teller machines (ATM)

A cashier's check. (Source: *Texas Bank of Austin.*)

Figure 4–3

deposits or allow withdrawals. A special card is issued that has a magnetic strip on the back on which the customer's bank account number has been placed. The machine is activated by placing the card in a slot and punching in a code on the keyboard. The automated teller then carries out the desired transaction. These automated teller machines are placed outside the building of the institution issuing the card and are accessible at all times. In recent years they have also been placed in shopping centers, office buildings, and other places.

Automatic funds transfer (AFT): The sweep accounts

In recent years many institutions have established automatic funds transfer accounts, which permit the transfer from a higher-interest-paying savings account to a lower-paying checking account, and vice versa. This permits a person to hold the bulk of his or her money in a higher-paying savings account and minimize the amount of money in a lower-paying checking account. Then as checks are written and come into the bank for clearing, the needed funds are transferred into the checking account by computer.

An agreement is made that the checking account is not to fall below a certain minimum, a minimum that will vary according to the desires and needs of the customer. When checks come in which reduce the checking account below the minimum, funds are transferred. Some institutions will also provide two-way transfers. That is, if the checking account climbs above the minimum, the computer transfers funds from it to the savings account. How often the computer sweeps the account varies from institution to institution as well as with the size of the deposits. Some are swept daily, others weekly. The various institutions charge varying fees for these services. The AFT system, then, provides overdraft protection, and is also a means of keeping most of the customer's deposits in higher interest-bearing accounts.

Automatic (computer-assisted) payment of bills

In those cases where the customer has a regular monthly bill of a uniform size (like a mortgage or rent payment) he or she may authorize the payee to write a draft on the checking account on a certain day.

More recently some banks and savings and loan associations have gone one step further and have developed computer-assisted check writing and bill payment systems. Sometimes these are also tied in with the automatic funds transfer system discussed above, and hence most of the individual's funds can be kept in an interest-bearing savings account until the bills are due. The customer has access to the institution's computer by telephone, and checks are generated by the computer and mailed to the desired recipient upon punching the correct sequence of numbers on the telephone.

Electronic debit

Similar to the automatic payment of bills is the electronic debit. Under this system a computer pays the customer's bills automatically at the time of a purchase, usually through the use of a debit card. A debit card, unlike a credit card, transfers funds immediately and automatically, and no check need ever be written. The debit card is discussed in greater detail in the next chapter.

Deposit safety

What would happen to a depositor's money if an institution should fail? In nearly all cases depositors are protected against such possibilities. The Federal Deposit Insurance Corporation (FDIC), a federal agency, insures deposits up to $100,000 against such loss. Virtually all banks in the United States are insured by the FDIC. Savings and loan associations, credit unions, and mutual savings banks have the same insurance, either with the FDIC or with a similar U.S. government agency. Only a few institutions have chosen not to have this deposit insurance. All insured institutions have metal signs indicating that they have insurance in prominent places or near the tellers' counters. If an insured bank should fail, depositors would be reimbursed by an agency of the U.S. government. Even if an institution is robbed or burns down, depositors do not lose their money because depository institutions carry private insurance against losses from such risks.

A married couple may have insurance covering a total of $300,000 per institution—$100,000 deposit in the wife's name, $100,000 in the husband's name, and $100,000 held jointly.[3] Table 4–1 shows the insuring agencies for the various depository institutions.

OTHER SERVICES PROVIDED BY DEPOSITORY INSTITUTIONS

There are a number of other services provided by depository institutions,[4] including: (1) accepting savings accounts, (2) selling travelers' checks, (3) providing safety deposit boxes, and (4) providing trustee services (discussed in greater detail in a later chapter).

Savings accounts

While savings deposits are discussed in greater detail in Chapter 13 on thrift institutions, a few words about them are in order here. Savings accounts are not as liquid as checking accounts and consist, in general, of funds that can be invested by the banks for the long run.[5] For this reason institutions pay higher interest on savings than on checking deposits and do not assess service fees, as is often the case on checking accounts.

---

3. In some cases couples have a trust account. In most cases a trust account is considered to be a joint account and it serves as the joint account mentioned in the text insofar as insurance is concerned.

4. Loans are not included in this discussion. These institutions make all kinds of loans, and they are discussed in a later chapter.

5. Liquidity is a relative term, but it refers to how close something is to money, i.e., how easily and quickly it can be converted to money. While anything of value can be sold and converted into money, some things can be converted more quickly and easily than others; hence, they are more liquid. Money is the most liquid commodity of all.

Table 4–1   *Deposit insurance*

Institution	Government insuring agency	Dollar amount*
Commercial bank	Federal Deposit Insurance Corporation (FDIC)	$100,000
Credit union	National Credit Union Administration (NCUA)	$100,000
Mutual savings bank	Federal Deposit Insurance Corporation (FDIC)	$100,000
Savings and loan association	Federal Deposit Insurance Corporation (FDIC)**	$100,000

*The maximum dollar amount of insurance is per depositor per institution. Since there are thousands of insured institutions in the U.S., no one needs to keep deposits in any uninsured institution.

**In 1990 the law was changed and the FDIC now insures all S&L deposits using a newly-established special fund (the Savings Association Insurance Fund—SAIF), which replaced the former Federal Savings and Loan Insurance Fund (FSLIC) as the insuring agency.

There are a number of different savings deposits with which you should be familiar. First, there is the passbook savings account, which up until a few years ago was the major savings deposit. While withdrawals may be made from it at any time—hence, it is highly liquid—it is not as liquid as a checking account because checks may not be written on it. In order to make a withdrawal from a passbook savings account, it is sometimes necessary to make a trip to the institution; although most institutions provide for withdrawals by mail and telephone.

In addition there are various savings certificates of deposit (CDs). In some cases CDs run over several years before they mature and may not be withdrawn before that time without a penalty. For this reason they are considered less liquid than passbook or checking accounts, and for this reason they also receive a higher rate of interest. They are discussed in greater detail in Chapter 13.

There are also several other specialized savings accounts not yet discussed, and checks may be written on some of them. They may also pay a higher rate of interest than the passbook account. They too will be discussed in detail in Chapter 13 which deals with saving and investing through savings institutions.

Money orders and travelers' checks

Although in terms of dollar volume these instruments rank low compared with checks, money orders and travelers' checks should be mentioned briefly because some disbursements are made in this way. Money orders are a means of transmitting funds and serve much the same function as checks. There are three parties to the money order: the **payer,** who buys the money order; the **payee,** who receives it; and the **drawee,** which is the institution ordered to make the payment. One such institution is the U.S. Post Office. Postal money orders, which are purchased for a small fee from any United States Post Office, permit only one endorsement and are collected by presentation at either a post office or a commercial bank. Although postal money orders are very safe, they are not as convenient to use in paying bills as checks because they require a trip to the post office. In recent years, other institutions—such as banks, savings and loan associations, and even some convenience stores and major food chains—have begun to sell money orders.

The money orders sold by these institutions are not considered quite as safe as those issued by the post office and hence are not as convenient a means of payment. The money orders issued by the post office are an obligation of the U.S. government. As such they are universally acceptable. The money orders issued by other institutions are usually accepted but sometimes not until they have cleared through a bank.

Travelers' checks were at one time issued only by the American Express Company and by Thomas Cook Company, both private corporations. They are issued in much the same manner as money orders; the basic difference between the two is that the express money order can pass from hand to hand by continuous endorsement. Traveler's checks are sold by many depository institutions, most travel agencies, and at the offices of the American Express Company, which can be found in any large city. They come in denominations of $10, $20, $50, $100, and $500. The fee charged is $1 per $100 of checks purchased. They are often used by people who travel, since they are universally known and accepted almost everywhere just like money itself. They are very safe because they must be endorsed before they can be exchanged. If they are lost or stolen, the original issuer will replace them. The checks are numbered, and the buyer should make a separate copy of these numbers since they will be needed if a lost or stolen claim is to be filed. The American Express Company has offices in most foreign countries, and their checks are widely accepted abroad.

In recent years a number of competitors (mostly large city banks) have entered this field. The Bank of America now has its own negotiable and nearly universally accepted travelers' checks. The First National City Bank of New York and a number of other large city banks now also provide this service. These travelers' checks are sold to the public nationally by banks and travel agencies having ties to the issuing banks. The purchase and use conditions of the American Express travelers' checks also apply to these competitors' checks.

Safety deposit boxes are heavy steel boxes inside a special walk-in vault. The vault door is locked when the bank is closed. Inside the walk-in vault

Safety deposit box

are individual boxes, each with its own separate lock, that may be rented by the bank's customers. These boxes come in several sizes, and rental fees vary with the size and range from about five dollars to about sixty dollars per year. Each customer has a key to the box he or she rents and the bank has a second key; both are needed to open the box. Safety deposit boxes are protected by alarms and heavy metal, and are fireproof insofar as possible. All valuables that could be lost by fire or burglary and that are compact should be kept in a safety deposit box. This includes such things as stock certificates, bonds, wills, insurance policies, and savings account passbooks. Safety deposit boxes are normally sealed upon the death of an owner; therefore, it is sometimes appropriate that a married couple hold the box in a joint name. Thus, the box is accessible to the survivor upon the death of a spouse.

Trustee services

Commercial banks are authorized by law to perform the role of a trustee. This involves managing the assets of someone else. Sometimes a will of a deceased person will set up an estate for the heirs. The trust department of a bank can manage the estate. The bank will also look after the financial affairs of a minor. Large banks have well-established trust departments that invest billions of dollars of other people's money. The trustee service is discussed in greater detail in a later chapter. Recently, savings and loan associations have also been authorized to provide trustee services.

SUMMARY REVIEW QUESTIONS

These questions serve as a summary and a review of the chapter. If you are able to answer them all, you have a good understanding of the material covered by the chapter.
1. What is liquidity?
2. Are cash balances highly liquid?
3. What (or whom) are the three parties to a check?
4. How do the "new" checking accounts differ from the traditional accounts?
5. What role do the depository institutions perform?
6. What are the advantages of joint checking account between husband and wife?
7. How does a certified check differ from a cashier's check?
8. What is truncation?
9. Explain the value of a safety deposit box.
10. What are money orders and travelers' checks?
11. How does the automatic funds transfer work?
12. How is a depository institution able to pay bills automatically?
13. What are the trustee services which some banks provide?
14. Comment on the safety of funds deposited in the institutions discussed in this chapter.

1. Ruth Bullock has decided to open a checking account. The bank explained the three different accounts they provide as follows:

	Minimum balance	Monthly fee	Interest paid	Cost for checks	Charge per check
NOW Account	$1,000	$7.00	5½%	$6 per 200	0
Regular Account	$500	$5.00	0	$6 per 200	0
Special Checking	no minimum	$7.95	0	Free checks	0

The monthly fee is waived if the average monthly balance does not fall below $500 in the case of the regular checking account. In the case of the NOW account the monthly fee is waived only if the account never falls below $1,000, but the 5 1/2 percent interest is always paid. Ruth believes her average monthly balance will be just over $500, and she expects to write about thirty checks per month.

   (a) How much interest would she forgo by taking a regular checking account?

   (b) What would Ruth's cost be per month if she established a regular checking account?

   (c) What would her cost be if she established a NOW account?

   (d) What would her cost be for all of the above (a through c) if she wrote fifty checks per month?

   (e) Which account would you recommend for Ruth?

2. Jim and Katherine Center are a young couple who have recently moved to town. They have decided to open a checking account but are undecided whether they should open a joint account or whether each should have a separate account. Can you outline the advantages and disadvantages of each?

3. Wilfred and Dorothea Brown have just moved to Omaha, Nebraska, and their furniture is due tomorrow. The truck driver has phoned them explaining he will have to be paid $1,050 before he can unload it and that an ordinary check will not do. He has agreed, however, to accept either a cashier's check or a certified check. What is the difference between an ordinary check, a cashier's check, and a certified check?

4. Rebecca Ann Wagoner has both a savings account and a checking account at the First National Bank, and transfers funds from one to the other as needed. She would like to minimize her checking account balance and maximize her savings deposit balance so as to maximize her interest yield. Recently she learned about the NOW account which has been described as both an interest-bearing checking account and a savings account on which checks can be written. Ann is a bit confused. Could you explain the difference between a savings account, a checking account, and a NOW account?

SUGGESTED READINGS

Bankers Magazine. Boston: Warren, Gorham and Lamont. Published every other month.

Dalgaard, Bruce R. *Money, Financial Institutions and Economic Activity.* Glenview, Ill: Scott Foresman and Company, 1987.

The Electronic Fund Transfer Commission and Finance Companies: Report of the NCFA Task Force. Washington, D.C.: National Consumer Finance Association.

Electronic Fund Transfers: Current Legal Developments, New York: Practicing Law Institute.

Finance Facts Yearbook. Washington, D.C.: Research Services Division, National Consumer Finance Association. Annual publication.

Garcia, F. L. *How to Analyze a Bank Statement.* Boston: Bankers Publishing, 1985.

Hutchinson, Harry D. *Money, Banking, and the U.S. Economy.* Englewood Cliffs, N.J.: Prentice-Hall, 1988.

Journal of Bank Research. Published quarterly by the Bank Administration Institute, 303 South Northwest Highway, Park Ridge, Ill.

Money and Credit Management Education: A Descriptive Catalogue of Educational Materials for the Classroom Teacher or Counselor. Washington, D.C.: National Consumer Finance Association.

"Money, Master or Servant." New York: The Federal Reserve Bank of New York.

Money and Your Marriage. Washington, D.C.: Educational Services Division, National Consumer Finance Association.

"Monitor, A Summary of Current Research in Consumer and Mortgage Credit," West Lafayette, Ind.: Credit Research Center, Krannert School of Management, Purdue University. Semimonthly report.

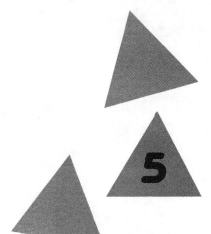

5 Consumer credit

HIGHLIGHTS

In order to provide a fundamental understanding of consumer credit and how it is used, this chapter discusses the following:

1   The various types of consumer credit
2   How credit is established
3   Why consumers borrow
4   The benefits and disadvantages of consumer credit
5   How to calculate the dollar amount and the interest rate on consumer credit
6   Where consumer credit may be obtained
7   Credit cards
8   A number of other things a person should know about consumer credit
9   The financial documents that accompany consumer loans

INTRODUCTION

Financial planners evaluate the income and debt of clients in considering barriers to and opportunities for achieving client goals, and therefore should be familiar with consumer credit issues. For most of the things that can be purchased by consumers, there are a number of choices as to the best method of payment. In the case of such items as food, clothing, and monthly bills, payments are generally made using the checking account discussed in the previous chapter. However, for larger items, such as automobiles, consumer credit may be used to buy them on the installment plan. In this chapter we will examine the relevant issues associated with using credit to finance consumer transactions.

THE FUNDAMENTALS OF CONSUMER CREDIT

Why do people buy on the installment plan? It would be cheaper to pay cash for all items because interest and service charges would be eliminated. Interest costs are also incurred when you borrow money at a bank in order to buy an item. Why do most people not save enough money through a budget to pay cash for large items like cars or household furniture? They are impatient. The money for a car would probably take several years to save. Some people, even if they had a budget, would never be able to save enough to pay cash for a car. So they go into debt, buy the car, and then engage in a negative form of savings when liquidating the debt.

To be sure, some people's incomes are so high that they can easily pay cash for any purchase and this group borrows little money. At the other extreme are the very low-income groups who are unable to borrow much money because their credit ratings are such that lenders are hesitant to lend to them. The great bulk of consumer credit, as it is called, is extended to the middle class, those whose incomes are high enough to give them a good credit rating and enable them to borrow, but too low to allow them to pay cash.

The classification of consumer credit

Consumer credit is credit extended to individuals for the purchase of final consumer items. Consumer credit is sometimes classified into sales credit and loan credit. **Sales credit** is extended by a merchant, and the person gets goods and promises to pay later. **Loan credit** is extended by a financial institution, and the person gets money (credit) with which to buy something and must then repay the loan. A second classification is perhaps superior; it is used by the Federal Reserve Board and consists of (1) installment credit and (2) noninstallment credit. Most of the credit extended by merchants is installment credit. Financial institutions make both installment loans and what is referred to as noninstallment single repayment loans.

In addition, consumer credit is extended through the use of credit cards. Credit card credit is classified as installment credit, even though many people liquidate their bill every month when due.

Installment credit consists of all credit extended to individuals that is to be repaid in two or more installments. It can be broken down into the type of product that it finances, such as:

1. Automobile loans
2. Revolving charge accounts (credit cards)
3. Mobile homes
4. Other

Credit extended for the purchase of autos is the largest single category. Most automobiles sold in the United States are financed through the use of installment credit. Revolving consumer credit is that which is extended through the use of credit cards. The balance due on most credit cards need never be fully liquidated; only a certain proportion of the principal and the interest need be paid each month when billed. Credit cards finance a wide variety of goods such as gasoline, clothing, and some household items.

Credit extended for the purchase of mobile homes is self-explanatory. Most of this credit is extended by commercial banks and finance companies, but in some states savings and loan associations also make it available.

Other consumer credit finances all other durable goods such as television sets, household appliances, home improvements, and other items. It also includes personal loans which may be made to individuals to purchase other goods and services, even a vacation. Table 5–1 shows these classifications, the dollar amounts, and the institutions that extended the credit, over the past few years. Figure 5–1 shows the relative shares of the major consumer lenders, and Figure 5–2 shows the types of installment debt by major types.

Noninstallment credit consists primarily of single payment loans and service credit. It also, however, consists of those few charge accounts in which the entire sum charged is due and payable at the end of each month.

Substantial interest savings may be available to a consumer who borrows if he or she agrees to repay the loan, together with interest, in one lump sum at a specific future time. The major reason why a person can obtain a much lower rate on a noninstallment-type consumer loan is because the lender incurs fewer bookkeeping, recordkeeping, and collection costs. If one borrows from an insurance company on a noninstallment basis, the annual percentage rate may be about 8 percent. If the individual then sets aside a sum every week or month in a passbook savings account, he or she will earn about 5 percent for a net cost of about 3 percent. A single repayment loan from a bank, savings and loan association, mutual savings bank, or credit union will cost about 13 to 15 per-

Managing income and assets

Table 5—1   *Source: Federal Reserve Bulletin, September 1990, Board of Governors of the Federal Reserve System, p. A39.*

CONSUMER INSTALLMENT CREDIT[1] Total Outstanding, and Net Change, seasonally adjusted

Millions of dollars, amounts outstanding, end of period

Holder, and type of credit	1988	1989	1989				1990				
			Sept.	Oct.	Nov.	Dec.	Jan.	Feb.	Mar.'	Apr.'	May
						Seasonally adjusted					
1 Total	664,701	716,624	705,703	710,133	713,903	716,624	717,829	717,869	720,445	720,835	724,745
2 Automobile	284,556	290,770	288,839	290,210	290,972	290,770	290,904	289,629	290,932	288,936	288,849
3 Revolving	174,057	197,110	190,378	191,734	194,679	197,110	199,146	199,927	202,263	203,965	207,104
4 Mobile home	25,201	22,343	22,661	22,621	22,197	22,343	22,604	22,633	22,708	22,702	23,027
5 Other	180,887	206,401	203,825	205,568	206,055	206,401	205,175	205,680	204,543	205,232	205,765
						Not seasonally adjusted					
6 Total	674,719	727,561	708,370	711,295	715,145	727,561	721,026	717,062	713,138	715,801	720,304
By major holder											
7 Commercial banks	324,792	343,865	332,502	335,657	337,285	343,865	342,266	339,418	334,645	337,576	339,631
8 Finance companies	146,212	140,832	146,296	143,293	142,802	140,832	140,740	139,115	137,857	138,174	138,384
9 Credit unions	88,340	90,875	91,285	91,291	90,965	90,875	90,452	90,127	89,556	89,689	89,869
10 Retailers[4]	48,302	42,638	37,400	37,045	37,906	42,638	39,959	37,904	37,302	37,207	37,347
11 Savings institutions	63,399	57,228	59,556	58,720	58,236	57,228	55,425	54,771	54,095	53,606	53,301
12 Gasoline companies	3,674	3,935	4,052	3,947	3,853	3,935	4,013	3,803	3,792	3,928	4,024
13 Pools of securitized assets[2]	n.a.	48,188	37,279	41,342	44,098	48,188	48,171	51,924	55,891	55,621	57,748
By major type of credit[3]											
14 Automobile	284,328	290,421	293,114	293,664	292,543	290,421	288,984	288,036	286,539	286,220	287,058
15 Commercial banks	123,392	126,613	126,972	128,213	128,111	126,613	127,075	127,149	126,289	126,483	126,997
16 Finance companies	97,245	82,721	90,217	86,655	85,725	82,721	81,918	80,227	79,523	79,295	78,927
17 Pools of securitized assets[2]	n.a.	18,191	11,785	15,024	15,376	18,191	17,827	18,931	19,563	19,406	20,151
18 Revolving	183,909	208,188	188,684	189,913	194,640	208,188	203,288	200,147	199,306	201,783	204,805
19 Commercial banks	123,020	130,956	119,413	120,484	122,728	130,956	128,384	124,821	122,024	124,039	125,386
20 Retailers	43,697	37,967	32,961	32,618	33,432	37,967	35,359	33,378	32,794	32,721	32,857
21 Gasoline companies	3,674	3,935	4,052	3,947	3,853	3,935	4,013	3,803	3,792	3,928	4,024
22 Pools of securitized assets[2]	n.a.	22,977	19,731	20,371	22,186	22,977	23,450	26,204	29,542	29,403	30,913
23 Mobile home	25,143	22,283	22,808	22,849	22,319	22,283	22,717	22,726	22,426	22,484	22,820
24 Commercial banks	9,025	9,155	9,121	9,130	9,144	9,155	9,109	9,162	9,142	9,231	9,505
25 Finance companies	7,191	4,716	5,106	5,205	4,682	4,716	5,411	5,410	5,178	5,168	5,224
26 Other	181,339	206,669	203,764	204,869	205,643	206,669	206,037	206,153	204,236	205,314	205,621
27 Commercial banks	69,355	77,141	76,996	77,830	77,302	77,141	77,698	78,286	77,190	77,823	77,743
28 Finance companies	41,776	53,395	50,973	51,433	52,395	53,395	53,411	53,478	53,156	53,711	54,233
29 Retailers	4,605	4,671	4,439	4,427	4,474	4,671	4,600	4,526	4,508	4,486	4,490
30 Pools of securitized assets[2]	n.a.	7,020	5,763	5,947	6,536	7,020	6,894	6,789	6,786	6,812	6,684

1. The Board's series cover most short- and intermediate-term credit extended to individuals that is scheduled to be repaid (or has the option of repayment) in two or more installments.
These data also appear in the Board's G.19 (421) release. For address, see inside front cover.

2. Outstanding balances of pools upon which securities have been issued; these balances are no longer carried on the balance sheets of the loan originator.
3. Totals include estimates for certain holders for which only consumer credit totals are available.

cent depending upon the size of the loan and the borrower's credit rating. This amounts to a net cost of about 8 to 10 percent if a passbook savings account is used to budget the repayment. It should be noted that in order to borrow from many lenders on a noninstallment basis, the borrower's credit rating must be better than that of many installment borrowers.

Service credit   Service credit is that which is extended by professional practitioners and some establishments such as hospitals. Because of the growing use of medical insurance this type of credit is not as important as formerly, but

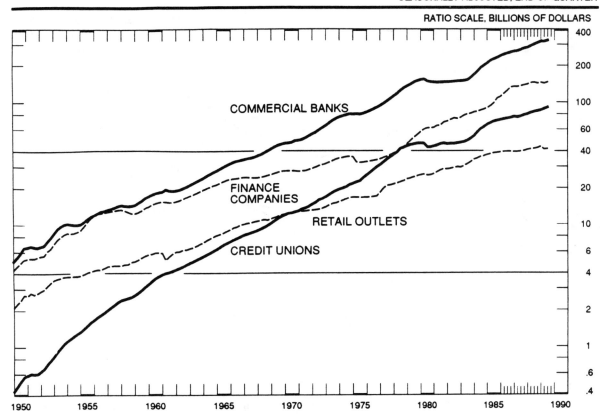

CONSUMER INSTALLMENT CREDIT
MAJOR HOLDERS
SEASONALLY ADJUSTED, END OF QUARTER

RATIO SCALE, BILLIONS OF DOLLARS

COMMERCIAL BANKS

FINANCE
COMPANIES

RETAIL OUTLETS

CREDIT UNIONS

Relative shares of the major consumer lenders. (Source: 1989 Historical Chart Book,   Figure 5–1
Board of Governors of the Federal Reserve System, p. 67.)

it includes unpaid medical and dental bills and monies owed to hospitals
or to the accountant who prepared the individual's tax returns. The
amounts owed to utilities after deducating deposits are also part of the
statistics of service credit. Figure 5–3 shows how total consumer installment debt has risen over the last few years.

Loans to consumers may be secured or unsecured. If the loan is secured,   *Secured and*
usually that which is financed is pledged as collateral, such as an auto-   *unsecured loans*
mobile or household furniture. This is accomplished by having the bor-
rower give a security agreement to the lender. (See the end of the chapter
for an example of a security agreement.) An unsecured loan is called a

CONSUMER INSTALLMENT CREDIT
MAJOR TYPES
SEASONALLY ADJUSTED, END OF QUARTER

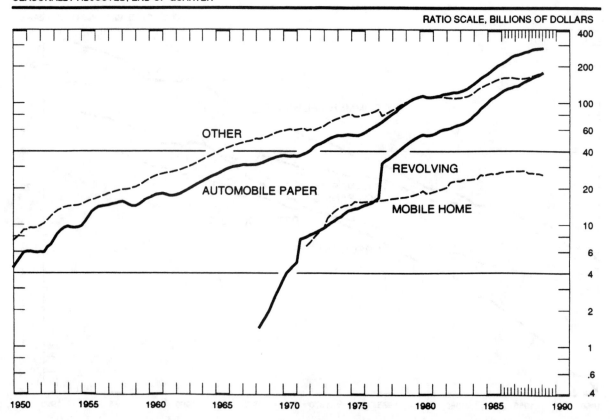

Figure 5—2   *Consumer installment credit: Major types. Seasonally adjusted, end of quarter.* (Source: 1989 Historical Chart Book, *Board of Governors of the Federal Reserve System, p. 66.*)

signature loan; no collateral is pledged, and the borrower has a good enough credit rating to obtain the loan by merely signing a promissory note to repay it.

Sometimes a borrower will pledge other assets as security such as marketable bonds or stock. In such a case the risk to the lender is reduced substantially because if the lender defaults on the loan, the securities may be sold and the proceeds used to liquidate the loan. Therefore, the interest rate charged is lower. Or if an individual borrows from a financial institution in which he or she has a savings account, pledging it as security may lower the interest rate.

Establishing credit   Lenders' willingness to extend credit is based on their appraisal of the potential borrower's credit-worthiness; that is, how much of a credit risk is he or she? This in turn is based on their appraisal of the ability to

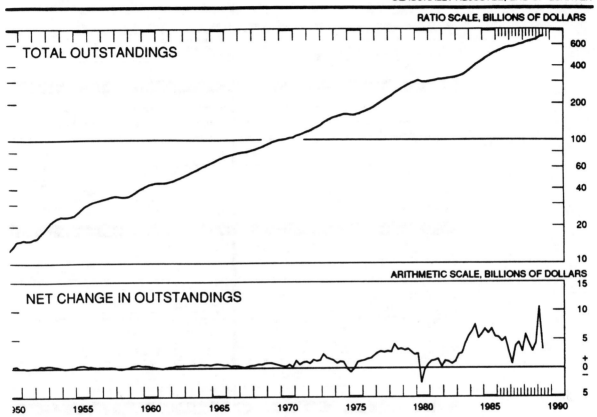

CONSUMER INSTALLMENT CREDIT
TOTAL
SEASONALLY ADJUSTED, END OF QUARTER

Consumer installment credit: Total. Seasonally adjusted, quarterly averages. (Source: 1989 Historical Chart Book, Board of Governors of the Federal Reserve System, p. 65.)

Figure 5–3

repay; and the past credit repayment is one of the factors lenders take into account. However, the following other factors are considered as well: income, savings, and other debts if any, and net worth of the borrower.

The credit (or loan) application

Whether one is going to open a charge account or apply for any other type of installment loan, one must make an application for credit. The credit application is a request for information concerning place of employment, address, size of income, bank account, assets and liabilities, and whether or not one has ever had credit (see Figure 5–4). From this information, the credit investigation is made.

The credit bureau's report

After one has applied for credit, the information is generally forwarded to a local credit bureau for verification. Every credit bureau maintains rec-

UNIVERSITY FEDERAL CREDIT UNION

P.O. Box 4069
4611 Guadalupe
Austin, Texas 78765
(512) 467-8080

Medical Branch
428 Postoffice Street
Galveston, Texas 77550
(409) 765-9999

NOTICE: Married applicants may apply for a separate account. Check the box indicating the type of credit you are applying for:
☐ **Individual Credit:** 1) Complete applicant section if you are relying only on your own income and assets to establish credit. 2) Complete other applicant section providing information about your spouse or former spouse if you reside in a community property state (AZ, CA, ID, LA, NM, TX, WA, WI) or if you are relying on alimony, child support or separate maintenance payments to establish credit.
☐ **Joint Credit:** 1) Complete applicant and co-applicant section providing information about you and the other party.

Amount Requested $	Purpose and Collateral

Applicant	■ **Co-Applicant** ■ **Spouse** ■ **Guarantor**

Name	Name
Account Number / Drivers License Number / Social Security Number	Account Number / Drivers License Number / Social Security Number
Birth Date / Home Phone ( ) / Business Phone ( )	Birth Date / Home Phone ( ) / Business Phone ( )
Present Address (Street, City, State, Zip) / Years at this address / ☐ Own ☐ Rent	Present Address (Street, City, State, Zip) / Years at this address / ☐ Own ☐ Rent
Previous address (Street, City, State, Zip) (if at present address less than 5 years) / Years at this address / ☐ Own ☐ Rent	Previous address (Street, City, State, Zip) (if at present address less than 5 years) / Years at this address / ☐ Own ☐ Rent
Complete for joint credit, secured credit or if you live in a community property state: ☐ Married ☐ Separated ☐ Unmarried (Single, Divorced, Widowed)	Complete for joint credit, secured credit or if you live in a community property state: ☐ Married ☐ Separated ☐ Unmarried (Single, Divorced, Widowed)
Number of Dependents other than listed by Co-Applicant (exclude self) / Ages	Number of Dependents other than listed by Applicant (exclude self) / Ages

Employment and Income Information	**Employment and Income Information**
Name and address of employer	Name and address of employer
Position / Supervisor	Position / Supervisor
Starting Date / Self Employed ☐ Yes ☐No / Type of Business	Starting Date / Self Employed ☐ Yes ☐No / Type of Business
Military: Is duty station transfer expected during next year? ☐ Yes ☐ No / Where	Military: Is duty station transfer expected during next year? ☐ Yes ☐ No / Where
NOTICE: Alimony, child support, or separate maintenance income need not be revealed if you do not choose to have it considered.	NOTICE: Alimony, child support, or separate maintenance income need not be revealed if you do not choose to have it considered.
Employment income ☐ Gross ☐ Net $ per / Other income $ per / Source	Employment income ☐ Gross ☐ Net $ per / Other income $ per / Source
If employed in current position less than five years, complete the following:	If employed in current position less than five years, complete the following:
Previous employer name & address / Starting date / Ending date	Previous employer name & address / Starting date / Ending date
Position / Supervisor	Position / Supervisor

These Questions Apply to Both Applicant & Co-Applicant									
If a "Yes" answer is given to a question, explain on an attached sheet	Applicant Yes	No	Co-Applicant Yes	No	If a "Yes" answer is given to a question, explain on an Attached Sheet	Applicant Yes	No	Co-Applicant Yes	No
Have you any outstanding judgments?					Is your income likely to reduce in the next two years?				
In the last 10 years, have you been declared bankrupt or filed a petition for Chapter 13?					Are you a co-maker or co-signer on any loan?				
Have you had property foreclosed upon or given title or deed in lieu thereof, in the last 7 years?					For whom (name of others obligated on loan):				
Are you a party in a law suit?					To whom (name of creditor):				
Are you other than a U.S. Citizen or Permanent Resident alien?									

References		**References**	
Name & address of nearest relative not living with you	Relationship / Home phone	Name & address of nearest relative not living with you	Relationship / Home phone
Name & address of personal friend—not a relative	Home phone	Name & address of personal friend—not a relative	Home phone

Continued on Reverse Side

Figure 5—4   *Loan application*

ords containing information on many individuals, much of it obtained from the office of the clerk of the county in which one lives. For example, the fact that any judgments have been recorded against one is entered in the record. In addition, home ownership and all existing mortgages and recorded bills of sale are included.

Assets

A-Applicant C-Co-Applicant		Name of Depository	Address	Balance
□A □C	Checking Account(s)			
□A □C	Savings Account(s)			
□A □C	Certificate(s) of Deposit			
□A □C	IRA			
□A □C	Annuities			
□A □C	Stocks/ Bonds			
□A □C	Life Insurance			
□A □C	Other			
□A □C	Other			
□A □C	Other			
□A □C	Other			
□A □C	Auto(s) Owned	Make	Model	Year

Outstanding Debts
(List everything-attach other sheets if necessary.)

A-Applicant C-Co-Applicant		Creditor Name & Address	Account Number	Present Balance	Monthly Payment	Number of Months Past Due
□A □C	Rent					
□A □C	Home Mortgage	Market Value $				
□A □C	Second Mortgage					
□A □C	Real Estate Other Than Home					
□A □C	Auto Loan	Make Year				
□A □C	Auto Loan	Make Year				
□A □C	UFCU					
□A □C	Other Credit Union					
□A □C	Finance Company					
□A □C	Credit Card					
□A □C	Credit Card					
□A □C	Credit Card					
□A □C	Credit Card					
□A □C	Alimony					
□A □C	Other					
□A □C	Other					
□A □C	Other					
□A □C	Other					

List any names under which credit has previously been received — **Totals**

I (we) certify that all information contained in this application is correct to the best of my (our) knowledge and I (we) have disclosed all outstanding obligations currently owed. I (we) agree to give the Credit Union authorization to check on my (our) credit; employment history; obtain a credit report; and to answer questions about our credit experience with you. I (we) understand that it may be a federal crime punishable by fine or imprisonment (or both) to knowingly make any false statements concerning any of the above facts as applicable under the provisions of the United States Criminal Code.

Applicant's Signature	Date	Co-Applicant's Signature	Date
X	Seal	X	Seal

Do Not Write Below—For Credit Union Use Only
Credit Committee/Loan Officer Action

Loan Officer: Date

Secured	Unsecured	Line of Credit	Overdraft Protection
$	$	$	$

☐ I approve the advance as submitted.
☐ Advance referred to CC.
☐ Advance rejected (where permissible.)
☐ Counter-offer will be made, if accepted advance approved.

Reason loan referred to Credit Committee   Loan Officer Signature

Credit Committee: Date   Describe Counter-Offer

☐ We approve the advance as submitted.
☐ We reject the advance as submitted.
☐ Counter-offer will be made, if accepted advance approved.

Specific reason(s) for rejection

Outside information considered   ☐ Yes   ☐ No   Describe

Signature	Date	Signature	Date	Signature	Date

☐ ECOA Notice and Reason for Rejection set or delivered on   Date   Signature

Credit bureaus also keep records of all previous credit extended, going back generally seven years. Credit bureaus are the "middle men;" they receive information from all merchants and institutions that extend credit, store it, and then sell it to any legitimate third party. A legitimate third party is anyone entering into a business transaction involving credit with the person on whom a credit report is requested. If the person requesting credit has established credit elsewhere locally, generally a phone call to the credit bureau is all that is necessary. The bureau will give the merchant the necessary information over the phone, and the fee for this service is only a few dollars. If the person requesting credit is newly arrived in town, it may be necessary for the credit bureau to telephone a bureau in some other town. In such cases, the cost of a credit report can grow quickly.

When a credit bureau receives a request from a merchant or lending institution, it will pass on what information it has gathered; but the bureau usually will not assign a credit rating such as poor, fair, good, or excellent. Generally, the information the credit bureau will pass on includes the following:

1. The person's place of employment
2. Length of time with employer
3. Position with the firm
4. Income
5. Husband or wife's income, if any
6. All credit extended over the past seven years and the date it was extended
7. The dollar amount of the extension
8. How the loan was paid off (whether in accordance with the agreement)
9. What kind of security, if any, was required on past loans
10. Whether the person rents or owns his or her own home
11. Judgments, if any, recorded against the person
12. Bankruptcies, if any, that the person has filed

In the case of a young person requesting credit for the first time, no record exists and the credit bureau cannot help as much. The merchant must make a decision based on the person's place of employment, position, income, bank accounts, and any other information the merchant can obtain. Generally, if the person has a responsible position and is not asking for more credit than his or her income warrants, it will be granted. Then a person begins to build a "track record;" if he or she repays credit in accordance with the agreement, these regular payments will be reported by the merchant and recorded by the credit bureau.

Generally, a credit investigation is made only the first time one applies for credit. Once one has used credit one will have established what is known as a "line of credit." The lending institution and merchants keep their own records and will extend credit up to a maximum amount almost routinely. In such cases, one may still have to fill out an application form but will not have to wait for a credit investigation.

Why consumers borrow

Consumers borrow or use consumer credit for different reasons, just as savers save for different reasons. One individual may save to pay her son's tuition, while another may have to borrow to pay the tuition; some people pay cash while on vacation, others use credit cards.

1. *High cost of durables.* A main reason for the use of consumer credit is the high unit cost of durable consumer goods. A ***consumer durable*** is a good having a relatively long life, such as a television set, a household appliance, or an automobile. Of the $700 billion consumer debt in 1990, over one-third resulted from the extension of automobile credit. The cheapest and possibly the best way to buy this type of durable good would, of course, be to save and pay cash. But to save, one must abstain from present consumption. Many consumers find this to be difficult. Suppose, for example, we planned to save to buy an auto priced at $14,000; we would have to defer the use of the car and put aside, say, $2,800 per year for five years before we would be able to buy the car. For most people, saving $2,800 per year for five years for the purpose of buying a car is a formidable task. So when it comes to high unit cost durable goods, most people buy on time. The product may be used immediately instead of being deferred until a future date and perhaps not being obtained at all. For this current use, many people are willing to pay interest.

2. *Financial emergencies.* Unfortunately, many people frequently are forced to borrow because of unforeseen emergencies. Unusually high medical and dental bills not completely covered by insurance are examples. Noninsured flood damage to a home is another. There are dozens of types of emergencies and other reasons for which consumer loans may be necessary.

3. *Financing vacations.* Many people finance their vacations with consumer credit. Not only do they make extensive use of credit cards while on their trips, but often they borrow money at a financial institution to spend at their destination and to finance their transportation costs.

There are some benefits but also some possible dangers stemming from the use of consumer credit.

Benefits and dangers of consumer credit

1. *Obtaining goods more quickly.* As noted above, consumer credit will enable the borrowers to consume certain items more quickly than otherwise would be possible. If a person goes into debt to buy an automobile, he or she is then forced to save out of future income to repay the loan. Without consumer credit the person may end up with neither savings nor the car. With consumer credit he or she at least has the car.

2. *Benefits to society.* Society as a whole may benefit from consumer credit provided that those granting it do not overdo it. Credit extension may lead to increased demand and hence increased production

of goods and services, and help to maintain full employment. The extension of consumer credit can lead to a lower unit cost of goods. For example, as a result of increased effective demand created by the extension of credit, certain firms are led to large-scale production. Up to a point, large-scale production brings about certain efficiencies that result in lower costs; and in a competitive economy these savings are frequently passed on to the consumer.

3.   *Higher cost.* One argument against extension of consumer credit is that the resultant interest costs actually reduce the amount of consumer goods persons might have purchased had they saved the money in the first place. As has been previously pointed out, however, it may be that the cost of borrowing is offset because credit extension increases sales and consequently has a tendency to lower unit costs as a result of mass production. This depends to some extent on the amount of competition involving a particular product, and on whether any cost savings are actually passed on to the consumer in the form of lower prices.

4.   *Getting in over one's head.* When an individual borrows money, he or she takes on an obligation of making a fixed payment on a time schedule. This payment is interest and repayment of the principal. Such a fixed payment comes off the top of the budget before the remainder of the individual's income is allocated among alternative wants. How large a fixed payment an individual can accept is determined largely by his or her income. But if credit is easy to obtain and a person lacks discipline, it is possible that he or she will have so many debts that it becomes impossible to meet the fixed monthly payments because they take too large a portion of income. Those who miss a payment or two may have their car or furniture repossessed. Worse still, they may be forced into bankruptcy. This is not really a danger of consumer credit, but rather a danger that comes from *abusing* consumer credit. It is the unwise and excessive use of consumer credit that gets people in over their heads. Frequently, this may be just as much the lender's fault as the borrower's. Consumer credit should not be feared, but it should be used when needed, after careful planning, and when one can take on the additional fixed payment required.

INTEREST RATES

It is often less costly for consumers to purchase those items of merchandise they need for cash; however, for most people, installment purchases or cash borrowing are often the alternatives. The financial planner should be aware of the costs associated with borrowing to help clients minimize expenses consistent with their goals.

Interest rate calculations

One of the fundamental problems of borrowing is to determine just how much interest is being charged. The borrower should be able to answer the question: What is the effective rate of interest that I must pay? or What is the real cost in percentage of interest charged?

Although the mathematics of obtaining a precise answer to "How much interest am I paying?" is complex, there is a formula that will provide the approximate answer. The formula is:

$$R = \frac{2 \times m \times I}{P(n + 1)} \text{ or, transposed, } I = \frac{R \times P(n + 1)}{2 \times m}$$

In the above formula:

R = annual interest rate in decimal form
I = dollar cost of the credit
m = the number of payment periods in a year
(twelve if paying monthly and fifty-two if weekly)
n = the number of payments scheduled in total
P = the net amount of credit or principal advanced

At this point it is useful to distinguish between simple interest, discounted interest, add-on interest, and annual percentage rate.

In the case of **simple interest,** interest is charged only on the actual loan balance outstanding. If a person borrows $1,000 for one year at 12 percent to be paid back in one lump sum, the interest would be $120. The interest rate is:

Simple interest

$$\frac{\$120}{\$1,000} = 12 \text{ percent.}$$

Discounted interest is paid in advance; it is deducted from the principal or amount borrowed. For example, if a person borrowed $1,000 for one year discounted at 12 percent to be paid back in one lump sum, he or she would receive $880 of borrowed funds. One year later, the individual would repay $1,000; of this $120 would be interest. Hence the true rate is:

Discounted interest

$$\frac{\$120}{\$880} = 13.6 \text{ percent.}$$

Discounting results in a higher interest rate than does simple interest.

Add-on interest is applied to the original balance owed even though on an installment loan the balance owed declines as the months pass and payments are made. For example, if a $1,000 loan at 12 percent is to be repaid in twelve equal monthly installments over a year, it is referred to as a 12 percent add-on loan. The so-called add-on interest must be converted to simple interest, a better measure of the true interest burden. The above-mentioned formula will approximate this conversion.

Add-on interest

The annual percentage rate (APR), which is the actual true actuarial interest rate, is the best (and real) measure of the interest rate. The above formula will convert the discounted interest rate and the add-on rate to the simple interest rate, which is an approximation of the annual per-

Annual percentage rate (APR)

centage rate. The formula will do this whether the loan is discounted or not and whether it is an installment loan or a single repayment loan.

The formula to calculate the annual percentage rate of interest precisely is very complex. However, there are tables that will permit you to convert the add-on rate to the APR as we shall see below.

Some examples

Suppose that Ms. Stein borrows $1,000 at 12 percent, and must pay back $1,120 in twelve equal monthly installments of $93.33. The total cost is $120, but what is the interest rate? Substituting the figures into the formulas above:

$$I = \$120$$
$$m = 12$$
$$n = 12$$
$$P = \$1,000$$

$$R = \frac{2 \times 12 \times \$120}{\$1000 \ (12 + 1)} = \frac{2880}{13,000} = 22.15 \text{ percent}$$

As noted above, the formula only approximates the true annual percentage rate (APR).

A loan can be both discounted and repaid in installments; but the above formulas will still approximate the APR if you use the net amount of the principal advanced. If the above $1,000 installment loan had also been discounted at 12 percent, the formula would use:

$$I = \$120$$
$$m = 12$$
$$n = 12$$
$$P = \$880$$

and the result is:

$$R = \frac{2 \times m \times I}{P(n+1)} = \frac{2 \times 12 \times 120}{880 \times (12+1)} = \frac{2880}{11440} = 25.17 \text{ percent}$$

The reason why the true interest rate (APR) is so much higher than the add-on rate is because when repaying a loan on an installment basis, the add-on interest applies to (and must be paid) on the original balance throughout the entire period of the loan. When loans are repaid on the installment basis, the amount of money actually owed declines with each repayment. To calculate the true interest rate, one must take into account this declining balance; otherwise the borrower is paying interest on money even after he or she has already repaid it. The formulas discussed above do this, but to understand the logic of how interest rates work a person must think in terms of the declining balance. An illustration will make this clear.

When an individual borrows money that is repaid on an installment basis, there are three balances: an original balance, a declining balance, and an average balance. We can illustrate this system with another method of calculating the true interest rate. Remember, however, that this second method of calculating the interest rate is somewhat cruder and hence a little less accurate than the formula explained above.

Let us assume that the individual borrows $1,200 from a bank to purchase a used automobile and agrees to repay it in twelve equal monthly installments of $110. A total of $1,320 will be paid back; $120 of that total is interest (the *I* in the formula above). This at first glance appears to be 10 percent, and insofar as add-on interest is concerned, it is. However, while the original balance owed is $1,200, after one month the first payment is made and the loan balance now due (the declining balance) is $1,100; a month later another $100 is paid on the principal and the balance now owed is $1,000; and so on. The balance owed declines each month, as shown in Table 5-2.

At the end of six months, $600 has been repaid and only $600 is now owed; the borrower is still paying 10 percent interest on the full $1,200. To calculate and pay interest monthly, take 10 percent of the declining balance and divide it by twelve to get the true interest cost at 10 percent. But to approximate the rate actually being paid, average the balance over the year (the first and last month's balance divided by two, or $650) and calculate the interest rate on it. Since interest charges are $120 and the amount really borrowed is only $650, the interest rate is 18.46 percent.

Let us take another case, in which $1,800 is borrowed at 10 percent add-on, to be repaid in eighteen equal monthly installments. Ten percent of $1,800 is $180 per year, but since the loan is for a year and a half, an additional interest payment of $90 is called for. The total interest cost, dollarwise, is $270. An average balance could be calculated for the first year and again for the next six months to get the true interest rate, but the formula introduced above provides us with an easier way.

Table 5—2   *Estimating interest costs*

Original balance: The amount originally borrowed	Month	Balance	Average balance: The amount of money you actually have on the average for the full year
$1200	1	$1,200	
	2	1,100	
	3	1,000	
	4	900	
	5	800	$650
	6	700	
	7	600	
	8	500	
	9	400	
	10	300	
	11	200	
	12	100	

$$I = \$270$$
$$m = 12$$
$$n = 18$$
$$P = \$1800$$

Thus:

$$\frac{24 \times 270}{1800 \times 19} = \frac{6480}{34200} = 18.95 \text{ percent}$$

In the past, lenders and merchants offering installment contracts found all kinds of devious ways of disguising the true interest rates. Often they would merely say, "so much down and so much per month," and the true interest cost (the I in the formula) or the net amount of credit advanced (the P in the formula) could not always be ascertained. If asked what the interest rate amounted to, lenders would often become evasive and sometimes even tell outright lies. In many cases, the borrower paid 12, 30, or 42 percent or even more without knowing it. All of this changed with the passage of the federal truth-in-lending law in 1968 (the Consumer Credit Protection Act). This law does not limit the rate that may be charged; it merely requires that the lender tell the borrowers what they are paying, both dollarwise and as a percentage of the loan. (A number of different agencies enforce truth in lending. See Chapter 6 for a complete list.) Lenders and merchants who extend credit do not work through the formulas presented above to determine the interest rates they charge. Rather they use tables that have been worked out in advance to tell the buyer the dollar amount of the finance charge and the annual percentage rate (APR) of these charges. Table 5—3 is such a table that can be used to obtain the true (APR) interest cost of any add-on rate. The various add-on rates are shown in the first column; to the right are shown the true rates for the various installment loans repaid monthly. For example, a 10 percent add-on rate is really 14.94 percent if paid back in three installments; 17.97 percent if paid back in twelve; and 17.92 percent if repaid in thirty-six.

Interest rates on consumer loans and credit cards

State laws set the maximum rate that may be charged on consumer credit transactions, hence there is variation from state to state. Some states have a number of different laws covering specific lending institutions, while others have just one or two to regulate all consumer lending. The laws also allow for different rates on different items. For example, rates on auto loans generally run from 12 to 18 percent, depending on whether a new or used car is being financed. Conversely, on very small loans for short periods of time, some states allow rates in excess of 100 percent on an annual basis. To illustrate this, consider borrowing $100 for thirty days with a fixed minimum interest charge of $10. This represents a monthly charge of 10 percent, which annualizes to 120 percent.

Credit card charges also vary somewhat depending on the issuing institution and the applicable state usury laws (which set the maximum allowable rate). Generally, interest rates on bank credit cards, such as Visa and MasterCard, run up to 1.5 percent per month.

The interest charge is assessed to any unpaid balance in the customer's account. For instance, if a credit card was used to pay for a $600 stereo but the borrower was only able to pay $200 when the bill came, a charge of $6 (i.e., [$600 − $200 × .015]) would be added to the next monthly statement. However, the interest cost could be higher than it is in the above example. Although some merchants still charge only on the unpaid balance at the end of the month, more and more of them are assessing interest on the average daily balance from billing date to billing date. For example, suppose an individual is billed $200 on his or her credit card but forgets to pay for twenty days. If he or she then makes another $100 credit purchase on the same day that the last month's statement is finally paid, then the unpaid balance at the end of the current month would be $100. However, to calculate the average daily balance, the bank would multiply $100 by ten days and $200 by twenty days. These figures are added together ($5,000) and divided by thirty, which gives us the average daily balance of $166.67, on which interest is calculated. Many credit cards are now calculating their interest rates on some version of this average daily balance method. Credit cards are discussed more fully below, under "Sources of Consumer Credit."

Interest rates on all consumer loans are usually higher than on business or mortgage loans. One reason for this is that consumer loans are smaller and the cost of making them is higher per dollar lent. The second reason for higher rates on consumer loans is that most individuals represent riskier customers than established corporations or merchants.

Table 5—3   *Actuarial equivalents of add-on rates. The annual add-on rate is shown as the left hand index. If this rate is applied to the original amount for the full term and the loan is repaid monthly, then the body of the table shows the actuarial rate of return on the money actually outstanding.*

Add-on rate per year	Term months							
	3 mo.	6 mo.	9 mo.	12 mo.	15 mo.	18 mo.	24 mo.	30 mo.
1.00	1.50	1.71	1.80	1.84	1.87	1.89	1.91	1.92
2.00	3.00	3.42	3.59	3.67	3.72	3.76	3.79	3.81
3.00	4.49	5.12	5.37	5.49	5.56	5.61	5.66	5.68
3.50	5.24	5.98	6.26	6.40	6.48	6.53	6.58	6.60
4.00	5.99	6.82	7.14	7.30	7.39	7.45	7.50	7.52
4.25	6.36	7.25	7.59	7.75	7.85	7.91	7.96	7.97
4.50	6.74	7.67	8.03	8.21	8.30	8.36	8.41	8.42
4.75	7.11	8.10	8.47	8.66	8.76	8.82	8.87	8.88
5.00	7.48	8.52	8.91	9.10	9.21	9.27	9.32	9.33
5.25	7.86	8.94	9.36	9.55	9.66	9.73	9.78	9.78
5.50	8.23	9.37	9.79	10.00	10.11	10.18	10.23	10.23
5.75	8.60	9.79	10.23	10.45	10.57	10.63	10.68	10.67
6.00	8.98	10.21	10.67	10.90	11.02	11.08	11.13	11.12
6.25	9.35	10.64	11.11	11.34	11.45	11.53	11.57	11.56
6.50	9.72	11.06	11.55	11.79	11.91	11.98	12.02	12.00
6.75	10.10	11.48	11.99	12.23	12.36	12.43	12.47	12.44
7.00	10.47	11.90	12.43	12.68	12.81	12.87	12.91	12.88
7.25	10.84	12.32	12.87	13.12	13.25	13.32	13.35	13.32
7.50	11.22	12.74	13.30	13.57	13.70	13.77	13.80	13.76
7.75	11.59	13.17	13.74	14.01	14.14	14.21	14.24	14.19
8.00	11.96	13.59	14.18	14.45	14.59	14.65	14.68	14.63
8.25	12.33	14.01	14.61	14.89	15.03	15.10	15.12	15.06
8.50	12.71	14.43	15.05	15.34	15.48	15.54	15.55	15.49
8.75	13.08	14.85	15.49	15.78	15.92	15.98	15.99	15.92
9.00	13.45	15.27	15.92	16.22	16.36	16.42	16.43	16.35
9.25	13.82	15.69	16.35	16.66	16.80	16.86	16.86	16.78
9.50	14.19	16.11	16.79	17.10	17.24	17.30	17.29	17.21
9.75	14.57	16.53	17.22	17.53	17.68	17.74	17.73	17.63
→10.00	14.94	16.94	17.66	17.97	18.12	18.17	18.16	18.06
10.25	15.31	17.36	18.09	18.41	18.56	18.61	18.59	18.48
10.50	15.68	17.78	18.52	18.85	18.99	19.05	19.02	18.90
10.75	16.05	18.20	18.95	19.28	19.43	19.48	19.44	19.32
11.00	16.43	18.62	19.39	19.72	19.36	19.91	19.87	19.74
11.25	16.80	19.04	19.82	20.15	20.30	20.35	20.30	20.16
11.50	17.17	19.45	20.25	20.59	20.73	20.78	20.72	20.57
11.75	17.54	19.87	20.68	21.02	21.17	21.21	21.15	20.99
12.00	17.91	20.29	21.11	21.46	21.60	21.64	21.57	21.41
12.25	18.28	20.70	21.54	21.89	22.03	22.07	21.99	21.82
12.50	18.65	21.12	21.97	22.32	22.47	22.50	22.42	22.23
12.75	19.03	21.54	22.40	22.76	22.90	22.93	22.84	22.64
13.00	19.40	21.95	22.83	23.19	23.33	23.36	23.26	23.05
13.50	20.14	22.79	23.68	24.05	24.19	24.21	24.09	23.87
14.00	20.88	23.62	24.54	24.91	25.04	25.06	24.92	24.68
14.50	21.62	24.45	25.39	25.77	25.90	25.91	25.75	25.49
15.00	22.36	25.28	26.24	26.62	26.75	26.75	26.58	26.30
15.50	23.10	26.10	27.09	27.48	27.60	27.60	27.40	27.10
16.00	23.84	26.93	27.94	28.33	28.45	28.43	28.22	27.89
16.50	24.58	27.76	28.79	29.18	29.29	29.27	29.03	28.69
17.00	25.32	28.58	29.64	30.03	30.14	30.10	29.85	29.48
18.00	26.80	30.23	31.32	31.72	31.81	31.76	31.46	31.04
19.00	28.28	31.88	33.01	33.40	33.48	33.41	33.06	32.60
20.00	29.76	33.52	34.68	35.07	35.14	35.05	34.65	34.14

Term-months

36 mo.	42 mo.	48 mo.	54 mo.	60 mo.	72 mo.	84 mo.	96 mo.	108 mo.	120 mo.
1.93	1.93	1.93	1.94	1.94	1.94	1.93	1.93	1.93	1.92
3.82	3.82	3.82	3.82	3.82	3.80	3.79	3.77	3.75	3.74
5.68	5.68	5.67	5.66	5.64	5.61	5.57	5.54	5.50	5.46
6.60	6.59	6.58	6.56	6.54	6.49	6.44	6.39	6.34	6.29
7.51	7.50	7.47	7.45	7.42	7.36	7.30	7.23	7.17	7.11
7.96	7.94	7.92	7.89	7.86	7.79	7.72	7.65	7.58	7.51
8.41	8.39	8.36	8.33	8.29	8.22	8.14	8.06	7.98	7.91
8.86	8.84	8.80	8.77	8.72	8.64	8.55	8.47	8.38	8.30
9.31	9.28	9.24	9.20	9.15	9.06	8.97	8.87	8.78	8.69
9.76	9.72	9.68	9.63	9.58	9.48	9.37	9.27	9.17	9.08
10.20	10.16	10.11	10.06	10.01	9.89	9.78	9.67	9.56	9.46
10.64	10.60	10.54	10.49	10.43	10.31	10.18	10.06	9.95	9.84
11.08	11.03	10.97	10.91	10.85	10.72	10.58	10.46	10.33	10.21
11.52	11.47	11.40	11.34	11.27	11.12	10.98	10.85	10.71	10.59
11.96	11.90	11.83	11.76	11.68	11.53	11.38	11.23	11.09	10.96
12.39	12.33	12.25	12.17	12.09	11.93	11.77	11.61	11.47	11.32
12.83	12.76	12.68	12.59	12.50	12.33	12.16	11.99	11.84	11.69
13.26	13.18	13.10	13.01	12.91	12.73	12.55	12.37	12.21	12.05
13.69	13.61	13.51	13.42	13.32	13.12	12.93	12.75	12.57	12.41
14.12	14.03	13.93	13.83	13.72	13.52	13.31	13.12	12.94	12.76
14.55	14.45	14.35	14.24	14.13	13.91	13.69	13.49	13.30	13.12
14.97	14.87	14.76	14.64	14.53	14.29	14.07	13.86	13.66	13.47
15.40	15.29	15.17	15.05	14.92	14.68	14.45	14.23	14.02	13.82
15.82	15.70	15.58	15.45	15.32	15.07	14.82	14.59	14.37	14.16
16.24	16.12	15.99	15.85	15.71	15.45	15.19	14.95	14.72	14.51
16.66	16.53	16.39	16.25	16.11	15.83	15.56	15.31	15.07	14.85
17.08	16.94	16.80	16.65	16.50	16.21	15.93	15.67	15.42	15.19
17.50	17.35	17.20	17.04	16.89	16.58	16.29	16.02	15.77	15.53
17.92	17.76	17.60	17.44	17.27	16.96	16.66	16.38	16.11	15.86
18.33	18.17	18.00	17.83	17.66	17.33	17.02	16.73	16.45	16.20
18.75	18.58	18.40	18.22	18.04	17.70	17.38	17.08	16.79	16.53
19.16	18.98	18.79	18.61	18.42	18.07	17.74	17.42	17.13	16.86
19.57	19.38	19.19	19.00	18.80	18.44	18.09	17.77	17.47	17.19
19.98	19.78	19.58	19.38	19.18	18.80	18.45	18.11	17.80	17.52
20.39	20.18	19.97	19.77	19.56	19.17	18.80	18.46	18.14	17.84
20.79	20.58	20.36	20.15	19.94	19.53	19.15	18.80	18.47	18.17
21.20	20.98	20.75	20.53	20.31	19.89	19.50	19.13	18.80	18.49
21.60	21.37	21.14	20.91	20.68	20.25	19.85	19.47	19.13	18.81
22.01	21.77	21.53	21.29	21.05	20.61	20.19	19.81	19.45	19.13
22.41	22.16	21.91	21.66	21.42	20.96	20.54	20.14	19.78	19.44
22.81	22.55	22.30	22.04	21.79	21.32	20.88	20.47	20.10	19.76
23.61	23.33	23.06	22.79	22.52	22.02	21.56	21.14	20.75	20.39
24.40	24.11	23.82	23.53	23.25	22.72	22.24	21.79	21.38	21.01
25.19	24.88	24.57	24.26	23.97	23.41	22.91	22.44	22.02	21.63
25.98	25.64	25.32	24.99	24.68	24.10	23.57	23.09	22.64	22.24
26.76	26.41	26.06	25.72	25.39	24.79	24.23	23.73	23.27	22.85
27.53	27.16	26.80	26.44	26.10	25.46	24.88	24.36	23.88	23.45
28.30	27.91	27.53	27.16	26.80	26.14	25.54	24.99	24.50	24.05
29.07	28.66	28.26	27.87	27.50	26.81	26.18	25.62	25.11	24.65
30.59	30.14	29.70	29.28	28.88	28.13	27.46	26.86	26.31	25.82
32.10	31.61	31.13	30.67	30.24	29.44	28.72	28.08	27.51	26.99
33.60	33.06	32.54	32.05	31.58	30.73	29.97	29.29	28.69	28.14

SOURCES OF CONSUMER CREDIT

Consumer credit is made available by a number of financial institutions either directly or indirectly—directly when the borrower goes to an institution and borrows money and indirectly when he or she goes to a merchant and buys something on the installment plan.

Merchants

If an individual goes to a merchant and buys a car or some household furniture, all he or she need do is sign the papers. The merchant arranges the financing because he or she has an agreement with some financial institution. Sometimes the latter happens without the consumer's knowledge until after it takes place. For example, the consumer signs papers promising to pay so much per month for so many months. Then, the merchant takes this paper to a financial institution, turns it over to the institution, and gets his or her money. This is called "selling the paper" or, more properly, discounting it. The institution gets the interest as the monthly payments are made, and the borrower is told to make the monthly payments to the institution.

Financial institutions may also be extending credit indirectly when a consumer uses his or her credit card. This is because some banks issue credit cards, and also because merchants who have issued credit cards (e.g., Sears or a gasoline company) must borrow more money at a bank to carry the user until he or she pays the bills on the card.

Financial institutions

There are a number of financial institutions that deal with consumer credit in the form of cash. The major ones are:

1. Commercial banks
2. Savings and loan associations
3. Mutual savings banks
4. Credit unions
5. Life insurance companies
6. Small loan companies
7. Pawnshops

Commercial banks, savings and loan associations, and mutual savings banks are similar in their consumer lending activities. They all make installment and single repayment loans. Rates will vary depending on the borrower's credit rating, the amount borrowed, whether the loan is secured, and whether it is on an installment or single-payment basis. The interest rates charged by these institutions are a bit lower than those charged by some other lenders because they screen the borrower more carefully and make loans to people with better credit ratings. Rates generally run from 12 to 15 percent.

Credit unions are voluntary associations whose members have a common bond, usually that of a common employer. They will accept deposits and make consumer loans only to their members. Traditionally, credit unions paid a bit more on deposits and charged a bit less on loans than even banks and savings and loan associations (S&Ls). To some extent this is still true, but not to the extent that it was a few years ago. Their rates, however, are competitive with banks and S&Ls.

Life insurance companies make loans to their policyholders if the policy has a cash surrender value (see Chapter 10). Life insurance policy loans need never be repaid. If the policy owner were to die, the loan would be deducted from the face value, which would then be paid to the beneficiaries. Interest rates charged by life insurance companies are usually the lowest available anywhere—generally from 5 to 8 percent, although some insurance companies do charge variable rates based on current money market rates.

The small loan company, also known as the consumer finance company or personal finance company, is a firm specializing in loans to consumers. Interest rates charged by finance companies are generally a bit higher than those charged by banks and S&Ls because their loans are often smaller, and they lend to poorer credit risks. These companies make loans for almost any conceivable purpose, but personal loans and automobile loans constitute the bulk of their business. Pawnshop operators accept personal property that is pledged as collateral for the loan. The loans are never for more than 40 to 50 percent of the value of the property. The borrower receives a pawn ticket and has a certain period of time in which to repay the loan and redeem his property. If he or she doesn't do so, the pawnbroker may sell the article. The interest rate charged generally runs from 25 to 42 percent per year.

Credit cards

No discussion of consumer credit is complete without comments about credit cards. Traditionally, the credit card permitted consumers to obtain merchandise without paying and at the end of the month one bill was sent for all purchases. Credit was extended for a few weeks at most. Now, however, most credit cards are using what is referred to as a rotating or revolving charge account, where the buyer is still permitted to liquidate the bill monthly but need not do this. Those who choose not to do so move into an automatic monthly payment plan. While these plans vary somewhat, they all are similar. They require a minimum monthly payment (usually $10 or 10 percent of the total amount due). They also have a maximum amount (usually $500 to $3,000) beyond which credit will not be extended unless special arrangements are made. Under these rotating charge accounts consumers need never liquidate their total bill. The only requirement is that they make the minimum monthly payment and do not exceed the maximum. In the case of gasoline credit cards, however, most companies exclude gasoline from the credit that need not be liquidated monthly. They permit only items such as tires, batteries, and so forth to be financed on a rotating basis.

Table 5—4   *Sources of consumer credit*

	Type of loan	Cost and lending policies
Commercial banks	Single payment Installment Secured Signature Passbook Home improvement	Lower interest than some Make lower risk loans Make larger loans
Savings and loan associations	Same as commercial banks	Same as commercial banks
Mutual savings banks	Same as commercial banks	Same as commercial banks
Credit unions	Single payment Installment Share draft secured Home improvement	Lower interest than most others Lend only to member Make lower risk loans
Life insurance companies	Single payment	Lowest interest Lend policyholders their own money Assume no risk
Finance companies	Installment Second mortgages Home improvement	Higher interest than some Assume more risk Make smaller loans

Some merchants still charge interest only on the unpaid balance. This has the effect that if you liquidate your charge in full every month when due, you never have any finance charges. But more and more of them are charging interest on the average daily balance from billing date to billing date; this results in charging interest on future purchases. For example, suppose an individual is billed $200 on his or her credit card and pay $100. If he or she makes no further purchases for, say, 10 days, the average daily balance for those 10 days is $100. If the individual now charges another $100, the average daily balance for the next 20 days is $200. To calculate the average daily balance, the bank would multiply $100 by 10 days and $200 by 20 days. These figures are added together ($5,000) and divided by 30, which gives us the average daily balance of $166.67, on which interest is calculated. Many credit cards are calculating their interest rates on some version of this average daily balance method. The rates they charge vary from state to state because of state usury laws. But rates from 14 to 21 percent are typical.

There are two major credit cards that have been developed by banks: Visa issued by the Bank of America and MasterCard by CitiBank of New York. Many financial institutions throughout the country have entered into an agreement with these two banks and provide these cards.

Until recently most of these institutions charged only interest, and not an annual fee. More recently, however, more and more have added an annual fee as well. Most of the institutions providing Visa or MasterCard calculate their interest charges on the average daily balance or some version of it. Interest rates typically run from up to 21 percent. In some states, however, usury ceilings prevent charges this high, and consequently some of the financial institutions issuing these cards have moved their credit card operations to Delaware or South Dakota, which have no interest ceilings.

With certain national credit cards such as American Express, the credit card holder pays an annual fee of about $45. The card holder is billed monthly and must liquidate the bill monthly except for bills for airline tickets, where a twelve-month payoff is permitted. If a twelve-month payoff is chosen, an additional 1 percent per month interest on the declining balance is added. If the bill is paid every month, American Express does not assess interest.

The national credit card firms receive about 5 or 6 percent of the amount collected from the merchant for whom they collect it. This is their service charge and should be looked upon as a cost of credit. This fee is included in the price of the final goods and services, and, to a slight extent, those who do not have these credit cards subsidize those of us who do.

At one time credit cards were sent to people on an unsolicited basis, but this is no longer so. Now persons who want a credit card not only must apply, but most qualify. The criterion used to determine whether a person qualifies is primarily income; however, nearly anyone who has an annual income of $12,000 or more can obtain a national credit card upon application, if he or she has a good credit record.

The selection of a credit card

All credit cards are not the same. Some charge higher interest rates than others, and in addition some have annual fees (and those fees vary) and some do not. However, some cards with no annual fees charge a higher interest rate; hence, give that some consideration. Some cards have a longer grace period (often up to 30 days) than others; if the bill is paid in full by then, interest is not charged.

Not all credit card companies calculate the balance to which the interest rate is applied the same way. Some use the average daily balance from billing date to billing date, some the previous unpaid balance, some the ending balance (balance at the billing date), and some have an interest-free grace period if bills are paid promptly.

State usury laws set the maximum interest rate that credit card companies may charge, and these charges vary. Consumers may save money by obtaining an out-of-state card. However, even within a state some cards have a lower rate than others.

There are still some cards around that have no annual fees, low interest rates (but 14 to 18 percent is about as low as one can expect), have a grace period in which bills that are paid on time have no interest charges whatsoever. There are fewer and fewer of these, however. But if the consumer shops around, he or she can minimize credit card expenses; indeed these expenses can be zero in some cases. It is important that the financial planner be aware of this in order to minimize his or her client's credit card expenses.

The checkless society: The debit card

Now that banks have developed national credit cards and they have been widely accepted, the next step will be to use the electronic computers of these banks to pay bills automatically. The result will be to do away with checks almost completely. This involves the use of what is known as the **debit card.**

With a debit card, when an individual makes a purchase, the card is put into a machine that is tied to the computers of the individual's bank and the merchant's bank. The computer will automatically transfer the amount out of the individual's bank account and into the merchant's bank account. The computer can do this immediately at the time of the purchase or at the end of the month in accordance with whatever arrangement is made. The computer, through the merchant's machine, will give the individual a receipt and a bank statement. He or she will get a bank statement each time a purchase is made rather than monthly. If the transfer of accounts is made at the end of the month rather than when purchases are made, the individual still gets a monthly statement rather than a statement with each purchase.

Automatic loans will be granted by the computer as needed, in accordance with predetermined maximums. The need for checks will virtually be over.

The debit card, however, is not popular as yet. While some people use debit cards, there is some concern over how a consumer could do the equivalent of stopping the payment of a check if purchased goods were defective. Other critics are concerned about electronic fraud. Someone might be able to manipulate the computer and steal almost limitless funds.

Electronic debit

Electronic debit is similar to the debit card, but with certain differences. With this method the bank automatically pays the customer's regular fixed monthly bills such as the mortgage, rent, or car loan payment. In order to do this, an authorization form must be completed and the computer does the rest. The customer's weekly or monthly paycheck may also be automatically deposited in the individual's bank by the employer.

OTHER THINGS A PERSON SHOULD KNOW ABOUT CONSUMER CREDIT

The preceding discussion has concentrated on the availability and direct costs of using consumer credit. However, there are several other related matters of which a consumer should be aware. The most important of these matters are considered below.

Sometimes the lender will insist that the installment buyer purchase life insurance in an amount equal to the debt. The lender is the beneficiary; and in the event of the death of the buyer, the balance of the debt is paid off by the insurance company. The cost of this life insurance is passed on to the installment buyer. In the case of lending institutions, this cost often shows up in the form of an extra 0.5 percent interest per month. In arrangements made with merchants, it either shows up as an added service charge or is included in the price of the item. In some cases, the lender actually keeps a portion of the insurance premiums; only part of them is necessary to buy insurance. This is another illustration of a price pack to enhance the return of the lender or dealer.

Credit life insurance

Not all lenders and dealers will insist that the buyer take the credit life insurance. In some states, it is against the law to require that the installment buyer buy credit life insurance. However, the buyer seldom knows this, and the law is very difficult to enforce. The lender can simply let it be known that the credit life insurance will have to be purchased as a condition to granting the loan.

It is possible to buy credit card insurance. This protects the consumer from fraudulent use of the card in case it is lost or stolen. However, this is not as necessary as it once was because now, by federal law, a cardholder's liability is limited to $50 per card even if it is not reported right away. Nevertheless, this insurance appeals to some people who have numerous cards. Once a card has been reported as lost or stolen, the consumer may not be held responsible for any fraudulent use. All credit card numbers should be recorded in a safe place, and loss of cards should be reported promptly.

Credit card insurance

Many financial planners believe that credit cards are most appropriately used as a convenience. Misuse or overuse of credit cards can lead to significant financial problems. In general, credit card balances should be paid in full each month. This is particularly true since consumer interest will no longer be tax deductible after 1990.

Credit card abuse

Why do interest rates on consumer loans vary from one institution to another? Aside from reasons involving legislative permissions enabling the various institutions to charge different rates for small loans, there are other considerations. Management expenses tend to vary greatly among the lending institutions. For a small loan company management expenses are fairly high, because many of their loans are small, and it costs just as much to manage a $200 or $300 loan as it does for a $2,000 or $3,000 loan. In addition, small loan companies make loans to people who are poorer credit risks. Because of this risk, they charge higher interest rates.

Why interest rates vary

Interest rates charged by credit unions are among the lowest. They are voluntary cooperatives, and as such they have eliminated the middleman. Members lend to members. Their philosophy is to give the depositor a fair return and charge the borrower a fair rate. Their record of losses is very low, and they are given a tax advantage over other lending institutions.

The insurance company suffers no risk of loss when making a policy loan, and its cost of collection is very low because these loans are similar to single-payment loans that will eventually be repaid.

Commercial banks generally make loans only to the better credit risks. Because of this circumstance, their loss record is low, a fact that their interest charges reflect. Savings and loan associations also accept only the better risks. Hence their rates are usually below those of finance companies and are comparable to those of commercial banks.

The maximum interest rate permitted on small loans (consumer loans) is higher than the rate permitted under the general usury laws. There are three reasons for this difference in interest rates:

1. Usually the cost of the credit investigation is higher per dollar lent. It takes just as much time to run a credit check and determine the credit-worthiness of a person borrowing $100 or $1,000 as it does of a person borrowing $10,000 or $20,000.
2. The bookkeeping and record-keeping costs are higher on a small loan than on a larger loan per dollar loaned.
3. There is often more risk to the lender because of the credit rating of many of the people borrowing from small loan companies. Because of the higher risk of default, the lender insists upon a higher rate of interest as compensation for assuming the greater risk.

Early repayments: the rule of 78

Suppose that sometime soon after assuming some consumer debt, a consumer experiences good fortune and discovers that he or she is able to repay it far in advance of the installment schedule. The question is, if the debt is paid off in advance, is an interest rebate given? The answer is yes, in most cases. Generally the method used to calculate this rebate is referred to as the **rule of 78,** but this figure is misleading. It could just as well be called the rule of 21 or the rule of 171. A few examples will make this clear.

Suppose that Mr. Wilson borrowed $1,200 to be paid off in twelve equal monthly installments at 6 percent add-on interest. This makes his true interest rate just over 11 percent over the entire twelve months and his monthly payments $106. Then, when the third monthly payment is due he decides to liquidate the entire debt. How is the interest recalculated?

First, take the sum of all numbers from 1 to 12; they equal 78. If the loan is repaid in full after one month, the lenders receive 12/78 of the interest that they would have received had the loan been outstanding the entire year; if it is liquidated after two months, the lenders receive 12 + 11 or 23/78; if after three months, 12 + 11 + 10 or 33/78 and so on. Only if the loan is outstanding the full twelve months does the lender receive the full 78/78 of the agreed-upon interest. Calculating the interest for early repayments by this method results in the lender getting somewhat more than a strictly pro rata distribution of interest. For example, after three months on a pro rata basis, the lender would get only one-fourth of the total interest, which would be 19.5/78 in the example used above. This would be a true interest rate of about 6.6 percent for these three months. It is less than the annual 11 percent that would have applied if the loan had been amortized normally because the declining balance (and hence the average balance) is relatively high during the early months of the loan. But because of the sum-of-the-digits method, the lender gets 33/78, which in our example is 33/78 of $72 or a total interest payment of $30.45. This is about 11 percent per year simple interest over these three months. What the sum of the digits does is to increase the interest rate on installment loans to put it back up where it would have been had the loan been amortized normally.

Suppose that in another case $900 is borrowed to be paid back in six monthly installments of $150, but after two months the entire loan is liquidated. This could be called the rule of 21 (the sum of the digits from 1 to 6 = 21). The lenders would receive 11/21 of the total interest if the loan is repaid after two months. The sum of the digits is the rule, and it can be used to calculate the interest on an early repay for a loan of any length. All that is needed is to know the total number of payments and the total interest, in dollars, that would be paid if the loan were not liquidated early.

Assume, for example, that an eighteen-month installment loan is repaid in full after six months. The sum of the digits here gives us 171 (18 + 17 + 16 + 15, etc.). Since six months have elapsed, the lender receives 93/171 (18 + 17 + 16 + 15 + 14 + 13 = 93) of the interest that would have been received had the loan been outstanding the entire eighteen months.

To be sure, lenders do not calculate these rebates in this manner because tables have been prepared and the lender merely looks up the rebate from the tables. These tables have been prepared, however, by using the sum-of-the-digits method described above.

Credit counselors

As a financial planning practitioner, you may encounter individuals with substantial financial difficulties arising from abuse of credit. It may be wise to refer these people to credit advisors or credit counselors. Credit advisors are not a source of credit and they do not lend any money. They provide two useful services.

First, they help a person to manage his or her personal affairs; they may set up a budget and persuade the client to live within it. For example, if a person has monthly payments in excess of his or her ability to pay, the credit counselor will attempt to stretch out the debt over a longer time period and in this way reduce the monthly payments. Second, after having worked out a new payment plan that the individual can meet, the credit advisor will act as the middleman and attempt to persuade the lender to accept the new reduced monthly payments. As a disinterested third party, he or she can often do this more easily than can the person involved.

Some cities provide free counseling services under their consumer protection division. In some cases they will have the counselee send them one weekly or monthly check as soon as they receive their wage or salary. The counselor will then disburse it to the various creditors. Many lenders too will act as credit counselors and in many cases will stretch out payments to keep the borrower afloat.

A typical installment contract

When a consumer buys something or borrows money on the installment plan, he or she must sign some papers. The financial planner must be acquainted with the client's liabilities to make an accurate assessment of his or her financial situation. This requires a familiarity with contracts used to establish credit. Figures 5–5, 5–6, 5–7, and 5–8 show several such agreements. The first is a combined promissory note, disclosure statement, and security agreement. It is used to finance the purchase of automobiles. The security agreement part of it is on the back side and is shown separately as Figure 5–6. The security agreement permits the lending institution to repossess the car in the event the buyer misses payments. It provides that the borrower pay all court and attorney's fees if they are necessary to collect payments.

The promissory note lists the car. It is a Toyota. It had a list price of $14,000, but after a 20 percent down payment, $11,200 was financed. The note shows the terms of the loan as required by law. The interest rate is 9.9 percent; the 36 monthly payments are $360.91, except for the last one, which is a few pennies less. It also stipulates the penalty for late payments. The total dollar interest cost is $1,792.53.

This is a **closed-end note,** which means it has a specific period of time (thirty-six months) to maturity. The note is drawn up in accordance with the Uniform Commercial Code and also conforms to the federal truth-in-lending law. Consequently, with slight variations, contracts similar to it are used for new cars throughout the United States. This type of contract is also employed to finance other durable goods. However, sometimes an **open-end note** is used to finance less expensive items. Figure 5–7 shows such a note (open-end loan advance request voucher and security agreement). It finances $5,000 worth of furniture. It is a signature loan, which means there is no collateral behind the note. However, the furniture could be used as collateral, in which case the security agreement on the back of the note would be used. The note shows the monthly payment ($240.10) and the interest rate (14 percent). There are twenty-four monthly payments, which make the interest rate dollar-wise

**COMBINED PROMISSORY NOTE, DISCLOSURE STATEMENT AND
SECURITY AGREEMENT (Closed End)**

University Federal _____ Credit Union, __September 1__, 19__87__

Borrower(s): __John J. Member__ Account No: __000-00-0000__ Note No: __-00__

Address: __Some Where__ __Austin__ __Texas__ __78701__
City / (State) / (Zip Code)

Items preceded by a box ☐ applicable only if checked.

ANNUAL PERCENTAGE RATE — The cost of your credit as a yearly rate.	FINANCE CHARGE — The dollar amount the credit will cost you.	Amount Financed — The amount of credit provided to you or on your behalf.	Total of Payments — The amount you will have paid after you have made all payments as scheduled.
9.9 %	$1,792.53	$11,200.00	$12,992.53

You have the right to receive at this time an itemization of the Amount Financed. ☐ I want an itemization.
☐ I do not want an itemization.

Your payment schedule will be:

Number of Payments	Amount of Payments	When Payments are Due
35	$360.91	Starting Oct 1, 1987 every 1st thereafter
1	$360.68	Final

Security: You are giving a security interest in: your shares and/or deposits.
☐ the goods or property being purchased.
☒ other _____
__1987 Toyota Tercel 4dr. VIN: JTM10435H5201BM56__
Collateral securing other loans with us may also secure this loan.
☒ Filing fees $ __N/A__ ☐ Non-Filing Insurance $ __N/A__
☒ **Late Charge:** If a payment is late, you may be charged __25% of the interest due if more than 7 days late__ __$10.00 minimum and $25.00 maximum__
Prepayment: If you pay off early, you will not have to pay a penalty.
See the rest of this credit document for any additional information about nonpayment, default, any required repayment in full before the scheduled date, and prepayment refunds and penalties.

_____
e means an estimate

PROMISE TO PAY: By signing this document and receiving the money advanced and/or the benefits received, you promise to pay to the credit union or its order, the sum of $ __11,200.00__ Dollars plus interest on the unpaid balance until it is paid in full at __9.9__ % per year in the amounts and on the dates disclosed above. When received, your payment will be applied in this order: Collection costs, late charges, interest due, and unpaid principal balance. Any unpaid interest will be paid by later payments and will not be added to your unpaid principal balance. If any payment is made late, you may be charged a late charge as disclosed above. In the event that applicable law is interpreted so that the interest or other charges collected or to be collected in connection with this loan would exceed permitted limits, any such charge shall be reduced by the amount necessary to reduce the total charge to the permitted limit and any sums already collected which exceeded permitted limits shall be credited to the principal amount of your loan or refunded at the discretion of the credit union.

SECURITY: You are giving the credit union a security interest in all present and future shares and/or deposits in any account in the credit union in which you have an interest. You authorize the credit union to take that money and apply it to what you owe if you are in default. The credit union may, but does not have to, allow you to withdraw a portion of your shares or deposits without affecting its security interest.

No withdrawal will be permitted if it will reduce the amount of your total shares and/or deposits in the credit union below $ __50.00__ or the amount you owe the credit union at the time of the withdrawal, whichever is less. You are not giving a security interest in any shares or deposits in an IRA, SEP, KEOGH, or any other account which, if pledged, would result in the loss of special tax treatment under the Internal Revenue Code.
☐ As additional security you are giving the credit union a security interest in the following goods or property _____

____ N/A ____

In signing the security agreement on the reverse side of this document, you agree to all its terms and conditions.

PROPERTY INSURANCE: You may obtain property insurance from anyone you want that is acceptable to the credit union.
☐ If you get the insurance through the credit union you will pay $ __N/A__ for a term of __N/A__.

CREDIT INSURANCE: If available, credit life insurance and credit disability insurance are not required to obtain credit and will not be provided unless you sign and agree to pay the additional cost. You may select any insurance company of your choice.

Type	Premium	Signature
Credit Life		I want credit life insurance ☐ Yes ☒ No Signature:
Credit Disability		I want credit disability insurance ☐ Yes ☒ No Signature:
Credit Life and Disability		I want credit life and disability insurance ☐ Yes ☒ No Signature:

DEFAULT: You will be in default if you break any promise made in this document, if you fail to make a payment when due, if anyone tries by any legal means to take any money you have which is in the possession of the credit union, if you are the subject of an order for relief under the Federal Bankruptcy Code, or if anything happens which the credit union reasonably believes endangers the collateral or your ability to repay what you owe. If you are in default, the credit union can require immediate payment of all you owe. That means you will have to pay your entire unpaid principal balance plus any interest earned as well as unpaid late charges and collection costs. The credit union has the right to file suit to collect what you owe. This document and applicable law authorize the credit union to take this action, and the credit union may rely on any or all of those sources. If the credit union incurs any expenses in taking these actions, you promise to reimburse the credit union and pay for all reasonable attorney's fees, court costs and disbursements. You waive any right to advance notice before the credit union takes any action resulting from your default unless the waiver is expressly prohibited by law.

CREDIT UNION RIGHTS: The credit union may delay taking any action to protect its rights as many times as it wants and as long as it wants without losing them. If the credit union agrees to change any of the terms of this loan, you agree that any security interest will continue to protect the credit union. Use of the term "you" includes any person who signs this document. By signing, any such person agrees to all the terms and conditions and promises to perform all the obligations, requirements and duties contained in this document.

ACKNOWLEDGEMENT: I(we) acknowledge receipt of a copy of the credit document completely filled in.

_____   _____
Borrower   Comaker/Guarantor

_____   _____
Date Signed   Date Signed
C.E.—2 (TX 1-82)

Combined promissory note, disclosure statement and security agreement (closed end)   Figure 5—5

SECURITY AGREEMENT

SECURITY INTEREST: By signing this document and receiving the benefits of your loan described on the reverse side, you are giving the Credit Union a security interest in the property described on the reverse side. This security interest covers not only that property but all proceeds, substitutions or replacements, accessions, improvements, all proceeds from insurance and all refunds of unearned premiums. Any time this agreement refers to collateral, it means any or all of the property described above. You are giving this interest to secure repayment of your loan as well as any other amounts you now owe or will owe the Credit Union. The collateral also secures your performance of all other obligations under your loan, this security agreement and any other agreement you have with the Credit Union.

OWNERSHIP OF COLLATERAL: You promise that you will use the proceeds of the loan advance to buy the collateral or that you own the collateral and that no one else has any interest in it or claim against it. You agree not to sell, lease it, or give it as collateral to anyone else until you have repaid what you owe the Credit Union or the Credit Union gives its written permission.

USE OF COLLATERAL: Until what you owe the Credit Union is fully repaid, you promise: To defend the collateral from third-party claims and protect it from forced sale by such persons; to protect the collateral and keep it in good repair; not to use the collateral for any unlawful purpose; to obtain written permission from the Credit Union before making major alterations or improvements; to notify the Credit Union in writing before changing your mailing address or the location of the collateral; and to help the Credit Union to protect the rights you have given it.

PROPERTY INSURANCE AND TAXES: You are required to fully insure the collateral against loss and damage. You may obtain this insurance through any insurance company of your choice, unless the Credit Union, for good cause, refuses to accept it. If you obtain insurance through the Credit Union, the cost and the term is disclosed on the reverse side of this document. If you fail to obtain or maintain insurance, the Credit Union may buy any type of insurance it feels is necessary to protect its interest in the collateral. This could result in less protection for you and at a higher cost. The credit union will add the premium for this insurance to the applicable loan account and charge you a **FINANCE CHARGE** at the applicable rate. You promise to have any insurance policy payable to the Credit Union, and, if asked, to deliver it to the Credit Union. You also promise to pay all taxes due on the collateral. If you fail to do so, the Credit Union may, but does not have to, pay the taxes and add the amount to the unpaid principal balance of the loan and charge you a **FINANCE CHARGE** at the same rate as your loan.

DEFAULT AND REPOSSESSION: You will be in default if you break any promise made under this agreement, if you are in default on your loan, if you fail to obtain or maintain the required insurance, or if anything happens which the Credit Union reasonably believes endangers the collateral or your ability to repay what you owe.

If you are in default, the Credit Union may require that you deliver the collateral to it at a time and place of its choosing. You agree that the Credit Union can take possession of the collateral without judicial process and without giving you advance notice unless waiver of the notice is otherwise expressly prohibited by law. This agreement, the Texas Business and Commerce Code, and other applicable law, authorize the Credit Union to take various actions, and the Credit Union may rely on any or all of those sources.

The Credit Union may also file suit to recover the collateral and/or collect what you owe. If the Credit Union incurs any expenses in taking these actions, or in protecting its rights to the collateral, you promise to reimburse it and pay for all reasonable attorneys' fees, court costs and disbursements. If the Credit Union repossesses the collateral, you promise to also pay for actual and reasonable out-of-pocket expenses incurred by the Credit Union in connection with repossession or foreclosure, including costs of storing, reconditioning, and reselling the collateral. Any disposition of the collateral will be in accordance with the standards of good faith and commercial reasonableness as well as the procedures set by the Texas Business and Commerce Code, as amended.

OTHER RIGHTS: The Credit Union may delay taking any action to protect its rights as many times as it wants and as long as it wants without losing them. If the Credit Union changes any of the terms of this agreement or the loan, you agree that the security interest will continue to protect the Credit Union. Use of the term "you" includes any person who signs this document. By signing, any such person agrees to all the terms and conditions and promises to perform all the obligations, requirements and duties contained in this agreement.

Date _____ Borrower _____

Date _____ Borrower _____

Figure 5—6   *Security agreement*

$762.40. The number of monthly payments and the total dollar interest cost, however, are generally not shown on an open-end note. This is because additional items may be added and financed with the same note. For example, if after a year, with twelve payments ($2,881.20) remaining, the buyer wanted to buy a $500 refrigerator, the monthly payments could be increased to include that. This could go on forever in theory; hence the term "open end." When using an open-end note, the law requires that an additional form (Figure 5—8, open-end credit plan disclosure for fixed rate loans) be used. This spells out the exact dollar cost of the note, as well as the annual percentage rate.

OPEN-END LOAN ADVANCE
REQUEST VOUCHER AND SECURITY AGREEMENT

UNIVERSITY FEDERAL CREDIT UNION

(COMPLETE SHADED PORTION ONLY)

MAIN OFFICE
1611 GUADALUPE
P.O. Box 4069
AUSTIN, TX 78765
(512) 467-8080

MEDICAL BRANCH
428 Postoffice St.
GALVESTON, TX 77550
(409) 765-9999

INFORMATION CONCERNING CREDIT INSURANCE

Group Credit Insurance is available on loans made to Credit Union members. Insurance is voluntary and not required to obtain credit. If you would like your loan protected by Group Credit Insurance check below.

☐ SINGLE CREDIT LIFE INSURANCE   ☐ JOINT CREDIT LIFE INSURANCE   ☐ CREDIT DISABILITY INSURANCE
The Credit Union will disclose the cost of this voluntary insurance to you if checked above. A separate insurance election disclosing the term and conditions of the credit insurance must be signed for the coverage to become effective.

MEMBERS NAME (Please Print)		ACCOUNT NO. (Soc. Sec. No.)
STREET ADDRESS	CITY STATE ZIP	

HOME PHONE	MARITAL STATUS — Do not complete unless you reside or are relying on property located in a community property state (AZ, CA, ID, LA, NM, NV, TX, WA)	☐ MARRIED ☐ UNMARRIED ☐ SEPARATED

HAVE YOU CHANGED EMPLOYERS SINCE YOUR LAST LOAN? ☐ YES ☐ NO	EMPLOYER AND ADDRESS		EMPLOYMENT PHONE NO.
Your monthly income (net) $	Income from Alimony, Child Support or maintenance payments need not be revealed if you choose not to disclose or list this income in this application.	Source of other income:	Amount of other income $

SUBJECT TO THE TERMS AND CONDITIONS OF YOUR OPEN-END CREDIT PLAN AGREEMENT, YOU HEREBY REQUEST A LOAN IN THE AMOUNT OF: $ *5000⁰⁰*   YOU MAY REQUEST A PAYMENT OF: $

PURPOSE OF THIS ADVANCE IS: *Buy Furniture*   SECURITY (IF ANY)

I WOULD LIKE THE FUNDS FROM THIS ADVANCE AS:	I WOULD LIKE TO MAKE PAYMENTS BY:
☐ CASH ($1,000 maximum)	☐ CASH (Counter or Mail Payments)
☐ CREDIT TO MY UFCU SHARE DRAFT ACCT.	☐ DEDUCTED FROM UT CHECK (Net pay only)
☐ CREDIT TO MY REGULAR SHARES	☐ TRANSFER FROM REGULAR SHARES
☐ CHECK	☐ TRANSFER FROM SHARE DRAFT
☐ DEALER DRAFT (Auto purchases only)	☐ BANK DRAFT ON MY BANK ACCOUNT
☐ CREDIT TO ACCT. NO. _____	☐ TRANSFER FROM ACCOUNT NO. _____
	☐ PAYROLL DEDUCTION (Medical Branch only)

— SECURITY —

Item	MAKE	MODEL	YEAR	I.D. NUMBER	LOAN VALUE OR PURCHASE PRICE
1.					
2.					
3.	Other (Describe): _____ *Signature* _____				

By accepting this advance you agree to pay the Credit Union according to the terms of your Open End Credit Plan Agreement and this Advance Voucher. You are giving the Credit Union a security interest in the collateral described above. The terms and conditions of the security agreement are shown on the reverse side of this voucher and incorporated in your Open End Credit Plan Agreement.

TLR. I.D.	SEQUENCE NUMBER	CURRENT DATE	EFFECTIVE DATE	ANNUAL PERCENTAGE RATE	To obtain this advance, you agree to maintain a minimum regular share balance of:	Total filing fees deducted from proceeds are:
		09/01/87	09/01/87	14 %	$ 50⁰⁰	$ –0–

SUB-ACCOUNT TYPE								
TRANS. CODE	PAYMENT AMOUNT	FIRST PAYMENT DATE	PREVIOUS LOAN BALANCE	NEW MONEY	INTEREST ADJUSTMENT	NEW LOAN BALANCE		
	240.10	10/1/87	–0–	5000.00		5000.00	☐ OPEN END ADV. ☑ INSTALLMENT LN.	

SUB-ACCOUNT TYPE						
TRANS CODE	PREVIOUS SHARE BALANCE	SHARE AMOUNT	NEW SHARE BALANCE	FEE	LOAN OFFICER APPROVAL	DATE APPROVED
					DISAPPROVED BY CR. COMMITTEE APPROVED	DATE DISAPPROVED APPROVED
					CREDIT COMMITTEE	
SIGNATURE OF BORROWER			DATE		CREDIT COMMITTEE	
SIGNATURE OF SPOUSE, JOINT APPLICANT OR OTHER PARTY			DATE			

SEE REVERSE SIDE FOR TERMS AND CONDITIONS OF THE SECURITY AGREEMENT.

Open-end loan advance: Request voucher and security agreement   Figure 5–7

OPEN-END CREDIT PLAN SECURITY AGREEMENT

SECURITY INTEREST: By signing this document and receiving the benefits of your open-end advance described on the reverse side, you are giving the Credit Union a security interest in the property described on the reverse side. This security interest covers not only that property but all proceeds, substitutions or replacements, accessions, improvements, all proceeds from insurance and all refunds of unearned premiums. Any time this agreement refers to collateral, it means any or all of the property described above. You are giving this interest to secure repayment of your Open End Advance Loan, as well as any other amounts you now owe or will owe the Credit Union. The collateral also secures your performance of all other obligations under the Open End Credit Plan Agreement, this security agreement and any other agreement you have with the Credit Union. If the collateral is household goods as defined in the Federal Trade Commission Fair Credit Practices Rule, it only secures obligations for the purchase money for that collateral or a refinancing or consolidation of such obligations.

OWNERSHIP OF COLLATERAL: You promise that you will use the proceeds of the loan advance to buy the collateral or that you own the collateral and that no one else has any interest in it or claim against it. You agree not to sell, lease it, or give it as collateral to anyone else until you have repaid what you owe the Credit Union or the Credit Union gives its written permission.

USE OF COLLATERAL: Until what you owe the Credit Union is fully repaid, you promise: To defend the collateral from third-party claims and protect it from forced sale by such persons; to protect the collateral and keep it in good repair; not to use the collateral for any unlawful purpose; to obtain written permission from the Credit Union before making major alterations or improvements; to notify the Credit Union in writing before changing your mailing address or the location of the collateral; and to help the Credit Union to protect the rights you have given it.

PROPERTY INSURANCE AND TAXES: You are required to fully insure the collateral against loss and damage. You may obtain this insurance through any insurance company of your choice, unless the Credit Union, for good cause, refuses to accept it. If you obtain insurance through the Credit Union, the cost and the term will be disclosed to you at that time. If you fail to obtain or maintain the insurance, the Credit Union may buy any type of insurance it feels is necessary to protect its interest in the collateral. This could result in less protection for you and at a higher cost. The Credit Union will add the premium for this insurance to the applicable loan account and charge you a **FINANCE CHARGE** at the applicable rate. You promise to have any insurance policy payable to the Credit Union, and, if asked, to deliver it to the Credit Union. You also promise to pay all taxes due on the collateral. If you fail to do so, the Credit Union may consider this failure as a request for a loan advance under your Open-End Credit Plan Agreement. In that event, the Credit Union may, but does not have to, pay the taxes and add the amount to the appropriate loan account and charge you a **FINANCE CHARGE** at the applicable rate.

DEFAULT AND REPOSSESSION: You will be in default if you break any promise made under this Agreement or if you are in default under the Open-End Credit Plan Agreement.

If you are in default, the Credit Union may require that you deliver the collateral to it at a time and place of its choosing. You agree that the Credit Union can take possession of the collateral without judicial process and you authorize a right of entry for that purpose and said repossession may occur without giving you advance notice unless waiver of the notice is otherwise prohibited by law. This agreement, The Texas Business and Commerce Code, and other applicable law, authorize the Credit Union to take various actions, and the Credit Union may rely on any or all of those sources.

The Credit Union may also file suit to recover the collateral and/or collect what you owe. If the Credit Union incurs any expenses in taking these actions, or in protecting its rights to the collateral, you promise to reimburse it and pay for all reasonable attorneys' fees, court costs and disbursements. If the Credit Union repossesses the collateral, you promise to also pay for actual and reasonable out-of-pocket expenses incurred by the Credit Union in connection with respossession or foreclosure, including costs of storing, reconditioning, and reselling the collateral. Any disposition of the collateral will be in accordance with the standards of good faith and commercial reasonableness as well as the procedures set by the Texas Business and Commerce Code, as amended.

OTHER RIGHTS: The Credit Union may delay taking any action to protect its rights as many times as it wants and as long as it wants without losing them. If the Credit Union changes any of the terms of this Agreement or the Open-End Credit Plan Agreement, you agree that the security interest will continue to protect the Credit Union. Use of the term "you" includes any person who signs this document. By signing, any such person agrees to all the terms and conditions and promises to perform all the obligations, requirements and duties contained in this Agreement.

Date   Borrower

Date   Borrower

ATTACHMENT "A" — OPEN-END CREDIT PLAN DISCLOSURES FOR FIXED RATE LOANS

University Federal Credit Union

P.O. Box 4069
4611 Guadalupe
Austin, Texas 78765
(512) 467-8080

Medical Branch
428 Post Office Street
Galveston, Texas 77550
(409) 765-9999

ADDITIONAL DISCLOSURES ● FIXED RATE LOANS

Your minimum periodic payment is calculated after each advance as described below:
UNSECURED OPEN-END/LINE OF CREDIT LOANS — $3.50 per $100, or fraction of $100, of your balance.
ALL OTHER LOANS — Payment based on available terms, and your loan officer.

FIXED RATE SUB-ACCOUNT LOANS

LOAN SUB-ACCOUNT DESCRIPTION	ESTIMATED TERM	BASIC MONTHLY PAYMENT	% ABOVE INDEX	DAILY PERIODIC RATE	ANNUAL PERCENTAGE RATE
NEW VEHICLES					
20% Down Payment	12 months			.0189041%	6.9%
20% Down Payment	18 months			.0216438%	7.9%
20% Down Payment	24 months			.0243836%	8.9%
20% Down Payment	36 months			.0271233%	9.9%
20% Down Payment	42 months	Minimum payment due		.0284932%	10.4%
20% Down Payment	48 months	will always be at least		.0298630%	10.9%
20% Down Payment	60 months	$30.00.		.0326027%	11.9%
20% Down Payment	84 months			.0353425%	12.9%
USED VEHICLES					
20% Down Payment					
Current, Plus 6 years	42 months			.0315068%	11.5%
7 years and older	30 months			.0383561%	14.0%
Share/Certificate Loans			3%	_____ %	____ %
All other secured loans				.0434658%	15.50%
Unsecured Loans					
($0 - $2,500)	60 months max.			.0452055%	16.5%
($2,501 - $4000)	60 months max.			.0424658%	15.5%
($4,001 - OVER)	60 months max.			.0383561%	14.0%
Real estate (all)	180 months max. per policy limits			.0369863%	13.5%
COMPUTERS					
20% Down Payment	36 months max			.0369863%	13.5%
Home Improvement $5,000 - $25,000	180 months max.			.0369863%	13.5%
80% of Equity or $25,000 - OVER	180 months max.			.0315068%	11.5%
80% Market Value $0 - $5,000	60 months max.			.0369863%	13.5%

For Certificate Secured advances the **ANNUAL PERCENTAGE RATE** will be the dividend rate being paid on the certificate on the date of the advance (Index) plus the percentage shown in the "% Above Index" column above. The certificate offered as security must be renewed until the advance is completely paid. When the certificate is renewed the **ANNUAL PERCENTAGE RATE** on existing balances will be 3% above the rate being paid on the new certificate. Failure to renew the certificate will result in default under the plan. The **ANNUAL PERCENTAGE RATE** will never exceed the rate permitted under the Federal Credit Union Act or a minimum of 10.8%. Any increase in the **ANNUAL PERCENTAGE RATE** will take the form of more payments of the same amount.

Borrower's Signature _____

FIXED RATE LOANS: When the Annual Percentage Rate I select is a Fixed Rate, this is the rate I will pay for the life of my loan, subject to the terms previously agreed to in the Open-End Credit Plan Agreement.

Figure 5—8

SUMMARY REVIEW QUESTIONS

These questions serve as a summary and a review of the chapter. If you are able to answer them all, you have a good understanding of the material covered by the chapter.

1. How is consumer credit classified for statistical purposes by the Federal Reserve Board?
2. Distinguish between an installment loan and a single-payment loan.
3. What is a credit bureau? What does it do?
4. The text gives a number of reasons for consumer borrowing; list three and explain each in detail.
5. How do individual savers benefit by consumer borrowing?
6. It is said that society as a whole may benefit from consumer credit. Rationalize this statement.
7. Explain how easy credit and the careless use of it may actually wreck the client's budget.
8. Explain in detail whether consumer credit "costs" anything.
9. How may it be said that borrowing on a life insurance policy has a psychological drawback for many consumers?
10. Explain in detail the workings of the revolving credit plan.
11. Do you think the checkless society will be a reality soon? What are your views regarding it?
12. What is credit life insurance?
13. Aside from permissive legislation, discuss the reasons for variations in loan charges among the various financial institutions that grant consumer loans.
14. If an individual pays off a loan early, is there an interest refund?
15. What are credit counselors, and how do they differ from sales finance companies?

CASES

1. Helen Walker has decided to buy a sofa that is priced at $1,200. She has found the identical sofa at two different stores, but they have different financing arrangements, as shown below:

	Down payment	Payment	Number of payments
Store one	$100	$20 per week	65
Store two	0	$100 per month	14

(a) Which store is offering Helen the best deal?

(b) What is the effective interest rate in both cases?

(c) Can you offer any suggestion that may save Ms. Walker some money?

2. Betty Canfield has a choice in financing her $4,000 used car:

	Down payment	Amount Financed	Payment per month	Number of payments
Choice one	$1,500	$2,500	$72.45	42
Choice two	800	3,200	93.12	42

(a) What is the approximate interest rate in each case?

(b) Why is the monthly payment lower in one case?

(c) Which loan is the cheaper?

(d) Which one would you recommend?

(e) What is the total dollar amount of interest?

3. Mary Rupp recently opened a revolving charge account at a large department store. The clerk told her she could always have some balance outstanding. However, every month she is billed for her entire account. She cannot reconcile these two facts. Can you help her?

4. In order to obtain consumer credit, it is generally necessary to make an application and undergo a credit investigation. What information is requested when an individual applies for credit? What will the credit investigation attempt to reveal?

5. Jim Hoffman earns $300 per week take-home pay. He has the following installment loans to pay off:

car $75 per month for ten months

refrigerator $25 per month for eight months

furniture $30 per month for twelve months

loan from bank $30 per month for six months

Jim's budget cannot meet these payments. Can you prepare a plan whereby Jim can pay off his debts? The most he can pay is $80 per month. Where can he go for such service?

6. Dorothy Jenkins is a young schoolteacher in Santa Ana, California, who borrowed $600 to repair her car after an accident and to meet other expenses. She agreed to pay it back in nine monthly installments of $74.70. What interest rate is this? However, after two months, Dorothy was reimbursed by an insurance company and was able to liquidate the entire loan. Calculate the actual dollar amount of interest Dorothy paid. What true annual percentage rate is this?

SUGGESTED READINGS

Banking Journal of the American Bankers Association. New York: American Bankers Association. Monthly publication.

"Borrowers, Lenders and Interest Rates." Richmond, VA.: The Federal Reserve Bank of Richmond.

Cole, Robert H. *Consumer and Commercial Credit Management,* 4th ed. Homewood, Ill: Irwin, 1980.

"Consumer Credit Counseling." Silver Springs, Md.: The National Foundation for Consumer Credit.

"Consumer Credit Terminology Handbook." New York: The Federal Reserve Bank of New York.

Consumer Credit and You. Greenfield, Mass: Channing I. Bete Company.

Consumer Finance News. Washington, D.C.: National Consumer Finance Association. Monthly publication.

Consumer Finance Rate and Regulation Chart. Washington, D.C.: National Consumer Finance Association. Revised annually.

Consumer Loan and Sales Finance Rate and Regulation Chart. Washington, D.C.: National Consumer Finance Association Revised annually.

Consumer Reports. Mt. Vernon, N.Y.: Consumer's Union of the United States. Monthly publication.

Cost of Personal Borrowing in the United States. Boston: Financial Publishing Company. Annual publication.

Credit. Washington, D.C.: National Consumer Finance Association. Bimonthly publication.

"Credit Research Center Working Papers." West Lafayette, Ind.: Credit Research Center, Purdue University. A series of research studies on topics significant to consumer credit.

Family Budget Guide. Washington, D.C.: National Consumer Finance Association.

Finance Facts Yearbook. Washington, D.C.: National Consumer Finance Association. Annual publication.

"Getting a Hold on Credit." Silver Springs, MD.: The National Foundation for Consumer Credit.

"How Much Are You Really Worth?" Silver Springs, MD.: The National Foundation for Consumer Credit.

"How Much Credit Can You Afford?" Silver Springs, MD.: The National Foundation for Consumer Credit.

"How to Establish and Use Credit." Philadelphia: The Federal Reserve Bank of Philadelphia.

International Credit Union Yearbook, 1981. Madison, Wis.: CUNA International, Inc. Annual publication.

"Monitor: A Summary of Current Research in Consumer and Mortgage Credit." West Lafayette, Ind.: Credit Research Center of the Krannert Graduate School of Management, Purdue University. Bimonthly publication.

NCFA Research Report on Finance Companies. Washington, D.C.: Research Services Division, National Consumer Finance Association. Annual publication.

"The Rule of 78's or What May Happen When You Pay Off a Loan Early." Philadelphia: The Federal Reserve Bank of Philadelphia.

"The Story of Consumer Credit." New York: The Federal Reserve Bank of New York.

Taylor, John. *Consumer Lending.* Reston, VA.: Reston Publishing Company, 1982.

U.S. Department of Agriculture, *Consumers All, The Yearbook on Agriculture.* Washington, D.C.: U.S. Department of Agriculture. Annual publication.

Wood, Oliver G., Jr., and Barksdale, William C. *How to Borrow Money.* New York: Van Nostrand Reinhold, 1981.

"Your Credit Rating." Philadelphia: The Federal Reserve Bank of Philadelphia.

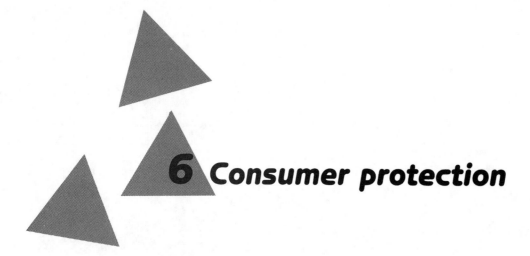

6 Consumer protection

HIGHLIGHTS   In order to provide an understanding of protection available to the consumer, we will examine the following:

1   The various federal consumer protection laws and what they do
2   Private, voluntary consumer organizations that sometimes help, especially in giving advice
3   The holder-in-due-course doctrine
4   The federal and state agency to which the consumer should go if a federal law has been violated

INTRODUCTION

In recent years legislation has been passed to protect the consumer. There is, however, no uniformity among various states' laws. Many states have usury laws that have been on the books for years. In some states these usury laws apply to consumer credit, and in some they do not; and special laws have been passed that set the upper limits on consumer credit interest rates. Regular usury laws do, however, usually apply to mortgage loans made to individuals and to business loans.

In most states there is a consumer credit commission or a similar office that regulates consumer credit lenders and enforces state laws that cover, among other things, the maximum interest rate that may be charged. In a few states this office may listen to consumer complaints and even take action if the complaint is legitimate. But an official state agency to help the consumer is the exception rather than the rule, and generally an individual must initiate legal action unless a federal or state statute has been violated. Private voluntary consumer organizations also exist in some areas. Some groups may aid an individual and bring strength of numbers to bear, or they may provide financial and legal aid in the event of a lawsuit. These groups may also lobby for stronger consumer protection laws. But unless a law has been violated there is often little that can be done, even if one has been treated shabbily. Consequently, the consumer should read carefully any installment contract before signing it.

FEDERAL CONSUMER PROTECTION LAWS

When a consumer borrows money or buys something on the installment plan, there are certain federal laws that protect him or her. As a finanacial planner, you should be familiar with this protection and know where consumers can go if a law has been broken. Currently, federal legislation covers the following general areas:

Truth in lending
Fair credit reporting
Equal credit opportunity
Fair credit billing
Consumer leasing
Fair debt collection practices

Truth in lending

Officially known as the Consumer Credit Protection Act, the federal truth-in-lending law was passed in 1968 and has been amended several times since then. "Truth in Lending" does what its title suggests: it requires that certain facts be disclosed when consumer loans are made.

Interest costs

The lender must inform the borrower of the "true" or actuarially correct percentage interest rate that he or she is paying. As pointed out in a previous chapter, this is called the annual percentage rate (APR) and must be distinguished from the so-called add-on interest rate. The add-on rate is misleading because it is calculated on the original balance, which is actually declining if paid off in installments. The borrower must also be told the total dollar amount of interest together with any service charges, extra loading fees, and points. If a product is being financed (rather than money being borrowed at a bank), the cash price as well as credit price must be spelled out.

The cost of any credit life insurance must be explained; the same is true of accident, health, or disability insurance written in connection with any credit transaction. While the lender may require that the borrower accept credit life insurance, if he or she does, its premium is included in the cost of the load (APR), which is subject to the various states' usury laws.

Credit life

The truth-in-lending law also requires that the "right of rescission" clause be inserted into every contract in which the borrower's home is used as collateral (including mobile homes). This gives the borrower three business days in which to nullify any such contract. The borrower's home is frequently used as collateral when a major repair or remodeling job is being done. In such a case, work may not begin until the three days have passed unless the borrower, in writing, waives the right of rescission. If the borrower cancels during the three days, this must also be done in writing.

Right of rescission

This law also protects the borrower in the event a credit card is lost or stolen. Once the missing card has been reported, the cardholder is not liable for bills stemming from its unauthorized use. It is up to the issuer to block its illegal use. Even if the missing card is not reported, the maximum liability is $50 per card. Consequently, any missing cards should be reported immediately, first by telephone and then by certified or registered letter.

Lost or stolen credit or debit cards

In 1980, Congress passed the Electronic Funds Transfer Act which covered lost or stolen debit cards. However, there are some differences. On a debit card the consumer's loss is limited to $50, only if it is reported within two business days after learning of the loss. If the customer does not inform the card issuer within two days after learning of the loss, his or her liability could be as much as $500. It cannot be proven when one learned of the loss; hence it is assumed the customer learned of it at the latest when he or she received the bank statement. If unreported within two days after that, the loss is now limited to $500. For an individual who is out of the country and doesn't report the loss within sixty days after receiving the bank statement, the loss is unlimited.

In 1970 an amendment to the truth-in-lending law spelled out the maximum amount of a person's income that may be garnished to meet unpaid debts. This maximum is now either 25 percent of a person's weekly take-home pay or the amount by which his or her weekly take-home pay exceeds 30 times the minimum hourly wage, whichever is smaller.

Garnishment of wages

The federal law then sets the maximum penalty with respect to garnisheeing wages. Moreover, it provides that in those states that have a garnisheeing law more lenient to the debtor than the federal law, the state law shall prevail. The law also prohibits an employer from firing an employee whose wages were garnisheed to satisfy any one debt. Formerly, firing was frequent because garnisheeing wages meant extra bookwork for the employer.

Fair credit reporting act

The Fair Credit Reporting Act guarantees certain consumer rights in reporting credit information about consumers to credit granters. For example, it gives the consumer the right to see his or her credit file. All cities of any size have professional credit bureaus that collect and store pertinent financial data on virtually all individuals in the community. They then sell these data (know as "inspection reports") to institutions and individuals who extend credit. They also sell reports to prospective employers and life insurance companies that are considering an individual for life insurance. The credit file includes personal data as well as data on where the individual works, his or her position, how long the individual has held that position, annual income, spouse's income, assets, whether he or she rents or owns the home, previous job and address, number of dependents, credit history and experience, and any judgments that may have been recorded against the individual.

Checking the file

If an individual merely wishes to check his or her credit file routinely, he or she will have to pay the regular fees a lender pays—a few dollars. If credit has been denied because of a credit report, the lender or merchant must disclose this. In such a case the individual has thirty days during which he or she may see the credit report free of charge; all data in it must be revealed and its source disclosed. Any errors found must be corrected, and any falsehoods deleted. If the file contains information subject to two or more interpretations, the individual's interpretation must be added and included in all future reports. The corrected version must also be sent to all possible creditors who have received a report on the individual during the last six months, and all prospective employers who have received a report during the past two years, at no cost to the individual.

Adverse information limitation

The limits to how long adverse information in the credit file may be made available in a credit report are as follows:

Information on bankruptcies—14 years
Suits and judgments against the consumer—7 years or until the statute of limitations has expired, whichever is the longer
Paid tax liens, collection accounts, accounts charged to bad debts, arrests, indictments, convictions, and other damaging information—7 years

However, none of these limitations applies if the credit reports are to be used in connection with a credit or life insurance transaction involving $50,000 or more, or employment involving an annual salary of $20,000 or more.

Although the consumer may see his or her credit file, it is strictly confidential to almost all others. Those who have a legitimate need may see a credit report as may those whom the consumer authorizes. Those who may receive a report without consumer authorization because they have a legitimate need are: prospective creditors, creditors or their agents trying to collect past debts, prospective employers, and employees of life insurance companies considering the individual for life insurance. For anyone else a court order is needed. Even the government cannot see your file or receive a report unless it is considering employing the individual, granting a license of some kind, considering him or her for security clearance, or thinks back taxes are owed. For the IRS to receive a report, it must have a legitimate case.

Who may see the file

The Equal Credit Opportunity Act (ECOA) became effective in October, 1975, and it banned discrimination in the granting of credit on the basis of sex or marital status. In 1976 this act was amended so that it now also prohibits discrimination on the basis of race, color, religion, and age. The act also bans discrimination against welfare or other public assistance recipients and borrowers who exercise their rights under consumer protection laws. Moreover, it provides that if people are denied credit, they must be told why in writing.

Equal Credit Opportunity Act

Prior to the passage of ECOA, women had more difficulty getting credit than men. A married woman often had to rely on her husband's credit. In addition, single and divorced people often had a more difficult time getting credit than married couples. Now this discrimination as well as other types is unlawful.

Women should establish credit in their own names if they have an income, even if they are married. If a woman relies upon her husband's credit, then upon death or divorce she may be without it temporarily. To be sure, ECOA will permit her to establish credit in her own name in such a case, but this takes time.

Women and credit

Prior to the passage of ECOA, it was alleged that lenders sometimes refused to grant credit to older people. This act prevents the arbitrary denial of credit to the elderly, who for the purpose of the provision in this act are defined as persons 62 and older. Credit may still be denied on the basis of inadequate income, excessive debts, a person's credit record, and the like, but the reason for refusing credit must be spelled out in writing.

Age and credit

Fair credit billing act

The Fair Credit Billing Act (FCBA) does three things: It permits merchants who so desire to grant cash discounts, it permits the consumer to withhold payments for defective merchandise purchased with credit cards, and it provides some safeguards in the case of billing errors.

Cash discounts

Twenty or thirty years ago cash discounts were often granted by merchants to people who paid cash. This practice had all but ceased until very recently when there has been a reemergence of the cash discount. Because of this, some major credit card companies included a provision in their contract with retail merchants prohibiting cash discounts. The FCBA prohibits such "no cash discounts" provisions. The act does not require cash discounts; it merely says that merchants may grant them if they wish. Obviously, expenses are minimized if the individual uses cash in instances where a cash discount is available. This discount is limited to 5 percent because otherwise it would be in violation of the truth-in-lending law.[1]

Merchants granting cash discounts must have signs so stating in clear sight, such as near cash registers or on doors at entrances. Moreover, merchants granting cash discounts must grant them to all buyers, not just to credit card holders.

Withholding payments

The FCBA permits the consumers to stop making payments for defective merchandise or service purchased with credit cards. If the merchant who sold the merchandise is also the issuer of the credit card, all the consumer need first do is make a good faith effort to return the merchandise or resolve the problem by having the merchant replace or repair the item. In the event that a third party issued the credit card (for example, Visa or MasterCard), the consumer may still withhold payment, but now there are two additional restrictions. First, the purchase must have exceeded $50, and, second, it must have taken place in his or her state or within 100 miles of his or her current address.

By withholding payments the consumer can generate pressure to have the grievance resolved. If a third party's credit card is involved, the consumer can, by withholding payment, enlist that party as an ally in bringing pressure on the retailer.

Billing errors

In some cases the consumer may be billed incorrectly because of accounting errors, goods that were delivered to the wrong address, goods returned or not accepted, or other reasons. The FCBA makes it easier to settle such disputes. The consumer has sixty days after receiving such a bill to report an error. This must be done in writing and the nature of the dispute explained. The creditor has thirty days in which to send a written reply. While the dispute is being settled, the creditor may not collect any

---

1. Discounts in excess of 5 percent would constitute a finance charge under the truth-in-lending law and hence would necessitate further regulations and red tape.

disputed amount, nor add interest charges. During this time the creditor may not close the account nor give the consumer a bad credit rating because of the claim.

What these provisions of the FCBA have done is to make the creditor more cooperative in settling disputes; complaints must now be investigated. Even though legally complaints must be in writing, in many cases disputes can be settled on the telephone. National credit card companies have established regional offices throughout the country with full-time people who handle only complaints. Often the address and phone numbers for complaints are listed on the monthly bills, and the numbers are often toll-free.

While fewer consumers are involved in leasing than in purchasing, there is some legal protection for those who do lease automobiles, furniture, and other items.

Consumer leasing act

There are two types of leases and both are covered by the Federal Consumer Leasing Act. Under a **closed-end lease** the consumer pays so much per month, and when the lease is over he or she may return the car or furniture and the lease is terminated. As a result of this simplicity, closed-end leases usually have a higher monthly payment than open-end leases.

An **open-end lease** is a bit more complicated. The consumer has the option of buying the car or other item when the lease expires. The car must be depreciated according to a schedule calculated in advance, and its estimated value at the expiration of the lease must be stated in advance. If the car is worth more than that, the consumer may keep it, sell it, and pocket the difference. If the car is worth less than that, the consumer needs to make up the difference. However, this difference cannot be more than three times the monthly payment. There is a penalty, then, if the individual has been overly hard on a car.

The leasing law covers personal property leased by an individual for more than four months for personal family or household use. The law does not cover the following:

- Daily, weekly, or monthly car rentals
- Houses or apartments, or furniture that comes with these residential units
- Property leased to companies or individuals for business use

The Fair Debt Collection Practices Act (FDCPA) spells out the maximum amount of harassment that may be used to collect bills. It limits the number of phone calls that may be made and the time of day during which they may be made. Phone calls must be made at convenient times, which generally are defined as between 8:00 A.M. and 9:00 P.M. The debtor, however, cannot be contacted at his or her place of employment, if it is

Fair debt collection practices act

"It says, 'This is your final notice. If you do not pay immediately, we will destroy your credit and have you thrown in jail. Have a happy day.'" (Source: Permission Cartoon Features Syndicate; from the Wall Street Journal.)

known that the employer prohibits or discourages this. The total amount of contacts of any sort is fixed, and of course threats, overt or implied, are prohibited. This act, however, has one loophole. It does not apply to the lenders directly, but only to third parties collecting for them. A creditor can call a debtor anytime but a collection agency cannot.

Holder-in-due-course doctrine

The Federal Trade Commission (FTC), which enforces many of the federal consumer protection laws, has by means of regulations weakened (but not completely eliminated) the holder-in-due-course doctrine. Holder-in-due-course is the legal concept that, if a merchant entered into a credit relationship with a consumer to finance, say, a refrigerator and then sold the installment contract to a third party (say, a finance company), a legally binding contract existed between the consumer and the finance company. The payments were then made to the finance company which bought the paper on good faith and was not a party to the agreement. In short, under the old holder-in-due-course doctrine you had to pay for the refrigerator even if it was defective. Normally you can generate great pressure to have a defective item repaired or replaced by withholding payments; this was not possible formerly if a third party was involved.

FTC regulations now permit the consumer to stop making payments to third parties (even if a credit card is not involved) for defective merchandise or services. Both the seller and the third party may now be held partly liable. This permits the consumer to generate greater pressure. If it comes to legal court action, he or she can go after both the seller and the financial institution, since both are equally liable. The person now has the same rights against the third party as against the seller.

The FCBA strengthens the hand of the consumer somewhat by permitting payments to be withheld. However, if it comes to a legal battle, sellers and creditors are often not liable. This is because often the warranty is granted by the manufacturer, not the seller. While the lender and the retailer share any warranty granted at that level, neither is liable if it is granted by the manufacturer. This is especially true if a disclaimer clause is inserted into a contract. The retailer and creditor are then freed of liability for defective products if there is a court case. Nevertheless, the new law is a plus for the consumer because he or she can now withhold payments, generate some additional pressure on the retailer and creditor, and enlist them as allies against the manufacturer.

The FTC's regulations now also prohibit the waiver of defense clauses in installment contracts. These were formerly used by some retailers and protected them against action on the part of the consumer.

The Federal Consumer Credit Laws offer these major protections:

Summary of consumer credit laws

1. The *Truth in Lending Act* requires disclosure of the "finance charge" and the "annual percentage rate"—and certain other costs and terms of credit—so that prices of credit from different sources can be compared. It also limits liability on lost or stolen credit cards.

2. The *Equal Credit Opportunity Act* prohibits discrimination against an applicant for credit because of age, sex, marital status, race, color, religion, national origin, or receipt of public assistance. It also prohibits discrimination because a consumer has made a good faith exercise any of his or her rights under the federal consumer credit laws. If the consumer has been denied credit, the law requires that he or she be notified in writing and that he or she have the right to request the reason for the denial.

3. The *Fair Credit Billing Act* sets up a procedure for the prompt correction of errors on a credit account and prevents damage to the consumer's credit rating while he or she is settling a dispute.

4. The *Fair Credit Reporting Act* sets up a procedure for correcting mistakes on the credit record and requires that the record be kept confidential.

5. The *Consumer Leasing Act* requires disclosure of information that helps the consumer compare the cost and terms of one lease with another and with the cost and terms of buying on credit or with cash.

6. The *Fair Debt Collection Practices Act* spells out the amount of pressure collection agencies may use to collect past due bills.

7. The *Real Estate Settlement Procedures Act* requires that the consumer be given information about the services and costs involved at settlement, when real property transfers from seller to buyer.

8. The *Home Mortgage Disclosure Act* requires most lending institutions in metropolitan areas to let the public know where they make their mortgage and home improvement loans.

Pamphlets describing some of these laws in more detail are available from the Federal Reserve Bank in your district.

ENFORCING AGENCIES AND OTHER COURSES OF ACTION

When a consumer has a grievance with a merchant or financial institution, there are several courses of action available, including legal action. First, he or she should attempt to settle the dispute himself or herself. Legal action should be seen as a last resort, and then only if a substantial amount of money is involved.

Voluntary consumer organizations

If the consumer does not receive satisfaction from working directly with the company, another course of action is working through voluntary organizations. While voluntary organizations are not enforcing agencies because they have no power, they can sometimes bring pressure to bear because of the power of numbers. In many states and communities, voluntary groups of consumers have developed various programs to help themselves and advance their version of the consumers' cause. These groups generally have been assisted in their growth and activities by the Consumer Federation of America (CFA), a Washington, D.C. based coalition of over two hundred national, state, and local organizations. CFA's affiliates have their own memberships of more than thirty million persons in consumer, farmer, cooperative, labor, and other endeavors. Ralph Nader has founded a number of specialized consumer organizations, and others have arisen in recent years to deal with problems in individual industries such as food, electric utilities, broadcasting, and housing.

Consumer groups developed rapidly following the activities of homemakers a few years ago in a well-publicized eruption of sentiment, pickets, and boycotts of supermarkets over rising prices. The activities of the groups that emerged reflect particular interests and special conditions of the urban, suburban, or rural areas in which they flourish.

Some groups make frequent statewide and local area comparisons of store prices for drugs, household items, and food. Others demand financial settlement for members who have received poor treatment. Voluntary consumer organizations generally do three things: (1) they engage in lobbying at all levels of government to obtain stronger consumer protection laws; (2) they engage in consumer education by sponsoring seminars and lectures on many topics of interest to consumers; (3) they provide consumer counseling.

Federal agencies

There are a number of federal and state enforcing agencies. If the consumer has a complaint and the law has been violated, the correct agency to use depends on the creditor involved. Figure 6–1 illustrates where a consumer may go for help. The following list summarizes agencies responsible for enforcing federal laws:

Creditor	Federal agency
National commercial banks	The Comptroller of the Currency United States Treasury Department Washington, D.C. The Comptroller has regional offices in a number of major cities. Check the telephone directory.
State banks that are members of the Federal Reserve System	The Federal Reserve Bank serving the area in which the bank is located. The Federal Reserve has 12 regional offices
State nonmember banks that are insured by the Federal Deposit Insurance Corporation	The Federal Deposit Insurance Corporation Washington, D.C. The FDIC has regional offices in a number of major cities. Look in the telephone directory.
State nonmember noninsured banks	Division of Consumer Credit The Federal Trade Commission Washington, D.C. The Federal Trade Commission has regional offices in a number of major cities. There are very few such noninsured banks, however.
Federal savings and loan associations	The Federal Home Loan Bank Board Washington, D.C. The FHLBB has regional offices in a number of major cities.
State savings and loans associations insured by the Federal Deposit Insurance Corporation (FDIC)	The Federal Deposit Insurance Corporation (FDIC) Washington, D.C. The FDIC has regional offices in a number of major cities.
State savings and loan associations that are not insured	Division of Consumer Credit The Federal Trade Commission Washington, D.C. The FTC has regional offices in a number of major cities. Look in the telephone directory. There are very few such noninsured savings associations.
Mutual savings banks	The Federal Deposit Insurance Corporation Washington, D.C. The FDIC has regional offices in a number of major cities. Virtually all mutual savings banks are insured by the FDIC and hence regulated by them.

Creditor	Federal agency
Federally chartered credit unions and insured state-chartered credit unions	The National Credit Union Administration Washington, D.C. The NCUA has regional offices in a number of major cities.
State-chartered noninsured credit unions	Division of Consumer Credit The Federal Trade Commission Washington, D.C. The FTC has a number of regional offices. There are very few noninsured credit unions.
Retail merchants, including department stores, finance companies, nonbank credit card issuers, and most others	Division of Consumer Credit The Federal Trade Commission Washington, D.C. The FTC has a number of regional offices.
Airlines and other creditors subject to Civil Aeronautics Board	Director, Bureau of Enforcement Civil Aeronautics Board
Meat packers, poultry processors, and other creditors subject to Packers and Stockyards Act	Nearest Packers and Stockyards Administration area supervisor.
Creditors subject to Interstate Commerce Commission	Office of Proceedings Interstate Commerce Commission Washington, D.C.

The Federal Reserve System and the Comptroller of the Currency have established an Office of Consumer Affairs at all of their regional offices, as have many of the other federal agencies, where complaints can be taken by mail. The Office of Consumer Affairs at the Regional Federal Reserve Bank of your district of the Federal Reserve System will send the consumer a complaint form that can be filled out and returned to them. A sample of such a complaint form is shown in Figure 6–2.

The Department of Health, Education and Welfare (HEW) established an Office of Consumer Affairs some time ago. Although this office has no power of enforcement, it listens to complaints from consumer organizations. It plays the role of advocate and will report any violations of federal law to the proper enforcement agencies.

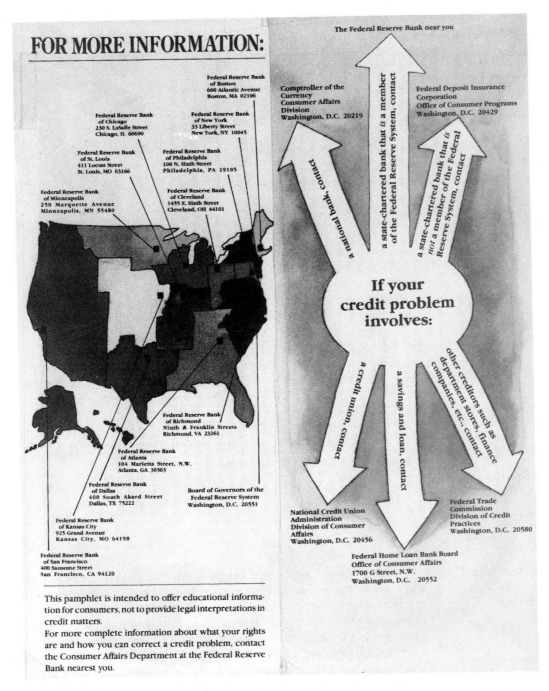

Where to go for help. (Source: *Board of Governors of the Federal Reserve System.*)   Figure 6—1

COMPLAINT FORM   **Federal Reserve System**

Name _____   Name of Bank _____

Address _____   Address _____
           Street   City   State   Zip

     City   State   Zip

Daytime telephone _____   Account number (if applicable) _____
           (include area code)

The complaint involves the following service: Checking Account ☐   Savings Account ☐   Loan ☐

     Other: Please specify _____

I have attempted to resolve this complaint directly with the bank: No ☐   Yes ☐

     If "No", an attempt should be made to contact the bank and resolve the complaint.

     If "Yes", name of person or department contacted is _____
                                                          Date

MY COMPLAINT IS AS FOLLOWS (Briefly describe the events in the order in which they happened, including specific dates and the bank's actions to which you object. Enclose copies of any pertinent information or correspondence that may be helpful. Do not send us your only copy of any document.):

_____
_____
_____
_____
_____
_____
_____
_____
_____
_____
_____

This information is solicited under the Federal Trade Commission Improvement Act. Providing the information is voluntary; complete information is necessary to expedite investigation of your complaint. Routine use of the information may include disclosing it to bank(s) or others involved or to other governmental agencies as deemed appropriate.

Date _____   Signatures _____

                                                     _____

Figure 6—2   *Complaint form. (Source: Board of Governors of the Federal Reserve System.)*

State agencies

There are state agencies to enforce state laws. All states have banking commissioners by that or some other name. Some have credit union commissioners, savings and loan commissioners, and consumer credit commissioners. Some have a similar state agency to enforce all state laws dealing with consumer credit including the maximum interest rates that may be charged. Some states also have deceptive trade legislation on the books, and some have established offices of consumer protection or consumer affairs, either within the Attorney General's office or elsewhere.

**Small claims court:
Legal action**

Legal action should probably be used as a measure of the last resort. In most cases where small dollar amounts are involved, such action should be taken through a small claims court, which is often able to handle claims effectively, quickly, and at a much lower cost than regular legal action. However, the amount of damages for which a person may sue is limited in a small claims court, in most states to under $1,000. If the consumer has suffered damages (and would like to collect) in excess of that amount, he or she will probably have to hire an attorney and go to a regular court. The effectiveness of a small claims court depends on particular state laws and on the availability of the courts in particular locations. In most states hiring a lawyer is not required. Procedures are usually handled in an informal manner and the legal rules of evidence and procedure are often waived. The consumer simply tells the magistrate what happened in his or her own words.

In some states the small claims courts are under the jurisdiction of the justice of the peace (JP), and in others under the alderman. Both of these are elected officials at the lowest (precinct) political subdivision.

The cost of filing a claim in a small claims court is only a few dollars. Actual court costs are also modest. More information about the small claims court in your area may be obtained by calling your county clerk, the justice of the peace or alderman for your precinct.

SUMMARY REVIEW QUESTIONS

These questions serve as a summary and a review of the chapter. If you are able to answer them all, you have a good understanding of the material covered by the chapter.

1. Does the federal law or state law govern the maximum interest rate that may be charged on consumer loans?
2. Discuss the truth-in-lending law. What is its purpose?
3. What does the truth-in-lending law say about credit life insurance?
4. What is meant by the right of rescission? What law grants it?
5. What should the consumer do if his or her credit card is lost or stolen?
6. Which federal law deals with garnishment of wages? Summarize briefly what it provides.
7. What does the Fair Credit Reporting Act do?
8. Is an individual permitted to see his or her credit file?
9. How long may adverse information be kept in the credit file?
10. Who besides the consumer may obtain a credit report on an individual without a court order?
11. What happens if a woman relies on her husband's credit and they then separate?
12. Which law covers cash discounts? What does it provide?
13. May a consumer legally withhold payments for defective merchandise?
14. What should be done if there is a billing error on an account?
15. What is the holder-in-due-course doctrine?
16. What groups are covered by the Fair Debt Collection Practices Act? Which groups are not covered?
17. What types of activities do voluntary consumer organizations perform?

CASES

1. Barbara Hudson applied for a loan at a bank so that she could buy a car. If the loan is granted, what information must the bank provide Barbara? If Barbara is turned down, what must the bank do?

2. Philip and Virginia Kidd recently purchased a new Cadillac. One day while Virginia was driving it, the motor literally exploded. Upon examination the dealer discovered a push rod had come through the block and the motor was damaged beyond repair. What recourse does Virginia have?

3. Dee Van Antwerp of Ogallala, Nebraska has been admitted to the Nebraska bar and has joined her husband in the practice of law. Dee doesn't have any credit cards of her own but uses her husband's. She feels perhaps she should get some cards in her own name, and seeks your advice.

4. Anita Garcia had a flight reservation from Austin, Texas to New Orleans via Dallas. But the flight to Dallas was late, so to avoid missing her connection there she purchased a ticket from another airline via Houston. There was not time to cancel her flight via Dallas at the time but she did so later. She had charged all these flights on her Visa card and later both airlines billed her. What should Anita do?

5. Rusty Snow lost her purse, which had little of value in it except three credit cards. Rusty is concerned that someone might find them and run up a lot of bills. What should she do?

6. Blanche Wright wanted to buy some furniture for her apartment, but the store would not sell it to her on the installment plan because of an unfavorable report from the credit bureau. What are Blanche's rights?

SUGGESTED READINGS

Alice in Debitland; Consumer Protection and the Electronic Fund Transfer Act. Washington, D.C.: Board of Governors of the Federal Reserve System.

"The American Lawyer: How to Choose and Use." Chicago: The American Bar Association.

Annual Buying Guide, Consumer Reports. Published in December of each year by Consumer's Union of the United States.

Changing Times. The Kiplinger Magazine. A weekly publication with a good deal of material of interest to the consumer.

Charting Mortgages. Department of Consumer Affairs, Federal Reserve Bank of Philadelphia.

Consumer Handbook to Credit Protection Laws. Washington, D.C.: Board of Governors of the Federal Reserve System.

Consumer Information Catalog. Pueblo, Col.: Consumer Information Center. Quarterly publication.

Consumers, Credit Bureaus, and the Fair Credit Reporting Act. Associated Credit Bureaus. Check with your local credit bureaus; they may have similar publications by credit bureaus near you.

Consumer News. Washington, D.C.: Office of Consumer Affairs.

Consumer Reports. Mt. Vernon, N.Y.: Consumer's Union of the United States. Monthly publication.

Credit Guide. Federal Reserve Bank of Chicago.

Equal Credit Opportunity Act . . . and Age. Washington, D.C.: Board of Governors of the Federal Reserve System.

Equal Credit Opportunity Act and . . . Credit Rights in Housing. Washington, D.C.: Board of Governors of the Federal Reserve System.

Equal Credit Opportunity Act and . . . Doctors, Lawyers, Small Retailers, and Others Who May Provide Incidental Credit. Washington,

D. C.: Board of Governors of the Federal Reserve System.

Equal Credit Opportunity Act and . . . Women. Washington, D.C.: Board of Governors of the Federal Reserve System.

Fair Credit Billing. Washington, D.C.: Board of Governors of the Federal Reserve System.

Fair Debt Collection Practices Act. Department of Consumer Affairs, Federal Reserve Bank of Philadelphia.

How to File a Consumer Credit Complaint. Washington, D.C.: Board of Governors of the Federal Reserve System.

If You Borrow to Buy Stock. Washington, D.C.: Board of Governors of the Federal Reserve System.

If You Use a Credit Card. Washington, D.C.: Board of Governors of the Federal Reserve System.

Myerson, Bess. *Consumer Guidelines to Shopping by Mail.* New York: Direct Mail Marketing Association.

Richardson, Lee. *Consumer Newsletter.* Columbia, Md.

Rosenbloom, Joseph. *Consumer Complaint Guide.* New York: Macmillan, 1984.

Truth in Leasing. Prepared jointly by the Federal Trade Commission and the Board of Governors of the Federal Reserve System.

U. S. Office of Consumer Affairs. *A Consumer's Shopping List of Inflation-Fighting Ideas.* Pueblo, Col.: Consumer Information Center.

What Truth in Lending Means to You. Revised ed. Washington, D.C.: Board of Governors of the Federal Reserve System.

"When You Move—Do's and Don'ts." Pueblo, Col.: Consumer Information Center.

Your Credit Rating. Department of Consumer Affairs, Federal Reserve Bank of Philadelphia.

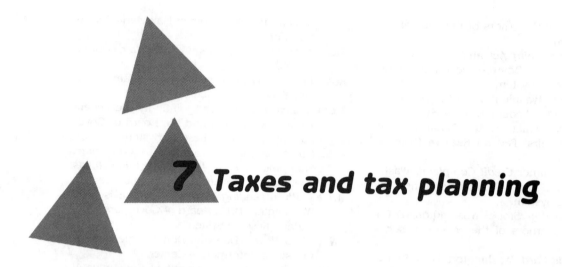

7 Taxes and tax planning

HIGHLIGHTS   In order to help the reader understand the tax regulations, this chapter examines the following:

1   State and local taxes
2   The federal income tax and how it works
3   Who must file a return and pay a tax
4   The standard deduction
5   The personal exemptions
6   The tax forms
7   A thumbnail sketch of the 1990 Tax Act
8   Income that is and is not taxable
9   Adjusted gross income and the deductions allowed to arrive at adjusted gross income
10 Allowable itemized deducations
11 Certain tax credits that can reduce taxes
12 The alternative minimum tax
13 The course of action to follow in the event of an audit

INTRODUCTION

Individuals cannot avoid paying taxes, but with proper planning they can lessen the amount they would otherwise pay. There are state, local, and federal taxes, and each one of them can take a significant part of a person's income. There are also Social Security taxes, but they will be discussed in Chapter 18. In this chapter we will discuss taxes of all the three above-mentioned levels of taxing entities; but we will concentrate on federal income taxes because they are the most complex, and for many of us they take away the largest dollar amount of our income. After a brief analysis of state and local taxes, we will work through the current federal personal income tax law, with an emphasis on legally minimizing taxes. Many people overpay income taxes because of lack of knowledge or carelessness.

There is a difference between evading and avoiding taxes. Evading taxes is deliberately cheating and not paying taxes that are due. It is illegal and a person guilty of this is subject to penalties, fines, and even confinement in a federal penitentiary. Avoiding taxes is legal; it consists of using a knowledge of the law to minimize taxes. Chief Justice Oliver Wendell Holmes said that "every man has a right to so arrange his affairs as to minimize his taxes."

TAXES, EXPENDITURES, AND NATIONAL INCOME

Government expenditures at all levels have risen sharply in recent years. Federal expenditures were $96.5 billion in 1965. In 1990 they exceeded one trillion dollars. In 1991 they are expected to be $1.31 trillion. Among the reasons are growth in population and the increase in the demand for

"Your return was neat and accurate and indicated that you understood the forms completely . . . what we want to know is how?" (Source: Permission Cartoon Features Syndicate; from The Wall Street Journal.)

more government services. Along with greater government expenditures came an increase in taxes.

Comparing taxes and expenditures with national income and gross national product is one indicator of the cost (or burden) of government, since taxes are paid out of income. Table 7–1 shows federal taxes and expenditures, together with national income figures. The figures in Table 7–1 are aggregates.

At the personal level a person can compare his or her total taxes paid with his or her income. The percent of one's income paid to the government in the form of taxes is called the effective tax rate, and it can be considered as the person's personal tax burden—or cost of government. The figures below only include federal tax. In order to get the total cost of all governments, the taxpayer must make the same analysis of state and local taxes. This calculation can be made quite accurately for state and city income taxes and for property taxes. In the case of sales

U.S. taxes, expenditures, and national income   Table 7–1

Year	Taxes	Expenditures	National income	Taxes as a % of National Income	Expenditures as a % of National income
1971	$ 188.4	211.4	858.1	22.0%	24.6%
1972	208.6	232.0	951.9	21.9	24.4
1973	232.2	247.1	1,064.6	21.8	23.2
1974	264.9	269.6	1,136.0	23.3	23.7
1975	281.0	326.2	1,215.0	23.1	26.9
1976	300.0	366.4	1,359.8	22.1	27.0
1977	357.8	402.7	1,525.8	23.5	26.4
1978	402.0	450.8	1,724.3	23.3	26.1
1979	465.9	493.6	1,924.8	24.2	25.6
1980	532.2	572.7	2,117.1	25.1	27.1
1981	599.3	657.2	2,352.5	25.4	27.9
1982	617.8	728.4	2,436.6	25.3	29.8
1983	600.6	808.5	2,718.3	22.9	29.7
1984	666.5	851.1	3,039.3	21.9	28.0
1985	734.0	945.9	3,104.4	23.6	30.5
1986	769.1	989.8	3,386.4	22.7	29.2
1987	854.1	1,004.6	3,635.3	23.5	27.6
1988	909.2	1,055.9	3,849.8	23.6	27.4
1989	990.7	1,142.6	4,223.3	23.5	27.1
1990	1,044.2	1,264.3	4,651.5	22.5	27.2
1991*	1,135.4	1,311.7	—	—	—

*Estimates

Source: *Economic Indicators,* Council of Economic Advisors, September 1990, p. 32.

taxes, however, the taxpayer will probably have to rely on an estimate as to total sales-tax dollars.

State and local taxes

While some states and even some cities impose income taxes, the bulk of state and local tax revenues are from sales and property taxes. The largest single portion of the property tax goes to support the schools, but city and county governments also derive some revenue from it. Many cities today also have a sales tax. The bulk of sales tax receipts, however, flow into state treasuries. Other major sources of revenue for states in addition to income taxes are excise taxes, such as gasoline, liquor, and cigarette taxes.

Sales taxes

Sales taxes are imposed at the retail level. In some states, there are certain exempted or nontaxed items, and in others there are none. The most commonly exempted items are food consumed in the home and services such as doctors' fees, haircuts, laundry bills, and the like. Generally, rates vary from 4 to 7 percent for the states' share, and some cities add a bit more to this, usually 1 or 2 percent. The retail merchant must collect this tax and usually can keep a small part of it (this varies from state to state but generally is 1 percent of the taxes due) to cover collection cost.

The sales tax is considered to be regressive because it takes away a larger portion of a low income than a high one. It is a tax on consumption, and low-income persons consume a higher percentage (save less) of their income than do high-income persons. For example, let us assume that Mr. A has $20,000 after withholding tax take-home income per year, and let us say he saves $500 and consumes $19,500 and lives in an area that levies a 7 percent sales tax. Depending on whether or not food and services are taxed, he will pay about $1,365 in sales taxes per year. This is 6.82 percent of his take-home pay. Let us assume Ms. B is earning $50,000 take-home pay per year and lives in the same town. But she consumes $45,000 and saves $5,000 of it; hence, she pays about $3,150 in sales taxes, which is 6.3 percent of her income.[1] As incomes rise further, the percentage taken away under the sales tax generally declines further. Even though sales taxes are taxes on consumption, many citizens seem to prefer this kind of tax to a state or local income tax. This may be because it is paid in small amounts and seems more painless. The sales tax has the virtues of being broad-based and raising a lot of revenue; the administrative and collection cost is low relative to the revenue it raises.

---

1. A sales tax of 7 percent may result in taxes of more than 7 percent of total consumption, because most purchases are in small amounts and fractional dollars are taxed at a higher rate. There are breaking points on the tables that the merchants use to calculate the tax and often the seven cents per dollar tax is reached at seventy cents.

While some state and local governments impose a personal property tax (on automobiles, boats, and the like) and some even on intangible personal property (on bank accounts and securities), these taxes do not raise much revenue. The biggest single property tax for most individuals is on real estate—that is, on the person's home. The real property tax is an ancient device. It is not considered the best tax, but it will no doubt remain with us because it raises a good deal of revenue. Some states have abandoned the property tax levying, leaving it as a source of revenue for the local taxing units.

The property tax is generally shared by the city government, the county government, and in some cases the state government, and the school system, with the latter getting the largest share. Sometimes, however, a portion of the tax is also earmarked for specific items such as a sewer or water district. In some areas, the tax is paid to one of the above governments (usually the city or the county) and is then disbursed to the other units in accordance with the predetermined percentage share each is to get. In other areas, various local governments cannot get together and the home owner must write two (or more) checks and pay the county's share and the city's share separately. In most cases, if a client is paying off a mortgage loan on a home, the lending institution will add one-twelfth ($1/12$) of the estimated annual tax to the monthly payment and then pay this tax for the home owner when due.

The computation of the property tax is roughly the same everywhere. The only variables are the appraised (or assessed) value and the tax rate or millage rate. The assessed value generally varies from about 20 percent to 75 percent of the market value of the property.

The tax rate applied to assessed value to obtain the actual tax liability is stated either as a percentage (so much dollarwise per $100 of assessed valuation) or in mills (a mill is one-tenth of one cent). A house with a $100,000 assessed value could be taxed at 6 percent of its assessed valuation or 60 mills per hundred dollars of assessed valuation. In both cases the tax on it is $6,000. Generally speaking, real estate is reappraised every few years to take into account appreciation in the market value. Periodically, too, the tax rate is raised.

A growing number of states and a few cities have an income tax. A few years ago most of the states having income taxes had laws that did not take advantage of the federal income tax. Therefore, after filing federal taxes, one had to go file again at the state level. Recently, more states have tied their income taxes into the federal government's. Consequently, after filing the federal form, a copy of it could be sent to the state authorities as verification of earned income and only a relatively simple additional state form would be needed.

*Other state and
local taxes*

A number of other taxes are levied by state and local governments. The most important of these are gasoline and tobacco taxes, taxes on liquor and hotel rooms, the personal property tax, personal intangible property tax, license and fees on a car, estate and inheritance taxes, and corporate income taxes. These are the major ones in use today.

FEDERAL PERSONAL INCOME TAXES

Although there are other federal taxes (for example, on corporations), the federal personal income tax is the largest revenue producer and the tax that has the biggest impact on the average citizen. In fiscal 1991 the federal government is expected to collect about $508.4 billion through personal income taxes.[2] This will be about 43 percent of total tax receipts. (The second largest source of revenue is the Social Security tax; and the third largest, the corporate income tax.) Figure 7–1 illustrates where the federal dollar comes from and where it goes for the year 1990 and provides an estimated graph for 1991.

In 1986, Congress passed and the president signed The Tax Reform Act of 1986. It contained massive changes in the tax code. It was intended to be revenue neutral in that it was not to increase aggregate tax receipts. In order to do this, it was inevitable that it would change the burden of who pays how much tax. There was also a Technical Tax Correction Act of 1988, which made some modest changes. The most recent change in tax law occurred in October 1990.

*Who must file a
return?*

Generally speaking, any individual must file an income tax return in 1990 if he or she had a gross income of $5,300 or more, if single. If married and filing jointly, the figure is $9,550, and for a head of household it is $6,800.[3] If married and filing separately, the magic figure is $4,775. This is because of the standard deduction and the personal exemption. These deductions and exemptions are indexed annually to offset inflation.

---

2. The fiscal year differs from the calendar year. The fiscal year runs from October 1 through September 30. The fiscal year 1991, then, covers October 1, 1990, through September 30, 1991.

3. See section on head of household in this chapter.

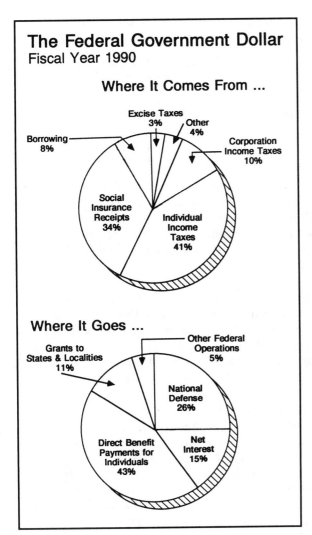

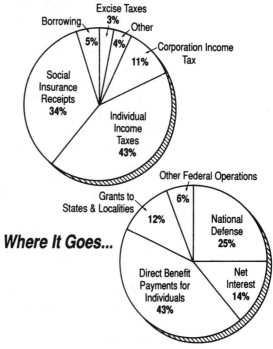

The budget dollar, fiscal year 1990 and estimates for 1991. (Source: The United States Budget, Fiscal Year 1990, Office of Management and the Budget, Washington, D.C.)   Figure 7—1

The standard deduction

There is a standard deduction for taxpayers who do not itemize their deductions. The following table shows the standard deduction for 1990.

	Standard deductions
	1990
Married filing jointly	$5,450
Unmarried	3,250
Heads of household	4,750
Married filing separately	2,725

These standard deductions are adjusted annually for inflation. Taxpayers age sixty-five and over and those who are blind are allowed an additional deduction of $750 if single and $600 if married. If the taxpayer is both blind and over 65, the above figures become $1,500 and $1,200.[4] These additional deductions are also adjusted occasionally for inflation.

The personal exemption

Each taxpayer also has a personal exemption of $2,000 for tax years after 1988 (adjusted annually for inflation) for every qualifying dependent. In 1990 the personal exemption is $2,050. A married taxpayer with two children (four total qualifying exemptions), filing jointly, and taking the standard deduction would not pay any taxes in 1990 until his or her income exceeded $13,650 (the exemptions of $8,200 plus the standard deduction of $5,450).

A person receives an exemption for himself or herself, his or her spouse, and for each person qualifying as a dependent for tax purposes. To qualify as a dependent, the person must meet the requirements of five different tests, one of which is that he or she must receive more than one-half of his or her support from the taxpayer. Married taxpayers may file jointly and claim two personal exemptions (assuming no other dependents), or separately and each claim only himself or herself. Table 7–2 illustrates who must file a tax return and possibly pay a federal income tax.

If a person does not owe a tax but has had taxes withheld and is entitled to a refund, he or she must, of course, file a return to obtain the refund.

The tax forms

There are three basic forms from which certain individuals may choose when filing their taxes. These are (1) 1040EZ, which is very short; (2) the 1040A, which is also quite short; and (3) the 1040, which is longer and is required for more complex returns.

---

4. The additional allowance for the elderly and the blind was converted from an additional exemption to an additional deduction by the 1986 tax change. This means that the taxpayers who itemize deductions do not receive it as an additional benefit.

Deductions and exemptions, 1990   Table 7—2

Category	Standard deduction*	Exemptions*	Income not taxed*
Single	$3,250	$ 2,050	$ 5,300
Single over 65	4,000	2,050	6,050
Married joint return	5,450	4,100	9,550
Married joint return—one spouse over 65	6,050	4,100	10,150
Married filing separately**	2,725	2,050	4,775
Married joint return—3 children	5,450	10,025	15,075
Unmarried head of household	4,750	2,050	6,800

*These figures will be adjusted annually for inflation.

**Each spouse receives that amount.

The 1040EZ form may only be used if the taxpayer:

- is single and claims *only* his or her own personal exemption.
- has income *only* from wages, salaries and tips, taxable scholarships and fellowships, and interest of $400 or less.
- has taxable income of less than $50,000.
- does not itemize deductions or claim any adjustments to income or tax credits.
- is not liable for any special taxes
- is neither blind nor age 65 or older

Form 1040A may be used if the taxpayer:

- had income *only* from wages, salaries, tips, taxable scholarships and fellowships, taxable IRA distributions, taxable pensions and annuities, taxable social security benefits, unemployment compensation, interest, or dividends.
- has taxable income of less than $50,000.
- does not itemize deductions.
- claims as an adjustment *to* income only the deduction for an IRA contribution.
- claims only the child and dependent care credit, the credit for the elderly or the disabled, or the earned income credit.
- is not liable for any special taxes.

Another difference between Form 1040A and 1040EZ is that married taxpayers may use 1040A, but not 1040EZ. In other words, all taxpayers may use 1040A. This is a two-page form and is easy to fill out.

All others must use Form 1040. The 1040 is a two-page form and may be used without any attachments by many taxpayers. If a person has income solely from wages, salaries, tips, interest and dividends, or certain miscellaneous income and does not itemize deductions, the basic two-page form is all that need be completed. If the taxpayer has income from other sources, wishes to itemize deductions, or wishes to claim certain credits, supplementary schedules must be filled out and attached to the 1040. After having calculated his or her taxable income, the taxpayer must use the appropriate tax table to obtain the tax liability if his or her taxable income is less than $50,000. These tables are found in the "Tax Forms and Instructions" booklet made available by the IRS. This booklet, incidentally, is a very valuable source of information when filing taxes, because it contains the answers to many questions the taxpayer may have. (A number of tax booklets and guides to assist the taxpayer may be obtained free of charge from the IRS.)

If the taxpayer has an adjusted gross income of more than $50,000, he or she cannot use the tax tables, but must use the appropriate Tax Rate Schedule (either Schedule X, Y-1, Y-2, or Z) furnished by the IRS and included in the 1040 "Tax Forms and Instructions" booklet.

If deductions are itemized, the individual should compare them with the standard deduction, and take whichever is the larger. The itemized deduction (or standard deduction) is subtracted from adjusted gross income (AGI); then the personal exemptions are subtracted from that; this brings the taxpayer to taxable income on which taxes are calculated.

An example of one page of the tax tables is shown in Table 7–3. Shown, too, are the tax forms 1040EZ, 1040A, 1040, and the Tax Rate Schedules X, Y-1, Y-2, and Z (for single taxpayers, married taxpayers, and qualifying heads of household). These sample forms follow as Tables 7–4 through 7–7.

The IRS requires that certain other forms be attached to the 1040 return in some cases. For example, Schedule A, which shows itemized deductions, must be attached if the taxpayer itemizes. This form, too, is shown as Table 7–8. If the taxpayer has farm income, sole proprietorship business income, capital gains, or certain other income or tax credits, additional schedules and forms would need to be submitted. These additional forms are explained in the IRS "Forms and Instructions" booklet.

A thumbnail sketch of the 1990 Tax Act

In October 1990, Congress passed and the president signed a new tax law. These changes, to become effective mostly in 1991, are integrated into this chapter, but below is a summary of the major changes.

The new law raised federal tax in three general areas that are important for financial planners. They include certain excise taxes; the Medicare part of Social Security taxes, together with payments to be made by Medicare beneficiaries; and personal income taxes. The new taxes become effective in 1991, except where noted to the contrary.

*1989 tax table**   *Table 7—3*

1989 Tax Table—Continued

41,000 / 42,000 / 43,000

If line 37 (taxable income) is— At least	But less than	Single	Married filing jointly *	Married filing separately	Head of a household
41,000					
41,000	41,050	9,076	7,464	9,655	8,257
41,050	41,100	9,090	7,478	9,672	8,271
41,100	41,150	9,104	7,492	9,688	8,285
41,150	41,200	9,118	7,506	9,705	8,299
41,200	41,250	9,132	7,520	9,721	8,313
41,250	41,300	9,146	7,534	9,738	8,327
41,300	41,350	9,160	7,548	9,754	8,341
41,350	41,400	9,174	7,562	9,771	8,355
41,400	41,450	9,188	7,576	9,787	8,369
41,450	41,500	9,202	7,590	9,804	8,383
41,500	41,550	9,216	7,604	9,820	8,397
41,550	41,600	9,230	7,618	9,837	8,411
41,600	41,650	9,244	7,632	9,853	8,425
41,650	41,700	9,258	7,646	9,870	8,439
41,700	41,750	9,272	7,660	9,886	8,453
41,750	41,800	9,286	7,674	9,903	8,467
41,800	41,850	9,300	7,688	9,919	8,481
41,850	41,900	9,314	7,702	9,936	8,495
41,900	41,950	9,328	7,716	9,952	8,509
41,950	42,000	9,342	7,730	9,969	8,523
42,000					
42,000	42,050	9,356	7,744	9,985	8,537
42,050	42,100	9,370	7,758	10,002	8,551
42,100	42,150	9,384	7,772	10,018	8,565
42,150	42,200	9,398	7,786	10,035	8,579
42,200	42,250	9,412	7,800	10,051	8,593
42,250	42,300	9,426	7,814	10,068	8,607
42,300	42,350	9,440	7,828	10,084	8,621
42,350	42,400	9,454	7,842	10,101	8,635
42,400	42,450	9,468	7,856	10,117	8,649
42,450	42,500	9,482	7,870	10,134	8,663
42,500	42,550	9,496	7,884	10,150	8,677
42,550	42,600	9,510	7,898	10,167	8,691
42,600	42,650	9,524	7,912	10,183	8,705
42,650	42,700	9,538	7,926	10,200	8,719
42,700	42,750	9,552	7,940	10,216	8,733
42,750	42,800	9,566	7,954	10,233	8,747
42,800	42,850	9,580	7,968	10,249	8,761
42,850	42,900	9,594	7,982	10,266	8,775
42,900	42,950	9,608	7,996	10,282	8,789
42,950	43,000	9,622	8,010	10,299	8,803
43,000					
43,000	43,050	9,636	8,024	10,315	8,817
43,050	43,100	9,650	8,038	10,332	8,831
43,100	43,150	9,664	8,052	10,348	8,845
43,150	43,200	9,678	8,066	10,365	8,859
43,200	43,250	9,692	8,080	10,381	8,873
43,250	43,300	9,706	8,094	10,398	8,887
43,300	43,350	9,720	8,108	10,414	8,901
43,350	43,400	9,734	8,122	10,431	8,915
43,400	43,450	9,748	8,136	10,447	8,929
43,450	43,500	9,762	8,150	10,464	8,943
43,500	43,550	9,776	8,164	10,480	8,957
43,550	43,600	9,790	8,178	10,497	8,971
43,600	43,650	9,804	8,192	10,513	8,985
43,650	43,700	9,818	8,206	10,530	8,999
43,700	43,750	9,832	8,220	10,546	9,013
43,750	43,800	9,846	8,234	10,563	9,027
43,800	43,850	9,860	8,248	10,579	9,041
43,850	43,900	9,874	8,262	10,596	9,055
43,900	43,950	9,888	8,276	10,612	9,069
43,950	44,000	9,902	8,290	10,629	9,083

44,000 / 45,000 / 46,000

If line 37 (taxable income) is— At least	But less than	Single	Married filing jointly *	Married filing separately	Head of a household
44,000					
44,000	44,050	9,916	8,304	10,645	9,097
44,050	44,100	9,930	8,318	10,662	9,111
44,100	44,150	9,944	8,332	10,678	9,125
44,150	44,200	9,958	8,346	10,695	9,139
44,200	44,250	9,972	8,360	10,711	9,153
44,250	44,300	9,986	8,374	10,728	9,167
44,300	44,350	10,000	8,388	10,744	9,181
44,350	44,400	10,014	8,402	10,761	9,195
44,400	44,450	10,028	8,416	10,777	9,209
44,450	44,500	10,042	8,430	10,794	9,223
44,500	44,550	10,056	8,444	10,810	9,237
44,550	44,600	10,070	8,458	10,827	9,251
44,600	44,650	10,084	8,472	10,843	9,265
44,650	44,700	10,098	8,486	10,860	9,279
44,700	44,750	10,112	8,500	10,876	9,293
44,750	44,800	10,126	8,514	10,893	9,307
44,800	44,850	10,140	8,528	10,909	9,321
44,850	44,900	10,154	8,542	10,926	9,335
44,900	44,950	10,169	8,556	10,942	9,349
44,950	45,000	10,185	8,570	10,959	9,363
45,000					
45,000	45,050	10,202	8,584	10,975	9,377
45,050	45,100	10,218	8,598	10,992	9,391
45,100	45,150	10,235	8,612	11,008	9,405
45,150	45,200	10,251	8,626	11,025	9,419
45,200	45,250	10,268	8,640	11,041	9,433
45,250	45,300	10,284	8,654	11,058	9,447
45,300	45,350	10,301	8,668	11,074	9,461
45,350	45,400	10,317	8,682	11,091	9,475
45,400	45,450	10,334	8,696	11,107	9,489
45,450	45,500	10,350	8,710	11,124	9,503
45,500	45,550	10,367	8,724	11,140	9,517
45,550	45,600	10,383	8,738	11,157	9,531
45,600	45,650	10,400	8,752	11,173	9,545
45,650	45,700	10,416	8,766	11,190	9,559
45,700	45,750	10,433	8,780	11,206	9,573
45,750	45,800	10,449	8,794	11,223	9,587
45,800	45,850	10,466	8,808	11,239	9,601
45,850	45,900	10,482	8,822	11,256	9,615
45,900	45,950	10,499	8,836	11,272	9,629
45,950	46,000	10,515	8,850	11,289	9,643
46,000					
46,000	46,050	10,532	8,864	11,305	9,657
46,050	46,100	10,548	8,878	11,322	9,671
46,100	46,150	10,565	8,892	11,338	9,685
46,150	46,200	10,581	8,906	11,355	9,699
46,200	46,250	10,598	8,920	11,371	9,713
46,250	46,300	10,614	8,934	11,388	9,727
46,300	46,350	10,631	8,948	11,404	9,741
46,350	46,400	10,647	8,962	11,421	9,755
46,400	46,450	10,664	8,976	11,437	9,769
46,450	46,500	10,680	8,990	11,454	9,783
46,500	46,550	10,697	9,004	11,470	9,797
46,550	46,600	10,713	9,018	11,487	9,811
46,600	46,650	10,730	9,032	11,503	9,825
46,650	46,700	10,746	9,046	11,520	9,839
46,700	46,750	10,763	9,060	11,536	9,853
46,750	46,800	10,779	9,074	11,553	9,867
46,800	46,850	10,796	9,088	11,569	9,881
46,850	46,900	10,812	9,102	11,586	9,895
46,900	46,950	10,829	9,116	11,602	9,909
46,950	47,000	10,845	9,130	11,619	9,923

47,000 / 48,000 / 49,000

If line 37 (taxable income) is— At least	But less than	Single	Married filing jointly *	Married filing separately	Head of a household
47,000					
47,000	47,050	10,862	9,144	11,635	9,937
47,050	47,100	10,878	9,158	11,652	9,951
47,100	47,150	10,895	9,172	11,668	9,965
47,150	47,200	10,911	9,186	11,685	9,979
47,200	47,250	10,928	9,200	11,701	9,993
47,250	47,300	10,944	9,214	11,718	10,007
47,300	47,350	10,961	9,228	11,734	10,021
47,350	47,400	10,977	9,242	11,751	10,035
47,400	47,450	10,994	9,256	11,767	10,049
47,450	47,500	11,010	9,270	11,784	10,063
47,500	47,550	11,027	9,284	11,800	10,077
47,550	47,600	11,043	9,298	11,817	10,091
47,600	47,650	11,060	9,312	11,833	10,105
47,650	47,700	11,076	9,326	11,850	10,119
47,700	47,750	11,093	9,340	11,866	10,133
47,750	47,800	11,109	9,354	11,883	10,147
47,800	47,850	11,126	9,368	11,899	10,161
47,850	47,900	11,142	9,382	11,916	10,175
47,900	47,950	11,159	9,396	11,932	10,189
47,950	48,000	11,175	9,410	11,949	10,203
48,000					
48,000	48,050	11,192	9,424	11,965	10,217
48,050	48,100	11,208	9,438	11,982	10,231
48,100	48,150	11,225	9,452	11,998	10,245
48,150	48,200	11,241	9,466	12,015	10,259
48,200	48,250	11,258	9,480	12,031	10,273
48,250	48,300	11,274	9,494	12,048	10,287
48,300	48,350	11,291	9,508	12,064	10,301
48,350	48,400	11,307	9,522	12,081	10,315
48,400	48,450	11,324	9,536	12,097	10,329
48,450	48,500	11,340	9,550	12,114	10,343
48,500	48,550	11,357	9,564	12,130	10,357
48,550	48,600	11,373	9,578	12,147	10,371
48,600	48,650	11,390	9,592	12,163	10,385
48,650	48,700	11,406	9,606	12,180	10,399
48,700	48,750	11,423	9,620	12,196	10,413
48,750	48,800	11,439	9,634	12,213	10,427
48,800	48,850	11,456	9,648	12,229	10,441
48,850	48,900	11,472	9,662	12,246	10,455
48,900	48,950	11,489	9,676	12,262	10,469
48,950	49,000	11,505	9,690	12,279	10,483
49,000					
49,000	49,050	11,522	9,704	12,295	10,497
49,050	49,100	11,538	9,718	12,312	10,511
49,100	49,150	11,555	9,732	12,328	10,525
49,150	49,200	11,571	9,746	12,345	10,539
49,200	49,250	11,588	9,760	12,361	10,553
49,250	49,300	11,604	9,774	12,378	10,567
49,300	49,350	11,621	9,788	12,394	10,581
49,350	49,400	11,637	9,802	12,411	10,595
49,400	49,450	11,654	9,816	12,427	10,609
49,450	49,500	11,670	9,830	12,444	10,623
49,500	49,550	11,687	9,844	12,460	10,637
49,550	49,600	11,703	9,858	12,477	10,651
49,600	49,650	11,720	9,872	12,493	10,665
49,650	49,700	11,736	9,886	12,510	10,679
49,700	49,750	11,753	9,900	12,526	10,693
49,750	49,800	11,769	9,914	12,543	10,707
49,800	49,850	11,786	9,928	12,559	10,721
49,850	49,900	11,802	9,942	12,576	10,735
49,900	49,950	11,819	9,956	12,592	10,749
49,950	50,000	11,835	9,970	12,609	10,763

* This column must also be used by a qualifying widow(er).

50,000 or over—use tax rate schedules

Page 50

*1990 Tax Tables were not available from the IRS at the time of publication of this book. The 1990 figures will change slightly.

Table 7—4 *1040 EZ sample*

Department of the Treasury - Internal Revenue Service

Form 1040EZ

Income Tax Return for Single Filers With No Dependents **1990**

OMB No. 1545-0675

Name & address

Use IRS label (see page 8). If you don't have one, please print.

Print your name (first, initial, last)

JOHN   Q.   DOE

Home address (number and street). (If you have a P O. box, see page 9.)   Apt. no.

1234   KAY ST.

City, town or post office, state, and ZIP code. (If you have a foreign address, see page 9.)

ANYTOWN   USA   99900

Please print your numbers like this:

9 8 7 6 5 4 3 2 1 0

Your social security number

1 2 3 4 5 6 7 8 8

See the back. Also, see the Form 1040EZ booklet.

Presidential Election Campaign (see page 9)
Do you want $1 to go to this fund?

Note: Checking "Yes" will not change your tax or reduce your refund. ▶

Yes No

X

Dollars   Cents

Report your income

Attach Copy B of Form(s) W-2 here. Attach tax payment on top of Form(s) W-2.

Note: You must check Yes or No.

1 Total wages, salaries, and tips. This should be shown in Box 10 of your W-2 form(s). (Attach your W-2 form(s).)   **1**   12,750.00

2 Taxable interest income of $400 or less. If the total is more than $400. you cannot use Form 1040EZ.   **2**   25.25

3 Add line 1 and line 2. This is your adjusted gross income.   **3**   12,775.25

4 Can your parents (or someone else) claim you on their return?
☐ **Yes.** Do worksheet on back; enter amount from line E here.
☒ **No.** Enter 5,300.00. This is the total of your standard deduction and personal exemption.   **4**   5,300.00

5 Subtract line 4 from line 3. If line 4 is larger than line 3, enter 0. This is your taxable income.   **5**   7,475.25

Figure your tax

6 Enter your Federal income tax withheld from Box 9 of your W-2 form(s).   **6**   1,110.00

7 **Tax.** Use the amount on **line 5** to find your tax in the tax table on pages 14-16 of the booklet. Enter the tax from the table on this line.   **7**   1,121.00

Refund or amount you owe

8 If line 6 is larger than line 7, subtract line 7 from line 6. This is your **refund.**   **8**

9 If line 7 is larger than line 6. subtract line 6 from line 7. This is the **amount you owe.** Attach your payment for full amount payable to "Internal Revenue Service." Write your name, address, social security number, daytime phone number, and "1990 Form 1040EZ" on it.   **9**   11.00

Sign your return

(Keep a copy of this form for your records.)

I have read this return. Under penalties of perjury, I declare that to the best of my knowledge and belief, the return is true, correct, and complete.

Your signature   Date

X

For IRS Use Only—Please do not write in boxes below.

NOTE: Because the 1990 Tax Tables were unavailable from the IRS at the time of publication of this book, the taxes were calculated from the 1990 Tax Rate Schedules. A very slight variation may occur.

For **Privacy Act and Paperwork Reduction Act Notice,** see page 3 in the booklet.   Form 1040EZ (1990)

1990   **Instructions for Form 1040EZ**

Use this form if	• Your filing status is single. • You were under 65 and not blind at the end of 1990.

• Your filing status is single.

• You do not claim any dependents.

• You were under 65 and not blind at the end of 1990.

• Your taxable income (line 5) is less than $50.000.

• You had **only** wages. salaries. tips, and taxable scholarships or fellowships, and your taxable interest income was $400 or less. *Caution: If you earned tips (including allocated tips) that are not included in Box 13 of your W-2, you may not be able to use Form 1040EZ. See page 10 in the booklet.*

If you are not sure about your filing status or dependents. **see page 4 in the booklet.**

If you can't use this form. see Tele-Tax *(topic no. 152)* on page 23 in the booklet.

Completing your return

Please print your numbers inside the boxes. Do not type your numbers. Do not use dollar signs.

Most people can fill out the form simply by following the instructions on the front. But you will have to use the booklet if you received a scholarship or fellowship or tax-exempt interest (such as on municipal bonds). Also use the booklet if you received a 1099-INT showing income tax withheld (backup withholding) or if you had two or more employers and your total wages were more than $51.300.

Remember, you must report your wages. salaries. and tips even if you don't get a W-2 form from your employer. You must also report all your taxable interest income from savings accounts at banks. savings and loans. credit unions. etc., even if you don't get a Form 1099-INT.

Standard deduction worksheet for dependents who checked "Yes" on line 4

If you checked "Yes" because someone can claim you as a dependent. fill in this worksheet to figure the amount to enter on line 4.

A.	Enter the amount from line 1 on front.	A. _____
B.	Minimum amount.	B. _____ 500.00
C.	**Compare** the amounts on lines A and B above. Enter the LARGER of the two amounts here.	C. _____
D.	Maximum amount.	D. _____ 3.250.00
E.	**Compare** the amounts on lines C and D above. Enter the SMALLER of the two amounts here and on line 4 on front.	E. _____

If you checked "No" because no one can claim you as a dependent. enter 5.300.00 on line 4. This is the total of your standard deduction (3.250.00) and personal exemption (2.050.00).

Avoid common mistakes

This checklist is to help you make sure that your form is filled out correctly.

1. Are your name and address correct on the label? If not, did you correct the label?

2. Is your social security number correct?

3. Did you attach your W-2 form(s) to the left margin of your return?

4. Did you add and subtract correctly?

5. If someone (such as your parent) can claim you as a dependent on his or her tax return, did you check the "Yes" box on line 4 and fill out the worksheet above?

6. Did you enter an amount on line 4?

7. Did you use the amount from **line 5** to find your tax in the tax table?

8. Did you sign and date your return? If you paid someone to prepare your return, did that person sign it and show other information? See page 13 in the booklet.

Mailing your return

Mail your return by **April 15, 1991.** Use the envelope that came with your booklet. If you don't have that envelope, **see page 17 in the booklet for the address to use.**

Table 7—5   1040A sample

1040A	U.S. Individual Income Tax Return	1990		OMB No. 1545-0085

Step 1
Label
(See page 14.)

Use IRS label. Otherwise. please print or type.

Your first name and initial: JOHN J. — Last name: DOE

If a joint return, spouse's first name and initial: JANE J. — Last name: DOE

Home address (number and street). (If you have a P.O. box. see page 15.): 1111 JAY St. — Apt. no.

City. town or post office. state and ZIP code. (If you have a foreign address. see page 15.): ANYTOWN, USA 99999

Your social security no.: 123 45 6789
Spouse's social security no.: 987 65 4321

For Privacy Act and Paperwork Reduction Act Notice, see page 3.

Presidential Election Campaign Fund (see page 15)
Do you want $1 to go to this fund?. . . . . ☒ Yes ☐ No
If joint return. does your spouse want $1 to go to this fund? ☐ Yes ☒ No

Note: *Checking "Yes" will not change your tax or reduce your refund.*

Step 2
Check your filing status
(Check only one.)

1 ☐ Single. (See page 16 to find out if you can file as head of household.)
2 ☒ Married filing joint return (even if only one had income)
3 ☐ Married filing separate return. Enter spouse's social security number above and spouse's full name here ▶
4 ☐ Head of household (with qualifying person). (See page 16.) If the qualifying person is your child but not your dependent, enter this child's name here ▶
5 ☐ Qualifying widow(er) with dependent child (year spouse died ▶ 19 ___). (See page 17.)

Step 3
Figure your exemptions
(See page 17.)

6a ☒ Yourself   If someone else (such as your parent) can claim you as a dependent on his or her tax return. do not check box 6a. But be sure to check the box on line 18b on page 2.
6b ☒ Spouse

No. of boxes checked on 6a and 6b: **2**

c Dependents:

1. Name (first, initial. and last name)	2. Check if under age 2	3. If age 2 or older. dependent's social security number	4. Relationship	5. No. of months lived in your home in 1990
SUSIE K. DOE		111 12 1234	child	12

If more than 7 dependents. see page 20.

No. of your children on 6c who:
● lived with you: **1**
● didn't live with you due to divorce or separation (see page 20)
No. of other dependents listed on 6c

d If your child didn't live with you but is claimed as your dependent under a pre-1985 agreement, check here . . . . ▶ ☐
e Total number of exemptions claimed.

Add numbers entered on lines above: **3**

Step 4
Figure your total income

Attach Copy B of your Forms W-2 and W-2P here.

Attach check or money order on top of any Forms W-2 or W-2P.

7 Wages, salaries, tips, etc. This should be shown in Box 10 of your W-2 form(s). (Attach Form(s) W-2.) — 7 | 38060 | 55
8a Taxable interest income (see page 23). (If over $400, also complete and attach Schedule 1, Part I.) — 8a | 231 | 25
b Tax-exempt interest. (DO NOT include on line 8a.) 8b
9 Dividends. (If over $400, also complete and attach Schedule 1, Part II.) — 9
10a Total IRA distributions. 10a — 10b Taxable amount (see page 24). 10b
11a Total pensions and annuities. 11a — 11b Taxable amount (see page 24). 11b
12 Unemployment compensation (insurance) from Form(s) 1099-G. 12
13a Social security benefits. 13a — 13b Taxable amount (see page 27). 13b
14 Add lines 7 through 13b (far right column). This is your **total income.** ▶ 14 | 38291 | 80

Step 5
Figure your adjusted gross income

15a Your IRA deduction from applicable worksheet. 15a | 200
b Spouse's IRA deduction from applicable worksheet.
Note: *Rules for IRAs begin on page 29.* 15b | 200
c Add lines 15a and 15b. These are your **total adjustments.** 15c | 400 | 00
16 Subtract line 15c from line 14. This is your **adjusted gross income.** (If less than $20,264, see "Earned income credit" on page 39.) ▶ 16 | 37891 | 80

1990   Form 1040A   Page 2

Step 6	17	Enter the amount from line 16.	17 37891 80

Figure your standard deduction,

18a Check { ☐ **You were 65 or older**   ☐ **Blind** } Enter number of
if: { ☐ **Spouse** was 65 or older ☐ **Blind** } boxes checked ▶18a ☐

b If someone else (such as your parent) can claim you as a
dependent, check here . . . . 18b ☐

c If you are married filing separately and your spouse files Form
1040 and itemizes deductions, see page 33 and check here . . . ▶18c ☐

19 Enter your standard deduction. See page 33 for the chart (or worksheet)
that applies to you. Be sure to enter your standard deduction here.   19 5450 00

exemption amount, and

20 Subtract line 19 from line 17. (If line 19 is more than line 17, enter -0-.)   20 32441 80

21 Multiply $2,050 by the total number of exemptions claimed on line 6e.   21 6150 00

taxable income

22 Subtract line 21 from line 20. (If line 21 is more than line 20, enter -0-.) This
is your **taxable income.**   ▶ 22 26291 80

Step 7

Figure your tax, credits, and payments

23 Find the tax on the amount on line 22. Check if from:
☒ Tax Table (pages 48–53) or ☐ Form 8615 (see page 36)   23 3944

24a Credit for child and dependent care expenses.
Complete and attach Schedule 2.   24a

b Credit for the elderly or the disabled.
Complete and attach Schedule 3.   24b

c Add lines 24a and 24b. These are your **total credits.**   24c

25 Subtract line 24c from line 23. (If line 24c is more than line 23, enter -0-.)   25

(If you want IRS to figure your tax, see page 35.)

26 Advance earned income credit payments from Form W-2.   26

27 Add lines 25 and 26. This is your **total tax.**   ▶ 27 3944

28a Total Federal income tax withheld. (If any is
from Form(s) 1099, check here ▶ ☐.)   28a 4089

b 1990 estimated tax payments and amount
applied from 1989 return.   28b

c **Earned income credit.** See page 39 to find
out if you can take this credit.   28c

d Add lines 28a, 28b, and 28c. These are your **total payments.** ▶ 28d 4089

Step 8

Figure your refund or amount you owe

29 If line 28d is more than line 27, subtract line 27 from line 28d.
This is the amount you **overpaid.**   29 145

30 Amount of line 29 you want **refunded to you.**   30 145

31 Amount of line 29 you want **applied to your
1991 estimated tax.**   31

Attach check or money order on top of Form(s) W-2, etc. on page 1.

32 If line 27 is more than line 28d, subtract line 28d from line 27. This is the
amount you owe. Attach check or money order for full amount payable to
"Internal Revenue Service." Write your name, social security number,
address, daytime phone number, and "1990 Form 1040A" on it.   32

33 Estimated tax penalty (see page 43).   33

Step 9

Sign your return

Under penalties of perjury, I declare that I have examined this return and accompanying schedules and statements, and to the best of my knowledge and belief, they are true, correct, and complete. Declaration of preparer (other than the taxpayer) is based on all information of which the preparer has any knowledge.

Keep a copy of this return for your records.

Your signature	Date	Your occupation
Spouse's signature (if joint return. BOTH must sign)	Date	Spouse's occupation

NOTE: Because the 1990 Tax Tables were unavailable from the IRS at the time
of publication of this book, the taxes were calculated from the 1990
Tax Rate Schedules. A very slight variation may occur.

Table 7—6   Form 1040 sample

ISSUED AS A SUPPLEMENT To FEDERAL TAXES 2nd and FEDERAL TAX GUIDE

Drafts of Forms 1040 with Schedules A & B, D, E, F, R, and SE, Form 1040A with Schedules 1, 2, and 3, Forms 1040EZ, 2106, 2441, 4562, 8815, 8822 and 1990 Tax Tables and Rate Schedules

Form 1040 Department of the Treasury—Internal Revenue Service

U.S. Individual Income Tax Return 1990

For the year Jan.–Dec. 31, 1990, or other tax year beginning , 1990, ending , 19

OMB No. 1545-0074

Label
(See Instructions on page 8.)
Use IRS label. Otherwise, please print or type.

Your first name and initial: JOHN R. Last name: DOE

Your social security number: 111 11 1112

If a joint return, spouse's first name and initial: JANE L. Last name: DOE

Spouse's social security number: 222 22 2221

Home address (number and street). (If you have a P.O. box, see page 8.): 1000 JOY AVE   Apt. no.

City, town or post office, state and ZIP code. (If you have a foreign address, see page 8.): ANYTOWN USA 11111

For Privacy Act and Paperwork Reduction Act Notice, see Instructions.

Presidential Election Campaign (See page 9.)

Do you want $1 to go to this fund? Yes [ ] No [X]
If joint return, does your spouse want $1 to go to this fund? Yes [X] No [ ]

Note: Checking "Yes" will not change your tax or reduce your refund

Filing Status

Check only one box.

1 [ ] Single. (See page 9 to find out if you can file as head of household.)
2 [X] Married filing joint return (even if only one had income)
3 [ ] Married filing separate return. Enter spouse's social security no. above and full name here.
4 [ ] Head of household (with qualifying person). (See page 9.) If the qualifying person is your child but not your dependent, enter this child's name here.
5 [ ] Qualifying widow(er) with dependent child (year spouse died ▶ 19) (See page 9.)

Exemptions
(See Instructions on page 10.)

6a [X] Yourself If someone else (such as your parent) can claim you as a dependent on his or her tax return, do not check box 6a. But be sure to check the box on line 33b on page 2.
b [X] Spouse

No. of boxes checked on 6a and 6b: **2**

c Dependents:

(1) Name (first, initial, and last name)	(2) Check if under age 2	(3) If age 2 or older, dependent's social security number	(4) Relationship	(5) No. of months lived in your home in 1990
MARK H. DOE		444 45 6666	child	12
SUELLEN F. DOE		777 66 8888	child	12

No. of your children on 6c who:
• lived with you: **2**
• didn't live with you due to divorce or separation (see page 11)

No. of other dependents on 6c

If more than 6 dependents, see Instructions on page 11.

d If your child didn't live with you but is claimed as your dependent under a pre-1985 agreement, check here ▶ [ ]
e Total number of exemptions claimed

Add numbers entered on lines above ▶ **4**

Income

Attach Copy B of your Forms W-2, W-2G, and W-2P here.

If you do not have a W-2, see page 8.

Attach check or money order on top of any Forms W-2, W-2G, and W-2P.

7	Wages, salaries, tips, etc. (attach Form(s) W-2)	7	80000 00
8a	Taxable interest income (also attach Schedule B if over $400)	8a	390 50
b	Tax-exempt interest income (see page 13). DON'T include on line 8a	8b	
9	Dividend income (also attach Schedule B if over $400)	9	378 50
10	Taxable refunds of state and local income taxes, if any, from worksheet on page 13	10	
11	Alimony received	11	
12	Business income or (loss) (attach Schedule C)	12	
13	Capital gain or (loss) (attach Schedule D)	13	
14	Capital gain distributions not reported on line 13 (see page 14)	14	
15	Other gains or (losses) (attach Form 4797)	15	
16a	Total IRA distributions 16a	16b Taxable amount (see page 14)	16b	
17a	Total pensions and annuities 17a	17b Taxable amount (see page 14)	17b	
18	Rents, royalties, partnerships, estates, trusts, etc. (attach Schedule E)	18	
19	Farm income or (loss) (attach Schedule F)	19	
20	Unemployment compensation (insurance) (see page 15)	20	
21a	Social security benefits. 21a	21b Taxable amount (see page 16)	21b	
22	Other income (list type and amount—see page 16) PRIZE	22	250 00
23	Add the amounts shown in the far right column for lines 7 through 22. This is your total income ▶	23	81019 00

Adjustments to Income

(See Instructions on page 16.)

24a	Your IRA deduction, from applicable worksheet on page 17	24a	2000 00	
b	Spouse's IRA deduction, from applicable worksheet on page 17	24b	2000 00	
25	Deduction for self-employment tax, from worksheet on page 18	25		
26	Self-employed health insurance deduction, from worksheet on page 18	26		
27	Keogh retirement plan and self-employed SEP deduction	27		
28	Penalty on early withdrawal of savings	28		
29	Alimony paid. Recipient's SSN ▶	29		
30	Add lines 24a through 29. These are your total adjustments ▶			4000 00

Adjusted Gross Income

31 Subtract line 30 from line 23. This is your adjusted gross income. If this amount is less than $20,264 and a child lived with you, see page 22 to find out if you can claim the "Earned Income Credit" on line 57 ▶ | 31 | 77019 00 |

Form 1040 (1990)　　　　　　　　　　　　　　　　　　　　　　　　　Page **2**

Tax Computation If you want IRS to figure your tax, see instructions on page 19.	32	Amount from line 31 (adjusted gross income)	32	77019	00

33a	Check if: ☐ You were 65 or older ☐ Blind; ☐ Spouse was 65 or older ☐ Blind.	
	Add the number of boxes checked and enter the total here ▶ 33a ☐	
b	If someone else (such as your parent) can claim you as a dependent, check here 33b ☐	
c	If you are married filing a separate return and your spouse itemizes deductions, or you are a dual-status alien, see page 19 and check here . . . . ▶ 33c ☐	
34	Enter the larger of: • Your **standard deduction** (from applicable chart (or worksheet) on page 20), **OR** • Your **itemized deductions** (from Schedule A, line 27). If you itemize, attach Schedule A and check here . . . . ▶ ☒	34	15549	35
35	Subtract line 34 from line 32	35	61469	65
36	Multiply $2,050 by the total number of exemptions claimed on line 6e .	36	8200	00
37	**Taxable income.** Subtract line 36 from line 35. (If line 36 is more than line 35, enter -0-.)	37	53269	65
38	Enter tax. Check if from: a ☐ Tax Table, b ☐ Tax Rate Schedules, or c ☐ Form 8615 (see page 20). (If any is from Form(s) 8814, enter that amount here ▶ d ___	38	10697	00
39	Additional taxes (see page 21). Check if from: a ☐ Form 4970 b ☐ Form ____	39		
40	Add lines 38 and 39 . . . . ▶	40	10697	00

Credits
(See Instructions on page 21.)

41	Credit for child and dependent care expenses (attach Form 2441)	41	
42	Credit for the elderly or the disabled (attach Schedule R)	42	
43	Foreign tax credit (attach Form 1116)	43	
44	General business credit. Check if from a ☐ Form 3800 or b ☐ Form (specify)	44	
45	Credit for prior year minimum tax (attach Form 8801)	45	
46	Add lines 41 through 45	46		
47	Subtract line 46 from line 40. (If line 46 is more than line 40, enter -0-.) ▶	47	10697	00

Other Taxes

48	Self-employment tax (attach Schedule SE)	48		
49	Alternative minimum tax (attach Form 6251)	49		
50	Recapture taxes (see page 21). Check if from: a ☐ Form 4255 b ☐ Form 8611 .	50		
51	Social security tax on tip income not reported to employer (attach Form 4137)	51		
52	Tax on an IRA or a qualified retirement plan (attach Form 5329)	52		
53	Advance earned income credit payments, from Form W-2 . . .	53		
54	Add lines 47 through 53. This is your **total tax** . . . . ▶	54	10697	00

Payments

Attach Forms W-2, W-2G, and W-2P to front.

55	Federal income tax withheld (**if any is from Form(s) 1099,** check ▶ ☐) . . .	55	10800	00
56	1990 estimated tax payments and amount applied from 1989 return	56		
57	**Earned income credit** (see page 22)	57		
58	Amount paid with Form 4868 (extension request)	58		
59	Excess social security tax and RRTA tax withheld (see page 23) .	59		
60	Credit for Federal tax on fuels (attach Form 4136)	60		
61	Regulated investment company credit (attach Form 2439) . .	61		
62	Add lines 55 through 61. These are your **total payments** . . ▶	62	10800	00

Refund or Amount You Owe

63	If line 62 is more than line 54, enter amount **OVERPAID** . . . ▶	63	103	00
64	Amount of line 63 to be **REFUNDED TO YOU** . . . . . ▶	64	103	00
65	Amount of line 63 to be **APPLIED TO YOUR 1991 ESTIMATED TAX** ▶ 65			
66	If line 54 is more than line 62, enter **AMOUNT YOU OWE.** Attach check or money order for full amount payable to "Internal Revenue Service." Write your name, social security number, address, daytime phone number, and "1990 Form 1040" on it	66		
67	Estimated tax penalty (see page 24) 67			

Sign Here

(Keep a copy of this return for your records.)

Under penalties of perjury, I declare that I have examined this return and accompanying schedules and statements, and to the best of my knowledge and belief, they are true, correct, and complete. Declaration of preparer (other than taxpayer) is based on all information of which preparer has any knowledge.

Your signature	Date	Your occupation
Spouse's signature (if joint return, BOTH must sign)	Date	Spouse's occupation

Paid Preparer's Use Only

Preparer's signature	Date	Check if self-employed ☐	Preparer's social security no.
Firm's name (or yours if self-employed) and address		E.I. No.	
		ZIP code	

Table 7—7   Tax rate schedules

1990 Tax Rate Schedules

Caution: *Use ONLY if your taxable income (Form 1040, line 37) is $50,000 or more. If less, use the Tax Table. (Even though you cannot use the tax rate schedules below* because your taxable income is less than $50,000, we show all levels of taxable income so that taxpayers can see the tax rate that applies to each level.)

Schedule X—Use if your filing status is Single

If the amount on Form 1040, line 37, is: Over—	But not over—	Enter on Form 1040, line 38	of the amount over—
$0	$19,450	.......15%	$0
19,450	47,050	**$2,917.50 + 28%**	19,450
47,050	97,620	**10,645.50 + 33%**	47,050
97,620	....	Use Worksheet below to figure your tax.	

Schedule Z—Use if your filing status is Head of household

If the amount on Form 1040, line 37, is: Over—	But not over—	Enter on Form 1040, line 38	of the amount over—
$0	$26,050	.......15%	$0
26,050	67,200	**$3,907.50 + 28%**	26,050
67,200	134,930	**15,429.50 + 33%**	67,200
134,930	....	Use Worksheet below to figure your tax.	

Schedule Y-1—Use if your filing status is Married filing jointly or Qualifying widow(er)

If the amount on Form 1040, line 37, is: Over—	But not over—	Enter on Form 1040, line 38	of the amount over—
$0	$32,450	.......15%	$0
32,450	78,400	**$4,867.50 + 28%**	32,450
78,400	162,770	17,733.50 + 33%	78,400
162,770	....	Use Worksheet below to figure your tax.	

Schedule Y-2—Use if your filing status is Married filing separately

If the amount on Form 1040, line 37, is: Over—	But not over—	Enter on Form 1040, line 38	of the amount over—
$0	$16,225	.......15%	$0
16,225	39,200	**$2,433.75 + 28%**	16,225
39,200	123,570	**8,866.75 + 33%**	39,200
123,570	....	Use Worksheet below to figure your tax.	

Worksheet (Keep for your records)

1. If your filing status is: Single, enter $27,333.60 / Head of household, enter $37,780.40 / Married filing jointly or Qualifying widow(er), enter $45,575.60 / Married filing separately, enter $36,708.85 .... 1. _____

2. Enter your taxable income from Form 1040, line 37 . . . . 2. _____

3. If your filing status is: Single, enter $97,620 / Head of household, enter $134,930 / Married filing jointly or Qualifying widow(er), enter $162,770 / Married filing separately, enter $123,570 . . 3. _____

4. Subtract line 3 from line 2. Enter the result. (If the result is zero or less, use the schedule above for your filing status to figure your tax. DO NOT use this worksheet.) 4. _____

5. Multiply the amount on line 4 by 28% (.28). Enter the result . . . . 5. _____

6. Multiply the amount on line 4 by 5% (.05). Enter the result . . . . 6. _____

7. Multiply $574 by the number of exemptions claimed on Form 1040, line 6e. (If married filing separately, see the **Note** below.) Enter the result . . . . 7. _____

8. Compare the amounts on lines 6 and 7. Enter the **smaller** of the two amounts here . . . . 8. _____

9. **Tax.** Add lines 1, 5, and 8. Enter the total here and on Form 1040, line 38 . . . . 9. _____

Note: If married filing separately and you did not claim an exemption for your spouse, multiply $574 by the number of exemptions claimed on Form 1040, line 6e. Add $574 to the result and enter the total on line 7 above.

Page 56

Schedule A   *Table 7—8*

	Schedule A—Itemized Deductions	OMB No. 1545-0074
SCHEDULES A&B **(Form 1040)** Department of the Treasury Internal Revenue Service	(Schedule B is on back) ► Attach to Form 1040. ► See Instructions for Schedules A and B (Form 1040).	**1990** Attachment Sequence No. **07**

Name(s) shown on Form 1040 — JOHN R. AND JANE L. DOE   Your social security number — 111 11 1112

Medical and Dental Expenses	**Caution:** *Do not include expenses reimbursed or paid by others.*		
	1 Medical and dental expenses. (See page 24 of the Instructions.)	1	5950 50
	2 Enter amount from Form 1040, line 32. 2 77019		
	3 Multiply the amount on line 2 by 7.5% (.075). Enter the result	3	5776 42
	4 Subtract line 3 from line 1. Enter the result. If less than zero, enter -0- ►	4	174 08
Taxes You Paid (See Instructions on page 26.)	5 State and local income taxes	5	
	6 Real estate taxes	6	3050 00
	7 Other taxes. (List—include personal property taxes.) ►	7	
	8 Add the amounts on lines 5 through 7. Enter the total ►	8	3050 00
Interest You Paid (See Instructions on page 26.)	9a Deductible home mortgage interest paid to financial institutions and reported to you on Form 1098. Report deductible points on line 10	9a	9050 45
	b Other deductible home mortgage interest. (If paid to an individual, show that person's name and address.) ►	9b	
	10 Deductible points. (See Instructions for special rules.)	10	
	11 Deductible investment interest (attach Form 4952 if required). (See page 27.)	11	
	12a Personal interest you paid. (See page 27.) 12a		
	b Multiply the amount on line 12a by 10% (.10). Enter the result	12b	
	13 Add the amounts on lines 9a through 11, and 12b. Enter the total ►	13	9050 45
Gifts to Charity (See Instructions on page 26.)	**Caution:** *If you made a charitable contribution and received a benefit in return, see page 28 of the Instructions.*		
	14 Contributions by cash or check	14	2945 00
	15 Other than cash or check. (You **MUST** attach Form 8283 if over $500.)	15	
	16 Carryover from prior year	16	
	17 Add the amounts on lines 14 through 16. Enter the total ►	17	2945 00
Casualty and Theft Losses	18 Casualty or theft loss(es) (attach Form 4684.) (See page 28 of the Instructions.) ►	18	250 20
Moving Expenses	19 Moving expenses (attach Form 3903 or 3903F). (See page 29 of the Instructions.) ►	19	
Job Expenses and Most Other Miscellaneous Deductions (See Instructions on page 29 for expenses to deduct here.)	20 Unreimbursed employee expenses—job travel, union dues, job education, etc. (You **MUST** attach Form 2106 in some cases. See Instructions.) ► UNION DUES	20	700 00
	21 Other expenses (investment, tax preparation, safe deposit box, etc.). List type and amount ► INVESTMENT MNGMT FEE 100 SAFETY DEPOSIT BOX 120 INVESTMENT EXPENSE 700.	21	920 00
	22 Add the amounts on lines 20 and 21. Enter the total	22	1620 00
	23 Enter the amount from Form 1040, line 32 23 77019		
	24 Multiply the amount on line 23 by 2% (.02). Enter the result	24	1540 38
	25 Subtract line 24 from line 22. Enter the result. If less than zero, enter -0- ►	25	79 62
Other Miscellaneous Deductions	26 Other (from list on page 29 of Instructions). List type and amount ►	26	
Total Itemized Deductions	27 Add the amounts on lines 4, 8, 13, 17, 18, 19, 25, and 26. Enter the total here. Then enter on Form 1040, line 34, the LARGER of this total or your standard deduction from page 20 of the Instructions ►	27	15549 35

For Paperwork Reduction Act Notice, see Form 1040 Instructions.   Schedule A (Form 1040) 1990

Proofs only (May 16, 1990) (subject to change!)

1. Excise taxes
   a. Gasoline. Taxes were increased from $0.09 to $0.14 per gallon effective December 1, 1990.
   b. Cigarettes. Taxes were increased by $0.04 per pack effective January 1, 1991. On January 1, 1993 this tax will rise by another $0.04.
   c. Alcoholic beverages. Increased the tax on beer from $0.16 per six pack to $0.32; on wine by $0.90 per wine gallon; and on liquor from $12.50 per proof gallon to $13.50.
   d. Airline tickets. Taxes were increased from 8 percent to 10 percent, effective December 1, 1990.
   e. Luxury items. Imposed a tax of 10 percent on that portion of the price in excess of $30,000 on cars, $10,000 on furs, $10,000 on jewelry, $100,000 on boats, and $250,000 on airplanes.
2. Medicare
   a. Increased the deductible from $75 to $100.
   b. Raised the monthly premiums from $28.60 in 1990 to $29.90 in 1991, and to $46.10 starting in 1995.
   c. Increased the base from $53,400 to $125,000 on which the 1.45 percent Medicare part of the Social Security tax is calculated. (The base on which the remainder of the Social Security tax is imposed—retirement and disability—will remain at $53,400, which was automatically increased from $51,300 in 1990).
3. Personal Income Taxes

The new law establishes a new 31 percent marginal tax bracket to apply to taxable income in excess of $82,150 on a joint return, $70,450 for a head of household, $49,300 for a single person, and $41,075 for a married person filing separately.

Capital gains, currently taxed as high as 33 percent for some taxpayers, are now taxed at a maximum rate of 28 percent.

The personal exemption was raised from $2,050 in 1990 to $2,150 in 1991. Both the standard deduction and the personal exemption will continue to be indexed for inflation in future years. The personal exemption and itemized deductions will both be phased out for certain high-income taxpayers. The itemized deduction phaseout starts at an AGI (adjusted gross income) of $100,000 (adjusted for inflation after 1991) for both individuals and couples. The new law disallows itemized deductions at a rate of 3% of the excess adjusted gross income over the threshold level. Deductions for medical expenses, casualty losses, and investment interest, however, are exempt from this provision. There is a cap on this phaseout, however, which provides that no taxpayer would lose more than 80 percent of his or her deductions. The personal exemption phaseout begins at an AGI level above $150,000 for marrieds and $100,000 for single taxpayers.

There is then an overlap for these two phaseouts. A single taxpayer is subject to both phaseouts at an AGI level of $100,000. A married couple is subjected to the deduction phaseout at $100,000 and the personal exemption phaseout at $150,000.

The alternative minimum tax (AMT) was increased in 1990 from 21 to 24 percent. The AMT is triggered by a number of tax preference items, which are included when calculating the AMT but not the regular tax liability. The alternative minimum tax is discussed in greater detail below.

At one time it was possible for a child to be counted as a double exemption, especially if he or she were a student. This is no longer possible. Either the child or the parent gets the exemption, but not both. If the child is eligible to be claimed as a dependent on the parent's return, then he or she cannot use an exemption on his or her return.

When a taxpayer loses a child as an exemption

If the child has income, then, even though a dependent and not allowed to take the personal exemption, he or she may take the standard deduction in some cases, as will be explained below.

A child with earned income is allowed to use his or her standard deduction, and the income is taxed at the child's presumably lower rate. However, if a child under the age of fourteen has unearned income (i.e., investment income) in excess of $1,100, the amount over $1,100 is taxed at the parent's higher rate.[5] The child, while he or she may not have the personal exemption, does have a special $550 standard deduction. This special $550 deduction applies to the unearned income of a child under 14. The first $550, then, is not taxed. The next $550 of unearned income is taxed at the child's rate and the remainder at the parents' rate. The following table illustrates this.

A child with unearned income

Unearned income	$1,100
Standard deduction	550
Net unearned income	$ 550
Taxed at child's rate	× 15%
Tax	$ 82.50

Congress did this to prevent people from transferring substantial earning assets to their children and saving taxes for the family. However, modest amounts of tax savings are still possible. This is important if a parent wishes to establish a college trust fund for his or her children, and it is explained in greater detail in Chapter 19.

---

5. The IRS defines unearned income as that income from investments such as interest and dividends, and earned income such as wages and salaries.

If a child is fourteen or over, then the child's entire unearned income (as well as earned income) is taxed at his or her rate rather than at the parents' rate. In addition, the child may apply the full standard deduction to all income at the age of 14 or older.

A child with both earned and unearned income

A child with earned income who is taken as a dependent by his or her parents cannot, of course, claim his or her own personal exemption on his or her tax return. However, he or she may still qualify for the standard (or itemized) deduction, but it may be less than the regular standard deduction. Rather, the child must take a special standard deduction which is equal to $550 or earned income, whichever is the greater up to the maximum of $3,400 in 1991.

Income subject to tax

All income, unless specifically excluded by law, is subject to tax. This includes wages, salaries, bonuses, tips, commissions, royalties, farm and business income, gambling winnings, interest, rental income, dividends, the value of prizes won, and alimony received—in other words, nearly everything.

Moreover, in most cases the taxpayer must report the income when he or she earned it and could have received it. For example, interest on a savings account must be reported in the year in which it was earned and credited to his or her account, not when actually withdrawn. On the other hand, interest on U.S. Government savings bonds (called series EE bonds and discussed in Chapter 13) need not be reported and is not taxed until received some years later.

Unemployment benefits are fully taxable. So too are prizes and awards. Nobel Prizes were formerly not taxed; now they are. So too are college scholarships and fellowships—but only to the extent that the money is not spent on tuition, course-related equipment or expenses such as travel, research, and clerical help and equipment by degree candidates.

In the case of farm, business, and certain other professional income, there are certain expense items that the person may first deduct before reporting the income. These will be discussed below.

Income from a pension (including social security) receives special treatment, but in many cases is taxed, as will be explained in Chapter 18.

Nontaxable income

The major item not taxable today is the interest income on many state and local bonds. Even here not all state and local bonds are tax exempt. All such bonds issued prior to August 7, 1986, are exempt in all cases. Municipal bonds issued since August 7, 1986, have been classified, for tax purposes, as public activity bonds and private activity bonds. The interest on public activity bonds is tax exempt; the interest on some private activity bonds is tax exempt, on others it is not. The investor should verify this if purchases are contemplated. The income on private activity non-taxable bonds is considered a tax preference item by the IRS and as such may be subject to the alternative minimum tax (AMT), which is discussed below.

Certain other items, too, need not be included as income. Most government payments made to veterans and their families, worker's compensation payments, casualty insurance payments received, gifts, life insurance proceeds received by the beneficiary, disability and death payments awarded by the courts, and inheritances are not subject to the income tax. Rebates for the overpayment of federal income taxes are not taxable but the interest paid on them is. On the other hand, refunds on state and local income taxes may be subject to the federal tax. There are separate gift and inheritance taxes at both the state and federal levels, but at the federal level there are high exemptions. Moreover, loopholes exist by which inheritance and gift taxes can be avoided legally. Gift and inheritance taxes are explained in Chapter 19. Table 7–9 illustrates various sources of income not subject to the federal income tax.

Checklist of nontaxable income (in most cases)   Table 7–9

Accident insurance proceeds
Bequests
Board furnished for convenience of employer
Child support received
Clergymen—rental value of parsonage furnished as part of compensation
Damages awarded by a court due to a physical injury
Dividends on life insurance policies
Gifts
Inheritances
Interest on bonds of a state, city, or other political subdivision*
Insurance benefit payments*
IRA contributions (in many cases, see Chapter 18)
Keogh contributions
Legacies
Marriage settlement, lump-sum payment received
Old age benefits under Railroad Retirement Act
Political campaign contributions received by candidates
Scholarships* (if spent by degree candidates on tuition or course-related
     expenses)
Sick pay (taxable in most cases)**
Social Security benefits***
Worker's compensation benefits

---

*In most cases.

**Sick pay is not taxable if it is financed through an insurance company and the premiums were paid by the individual rather than the employer. Otherwise sick pay is taxable as income.

***Social Security benefits are partially taxable in some cases, and not taxable in others.

The tax rates

For most people, there are just two tax rates in 1990—15 and 28 percent. However, for some high-income taxpayers there is a 5 percent surtax. (See Table 7—10 for a chart of various tax rates in 1990.) For a single taxpayer this would apply to all income in excess of $47,050 in 1990. The marginal tax rate is defined as that tax rate which is applicable to the last dollar of taxable income. This is also called the marginal tax bracket, and it, of course, applies to the last dollar in that bracket. For example, in the case of an unmarried taxpayer with a taxable income of $50,000 he or she would pay the following taxes for 1990.

$19,450 taxed at 15 percent	=	$ 2,917.50
$27,600 taxed at 28 percent	=	$ 7,728.00
$ 2,950 taxed at 33 percent	=	$ 973.50
TOTAL TAX		$11,619.00

Percent rate

Marginal Tax $ 973.5 ÷ $ 2,950 =   33.00%
Average Tax $11,619 ÷ $50,000 =   23.24%

There is also a concept called the effective tax rate which would be the total tax divided by taxable income. These taxes were obtained from the proper tables. If a person used the tax rate schedules, the tax liability might vary by a dollar or two.

Table 7—10   *The following table shows the various tax rates*

Married	Taxable Income	Tax Rate
Filing Jointly	Up to $32,450	15%
	$32,450–$78,400	28%
	$78,400–$162,770	33%
Filing Separately	Up to $16,225	15%
	$16,225–$39,200	28%
	$39,200–$123,570	33%
Unmarried	Up to $19,450	15%
	$19,450–$47,050	28%
	$47,050–$97,620	33%
Head of household	Up to $26,050	15%
	$26,050–$67,200	28%
	$67,200–$134,930	33%

Employers are required to withhold a portion of their employees' wages for income tax purposes. This is referred to as collection at the source, or pay-as-you-go. Its purpose is both to assure the government that the taxes will be paid and to make it easier for the taxpayer. Before the enactment of the withholding tax law, many taxpayers had to borrow to pay their income taxes on time. *Tax withholdings*

When persons begin work with an organization, they file with the employer a withholding tax exemption certificate (the W-4 form), which contains a statement of the number of exemptions to which they are entitled. The employer will then withhold a percentage of wages based on the number of exemptions and the level of the wage or salary. The greater the number of exemptions, the lower the amount withheld. The taxpayer should attempt to withhold as close to what the actual tax liability will be as possible. Substantial under-withholding could result in the taxpayer having to pay a penalty and interest. On the other hand, over-withholding results in the IRS holding funds that could be earning interest for the taxpayer elsewhere. Over-withholding is really an interest-free loan to the IRS. A W-4 withholdings allowance certificate is shown in Figure 7–2.

At the end of the year the employer gives the employee two or three copies of a W-2 form, showing the amount paid in wages, the amount of income tax withheld, and the amount of Social Security tax withheld, if any. The W-2 form is the basis for the tax returns of those persons working for wages and salaries. The original copy of the W-2 form is submitted by the employer to the IRS; the taxpayer's first copy is submitted with the tax return and a duplicate copy is retained for the taxpayer's files.

If the taxpayer has income not subject to withholding, he or she may have to file a declaration of estimated income (a 1040-ES) and pay a tax on it quarterly. People who are self-employed and those with substantial interest, dividend, or other so-called nonearned income have to do this. If there is only a small amount of income not subject to withholding, the taxpayer may avoid filing this form quarterly by increasing the amount withheld from his or her salary over what it normally would be. The rule is that if the withholdings are 90 percent or more of the total tax liability for the current year or 100% of the total tax liability for the prior taxable year, there is no penalty for not paying quarterly estimated taxes. *Payment of estimated tax*

If a person underpays and a late payment penalty is assessed, it is quite severe. It is currently one-half (1/2) of one percent *per month* on the unpaid amount. In addition to a late payment penalty, there is also an interest charge on any tax payment that is late. It was 11 percent at year end 1990, but it may be adjusted up or down quarterly as the market interest rates vary.

Figure 7—2   W-4 Withholding allowance certificate.

19**90** Form W-4

**Department of the Treasury
Internal Revenue Service**

Purpose. Complete Form W-4 so that your employer can withhold the correct amount of Federal income tax from your pay.

Exemption From Withholding. Read line 6 of the certificate below to see if you can claim exempt status. *If exempt, complete line 6; but do not complete lines 4 and 5.* No Federal income tax will be withheld from your pay. This exemption expires February 15, 1991.

Basic Instructions. Employees who are not exempt should complete the Personal Allowances Worksheet. Additional worksheets are provided on page 2 for employees to adjust their withholding allowances based on itemized deductions, adjustments to income, or two-earner/two-job situations. Complete all worksheets that apply to your situation. The worksheets will help you figure the number of withholding allowances you are

entitled to claim. However, you may claim fewer allowances than this.

Head of Household. Generally, you may claim head of household filing status on your tax return only if you are unmarried and pay more than 50% of the costs of keeping up a home for yourself and your dependent(s) or other qualifying individuals.

Nonwage Income. If you have a large amount of nonwage income, such as interest or dividends, you should consider making estimated tax payments using Form 1040-ES. Otherwise, you may find that you owe additional tax at the end of the year.

Two-Earner/Two-Jobs. If you have a working spouse or more than one job, figure the total number of allowances you are entitled to claim on all jobs using worksheets from only one Form

W-4. This total should be divided among all jobs. Your withholding will usually be most accurate when all allowances are claimed on the W-4 filed for the highest paying job and zero allowances are claimed for the others.

Advance Earned Income Credit. If you are eligible for this credit, you can receive it added to your paycheck throughout the year. For details, obtain Form W-5 from your employer.

Check Your Withholding. After your W-4 takes effect, you can use **Publication 919,** Is My Withholding Correct for 1990?, to see how the dollar amount you are having withheld compares to your estimated total annual tax. Call 1-800-424-3676 (in Hawaii and Alaska, check your local telephone directory) to order this publication. Check your local telephone directory for the IRS assistance number if you need further help.

Personal Allowances Worksheet

A	Enter "1" for **yourself** if no one else can claim you as a dependent	A _____
B	Enter "1" if: { **1.** You are single and have only one job; or **2.** You are married, have only one job, and your spouse does not work; or **3.** Your wages from a second job or your spouse's wages (or the total of both) are $2,500 or less. }	B _____
C	Enter "1" for your **spouse.** But, you may choose to enter "0" if you are married and have either a working spouse or more than one job (this may help you avoid having too little tax withheld)	C _____
D	Enter number of **dependents** (other than your spouse or yourself) whom you will claim on your tax return	D _____
E	Enter "1" if you will file as a **head of household** on your tax return (see conditions under "Head of Household," above) .	E _____
F	Enter "1" if you have at least $1,500 of **child or dependent care expenses** for which you plan to claim a credit . . .	F _____
G	Add lines A through F and enter total here . . . . ▶	G _____

For accuracy, do all worksheets that apply.
- If you plan to **itemize or claim adjustments to income** and want to reduce your withholding, turn to the Deductions and Adjustments Worksheet on page 2.
- If you are **single** and have **more than one job** and your combined earnings from all jobs exceed $25,000 OR if you are **married** and have a **working spouse or more than one job,** and the combined earnings from all jobs exceed $44,000, then turn to the Two-Earner/Two-Job Worksheet on page 2 if you want to avoid having too little tax withheld.
- If **neither** of the above situations applies to you, **stop here** and enter the number from line G on line 4 of Form W-4 below.

------------------------------ **Cut here and give the certificate to your employer. Keep the top portion for your records.** ------------------------------

Form W-4
Department of the Treasury
Internal Revenue Service

Employee's Withholding Allowance Certificate
▶ **For Privacy Act and Paperwork Reduction Act Notice, see reverse.**

OMB No. 1545-0010

19**90**

1 Type or print your first name and middle initial	Last name		**2** Your social security number
Home address (number and street or rural route)		**3** Marital status	☐ Single ☐ Married ☐ Married, but withhold at higher Single rate.
City or town, state, and ZIP code			**Note:** If married, but legally separated, or spouse is a nonresident alien, check the Single box.

4 Total number of allowances you are claiming (from line G above or from the Worksheets on back if they apply) . . . | **4** |
5 Additional amount, if any, you want deducted from each pay . . . . | **5** $ |
6 I claim exemption from withholding and I certify that I meet **ALL** of the following conditions for exemption:
- Last year I had a right to a refund of **ALL** Federal income tax withheld because I had **NO** tax liability; **AND**
- This year I expect a refund of **ALL** Federal income tax withheld because I expect to have **NO** tax liability; **AND**
- This year if my income exceeds $500 and includes nonwage income, another person cannot claim me as a dependent.

If you meet all of the above conditions, enter the year effective and "EXEMPT" here . . . . ▶ | **6** | 19
7 Are you a full-time student? **(Note:** Full-time students are not automatically exempt.) . . . . | **7** ☐ Yes ☐ No

Under penalties of perjury, I certify that I am entitled to the number of withholding allowances claimed on this certificate or entitled to claim exempt status.

Employee's signature ▶ _____   **Date** ▶ _____ , 19___

8 Employer's name and address (**Employer:** Complete 8 and 10 **only if sending to IRS**) | **9** Office code (optional) | **10** Employer identification number

Form W-4 (1990)   Page **2**

Deductions and Adjustments Worksheet

Note: *Use this worksheet only if you plan to itemize deductions or claim adjustments to income on your 1990 tax return.*

1 Enter an estimate of your 1990 itemized deductions. These include: qualifying home mortgage interest, 10% of personal interest, charitable contributions, state and local taxes (but not sales taxes), medical expenses in excess of 7.5% of your income, and miscellaneous deductions (most miscellaneous deductions are now deductible only in excess of 2% of your income) . . . . 1 $ _____

2 Enter: { $5,450 if married filing jointly or qualifying widow(er) / $4,750 if head of household / $3,250 if single / $2,725 if married filing separately } . . . . 2 $ _____

3 **Subtract** line 2 from line 1. If line 2 is greater than line 1, enter zero . . . . 3 $ _____

4 Enter an estimate of your 1990 adjustments to income. These include alimony paid and deductible IRA contributions . 4 $ _____

5 **Add** lines 3 and 4 and enter the total . . . . 5 $ _____

6 Enter an estimate of your 1990 nonwage income (such as dividends or interest income) . . . . . . 6 $ _____

7 **Subtract** line 6 from line 5. Enter the result, but not less than zero . . . . 7 $ _____

8 **Divide** the amount on line 7 by $2,000 and enter the result here. Drop any fraction . . . . . . 8 _____

9 Enter the number from Personal Allowances Worksheet, line G, on page 1 . . . . 9 _____

10 **Add** lines 8 and 9 and enter the total here. If you plan to use the Two-Earner/Two-Job Worksheet, also enter the total on line 1, below. Otherwise, **stop here** and enter this total on Form W-4, line 4 on page 1 . . . . 10 _____

Two-Earner/Two-Job Worksheet

Note: *Use this worksheet only if the instructions at line G on page 1 direct you here.*

1 Enter the number from line G on page 1 (or from line 10 above if you used the Deductions and Adjustments Worksheet) . 1 _____

2 Find the number in **Table 1** below that applies to the **LOWEST** paying job and enter it here . . . . . 2 _____

3 If line 1 is **GREATER THAN OR EQUAL TO** line 2, subtract line 2 from line 1. Enter the result here (if zero, enter "0") and on Form W-4, line 4, on page 1. **DO NOT** use the rest of this worksheet . . . . . . 3 _____

Note: *If line 1 is **LESS THAN** line 2, enter "0" on Form W-4, line 4, on page 1. Complete lines 4–9 to calculate the additional dollar withholding necessary to avoid a year-end tax bill.*

4 Enter the number from line 2 of this worksheet . . . . 4 _____

5 Enter the number from line 1 of this worksheet . . . . 5 _____

6 **Subtract** line 5 from line 4 . . . . 6 _____

7 Find the amount in **Table 2** below that applies to the **HIGHEST** paying job and enter it here . . . . . 7 $ _____

8 **Multiply** line 7 by line 6 and enter the result here. This is the additional annual withholding amount needed 8 $ _____

9 **Divide** line 8 by the number of pay periods each year. (For example, divide by 26 if you are paid every other week.) Enter the result here and on Form W-4, line 5, page 1. This is the additional amount to be withheld from each paycheck . . . 9 $ _____

Table 1: Two-Earner/Two-Job Worksheet

Married Filing Jointly		All Others	
If wages from **LOWEST** paying job are—	Enter on line 2 above	If wages from **LOWEST** paying job are—	Enter on line 2 above
0 - $4,000	0	0 - $4,000	0
4,001 - 8,000	1	4,001 - 8,000	1
8,001 - 19,000	2	8,001 - 14,000	2
19,001 - 23,000	3	14,001 - 16,000	3
23,001 - 25,000	4	16,001 - 21,000	4
25,001 - 27,000	5	21,001 and over	5
27,001 - 29,000	6		
29,001 - 35,000	7		
35,001 - 41,000	8		
41,001 - 46,000	9		
46,001 and over	10		

Table 2: Two-Earner/Two-Job Worksheet

Married Filing Jointly		All Others	
If wages from **HIGHEST** paying job are—	Enter on line 7 above	If wages from **HIGHEST** paying job are—	Enter on line 7 above
0 - $44,000	$310	0 - $25,000	$310
44,001 - 90,000	570	25,001 - 52,000	570
90,001 and over	680	52,001 and over	680

Joint or separate returns

In most cases, married couples have an option of filing separately or jointly. Ordinarily when a married couple files a joint return, as opposed to filing separately, they save substantially in taxes. Whether a couple is married for tax purposes is determined by their status on December 31 of the year in question. There is one exception to this rule: if one of the members of a marriage dies, the survivor may elect to file a joint return that year.

Occasionally it may be advantageous for each member to file a separate return. If there is any doubt, a married couple should calculate their taxes both jointly and separately to determine which is the most beneficial. Filing jointly will usually save taxes but there are exceptions. For example, sometimes filing separately will lower the AGI to the point where the itemized deductions will exceed the standard deduction.

Married couples living in community property states must apply special rules when filing separately. Anyone who is in this category should study the IRS guide very carefully or consult a tax specialist when considering filing separately. (The community property states are Arizona, California, Idaho, Louisiana, Nevada, New Mexico, Texas, and Washington.)

Head of a household

Persons qualifying as heads of household are granted approximately 50 percent of the benefits given to married couples filing a joint return.

To qualify as head of household, an individual must be unmarried or qualify as an abandoned spouse at the end of the tax year. Further, he or she must have maintained a household in which lives any closely related or non-related person for whom the taxpayer would ordinarily be entitled to a dependency deduction. The taxpayer must contribute over half the cost of maintaining the home, which has been interpreted to include property taxes, maintenance costs, mortgage payments or rent, and the like, plus the cost of food consumed on the premises.

ADJUSTMENTS TO INCOME: ADJUSTED GROSS INCOME

A number of items may be deducted from gross income to arrive at adjusted gross income (AGI); for example, a deductible IRA or a Keogh contribution, one-half of any self-employment tax paid, penalty on early withdrawal of savings, 25% of self-employed health insurance premiums, and alimony paid. These are taken on page one of the 1040 form. Many people do not have many page one deductions. Later, certain other expense deductions may be taken in order to reduce AGI to move toward taxable income; these are the personal exemptions, and either the itemized deductions or the standard deduction. These will be examined below; but first we will examine those items that can be taken in moving from gross income to adjusted gross income shown on the bottom of page one of form 1040 under "Adjustments to Income."

The Keogh plan and the Individual Retirement Account (IRA) are discussed in greater detail in Chapter 18. They are a means whereby an eligible taxpayer may set aside and earmark funds for retirement. A portion or all of the contributions made may be deducted from gross income to arrive at adjusted gross income. In addition the income they earn is tax deferred until withdrawn upon retirement. In some cases, however, IRA contributions may not be deductible; this is discussed further in Chapter 18. A Keogh plan is only for the self-employed and eligible employees. In some cases a person may have both an IRA and a Keogh plan; in others not.

Payments to a Keogh and an Individual Retirement Account (IRA)

There is a penalty assessed in some but not all cases when a person withdraws savings early from banks and savings and loan associations. The penalty is assessed in the form of reduced interest on early withdrawals, before maturity (see Chapter 13). The penalty is tax deductible and taken on page one of the 1040 form to obtain adjusted gross income.

Penalty on early withdrawal of savings

Periodic alimony payments or separate maintenance payments made under a court order may be deducted. Payments made under a written separation agreement may also be deducted. The taxpayer may not deduct lump-sum cash or property settlements, voluntary payments, or amounts specified as child support.

Alimony paid

Taxable income is the sum upon which taxes are calculated. Taxable income is calculated on page two of the form 1040 under the section titled "Tax Computation." Certain deductions may be taken by the taxpayer who qualifies in moving from **adjusted gross income** to **taxable income.** These are the itemized deductions. Some people do not need to itemize because their legitimate deductions do not exceed the standard deduction. The standard deduction was $5,450 in 1990 for marrieds and $3,250 for singles. This will be adjusted for inflation annually.

The itemized deductions that can be taken only on Schedule A are of no value unless they exceed the standard deduction. If the taxpayer has a few large items, however, such as interest on a home mortgage and property taxes, these alone will often give a deduction in excess of the standard amount. If this is the case, it is worthwhile to keep records so that all the various smaller items can be added. Table 7–8 shows Schedule A with the various itemized deductions.

ITEMIZED DEDUCTIONS: "SCHEDULE A" (AND OTHER) DEDUCTIONS

Taxes

Certain state and local taxes paid by the taxpayer during the taxable year are deductible. The major taxes involved are state and local income taxes and real estate taxes. Sales taxes are no longer allowed as a deduction.

Real estate taxes are probably the most important single tax for the average person. If an individual has an adjusted gross income of $50,000 per year and his or her real property tax is $4,000, that alone will reduce the taxable income to $46,000.

Interest

Interest is another big deduction for many taxpayers, especially if they are paying off a mortgage. Interest payments have been broken down into two varieties: mortgage interest and investment interest.

1. *Mortgage interest.* All mortgage interest is usually fully deductible if the home is the principal residence of the taxpayer. If a person has a second vacation home, the mortgage interest on it too is usually fully deductible. During the first few years when the individual is making payments on a mortgage, much of the money is for the payment of interest and will constitute a major deduction.

    On a $100,000 mortgage amortized over 30 years at 10 percent interest, the monthly payment (including only interest and reduction of principal and not insurance and taxes) is $877.57 per month. Of this, $833.33 is interest the first month. The interest portion then declines a bit each month, but over the first twelve months it amounts to $7,974.97. The interest portion then declines a bit each year in the future, but is still substantial and constitutes a major deduction.

    In the case of very expensive homes, there is a limit to the mortgage interest which may be deducted. It is tied to the total debt. The interest deductible limit is the interest on all debt up to $1,000,000. This $1,000,000 debt limitation applies to the combined debt on both the principal residence and the second vacation home.

    At one time consumer interest (interest on a car loan or credit card) could be deducted. In 1990, ten percent of consumer interest was deductible, but Congress eliminated it as a deductible item beginning in 1991. There is, however, a way to get around that interest exclusion if a person is a home owner. An individual may use his or her home as collateral and borrow on it (this is referred to as a home equity mortgage and is discussed in the next chapter). He or she may then use these funds to buy a car. Then instead of car payments, the person has home equity (second mortgage) payments to make and the interest is fully deductible.[6] There is a limit to how

---

6. In Texas and a few other states the law does not allow second (or home equity) mortgages on owner-occupied homes, except for home improvement loans.

much a person may borrow to take advantage of this deduction, and therefore there is a limit to the interest which is deductible. The debt limit is equal to the taxpayer's equity in the home or $100,000, whichever is less.

2. *Investment interest.* Interest paid on loans to finance investments, except to purchase securities which yield tax-free interest such as municipal bonds, is deductible. It is deductible, however, only by an amount equal to the taxpayer's investment income. Investment income here includes dividends, interest, and capital gains. The limit on this deduction is also phased in; interest in excess of the limit is allowed up to 40, 20, and 10 percent respectively for 1988, 1989, and 1990, after which the limit becomes the ceiling. For 1990 only, any excess investment interest expense over investment income may be deducted by an amount equal to the lesser of 1) 10% of $10,000 or 2) 10% of such excess.

Charitable contributions

Charitable deductions may be itemized and deducted on Schedule A. Contributions to approved institutions operated for religious, charitable, literary, scientific, educational, or eleemosynary purposes may be deducted, although such deductions generally may not exceed 50 percent of the taxpayer's adjusted gross income. However, there are different limits in some cases if the gifts were assets that had appreciated substantially since purchased by the donor.

Charitable contributions may include cash as well as assets or personal property (called "other than cash"). In addition, transportation expenses on behalf of charitable organizations may be deducted at 12 cents per mile.

Medical expenses

Medical expenses may be deducted only to the extent that they exceed 7.5 percent of adjusted gross income (AGI). Medical expenses include, but are not limited to, dental, doctors, hospitals, prescription drugs, and the cost of eyeglasses and hearing aids. Also included is the cost of medical insurance premiums paid by the taxpayer. However, all medical expenses should be reduced by insurance reimbursement before calculating the allowable deduction.

An often-overlooked medical deduction is transportation costs for medical purposes. Mileage to and from doctor's offices, etc., may be deducted at 9 cents per mile. Other medically-required transportation/travel expenses may be deducted, but have strict limitations by the IRS. If an individual has medical travel away from home, he or she should consult with the Federal Tax Guide for the requirements of this deduction.

The following table shows how the medical deduction works. Because of the 7.5-percent-of-AGI reduction, only fairly substantial medical bills may be deducted.

Adjusted Gross Income (AGI)	$30,000
Medical insurance premium	$ 875
Medical bills not covered by insurance	1,500
Prescription drugs	350
Dental bills	200
Total	$ 2,925
7.5 percent of AGI	2,250
Medical deduction	$675

Casualty and theft losses

A casualty is the destruction of property resulting from an identifiable event of a sudden, unexpected, or unusual nature. It must be due to an external cause and not a defect in the product itself.

Casualty and theft losses are tax deductible to some extent. The loss of personal (non-business) property as the result of accident, fire, theft, vandalism, hurricane, tornado, flood, or other casualty loss not reimbursed by insurance is sometimes deductible. The amount of loss is computed by determining the value of the property just before the loss (fair market value) less the amount of any insurance received. This total is then reduced by a $100 "floor," as it is called. The $100 floor is normally a reduction of each casualty established by the IRS. It is normally applicable to each separate casualty or theft loss of personal-use property that occurs during the tax year (except in the case where more than four items are involved in the same casualty or theft). The amount is further reduced by ten percent of AGI, to arrive at the deductible portion.

Unreimbursed losses of investment property such as notes, bonds, or collectibles held for potential increase in value are deductible on Schedule A, but such losses are not reduced by the $100 floor or the ten percent of AGI.

If casualty and theft losses are to be used on Schedule A, the taxpayer must fill out Form 4684 to determine the steps involved in the calculation.

Moving expenses

Moving expenses for job-related moves may be deducted in many cases (first-time employees may not use this deduction). If an individual moves to a new job location, he or she may be able to deduct some or all of the moving expenses. To obtain the deduction, however, two tests must be met: (1) the new job must be at least 35 miles farther from the old residence than was the old job, and (2) the individual must be employed full time at the new job for at least 39 weeks during the 12 months immediately following the move. Temporary moves do not count. If the person is self-employed, he or she must work full-time for at least 39 weeks during the first 12 months and 78 weeks during the 24 months right after the move.

If a person qualifies under these tests, most of the direct moving costs may be deducted on Schedule A, including the cost of moving household and personal goods and reasonable travel costs for the entire family, including lodging and 80% of meals. Auto expenses for driving to the new location may also be taken, either by keeping actual receipts or by using a 9 cents per mile transportation deduction.

Certain indirect moving costs may also be deducted, such as house-hunting trips and temporary quarters. After an individual has moved, the reasonable cost of lodging in temporary quarters up to 30 days and 80% of meals may be deducted as indirect moving costs. Costs of selling, buying, or leasing a home, including brokers' and attorneys' fees and the like are other examples of indirect moving costs which may be taken. There is, however, an overall limit on indirect moving cost deductions of $3,000, of which no more than $1,500 may be for house-hunting and temporary living expenses.

The deductions for moving expenses must be calculated on Form 3903 before transferring the deduction to Schedule A.

A number of other miscellaneous deductions may be included on Schedule A. These miscellaneous itemized deductions usually encompass expenses necessary for the production of income or the protection and enhancement of the taxpayer's wealth. These include such things as unreimbursed employee expenses, investment expenses, job-seeking expenses, tax preparation expenses, hobby expenses, gambling losses, etc. The total of most, but not all, of the miscellaneous itemized deductions are subject to a reduction of two percent of AGI before being summed on Schedule A.

Job expenses and other miscellaneous deductions

Let's look at an example of a miscellaneous itemized deduction which is NOT subject to the 2-percent-of-AGI reduction. Gambling losses to the extent of winnings are not subject to the reduction of 2 percent of AGI. All gambling winnings are taxable income on page one of Form 1040. The gambling losses associated with these winnings may be deducted on Schedule A, but only up to a limit of the amount of these winnings.

The miscellaneous itemized deductions discussed in the remainder of this section are, after totalled, subject to a reduction of 2 percent of AGI.

Unreimbursed ordinary and necessary employment expenses such as job travel, union dues and job education may be deducted on Schedule A under certain circumstances. Form 2106 is used to report many employee expenses, and must be completed if ANY of a person's employment-related expenses are reimbursed by the employer, or if claiming a deduction for any meal, entertainment, travel, or transportation ex-

Unreimbursed employee expenses

penses. For unreimbursed employment-related expenses, other than those listed above, Form 2106 is not necessary.

Employee business expenses

If a taxpayer's job requires travel, these travel costs may be deducted (including an allowance for car expenses, discussed below), meals and lodging, and necessary entertainment of clients. The employee may take portions of these expenses subject to IRS limitations (such as 80% of meals and entertainment) only to the extent that the employer does not provide reimbursements. The costs must be necessary business travel costs, and may not include commuting to and from work. These expenses are included on Form 2106. They are subject to the 2-percent-of-AGI reduction. (Only that portion in excess of 2 percent of AGI may be deducted).

Other types of employee business expenses include parking fees and tolls which are not reimbursed by the employer.

Transportation (auto) expenses

Transportation expenses to produce self-employment income are deducted from that income (on Schedule C). Transportation expenses to take care of rental property are deducted from rental income (on Schedule E). In some cases, transportation (auto) expenses of employees are deductible on Schedule A as part of miscellaneous itemized deductions subject to the 2-percent-of-AGI reduction.

If a car is used for business purposes, the expense of running it can be deducted. If the taxpayer's car is used for both business and pleasure, the expense must be prorated in accordance with the rules on Form 2106. The cost (or mileage) of driving to and from work (commuting) is not considered a business expense and hence is not deductible. If expenses are prorated, good records must be kept. Expenses for the vehicle such as oil and gas, repairs, taxes, insurance, etc., including an allowance for depreciation (explained in detail below) may be used. Accurate records must be kept of miles driven for both business and pleasure. All calculations must be made on Form 2106 for this auto deduction.

An alternative method of calculating auto expenses is to take so much per mile of business mileage driven. For 1990 the business mileage rate is 26 cents per mile used for business.

Travel expenses

Travel expenses away from home (or job site) are deductible only if they directly relate to a trade, business or employment, and only to the extent not reimbursed by the employer. Travel as a form of education is no longer allowed. Travel expenses to a luxury resort or on a cruise ship, even if directly related to a trade, business or employment, are limited.

Although most people have only one source of income, many have income other than that from wages and salaries and consequently may become involved with depreciation. A person who owns rental property may depreciate the home or apartment building and take the depreciation as a deduction on Schedule E. An accountant, lawyer, physician, or other professional or self-employed person may recover the cost of books and certain equipment through depreciation on Schedule C.

Depreciation is defined as wear and tear on property used in a trade or business as well as obsolescence. To take depreciation as a deduction on the income tax return, the taxpayer must have certain kinds of property; one cannot claim depreciation on land, stock, bonds, or securities. The taxpayer must also know the date the property was acquired or placed in service for business purposes, because its life is figured from that date. The cost or other basis of the property must also be known by the taxpayer.

Depreciation is generally computed on the cost of the property as of the date purchased or placed in service. The useful life of the asset generally is determined by IRS guidelines, and may be depreciated for tax purposes over this period of time, which varies from asset category to asset category. For example, furniture has a depreciable life of seven years; computers and computer peripherals, 5 years; automobiles, 5 years. The amount of depreciation deduction is determined by IRS tables or percentages, as defined by IRS regulations.

Depreciation

Office-in-home expenses of self-employed individuals are deducted on Schedule C. Certain office-in-home expenses of other employees are deductible only if deductions are itemized on Schedule A. Office-in-home expenses are very limited and must meet restrictive guidelines by the IRS. The office must be used exclusively and regularly as the principal place of the taxpayer's business or place to meet customers, patients, or clients. These expenses may be calculated on Form 2106 before being carried forward to Schedule A.

If an employee must maintain an office in part of his home, as a requirement of the job and not as a convenience of the employee, he or she may deduct expenses for an office in the home on Schedule A, if itemizing deductions. If a person qualifies under the rules set by the IRS, he or she may deduct depreciation (explained above), insurance, and utility bills; or if a person rents instead of owning a home, a portion of the rent may be used instead of depreciation. However, these items must be prorated by one of two methods—by number of rooms in the home or by square footage of the home. If the office comprises one-ninth of the home, then one-ninth of the expenses may be deducted—on Schedule C if self-employed, or on Schedule A under Miscellaneous Deductions if itemizing. The Schedule A deduction is subject to the 2-percent-of-AGI reduction.

Home office deduction

Other miscellaneous deductions

If a person is a member of a union or professional society, union and professional society dues may be deducted on Schedule A, as well as subscriptions to professional journals connected with one's job. The taxpayer may also deduct any fee paid to have his or her tax return prepared the previous year. A safety deposit box rental may be deducted if the box contains income-producing documents, such as stocks, bonds, or securities. Job-seeking fees are deductible, as are special uniforms required by the place of employment and not suitable for regular wear, including the cost of cleaning and repairing them. Investment expenses such as management fees of mutual funds are another example of a miscellaneous deduction. All of these miscellaneous items are subject to the 2-percent-of-AGI reduction.

TAX CREDITS

Itemized deductions, or the standard deduction, are used to reduce adjusted gross income (AGI). Personal exemptions are also subtracted from the adjusted gross income to arrive at taxable income. At this point, the tax liability is calculated. Then there *may* be **tax credits,** which reduce the actual tax itself. That is, after the actual tax liability has been calculated, each dollar of tax credit available will reduce taxes dollar for dollar.

Rehabilitation and low-income housing credits

Expenditures incurred in rehabilitating buildings built before 1936 will qualify for a 10 percent credit. If a person buys such an old building for $50,000 and spends $20,000 rebuilding, he or she may take a $2,000 credit and reduce taxes by that amount.

Buildings that have been certified by the IRS as being historical structures will earn a 20 percent credit. If the building in the above case were in this category, final taxes would be reduced by $4,000.

The low-income housing credit is designed for owners of residential rental projects providing low-income housing, and is available for property placed in service after December 31, 1986.

Child and other dependent care credit

Child care expense is another tax credit to which many taxpayers are entitled. The same is true of expenses for other dependents if they are disabled. The child care or care of other dependents must be incurred in order to enable the taxpayer to be gainfully employed. The person being cared for must be under thirteen years old or disabled. The credit may be taken by a couple even if only one works full-time, if the other works part-time, or is a full-time student. The credit also includes the cost of services received outside the taxpayer's home such as in a day care center. It is allowed even if the care is provided by a relative or member of the household if such person is not a dependent of the taxpayer.

There are, however, limits to how large a child care credit may be taken. First, the credit may not exceed 30 percent of the total cost of the care, up to $2,400 for one individual and $4,800 for two or more. This makes the maximum credit $720 and $1,440 respectively. The above amounts, however, apply only if adjusted gross income (AGI) is $10,000 or less. The 30 percent is adjusted downward by 1 percent for each $2,000 (or fraction thereof) of income in excess of $10,000. The maximum downward adjustment, however, will not go below 20 percent, which it becomes when the taxpayer's AGI exceeds $28,000. A person who uses this credit must calculate the credit on (and submit) Form 2441.

The earned income credit is available for low-income people who have a dependent child. It could be a married couple, a surviving spouse with a child, or the head of a household with a dependent child. Eligible taxpayers can claim the earned income credit if earned income and AGI were both less than IRS stated maximum levels. These figures are adjusted periodically for inflation. The IRS publishes EARNED INCOME TAX TABLES from which the credit must be calculated.

Earned income tax credit

The 1986 change in the tax law defined passive income (and losses) for the first time. Congress has defined the income (and losses) from such limited partnerships as "passive." **Passive income (and loss)** has been defined as any income (or loss) received from activity in which the taxpayer does not materially participate in the management of the enterprise. Passive income is, of course, fully taxable like any income. Passive losses, however, are not fully tax deductible. Passive losses may be deducted from passive income, but these losses may not be fully offset against other (say, salary) income as they once were. Congress's intent was to eliminate this form of tax shelter because too many people were using it, and the 1986 tax law did accomplish Congress's intent.

After 1990, passive losses may no longer be used to reduce active or portfolio income for tax purposes. In 1990, only 10 percent of passive losses may be used to offset salary income.

One way in which passive factors arise is if a person invests in a limited partnership. A limited partnership is a means whereby an investor and many other small investors put in a few dollars (usually the minimum is $5,000); the large sum generated this way is pooled and invested by the managing (or general) partner. The limited partners assume no risk over and above their own individual investment. The large sum of money

INCOME (LOSSES) FROM PASSIVE INVESTMENTS

generated this way is invested in shopping centers, apartment houses, office building warehouses, computer parts, and the like. Some limited partnerships are designed as income partnerships—rent and lease income—and some are designed as tax shelters; some have both income and tax shelters as their goal. The income comes about in the form of rental income. The tax-shelter aspect works primarily through depreciation (as discussed above) with respect to rental property.

ALTERNATIVE MINIMUM TAX (AMT)

If an individual is a high-income taxpayer, he or she may also have to pay an alternative minimum tax. It was imposed because Congress felt everyone should pay some taxes. A few high-income people had so arranged their affairs that they paid little or no taxes. Congress had provided certain beneficial provisions in the tax laws. Many of these were eliminated by the 1986 tax law changes, but some still remain. If a person takes excessive advantage of these, the tax law attempts to recapture part of the gain. The alternative minimum tax, then, generally affects people who have a lot of tax-sheltered income, through what are called ***tax preference items.*** Tax preference items include:

1. The appreciation in the market value of charitable gifts. For example, if a taxpayer donates $20,000 of stock, which was purchased for $10,000 five years ago, to the Ogalla School for Wayward Boys, the $10,000 capital gain is a tax preference item. It is taxed under the AMT but not under the regular income tax. (This item is not applicable for 1991; however, it is applicable for tax years after 1991.)
2. The tax exempt interest on certain private activity municipal bonds.
3. The bargain element of incentive stock options. This is the difference between the exercise price and the stock's trading price when the options are exercised.
4. Losses from passive activities.
5. The accelerated portion of depreciation on real and personal property. Personal property—such as a car used for business—may still be depreciated in excess of straight line, as may rental houses purchased before August 1986. You must add in here the difference between accelerated and straight-line depreciation.
6. Personal exemptions.
7. Standard deductions. Also, there are increased limits on some itemized deductions.

   In addition to the tax preferences, certain other items, too, have an impact on the AMT. For example, state and local income taxes are not deductible in computing the AMT. Taxpayers living in high state-income-tax states may be pushed into an AMT status by that fact alone.

The AMT rate is a flat 24 percent in 1991 (up from 21 percent in 1990), which is well below the top rate under the regular tax rules. Nevertheless, AMT will increase some taxpayer's tax liability because it (the tax base) applies to a greater amount of their income. The preference items and other adjustments are things that taxpayers can deduct or do not have to report on their regular returns.

In order to calculate the alternative minimum tax, the person must first calculate the alternative minimum tax income (AMTI). The taxpayer must begin by taking his or her regular taxable income and adding back the items noted above. There is, however, an AMT exemption which may be deducted.

There is an AMT exemption, which is $40,000 for couples filing jointly, $20,000 each if filing separately, and $30,000 for singles. However, the exemption is phased out for taxpayers with income above certain levels. The exemption is subtracted from the AMTI to obtain the AMT taxable income. In 1991 the AMT is a flat 24 percent (up from 21 percent in 1990) of the alternative taxable income. The alternative minimum tax is compared with the regular income tax, and the higher of the two is paid.

The calculation of AMT is complex. If a taxpayer believes he or she is subject to it, probably professional help should be sought.

Alternative minimum tax exemption

In 1990, national income was $4,651.5 billion and total personal income tax receipts were about $508.4 billion. This means that if the entire income had been subject to taxes, an average rate of only about 10.92 percent would have provided the same revenue. But the entire income is not subject to taxes.

OTHER THINGS THE TAXPAYER SHOULD KNOW ABOUT TAXES

The income from these sources is taxed differently than income currently being earned. Until a few years ago Social Security was not taxed at all, but now it is if it together with other income exceeds a certain level. There are several types of pensions, and the taxation of their benefits varies with the type. Life insurance annuities are also special and are taxed differently. The taxation of all these will be discussed in Chapter 18, Retirement Planning.

The taxation of annuities, Social Security, and pensions

Deductions for interest on mortgages, local property taxes, and income splitting apply to many individuals. Other ways of reducing taxes are to invest in rental property or certain state and local bonds on which the

Legal tax avoidance

interest is not taxable. Corporate pension plans, the personal service corporation, Keogh plans, and the IRA are other methods of sheltering income from taxes (see Chapter 18). Many of these tax shelters that permit legal tax avoidance (as opposed to illegal evasion) are complex. Any person to whom they apply should check with a competent tax accountant. After all, everyone should so arrange their affairs as to minimize taxes.

Capital gains on owner-occupied homes

Many assets, such as homes, appreciate in value as the years pass, and when sold the owner has a nice capital gain. Capital gains used to receive preferable tax treatment, but now they are taxed just like regular income. There is one exception, however. Capital gains on the sale of owner-occupied houses, if reinvested in another house within twenty-four months, are not taxed. However, if the former house sells for more than the cost of the new one, then the differential is taxable as income.

Congress also provided a once-in-a-lifetime exclusion in some cases. Any taxpayer, age fifty-five or over, may take a once-in-a-lifetime tax exclusion of $125,000 on the sale of a house that has been his or her principal residence for at least three years during the last five years ending on the date of sale of the house. This provision applies to homes sold after July 26, 1978.

IRS audits

If a taxpayer has filled out the tax return correctly, the chances of being audited are remote. There are three kinds of audits. First is the correspondent audit, where a few items might be questioned; this does not usually take much time. The IRS will write the taxpayer a letter. Usually such an audit can be handled by writing letters or making a telephone call. If the items are in a gray area, there may be some bargaining. The IRS may compromise and allow some deductions but not others. Second, there is an office audit, in which the taxpayer appears at the IRS office to discuss the items in question. Third, there is the field audit, in which the IRS comes to the taxpayer's home or office.

Returns selected for audit are based upon the IRS's discriminant functions system (DFS) program which is developed through Taxpayer Compliance Measurement Program (TCMP) audits. TCMP audits are an item-by-item examination of the taxpayer's entire return. People picked for the TCMP are chosen at random. The purpose of the TCMP is to give the IRS a feeling for the various legitimate expenses of various income groups in order to update their computer, which scans millions of tax forms to spot irregularities. Statistics obtained this way are fed into the IRS's discriminant functions system (DFS) program to determine norms. These statistics are then used to select returns for audit based upon variances from established norms.

The chances of being audited are small. Only about 1 percent of all returns are selected for an audit. If the taxpayer's income is above $100,000, the chances are about four percent.

How to avoid an audit

Generally speaking, if there are high itemized deductions on a return, the chances of being audited are greater. The IRS has average or acceptable dollar amounts of deductions for various levels of income. The greater a person's deductions are above the averages, the greater the likelihood of an audit. If some deductions are unusually high in a given year, the taxpayer might attach a note explaining why. For example, if there are unusually large dental bills because of treatment for orthodontia, this may be explained in an attached note. This may be done for any high deductible item that is legitimate.

Substantial declines in income, if the person is self-employed, too, may trigger an audit.

SUMMARY REVIEW QUESTIONS

These questions serve as a summary and a review of the chapter. If the reader is able to answer them all, he or she has a good understanding of the material covered by the chapter.

1. What proportion of national income is taxed away at the federal level?
2. How are state and local taxes on real estate calculated?
3. Why is it that two individuals with the same income and the same dependents do not necessarily pay the same amount of taxes?
4. Who must file a federal income tax return? Who might want to file even if they do not have to?
5. What is the earned income credit?
6. Is alimony subject to the federal personal income tax?
7. How does filing a joint return save the taxpayer money?
8. Are charitable contributions deductible?
9. Who may contribute to an individual retirement account (IRA)?
10. How are casualty and theft losses treated on the 1040 tax forms?
11. Are moving expenses deductible on the federal tax form?
12. What are tax credits? How are they applied?
13. Why is it that most people who do not own a home are better off taking the standard deduction than itemizing?
14. What are passive investments?
15. What is the alternative minimum tax? How does it work?
16. What are tax preference items? How may they affect taxes?
17. What is the alternative minimum tax exemption?
18. How is the capital gain on owner-occupied homes taxed?

CASES

1. Joe and Jean Sargeant have one child and would like you to calculate their taxes. The pertinent facts are as follows:

Income	$40,000
Mortgage interest	7,200
Property taxes	2,100
Other itemized deductions	1,000
Sales taxes	2,350

   (a) Calculate their taxes.
   (b) Calculate what their taxes would be if they were renting instead of buying a home.

   (c) What are their savings as home owners?

2. Bob and Joan Rider are a young couple with no dependents. Bob works as a salesman for a local manufacturer and earns $35,000 per year. Joan is a law student. They rent a modest apartment for $400 per month. They have never been able to itemize their deductions and earn more than the standard deduction. Calculate the tax liability of the Riders using the standard deduction.

3. Geraldean Fitzgerald invested $10,000 at 10 percent which is fully taxable, and

$10,000 in municipal bonds at 7 percent on which the interest is tax-free. She is in the 28 percent tax bracket.

(a) Which provides her with the higher after-tax yield and by how much?

(b) Her taxable investment, however, is expected to appreciate in value at 4 percent per year, while her bonds will not. If this proves to be the case, which is the better investment?

(c) If inflation is 4 percent, what is Ms. Fitzgerald's yield in both cases?

4. James and Mary Wingo are a two-income family. James has an annual salary of $35,000, and his employer withheld $6,400 for income taxes and $2,677.50 for Social Security taxes. James was ill for one week and did not work, but his employer had a sick-pay plan and James received his salary that week.

James's wife Mary is self-employed and earned $40,000. Mary also received $180 of dividends on stock she owned individually and $250 in interest income. During the year they had an accident in which Mary ran over an unfortunate man who stepped in front of her car. Mary suffered $600 damages to the grill and front end of her car. Her insurance policy has a $500 deductible clause.

Mary filed an estimated tax return and made four quarterly payments of $2,000 each on her estimated tax. As a self-employed person, Mary must pay Social Security taxes of $6,120.00.

In addition to their own exemptions, they are entitled to claim an exemption for their two children. These are their other deductible items:

Contributions	$ 500
Interest (mortgage)	5,422
Taxes	1,545
Medical expenses paid (including $125 for medicine & drugs)	500
Professional dues	60
Medical insurance	1,097

Compute James and Mary's additional tax or refund.

5. John and Bette Pasmack live on the West Coast, and John earned $35,000 last year. In addition, he received a bonus of $2,500 just before Christmas. His employer withheld $4,396 for income taxes and $2,677.50 for Social Security tax. John and Bette each had $60 of dividend income and, in addition, Bette received $500 interest income from a trust.

In addition to their own exemptions, John and Bette are entitled to exemptions for son Jack, daughter Jean, and Bette's seventy-year-old widowed mother. Their deductible items are:

Contributions	$ 510
Interest	4,695
Taxes	1,800
Loss on their summer cottage damaged by fire	1,200
Dues to professional societies	55
Medical expenses paid (including $225 for medicine and drugs and $750 for hospitalization insurance)	1,120

Compute their additional tax or refund.

SUGGESTED READINGS

Commerce Clearing House. *Federal Tax Return Manual.* Chicago: Commerce Clearing House. Annual publication.

"Federal Tax Course." Chicago: Commerce Clearing House. Annual publication.

"Federal Tax Courses." Englewood Cliffs, N.J.: Prentice-Hall. Annual publication.

"Highlights of the Tax Reform Act of 1986." Chicago: Arthur Andersen & Co.

Internal Revenue Service. "Employer's Tax Guide, Circular E." Washington, D.C.: Internal Revenue Service. Annual publication.

————. "Instructions for Preparing Form 1040." An annual IRS publication which can be obtained at any post office during tax time and at any regional IRS office at other times.

————. "Instructions for Preparing Form 1040A." An annual IRS publication which can be obtained at any post office during tax return time and at any regional IRS office at other times.

————. *Tax Guide for Small Business.* Washington, D.C.: U.S. Government Printing Office. Annual publication.

————. *Your Federal Income Tax.* An annual IRS publication which gives a far more detailed explanation than the "Instructions for Preparing Form 1040." It can be obtained at any IRS regional office.

"Master Tax Guide." Chicago: Commerce Clearing House. An annual publication.

"The National Debt." Philadelphia: The Federal Reserve Bank of Philadelphia.

"Price Waterhouse Guide to the New Tax Law." New York: Bantam Books, 1987.

Sommerfeld, Ray M., Anderson, Hershel M., and Brock, Horace R. *An Introduction to Taxation,* 4th ed. New York: Harcourt, Brace & World, 1988.

"Tax Reform 1998." Chicago: Arthur Andersen & Co.

"22 Ways to Save Money on Income Taxes." Dean Witter Reynolds, Inc. You may obtain this from your Dean Witter broker.

United States Budget. Washington, D.C.: U.S. Government Printing Office. Annual publication.

"Year-End Tax Strategy for Individuals; Planning for 1986 and Beyond." Chicago: Arthur Andersen & Co.

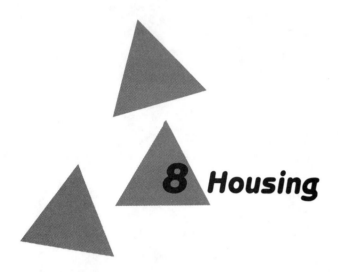

8 Housing

HIGHLIGHTS   In order to present the basic information needed for home ownership, this chapter examines the following:

1   The advantages and disadvantages of home ownership
2   Renting versus owning
3   How homes are financed, and the cost of financing them
4   How home mortgages are paid off or amortized
5   Refinancing a home
6   Large versus small down payments
7   The new innovative mortgages
8   The closing costs of buying a home

Home ownership is important in a budget. Most people who own homes must meet a monthly mortgage payment that is a substantial proportion of the budget, a fixed payment that must be paid for many years. In addition, many people consider part of this monthly payment to be forced saving because with each monthly payment the individual's equity or ownership in the home increases. Others relate home ownership to the family budget because the interest paid as well as the real property taxes constitute large tax-deductible items.

The popularity of home ownership is shown by the fact that currently about 64 percent of United States families own their own homes. The rate of increase, however, has slowed in the last few years, generally because of the greater availability of rental units and increases in construction costs.

FACTORS TO CONSIDER

Some people attach great importance to the peace of mind, pride, security, greater privacy, and convenience that owning a home provides. Some also feel that homes are often located in less congested areas than apartments, and provide a better environment in which to raise children.

Advantages of home ownership

There are several advantages of owning a home. Some of these are enumerated in the following discussion.

Tax advantages

There is a considerable tax advantage to home ownership. A home owner pays interest on the mortgage and local property taxes on the home, while a person who rents an apartment pays rent. The latter, however, includes a sum to enable the landlord to pay the interest and tax; hence the renter pays these costs indirectly. Because of this hidden cost for the renter, home owners have a tax advantage over renters. If their income, exemptions, and other deductions are the same as the renter's, they will usually pay lower taxes. This is because home owners may deduct from their incomes, when calculating their taxes, interest on their mortgage and property taxes. Rent, of course, cannot be deducted. This can best be illustrated by an example. Consider two childless couples whose circumstances are identical except that one rents and one owns a house. Both have adjusted gross incomes of $20,000, and total deductions because of medical expenses, contributions to charity, church, and so forth, amount to $2,000. The couple owning a home, however, has additional deductions of $6,900 due to interest and property taxes ($75 per month taxes and about $500 per month interest is not unreasonable for even a modest home). The couple owning a home will take a total deduction of $8,900, while the one renting can take only the $5,200 standard deduction that married couples may take if filing jointly.[1] The home

---

1. The standard deduction for married couples filing jointly for 1989 was $5,200. Beginning in 1990, the standard deduction will be adjusted for inflation based upon the Consumer Price Index.

owner's taxable income is $3,700 lower; at the 15 percent tax bracket they save $555 in taxes, using this 1989 example. At the 28 percent bracket the savings are $1,036. The nature of our tax laws enables the home owner to pass part of the interest and property taxes on to Uncle Sam, if they have enough total deductions to itemize deductions on their tax return.

In some states, laws have been enacted making it possible for persons to declare their home to be their homestead. This prevents the home from being seized to satisfy certain private debts. In some states, there is a dollar limit to the amount of real estate protected against seizure. The homestead act does not prevent the mortgage lender from foreclosing if mortgage payments are not made. Also, the government is not prevented from seizing the property if it has a valid claim against the owner. But with these two exceptions, the property is protected. In some areas, property taxes are also reduced by a modest amount if a homestead claim is filed.

Homestead

A home is often thought of as a good inflationary hedge. Generally, a home will appreciate as much as inflation, and sometimes more, than overall prices during times of inflation, because when prices rise, so too do building materials and labor costs. Consequently, during inflation, the cost of building new houses rises; this generally brings up the price of older houses as well.

A home as an inflationary hedge

During the decade of the 1970s the price of houses rose much more rapidly than the overall rate of inflation. However, by the middle 1980s this rapid home price escalation slowed; indeed in some depressed areas of the country, prices have actually declined. In most areas, however, the price of homes has still kept up with inflation and in many cases has exceeded it. In addition, the past few years is likely to prove an ephemeral phenomenon. If history is any guide, the future price of homes will more than keep up with inflation in the long run.

Table 8–1 shows the sale of one-family homes and median price since 1970.

Some people consider maintenance as a disadvantage of home ownership. The house must be painted every few years, and from time to time the roof will need repairs. Occasionally, a plumber will have to be called, and certain built-in appliances like the hot water heater, furnace, and air conditioner wear out and must be repaired or replaced. These things can be avoided by the apartment dweller, as well as work like raking leaves, cutting the lawn, and shoveling snow. Since most people do these chores themselves, little monetary cost is involved, but the home owner's time is committed.

Disadvantages of home ownership

It has been estimated that maintenance costs will be about 1 1/2 percent of the cost of the house per year. This is the average cost, and in some years the cost will be considerably higher. Some people consider

Table 8—1   *New and existing one-family homes sold*

Year	Number (thousands)			Dollar volume (billions)			Median price	
	New homes	*Existing homes*	*Total homes*	*New homes***	*Existing homes*	*Total homes*	*New homes*	*Existing homes*
1970	485	1,612	2,097	$12.9	$ 41.4	$ 54.3	$23,4000	$23,000
1971	656	2,018	2,674	18.6	56.5	75.1	25,200	24,800
1972	718	2,252	2,970	21.9	67.8	89.7	27,600	26,700
1973	634	2,334	2,968	22.5	76.8	99.3	32,500	28,900
1974	519	2,272	2,791	20.2	81.3	101.5	35,900	32,000
1975	549	2,476	3,025	23.4	96.6	120.0	39,300	35,300
1976	646	3,064	3,710	31.0	129.3	160.3	44,200	38,100
1977	819	3,650	4,469	44.4	174.8	219.2	48,800	42,900
1978	817	3,986	4,803	51.1	221.2	272.3	55,700	48,700
1979	709	3,827	4,536	50.9	245.7	296.6	62,900	55,700
1980	545	2,973	3,518	41.6	216.4	258.0	64,600	62,200
1981	436	2,419	2,855	36.2	189.4	225.6	68,900	66,400
1982	412	1,990	2,402	34.6	160.2	194.8	69,300	67,800
1983	623	2,719	3,342	55.9	225.9	281.8	75,300	70,300
1984	639	2,868	3,507	62.4	246.6	309.0	79,900	72,400
1985	688	3,214	3,902	69.4	291.9	361.3	84,300	75,500
1986	749	3,565	4,314	83.7	351.5	435.2	91,700	80,300
1987	671	3,526	4,197	85.4	374.8	460.2	104,500	85,600
1988*	677	3,594	4,271	93.6	405.4	499.0	112,500	89,300

*Preliminary.

**Computed from number of homes sold and average sales price.

Sources: Bureau of the Census; National Association of Realtors; Savings Institutions Sourcebook, 1989, p. 42.

the big investment required to be a home owner a disadvantage. The fact that a home is not very liquid and requires time to sell reinforces this disadvantage.

To rent or own a home

When comparing renting and buying, many people compare renting an apartment with buying a house. This is not completely valid because two different things are being compared. Usually (but not always), a house is larger than an apartment. In addition, the home owner has more privacy than a tenant in an apartment and a backyard, which the tenant lacks. Also, home owners are building up an equity in their houses. Consequently, you cannot compare the monthly mortgage payment on a house with the monthly rental payment and reach a decision. You must also give some weight to all the things discussed above under advantages and disadvantages of home ownership.

To be sure, houses can also be rented. If you were to compare the monthly rent on a house with the mortgage payment on a like (or similar) house, you would have a more meaningful comparison.

The two options must be compared in the long run and the short run. A home owner does not build up much equity during the first few years of home ownership, because most of the montly payments go for interest. Also, the first year will necessitate additional closing costs and possibly expenditures for putting in a lawn and other landscaping.

When buying a house as opposed to renting, an individual is almost certainly better off financially to buy, except possibly in the short run. That has been the case in the past, and it is likely to be so in the future. However, if a person is only going to live in a community a year or two, he or she might want to rent for the somewhat greater convenience and possibly less expense: for example, no maintenance cost, no landscaping (needed on new homes only), no closing costs, no possible realtor's fee when selling, and the like. In the long run, especially if the monthly mortgage payment is lower than the monthly rent, probably an individual should buy.

If it does not matter to the individual whether he or she lives in an apartment or buys a house, and the decision between buying or renting is made strictly on a financial basis, then the task is more complex. The following will need to be considered:

1. The monthly rent and the monthly mortgage payment
2. The dollar amount of property taxes and interest, as well as the individual's tax bracket, since these two items are tax deductible
3. How much the house is likely to appreciate in price per year
4. How long the individual is likely to be living in the community before moving
5. The cost of insurance and maintenance

Whether a person should buy or rent is a question that must be analyzed individually. It will vary from time to time and place to place and person to person. An individual might be living in an area that is overbuilt with apartments; hence, rents might be relatively low. If that is the case at a time when interest rates are very high and few homes are being built and hence are very costly, he or she could be better off to rent at least for a time. If, later, apartments are no longer overbuilt and rents rise and at the same time interest rates decline, this might be the time to investigate home ownership.

When an individual decides whether to rent or buy, the material on the personal budget and on housing expenditures in Chapter 2 should be reviewed. Housing expenses from renting and from buying should be compared. Table 8–2 is a place to begin in making the analysis.

In it we are assuming a $90,000 home with an $80,000 thirty-year mortgage at 12 percent. This will make the monthly mortgage payment $823. The annual rent for a comparable home is $8,400. However, it and some of the other items may differ according to geographical area.

In the case shown in Table 8–2, the cost of owning a home at the 15 percent tax bracket exceeds the cost of renting by $2,230 even after taking taxes into account. However, this $2,230 shrinks to $868 at the 28

Table 8—2   *Expenses of renting versus buying a home*

COST OF RENTING: $700/month × 12		$8,400 per year
COST OF BUYING A HOME:		
Mortgage payment $823/month × 12		$9,876 per year
Maintenance $50/month × 12		600
Interest foregone on $10,000 down payment		
($10,000 × 9%)	$900	
Less taxes at 15%	−135	
		765
Property taxes $75/month × 12		900
Insurance on house $30/month × 12		360
Total Cost		$12,501
Less tax benefits from deducting interest and		
property taxes:		
Interest $9,576		
Taxes 900		
$10,476 × 15% tax rate		−$1,571
Less equity build-up $25/month × 12		300
Net cost; $12,501 − $1,871		$10,630

Adjust further by price appreciation of house. To be sure, the value of homes do not always appreciate. However, generally homes have appreciated enough to keep up with inflation in the long run, and in many cases by more.

Net cost at the	
28% tax bracket: $12,501 − $3,233	$9,268

percent tax bracket. If we also consider appreciation to be 4 percent per year, then even the person in the 15 percent tax bracket might be better off by buying, because he or she has an inflationary hedge. In addition, the longer an individual owns a home, the better off he or she will be relative to the renter; because as the years pass, the total dollar cost of interest declines and the equity build-up increases. It should also be noted that as the years pass, rent is more likely to rise as a result of inflation; whereas house payments (on a fixed mortgage) will remain constant (although some portions may rise such as taxes and insurance).

How much house can an individual afford?

There used to be, and to some extent still are, five rules of thumb used by mortgage lenders to indicate how much of a house a prospective home owner could afford. They are:

1.   The price of the home (including the lot) should be no more than two and one-half times the purchaser's annual gross (before tax) income.

2. The amount borrowed to purchase a home should be no more than two times the purchaser's gross annual income.
3. The monthly mortgage payments of a home owner (which includes reduction of principal, interest, taxes, and insurance—PITI) should be no more than 25 percent of the home owner's gross income. This assumes a 10 percent down payment. If you pay down more than 10 percent, this 25 percent figure may be scaled up to as much as 28 percent.
4. Total monthly housing costs should not exceed one week's take-home pay (net, not gross, income).
5. Total monthly payment on all debts (including consumer installment debt) should not exceed 36 percent of gross monthly income. To be sure, the aforementioned percentage figures will vary some from state to state and between lenders.

The first three rules all work out about the same. Under the first rule, a person making $25,000 per year could buy a house worth $62,500. He or she could also finance about $50,000 of it under the second rule and hence would need a down payment of about $12,500. This is the often standard 20 percent.

Under the third rule, the person could pay $520 per month ($25,000 ÷ 12 = $2,083 × 25% = $520). Moreover, historically about 1 percent of the mortgage would cover the monthly payment needed for the reduction of principal, interest, taxes, and insurance. In the $50,000 mortgage noted above, this amounts to $500.

Rule four has more often been applied to renters, but sometimes to homeowners. Under it, the person would not quite qualify. One week's gross pay is $480 ($25,000 ÷ 52). The net after taxes would be even less.

Under rule five the person making $25,000 per year could assume debts requiring monthly payments of up to $750.

In recent years all of the rules have been stretched a bit, especially for two-income families. Obviously the higher a down payment you are able to make, the more house you can afford. But the rules have been modified in other ways. The 2½ times rule is now sometimes the 3 times rule. The 2 times rule is now sometimes the 2½ times rule, and the 25 percent has been modified to 28 percent in some cases. In such a case, the person making $25,000 could afford a monthly payment of $583. This has been done because interest costs and construction costs, and hence housing costs, have risen faster than income. In addition, many people have been willing to make a greater sacrifice to acquire a home because home ownership has proven to be a good investment. The individual who does this must do so with care, and budget wisely.

Some people prefer a condominium to a house. A condominium provides some of the benefits of owning a house and some of the benefits of

Condominium or house?

apartment living. Condominiums are apartmentlike structures, but residents receive *title* to their units. They must make a down payment and arrange their mortgage, if financed, just as for a house. Moreover, they can sell at any time. Condominium owners have the same tax benefits as home owners and build up equity like a home owner. They have all the building maintenance problems to take care of in their unit.

A condominium owner is more like an apartment dweller in that there is no yard work to perform. There may be a common yard that can be enjoyed with other condominium owners in the building. Sometimes this includes a common swimming pool, tennis court, and putting green. Instead of maintaining these facilities, the individual is assessed a fee each month, and a maintenance crew is hired.

When buying a condominium, the owner joins the condominium association, and all members have one vote in deciding matters in accordance with the provisions as set forth in the condominium agreement that all members must agree to abide by. Generally speaking, condominium owners may sell their unit to anyone they choose.

Choosing between a house and a condominium is a personal matter. Those who want some of the benefits of home ownership but not all of the problems might choose this compromise, although they give up some backyard privacy.

Co-ops

In some cities, there are co-op apartments and even co-op homes. These co-ops are nonprofit corporations, and the residents of a co-op housing unit, technically speaking, do not own their unit. The corporation owns it, and each resident owns some stock (certificates of ownership) of the corporation. Often the number of apartments in a co-op is large, and home co-ops may cover an entire city block. Generally, the homes are connected and are built facing the street on all four sides of the block. The center then becomes a courtyard and serves as a common backyard.

Since the apartments (or homes) in a co-op are of varying sizes (and values), the amount of stock a co-oper has is prorated accordingly. The price residents have to pay for the stock is then similar to the down payment on a house. The co-oper makes a monthly payment (which varies in accordance with the value of the individual unit) to the co-op; this includes interest, taxes, insurance, and reduction of principal, and the co-op makes one mortgage payment to the mortgage holder. There is one common mortgage on twenty or thirty different rental units rather than each one being financed separately. As the years pass and the mortgage is reduced, the theoretical value of the co-op shares rises.

Since co-op housing is a relatively new development, few of them have been around long enough to have their mortgage paid off. However, when the common mortgage is paid, there is usually some arrangement for the co-op to be dissolved and all co-opers to obtain title to their units. Each co-oper may be expected to help in doing yard work, or there may be a monthly fee to have this done.

A co-op is similar to a condominium, but legally different. In a condominium, each unit has a separate mortgage and each resident has title to his or her property. In a co-op, there is one mortgage and the resident owns shares in the co-op. However, co-op owners may sell their shares to qualifying buyers.

That portion of the co-oper's monthly payment for the payment of interest or property taxes is fully deductible for tax purposes, just as in the case of the home or condominium owner. The co-op may offer one advantage over the individual residential unit, since on a mortgage often for hundreds of thousands of dollars (or even millions) the interest rate may be a little lower.

One question may have occurred to you. Since a co-op is a nonprofit corporation, who would have an incentive to establish one? The answer is realtors, builders, and land developers, who would stand to make a profit due to realtors' fees or in the construction of the building. One possible disadvantage to owning a co-op is that since there is one mortgage and since the value of the co-op shares rises as equity is built up, the new prospective buyer would need a large down payment to buy a co-op unit. In the case of an individual mortgage, it can be refinanced, but with a common mortgage this is not possible. This problem can be solved in some states where banks and savings and loan associations can make long-term loans using co-op stock as security.

Mobile homes

Recently more and more people have been buying mobile homes. At one time these units appealed primarily to people whose jobs required that they move a good deal, such as construction workers. Today, however, primarily because they are so much cheaper than a conventional home, many young couples as well as older retired people are buying them.

There are two varieties of mobile homes. There is the true mobile home, which is on wheels and is moved from place to place. Many retired people have these trailers and go south during the winter. Then there is the so-called **mobile home,** which is on blocks and may have elaborate extensions built onto it. It can never again be moved and will remain permanently in a trailer or mobile home park.

In the past a mobile home was always a trailer with or without wheels. Recently, **motor homes** have been developed: self-propelled units generally built on a truck frame. Many of these units have become the second homes discussed below.

Mobile homes were financed like cars until a few years ago. Loans for them were considered consumer loans, the interest rates were similar to rates on cars, and they had to be amortized over several years like auto loans. Some lenders still feel this way; if they have wheels, they can be moved, and thus loans for them are similar to an auto loan. However, in the last few years, a number of changes have been made. Mobile home loans are now made for up to fifteen years. One reason is that the cost of a mobile home may now be as much as $50,000 and sometimes even more. Interest rates on mobile home loans are generally 2 to 3 points above regular home loans. In general at least a 15 percent down payment is required to obtain a mobile home loan.

Prefabricated houses

Until recently, the use of prefabricated homes was greatly restricted by zoning laws. While still true in many areas this is slowly changing. Often prefabricated homes are found in the low-income areas of the community or are used as vacation homes. Until recently lenders did not finance them over more than ten years. This too is slowly changing. Prefabricated homes, while still cheaper than others, now sell for up to $75,000 and are a much better product than a decade ago. An advantage of buying a prefabricated home is that it takes much less time to assemble it than to construct a conventional home. The major disadvantage is that the buyer will have less choice and flexibility as to style and design.

Second or vacation homes

Some of the more affluent members of society have summer or vacation homes. These are, if not mobile, usually located on a lake, at the beach, in the mountains, or at some other resort area. In some cases these homes are also an investment property. Arrangements can be made to rent them when they are not used by the owner. Most large resort areas have a service that makes the rental arrangements. People have purchased single-family units, condominiums, motor homes, prefabs, and trailers for their second homes. Of these single-family units, condominiums are the easiest to rent, since a service usually exists to do this for the property owner.

HOME FINANCING

About nine out of ten Americans who purchase or build a residence do so with the help of mortgage financing, the security for the debt. The borrower is called the mortgagor and the lender the mortgagee. The borrower gives the mortgage and the lender is said to take the mortgage. Most mortgage loans are made by financial institutions and a few by individuals. The institutions involved are savings and loan associations, mutual savings banks, life insurance companies, mortgage banks, and some commercial banks. In addition, the trust departments of some commercial banks may finance a few mortgages, and recently credit unions were authorized to do so. However, up to now very few credit unions have been active in mortgage financing.

Historically there were three types of mortgages; **conventional, FHA-insured,** and **VA-guaranteed.** These were all fixed mortgages. This means the interest rate was fixed the entire twenty or thirty years over which the mortgage runs. Recently, however, a number of innovative mortgages have been developed which will be discussed below.

In some states **deeds of trust** are used. This is a special kind of mortgage. The regular mortgage involves only two parties, the borrower (mortgagor) and the lender (mortgagee). In the deed of trust, the borrower conveys the realty not to the lender but to a third party, in trust, for the benefit of the lender, but for all practical purposes a deed of trust and a mortgage are the same.

A conventional fixed-payment mortgage is an arrangement solely between the lending institution and the buyer of the home. The institution lends its money and, until a few years ago, assumed the entire risk of loss, but now there is insurance that pays any losses suffered by the lender due to a default. Conventional mortgage loans may be made for as long as thirty years, but many of them last much less than this.

The conventional mortgage

In most states, savings and loan associations are now able to make loans up to 90 percent of the value of the home. At one time, 80 percent was the maximum amount in most states because there was no mortgage insurance available on conventional mortgages. However, with the coming of **private mortgage insurance** (PMI), lenders are willing to make larger loans and the law allows it in most states. PMI works just like any insurance plan. A premium is assessed against the home owner, and this goes into a fund used to pay any losses the lender might suffer if there is a default. To be sure, the interest charged on a 95 percent mortgage loan is usually a little higher than on a 90 percent loan, which in turn is higher than on an 80 percent one. While lenders may lend up to 95 percent of the value of the home, how much they actually advance varies. When money is scarce, they require a larger down payment than when money is plentiful.

The interest rate on mortgages varies from time to time and place to place. It varies from state to state because the demand for loans relative to the supply of mortgage money varies geographically. Generally speaking, all geographical areas have relative shortages of money at times and relatively plentiful supplies at others (but as noted above the relative degree varies regionally). Occasionally mortgage money is so scarce that it is difficult and sometimes even impossible to obtain at any interest rate.

The FHA mortgage is a loan secured by a mortgage and given by an approved lending institution, but the loan is insured by the Federal Housing Administration. The government does not do the lending but merely acts as an insurance company. The borrower pays a fee of about 3.8 percent (the fee varies a bit from time to time) of the loan for this insurance. However, the borrower need not pay this in one lump sum; rather it is added to the mortgage, and financed over thirty years. In the event of default in the payment of the loan by the buyer, the lending institution is paid for certain losses.

The FHA mortgage

There is an upper limit to the insurance provided by the FHA, but this upper limit is scaled upward periodically as the prices of homes rise. Check with a realtor to find the current maximmum.

For a prospective home buyer to qualify for an FHA-insured loan, he or she must meet certain credit and income requirements. In addition, the home must meet minimum appraisal standards as established by the FHA, providing the buyer with some protection. This necessitates FHA inspection of the home. This and other FHA "red tape" result in more time being required for a FHA loan to be approved than for a conventional loan. Although the maximum length of FHA loans changes from time to time, the current maximum maturity is thirty years. The minimum down payment required on an FHA mortgage varies as FHA regulations change and with the value of the house. Currently the minimum is between 5 and 10 percent depending on the value of the home. Because these loan-to-value ratios are frequently changed by the FHA commissioner, it is necessary to obtain the current figures by asking a real estate broker or lending institution.

The maximum interest rate on an FHA-insured loan is set by the federal housing commissioner, subject to statutory limitations, and it too is changed from time to time.

The VA-guaranteed mortgage

A VA-guaranteed mortgage is a loan on which the Veterans Administration guarantees payment to the lending institution or to an individual lender in the event of default by the veteran-buyer under the terms of the Servicemen's Readjustment Act of 1944 as amended. There are limits, however, to the dollar amount the VA will guarantee ($144,000 in 1990). These limits change from time to time; see a realtor for current figures. A VA loan does not require a down payment; consequently the entire price of the house may be financed, if it is within the upper limit. For homes above $144,000, a down payment is required.

To be eligible for a VA loan the person must be an honorably discharged veteran of the United States Armed Forces. The law also permits veterans who have had one VA loan who sold the house which it financed to obtain a second VA loan in certain cases.

The present legal ceiling on VA-guaranteed mortgages is 10 percent, but this changes periodically. The maximum maturity period is now thirty years. The VA borrower pays a small fee for this mortgage guarantee which varies a bit with the down payment but currently is about one percent.

Billions of dollars of investors' money are tied up in various types of mortgages. Figure 8–1 and Table 8–3 illustrate total residential mortgages outstanding over the years, as well as mortgages outstanding by type of lender.

Second mortgages

Sometimes second mortgages are needed to finance a home. Second mortgages come into existence when the purchaser does not have suffi-

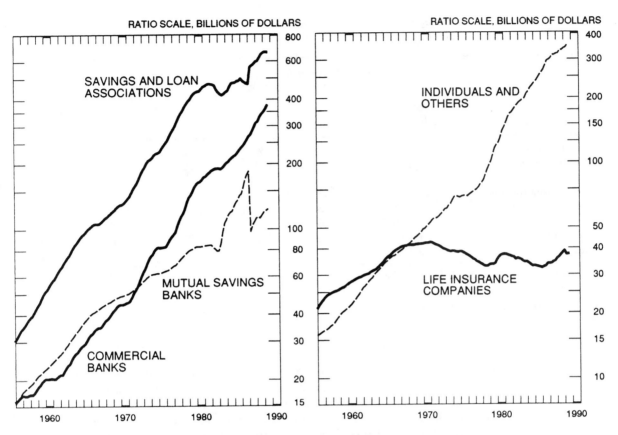

RATIO SCALE, BILLIONS OF DOLLARS

SAVINGS AND LOAN
ASSOCIATIONS

MUTUAL SAVINGS
BANKS

COMMERCIAL
BANKS

RATIO SCALE, BILLIONS OF DOLLARS

INDIVIDUALS AND
OTHERS

LIFE INSURANCE
COMPANIES

Residential mortgage debt: type of lender. Amount outstanding, end of quarter (Source: Figure 8–1
1989 Historical Chart Book, *Board of Governors of the Federal Reserve System, p. 75.*)

cient funds to make the necessary down payment to pay the owner his or
her equity in an existing (not a new) home. The purchaser pays off what
proportion of the equity he can and assumes a second mortgage for the
remainder.

Second mortgages are riskier than first mortgages. In the event of a
foreclosure and sale of a house on which the mortgagor has defaulted,
the second mortgage is not paid off until after the first mortgagee has
been completely repaid. An illustration will make the second mortgage
clear. Assume that a buyer wishes to buy a home for $100,000 and the
home has a $60,000 mortgage on it. If the buyer could pay the seller
$40,000 in cash, he could assume the old outstanding $60,000 mortgage. However, if he has only $30,000 for a down payment, he could pay
that and give the seller a $10,000 second mortgage. Second mortgages
are for smaller dollar amounts and run over fewer years than first ones.
Generally they are for four, five, or perhaps up to ten years. The new
home owner now has two monthly payments to make. Interest rates are
higher on second mortgages than on first because they are riskier.

Table 8—3   *Mortgage loans outstanding, by type of property and lender, year-end 1988**
(billions of dollars)

Lender	Residential properties			Commer-cial properties	Farm proper-ties	Total mortgage loans
	One- to four-family	Multi-family	Total			
Savings associations	$ 552.1	$ 87.5	$ 639.6	$119.5	$ 0.0	$ 759.1
Savings banks	104.9	19.3	124.2	29.4	0.0	153.6
Thrift institutions	$ 657.0	$106.8	$ 763.8	$148.9	$ 0.0	$ 912.7
Commercial banks	311.8	36.8	348.6	301.3	15.6	665.5
Life insurance companies	15.3	23.6	38.9	185.6	9.2	233.8
All others	1,143.7	126.0	1,269.7	77.7	62.0	1,409.0
Total	$2,127.8	$293.2	$2,421.0	$713.5	$ 86.8	$3,221.3

Note: components may not add to totals due to rounding.

*Preliminary.

Source: Federal Reserve Board; *Savings Institutions Sourcebook,* 1989.

Recently mortgages referred to as **home equity loans** have been developed. This is simply a fancy name for a second mortgage. However, these mortgages are not used to finance the purchase of a home like the traditional second mortgage described above. Rather they are used when a home owner has paid off a substantial part of his or her mortgage and also has a large price appreciation, and hence has a big equity in his or her home. The home owner borrows on his or her equity to finance vacations, luxury cars, trips abroad, home improvements, college education for the kids, and perhaps new investments.[2]

Amortizing a home loan

A mortgage loan is paid off or amortized by having the home owner make monthly payments, which pays off the mortgage loan in installments. A fixed monthly payment includes interest, reduction of principal, and perhaps taxes and insurance. A $50,000, 30-year mortgage at 12 percent would require a montly payment of $514.31 to be amortized in 30 years, exclusive of taxes and insurance. Since the interest is calculated each month on the unpaid balance, that balance and the interest paid declines a bit each month. Inasmuch as the $514.31 payment is constant, the savings in interest are applied to reduce the principal more each month. These calculations have been made and printed in table form, and such

---

2. As noted above in Chapter 7 such loans are illegal in Texas and a few other states except in the case of home improvement loans.

an amortization table may be obtained from most banks or savings and loan associations.

The first $514.31 monthly payment mentioned above includes interest of $500 the first month and $14.31 for the reduction of the principal. If we add $75 for taxes and $25 for insurance, the total monthly payment becomes $614.31. The second monthly payment would include less interest and a little more reduction of principal: for example, $499.86 and $14.45 respectively. The insurance and tax payments would presumably remain constant in the short run although every few years they are adjusted upward. These four monthly payments and the way they appear over time can be depicted graphically, as in Figure 8–2. Time is measured on the hoizontal axis and the monthly payments on the vertical axis. This same relationship can be shown in a different manner, as illustrated by Table 8–4. You will note that after the last payment (the 360th payment) is made a principal of $53.38 remains. This is because a mortgage payment this long cannot always be made to come out exactly even.

Assumptions versus refinancing

The prospective buyer who has the necessary down payment to buy the equity in a house can often take over or assume an older existing mortgage. He or she then assumes all the obligations of paying it off. This is often advantageous because by taking over an older existing mortgage the buyer may obtain funds at the interest rate prevailing several years before, which might have been lower. On the other hand, if rates were higher several years ago, the buyer might want to consider refinancing—that is, taking out a new mortgage that pays off the old one.

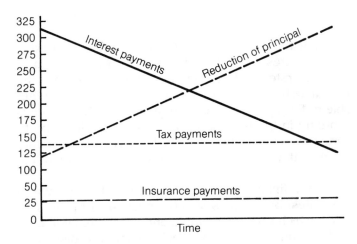

Relationships among the four payments included in single monthly loan payments. The graph is not geometrically accurate; it is only intended to illustrate the principle of amortization of mortgages. The tax and insurance payments may be adjusted upward periodically as taxes and premiums are raised.

Figure 8–2

Table 8–4   *Relationship between interest and principal*

Payment number	Interest	Principal	Balance
1	$500.00	$ 14.31	$49,985.69
2	499.86	14.45	49,971.24
3	499.71	14.60	49,956.64
4	499.57	14.74	49,941.90
5	499.42	14.89	49,927.01
6	499.27	15.04	49,911.97
7	499.12	15.19	49,896.78
8	498.97	15.34	49,881.44
9	498.81	15.50	49,856.94
10	498.66	15.65	49,850.29
351	49.20	465.11	4,454.40
352	44.54	469.77	3,984.63
353	39.85	474.46	3,510.17
354	35.10	479.21	3,030.96
355	30.31	484.00	2,546.96
356	25.47	488.84	2,058.12
357	20.58	493.73	1,564.39
358	15.64	498.67	1,065.72
359	10.66	503.65	562.07
360	5.62	508.69	53.38

Final payment	$53.38	Total no. payments	360
Total payment	$185,151.60	Total principal	$49,946.62
		Total interest	$135,204.98

Sometimes lending institutions will not let a buyer assume an existing mortgage at the old interest rate. They will insist on refinancing at today's presumably higher rate, or in some cases they will permit the assumption but will escalate the interest rate to the current level. Whether or not lenders are able to force refinancing or escalate the interest rate is determined by the wording in the mortgage (deed of trust). Many (probably most) of the mortgages written during the last few years have a due-on-sale clause that permits the lender to require refinancing. Some of the older ones do not.

If an individual has to refinance, not only must he or she pay today's (possibly high) interest rates, but there is also the necessity of paying all the added *closing costs,* which are considerable and which are avoided if a person is able to obtain an assumption. Closing costs are discussed below.

It should be noted that the escalation of interest rates and forced refinancing are not permitted on FHA and VA mortgages.

Since, in giving a mortgage loan, the lender has made an investment of a substantial amount of money at, say 10 percent for a long period of time, the lender wants to receive the interest income year by year. Over the years, interest on a mortgage may amount to thousands of dollars. Home owners, on the other hand, might like to save this interest cost; if in the future their incomes should rise, they might want to make extra mortgage payments. Or if they should inherit a large sum of money, they might want to pay off the mortgage—perhaps even before the ink is dry. Other extra or windfall income might be used to greatly reduce or pay off a mortgage early.

Penalties

To prevent or discourage the buyer from repaying the mortgage more quickly than agreed, the lender often insists on a penalty clause. Lending institutions defend these penalties on the basis that administrative and investment costs are involved in reinvesting early repayments, and that they partially compensate for lost income from interest.

In some cases, a penalty clause merely states that a fee, usually 1 or 2 percent, is charged for mortgage payments made in advance of the schedule. For example, if a person paid off in one payment a $20,000 mortgage, the penalty would be $200 or $400. Often, then, the penalty is small enough not to discourage greatly early repayment.

In other cases the penalty clause applies only to extra payments in excess of a given amount per year, say $1,000 or $2,000. In still other cases, penalties are calculated by applying the interest rate on the mortgage against the advance payment for so many months. There are three- and six-month penalty clauses. If a 10 percent $60,000 mortgage carried a six-month interest penalty and some was paid in advance, the penalty would be six months' interest on the amount paid off at 10 percent. If all of the $60,000 was paid off, the penalty would be $3,000. In some cases the penalty clause drops out completely and automatically after a given period of time. The home owner should, however, try to get a mortgage that does not contain a penalty clause. Usually the conditions in the money market will determine whether penalties are inserted into the mortgage. If funds are hard to obtain, not only will interest rates be higher but penalty clauses will more likely be inserted. If funds are plentiful, the home owner will receive a lower rate of interest and can more easily avoid a penalty clause.

If one succeeds in avoiding a penalty clause, and in some cases even if one does not, it may sometimes pay to refinance. If, for example, a person obtains a mortgage at a time when competitive conditions indicate a 15 or even 16 percent interest rate and a few years later rates are only 12 or 13 percent, it may pay to refinance. Remember that in doing this the individual has most of the closing costs to meet again, as well as the penalty; but if interest rates have declined enough, the saving may more than offset these two items. For example, if an individual had a 15 per-

When does it pay to refinance?

cent thirty-year, $75,000 mortgage, the principal and interest would come to $948.34 per month. If the mortgage could be refinanced at 12 percent, the comparable monthly payment would be $771.46, a savings of $176.88 per month. Over just ten years, this would amount to a savings of $21,226. Whether it would pay to refinance would depend on the size of the mortgage, the amount of decline in interest rates, and the dollar amount of closing costs. A sharp pencil would have to be put to each individual case to figure it out. The general rule of thumb, however, is if interest rates have come down 3 percent or more, it nearly always pays to refinance. In some cases refinancing is worthwhile even if rates have come down by less than 3 percent.

Early payoff options

Recently some mortgage lenders have offered home owners the option of paying off their mortgages early at rather attractive terms. These lenders offer substantial discounts to encourage early repayment to remove older, lower-yielding mortgages from their books. At first glance, both the lending institution and the home owner would benefit from this. A mortgage made twenty years ago and running over thirty years would yield about 7 or 8 percent as opposed to today's much higher rate. If the lender offered the home owner a 12 percent discount on a $20,000 mortgage, the home owner could pay it off completely for $17,860. He or she would have his or her home debt free and save $2,140 and all future interest. The lending institution, while it would be out $2,140, would have $17,860 to invest at today's higher market rate.

Large down payment versus small down payment

The size of the down payment individuals make is most often determined by the amount of cash available at the time they purchase the home. Assuming that one has a choice, however, the question is whether one should make a large or a small down payment. The buyer should consider the following factors:

1. *The cost.* With a large down payment an individual may be able to reduce the time the loan will run before maturity, resulting in considerable interest savings. In addition, even if an individual places a large down payment on a property and the time to maturity remains the same, he or she will still save money on interest. For instance, a home buyer who borrows $50,000 at 12 percent interest for a twenty-five-year period will pay $107,986 in interest during the life of the mortgage. On the other hand, if the same borrower needed only a $40,000 mortgage for the same number of years at the same interest rate, interest payments would drop to $86,387—the person would save $21,599. In other words, the $50,000 mortgage will cost the borrower about 25 percent more than the smaller $40,000 loan. In addition, if a larger down payment is made, often the interest rate is reduced somewhat.

2. *Possibility of moving.* Each year nearly one out of every five American families moves to a new location. If there is a possibility that a person is going to move, it is advisable to put as small a down payment on a home as possible when purchasing it. Many people consider that the competition between the sale of an older home and a new home to a large degree rests with the size of the down payment, for it is easier to sell a home requiring a $5,000 down payment than it is to sell a home requiring a $20,000 down payment. Therefore, if one has a small equity in a home, it may be easier to sell if one has to move.

Both FHA-insured and the VA-guaranteed loans have maximum rates of interest set by law. Sometimes the rates an individual has to pay are at this maximum level, and sometimes they are below it. The interest rate on conventional loans fluctuates from time to time and also varies from one part of the nation to another, depending on the supply of money available for mortgage loans. Interest rates may also vary slightly with the amount of the down payment. If there is a substantial down payment, interest rates may be reduced from one-quarter to one-half of 1 percent from what the rate would have been with a lower down payment. Over the years, a quarter or a half of 1 percent difference can amount to a good deal of money, especially on a big mortgage. One-half of 1 percent on $50,000, for example, is $250 per year. The total amount of interest paid over the years at different interest is truly amazing. This is shown in Table 8–5.

Interest on mortgages

For any given home, then, the size of the down payment will affect the size of the monthly payment as well as the total interest paid over the years. Table 8–6 shows a $60,000 home financed over twenty-five years

Monthly payments and total dollar interest costs at various interest rates on a 25-year, $50,000 mortgage

Table 8–5

Interest rate percent	Monthly payment	Total payments	Total interest
10	$454.36	$136,308	$ 86,308
11	$490.06	$147,018	$ 97,018
12	$526.62	$157,986	$107,986
12.5	$545.18	$163,554	$113,554
13	$563.92	$169,176	$119,176
13.5	$582.83	$174,849	$124,849
14	$601.89	$180,567	$130,567
14.5	$621.09	$185,327	$135,327
15	$640.42	$192,126	$142,126

Table 8—6   *Amortization of a $60,000 house with varying down payments over a twenty-five-year period as 12 percent interest*

	A	B	C
House	$ 60,000.00	$ 60,000.00	$60,000.00
Down payment	10,000.00	20,000.00	30,000.00
Mortgage	50,000.00	40,000.00	30,000.00
Monthly payment (interest & principal only)	526.62	421.29	315.97
Total dollars paid	157,986.00	126,387.00	94,791.00
Total interest over the 25 years	107,986.00	86,387.00	64,791.00

at 12 percent with a large, a medium, and relatively small down payment. The difference in total interest over the years is substantial.

Monthly payments   The monthly payment varies not only with the amount of the mortgage but also with the length of the mortgage, the interest rate, and usually with the level of taxes and insurance premiums. A higher interest rate, all else being equal, tends to increase the monthly payments. The longer the number of years for which the mortgage runs, the lower the monthly payments with any given interest rate and dollar amount of the loan. However, if one reduces the monthly payments by increasing the length of the mortgage, one pays more total dollars in interest over the years.

When buying a house, the down payment is now always subject to variation; usually a person must have the $2,000 or $10,000 in cash, or whatever the figure is. The exception has been discussed previously. Buyers have some control over the length of the mortgage and, to a slight extent, over the interest rate if they shop around. If the house buyer wishes to save total interest costs, the person should select the amortization time period that makes the monthly payments as large as he or she can easily bear. On a $40,000, twenty-year, 12 percent mortgage, monthly payment (not including insurance and property taxes) would be $440.44. Total payments over the twenty years would be $105,705.60 and interest over the years would amount to $65,705.60. The same mortgage financed over twenty-five years would have monthly payments of $421.29 and total payments of $126,387, of which $86,387 would be for interest. By reducing monthly payments by $19.15, the buyer pays an additional $20,682 in interest over the years. This is not to say that mortgages should never be stretched out to reduce monthly payments. Sometimes such a step is necessary; one of the benefits of a thirty-year mortgage is that it reduces monthly payments to the point where people can buy homes who otherwise could not do so. One should make the decision with eyes open and not lengthen the mortgage just to reduce monthly payments. Table 8–7 shows the monthly payments necessary to amortize a given loan at 12 percent interest over a given number of years. It includes interest and reduction of principal only; taxes and insurance are omitted.

Monthly payments can include four items: interest, reduction of principal, insurance premiums, and local property taxes (this is referred to as PITI). Nearly all lenders will insist that insurance to protect the house against loss due to fire or other physical damage be obtained. Even if the lending institution did not demand it, no property owner should be without fire insurance. In addition to fire insurance, sometimes a life insurance policy is bought on the mortgage so that if the borrower dies before paying off the mortgage, the insurance company will pay it.

Although property taxes vary from community to community, they must be paid annually or semiannually in most cases. Since they usually run to several hundred dollars or more, a person who does not budget for them may have difficulty paying them. Many lending institutions include one-twelfth of the annual tax liability and add it to the monthly payments. These funds then go into a special account called the escrow account, which is used by the institution to pay the taxes when due. It may do the same with insurance premiums (both mortgage credit life insurance and hazard insurance premiums).

Some people object to these monthly payments for insurance and property taxes on the ground that they are paying in advance, and the financial institution has the use of their money for a time before it pays the bills. This is the same as an interest-free loan to the bank. However, the lending institution is providing a real service. It is doing the individual's budgeting, and it also takes care of the paperwork involved in keeping the records and paying the taxes and insurance premiums. If a person objects to this advance payment, he or she should bargain with the lending institution and try to keep it out of the monthly payments. If the down payment is fairly large, a person can probably keep the life insurance and the tax payments out, but it is more difficult to avoid including fire insurance premiums, which are, however, relatively small.

If an individual succeeds in keeping some of the above items out of the monthly payments, budgeting should be done to set aside one-twelfth of the sum each month. Then not only would the person be sure of having the funds when they are due, but they can be put into a savings account (to accumulate until needed) and receive interest perhaps from the very bank that has the mortgage.

Normally mortgage payments are due the first of each month, although in most cases a grace period of from ten to fifteen days is granted the mortgagor by the lending institution.

Recently, however, a mortgage has been developed that requires a payment every other week. Instead of a $500 payment each month, the home owner would pay $250 every two weeks. More people are paid

The biweekly (semimonthly) mortgage

Table 8—7 *Monthly payment necessary to amortize a loan at 12 percent*

Term amount	15 years	16 years	17 years	18 years	19 years	20 years	21 years	22 years	23 years
$ 22500	270.04	264.09	259.03	254.69	250.97	247.75	244.96	242.54	240.43
23000	276.04	269.96	264.78	260.35	256.54	253.25	250.41	247.93	245.77
23500	282.04	275.83	270.54	266.01	262.12	258.76	255.85	253.32	251.12
24000	288.05	281.70	276.30	271.67	267.70	264.27	261.29	258.71	256.46
24500	294.05	287.57	282.05	277.33	273.27	269.77	266.74	264.10	261.80
25000	300.05	293.44	287.81	282.99	278.85	275.28	272.18	269.49	267.15
25500	306.05	299.30	293.56	288.65	284.43	280.78	277.62	274.88	272.49
26000	312.05	305.17	299.32	294.31	290.01	286.29	283.07	280.27	277.83
26500	318.05	311.04	305.08	299.97	295.58	291.79	288.51	285.66	283.17
27000	324.05	316.91	310.83	305.63	301.16	297.30	293.95	291.05	288.52
27500	330.05	322.78	316.59	311.29	306.74	302.80	299.40	296.44	293.86
28000	336.05	328.65	322.35	316.95	312.31	308.31	304.84	301.83	299.20
28500	342.05	344.52	328.10	322.61	317.89	313.81	310.28	307.22	304.55
29000	348.05	340.39	333.86	328.27	323.47	319.32	315.73	312.61	309.89
29500	354.05	346.25	339.61	333.93	329.04	324.83	321.17	318.00	315.23
30000	360.06	352.12	345.37	339.59	334.62	330.33	326.61	323.39	320.57
30500	366.06	357.99	351.13	345.25	340.20	335.84	332.06	328.78	325.92
31000	372.06	363.86	356.88	350.91	345.77	341.34	337.50	334.17	331.26
31500	378.06	369.73	362.64	356.57	351.35	346.85	342.95	339.56	336.60
32000	384.06	375.60	368.39	362.23	356.93	352.35	348.39	344.95	341.95
32500	390.06	381.47	374.15	367.89	362.51	357.86	353.83	350.33	347.29
33000	396.06	387.33	379.91	373.55	368.08	363.36	359.28	355.72	352.63
33500	402.06	393.20	385.66	379.21	373.66	368.87	364.72	361.11	357.97
34000	408.06	399.07	391.42	384.87	379.24	374.37	370.16	366.50	363.32
34500	414.06	404.94	397.17	390.53	384.81	379.88	375.61	371.89	368.66
35000	420.06	410.81	402.93	396.19	390.39	385.39	381.05	377.28	374.00
36000	432.07	422.55	414.44	407.51	401.54	396.40	391.94	388.06	384.69
37000	444.07	434.28	425.95	418.83	412.70	407.41	402.82	398.84	395.37
38000	456.07	446.02	437.47	430.15	423.85	418.42	413.71	409.62	406.06
39000	468.07	457.76	448.98	441.47	435.01	429.43	424.60	420.40	416.75
40000	480.07	469.50	460.49	452.79	446.16	440.44	435.48	431.18	427.43
41000	492.07	481.23	472.00	464.10	457.31	451.45	446.37	441.96	438.12
42000	504.08	492.97	483.52	475.42	468.47	462.46	457.26	452.74	448.80
43000	516.08	504.71	495.03	486.74	479.62	473.47	468.15	463.52	459.49
44000	528.08	516.44	506.54	498.06	490.77	484.48	479.03	474.30	470.17
45000	540.08	528.18	518.05	509.38	501.93	495.49	489.92	485.08	480.86
46000	552.08	539.92	529.56	520.70	513.08	506.50	500.81	495.86	491.54
47000	564.08	551.66	541.08	532.02	524.24	517.52	511.69	506.64	502.23
48000	576.09	563.39	552.59	543.34	535.39	528.53	522.58	517.42	512.92
49000	588.09	575.13	564.10	554.66	546.54	539.54	533.47	528.19	523.60
50000	600.09	586.87	575.61	565.98	557.70	550.55	544.35	538.97	534.29
51000	612.09	598.60	587.12	577.30	568.85	561.56	555.24	549.75	544.97
52000	624.09	610.34	598.64	588.62	580.01	572.57	566.13	560.53	555.66
53000	636.09	622.08	610.15	599.94	591.16	583.58	577.02	571.31	566.34
54000	648.10	633.82	621.66	611.26	602.31	594.59	587.90	582.09	577.03
55000	660.10	645.55	633.17	622.58	613.47	605.60	598.79	592.87	587.72
56000	672.10	657.29	644.69	633.90	624.62	616.61	609.68	603.65	598.40
57000	684.10	669.03	656.20	645.22	635.77	627.62	620.56	614.43	609.09
58000	696.10	680.77	667.71	656.54	646.93	638.63	631.45	625.21	619.77
59000	708.10	692.50	679.22	667.86	658.08	649.65	642.34	635.99	630.46
60000	720.11	704.24	690.73	679.18	669.24	660.66	653.22	646.77	641.14
61000	732.11	715.98	702.25	690.49	680.39	671.67	664.11	657.55	651.83
62000	744.11	727.71	713.76	701.81	691.54	682.68	675.00	668.33	662.52
63000	756.11	739.45	725.27	713.13	702.70	693.69	685.89	679.11	673.20
64000	768.11	751.19	736.78	724.45	713.85	704.70	696.77	689.89	683.89
65000	780.11	762.93	748.30	735.77	725.01	715.71	707.66	700.66	694.57
67500	810.12	792.27	777.08	764.07	752.89	743.24	734.88	727.61	721.29
70000	840.12	821.61	805.86	792.37	780.77	770.77	762.09	754.56	748.00
72500	870.13	850.96	834.64	820.67	808.66	798.29	789.31	781.51	774.71
75000	900.13	880.30	863.42	848.97	836.54	825.82	816.53	808.46	801.43
80000	960.14	938.99	920.98	905.57	892.31	880.87	870.96	862.36	854.86
85000	1020.15	997.67	978.54	962.16	948.08	935.93	925.40	916.25	908.29
90000	1080.16	1056.36	1036.10	1018.76	1003.85	990.98	979.83	970.15	961.71
95000	1140.16	1115.04	1093.66	1075.36	1059.62	1046.04	1034.27	1024.05	1015.14
100000	1200.17	1173.73	1151.22	1131.96	1115.39	1101.09	1088.70	1077.94	1068.57

24 years	25 years	26 years	27 years	28 years	29 years	30 years	35 years	40 years
238.59	236.98	235.57	234.33	233.24	232.29	231.44	228.50	226.92
243.89	242.25	240.80	239.54	238.43	237.45	236.59	233.58	231.96
249.19	247.51	246.04	244.75	243.61	242.61	241.73	238.66	237.00
254.50	252.78	251.27	249.95	248.79	247.77	246.87	243.74	242.04
259.80	258.04	256.51	255.16	253.98	252.93	252.02	248.81	247.09
265.10	263.31	261.74	260.37	259.16	258.09	257.16	253.89	252.13
270.40	268.58	266.98	265.57	264.34	263.26	262.30	258.97	257.17
275.70	273.84	272.21	270.78	269.52	268.42	267.44	264.05	262.21
281.01	279.11	277.45	275.99	274.71	273.58	272.59	269.13	267.26
286.31	284.38	282.68	281.20	279.89	278.74	277.73	274.20	272.30
291.61	289.64	287.92	286.40	285.07	283.90	282.87	279.28	277.34
296.91	294.91	293.15	291.61	290.26	289.07	288.02	284.36	282.38
302.21	300.17	298.39	296.82	295.44	294.23	293.16	289.44	287.43
307.52	305.44	303.62	302.03	300.62	299.39	298.30	294.51	292.47
312.82	310.71	308.86	307.23	305.81	304.55	303.45	299.59	297.51
318.12	315.97	314.09	312.44	310.99	309.71	308.59	304.67	302.55
323.42	321.24	319.33	317.65	316.17	314.87	313.73	309.75	307.60
328.72	326.50	324.56	322.85	321.36	320.04	318.87	314.83	312.64
334.03	331.77	329.80	328.06	326.54	325.20	324.02	319.90	317.68
339.33	337.04	335.03	333.27	331.72	330.36	329.16	324.98	322.72
344.63	342.30	340.26	338.48	336.90	335.52	334.30	330.06	327.77
349.93	347.57	345.50	343.68	342.09	340.68	339.45	335.14	332.81
355.23	352.84	350.73	348.89	347.27	345.85	344.59	340.21	337.85
360.53	358.10	355.97	354.10	352.45	351.01	349.73	345.29	342.89
365.84	363.37	361.20	359.30	357.64	356.17	354.88	350.37	347.94
371.14	368.63	366.44	364.51	362.82	361.33	360.02	355.45	352.98
381.74	379.17	376.91	374.93	373.19	371.65	370.31	365.60	363.06
392.35	389.70	387.38	385.34	383.55	381.98	380.59	375.76	373.15
402.95	400.23	397.85	395.76	393.92	392.30	390.88	385.91	383.23
413.55	410.76	408.32	406.17	404.28	402.62	401.16	396.07	393.32
424.16	421.29	418.79	416.58	414.65	412.95	411.45	406.22	403.40
434.76	431.83	429.26	427.00	425.02	423.27	421.74	416.38	413.49
445.37	442.36	439.73	437.41	435.38	433.60	432.02	426.54	423.57
455.97	452.89	450.19	447.83	445.75	443.92	442.31	436.69	433.66
466.57	463.42	460.66	458.24	456.11	454.24	452.59	446.85	443.74
477.18	473.96	471.13	468.66	466.48	464.57	462.88	457.00	453.83
487.78	484.49	481.60	479.07	476.85	474.89	473.17	467.16	463.91
498.38	495.02	492.07	489.49	487.21	485.21	483.45	477.31	474.00
508.99	505.55	502.54	499.90	497.58	495.54	493.74	487.47	484.08
519.59	516.08	513.01	510.31	507.95	505.86	504.03	497.62	494.17
530.20	526.62	523.48	520.73	518.31	516.18	514.31	507.78	504.25
540.80	537.15	533.95	531.14	528.68	526.51	524.60	517.94	514.34
551.40	547.68	544.42	541.56	539.04	536.83	534.88	528.09	524.42
562.01	558.21	554.89	551.97	549.41	547.16	545.17	538.25	534.51
572.61	568.75	565.36	562.39	559.78	557.48	555.46	548.40	544.59
583.22	579.28	575.83	572.80	570.14	567.80	565.74	558.56	554.68
593.82	589.81	586.30	583.22	580.51	578.13	576.03	568.71	564.78
604.42	600.34	596.77	593.63	590.87	588.45	586.31	578.87	574.85
615.03	610.88	607.24	604.05	601.24	598.77	596.60	589.02	584.93
625.63	621.41	617.71	614.46	611.61	609.10	606.89	599.18	595.02
636.23	631.94	628.18	624.87	621.97	619.42	617.17	609.33	605.10
646.84	642.47	638.65	635.29	632.34	629.74	627.46	619.49	615.19
657.44	653.00	649.12	645.70	642.71	640.07	637.74	629.65	625.27
668.05	663.54	659.59	656.12	653.07	650.39	648.03	639.80	635.36
678.65	674.07	670.06	666.53	663.44	660.71	658.32	649.96	645.44
689.25	684.60	680.52	676.95	673.80	671.04	688.60	660.11	655.53
715.76	710.93	706.70	702.98	699.72	696.85	694.32	685.50	680.74
742.27	737.26	732.87	729.02	725.63	722.66	720.03	710.89	705.95
768.78	763.59	759.05	755.06	751.55	748.47	745.75	736.28	731.17
795.29	789.92	785.22	781.09	777.46	774.27	771.46	761.67	756.38
848.31	842.58	837.57	833.16	829.30	825.89	822.90	812.44	806.80
901.33	895.25	889.91	885.24	881.13	877.51	874.33	863.22	857.23
954.35	947.91	942.26	937.31	932.96	929.13	925.76	914.00	907.65
1007.37	1000.57	994.61	989.38	984.79	980.75	977.19	964.78	958.08
1060.39	1053.23	1046.96	1041.45	1036.62	1032.36	1028.62	1015.55	1008.50

weekly or biweekly than monthly; hence, a biweekly mortgage is often easier to budget.

If a given traditional 30-year monthly mortgage were, instead, financed as a biweekly mortgage, it would be paid off in 20.29 years and would result in substantial interest savings. The mortgage is paid off more quickly because the principal is reduced a bit every two weeks rather than every month. This earlier reduction of principal lowers interest more quickly, making it possible to apply more of the biweekly payment to the principal in future payments. In addition, a biweekly mortgage would result in twenty-six payments per year, each of which woud be one-half the size of twelve regular monthly payments. This, of course, amounts to the same as one extra monthly payment per year, again reducing principal more quickly and saving interest.

Table 8–8 shows the differences in payments and total interest paid between some conventional 30-year and biweekly mortgages, which are amortized over 20.29 years.

The fifteen-year mortgage

Traditionally mortgages were financed over 30 years, although some were over 25 or even 20. Recently, however, the 15-year mortgage has become somewhat popular. While this increases the monthly payment, it saves on interest. The monthly payment on a $75,000 mortgage at 12 percent interest amortized over 30 years is $771.46; if amortized over 15 years this same mortgage would required a $900.13 monthly payment. The additional $128.67 per month would result in $115,702.20 in interest savings. That is why these shorter mortgages have become somewhat popular, especially with two-income couples Table 8–9 illustrates the savings achieved with shorter mortgages.

It should be noted, however, that the savings are not as great as the table suggests. This is because the differnces in the payments could be invested and earn interest if a longer mortgage were chosen. Also taxes must be taken into account, because mortgage interest paid, as well as interest earned, is tax deductible (or taxable, as the case may be).

Nevertheless, a shorter mortgage will save a great deal of interest cost. This is especially true if your after-tax mortgage interest rate is greater than the after-tax rate on your investments.

The graduated equity mortgage (GEM)

The graduated equity mortgage starts out as a straight conventional 30-year mortgage with a proviso that monthly payments will be escalated by a predetermined amount each month. This increased payment is applied entirely to the reduction of principal. The entire 30-year mortgage is then paid off over 13, 14, or 15 years rather than 30, saving a great deal of interest. This type of mortgage is fine for someone whose income is rising and who can afford the escalating monthly payments. This mortgage is no different than the traditional old-fashioned fixed 30-year mortgage

Differences between biweekly and conventional mortgages   Table 8—8

$75,000 mortgage based on 10.50% interest rate

	Conventional mortgage	Biweekly mortgage	Percent savings
Payments	$686.05 every month	$343.03 every 2 weeks	
Paid in full	30 years	20.29 years	
Total interest paid	$171,898.38	$106,352.98	
Interest saved		$65,636.40	38

$100,000 mortgage based on 10.50% interest rate

	Conventional mortgage	Biweekly mortgage	Percent savings
Payments	$914.74 every month	$457.37 every 2 weeks	
Paid in full	30 years	20.29 years	
Total interest paid	$229,304.00	$141.800.18	
Interest saved		$87,503.82	38

$150,000 mortgage based on 10.50% interest rate

	Conventional mortgage	Biweekly mortgage	Percent savings
Payments	$1,372.11 every month	$686.06 every 2 weeks	
Paid in full	30 years	20.29 years	
Total interest paid	$343,956.62	$212.700.18	
Interest saved		$131,256.44	38

Source: Commercial National Mortgage Corporation, Shreveport, La.

$75,000 mortgage at 12 percent   Table 8—9

	15-year mortgage	20-year mortgage	25-year mortgage	30-year mortgage
Monthly payment	$ 900.13	$ 825.82	$ 789.92	$ 771.46
Total payment	$162,023.40	$198,196.80	$236,976.00	$277,725.60
Total interest	$ 87,023.40	$123,196.80	$161,976.00	$202,725.60

which permits early repayments, except that a predetermined schedule of early repayment is worked out.

Seller-financed mortgages

Seller-financed mortgage loans are extended by the seller to the buyer, usually at lower than the going market rate, in order to expedite the sale of the home. These are sometimes called **purchase money loans.** Often these are second mortgages for five or ten years. Moreover, if they are for five years, they may have a final balloon payment. If this is the case, be certain that there is also a provision which will obligate the lender to refinance the balloon.

Reverse mortgages

Older people whose mortgage is paid off and who wish to reitre may sign a reverse mortgage whereby they sell their home back to a lending institution. Instead of making a monthly payment, they receive one. As time passes they own a smaller and smaller portion of their home; a larger and larger mortgage debt is built up on it again, as their equity in it declines. Usually only a portion of the value of the house (about 50 to 75 percent) can be reverse-mortgaged this way. While this can provide retirement income for a time, it is risky because after a number of years if the retirees are still living, they will have to sell their home to pay off the debt. Or they can try to refinance it and pay off another regular mortgage once again. Another option for individuals considering reverse mortgages might be to sell the home outright and move into a smaller home or apartment while investing the remaining proceeds of the sale in order to receive income.

INNOVATIVE MORTGAGES

In addition to the traditional fixed rate mortgage discussed above, a number of new innovative mortgages have been developed. These were popular during the 1970s and early 1980s because interest rates were very high and mortgage money was in short supply. They made it possible for people who otherwise might not qualify to qualify and afford a home. Recently some of these new mortgages have become less popular because rates have come down, and mortgage money is more plentiful again. However, two of them are still widely used. They are the Adjustable Rate Mortgage (ARM) and the Renegotiable Mortgage.

The adjustable (variable) rate mortgage

The **variable rate mortgage** (VRM) is also referred to as the "adjustable mortgage" (ARM). With variable interest mortgages, the rate can be adjusted every six months or so, but only if certain other rates such as marketable U.S. government (or corporate) bond rates change. Sometimes the lending institution will tie the adjustment to the average rate they pay on deposits. (The variable mortgage rate is usually one to three percentage points above the index to which it is tied.) Generally rates will only go up by a fraction of 1 percent every time they are adjusted. Normally there is also a limit (usually 3 to 5 percent) on the overall upward or downward movement during the life of the mortgage. There are three methods of adjusting the variable interest rate: The first is to change the monthly payment with the maturity remaining constant. The second is to change the length of the maturity with the monthly payment remaining constant. The third is a combination of the first two.

The difficulty in using a variable rate is that when rates are high the borrower may be willing to sign a variable contract and hope that rates come down, but the lending institution is reluctant to do so. During times when rates are low, the reverse is the case: the lender favors variable rates, the borrower does not. Another problem with the VRM is that in some states there is no limit to how high rates may go. In addition, if the rates are adjusted to the extent that the life of the mortgage is lengthened, the individual really has a negatively amortizing mortgage which would in theory never be paid off. Sometimes the VRM is written so that when interest rates are escalated, the monthly payment stays the same and the principal is reduced, but only for, say, three or five years. After this time, the original amortization schedule returns. When this is so, it may require a large increase in the monthly payment.

Usually, but not always, when the borrower has the choice between a fixed and variable mortgage, the variable one is a bit lower. Figure 8–3 illustrates a checklist to evaluate an adjustable rate mortgage.

Renegotiable mortgages

A modification of the variable interest rate mortgage is the **renegotiable mortgage,** sometimes called the rollover mortgage. Under it, interest rates are fixed but renegotiated every three, four, or five years as the case may be. There would be a negotiated rate change as the market changed, but it would not be an automatic adjustment tied to some money market indicator. Under this mortgage the lender is obliged to renegotiate and renew the mortgage; he cannot cancel it. The borrower, on the other hand, may pull out at renewal time and get a new mortgage elsewhere.

The rollover mortgage

The rollover mortgage is a variation of the renegotiable mortgage. It is generally written for five years, and it differs from the renegotiable in that when it comes due, the lender is not obliged to renew it. These are also sometimes referred to as "balloon" mortgages, because monthly payments are made for, say, five years, after which time the unpaid remainder is due in one large payment.

Other less common innovative mortgages

There are variations of the aforementioned mortgages which are less commonly used. Some examples include the wrap-around mortgage, the blended mortgage, the buy-down mortgage, the equity build-up mortgage and the shared appreciation mortgage.

An adjustable note mortgage should be looked at very carefully before finalization. If a person signs one, he or she is assuming the risk that the market interest rate will change—up or down. It is most important that the individual makes certain it has an overall cap for the life of the mortgage.

Original interest rate		_____%
Original monthly payment		$_____
Frequently of adjustment:	Yes	No
Every 6 months	____	____
Every year	____	____
Every 2 years	____	____
Maximum adjustment (cap):		
Per adjustment		_____%
Per year		_____%
Over the life of the mortgage		_____%
	Yes	No
Can the rate go down as well as up?	____	____
Is there a downward floor?	____	____
If the interest rate rises:		
Will the monthly payment rise?	____	____
Will the amount of the mortgage rise (negative amortization)?	____	____
Will a combination of the two occur?	____	____
What is the ARM tied to (index)?		
U.S. treasury securities?	____	____
Overall cost of deposits?	____	____
Other?	____	____
How much above the index is the rate?		_____%

Figure 8—3   *Checklist to evaluate an adjustable rate mortgage*

The wrap-around mortgage

One way of financing a home if the buyer does not have enough funds to assume an existing mortgage is to use the wrap-arond mortgage, often done if the seller is willing and able to finance the sale and assume the wrap-around mortgage; the new mortgage literally wraps around the old mortgage. This technique works particularly well if the existing mortgage is small. For example, suppose a seller has an older home for sale for $100,000 with only a $20,000 mortgage left on it. If the buyer has $40,000, he could pay that as a down payment, and the seller could take a $60,000 mortgage which includes (wraps around) the $20,000 due on the original. The seller would then continue to pay off the original $20,000 mortgage, and the buyer would need worry only about the new $60,000 one.

Wrap-arounds may also be illegal in some cases. Only if the mortgage is assumable or if the institution holding the original mortgages gives its permission is a wrap-around possible. Older mortgages often are assumable; but in the last seven or eight years, more and more institutions have placed due-on-sale clauses in their loan contracts, and in such a case wrap-arounds are not possible.

If a wrap-around is not possible, an individual might be able to negotiate a blended mortgage. In the above wrap-around case, for example, if it had not been legal, the home might not have sold if the entire mortgage of $80,000 had to be financed at a higher rate. To get the old 8 percent loan off the books, many institutions will negotiate a new one at a favorable rate. The above $80,000 new mortgage could be an average of the $40,000 at 8 percent and $40,000 at a bit above the current market rate. This would make the blend somewhat below the market rate.

The blended mortgage

The buy-down mortgage is a misnomer, but it is a means of reducing the interest rate from, say, 13 percent to 10 percent. In reality, the buyer pays a lump sum (usually at closing) in return for which the lender will reduce the interest rate. This amounts to prepaying some of the interest and, upon closer examination, may not be the best arrangement for the buyer. For example, a $50,000 mortgage at 13 percent over 30 years requires a $553.10 per month amortization payment. However, if the buyer pays an additional $4,115.16 at closing, the interest rate is reduced to 10 percent and the monthly amortization payment drops to $438.79. The buy-down was calculated by taking the difference between the two monthly payments ($553.10 − $438.79 = $114.31) and multiplying it by 36. The buy-down rate is therefore effective for three years, after which time the rate escalates to 13 percent or is renegotiated at the then market rate. The result may be that a buyer who did not qualify for a loan previously now does. Psychologically it may also be beneficial for the buyer to obtain 10 percent financing. In reality, however, it might have been better for the buyer to make a larger down payment and finance a smaller principal sum at a higher rate. If the buyer does not have the required buy-down charges, the seller may provide it by means of a second mortgage. Some builders do this.

The buy-down mortgage

At one time the equity build-up sharing mortgage was used. These are also called shared appreciation mortgages (SAM) and shared equity mortgages (SEM). With these, when the home owner sells his or her home, a portion (say, 20 to 25 percent) of the capital gain attributable to inflation is remitted to the mortgagee. For this, the buyer received a more favorable interest rate.

Equity build-up mortgage (EBM) and shared appreciation mortgage (SAM)

The major danger of innovative mortgages is that interest rates may escalate wildly. In the case of a fixed mortgage at least the individual knows what the cost is—and will remain. To be sure, ceilings may be placed on the amount of interest escalation, but this is not always done. In the case of a variable rate mortgage, there is also the problem of what the rate should be tied to, i. e., what determines when rates are to rise. Probably the best indicator is the long-term U.S. government bond rate. The variable mortgage rate could be 1.5 or 2 points above the government rate.

Some dangers of innovative mortgages

If a mortgage has a balloon on it and no guaranteed refinancing provision, the person may be in serious difficulty when it comes due. This is not to say that individuals should never use innovative mortgages; only they should go into such an arrangement with their eyes open, and be careful. A home owner should not expect a continued rise in home prices to bail him or her out if there is financial difficulty.

OTHER THINGS TO KNOW ABOUT HOME OWNERSHIP

When buying something as expensive as a home there may be certain hidden costs that might occur. Then there are the mechanics of making an offer on a home. The financial planner needs to be aware of the costs of purchasing a home and the home offer procedure in order to evaluate all options.

Points

Sometimes points are used when a loan is made. Generally, points are added during periods of tight money, and the tighter the money supply the greater the number of points added. A point is one percentage point of the mortgage loan and normally is paid by the buyer of the home. On a $60,000 mortgage loan on which two points are assessed, this amounts to $1,200 and is added to the closing costs if the buyer pays them (see below). However, sometimes points are paid, at least in part, by the seller. It depends on the market. If the market is tight and a shortage of homes exists in the area, the buyer will probably pay the points. If, on the other hand, there is a surplus of homes, the seller will almost invariably pay at least part of the points in order to make the sale. In short, points are negotiable.

The lending institution receives these "points," and it is a means of increasing interest rates the first year. If the seller pays these points, and an institution makes a $40,000 loan on a $50,000 house in which the seller has a $10,000 equity and assesses two points, then the institution advances the seller only $9,200. The buyer assumes a $40,000 mortgage at 10 percent, but the lender really receives 12 percent return the first year. In some cases these points are deductible for federal income tax purposes by the buyer if properly handled.

Making an offer on a house; earnest money

When a seller offers a house, he or she or the real estate agent draws up a sales contract. This piece of paper spells out the terms of the sale. It will describe the house, list the asking price and note the present mortgage. By signing this contract a prospective purchaser agrees to buy the house. However, usually the prospective buyer will make a counteroffer by changing the terms somewhat, perhaps lowering the price.

To ascertain whether or not the offering price is reasonably close to the true market value, ask a realtor, who can give a fairly good answer.

Also check the selling price (not the offered price) of other comparable homes that have been sold recently. Many sellers will price their house above the realistic market value in the hope that they will find a naive person who will pay it. In addition, some home owners have an inflated opinion of the value of the house. Often sellers will come down from their offering price. A buyer can negotiate with the seller but only indirectly through the realtor. It is also best to find out from the realtor whether selling prices generally have been close to asking prices.

When a buyer finally decides what he or she is willing to pay, a counteroffer is then made. This counteroffer is signed by the prospective buyer and conveyed to the seller by the realtor with a down payment (usually $500 to $1,000, depending on the price of the house) called **earnest money.** There may be several counteroffers between the buyer and seller; this is the negotiation over the price. The buyer must sign any counteroffer he or she makes and present earnest money with it. If the seller signs the buyer's counteroffer, it is a binding deal.

In some states this earnest money goes to the seller immediately and in others it goes into an escrow account until the transaction is closed. In any event, when both buyer and seller have signed the contract, it is binding and either can force the other to comply. However, in practice the seller can nearly always back out by returning the earnest money, because it would require a lawsuit to force compliance. A buyer who wanted to back out, however, would generally lose the earnest money. That is why the offer (sales contract) must carefully spell out all the conditions desired by both parties. For example, the buy offer will always be a conditional offer and effective only if satisfactory financing can be arranged. An earnest money contract is shown in Figure 8–4. Note that under the heading "special conditions," a number of provisions have been written into the contract. This is more often done on older homes than on new homes.

Closing costs

When the buyer and seller of a house have reached an agreement, they and the realtors involved get together to close the deal and sign the necessary papers. A representative of the lending institution also attends the closing which indeed may be held at the office of the lending institution. Up until recently, it was often at the closing that the surprised buyer first became aware that closing costs were involved. Now, however, the lending institution must disclose closing costs in advance. If the institution is not certain what they will amount to, a good-faith estimate must be made. Closing costs (not counting points) generally run from 2 to 3 percent of the mortgage.

The question is, what do these costs consist of? The totals generally vary with the section of the country in which the loan is being made. In addition to the points discussed above, closing costs generally include the following:

02-08-85

ONE TO FOUR FAMILY RESIDENTIAL EARNEST MONEY CONTRACT (RESALE)
ALL CASH, ASSUMPTION, THIRD PARTY CONVENTIONAL OR OWNER FINANCED

PROMULGATED BY TEXAS REAL ESTATE COMMISSION

NOTICE: Not For Use For Condominium Transactions

1. PARTIES: Samuel D. Seller and wife, Selina Ann Seller _____ (Seller) agrees to
sell and convey to ___ Peter D. Purchaser and wife, Penelope L. Purchaser _____ (Buyer) and Buyer
agrees to buy from Seller the property described below.

2. PROPERTY: Lot ___22___, Block ___G___ Brushy Creek North, Section 4
Addition, City of ___Austin___ Travis _____, County, Texas, known as
___10056 Forever Drive, Austin, Texas___ (Address); or as described on attached exhibit, together with the following items,
if any: curtains and rods, draperies and rods, valances, blinds, window shades, screens, shutters, awnings, wall-to-wall carpeting, mirrors fixed in place, ceiling
fans, attic fans, mail boxes, television antennas, permanently installed heating and air conditioning units and equipment, built-in security and fire detection
equipment, lighting and plumbing fixtures, water softener, trash compactor, garage door openers with controls, shrubbery and all other property owned by Seller
and attached to the above described real property. All property sold by this contract is called the "Property".

3. CONTRACT SALES PRICE:
A. Cash payable at closing .... $ 25,000.00
B. Sum of all financing described in Paragraph 4 below .... $ 125,000.00
C. Sales Price (Sum of A and B) .... $ 150,000.00

4. FINANCING: (Check applicable boxes below)
☐ A. ALL CASH: This is an all cash sale; no financing is involved.
☐ B. ASSUMPTION:
  (1) Buyer's assumption of the unpaid principal balance of a first lien promissory note payable to _____
  in present monthly installments of $_____, including principal, interest and any reserve deposits, with Buyer's first installment payment
  being payable on the first installment payment date after closing, the assumed principal balance of which at closing will be $_____.
  (2) Buyer's assumption of the unpaid principal balance of a second lien promissory note payable to _____
  in present monthly installments of $_____, including principal, interest and any reserve deposits, with Buyer's first installment payment
  being payable on the first installment payment date after closing, the assumed principal balance of which at closing will be $_____.
Buyer's assumption of an existing note includes all obligations imposed by the deed of trust securing the note.

If the total principal balance of all assumed loans varies in an amount greater than $350.00 at closing either party may terminate this contract and the Earnest
Money shall be refunded to Buyer. If the noteholder on assumption (a) requires Buyer to pay an assumption fee in excess of $_____ in
B(1) above or $_____ in B(2) above and Seller declines to pay such excess or (b) raises the existing interest rate above _____%
in B(1) above or _____% in B(2) above, Buyer may terminate this contract and the Earnest Money shall be refunded to Buyer. The cash payable at
closing shall be adjusted by the amount of any variance in the loan balance(s) shown above.
NOTICE TO BUYER: Monthly payments, interest rates or other terms of some loans may be adjusted after closing. Before signing the contract, examine the
notes and deeds of trust to determine the possibility of future adjustments.

☒ C. THIRD PARTY FINANCED:
  ☐ 1. A third party first lien note of $ 125,000.00 _____, due in full in ___30___ year(s), payable in initial monthly payments of principal
  and interest not exceeding $ 1,096.98 _____ for the first ___30___ year(s) of the loan.
  ☐ 2. A third party second lien note of $_____, due in full in _____ year(s), payable in initial monthly payments of principal
  and interest not exceeding $_____ for the first _____ year(s) of the loan.
NOTICE TO PARTIES: Before signing this contract Buyer is advised to determine the financing options from lenders. Certain loans have variable rates of
interest, some have monthly payments which may not be sufficient to pay the accruing interest, and some have interest rate "buydowns" which reduce the
rate of interest for part or all of the loan term at the expense of one or more of the parties to the contract.

☐ D. TEXAS VETERANS' HOUSING ASSISTANCE PROGRAM LOAN:
  This contract is also subject to approval for Buyer of a Texas Veterans' Housing Assistance Program Loan (the Program Loan) in an amount of
  $_____ for a period of at least _____ years at the interest rate established by the Texas Veterans' Land Board at the time
  of closing.

☐ E. SELLER FINANCED: A promissory note from Buyer to Seller in the amount of $_____, bearing _____% interest per annum,
  and payable:
  ☐ 1. In one payment due _____ after the date of the note with interest payable _____.
  ☐ 2. In installments of $_____ [ ] including interest [ ] plus interest beginning _____
  after the date of the note and continuing at _____ intervals thereafter for _____ year(s) when the entire balance of the
  note shall be due and payable.
  ☐ 3. Interest only in _____ installments for the first _____ year(s) and thereafter in installments of $_____
  [ ] including interest [ ] plus interest beginning _____ after the date of the note and continuing at _____
  intervals thereafter for _____ year(s) when the entire balance of the note is due and payable.
  ☐ 4. This contract is subject to Buyer furnishing Seller evidence of good credit within _____ days from the effective date of this contract. If notice
  of disapproval of Buyer's credit is not given within five (5) days thereafter, Seller shall be deemed to have approved Buyer's credit. Buyer hereby
  authorizes Buyer's credit report to be furnished to Seller.
  Any Seller financed note may be prepaid in whole or in part at any time without penalty. The lien securing payment of such note will be inferior to any
  lien securing any loan assumed or given in connection with third party financing. If an Owner's Policy of Title Insurance is furnished, Buyer shall furnish
  Seller with a Mortgagee's Title Policy.

Buyer shall apply for all third party financing or noteholder's approval of Buyer for assumption and waiver of the right to accelerate the note within ___7___
days from the effective date of this contract and shall make every reasonable effort to obtain the same. Such financing or assumption shall have been approved when
Buyer has satisfied all of lender's financial conditions, e.g., sale of other property, requirement of co-signer or financial verifications. If such financing
or noteholder's approval and waiver is not obtained within ___45___ days from the effective date hereof, this contract shall terminate and the Earnest Money
shall be refunded to Buyer.

5. EARNEST MONEY: $ 5,000.00 _____ is herewith tendered by Buyer and is to be deposited as Earnest Money with
___Gracy Title Company___ at ___220 West 7th at Lavaca, Austin___ (Address),
as Escrow Agent, upon execution of the contract by both parties. ☐ Additional Earnest Money of $ n/a _____ shall be deposited by Buyer with

101

TREC NO. 20-0

Figure 8—4 *One to four family residential earnest money contract (resale) all cash, assumption,
third party conventional or owner-financed*

One To Four Family Residential Earnest Money Contract — Page Two   02-08-85

the Escrow Agent on or before _____ n/a _____, 19____.

6. TITLE: Seller shall furnish to Buyer at Seller's expense either:

    ☒ A. Owner's Policy of Title Insurance (the Title Policy) issued by __Gracy Title Company__
        in the amount of the Sales Price and dated at or after closing: OR

    ☐ B. Abstracts of Title certified by an abstract company (1) from the sovereignty to the effective date of this contract (Complete Abstract) and (2) supplemented to the Closing Date (Supplemental Abstract).

    NOTICE TO SELLER AND BUYER: AS REQUIRED BY LAW, Broker advises Buyer that Buyer should have an Abstract covering the Property examined by an attorney of Buyer's selection, or Buyer should be furnished with or obtain a Title Policy. If a Title Policy is to be obtained, Buyer should obtain a Commitment for Title Insurance (the Commitment) which should be examined by an attorney of Buyer's choice at or prior to closing. If the Property is situated in a Utility District, Section 50.301 Texas Water Code requires the Buyer to sign and acknowledge the statutory notice from Seller relating to the tax rate and bonded indebtedness of the District.

7. PROPERTY CONDITION: (Check A or B)

    ☒ A. Buyer accepts the Property in its present condition, subject only to any lender required repairs and __repair of sprinkler system__

    ☐ B. Buyer requires inspections and repairs required by any lender and the Property Condition Addendum attached hereto.

    On Seller's receipt of all loan approvals and inspection reports, Seller shall commence repairs and termite treatment required of Seller by the contract, any lender and the Property Condition Addendum, if any, and complete such repairs prior to closing. Seller's responsibility for the repairs, termite treatment and repairs to termite damage shall not exceed $__500.00__. If Seller fails to complete such repairs, Buyer may do so and Seller shall be liable up to the amount specified and the same paid from the proceeds of the sale. If the repair costs will exceed the stated amount and Seller refuses to pay such excess, Buyer may (1) pay the additional cost or (2) accept the Property with the limited repairs unless such repairs are required by lender or (3) Buyer may terminate this contract and the Earnest Money shall be refunded to Buyer. Buyer shall make his election within three (3) days after Seller notifies Buyer of Seller's refusal to pay such excess. Failure of Buyer to make such election within the time provided shall be deemed to be Buyer's election to accept the Property with the limited repairs, and the sale shall be closed as scheduled; however, if lender required repairs prohibit Buyer's acceptance with the limited repairs, this contract shall terminate and Earnest Money shall be refunded to Buyer.

    If the repair costs will exceed five (5) percent of the Sales Price of the Property and Seller agrees to pay the cost of such repairs, Buyer shall have the option of closing the sale with the completed repairs, or terminating the sale and the Earnest Money shall be refunded to Buyer. Buyer shall make this election within three (3) days after Seller notifies Buyer of Seller's willingness to pay the cost of such repairs that exceed five (5) percent of the Sales Price. Failure of Buyer to make such election within the time provided shall be deemed to be Buyer's election to close the sale with the completed repairs.

    Broker(s) and sales associates have no responsibility or liability for inspections or repairs made pursuant to this contract.

8. BROKER'S FEE: __Wehelpu Realtors__, Listing Broker, and any Co-Broker represent Seller unless otherwise specified herein. Seller agrees to pay Listing Broker the fee specified by separate agreement between Listing Broker and Seller. Escrow Agent is authorized and directed to pay Listing Broker said fee from the sale proceeds.

9. CLOSING: The closing of the sale shall be on or before __November 30__, 19__87__, or within seven (7) days after objections to title have been cured, whichever date is later (the Closing Date); however, if financing or assumption approval has been obtained pursuant to Paragraph 4, the Closing Date shall be extended daily up to fifteen (15) days if necessary to complete loan requirements. If either party fails to close this sale by the Closing Date, the non-defaulting party shall be entitled to exercise the remedies contained in Paragraph 16 immediately and without notice.

10. POSSESSION: The possession of the Property shall be delivered to Buyer on __closing and funding__ in its present or required improved condition, ordinary wear and tear excepted. Any possession by Buyer prior to or Seller after closing that is not authorized by the Buyer's Temporary Residential Lease or Seller's Temporary Residential Lease Forms promulgated by the Texas Real Estate Commission shall establish a landlord-tenant at sufferance relationship between the parties.

11. SPECIAL PROVISIONS: (Insert factual statements and business details applicable to this sale.)

    Ceiling fans to convey.

12. SALES EXPENSES TO BE PAID IN CASH AT OR PRIOR TO CLOSING:

    A. Loan appraisal fees shall be paid by __buyer__

    B. The total of the loan discount and any buydown fees shall not exceed $__3,750.00__ of which Buyer shall pay the first $__937.50__ and Seller shall pay the remainder.

    C. Seller's Expenses: Prepayment penalties on any existing loans paid at closing, plus cost of releasing such loans and recording releases; tax statements; ½ of any escrow fee; preparation of deed; preparation and recording of any deed of trust to secure assumption; any Texas Veterans' Housing Assistance Program Participation Fee; other expenses stipulated to be paid by Seller under other provisions of this contract.

    D. Buyer's Expenses: Application, origination and commitment fees; private mortgage insurance premiums and any loan assumption fee; expenses incident to new loan(s) (e.g., preparation of any note, deed of trust and other loan documents, survey, recording fees, copies of restrictions and easements, Mortgagee's Title Policies, credit reports, photos); ½ of any escrow fee; any required premiums for flood and hazard insurance; any required reserve deposits for insurance premiums, ad valorem taxes and special governmental assessments; interest on all monthly installment payment notes from date of disbursements to one (1) month prior to dates of first monthly payments; expenses stipulated to be paid by Buyer under other provisions of this contract and any customary Texas Veterans' Housing Assistance Program Loan costs for Buyer.

    E. If any sales expenses exceed the maximum amount herein stipulated to be paid by either party, either party may terminate this contract unless the other party agrees to pay such excess.

13. PRORATIONS: Taxes, flood and hazard insurance (at Buyer's option), rents, maintenance fees, interest on any assumed loan and any prepaid unearned mortgage insurance premium which has not been financed as part of any assumed loan and which is refundable in whole or in part at a later date shall be prorated through the Closing Date. If Buyer elects to continue Seller's insurance policy, it shall be transferred at closing.

14. TITLE APPROVAL:

    A. If abstract is furnished, Seller shall deliver Complete Abstract to Buyer within twenty (20) days from the effective date hereof. Buyer shall have twenty (20) days from date of receipt of Complete Abstract to deliver a copy of the examining attorney's title opinion to Seller, stating any objections to title, and only objections so stated shall be considered.

    B. If Title Policy is furnished, the Title Policy shall guarantee Buyer's title to be good and indefeasible subject only to (1) restrictive covenants affecting the Property (2) any discrepancies, conflicts or shortages in area or boundary lines, or any encroachments, or any overlapping of improvements (3) taxes for the current and subsequent years and subsequent assessments for prior years due to a change in land usage or ownership (4) existing building and zoning ordinances (5) rights of parties in possession (6) liens created or assumed as security for the sale consideration (7) utility easements common to the platted subdivision of which this Property is a part and (8) reservations or other exceptions permitted by the terms of this contract. Exceptions permitted in the Deed and zoning ordinances shall not be valid objections to title. If the Title Policy will be subject to exceptions other than those recited above in sub-paragraphs (1) through (7) inclusive, Seller shall deliver to Buyer the Commitment and legible copies of any documents creating such exceptions that are not recited in sub-paragraphs (1) through (7) above at least five (5) days prior to closing. If Buyer has objection to any such previously undisclosed exceptions, Buyer shall have five (5) days after receipt of such Commitment and copies to make written objections to Seller. If no Title Commitment is provided to Buyer at or prior to closing, it will be conclusively presumed that Seller represented at closing that the Title Policy would not be subject to exceptions other than those recited above in sub-paragraphs (1) through (7).

    C. In either instance if title objections are raised, Seller shall have fifteen (15) days from the date such objections are disclosed to cure the same, and the Closing Date shall be extended accordingly. If the objections are not satisfied by the extended closing date, this contract shall terminate and the Earnest Money shall be refunded to Buyer, unless Buyer elects to waive the unsatisfied objections and complete the purchase.

    D. Seller shall furnish tax statements showing no delinquent taxes, a Supplemental Abstract when applicable, showing no additional title exceptions and a General

1.	Title insurance	$400	7. Tax reserve	$500
2.	Credit reports	50	8. Survey	50
3.	Attorney's fees	100	9. Recording fee	50
4.	Origination fee	500	10. Closing fee	100
5.	Appraisal fee	150	11. Points	
6.	Fire and other hazard insurance reserve	40		

Title insurance costs vary depending on the amount of the loan and the company with which the policy is placed. Fire insurance rates, credit reports, and attorney's fees all vary somewhat regionally. Furthermore, the closing costs differ depending on whether the loan is a conventional mortgage, a VA-guaranteed mortgage, or an FHA-insured mortgage; in general the same items are included.

In purchasing as important and expensive an item as a home, it is worthwhile for the first-time buyer to engage the services of an attorney. The $100 or $150 cost is usually well spent. When entering into a legal agreement, it is best to have an expert explain all of the fine print. This is over and above the attorney's fees shown on the closing costs statement. The latter are for the fees of the lender's attorney who draws up the papers.

In past years it was also necessary to have a title search, to confirm the fact that the legal title of the property was vested in the seller and that he or she could legally transfer it to you. Presently most people buy title insurance rather than have their attorney conduct such a search. This insurance policy protects the buyer against any loss because of a defect in the title. While this is typically paid for by the seller, sometimes the buyer also has to buy title insurance. In this latter case it is to protect the lender; that purchased by the seller protects only the buyer.

Another item under closing costs consists of what is called the **origination fee** (sometimes called finder's fee) or lender's fee. This is generally 1 percent of the mortgage, and if one is buying from a builder or a real estate broker it is supposedly a fee he or she receives for making the arrangements for the loan. Even if one is dealing directly with a financial institution, the fee is often charged. It is essentially then a means to increase the return to the broker, or the financial institution. Again conditions vary from one section of the country to another, but generally the only way to avoid paying the finder's fee is for the buyer to individually make the arrangement for the loan with a financial institution.

Other typical costs are appraiser's fees, credit reports, the cost of hiring a surveyor to survey the property and ascertain its exact boundaries, and a fee for an amortization table. There may or may not be a charge for these. Sometimes hazard insurance is shown twice on a closing statement, once for the first year's premiums, which must be paid in advance, and again for a one-or two-month premium, which goes into an escrow account for next year's premiums. Property taxes must also be

Form Approved
OMB NO 63-R1501

A.	U.S. DEPARTMENT OF HOUSING AND URBAN DEVELOPMENT		B. TYPE OF LOAN:	

B. TYPE OF LOAN:
1. ☐ FHA   2. ☐ FMHA   3. ☐ CONV. UNINS.
4. ☐ VA   5. ☑ CONV. INS.
6. FILE NUMBER   UTGAME   7. LOAN NUMBER 07208777
8. MORTG. INS. CASE NO.

SETTLEMENT STATEMENT

C. **NOTE:** This form is furnished to give you a statement of actual settlement costs. 'Amounts paid to and by the settlement agent are shown. Items marked "(p.o.c.)" were paid outside the closing; they are shown here for informational purposes and are not included in the totals.

D. NAME OF BORROWER	E. NAME OF SELLER	F. NAME OF LENDER
PETER D. PURCHASER AND WIFE, PENELOPE L. PURCHASER	SAMUEL D. SELLER AND WIFE, SELINA ANN SELLER	LIFETIME MORTGAGE COMPANY 1227 PAYMENT BLVD. SWEET HOME, WISCONSIN

G. PROPERTY LOCATION	H. SETTLEMENT AGENT	I. SETTLEMENT DATE:
LOT 22, BLOCK G, BRUSHY CREEK NORTH, SECTION 4, TRAVIS COUNTY, TEXAS 10056 FOREVER DRIVE AUSTIN, TEXAS 78754	GRACY TITLE COMPANY 220 W 7TH ST, AUSTIN TX 78701 PLACE OF SETTLEMENT GRACY TITLE COMPANY 220 W 7TH ST, AUSTIN TX 78701	9-09-87 Proration date: 9-10-87

J. SUMMARY OF BORROWER'S TRANSACTION		K. SUMMARY OF SELLER'S TRANSACTION	
100. GROSS AMOUNT DUE FROM BORROWER:		400. GROSS AMOUNT DUE TO SELLER:	
101. Contract sales price	150,000.00	401. Contract sales price	150,000.00
102. Personal property		402. Personal property	
103. Settlement charges to borrower (line 1400)	8,157.01	403.	
104.		404.	
105.		405.	
Adjustments for items paid by seller in advance:		Adjustments for items paid by seller in advance:	
106. City/town taxes to		406. City/town taxes to	
107. County taxes to		407. County taxes to	
108. Assessments to		408. Assessments to	
109. Maintenance to		409. Maintenance to	
110. School/Taxes to		410. Commitment Fee to	
111. to		411. to	
112. to		412. to	
120. GROSS AMOUNT DUE FROM BORROWER:	158,157.01	420. GROSS AMOUNT DUE TO SELLER:	150,000.00
200. AMOUNTS PAID BY OR IN BEHALF OF BORROWER:		500. REDUCTIONS IN AMOUNT DUE TO SELLER:	
201. Deposit or earnest money	5,000.00	501. Excess deposit (see instructions)	
202. Principal amount of new loan(s)	125,000.00	502. Settlement charges to seller (line 1400)	12,917.50
203. Existing loan(s) taken subject to		503. Existing loan(s) taken subject to	
204. Commitment Fee		504. Payoff of first mortgage loan	107,333.27
205.		505. Payoff of second mortgage loan	
206.		506.	
207. CREDIT FOR REPAIRS	325.00	507. CREDIT FOR REPAIRS	325.00
208.		508.	
209.		509.	
Adjustments for items unpaid by seller:		Adjustments for items unpaid by seller:	
210. City/town taxes 1-01-87 to 9-10-87	383.03	510. City/town taxes 1-01-87 to 9-10-87	383.03
211. County taxes 1-01-87 to 9-10-87	210.71	511. County Taxes 1-01-87 to 9-10-87	210.71
212. Assessments to		512. Assessments to	
213. School/Taxes 1-01-87 to 9-10-87	777.91	513. School/Taxes 1-01-87 to 9-10-87	777.91
214. to		514. Maintenance to	
215. to		515. to	
216. to		516. to	
217. to		517. to	
218. to		518. to	
219. to		519. to	
220. TOTAL PAID BY/FOR BORROWER:	131,696.65	520. TOTAL REDUCTION AMOUNT DUE SELLER:	121,947.42
300. CASH AT SETTLEMENT FROM/TO BORROWER:		600. CASH AT SETTLEMENT TO/FROM SELLER:	
301. Gross amount due from borrower (line 120)	158,157.01	601. Gross amount due to seller (line 420)	150,000.00
302. Less amounts paid by/for borrower (line 20)	131,696.65	602. Less total reductions in amount due seller (line 520)	121,947.42
303. CASH (☒ FROM) (☐ TO) BORROWER:	26,460.36	603. CASH (☒ TO) (☐ FROM) SELLER	28,052.58

HUD-1 (Rev. 5-76)
(10M 7-84)

Settlement statement   Figure 8—5

PAGE 2 OF OMB No. 2502-0265

L. SETTLEMENT CHARGES	GF # UTGAME		PAID FROM BORROWER'S FUNDS AT SETTLEMENT	PAID FROM SELLER'S FUNDS AT SETTLEMENT
700. TOTAL SALES/BROKER'S COMMISSION Based on price $ 150,000.00 @.00 %= 9,000.00				
Division of commission (line 700) as follows:				
701. $ 4,500.00 to	WEHELPU REALTORS			
702. $ 4,500.00 to	CLEAR TITLE REALTORS			
703. Commission paid at settlement				9,000.00
704.				
800. ITEMS PAYABLE IN CONNECTION WITH LOAN.				
801. Loan Origination fee 1.0000 %	LIFETIME MORTGAGE COMPANY		1,250.00	
802. Loan Discount 3.0000 %	LIFETIME MORTGAGE COMPANY		937.50	2,812.50
803. Appraisal Fee to	LIFETIME MORTGAGE COMPANY		275.00	
804. Credit Report $40 POC/BUYER to	LIFETIME MORTGAGE COMPANY			
805. Lender's inspection fee to	LIFETIME MORTGAGE COMPANY		30.00	
806. Mortgage Insurance application fee to				
807. Assumption Fee				
808. Commitment Fee				
809. XXXXXXXX DATA PROCESS to	LIFETIME MORTGAGE COMPANY		50.00	
810. XXXXX TAX SERVICE FEE to	LIFETIME MORTGAGE COMPANY		131.00	
811. UNDERWRITING FEE to	LIFETIME MORTGAGE COMPANY		100.00	
900. ITEMS REQUIRED BY LENDER TO BE PAID IN ADVANCE.				
901. Interest from 9-09-87 to 10-01-87 @$ 54.250 /day			1,193.50	
902. Mortgage insurance premium for 12.0 mo. to	TICOR		904.00	
903. Hazard insurance premium for 1 yrs. to	STATE FARM INSURANCE CO.		723.00	
904. Flood Insurance yrs. to				
905.				
1000. RESERVES DEPOSITED WITH LENDER				
1001. Hazard insurance 2 mo. @ $ 60.25 per mo.			120.50	
1002. Mortgage insurance 2 mo. @ $ 44.23 per mo.			88.46	
1003. City property taxes 11 mo. @ $ 46.23 per mo.			508.53	
1004. County property taxes 11 mo. @ $ 25.43 per mo.			279.73	
1005. Annual assessments (Maint.) mo. @ $ per mo.				
1006. School Property Taxes 11 mo. @ $ 93.89 per mo.			1,032.79	
1007. Water Dist. Prop. Tax mo. @ $ per mo.				
1008. Flood Insurance mo. @ $ per mo.				
1100. TITLE CHARGES:				
1101. Settlement or closing fee to				
1102. Abstract or title search to				
1103. Title examination to				
1104. Title insurance binder to				
1105. Document preparation to	VENUE, PROBATE & DEED		150.00	95.00
1106. Notary fees to				
1107. Attorney's fees to to				
(includes above items No.)				
1108. Title insurance to (includes above items No.)	GRACY TITLE COMPANY		60.00	936.00
1109. Lender's coverage $ 40.00 + $20.00				
1110. Owner's coverage $ 936.00				
1111. Escrow Fee to	GRACY TITLE COMPANY		40.00	40.00
1112. Restrictions				
1113. Messenger Service				
1200. GOVERNMENT RECORDING AND TRANSFER CHARGES				
1201. Recording fees: Deed $ 7.00 Mortgage $ 11.00 Releases $ 5.00			18.00	5.00
1202. City/county tax/stamps: Deed $ Mortgage $				
1203. State tax/stamps: Deed $ Mortgage $				
1204. Tax Certificates to	GRACY TITLE COMPANY			15.00
1205.				
1300. ADDITIONAL SETTLEMENT CHARGES				
1301. Survey to	SURV-TECH & ASSOCIATES		225.00	
1302. Pest inspection to	KILL-A-BUG		40.00	
1303. COURIER FEES-PAYOFF to	GRACY TITLE COMPANY			14.00
1304.				
1305.				
1400. TOTAL SETTLEMENT CHARGES (entered on lines 103, Section J and 502, Section K)			8,157.01	12,917.50

CERTIFICATION: I have carefully reviewed the HUD-1 Settlement Statement and to the best of my knowledge and belief, it is a true and accurate statement of all receipts and disbursements made on my account or by me in this transaction. I further certify that I have received a copy of HUD-1 Settlement Statement.

Borrowers _____ Sellers _____

To the best of my knowledge, the HUD-1 Settlement Statement which I have prepared is a true and accurate account of funds which were received and have been or will be disbursed by the undersigned as part of the settlement of this transaction.

Settlement Agent _____ Date _____

SELLER'S AND/OR PURCHASER'S STATEMENT Seller's and Purchaser's signature hereon acknowledge his/her approval of tax prorations and signifies their understanding that prorations were based on taxes for the preceding year, or estimate for the current year, and in the event of any change for the current year, all necessary adjustments must be made between Seller and Purchaser; likewise any default in deliquent taxes will be reimbursed to Title Company by the Seller. The parties have read the above sentences, recognize that the recitations herein are material, agree to same, and recognize Title Company is relying on the same.

Purchasers/Borrowers _____ Sellers _____

WARNING: It is a crime to knowingly make false statements to the United States on this or any other similar form. Penalties upon conviction can include a fine and imprisonment. For details see Title 18: U.S. Code Section 1001 and Section 1010.

Figure 8–5 (continued)

provided for. If it is an existing house, there may be extra funds in a tax escrow account which will have to be paid for.

We discussed points above. They are assessed at closing and are usually, but not always, paid by the buyer. All other closing costs except the premium on the title insurance, also discussed above, are paid by the buyer as well. Figure 8–5 shows a disclosure settlement statement.

SUMMARY REVIEW QUESTIONS

These questions serve as a summary and a review of the chapter. If you are able to answer them all, you have a good understanding of the material covered by the chapter.

1. Discuss the reasons for home ownership.
2. Explain in detail the current tax advantage of home ownership.
3. Discuss the merits of renting or owning a home.
4. Discuss the advantages and disadvantages of buying a condominium.
5. Discuss co-op housing.
6. Discuss the FHA mortgage.
7. How is a second mortgage different from a first mortgage? Does the second mortgage owner assume more risk than the first?
8. How is a home mortgage loan amortized?
9. When does it pay to refinance a mortgage?
10. What is a penalty clause in a mortgage?
11. Why is the size of the down payment on a house important?
12. How does the variable interest rate mortgage work?
13. How does the wrap-around mortgage work?
14. What is the buy-down mortgage?
15. What is earnest money?
16. What are closing costs?

CASES

1. Bill and Carol Calpepper have just bought a house and assumed an $80,000 conventional 30-year fixed mortgage at 10 percent.
   (a) What will be their monthly mortgage payment for interest and to amortize the loan?
   (b) What dollar amount of total interest will they pay over the 30 years?
   (c) If they had chosen a 20-year, 10 percent mortgage (rather than 30) what would their monthly payment be?
   (d) What dollar amount of total interest will they pay over 20 years?
   (e) Why are monthly payments lower on a 30-year loan but total payments so much higher?
   (f) If their property taxes are $2,200 per year and they itemize their deductions, what are their tax savings from owning this house at the 15 percent tax bracket?
2. Beckie and Don Garza are in the 28 percent tax bracket and own a home on which they have the following expenses:

Interest on mortgage	$7,200
Property taxes	1,950
Utilities	1,150
Interest lost on down payment	800
Homeowner's insurance	350
Maintenance	750

(a) What is the cost of owning this home?

(b) What are their tax savings from owning this home at the 28 percent tax bracket?

3. Ernie and Eloise Johansen are presently living in an unfurnished apartment renting for $500 per month. They have saved $10,000, which they think is enough for a down payment on a $80,000 home. One lending agency has told them it will give them a twenty-year mortgage of $70,000 at 10 percent. Another financial institution has offered them a loan at 9 percent for twenty years if they can raise another $5,000. They can borrow $5,000 on their life insurance policy at 6 percent. Which offer should they take? What will be the total interest charges in both cases? They believe they can pay back the loan on their insurance over a two-year period.

4. Timothy and Martha Hennessey have found a home selling for $100,000 which they would like to buy. They have discovered they could finance it with a 10 percent down FHA loan for thirty years at 10 percent. Under these conditions what would be their monthly payments for interest and reduction of principal? They are now renting at $600 per month. Would you recommend that they buy? The Hennesseys could, however, easily make a down payment of 20 percent and if they did, the lending institution would charge them only 9.5 percent interest. Which should they do? How much interest would they save if they financed with the 20 percent down payment? What would the monthly payments be for interest and reduction in principal if they bought the home with a 20 percent down payment?

5. Howard and Patricia Jones would like to buy a new house that is on the market for $95,000. The Joneses have two children, and Howard has an annual income after taxes of $30,000. They have $5,000 that they could use as a down payment and then assume a mortgage of $90,000. Can they afford to buy this home? Why or why not?

6. Carolyn and Bill Calkins have been renting a nice apartment for $500 per month. Most of their friends are home owners and therefore are enjoying certain tax benefits that Carolyn and Bill cannot obtain. What are these benefits and how do they work? While Carolyn and Bill would like the above benefits of home ownership, neither of them enjoys yard work and the like. Is there a solution to their problem?

SUGGESTED READINGS

Anosike, Benji O. *How to Buy or Sell Your Own Home Without a Lawyer or Broker.* New York: Do-It-Yourself Publishers, 1985.

The Appraisal Journal. Chicago: American Institute of Real Estate Appraisers. Quarterly publication.

Appraisal Review Journal. This journal is published three times per year by the National Association of Review Appraisers.

Arenea, Journal of the American Real Estate and Urban Economics Association. Quarterly publication.

"Before a House Becomes a Home." Hartford, CT.: Aetna Life Insurance Co.

Boroson, Warren. *How to Buy or Sell Your Home in a Changing Market.* Oradell, N.J.: Medical Economics Books, 1986.

"Buying and Selling Your Home." Chicago: American Bar Association Information Services.

Corgel, John, and Smith, Halbert C. *Real Estate.* Homewood, Ill.: Irwin, 1987.

Financial Real Estate Handbook. Boston: Financial Publishing Co. Annual publication.

Gritz, Robert D. *The Complete Home Buying Guide.* Beverly Farms, Mass.: Kay Publishing Co., 1986.

Harwood, Bruce. *Real Estate Principles.* Englewood Cliffs, N.J.: Prentice-Hall, 1986.

"Homes: Construction, Maintenance, Community Development." Washington, D.C.: U.S. Government Printing Office.

Kau, James B., and Sirmons, C.F. *Tax Planning For Real Estate Investors*, 3rd ed. Englewood Cliffs, N.J.: Prentice-Hall, 1985.

"Landlord and Tenants—Your Guide to the Law." Chicago: American Bar Association Information Services, 750 N. Lake Shore Dr., Chicago, Ill. 60611.

"Monthly Amortization Loan Schedule." Santa Monica, Cal.: Delphi Information Sciences Corporation.

Morton, Tom. *Real Estate Finance; A Practical Approach.* Glenview, Ill.: Scott, Foresman, 1986.

The Real Estate Appraiser and Analyst. Chicago: Society of Real Estate Appraisers. Bimonthly publication

"Real Estate Center Journal." College Station, TX.: Texas A & M University. Published quarterly.

Real Estate Review. Boston: Warren, Gorham and Lamont. Quarterly publication.

Savings and Loan Fact Book. Chicago: United States Savings and Loan League. Annual publication.

Seller Services. This is a bimonthly publication on home ownership published by the Federal National Mortgage Association.

The Story of Modern Home Financing. Chicago: United States League of Savings Associations, latest edition.

What You Should Know Before You Buy a Home. Chicago: United States League of Savings Associations. Obtain the latest edition of this annual publication.

Wiedemer, John P. *Real Estate Investments.* Reston, Va.: Reston Publishing Company, 1987.

Wofford, Larry E. *Real Estate.* New York: John Wiley and Sons, 1986.

Wurtzebach, Charles H., and Miles, Mike E. *Modern Real Estate.* New York: John Wiley and Sons, 1987.

Your Housing Dollar. Chicago: Money Management Institute, Household Finance Corp., 1985.

III Planning and managing an insurance program

The four chapters in this section cover all types of insurance. Chapter 9 is an introduction chapter that covers the risks and hazards we all face in this world. The risk of loss must be managed somehow and this chapter spells out how this can be done.

Chapter 10 develops in some detail how the risk of premature death may be planned for. Chapter 11 does the same thing for the risk that there may be a loss of income and high medical expenses because of illness or an accident.

Chapter 12 discusses protecting assets by means of property and liability insurance. Property may be destroyed because of fire or accident, and your client may be held liable for destroying other people's property or injuring them. This chapter illustrates how property and liability insurance can protect your client.

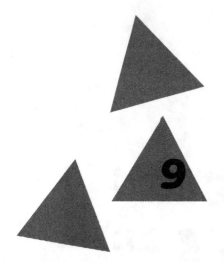

9 Risk and risk management: Introduction to insurance

HIGHLIGHTS   In order to present the principles of risk management and insurance, Chapter 9 analyzes the following:

1   Insurable risk
2   The various risks one faces in everyday life
3   The differences between gambling and insurance
4   Methods of successfully managing risk
5   How insurance companies spread risk over large numbers

INTRODUCTION: THE ELEMENTS OF RISK

Life is full of risks. Risk, moreover, is associated with loss. Loss may be defined as an unintentional decline in, or disappearance of, value arising from some contingency. We all face certain perils or hazards and they can inflict losses on us in our daily life.

There are some risks we face that, if the event happens, will not result in serious consequences, such as having a flat tire, or oversleeping, or the furnace's pilot light going out. However, there are other risks that can cause serious consequences, and these concern us here. There is the risk that a house will burn down, blow away in a hurricane, or wash away in a flood, causing financial hardship. One may become ill or have an accident and be unable to work. One may then lose income and have costly medical expenses. One's car may be wrecked or stolen. One's home may be burglarized and valuable possessions lost. An individual may become permanently disabled and unable to work and earn a livelihood. One may die prematurely, with the income stream cut off and the survivors left in dire financial straits. An individual may live too long; that is, he or she may outlive income and accumulated assets and spend old age in poverty. One may be sued for damages caused to others due to negligence or malpractice. The list of risks could continue, but we have covered the main ones. Risk, however, can often be insured against. Table 9-1 illustrates the major types of insurable risk, the penalty for not insuring, and the insurance protection available. Figure 9-1 shows life insurance purchases in the United States in recent years.

LEGAL CONCEPTS OF INSURANCE

Insurance companies are regulated by the state government, and all states have laws governing how the companies must operate. However, there is enough uniformity to make some general comments about insurance and the law.

Gambling versus insurance

To understand the bare fundamentals of insurable risk, it is necessary to distinguish between gambling and insurance. A horse player visits Churchill Downs in Kentucky for the purpose of betting on horses. Al-

Table 9-1 *Major insurance risk and protection available*

Risk	Penalty if event occurred	Protection
Premature death	Loss of income	Life insurance
Disability	Loss of income	Disability insurance
Illness or accident	Medical bills	Health insurance
Destruction of assets (car, home)	Monetary loss	Property insurance
Lawsuit (injuring others)	Monetary loss	Liability insurance

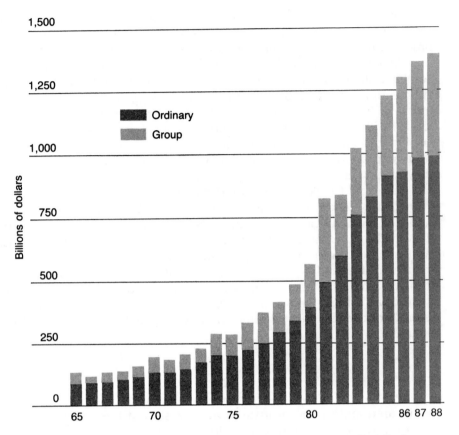

Life insurance purchases in the United States. (Source: Life Insurance Fact Book, 1989, p. 4)

Figure 9—1

though the gambler is becoming involved with the risk of loss, this risk is quite different from the risk borne by the person driving an automobile down an icy street or the risk assumed by everyone that he or she will die tomorrow. In the first instance, the individual has created his or her own hazard, namely, that of attempting to pick a winner, and in the latter case the individual has not created the hazard being faced. The driver is faced with a hazard inherent in the nature of things; so is every individual because no one knows when he or she is going to die. Here we have one important distinction between gambling and insurance. Gamblers create their risks, while those who face risks inherent in everyday living can make few choices about their fates.

The other difference between insurance and gambling is that the risk involved in insurance is predictable. Insurance actuaries can, if there are large numbers of drivers, predict to a high degree of accuracy how many of them will have accidents. They cannot predict which ones, but they can predict how many. They can also predict how many people will die each year, although they cannot tell which ones. The risk involved in gambling is not only self-created, but the possibility of winning is often sheer luck. How many times a person will win and lose, even over a long time, cannot be figured out mathematically with any precision.

Indeed, the authorities will not permit one to engage in gambling or semigambling activities by means of insurance. In the early 1600s, individuals did make insurance a form of gambling, mainly in the realm of maritime insurance policies. For example, a ship ready to set to sea and loaded with a valuable cargo would be inspected by various individuals hoping to make their fortunes. They would take out an insurance policy on a ship and a cargo in which they had no interest whatsoever. Then they would return home and hope, and probably sometimes pray, that the ship would sink. If they heard that the ship had sunk, they would immediately report to the insurance company, where they were paid the value of their policies. They had won their bet. This practice not only disturbed the insurance companies: it disturbed the members of the British Parliament even more. To prevent this sort of insured gambling, Parliament in the middle 1600s passed an act that prohibited individuals from obtaining insurance policies on *anything* unless they had in that thing what is today known as an "insurable interest." This "insurable interest" concept spread to other countries as well, including the United States.

Insurable interest

For there to be an **insurable interest,** a relationship must exist between the insured and the event insured against so that the happening of the event will cause the insured some injury or loss. A person insured must in some way be actually interested in the subject matter of the insurance at the time of loss. For example, let us consider a young lady who is a professional ice skater. Her professional life depends on the soundness of her limbs (oddly enough, the same is true for a race horse). If she falls and breaks a leg, she will be unable to earn any money for a long time. Therefore, she has an interest in insuring her leg: that is, an insurable interest. For someone else to insure the skater's legs would be in the nature of a gambling contract; such an individual ordinarily would not have an insurable interest in her legs. However, an impresario who is managing the ice show and who stands a risk of loss in the event the star's legs are broken alo may be said to have an insurable interest. The individual who can suffer no direct loss has no insurable interest whatever. For there to be insurance, therefore, one must have an interest in the thing or in the event being insured against.

The same is true of life insurance. One cannot, generally speaking, buy a policy on a stranger. (The exception is if one lends him money. Then one has an insurable interest up to the extent of the loan. This is discussed under credit life insurance.) One can, however, buy a policy on a direct member of one's family. Most life insurance is purchased by and on the breadwinner of a family.

The **principle of indemnity** applies primarily to property insurance. The indemnity concept prevents the insured from collecting *more* than the actual loss. If it were not for the principle of indemnity, the insured could make profit by buying two (or more) policies from different insurance companies. Therefore, insurance contracts contain a clause regarding other policies. Typically such clauses provide that all policies covering the same risk will share the loss pro rata. That is, if Jones carries $60,000 of coverage with Company A and $40,000 with Company B, the two companies will share any loss on a 60-percent/40-percent basis.

Principle of indemnity

There are two exceptions to the principle of indemnity. First, some companies will pay the entire face value of a policy, if, say, a home is completely destroyed, even though the value of the home may have fallen below the face value of the policy.

Second, replacment value insurance is becoming increasingly popular. Such policies do not take into account depreciation in the value of an asset. This is particularly true of the clause that provides for hail damage to a roof. A twenty-year-old roof destroyed by hail will be replaced by the insurance company, even though its value is far below its replacement cost.

Under the **principle of subrogation** the insurance company that has indemnified a person's loss is permitted to recover that loss from any liable third party. For example, if A damages B's property, and A is at fault, B's insurance company will pay (indemnify) B and then go after A to recover the amount it paid.

The principle of subrogation

The principle of subrogation does not apply in the case where the insured negligently damages his or her own property. In the above case, if A carelessly and negligently drove his or her car into a tree, the insurance company would have to pay. The company could not, then, turn around and sue A to recover, because that would defeat the entire concept of insurance. However, in such a case, the insurance company may refuse to sell insurance to A in the future; or it might raise A's premiums.

Like the principle of indemnity, the principle of subrogation applies only to property insurance and not to life or health insurance.

Some risk is insurable, some is not. The risk of loss while gambling is not insurable. Some risk is not worth insuring: for example, the risk of oversleeping. However, you can lower this risk by buying a good alarm clock.

RISK MANAGEMENT

For a risk to be insurable, the frequency of hazard insured against must be predictable. There are four methods of managing insurable risk: minimize the risk, bear the risk yourself, self-insure, or transfer the risk to an insurance company. We will examine all these things below.

Insurable risk

Minimizing risk

Risk may be minimized (or lessened) to some extent. For example, those individuals who neither drink nor smoke, and who exercise regularly and watch their diet, are minimizing the risk of a premature death. Those who don't drive during a blizzard are minimizing (or lessening) the likelihood of an accident. In general, being an alert and careful driver and keeping the car in good working order will reduce the risk of an accident. Keeping a portable fire extinguisher will reduce the risk of loss due to fire in the home. Where the house is located and the type of material used in its construction have a bearing on risk. Some insurance companies charge a lower premium if the insured has reduced insurable risk.

Assuming risk

Most people can and do assume some insurable risk themselves. For example, a deductibile on an automobile insurance policy indicates that the insured assumes some risk. Individuals who have an old car might drop collision insurance completely and assume the entire risk in this area.

For health insurance, the insured virtually always assumes a portion of the risk; insurance companies do not pay the entire medical bill.

How much risk to assume is a question only the individual can decide; but the more risk he or she assumes, the lower the premiums charged by insurance companies. Before deciding how much insurable risk to assume, planners can analyze their clients historical record and answer the following questions: In the case of health insurance, what have the medical expenses been in the past? What is the present condition of the client's health? For auto insurance, what kind of driver is he or she? Does he or she drive defensively? How many times has the client been involved in an accident? Has he or she ever killed or injured anyone with the car?

For home insurance, is it near the fire station? Is it an old frame house or a new brick structure? In the case of life insurance, what would be the financial consequences of a premature death? How many dependents are there? What are their ages? If the spouse is not now working, could she or he become employed if necessary? All of these factors will have a bearing on how much risk to assume. Finally, the client's financial strength will have a bearing how much risk he or she can assume. How much risk to assume and how much to transfer to an insurance company are discussed in greater detail in the next few chapters, where we will present some guidelines on how to determine the amount of the various kinds of insurance needed.

Self-insurance

It should be noted that when the client assumes some risk himself or herself, this is not **self-insurance**, although some people call it that. Risk assumed by the client is really no insurance, although that is a perfectly proper course of action at times—for example, when the risk of occurrence is low, and if the consequence (loss) of the unfortunate event is small.

Self-insurance technically requires that the person set aside (budget) a sum regularly to establish an insurance fund to pay for damages should an event occur.

Some doctors do this on a group basis for their malpractice insurance, through medical societies or a group of doctors setting up a pool. Some large corporations also self-insure for property and liability coverage. An individual could, but few actually do; rather some people have no insurance.

Individuals may manage insurable risk by transferring it to somebody else, usually an insurance company, which pools the insurable risk of many individuals and manages the aggregate risk. Insurance is a device by means of which one party through a contract (called the "policy") for a consideration (called the "premium") undertakes to assume for another party certain types of risk of loss. Insurance is social in nature since it represents cooperation for mutual protection. Through the payment of premium by many insured persons, the risk is spread over large numbers, and the few who suffer losses are reimbursed by the insurance company with the premiums paid by the many who do not suffer losses. The individual absorbs a small but certain loss (the premium), but avoids the burden of a less likely but potentially much larger loss.

Transferring risk: Buying insurance

There are numerous types of insurance; the main kinds are life insurance, disability, health, and property and liability insurance. Life and disability insurance protect a breadwinner's income stream. Health insurance provides protection from monetary loss due to illness or accident. For most people property and liability can be broken down into insurance on the home and on the car. The property portion is to reimburse the policyholder for the physical destruction of the home or the car. The liability aspect is to protect the insured against lawsuits by others in the event of damage to others—either bodily injuries or the destruction of their property.

PRINCIPLES OF INSURANCE

The underlying principle of any type of insurance is the **law of large numbers.** Highly trained and specialized mathematicians called **actuaries** can, with an amazing degree of accuracy, determine how many young men or women thirty years of age, out of a large number of thirty-year-olds, will die within the coming year. Figure 9–2 shows how the death rate has declined in recent years. Note that emphasis has been placed on large numbers. No actuary or any other mortal can predict when any one individual of thirty years of age is going to die. But an actuary working with large numbers can predict within limitations how many young men or women out of that large number will die within the year. In short, what cannot be predicted for the individual can be pre-

How life insurance companies spread risk: Mortality tables

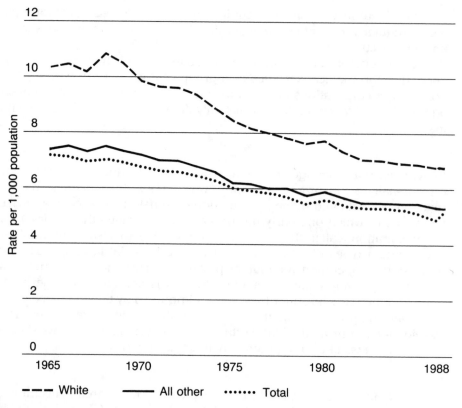

dicted in the mass. This can be done because we know a good deal about deaths at every age level from past experience.

Using past experience, insurance companies construct and use mortality tables to spread the risk of loss over large numbers. In this way they are able to absorb risk. Taking our thirty-year-old men again as an example, the actuaries who have for a great many years compiled life insurance statistics will predict that out of 100,000 thirty-year-old men in good health alive at the beginning of the year, 173 will die during the forthcoming year. For women the figure is 135. Life expectancy is calculated the same way. Table 9–2 shows part of a mortality table and illustrates deaths per 100,000; the table included in Figure 9–3 also shows life expectancy in years.

In the most simple case (without attempting to figure in anything for the company's operating cost, profit, and the like), the premium for a thirty-year-old woman under these circumstances would be $1.35 for every $1,000 of life insurance. The way this is calculated is simply that if 100,000 thirty-year-old women buy $1,000 of life insurance policies, they would pay in a total of $135,000. In this case, then, the amount going

Table 9–2   Mortality tables

	Commissioners 1980 standard ordinary (1970–1975)						Commissioners 1980 standard ordinary (1970–1975)			
	Male		Female				Male		Female	
Age	Deaths per 1,000	Expectation of life (years)	Deaths per 1,000	Expectation of life (years)		Age	Deaths per 1,000	Expectation of life (years)	Deaths per 1,000	Expectation of life (years)
0	4.18	70.83	2.89	75.83		56	11.46	20.51	7.57	24.49
1	1.07	70.13	.87	75.04		57	12.49	19.74	8.03	23.67
2	.99	69.20	.81	74.11		58	13.59	18.99	8.47	22.86
3	.98	68.27	.79	73.17		59	14.77	18.24	8.94	22.05
4	.95	67.34	.77	72.23		60	16.08	17.51	9.47	21.25
5	.90	66.40	.76	71.28		61	17.54	16.79	10.13	20.44
6	.86	65.46	.73	70.34		62	19.19	16.08	10.96	19.65
7	.80	64.52	.72	69.39		63	21.06	15.38	12.02	18.86
8	.76	63.57	.70	68.44		64	23.14	14.70	13.25	18.08
9	.74	62.62	.69	67.48		65	25.42	14.04	14.59	17.32
10	.73	61.66	.68	66.53		66	27.85	13.39	16.00	16.57
11	.77	60.71	.69	65.58		67	30.44	12.76	17.43	15.83
12	.85	59.75	.72	64.62		68	33.19	12.14	18.84	15.10
13	.99	58.80	.75	63.67		69	36.17	11.54	20.36	14.38
14	1.15	57.86	.80	62.71		70	39.51	10.96	22.11	13.67
15	1.33	56.93	.85	61.76		71	43.30	10.39	24.23	12.97
16	1.51	56.00	.90	60.82		72	47.65	9.84	26.87	12.28
17	1.67	55.09	.95	59.87		73	52.64	9.30	30.11	11.60
18	1.78	54.18	.98	58.93		74	58.19	8.79	33.93	10.95
19	1.86	53.27	1.02	57.98		75	64.19	8.31	38.24	10.32
20	1.90	52.37	1.05	57.04		76	70.53	7.84	42.97	9.71
21	1.91	51.47	1.07	56.10		77	77.12	7.40	48.04	9.12
22	1.89	50.57	1.09	55.16		78	83.90	6.97	53.45	8.55
23	1.86	49.66	1.11	54.22		79	91.05	6.57	59.35	8.01
24	1.82	48.75	1.14	53.28		80	98.84	6.18	65.99	7.48
25	1.77	47.84	1.16	52.34		81	107.48	5.80	73.60	6.98
26	1.73	46.93	1.19	51.40		82	117.25	5.44	82.40	6.49
27	1.71	46.01	1.22	50.46		83	128.26	5.09	92.53	6.03
28	1.70	45.09	1.26	49.52		84	140.25	4.77	103.81	5.59
29	1.71	44.16	1.30	48.59		85	152.95	4.46	116.10	5.18
30	1.73	43.24	1.35	47.65		86	166.09	4.18	129.29	4.80
31	1.78	42.31	1.40	46.71		87	179.55	3.91	143.32	4.43
32	1.83	41.38	1.45	45.78		88	193.27	3.66	158.18	4.09
33	1.91	40.46	1.50	44.84		89	207.29	3.41	173.94	3.77
34	2.00	39.54	1.58	43.91		90	221.77	3.18	190.75	3.45
35	2.11	38.61	1.65	42.98		91	236.98	2.94	208.87	3.15
36	2.24	37.69	1.76	42.05		92	253.45	2.70	228.81	2.85
37	2.40	36.78	1.89	41.12		93	272.11	2.44	251.51	2.55
38	2.58	35.87	2.04	40.20		94	295.90	2.17	279.31	2.24
39	2.79	34.96	2.22	39.28		95	329.96	1.87	317.32	1.91
40	3.02	34.05	2.42	38.36		96	384.55	1.54	375.74	1.56
41	3.29	33.16	2.64	37.46		97	480.20	1.20	474.97	1.21
42	3.56	32.26	2.87	36.55		98	657.98	.84	655.85	.84
43	3.87	31.38	3.09	35.66		99	1,000.00	.50	1,000.00	.50
44	4.19	30.50	3.32	34.77		100				
45	4.55	29.62	3.56	33.88		101				
46	4.92	28.76	3.80	33.00		102				
47	5.32	27.90	4.05	32.12		103				
48	5.74	27.04	4.33	31.25		104				
49	6.21	26.20	4.63	30.39		105				
50	6.71	25.36	4.96	29.53		106				
51	7.30	24.52	5.31	28.67		107				
52	7.96	23.70	5.70	27.82		108				
53	8.71	22.89	6.15	26.98		109				
54	9.56	22.08	6.61	26.14		110				
55	10.47	21.29	7.09	25.31						

Source: 1988 Life Insurance Fact Book, *American Council of Life Insurance*, p. 112.

Figure 9–3 (Source: Life Insurance Fact Book, 1987, p. 45)

	1984			1985*			1986**			1988		
	Male	Female	Total	Male	Female	Total	Male	Female	Total	Male	Female	Total
	71.2	78.3	74.7	71.2	78.2	74.7	71.5	78.5	75.0	71.4	78.3	74.9
	57.4	64.2	60.9	57.4	64.2	60.9	57.7	64.5	61.1	57.6	64.3	61.0
	48.2	54.5	51.4	48.1	54.5	51.4	48.5	54.8	51.7	48.4	54.6	51.6
	38.9	44.9	42.0	38.9	44.8	42.0	39.3	45.1	42.3	39.2	45.0	42.2
	29.9	35.5	32.8	29.9	35.4	32.8	30.2	35.7	33.1	30.3	35.5	33.0
	21.5	26.6	24.2	21.6	26.5	24.2	21.8	26.8	24.5	21.9	26.6	24.3
	14.6	18.6	16.8	14.6	18.6	16.8	14.7	18.9	17.0	14.8	18.6	16.9
	9.0	11.9	10.7	9.0	11.8	10.6	9.0	11.8	10.6	9.1	11.7	10.6
	5.2	6.5	6.1	5.0	6.5	6.0	NA	NA	NA	5.1	6.3	5.9

*Data are provisional from the National Center for Health Statistics.

**Data are estimated by Metropolitan Life Insurance Company.

N.A.—Not available.

Sources: National Center for Health Statistics. U.S. Department of Health and Human Services, and Metropolitan Life Insurance Company, *Statistical Bulletin*, July-September 1989.

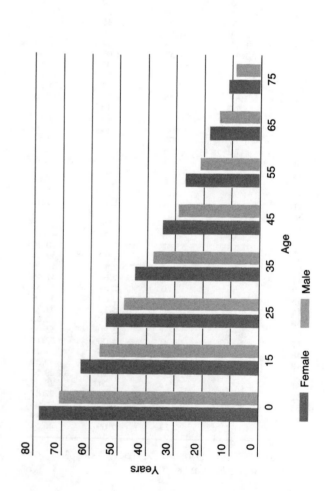

into the company would be equal to the amount paid out to the benefic-iaries of the 135 who died; and, at the end of the year, the company would have a total of zero remaining.

In real life things are not so simple. Just as in any other business, there must be additional sums included in the premium. In this case, the premiums include an amount to cover profits and operating costs.

The 100,000 thirty-year-olds referred to above must be in good physical condition. Statistics upon which the actuaries determine the probability of the number of deaths in any age group are based on the assumption that those persons insured are in good physical condition and good mental health to begin with. If it were not for the requirement of good physical and mental health, obviously anyone with a disease would immediately rush out to the company and buy insurance, in which case the predictions of the actuaries would fall short of their mark and the companies would rapidly go out of business.

Medical expenses may also be predicted fairly accurately based on past experience and estimated current cost of treatment. Using large numbers of individuals, insurance actuaries are able to calculate the number of, for example, appendectomies or heart attacks per 100,000 individuals. In the case of health insurance, however, there is an additional variable. It is the cost of treatment. Drugs, hospital charges, and doctors' fees rise periodically. Consequently, health insurance premiums rise almost yearly. Nevertheless, health insurance companies spread health care costs over large numbers of individuals and the premiums paid by indi-viduals who do not get sick and who are not injured are used to pay the claims of those individuals who do have medical bills.

How insurance companies spread medical expenses

Like health insurance, property and liability insurance are financed over a much shorter time period than is life insurance. Insurance on a house, for example, is sold for a one- or two-year period and then renewed. For an automobile, the insured period is six months or one year. The reason is that there are more variables. Inflation will cause rates to go up an-nually. Even without inflation, the cost of auto and home repairs could rise. Jury awards and how these awards may have risen in the recent past will also affect premiums. Like other insurance companies, property and liability insurance companies make an allowance for their expenses and the interest they can earn on premium dollars when setting rates. Just as in the case of other insurance, when one transfers the risk on a car or a home to an insurance company, it is spread over large numbers of peo-ple, and the premiums of those who do not suffer misfortunes pay for the damages of those who do. The insurance companies base premiums on a probability distribution for each of the various losses. Sometimes,

How property and liability companies spread risk

auto insurance companies will raise premiums for those drivers who have had two or more moving violation traffic tickets, on the theory that they are higher-risk drivers.

SUMMARY REVIEW QUESTIONS

These questions serve as a summary and a review of the chapter. If you are able to answer them all, you have a good understanding of the material covered by the chapter.

1. What are some risks that, if the event happens, will result in serious consequences? What are some that will not cause serious consequences?
2. What is insurable risk?
3. What are the four methods of managing risk?
4. What is the difference between gambling and insurance?
5. Explain insurable interest.
6. What is self-insurance?
7. How do insurance companies spread mortality risk?
8. How do property and liability insurance companies spread risk?

CASES

1. Geraldeen Baxter has analyzed the various risks she faces in order to determine her insurance needs. They are as follows:

	Likely dollar loss	Likelihood of occurring
Theft or other loss of personal property from apartment	$15,000	Not great
Medical expense:		
Minor	Up to $1,000	Substantial
Major	$10,000 or more	Not great
Credit card loss	$500	Not great
Automobile:		
Value of car	$10,000	
Minor damage	Up to $1,000	Moderate
Major damage	More than $1,000	Not great
Liability	Unknown	Not great

(a) Which risks should Ms. Baxter assume herself?
(b) Which risks should Ms. Baxter transfer?

2. Connie Brashear is a literary agent for a number of successful authors. She receives 10 percent of all of their earnings, and would like to take out a life insurance policy on several of the more successful ones. May she do that? Would it be a wise thing to do?

3. Joyce Faye Allen is a policewoman and wonders whether she should have malpractice insurance. Can you advise her?

4. Claire Baldwin is confused between minimizing risk, assuming risk, and transferring risk. Can you clarify this for Her?

SUGGESTED READINGS

Athearn, James L. *Risk and Insurance,* St. Paul, Minn.: West Publishing Co. 1984.

Best's Review, Life-Health Edition. Oldwick, N.J.: A.M. Best Company, Inc. Monthly publication.

Best's Review Property/Casualty Edition. Oldwick, N.J.: A. M. Best Company, Inc. Monthly publication.

Bickelhaupt, David L. *General Insurance,* 10th ed. Homewood, Ill.: R. Irwin, 1983.

Black, Kenneth, and Skipper, Harold. *Life Insurance,* 11th ed. Englewood Cliffs, N.J.: Prentice-Hall, 1987.

Cookerell, Hugh. *Lloyd's of London.* Homewood, Ill.: Dow Jones-Irwin, 1984.

Crane, Frederick G. *Insurance Principles and Practices.* New York: John Wiley and Sons, 1984.

Dorfman, Mark S. *Introduction to Insurance,* 3rd ed. Englewood Cliffs, N.J.: Prentice-Hall, 1987.

Greene, Mark R., and Trieschmann, James. "Risk and Insurance." Cincinnati: South-Western, 1984.

Harris, Louis. "Risk in a Complex Society." *The Journal of Insurance,* July-August, 1980.

Insurance Review, New York: The Insurance Information Institute. Monthly publication.

"Journal of Insurance." New York: The Insurance Information Institute. Bimonthly publication.

Life Insurance Fact Book. New York: The Institute of Life Insurance. Annual publication.

Mehr, Robert I., and Cammack, Emerson. *Principles of Insurance.* Homewood, Ill.: Irwin, 1985.

Mehr, Robert, and Gustavson, Sandra. *Life Insurance: Theory and Practice.* Plano, Tex.: Business Publications, Inc., 1987.

National Underwriter. Chicago, Ill.: The National Underwriter Co. Weekly publication.

"On the Way Up; A Description of Life Insurance and Annuities." Hartford, Conn.: Aetna Life Insurance Co.

"Property/Casualty Fact Book." New York: Insurance Information Institute. Annual publication.

Rejda, George E. *Principles of Insurance.* Glenview, Ill.: Scott, Foresman, 1986.

Vaughan, Emmet J. *Fundamentals of Risk and Insurance,* 4th ed. New York: John Wiley and Sons, 1986.

Williams, C. Arthur, Jr., and Heims, Richard M. *Risk Management and Insurance,* 4th ed. New York: McGraw-Hill, 1985.

Williams, C. Arthur, Jr., Herd, George L., and Glendenning, William. *Principles of Risk Management and Insurance.* Malvern, Pa.: American Institute for Property and Liability Underwriters, 1981.

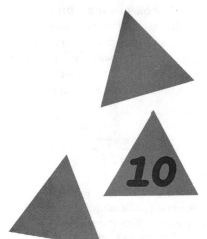

10 Life insurance

HIGHLIGHTS   In order to thoroughly understand insurance needs and how to satisfy them, a financial planner should be familiar with the following:

1   Why and when to buy life insurance
2   Some guidelines to help your client decide what kind and how much life insurance to buy
3   The various types of ordinary life insurance
4   How some life insurance builds up a cash value
5   Group life insurance as an alternative to an individual policy
6   Some things that will help you choose a life insurance company
7   Some other things that everyone should know about life insurance

WHY AND WHEN TO BUY LIFE INSURANCE

There are only two reasons for most people to buy life insurance: for protection and for savings. In most cases protection is primary. We discussed risk management, which is what we have in mind when we talk about protection, in Chapter 9.

Why buy life insurance at all?

While an individual may buy life insurance with a savings feature built in, insurance is usually a poor savings vehicle. Its return is modest and will be eroded by inflation. Only if one is not disciplined and finds it impossible to save in any other way should he or she consider entering into a contract with a life insurance company in which he or she is forced to save. Some investment advisors suggest that if a client is in a high tax bracket, insurance as a savings—and investment—scheme may be advantageous because of favorable tax treatment. (See "Taxes and Life Insurance Benefits" later in this chapter for a discussion of how insurance is taxed). That may be partially true, but in many cases one may be better off buying insurance for protection alone and then investing the difference in premiums; insurance that provides only protection is cheaper than insurance that includes a savings feature.

Insurance provides protection in the event of premature death: death that occurs before the person has reached his or her full life expectancy. Insurance protects the dependents of the insured against financial hardship in the event of death of the breadwinner. The income stream is being protected. Insurance dollars are being substituted for earned dollars. That gives us a clue as to how much insurance is needed. Figure 10–1 shows the amount of life insurance purchased, in force, and life insurance benefits paid over the last few years.

When to buy life insurance

The best time to buy life insurance is the day before death occurs, if one knows when that will be and if he or she can still buy it at that time. The person who is in ill health at an advanced age is probably uninsurable.

When should a person buy a refrigerator? Should one be bought for children when they are, say, ten years old, on the theory that the price will be lower when they are ten than when they are twenty years of age? That's the logic some insurance salesmen will use; premiums are cheaper at age ten than age twenty. Yes, but not that much cheaper. Besides, one does not buy something that is not needed just because it's cheaper. The only valid argument for buying insurance for children is that they may become uninsurable in young adulthood. Consequently, life insurance should be purchased when it is needed and can be afforded—just like a refrigerator—that is, when the individual becomes a young adult and takes on family responsibilities.

Probably your client won't be able to buy all the insurance he or she will need or want at one time; hence, he or she should consider buying several blocks over a few years as income rises. Review the insurance program periodically because needs will change as an individual grows

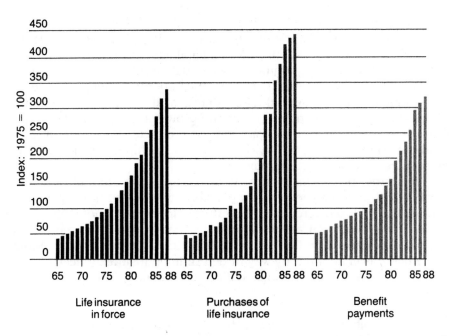

Relative growth of life insurance in force, purchases of life insurance, and benefit payments in the United States, 1965–1985. (Source: Life Insurance Fact Book, 1987, p. 6; 1989, p. 4.)

Figure 10–1

older. Sometimes a client will need more, and at other times the planner may recommend to let some term insurance expire, or that permanent insurance be surrendered for cash.

There are several ways to decide how much life insurance to buy. Some examples are the multiple income concept, the needs concept, the human life value concept—also called the present value of the total future income stream concept.

The multiple income approach is the simplest technique for calculating the amount of insurance that should be purchased. First, take the after-tax salary and adjust it down somewhat. After-tax salary is adjusted down to take into account two factors: (1) the income earner is also an income consumer, hence less income is required for a smaller family; and (2) the higher the income the greater the downward adjustment might be, because a lower percentage of it is required to enable the survivors to live well. Generally the after-tax earnings are adjusted down to 75, 65, or even 60 percent. On the other hand, as income rises, the client can afford more insurance; this may tend to lessen the downward adjustment. The percentage then selected is, in reality, at least in part determined by priorities and value judgments.

HELPING YOUR CLIENT DECIDE HOW MUCH LIFE INSURANCE TO BUY

Some multiple is then applied—the most common ones being 4, 5, 6, and even on up to 10. The multiple selected is determined by age, the age and number of dependents, assets, liabilities, income from property, and priorities and value judgments. Obviously the larger the number of dependents and the younger their ages, the larger the multiplier. The age of the spouse is also taken into consideration. If the spouse is relatively young, the multiple will rise as he or she grows older, on the theory that finding employment would become far more difficult at an older age. After about age forty-five or fifty, however, the multiple declines because fewer years of dependence remain.

The larger the Social Security benefits, the lower the multiple. If the client has other employer-provided pension benefits and high investment income, the multiple is reduced. Investment income will not decline with the insured's death. An assumption is also made regarding the income that could be earned on the insurance benefits in selecting the multiple.

While this is an arbitrary way of determining insurance needs, it can be considered a rule of thumb based on experience.

Family needs concept

Under the family needs approach, the first step is to estimate the total family needs. Next, ascertain the resources already available to meet those needs. Such things include savings accounts, securities, any other income-earning assets, Social Security, and other insurance already owned such as group insurance with an employer. The third step is to subtract the resources already available from the needs calculated in step one. The remainder shows the insurance needs.

Under the first step list all possible family needs.

1. Funeral and other final expenses

In addition to funeral expenses, there may be final medical and hospital bills to pay. There may also be administrative expenses and attorney's fees associated with probating a will and settling an estate. These expenses will probably be a minimum of $5,000 and may be much larger, especially if the estate is fairly large.

2. Paying off the mortgage and other debts

If there is a mortgage on the house, the client may wish to pay it off as well as liquidate any other installment debt outstanding. Special mortgage and credit life insurance is available for this, or it may be included in a regular insurance policy. There is no way of estimating the dollar amount of this item; it will vary greatly from person to person. An alternative way of handling the home mortgage is not to pay it off but to include the mortgage payments in regular family living expense needs. (See below).

3. Emergency fund

The client will no doubt want an emergency fund. He or she should already have this in a savings account, but in any event it is part of an individual's needs. Many experts suggest this fund should be at least 3 to 6 times the monthly take-home pay.

If there are college-bound children, college expenses become part of the insurance needs. An individual need not necessarily provide for full four-year college expenses because students can earn income to help defray the cost. On the other hand, it is difficult to calculate future college costs because of rapid inflation. College costs vary greatly even among state schools, but total costs (tuition, room and board, etc.) can easily reach $12,000 per year. At private schools this figure can go as high as or higher than $18,000 per year.

4. College fund

Annual family living needs consist of the day-to-day living expenses and is related to the personal or family budget discussed in Chapter 2. The amount will vary depending on the size of the family, its age makeup, and accustomed standard of living, or the level of livelihood that the insured would like to provide. Remember, however, this item will continue for a number of years. Moreover, this need will change (hopefully decline) as the children grow up and are on their own; this will be partly (or perhaps entirely) offset by inflation.

5. Annual family living needs

    The amount of insurance needed for family living would also need to be adjusted (presumably downward) to take into account other earning assets, Social Security benefits, and any private corporate pension payments to be received. Social Security benefits for children continue until the children reach age eighteen. The Social Security benefits paid to a surviving spouse do not begin until she or he reaches age sixty. (The time between when the benefits for the children end and when they begin again for the surviving spouse is known as "the blackout years.")

Part of the insurance proceeds would be invested to provide income to meet living (and retirement) needs. However, arrangements must be made to take into account future inflation. Consequently, an assumption must be made regarding future inflation as well as what the capital provided by insurance will earn. It is reasonable to assume that the investment return could exceed inflation by 2, 3, or even 4 percent in the long run. This would result in the amount available for living needs to rise a bit more than inflation as the years pass by. During periods of inflation, interest rates, generally speaking, also rise; hence the amount available to meet living needs rises.

6. Capital needed to provide annual desired living needs in real terms

    The amount of insurance to meet family needs could be designed so that only the interest income is utilized; hence the capital remains intact. It will pass to the heirs eventually. The amount of insurance could also be designed so that the capital would be depleted.

Adding up the six above-mentioned points will give you the answer to the total capital needed to provide for them. Table 10–1 summarizes this. As Table 10–1 shows, the total capital needs required for its hypothetical case are $447,000. It assumes capital remains intact.

7. Total capital needs

    However, the table also shows group insurance with the employer of $100,000 and $34,500 of other earning assets. Subtracting these from

Table 10–1   *Insurance needs for Kimberly and Bob Jacobs*

Present income		$ 42,000
Family needs:		
1. Final expenses		$ 10,000
2. Payment of debt		
a. mortgage	$ 50,000	
b. other	5,000	55,000
3. Emergency fund (twice monthly income		7,000
4. College fund		50,000
5. Annual living needs		
a. 55% of $42,000	$ 23,100	
b. less: Social Security	10,100	
c. net annual living needs	13,000	
6. Capital needed to provide $13,000 in real terms ($325,000 at 4%)		325,000
7. Total capital needed		$447,000
Other resources available at 4%		
1. Savings accounts	$ 12,500	
2. Securities	22,000	
3. Life insurance with employer (groups ins.)	100,000	$134,500
Insurance needs		$312,500

In the event of death, $50,000 of the insurance proceeds would be set aside to earn interest and to be used for future college expenses. The $7,000 emergency fund would also remain intact to earn interest, and $65,000 would be used to liquidate debt and final expenses. The remainder ($190,500)—together with the group insurance of $100,000 and Bob and Kimberly's other earning assets of $34,500—would (totaling $325,000) provide enough capital which, if invested at 4 percent, would provide the $13,000 of annual living needs. We are assuming that the $325,000 will earn 4 percent in real (after adjusted for inflation) terms. This will provide a slightly rising standard of living as the years pass.

the $447,000 of capital needs shows the additional insurance needed, which is $312,500.

Not all of the client's own personal entries will necessarily have a dollar figure. The individual may or may not have debts to pay off; he or she may or may not already have an emergency fund; and a college fund may or may not be needed. Remember also, however, that the item $13,000 for net family living, retirement living, or both, over and above Social Security is an annual and recurring expense.

If the capital provided by insurance is invested and earns a return equal to or in excess of inflation, there is no problem. If the reverse is the case, the family living standard may decline as the years pass, unless they dip into the capital. While the needs concept may suggest more insurance than the client can afford, nevertheless, it is a beginning.

Human life value: The future income stream

The human life value approach takes into account a person's entire future earnings. It is these lifetime earnings that need protecting because that is what would be cut off in the event of death. This requires an estimate of the future lifetime income, which cannot be made precisely but can be made accurately enough.

Let us assume a thirty-five-year-old individual is making $20,000 per year after taxes. Insurance benefit payments are not subject to the income tax, hence they are netted out. If the person continues at this income level until age sixty-five, he or she will earn $600,000 after taxes until retirement. However, the income will almost certainly rise above $20,000 per year, for two reasons. First, most people will probably keep up with inflation in the long run. In addition, historically salaries have on the average grown at about 2 to 3 percent in excess of inflation. Assuming inflation in the long run continues at its historical 4 to 5 percent level, it is reasonable to select 7 percent as the growth rate in the case of the $20,000 per-year income above. Compounding the $20,000 by 7 percent over the thirty-year period gives us a lifetime income stream of about $1,889,220. However, future dollars must be discounted because they are worth less than present dollars.

A present dollar will be worth more in the future because it will grow with interest ($1.00 will be worth $1.07 in a year if the interest rate is 7 percent). Using the same logic, a dollar to be received in the future is worth less than a dollar today, but it is worth something. Its value is again related to the interest rate, and at 7 percent, a dollar to be received in one year is worth about $.93 today. That is, the present value of future dollars takes interest away. Discounting $1,889,220 over thirty years at 7 percent (current interest rate) gives us $347,487. That figure is the human life value of the individual described above, making $20,000 after taxes and growing at 7 percent—it is the value of his or her lifetime income stream if received today.

That, in theory, is the upper-limit amount of insurance the individual in question should have to protect the income stream fully. Moreover, with each passing year, insurance needs decline because there is less and less future income to earn. When the person is sixty-four years old, the insurance needed to protect future income is exactly the same as the final year's earnings.

The human life approach has some shortcomings. It does not consider the other financial assets (savings accounts, securities, Social Security, and the like) that are available in the event of the breadwinner's death. The needs approach is probably the best method of determining insurance requirements.

The final decision

The methods we have discussed for determining insurance needs are only benchmarks. One still has to make a decision based on what the client can afford as well as the client's value judgments and priorities.

Reevaluating insurance needs

Insurance needs should be reevaluated at least every 5 years, if not more often. This is true regardless of which method is chosen to determine how much insurance to buy. Needs will change over the years. Single individuals need less insurance; hence, insurance needs will increase with marriage. When a child is born, insurance needs will again increase. When the children grow up and go out on their own, insurance needs may decline. In addition, as a person grows older, he or she will acquire more income-earning assets (securities and savings accounts) and will need less insurance. The heavy insurance needs are generally during the ages twenty-five to forty-five or fifty. After that the children are likely to be independent and earning assets larger. At retirement age (or near it), insurance needs may decline further. Insurance may be needed for estate planning purposes, in some cases, however.

Insurance for children

Insurance for children should be a low-priority item. Children are not breadwinners as a general rule. Some people buy insurance on their children, which builds up a cash value to give them a nest egg to start out when they reach young adulthood. If the budget can afford this, such a plan is fine. But saving via insurance should be compared with the yield on alternative investment outlets. In most cases, you could find an alternative that would yield more.

Insurance on a nonincome-earning spouse

Although a spouse may not contribute money income to the family, the time and skills he or she provides for the family are valuable and would be costly to replace in case of death or disability.

For example, while the death of one parent may not decrease family dollar income, it may necessitate an increase in family expenditures if the household is to be properly operated and the children are to receive adequate care. To be sure, if a nonworking spouse died, there would be one less consumer in the family, and expenses would decline. The client, with your help, must decide what the net effect would be in his or her individual case.

If there are two breadwinners in the family, there may be a reason for life insurance on both. Since there is a second income to protect, the analysis above regarding how much a person is worth applies to both husband and wife. In addition, with two incomes a more generous calculation of family needs would be possible.

Most people who buy individual life insurance policies buy what is referred to as "ordinary life," and buy it from legal reserve life insurance companies. The terminology covering ordinary life is a bit confusing because not all companies use the same designations. There are only a handful of kinds of ordinary policies: **term, whole life, endowment,** combinations that include two or more of the above, and the recently developed **universal** and **variable life policies.** In addition there are two types of whole life policies, the **straight life** and the **limited pay life** policies, and they are not the same. The following classification illustrates the various ordinary policies.

Ordinary life insurance
    Term
    Whole life
        Straight life
        Limited pay life
    Endowment
    Combinations of two or more of the above
    Universal life
    Variable life

Table 10–2 shows ordinary life insurance in force in the United States by type and average size. Figure 10–2 shows the average size insurance purchased. Term life insurance is the simplest type of ordinary life insurance, and is also the cheapest; it provides the most insurance coverage per dollar of premium. Term insurance is a contract that provides protection for a specific period of time, and, when that time has expired, the policy lapses. It has no savings feature built into it, hence no living ben-

Key life insurance statistics   Table 10–2

	1985	1986	1988	Percent change 1987–86	Percent change 1988–87
Life insurance in force in the United States (000,000 omitted)					
Ordinary	$3,247,289	$3,658,203	$4,511,608	13.1	9.0
Group	2,561,595	2,801,049	3,232,080	8.7	6.2
Industrial	28,250	27,168	25,456	−1.8	−4.5
Credit	215,973	233,859	251,015	3.9	3.3
Total	$6,053,107	$6,720,279	8,020,159	10.9	7.6
Average amounts of life insurance in force in the United States					
Per Household	$ 63,400	$ 69,100	$ 87,600	8.9	5.8
Per Insured Household	$ 74,600	$ 81,200	$108,200	9.0	5.9

Source: American Council of Life Insurance, 1989, page 4.

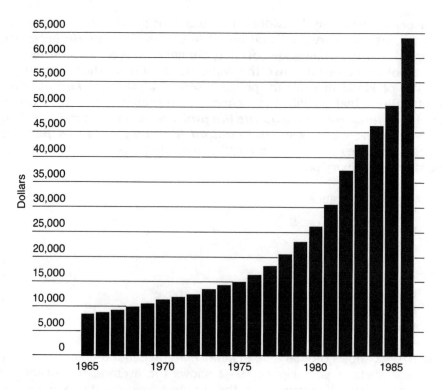

Figure 10–2   *Average size ordinary life insurance policy purchases in the United States.* (Source: Life Insurance Fact Book, 1989, p. 4.)

efits, only death benefits. Consequently, most of the premiums paid into the company are also paid out in the form of death benefits. For this reason, it is cheaper than all other insurance—which is also sometimes called "permanent" insurance as opposed to term. Many term policies are *renewable.* When the term for which it is written has expired, it may be renewed at the option of the insured without the need for a medical examination.

A term policy may also be **convertible.** It can be converted to a permanent policy without a medical examination. There are several types of term policies, but they are basically the same in that they are financed over a specific but variable number of years.

One-year renewable term

A one-year renewable term policy expires after one year; it is the cheapest type to buy. At the end of the year it may be renewed for another year, and so on. Each time it is renewed, however, the insured is one year older, and a higher premium will usually need to be paid. Refer to the mortality table in the previous chapter. You will see that for a person of age twenty, deaths per 1,000 are 1.90 for males and 1.05 for females. This indicates that for every $1,000 worth of life insurance the pure premium for a twenty-year-old female would be $1.05. If 1,000 twenty-year-olds paid that, it would raise just enough ($1,050) to pay the claims for those who died. To be sure, the premium would be more because the insurance companies add something for expenses and may even subtract a bit to take into account the interest they could earn before they had to pay it out in death claims. The mortality table referred to is a standard one, but not all companies use it. Each has developed its own, and it may be more favorable (lower premiums) because the company has had a more favorable mortality experience. Thus, individuals should shop around when buying life insurance.

The next year, the person is twenty-one years of age, and premiums would rise to $1.07 per $1,000 of insurance, and so on year after year with premiums rising. At age 40 they would still only be $2.42. Eventually premiums would get so high that they would be prohibitive. By then, however, one probably would no longer need insurance and would drop the policy. Individuals should consider dropping a policy any time they no longer need it even if the premiums are not prohibitive (e.g., if the children are grown and on their own).

Level premium term

Level premium term may run for five years, ten years, or even twenty years or more. Premiums are merely averaged. If a twenty year-old brought five-year level premium term, the deaths per thousand shown in the mortality table would be averaged for all ages 20 through 24. The premium ($1.87, adjusted for expenses and interest), which would be in excess of that needed in the early years, would build up a reserve to be used in later years when premiums would be deficient. Premiums can also be averaged over ten or twenty or any number of years, even over a lifetime. Figure 10–3 illustrates how a level premium policy works and how reserves are built up.

Until recently, ten- and twenty-year term policies were popular, but recently more people have switched to one-year renewable term. When a person buys level premium insurance he or she is paying some premiums in advance. Individuals can do their own budgeting and, in theory, bank the difference in premiums in the early years and develop their own reserve and earn interest, although the dollars saved in the early years by doing this may be small.

Decreasing term insurance

It is also possible to buy a term policy, the face value of which declines as the years or even the months pass. These are sometimes used to pay off a mortgage if the insured dies. Suppose one has a $50,000 mortgage on a home and desires to protect the family or to keep them from the necessity of playing that mortgage in the event of one's death. Under some circumstances it might be desirable for the individual to turn to the decreasing term policy for this purpose. In the amortizing type of mortgage, where part of the principal and interest is paid each month, the

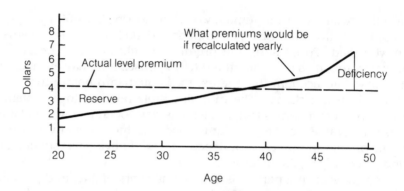

Figure 10–3   *Sample of a level premium policy, and what the premiums would be if they were recalculated on an annual basis.*

amount paid on the principal increases with each monthly payment. Hypothetically, let us assume that when individuals take out a $50,000 mortgage, they make a payment of $550 a month. Assume further that out of the $550 monthly payment, in the first month, $500 is paid in interest and $50 to reduce the principal. This leaves a balance due of $49,950. It is obvious that for purposes of protection, by the end of the first month a $50,000 policy is no longer necessary. The mortgage could be paid off at the end of that first month if the individual or the estate had $49,950. The decreasing term policy can take care of this.

For this purpose, the companies will typically write or issue a level premium policy on a decreasing term contract for as long as the mortgage runs, and the policy will decline with the mortgage. Any payoff turned over to the beneficiary will be sufficient to pay off the mortgage. In short, the contract states in effect that as each month passes, the amount the company will pay on the policy decreases. If the insured dies when only $1,000 is due on the mortgage, this balance will be paid off; or if the insured dies at the end of the first month with a balance due of $49,950, this amount will be paid to the beneficiary. The net result is to cause the average monthly premiums to be considerably lower than they would be if a policy with a fixed amount due is purchased because, as each month passes, the amount the beneficiary will receive is reduced roughly in the same amount that the balance due on the mortgage is reduced.

Cash value life insurance: Permanent insurance

Cash value life insurance (also called permanent insurance) has living benefits or a **cash value.** Consequently, if a person buys permanent insurance, he or she is developing a savings and investment program via insurance. These savings earn only a modest return and are eroded by inflation. We will discuss whole life: this in turn may be broken down into straight life and limited payment life, the endowment policy, plus the recently-developed variable life, and universal life.

Straight life builds up a cash surrender value and may pay dividends. If the dividends are left with the insurance company, a straight life policy may eventually become a paid-up policy. Otherwise premiums are paid for as long as the policy is in force.[1]

As was pointed out in the discussion of the term policy, the premium rates should rise each year as the insured grows older. However, to avoid changing the rates each year, insurance companies developed the idea of averaging the first five years' cost, the second five years' cost, and so forth. Thus in the five-year renewable policy, a constant level premium is paid during the first five years the policy is in force and a new and higher rate is paid during the second five years. The rate thus changes every five years. From this idea of averaging the rates every five years there grew the concept of averaging over an entire lifetime. For example, since it is possible to determine, on the average, the remaining life of a man aged thirty, it is possible to average what the cost of protection would be over the balance of his life. This is what is done. When the thirty-year-old man buys a whole life policy, his annual premium is greater than it would be if he were to purchase the same amount of term insurance. This, in part, is because the policy never expires. All term policies eventually expire. Hence, in the averaging process a straight life policy has to take into account some very high premiums because of advanced age.

As a result of averaging premiums over a lifetime on a policy that never expires, a higher reserve is built up than in the case of a term policy that eventually does expire. Some premiums are paid in advance and are called a **reserve,** which are invested by the insurance company to earn interest income. This is the savings feature of a straight life policy and, because of it, the policy builds up a cash surrender value as the years pass. **Cash surrender value** is the amount available in cash if the owner voluntarily terminates the policy. The policy itself never expires, and premiums continue to be paid until the policyholder dies, at which time the beneficiaries are paid the face value of the policy. However, policyholders may choose to take the cash value (their living benefits) and surrender their policy. Many people do this at an advanced age because they have no one financially dependent upon them. They have had insurance protection when they needed it and they have used insurance as a vehicle to generate savings for their retirement.

The savings feature built into a straight life policy can be described as modest, not heavy, but it is precisely this modest savings feature, together with insurance protection, that has made it appealing to some people. A straight life policy may become paid up if dividends are left with the company. A **dividend** is a return of part of the premium or participating insurance to reflect the difference between the premium

---

1. A straight life policy pays dividends only if it is a participating policy. Most policies purchased from mutual companies and some purchased from stock companies are participating policies.

charged and the combination of actual mortality, expense, and investment experience.

Limited payment life policy

The limited payment life insurance policy is the second type of whole life policy. It carries the idea of the straight life policy a step further. If it can be determined what the annual rates or premiums should be for the straight life policy and what the average lifetime premiums will be, why not divide the lifetime premiums by twenty or thirty and get paid-up insurance? This really amounts to a limited number of installment payments of the premium on such a policy for ten, twenty, thirty years, or to age sixty-five.

This policy provides for permanent protection, but the premiums are paid only for a certain number of years though the protection afforded is for the *whole life* of the individual. The most popular forms are twenty-pay life and thirty-pay life policies. The premium calculation is the same as that for the straight life policy, but, because the payments are made over a shorter period, the yearly or monthly premiums have to be greater. The insured pays much less than the face value of the policy during the limited payment period because the company is able to invest the funds at compound interest from the time the initial payment is made until the time, on the average, when those insured will die. For example, an individual at the age of twenty might be said to have a life expectancy of an additional 51.20 years. Thus, on the average, the company will have the use of the money for many years before it has to pay it out. This also means that the cash value of the policy will continue to rise even after the period for payment of premiums has expired, until eventually, if the insured does not die first, the cash value will equal the face value, and could even rise above it. The main reason for purchasing this type of policy is that some people want to pay for their insurance during the time when their earnings are the highest.

The endowment policy

The endowment policy provides protection for a specified number of years, at the end of which the insured will receive the face amount of the policy. If an individual purchases a $10,000 endowment policy and dies before the end of the specified number of years, his or her beneficiaries will receive the face amount of the policy. If this person lives for the number of years specified in the policy, the policy has matured and he or she will be paid the face value of the policy. At maturity, the face value and the cash surrender value are the same. An endowment policy has a limited number of payments.

People who buy endowments usually do so because they want a specific number of dollars for a specific purpose sometime in the future. Funds to send a child to college or to provide for retirement income or a trip around the world might be financed through an endowment policy.

When the endowment plan is paid up, it is like money in the bank rather than like insurance. When endowments become paid up, they are usually surrendered and the money used for some specific purpose. However, the policy can be left with the insurance company, where the cash surrender value builds up above the face value at some specified interest rate.

The emphasis in an endowment policy is on savings. Premiums on endowment policies are even higher than on the limited payment life policy. Because these premium funds are then invested and earn interest, the amount paid by the company when the policy matures—or to the beneficiaries if the policyholder dies—is greater than the amount paid in as premiums by the individual.

In summary, one can state that in progression from term, to straight life, to limited payment life, to endowments, the premiums rise with any given age because the savings feature also rises greatly. A second reason why the limited payment life and limited payment endowment policies have higher premiums than equal amounts of a straight life policy is because premiums are, in part, paid in advance.

In recent years, two new life insurance policies have been developed: universal life and variable life policies. Both are attempts to protect both the cash value (e.g., the savings feature) and the death benefits of the policy from inflation by investing part of the premiums in high-yielding money market funds or common stock. If the investments do well and the return exceeds inflation, the cash value and the death benefits are increased. In this way, both living and death benefits, it is hoped, will be inflation proof. But it doesn't always work that way. With the premiums invested in common stock, there may be losses as well as gains, and both the cash value and the death benefit can decline. Some policies have a guarantee that the death benefit will never fall below the face value. Even if the premiums are invested primarily in high-yielding securities funds, the return may not be as high as it should be, because there may be high commissions and brokerage or loading fees. Also, money market interest rates may decline.

Universal and variable life insurance

Universal life is a combination of annual renewable term insurance tied to an investment program. The premiums must more than cover the cost of the term insurance for there to be a surplus to invest on the insured's behalf. Moreover, this premium rises as one grows older. Often a universal life policy is set up by making a fairly large lump sum payment, and the insurance company deducts from that deposit once a month enough money from the fund to pay the premiums for the life insurance. Periodic payments may be made into the fund at any time. The face value of term life insurance may also be increased; however term life monthly premium withdrawals will also be increased. This makes the universal policy more flexible than most others. This is an investment fund that is managed by the insurance company and from which the insurance premiums are withdrawn.

Universal life

Such a fund has certain tax benefits; the interest that it earns is not taxed until withdrawn. To be sure, this is true of all insurance policy interest income.

Is universal life a good investment? That depends on how well the company manages the funds, and whether or not the company earns more than individuals could with their own investment program. Generally universal life policies are superior to other cash value insurance policies—such as straight life, limited pay life, and endowments.

Variable life

Variable life is similar to universal life and straight life. It differs from straight life in that premiums are invested primarily in variable assets—such as common stock—that fluctuate in price with inflation. It differs from universal life in that premiums are fixed. Variable life also was developed to protect the policyholder from inflation. Both its face value and its cash value will rise (or fall) if the insurance company is successful in investing in assets that appreciate pricewise with inflation.

What kind of insurance—cash value or term?

What type of life insurance should be bought depends on the individual. Is it being bought primarily for protection or for a savings program? Persons who need protection primarily should weight their insurance program toward term, which gives the maximum amount of insurance for the money. It often appeals to young people who have small children and need a good deal of insurance but have a limited income. However, term insurance eventually expires.

It has been stated that one who can save on one's own should buy term insurance and then bank the differential in premiums between term and straight life. Would a person who did this be better off in twenty years? Whether this is true would depend upon how much interest one could earn. Probably in most cases one could earn a little more in a savings and loan association than in an insurance company, but this is not always true. Also, in some cases there is as tax advantage in saving through life insurance, because any interest earned in a savings and loan association is fully taxable as income, while interest earned via a life insurance policy may not be.[2]

Cash value buildup and net risk to the insurance company

We have seen why and how insurance policies, with the exception of term, build up cash surrender values. The cash surrender value should be looked on as savings by the policyholder; it is like money in the bank because the policyholder may surrender his or her policy, take the cash surrender value (the living benefits), and call it quits at any time. This cash surrender value and the risk the insurance company assumes are

---

2. How life insurance is taxed will be discussed later in the chapter.

illustrated in Figure 10—4. The two bottom curves are for a straight life policy, the two middle are for a twenty-pay life, and the two top are for a twenty-year endowment. The cash surrender value was calculated for a $25,000 face value policy on a twenty-year-old person in each case. The annual premiums are $322.25, $539.75, and $1,047.25, respectively. Each policy has two possible buildups: one (the lower curve) if the annual dividends are taken in cash, and one (the upper curve) if they are left to accumulate more interest. The cash surrender value builds up over the years, as depicted by the curves, and the savings are represented by the surface under the curve. The risk assumed by the insurance company is depicted by the area above the curve, and this risk declines as the years pass.

If the dividends are left with the company, the cash surrender value will build up more quickly and will equal the face value more quickly.

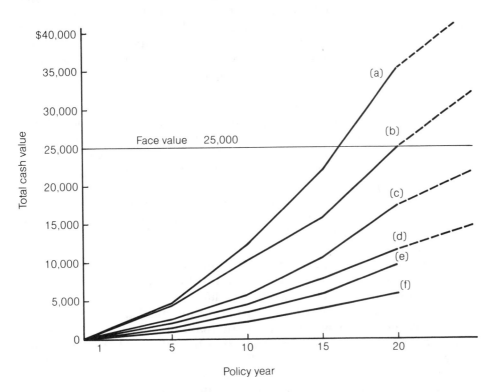

The relationships between cash surrender value and face value for each of three insur-   Figure 10—4
ance policies for a female aged twenty: (a) twenty-year endowment, dividends accumulated; (b) twenty-year endowment, dividends withdrawn; (c) twenty-pay life, dividends accumulated; (d) twenty-pay life, dividends withdrawn; (e) straight life, dividends
accumulated; (f) straight life, dividends withdrawn. Dividends accumulated at interest
are based on a recent dividend scale and are not guaranteed. This figure was furnished
by a large eastern mutual life insurance company.

(If there is a death claim, the companies pay the face value or the cash value, whichever is the larger.) The amount of insurance a person has then declines as the years pass and the cash surrender value builds up.

At the end of twenty years the limited pay life (LPL) and the endowment policy are paid up and premiums are no longer paid. The cash surrender value if not taken by the policyholder will now build up more slowly because only interest return adds to cash value. This is depicted by the dotted line in Figure 10–4. In the case of a whole life policy, the cash surrender value continues at a more uniform rate because in theory this type of policy is never paid up. There are two exceptions to this statement, however. First, if the policyholder outlives the mortality tables—which happens when one reaches the age of one hundred—the policy is paid up. At age one hundred one is actuarially dead, and insurance companies will pay off the policy. One has not won without dying, however, because cash surrender value is equal to face value. The other exception is when dividends are left with the company. In such a case, a straight life policy may become paid up before a person dies even though the person is not one hundred years of age. Whether it does depends on the age of the person when the policy was bought and upon the interest rate the insurance company is able to earn. Any policy will build up more quickly if dividends are left with the company.

OTHER TYPES OF LIFE INSURANCE
Group life insurance

The major difference between life insurance sold to an individual and that sold to a group is one of administration. Insurance is often sold by the life insurance company to a business firm, and the business firm provides each insured employee with an insurance certificate. The premiums may be withheld from the employees' salaries, they may be paid entirely by the employer, or they may be shared. A second difference between group life insurance and insurance sold to an individual is that group life involves neither an individual medical examination nor an individual application for insurance.

The group insurance package commonly consists of some term, which provides for benefits on the death of the policyholder, and some medical insurance (which is health, not life, insurance and is discussed in the next chapter) to pay for all or part of the medical bills of the employees covered. Usually employees automatically lose this group insurance when they leave the company, even by retirement. However, employees have the right to convert their group insurance to an individual policy after leaving the employer, without a medical examination. If they do convert, they pay the higher premiums that individual policies require.

Group insurance is nearly always cheaper than individual insurance, for several reasons. First, the employer may pay all or part of the premiums. Even if not, the administrative cost to the insurance company is less, and part of these savings are passed on to the policyholder. Since only one policy is written for many individuals, underwriting costs are reduced. Clerical and accounting costs are less for the same reasons, and

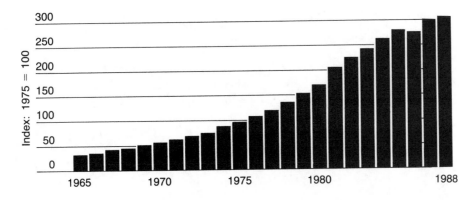

Growth of group life insurance in the United States. (Source: Life Insurance Fact Book,   Figure 10−5
1989, p. 4.)

the costs of premium collection also are less because the company involved remits one check per month for all the employees. In addition, commissions to insurance salespeople are eliminated or greatly reduced, the contract being often negotiated directly by the insurance company and the business whose employees are to be covered. Finally, in some cases a person saves because the premiums are determined by the average of the employees covered. Because of this the younger members of the group subsidize the older in some cases. In other cases, the group is broken into six or eight age categories, and the premium for each category is determined by the average age therein. Most group plans are sold via a common employer; self-employed individuals should check their professional organizations, which often have a group plan. Group life insurance is the modern way to buy life insurance because it is cheaper. However, there are limits, imposed by state law, on the maximum amount of group life insurance a person may buy—usually some multiple of the person's annual income. Because of this limit, group insurance cannot be looked on as a complete insurance plan. Figure 10−5 shows the growth of group life insurance in recent years.

Credit life insurance

Another type of life insurance policy is the ***credit life policy.*** Many financial institutions require that anyone borrowing money on a personal note be insured for the amount of the note. Thus a bank or other lending institution will automatically sell a creditor enough insurance to cover the amount of the loan in the event the borrower dies before the debt is paid. The lender merely sells the borrower the credit insurance; the institution has an arrangement with an insurance company that actually carries the policy.

Credit life insurance is a specialized type of term policy. It is also most often sold on a group basis; the lender has an arrangement with an

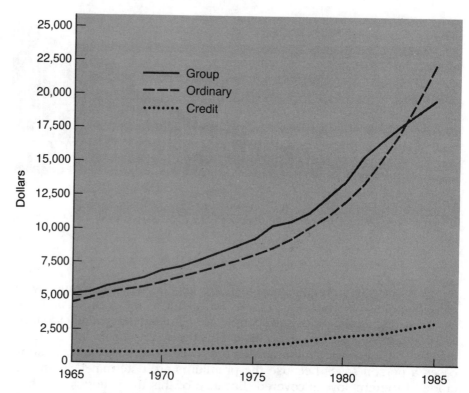

Figure 10–6   *Average size life insurance policy in force in the United States.* (Source: Life Insurance Fact Book, 1986, p. 22.)

insurance company whereby all of its borrowing customers are covered by one plan. Figure 10–6 illustrates the average size of the various types of life insurance in effect.

GI life insurance (government insurance)

Military persons are eligible to buy up to $50,000 of term life insurance from the government. It is a group policy officially called Servicemen's Group Life Insurance, administered by the Veteran's Administration, with insurance provided by private insurance companies. The government acts just like an employer and buys a group plan for all service personnel. When people leave the service, they have one hundred twenty days in which to convert their insurance with a civilian insurance company without taking a medical examination. If they do not convert, the insurance lapses. The government underwrites this insurance by paying part of the premiums, but the service men and women pay 80¢ per month per $10,000 of insurance. This permium is fixed and does not rise with the age of the insured.

First, an insurance company must be selected. Not all companies are the same; premiums vary for a number of reasons. Life insurance benefits are taxed differently, and there are certain other benefits and options that a policyholder enjoys.

There are more than 2,100 life insurance companies in the United States, and they are not all the same. There are big and small, and stock and mutual companies. Therefore, when buying something so important, one should shop around.

Selecting a company: why premiums vary

Premiums of course vary with the type of policy and the age of the insured. Table 10–3 shows this variation; the premiums shown are annual premiums per $1,000 of insurance. Premiums must be set high enough to meet the expenses of running the company, expenses that are largely wages and salaries of the insurance company employees.

Premiums also vary from company to company for like policies on individuals of the same age. The following factors help explain this variation.

1. Some companies have a more favorable mortality experience, that is, their death claims are fewer (or come later) per ten thousand policyholders, and hence their mortality tables are more favorable than those of other companies.

Annual premiums per $1,000 insurance   Table 10–3

Age	Term 1 yr	Straight life SL	LPL 20L	LPE 20E
Male				
18	$1.79	$ 8.26	$19.15	$44.93
19	1.79	8.44	19.47	44.94
20	1.79	8.52	19.68	44.96
30	1.91	11.88	24.68	45.33
40	2.76	17.82	30.58	47.24
50	6.51	28.22	44.45	52.90
Female				
18	$1.58	$ 7.74	$18.63	$44.77
19	1.58	7.91	18.94	44.77
20	1.58	8.92	19.13	44.79
30	1.77	12.95	23.21	45.09
40	2.24	15.77	28.53	46.34
50	5.11	24.40	36.63	51.06

Figures furnished by a large eastern mutual life insurance company.

2. Not all companies are equally efficient. Some have higher administrative and clerical costs than others.

3. Some companies earn a higher rate of return on their investments than others.

While there is an official mortality table (the Commissioners Standard Ordinary [CSO]), insurance companies are permitted to use their own mortality experience with only the proviso that it cannot be less favorable to the policyholder than the CSO. Consequently, with different mortality tables, premiums can vary somewhat from company to company.

Furthermore, not all companies are equally well managed and hence their costs are not the same. Even with companies that are equally well managed, the expense of running the insurance company, per $1,000 of life insurance in force, may vary with the size of the company and how fast it is growing. Generally newer and smaller companies have higher costs than older and larger companies, but there are exceptions. The percentage yield on the investments that a company earns will vary from company to company. A company that consistently earns more can either pay a higher dividend or charge a lower premium.

A final reason why insurance premiums vary is that two different policies from two different companies, while they appear about the same, may not be. Only one of them may have a dismemberment clause, which provides so much for the loss of an arm or a leg. A person may or may not want this coverage; but if the policy has it, he or she will pay more. Also the guaranteed cash surrender value buildup over the years may differ on two otherwise like policies. In such as case, different amounts of savings are built into otherwise similar policies. This can, of course, be done by varying premiums or dividends.

Thus, a better bargain may be obtained by shopping around and comparing companies' policies. Some weight should also be given to the financial strength and soundness of the insurance company. While total assets of the insurer are important, they are not the only factor to consider because there are also liabilities. It is difficult to compare the financial soundness of the various insurers, but one meaningful bench mark is referred to as the policyholder's "surplus ratio." It is simple—the insurance company's net worth (assets less liabilities) divided by liabilities. It can easily be calculated from an insurance company's balance sheet.

Another suggestion is to check with an insurance agent or local library for a copy of *Best's Insurance Guide* published by A. M. Best Company, a "watchdog" of the insurance industry. Its *Guide* can give information on the company's background, financial strength, and overall rating.

Insurance companies are regulated by the states. It is the task of the regulatory agencies to make sure that the insurers are sufficiently sound. However, the rigor of these agencies (and the stringency of the laws under which they operate) varies from state to state. More confidence may be placed in an insurance company if it operates in many, and especially in all, states. Since New York state has the toughest (best from the consumer's point of view) insurance laws, some financial advisers suggest that a bit more confidence may be placed in an insurance company that operates in New York.

Comparing term policies is usually simple enough. Since often no dividend is involved and there is no cash surrender value, a simple comparison of premiums per $1,000 of face value is all that is required.

Comparing different companies' policies

In the case of cash value insurance, the analysis is more complex, but two or more similar policies can be analyzed to see which appears to be the better buy. This can only be approximated. First, subtract the likely dividends from the gross annual premiums. Since future dividends are unknown, they must be estimated based on past experience. This calculation will give the approximate net annual premiums. Next, multiply this by, say, 5, and 10, and 20, to get the total premiums over the years. Then compare that to what the cash surrender value (which can be predicted with accuracy and which is stated in the policy) of the policy will be in 5, and 10, and 20 years. If this is done with several policies, an individual will be able to spot the better buy. However, while this can give a comparison among several policies, it ignores the interest which could have been earned if the premium dollars had been invested elsewhere. It also ignores the present value of dollars payable in the future, and future dollars are likely to be worth less than present dollars.

The recently developed interest-adjusted indexes attempt to consider factors and in so doing compare the cost of different policies. In the interest-adjusted method of calculating costs, each year's premium is assumed to earn interest (at, say, 5 percent). In calculating the index we first obtain the total (say 20 years) accumulation of premiums plus interest. From this we subtract, first, all dividends plus interest on them, and, second, the cash value of the policy at the end of twenty years. The result is the total (20 year) cost of the policy. It is then divided by the number of $1,000 units of coverage to get the 20-year cost per $1,000 of insurance. This cost per $1,000 is then divided again by a factor (34.57 in our case).[3] The final result is a dollar figure that if set aside each year at 5 percent would equal the net dollar cost of the policy. This will vary from company to company, but a recent random sample of nine different companies indicated that this interest-adjusted cost figure on a straight life policy on a thirty-five-year-old man varied from a low of $4.33 to a high of $6.68. While this interest-adjusted index is only an approximation, it is a useful measure of the difference in the cost of a policy.

---

3. This ($34.57) is the amount of money a person would have if one dollar were added per year for twenty years and these dollars were earning interest at 5 percent. In many tables this figure is 33.066, but this is because most tables accrue no interest until the end of the year, whereas in our case we earn interest continuously over the entire year.

Grace period

After a premium is due but not paid, there is generally **grace period** of twenty-eight to thirty-one days during which the premium may be paid without penalty. In the event that a policyholder dies during the grace period, the unpaid premium is collected from the amount paid to the beneficiary.

Reinstatement

Most policies contain a provision for reinstatement. If a policy has lapsed, it may, within a stated period, be put into effect again provided the policyholder is insurable, and of course this implies another physical examination. If the physical is passed, the overdue premiums together with interest must then be paid.

Incontestability

After one or two years, a policy will ordinarily be incontestable. This means that the company is given one or two years in which to check certain information given by the policyholder when he or she made the original application for the policy. If the company discovers that a materially false statement was made, it may seek to have itself released from the policy. After the incontestable period has passed, however, the company can no longer seek such release.

Nonfortfeiture value

What happens if one can no longer pay the premiums for some reason? Term insurance, which has no cash surrender value, will lapse after the grace period. If it is permanent life insurance and has built up a cash surrender value, one has four options. (Recall from the discussion that generally all policies except term build up a cash value after they have been in force for a few years and that this cash value increases as the years pass.) One's options are assured by the nonfortfeiture values that in a sense guarantee the cash surrender value of the policy. These four options are:

1. *Cash value.* A policy can be surrendered for its cash value. This cash surrender value can be taken in one lump sum or in a number of regular payments if it is large enough (usually $1,000 or more).
2. *Extended term insurance.* Often a policy includes a provision that if the holder fails to pay the premiums after the grace period, the policy automatically will remain in force as a term policy for as long as the cash surrender value of the policy will permit. For example, suppose one has a $4,000 cash surrender value in a $20,000 ordinary life insurance policy and he or she has failed to pay the premium after the grace period. Under the terms of the policy, the amount of cash surrendered value ($4,000) may be enough to keep that policy in force as term insurance for nine or ten years. The $4,000 equity in the policy actually is used to pay the premium on what will now be an **extended term policy.**

3. *Reduced paid-up insurance.* If one no longer wishes to pay premiums, one can reduce the face value of life insurance but keep it in force as paid-up permanent insurance. Then the $4,000 cash surrender value on the $20,000 policy might provide a paid-up policy with a face value of $10,000. This is now paid up and in force, and the death payment would become $10,000 but the individual no longer needs to pay premiums.
4. *Automatic premium loan* (APL). Some insurance policies have a provision that grants the insured an automatic loan used to pay the premiums after the grace period has expired if the policy has a cash value. This is designed to prevent the policy from lapsing due to the insured accidentally forgetting to pay the premiums, which might happen if he or she is on an extended trip. Then upon the policyholder's return the loan could be repaid and the insurance continue in its original form.

A person may borrow the cash surrender value of his or her life insurance policy from the company. Most states have laws requiring these loans to be made by insurance companies. However, insurance companies may wait as long as several months before making the loan. In practice, however, they make the money available almost immediately.

Borrowing on a life insurance policy

Insurance companies charge about 8 percent (annual percentage rate) interest on these loans, which is as low a rate as a person can get anywhere. The insurance companies must obtain the small interest which they charge because were it not for the policy loan they would invest the money elsewhere and their investment income would be greater. Since the insurance contract is made with an assumption of certain interest income, they have to charge a rate on policy loans.

There can be a danger in borrowing from one's insurance company. First of all, these loans are single repayment rather than installment loans. Therefore, some budgeting must be done and a sum set aside every week or month in order to liquidate the loan eventually. Moreover, there is no obligation ever to repay the loan. Some people just continue to pay the interest. If there is a death claim on a policy with a loan outstanding, it is deducted before the face value is paid. In some states the borrower is not even required to pay the loan interest.

It is frequently possible to use one's life insurance policy as collateral (and hence reduce the interest rate) when borrowing money from banks and others. Lenders may feel it desirable for them to be assigned the policy, so that if the borrower dies before repaying the obligation, the debt will be paid from the proceeds of the policy. To assign a policy, however, one must have the right to change the beneficiary; otherwise, it will be necessary to obtain the beneficiary's consent. Furthermore, the policy specifically states that no assignment will be binding on the company until the company has been notified.

Assignment

Ownership of the policy

In a life insurance contract, there are the insured, the beneficiaries, and the owner of the policy. The meaning of *insured* and *beneficiary* is clear and needs no further elaboration, but the term *owner* requires explanation.

Usually, but not always, the insured is also the owner. The insured can turn ownership over to the beneficiary. The owner of the policy, while living, has the right to modify the policy, change the beneficiary (if he or she has reserved that right in the policy), select the settlement options, surrender or cancel the policy, receive any insurance dividends, and any other rights which may exist. On the death of the insured (who may or may not be the owner) ownership of the policy is immediately and automatically transferred to the beneficiary.

One reason why a person may want to transfer ownership to the beneficiary prior to death is to avoid estate taxes. (Estate taxes are discussed in Chapter 19.) If the beneficiary is not the owner prior to the death of the insured, then, although the beneficiary receives the insurance claim upon the death of the insured, it is subject to the deceased's estate tax (not income tax, but estate tax). If the beneficiary is the owner, this tax is avoided. To make certain that this tax savings is realized, however, the owner-beneficiary should have his or her own checking account and pay the insured's premiums with his or her own personal checks. The actual transfer of ownership to the beneficiary is also a gift, and if the cash surrender value of the policy is large, this could have gift tax implications. (See Chapter 19 for a discussion of gift taxes.)

One word of warning: if ownership of a policy is transferred to the beneficiary, the insured loses all control over it and can never change the beneficiary or the settlement options, nor will he or she receive the dividends it may pay. In addition, if the owner-beneficiary dies before the insured, the cash value of the policy becomes part of the beneficiary's estate.

Change of beneficiary: Third party rights

There may be many reasons why one might want the beneficiary in a policy changed, such as marriage, divorce, or newborn children. To effect such a change at any time, one must have reserved the right to change the beneficiary when originally taking out the policy; most policies contain a clause giving this right. The company will furnish the proper forms. In some cases, where the insured has failed to reserve the right to change the beneficiary when taking out the policy, he or she must first obtain the consent of the present beneficiary in writing before the company will permit the change to be made.

What happens if a named beneficiary dies before the policyholder? Normally the company pays the money directly to one's estate when the insured dies. However, one or more persons can be, and usually are, named in the policy as contingent beneficiaries. In this case, the contingent beneficiary or beneficiaries receive the proceeds of the policy should the first-named beneficiary die before the insured.

Several different settlement options may be chosen that will determine how insurance benefits are to be paid. These options may be selected by the insured or the beneficiary, depending on the circumstances. The insured has first choice, and may choose the settlement option during his or her lifetime, and he or she may change it at any time. After the insured dies, the beneficiary must live with whatever options have been chosen. If the insured dies before having chosen the options, however, then the beneficiary may choose them.

There are four general options from which to choose:

1. *Lump sum.* In this case the entire sum is paid at once, and the beneficiary has the money management problem. However, when interest rates are high, this person might be able to earn more on his or her lump sum settlement than the insurance company.

2. *Interest payment only.* Under this option the insurance company retains the principal sum and pays the beneficiary the interest earned. These payments could be made for a specific period of years or for life. Eventually the principal would have to go to someone. It could go to the primary beneficiary if still alive and if the interest is paid for only a limited number of years. Otherwise the principal would go to the secondary beneficiary. If only interest is paid, the principal is never exhausted, and some provisions must be made to pay it to someone eventually. Sometimes arrangements are made whereby the beneficiary can dip into the principal within limits. This would reduce future interest payments, but would provide flexibility and an additional source of money for the beneficiary in the event of an emergency.

3. *Installment payments.* The company makes regular payments in equal amounts until the fund is exhausted. During the time that such regular payments are being made, the company will add interest to the part of the money not paid out. There are two ways this option could be set up. One would provide for a specific amount, say, $500 per month. In such a case the length of time for which the payments could be made would depend on the amount of the payment, the dollar cash value of the policy, and the rate of interest earned by the company.

   The second method is to set up the payments for a specific number of years—say, ten or fifteen. Then the amount of each payment depends on the amount of the dollar cash value, the number of years selected, and the rate of interest earned.

   Thus, one can decide the payments are to be made as a stated sum per month or for a stated number of years. The installment option may also have a provision to permit the beneficiary to "commute" the remaining payments, or to stop the income payments and choose to take all the money that remains in one final payment. The policyholder may also arrange that any money left when the first beneficiary dies shall be paid in one sum or continued as income to one or more secondary beneficiaries.

4. *Life annuity income.* One may elect to receive as a settlement a life annuity income. Briefly, a life annuity gives the beneficiary, or annuitant, a stated income for as long as he or she lives. (See Chapter 18.)

In some annuity plans, if the annuitant dies before the payments reach a stated total amount or before the payments have been made for a stated period of time, arrangements can be made to have the payments made to a secondary beneficiary. Under the annuity option the amount of each payment depends on several factors, including the age of the annuitant when payment begins, his or her life expectancy, the rate of interest earned, the form of life annuity settlement used, and the amount of the policy's cash value. Figure 10–7 shows how life insurance benefits have grown over the last few years.

Another variation of this option is sometimes chosen if there are two or more primary beneficiaries—the joint survivorship life income annuity. It is the same as life annuity income just described, except that payments are made until both beneficiaries are deceased.

Disability premium waiver

The waiver of premium, or what is more commonly referred to as a "disability clause" in a life insurance policy, means that any premiums that fall due after the beginning of a total and permanent disability will be waived. Thus if one is disabled, the life insurance policy will continue in

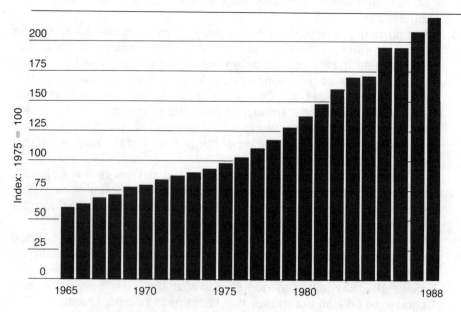

Figure 10–7   *Relative growth in average size life insurance death benefit payments in the United States. (Source: Life Insurance Fact Book, 1989, p. 17.)*

force because the company will make the premium payments. Disability must occur before one has reached a certain age, generally age sixty, and before the policy is paid up. In some cases, the disability must last for at least six months before premiums will be waived.

To have such a disability clause written into the policy, the insured must request it and must pay a small additional premium. The disability clause written into a policy really amounts to taking out additional insurance to insure that the premiums will continue to be paid if the policyholder is disabled. The addition to the premium is so small that its inclusion is recommended.

The clause relating to accidental death benefits is sometimes also called "double indemnity." Under the provisions of this clause, the company promises to pay twice the face value of the policy if death occurs by accidental means. If the death is to be construed as "accidental," it must occur within a certain time after one is injured. Suppose, for example, that an injury occurs that causes hospitalization for, say, one year, and after a year death can be directly attributed to the accident. In such a case, the accidental death benefit clause of the policy will probably not apply. Most policies state that death must occur within ninety days after the accident to be construed as accidental death. Furthermore, there is commonly a second limitation to the accidental death clause: the accidental death must have occurred before age sixty or sixty-five, depending on the policy.

Accidental death benefits

The double indemnity clause further excludes from the meaning of "accidental" death death arising from certain kinds of accidents. The reason is either that these deaths result from risks that cannot be calculated or that the cause of death is not accidental in the legal sense. For instance, if a person jumps from a moving car, his or her death is suicide, not an accident, and the double indemnity will not hold. Or if a person has a heart attack while driving a car and is killed in an accident caused by the attack, that person is not covered even though the death is caused by the accident, not the heart attack.

It is even possible to obtain a triple indemnity clause in an insurance policy. In such a case, the company pays three times the face value in the event of accidental death as defined above. An added premium must be paid in order to obtain either a double or a triple indemnity clause.

There has been much discussion over the respective merits of these companies. The **stock company** is a corporation, the ownership of which is in the hands of stockholders, and, as in any other corporation, the business affairs of the corporation are run by a board of directors. The profit, if any, is distributed to the stockholders much in the same manner as that of any corporation.

Stock insurance companies versus mutual companies

A ***mutual life insurance company,*** on the other hand, is owned by the policyholders. No stock is issued. The management of the mutual company is entrusted to experts in the insurance business just as the management of the stock company is placed in the hands of experts.

Insurance dividends

The distinction between stock and mutual companies is important because of dividends. Historically, insurance dividends have been paid by mutual companies to their policyholders. These should not be confused with the stock dividends given as a share of the profits to the stockholders of the stock companies. In the mutual company, if the income exceeds the amount needed to pay beneficiaries and expenses, part of it is returned to the policyholders in the form of dividends. The policyholder is generally given a choice of receiving the cash, applying the amount to subsequent premiums, buying paid-up additional insurance, or leaving it with the company at interest.

To compete with dividends paid to mutual policyholders, some stock companies issue a participating type of policy, which provides that the policyholder will share in the profits of the corporation along with the shareholders. Generally the premium rates of the participating policies are higher than those of the nonparticipating policies.

Frequently, the premiums on policies issued by stock companies are lower than those issued by mutual companies. These are the nonparticipating policies. Some stock companies, then, issue both participating and nonparticipating policies. Both of these are a competitive device to offset wholly or partially the dividends paid by the mutual companies to their policyholders. Some stock companies argue that the dividends paid by the mutual companies are not all earnings being paid to the policyholders; these critics say that mutual companies charge too much in premiums in the first place and are thus merely returning the excess premiums. Mutual companies are quick to deny this charge.

When buying life insurance and trying to choose between mutual and stock companies, keep in mind both the premiums and the dividends. The problem is often difficult because dividends are not guaranteed; however, a record of past dividends is usually available.

Keep in mind, when deciding between buying a policy from a mutual or stock company, the guaranteed buildup of cash surrender value. While the guaranteed cash buildup of stock companies is often somewhat higher than that guaranteed by mutual companies, the actual achieved cash buildup of the mutuals is usually better, especially in the long run. This is because if mutual companies earn more than they guarantee, they add it to the cash value, and in recent years this has happened. In the case of stock companies, any earnings in excess of that guaranteed may go to the stockholders, not the policyholders. Hence, the actual and the guaranteed cash buildups of a policy from a stock company are more likely to be the same, or at least closer to each other.

Regardless of whether insurance dividends are a return of premiums or shared interest which the company earned with the policyholders' premiums, a policyholder receiving them must decide what to do with them.[4] There are several alternatives from which to choose.

1. Take the dividend in cash and use as any other income.
2. Apply the dividend toward the payment of future premiums. The dividend will usually grow larger as the years pass because the cash surrender value grows larger, and after a time the dividends alone may pay the entire premium.
3. Leave the dividend with the company to be compounded at the going interest rate and continue to pay the regular premiums; then the cash surrender value of the policy will build up more rapidly than if option 1 or 2 were selected. However, under option 3 the policyholder will have to declare on his or her federal income tax the *added* interest that the company earns with the dividends. The dividend itself, however, is not taxable, but the interest earned with it is; the company will send a statement indicating the amount of the interest.
4. Use the dividends to buy paid-up additional insurance. Then the face value of the policy goes up some every year, and this incremental amount is paid up. A person who needs more life insurance may want to select this fourth option because it will save commissions. However, buying paid-up additions is like buying a single-premium-payment life insurance policy. One is really paying all future premiums in advance, and while the companies make an allowance for this, it is not very high. Consequently, a single-premium paid-up policy is more expensive than buying insurance the usual way. However, one's dividends might very well add several hundred dollars of paid-up additions each year. This fourth option also results in the cash surrender value rising more rapidly than if option 1 or 2 were selected but less rapidly than if option 3 were selected. Selecting option 4 also relieves the policyholder from having to pay federal income taxes on the interest that the dividend earns as in the case of option 3, because the dividend earns no interest. It is spent on more insurance. The dividend earns no interest if option 1 or 2 were selected. Only under option 3 does the dividend earn interest. If option 4 were selected, more dividends will be earned on the insurance purchased with previous dividends.
5. Use the annual dividend to buy one-year term. This will increase the face value of the policy by more than option 4 will for a number of

---

4. The Internal Revenue Service has ruled that the entire dividend is a return of premiums for tax purposes. Hence, insurance policy dividends are not taxable.

years. After a time, however, option 5 may no longer be a means of providing the maximum amount of insurance because under option 4 the added insurance is permanent and the cumulative amount of it may surpass the amount of annual term which may be purchased. If this option were selected, the cash surrender value will build up at the same rate as under options 1 and 2.

**Box 10—1
The seven don'ts
for your client**

After taking out insurance policies many people handle them poorly. The following suggests that there are proper ways of handling policies.

1. *Don't let insurance go to the wrong people.* In the event of a divorce, it is necessary that the beneficiary be changed. If a person remarries and forgets to change the beneficiary, then the first spouse will receive the proceeds of the policy in the event of the insured's death. Everyone's insurance program should be periodically reviewed. Every time a situation arises that changes the insurance needs, an individual should review his or her insurance program to make it conform with the changed circumstances.

2. *Don't let insurance dollars be foolishly dissipated.* The problem here is whether or not the beneficiaries should be given lump-sum payments or monthly payments. Some people cannot handle large sums properly.

3. *Don't forget to pay the premiums when they come due.* Most policies carry a thirty-one-day grace period, which means that even if one fails to pay on time, the policy will stay in force during that period. After that period, however, in order to reinstate the contract it may be necessary to take a new physical examination. In the event that an unsuspected change in one's health occurs, it may be impossible to reinstate the policy.

4. *Don't give up policies thoughtlessly.* Changing the kind of insurance one has by taking advantage of conversion privileges in one's policy is often a wise move but not so dropping one policy and buying another. A change in policies is very likely to turn out disadvantageously. Irreplaceable guarantees may be lost. Moreover, the cost of setting up policies is substantial, and since the insurance company applies this to the policyholder in the early years, no cash surrender value is built up on a new policy for a while.

5. *Don't hide policies in out-of-the-way places.* A mislaid policy delays prompt settlement of a death claim. Make sure the family knows where policies are kept.

6. *Don't ever throw away a policy, even if the premiums become unafford-able.* Many a supposedly worthless policy has been discovered to contain valuable benefits available to an individual or his or her heirs.

7. *Don't ever overlook the borrowing power of policies.* Insurance companies will lend money against the cash value of a policy at relatively low rates of interest.

Death benefits are not subject to the personal income tax but may be subject to estate taxes. Living benefits from a traditional policy are not taxable most of the time, but there are a few exceptions. There is no tax while the cash value builds up; when it is surrendered the cash value is taxable only if it is greater than the sum of the three following items:

Taxes and life insurance benefits

1. The total of all of the premiums paid over the years, less any dividends taken in cash over the years.
2. The total of all of the dividends left with the company over the years.
3. The total of all the interest earned by dividends over the years and which was taxed along the way.

In such a case, the tax is on the excess. For example, if a policyholder surrenders his or her policy for $15,000, after having paid over the years premiums—less dividends taken in cash over the years—totaling $12,000, and having left dividends with the company of $2,000, and having earned $500 with those dividends, the tax is levied on $500.

SUMMARY REVIEW QUESTIONS

These questions serve as a summary and a review of the chapter. If you are able to answer them all, you have a good understanding of the material covered by the chapter.

1. What are the reasons why people buy life insurance? Who should buy it?
2. When is the best time to buy life insurance?
3. What is the only valid reason for buying life insurance on a child?
4. What are the two main factors to consider in determining how much life insurance to buy?
5. Why should a family's principal wage earner think of insuring his or her partner's life?
6. What is term insurance?
7. If insurance premiums rise with age, how can life insurance companies sell level premium insurance?

8. What is cash value or permanent insurance?
9. How is term insurance different from (1) straight life, (2) limited payment life, (3) an endowment policy?
10. What are variable and universal life insurance?
11. What is meant by guaranteed cash buildup? How do life insurance companies guarantee this?
12. Why is group insurance cheaper than ordinary life?
13. Why do premiums vary from company to company?
14. How does the grace period in a life insurance policy relate to a policy lapse?
15. Explain the nonforfeiture value and how it works.
16. How does a person change the beneficiary of his or her life insurance policy?
17. Discuss the method and possible reason for an assignment of a policy.

18. What is a waiver of premium in a life insurance policy?
19. Discuss life insurance policy dividends. What alternatives does a person have as to how he or she disposees of dividends? Are they taxable?
20. How are life insurance benefits taxed?

CASES

1. Bill Rider is 25 years of age and believes his insurance needs will be low or nonexistent in 30 years. His current needs, however, are great because he has 3 dependents. He is considering one of the following policies:

Type of policy	Face amount	Actual premium	Cash value in 30 years
30-yr. term	$100,000	$ 580	0
Straight life	50,000	595	$25,860
Straight life	100,000	1,190	51,740

(a) If Bill were to die before 30 years, what would each policy pay?
(b) What would each policy pay if surrendered after 30 years?
(c) Would Bill be better off buying the term policy and banking the difference in premiums?
(d) What policy would you recommend?

2. Myrtle and Alfred Newman are in their early thirties and have two children—a boy of six and a girl of four. Myrtle has not worked outside the home since their son was born. Alfred, who works for a large retail store, earns $30,000 per year take-home pay. They are buying their home and have a monthly payment of $800. Alfred has converted his $10,000 GI life insurance policy and is paying premiums on it. Also he has a $100,000 group life insurance policy on which his employer pays all the premiums. Recently an insurance agent suggested that Alfred buy more insurance and recommended term insurance. Should they take the agent's advice and buy more? If so, should they buy term? If more insurance is required, how much more would you recommend?

3. Donald and Sally McLaughlen are aged forty and thirty-five, respectively, and they have two children, ten and eight. Donald has an annual income after taxes of $32,000 per year and feels that his $35,000 of life insurance is adequate. However, Sally, who earns $22,000 a year, and the children have no life insurance. Do you recommend life insurance for them? Why or why not? If insurance should be purchased, how much?

4. Barbara Kidd is a 21-year-old senior in college. She is single and has no immediate plans to marry. She has accepted a job at $28,000 a year as an accountant with a large CPA firm when she graduates in June. She has no life insurance at present, but will have a health insurance plan and $50,000 of group term life with her employer. Barbara is uncertain whether or not she should buy an individual plan for either savings or pro-

tection. Work out an insurance plan for Barbara, and advise her as to how much and what kind of insurance she should buy.

5. Mary Rupp has decided she should buy an additional $40,000 of life insurance. The insurance agent has told her she could have term, straight life, limited pay life, or a limited pay endowment plan. Mary has noticed a difference in the premiums and requests your clarification.

6. Peter Calcins has a $20,000 straight life policy which has been paying dividends of about $100 per year recently. Peter has been taking the dividend in cash rather than leaving it to accumulate with the company because of tax reasons. What is this tax reason? What else could Peter do with his dividends? What else could he do and still not pay taxes on them?

7. Wesley and Mary Roberts are a young couple in their early twenties. They have two children, a girl aged four and a boy aged six. Wesley earns $18,000 at his job with a local manufacturing plant. Mary is a former schoolteacher and will probably go back to work when their daughter starts school. Wesley has a good group medical plan where he works but no life insurance; however, he is a veteran of the armed forces and has $10,000 of government life insurance. He is wondering whether he should buy more life insurance, and if so, what kind and how much. Can you help him?

8. Alfred and Ruth McLain are a young couple in their early twenties who have just graduated from college. They have no children yet but hope to in the future. Alfred has just taken a job as a traveling representative with a large book publisher. Alfred and Ruth would like to begin planning their insurance program now, even though they do not feel they can at this time afford all the insurance they would like. Alfred makes $26,000 per year. Although Alfred's salary is modest at present, he feels he will double it over the next ten years, after which time it will probably level off. Can you plan an insurance program for them? Note the kind and amount of insurance they should have today and ten years from today.

SUGGESTED READINGS

American Society of Chartered Life Underwriters (CLU) Journal. Bryn Mawr, Pa.: The American Society of Chartered Life Underwriters. Quarterly publication.

Best's Review, Life-Health Edition. Oldwick, N.J.: A.M. Best Company, Inc. Monthly publication.

Black, Kenneth, and Skipper, Harold. *Life Insurance,* 11th ed. Englewood Cliffs, N.J.: Prentice-Hall, 1987.

Cockerell, Hugh. *Lloyd's of London.* Homewood, Ill.: Dow Jones-Irwin, 1984.

Consumer Reports Editors. *The Consumer's Union Report on Life Insurance: A Guide to Planning and Buying the Protection You Need.*

Dorfman, Mark S. *Introduction to Insurance,* 3rd ed. Englewood Cliffs, N.J.: Prentice-Hall, 1987.

Finance Facts Yearbook. Washington, D.C.: National Consumer Finance Association. Annual publication.

Greene, Mark R., and Trieschmann, James. "Risk and Insurance." Cincinnati: South-Western, 1984.

Huebner, Solomon S., and Black, Kenneth, Jr. *Life Insurance,* 8th ed. Englewood Cliffs, N.J.: Prentice-Hall, 1987.

Insurance Review. New York: The Insurance Information Institute. Monthly publication.

"The Journal of Insurance." New York: The Insurance Information Institute. Bimonthly publication.

Kenton, Walter S., Jr. *How Life Insurance Companies Rob You and What You Can Do About It.* New York: Random House, 1984.

Life Insurance Fact Book. New York: Institute of Life Insurance. Annual publication.

Mehr, Robert, and Gustavson, Sandra G. *Life Insurance; Theory and Practice.* Plano, Tex.: Business Publications, Inc., 1987.

National Underwriter. Chicago: The National Underwriter Co. Weekly publication.

"On the Way Up; A Description of Life Insurance and Annuities." Hartford, Conn.: Aetna Life Insurance Co.

A Shopper's Guide to Life Insurance; A Shopper's Guide to Term Life Insurance. Harrisburg, Pa.: Pennsylvania Insurance Dept.

Understanding Life Insurance, A Basic Guidebook. Milwaukee: Northwestern Mutual Life Insurance Co.

Vaughan, Emmet J. *Fundamentals of Risk and Insurance,* 5th ed. New York: John Wiley and Sons, 1988.

11 Health care and health insurance

HIGHLIGHTS

Health care is vital; health care is also expensive. In order to help the client manage the risk of sickness and injury and learn how to finance its high cost, this chapter will examine the following:

1   The expense involved in health care
2   The various types of health insurance, both medical insurance and disability insurance, and explain what they are intended to do
3   Major medical insurance to cover larger costs
4   How much health insurance to buy
5   Certain other things about health insurance
6   Some nonprofit health plans
7   A checklist to enable a person to evaluate his or her health insurance

INTRODUCTION

There are two major risks involved insofar as health is concerned. They are:

1. Loss of assets (savings) due to heavy medical expenses, and
2. Loss of earnings when unable to work.

These risks may both be managed by buying insurance. Hospital and medical expense insurance is needed to pay for the high cost of medical care, and disability insurance to replace lost income due to accident or illness.

Physicians' fees and hospital costs have been rising rapidly in recent years and will no doubt continue to do so. It is possible, in the absence of insurance, for a major illness quickly to exhaust the savings of even the upper-middle income groups and force them deeply into debt.

The cost of a hospital room can easily run in excess of $300 per day. Expensive laboratory tests and the use of other expensive equipment are extra. Doctors' and surgeons' fees can in some cases amount to thousands of dollars. The American public spent over $590 billion on health care in 1989. In recent years the cost of health care has been rising more rapidly than the overall price level because of new, expensive, sophisticated equipment; more skilled personnel; better care; and an enormous increase in the demand for medical services generated by government programs. Figure 11–1 shows national health expenditures as a percent of gross national product over the last few years.

Table 11–1 shows how health care costs have risen relative to other items.

Medical expense insurance

Medical expense insurance has been developed to protect the individual from such high medical costs. **Medical insurance** covers medical expenses, including doctors' fees, cost of drugs, hospital bills, and surgical fees. In addition, there is sometimes major medical insurance to cover expenses over and above what regular medical insurance covers.

Disability: Loss of income insurance

Disability insurance protects against loss of income while one is sick or disabled. Generally there is a waiting period before disability insurance pays a benefit. Short-term illnesses, then, are not covered. The length of time for which benefits are paid varies as well. All these factors will be discussed below.

Group or individual insurance

Health insurance can be purchased on a group or individual basis. To buy group insurance, however, one must be eligible, and usually group insurance is available to the employees of a firm. The premiums on group insurance are lower than on individual policies, and for this reason people who are able to take advantage of a group plan should do so.

272

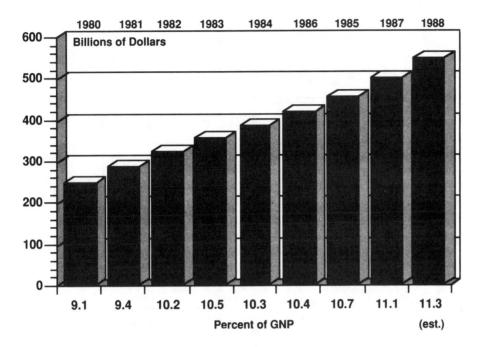

National health expenditures and percent of gross national product (Source: *Source Book of Health Insurance Data, 1989, Health Insurance Institute, p. 40.*)

Estimated expenditures for 1989 and 1990 are $597.2 billion and $647.3 billion, respectively.

Figure 11–1

Most insurance companies have several plans to choose from, differing in various amounts of coverage and various deductible and coinsurance features. Some policies have limits to the amount they will pay for a hospital room, others do not. Some will not cover certain ailments, others will. The better the coverage, the higher the premium. Each of the various policies may be purchased to cover an individual or an entire family. There are generally as many as four different premiums quoted for any given policy—one for a single person, another for a couple with no children, a third for a couple with children, perhaps even a fourth for an employee and children.

Types of health coverage can be classified into the following categories:

TYPES OF HEALTH INSURANCE COVERAGE

- Medical expense
    Hospital
    Surgical
    Medical
    Major medical or comprehensive
    Other
    Dental
- Disability insurance or loss of income

Table 11–1   Consumer prices

[1982–84 = 100, except as noted; monthly data seasonally adjusted, except as noted]

Period	All items — Not seasonally adjusted (NSA)	All items — Seasonally adjusted	Food	Housing Total	Shelter Total	Shelter — Renters' costs (Dec. 1982 = 100)	Shelter — Homeowners' costs (Dec. 1982 = 100)	Shelter — Maintenance and repairs NSA	Shelter — Fuel and other utilities	Apparel and upkeep	Transportation Total	Transportation — New cars	Transportation — Motor fuel	Medical care	Energy	All items less food, shelter, and energy
Rel. imp.	100.0	.....	16.3	42.0	27.9	7.9	19.8	0.2	7.5	6.1	17.1	4.2	3.2	6.2	7.4	48.4
1980	82.4	.....	86.8	81.1	81.0	.....	.....	82.4	75.4	90.9	83.1	88.4	97.4	74.9	86.0	80.6
1981	90.9	.....	93.6	90.4	90.5	.....	.....	90.7	86.4	95.3	93.2	93.7	108.5	82.9	97.7	88.3
1982	96.5	.....	97.4	96.9	96.9	.....	.....	96.4	94.9	97.8	97.0	97.4	102.8	92.5	99.2	95.1
1983	99.6	.....	99.5	99.5	99.1	103.0	102.5	99.9	100.2	100.2	99.3	99.9	99.4	100.6	99.9	100.0
1984	103.9	.....	103.2	103.6	104.0	108.6	107.3	103.7	104.8	102.1	103.7	102.8	97.9	106.8	100.9	105.0
1985	107.6	.....	105.6	107.7	109.8	115.4	113.1	106.5	106.5	105.0	106.4	106.1	98.7	113.5	101.6	109.0
1986	109.6	.....	109.0	110.9	115.8	121.9	119.4	107.9	104.1	105.9	102.3	110.6	77.1	122.0	88.2	112.7
1987	113.6	.....	113.5	114.2	121.3	128.1	124.8	111.8	103.0	110.6	105.4	114.6	80.2	130.1	88.6	117.0
1988	118.3	.....	118.2	118.5	127.1	133.6	131.1	114.7	104.4	115.4	108.7	116.9	80.9	138.6	898.3	121.9
1989	124.0	.....	125.1	123.0	132.8	138.9	137.3	118.0	107.8	118.6	114.1	119.2	88.5	149.3	94.3	127.3
1989:																
July	124.4	124.4	125.6	123.3	133.2	139.6	137.6	118.4	107.8	118.3	115.3	118.8	92.9	149.6	95.9	127.7
Aug.	124.6	124.5	125.9	123.5	133.5	139.1	138.2	118.5	107.8	116.9	114.2	118.5	88.4	150.8	93.8	127.8
Sept.	125.0	124.8	126.3	123.7	133.7	138.7	138.7	118.6	108.0	118.6	113.9	118.1	87.1	151.9	93.2	128.3
Oct.	125.6	125.4	126.8	124.2	134.4	139.8	139.4	118.6	108.1	119.4	114.5	118.8	88.4	153.0	94.1	128.8
Nov.	125.9	125.8	127.4	124.7	135.0	140.5	140.0	119.3	108.7	119.4	114.6	119.8	86.8	154.2	93.8	129.3
Dec.	126.1	126.3	128.0	125.2	135.6	141.0	140.6	119.5	109.4	119.0	115.0	120.8	86.3	155.1	94.1	129.7
1990:																
Jan.	127.4	127.7	130.5	126.1	136.3	142.3	141.1	120.4	111.6	119.0	117.4	121.6	93.4	156.1	98.9	130.4
Feb.	128.0	128.3	131.1	126.3	136.6	143.4	141.0	120.8	110.9	122.9	117.7	121.4	93.6	157.3	98.2	131.5
Mar.	128.7	128.9	131.5	126.9	137.6	143.8	142.4	121.2	111.0	124.9	117.6	121.2	92.2	158.5	97.4	132.2
Apr.	128.9	129.1	131.2	127.0	137.9	143.9	142.8	121.2	110.5	125.0	117.7	120.9	92.5	159.8	97.0	132.6
May	129.2	129.3	131.2	127.2	138.2	143.9	143.2	122.2	110.5	124.6	117.5	120.7	91.2	161.0	96.3	132.9
June	129.9	130.0	132.2	128.0	139.5	144.5	144.8	121.8	110.3	124.5	118.0	120.5	93.2	162.1	96.9	133.2
July	130.4	130.5	132.7	128.6	140.7	146.6	145.7	122.1	109.4	124.2	118.3	120.1	92.8	163.5	96.2	133.8

Source: Economic Indicators, August 1990, Council of Economic Advisers, p. 23.

Table 11—2 shows the number of people in the United States who are covered under some form of the more popular type of health insurance.

Hospital expense insurance covers basic hospital costs such as room and board, nursing care, X-ray costs, drugs, anesthetists and oxygen, laboratory work such as blood tests and urinalysis, and certain other miscellaneous costs. Many hospital policies also cover other costs, for example, expenses incurred when the insured is treated in a nursing care facility. Also often covered is emergency room treatment in a hospital on an outpatient basis.

Hospital expense insurance

Room and board charges sometimes are limited to a stated maximum amount, and a maximum number of days per illness may be stipulated. A person could choose a $100, $150, or $200 per day hospital room allowance with premiums varying accordingly. More and more plans, however, provide for payment of a semiprivate room. Generally, most other hospital fees such as laboratory work are covered. If the patient is in intensive care, room costs are much higher; some policies provide for a higher daily limit, others do not.

As noted above, hospital care is very expensive and is continuing to rise rapidly. For this reason hospital insurance is considered a must by most people. Figure 11—2 illustrates the average cost per day for a semiprivate hospital room by region.

Payment of surgical fees is not included in policies that cover hospital fees, and separate insurance plans have been developed to take care of them. Sometimes the company pays a given amount of dollars for certain types of operations. If the fee is above this figure, the person must pay the residual. The amount the policy will pay varies in accordance with the contract. Some policies state that reimbursable surgical fees will be based on reasonable, customary or prevailing charges for the particular procedure in that area. This makes for uncertainty, but usually a reimbursement schedule is developed based on charges normally or most frequently made by doctors in the area for a similar procedure.

Surgical expense insurance

Some plans require that a second medical opinion be obtained before they will pay the normal rate for a given operation. If a second opinion regarding the need for surgery is not obtained, a lesser amount is paid.

Medical expenses insurance, meant to provide for general medical expenses not covered by surgical and hospital plans, covers such items as drugs and visits to a doctor's office, as well as laboratory work. There may be provision for a maximum number of visits to a doctor per year, and there are also maximum dollar amounts—if not per illness or acci-

Medical expenses insurance

Table 11—2   Number of persons with private health insurance protection in the United States by type of coverage (000 omitted)

| End of year | Hospital expense | Major medical expense | Disability income | | Dental expense[†] |
			Short-term	Long-term	
1940	11,962	—	N.A.	N.A.	—
1945	32,072	—	N.A.	N.A.	—
1950	76,639	—	37,793	*	—
1955	101,400	N.A.	39,513	*	—
1960	122,500	32,590	42,436	*	N.A.
1961	125,825	41,974	43,055	*	N.A.
1962	129,407	48,393	45,002	*	N.A.
1963	133,472	55,382	44,246	3,029	N.A.
1964	136,304	62,112	45,092	3,363	N.A.
1965	138,671	69,666	46,927	4,514	N.A.
1966	142,369	73,843	49,931	5,068	N.A.
1967	146,409	81,550	51,975	6,778	4,570
1968	151,947	87,641	55,636	7,836	5,867
1969	155,025	95,528	57,770	9,282	8,858
1970	158,847	103,544	58,089	10,966	11,972
1971	161,849	108,813	59,280	12,284	15,263
1972	164,098	113,837	61,548	14,538	16,853
1973	168,455	124,627	64,168	17,011	20,418
1974	173,140	131,438	65,282	17,799	27,855
1975	178,180	134,092	62,971	18,396	30,337
1976	176,858	138,657	62,250	17,779	41,703
1977	179,853	139,884	64,627	19,364	50,737
1978	185,690	142,158	68,307	19,100	55,462
1979	185,743	148,805	65,808	19,920	61,608
1980	187,375	153,564	68,831	22,051	79,433
1981	186,193	153,676	65,301	22,582	83,245
1982	188,337	160,056	68,638	25,313	93,112
1983	186,644	159,612	64,146	24,655	100,828
1984	184,403	N.A.	59,332	22,944	102,159
1985	181,329	N.A.	N.A.	25,511	99,768
1986					
Under 65	158,635	155,462	N.A.	N.A.	N.A.
65 and over	21,204	N.A.	N.A.	N.A.	N.A.
Total	179,839	N.A.	N.A.	23,661	94,976

N.A.—Not available.

*Included in "Short-term," with the possibility of some duplication of disability income coverage for these years.

†Estimates on dental expense include fully-insured group plans, self-administered plans, plans employing third party administrators, and health maintenance organizations.

Note: Some data are revised from previous editions. Data for 1978 and later have been adjusted downward due to new data on average family size. For 1975 and later, data include the number of persons covered in Puerto Rico and U.S. territories and possessions. The data refer to the net total of people protected, i.e., duplication among persons protected by more than one kind of insuring organization or more than one insurance company policy providing the same type of coverage has been eliminated.

Source: Source Book of Health Insurance Data, 1988, Health Insurance Institute, p. 3.

	Northeast		Midwest		South		West	
	Jan. 1986	Jan. 1987	Jan. 1986	Jan. 1987	Jan. 1986	Jan. 1987	Jan. 1986	Jan. 1987
Dollars	241.00	260.83	212.16	242.38	179.60	195.02	265.54	293.34

NOTE: Northeast includes New England and Middle Atlantic states; Mideast, East North Central and West North Central states; South, South Atlantic, East South Central and West South Central states; and West, Mountain and Pacific states. Data exclude Puerto Rico.

Average cost to patient per day for semiprivate hospital room by region (Source: Source Book of Health Insurance Data, 1986–1987, *Health Insurance Institute, p. 41.*)   Figure 11–2

dent, then per year. Many of these plans have a schedule of fees indicating what they will pay for a given service. Others will pay what they consider to be the customary and reasonable charges for the services provided in that area.

Often these plans have a deductible of, say, $500 per year. The patient pays the first $500 of medical expenses per year and after that costs are usually shared, with the insurance company paying perhaps 80 percent and the patient 20 percent. This insurance will not usually cover visits to the doctor for regular checkups.

There are generally limits to the coverage provided by the basic hospital-surgical-medical plans discussed above. In such a case major medical takes over.   *Major medical expense or comprehensive insurance*

Major medical insurance covers virtually all medical expenses except dental work. It covers hospital fees, physicians' and surgeons' fees, laboratory work, drugs, and nursing care. It is in effect catastrophe insurance; if a person has very high medical bills because of a serious illness or accident, major medical coverage comes into force. Major medical insurance can be purchased on a group or individual basis, and can cover not only the individual but the entire family.

There are really two types of major medical plans. One supplements the basic hospital-surgical-medical plan discussed above. The other provides comprehensive protection, and the basic coverage and the major coverage are integrated. Indeed the term "major medical" is not even used any more in some policies.

"Don't worry, we'll have you on your feet and out of here in no time. Your hospital insurance doesn't cover much." (Source: *Permission Cartoon Features Syndicate; from The Wall Street Journal.*)

Some major medical plans have lifetime limits on the amounts that can be collected, but these limits go up to $1 million or more.

Some of the comprehensive plans even include dental coverage. More and more of the health insurance sold today is put into one comprehensive plan, reducing administrative and clerical costs and usually providing the policyholder with a better return on his or her premium dollar.

Other (supplemental) coverage

There are several other coverages that a few people buy. These are over and above the regular coverage just discussed, and are additional or supplemental coverage.

Hospital confinement indemnity provides for the payment of a specific cash sum of so much per day, per week, or per month while the person is in the hospital. It is similar to—but should not be confused with—disability insurance discussed below. Indemnity insurance payments are short-term and often there is no waiting period before the payment is made, whereas disability insurance does have a waiting period and payments may be long-term. In addition, indemnity insurance pays a predetermined fixed amount per period, whereas the payment under disability insurance is usually a certain percentage of the person's income.

Insurance that covers only accidents may be purchased. Such a policy is not recommended because virtually all regular health policies include this.

Coverage may be obtained for one or a few specific diseases. It might cover such catastrophic and devastating diseases as cancer or heart disease.

There is also short-term coverage of a few months; this takes care of the gap between permanent coverage being arranged for and the termination of previous coverage. This gap could arise during moves from one job to another, or for graduating students who have not yet taken their first job.

Dental insurance

Many companies are now offering dental insurance covering examinations, fillings, extractions, root canals, oral surgery, and most other dental work. There may be a limit to payments (usually $1,000) for expensive work such as orthodontics. There may also be yearly limits applied separately to each member of the family. The plans have a deductible amount; usually 80 percent of the costs above the deductible are paid by the insurance company and 20 percent by the insured. Some plans also have a proviso that they will not cover a routine examination more often than once every six months. Figure 11–3 shows dental expense protection in the United States.

Most health insurance policies have a number of other provisions you should be aware of.

COMMON PROVISIONS OF HEALTH INSURANCE

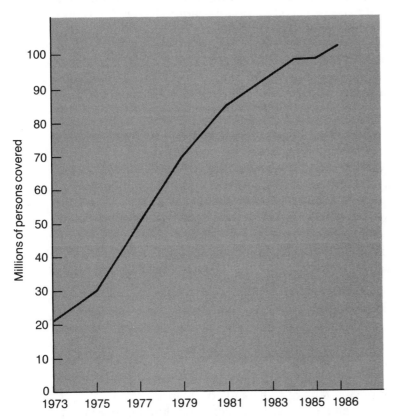

Dental expense protection in the United States. (Source: Source Book of Health Insurance Data, 1986–1987, *Health Insurance Institute, p. 15.*)

Figure 11–3

Deductible feature

Generally health insurance policies have a **deductible** that the policy-holder must pay, which may range anywhere from $100 to $500 or even higher. The higher the deductible, the lower the premium. If a policy has a $500 deductibility clause, this means the policyholder pays the first $500 of a medical bill. In most policies, the deductible feature applies on a yearly rather than on an illness basis. Therefore, once the person has paid a $500 deductible medical bill, all future medical expenses for the remainder of the year are submitted to the insurance company. Some-times there is also a family deductible which may be less than the sum of the deductibles of the individual family members. For example, if a family of four is covered and the policy has a $500 individual deductible, every member does not need to meet the $500 before he or she is cov-ered. Rather, once that family as a group has reached $2,000 (and some-times even less), the deductible is considered satisfied for all family members.

Copayments

Most of the medical policies contain a **coinsurance** as well as a deducti-ble feature, in accordance with which the company agrees to pay only a part of the total expense. Most companies agree to pay up to 80 percent of the cost, with the insured paying the remaining 20 percent. For exam-ple, assume a bill of $2,500 with a $500 deductible clause and an agree-ment on the part of the company to pay 80 percent of the total cost above the deductible; the company would pay $1,600, with the remainder to be paid by the insured ($2,500 total bill, minus $500, or $2,000 × .80 or $1,600, which is to be paid by the company).

Copayment cap

Some medical plans will pay 100 percent of all medical costs after a spe-cific dollar amount has been achieved. The policy may pay 80 percent of the cost in excess of $500, and then 100 percent after the total yearly cost to the patient has reached, say, $1,000. The $1,000 then becomes the "cap" or what some call the "out-of-pocket" limit. For a person with a $500 deductible and a 20 percent copayment, this limit is reached when his or her medical bills reach $3,000. The insurance company pays

$$\$3,000 - \$500 = \$2,500 \times 80\% = \$2,000$$

and then 100 percent of any additional medical bills for the rest of the year.

This cap is very important. For example, a catastrophic illness can easily run your medical bills up to and even over several hundred thou-sand dollars. A 20 percent coinsurance feature without a cap could result in the insured paying tens of thousands of dollars.

Tables 11–3 and 11–4 show typical premiums on various types of policies and the possible out-of-pocket limits.

Monthly premiums of various health plans

Table 11–3

	Monthly premiums	
	Plan 1 $200 ded. 20% copayment	Plan 2 $500 ded. 20% copayment
Employee	$123.47	$101.92
Employee and spouse	275.88	230.61
Employee and children	250.81	193.07
Employee and family	397.99	321.78

Medical expense coverage

Table 11–4

	Plan 1	Plan 2
Deductible	$200	$ 500
Coinsurance limit	500	500
Out-of-pocket limit	700	1,000

Limitations

Most of the medical policies contain a maximum amount that the company will pay. Generally, this figure ranges from $50,000 to $100,000, but it may go as high as $500,000 or $1,000,000. These are usually lifetime limits. The limitation may also be written to cover any single illness or it may be written as a limitation for a year. The policy may read, for instance, that it will cover only $50,000 for any one illness, meaning that no matter how long the individual is hospitalized, the company will cease paying after the $50,000 has been used up. If the limitation applies to a policy year, then the company would make payments the following year in the event the policyholder was so unfortunate as to be hospitalized for that long.

Generally policies are written so that as the second policy year starts, the insured must first pay the deductible amount before the company becomes liable. In addition, as noted above, most policies have a lifetime limit. This lifetime limit is often several times the single illness or yearly limit, but may be much more. Figure 11–4 shows the growth of major medical insurance over the past few years.

One of the hazards we all face is the possibility that we will lose our ability to earn a livelihood temporarily or permanently due to a serious accident or illness. Some jobs themselves are dangerous; some on-the-job accidents could cripple a person for life. Certain illnesses can render a person incapable of working even after recovery. Even people in relatively safe

**DISABILITY
INSURANCE
OR LOSS OF
INCOME**

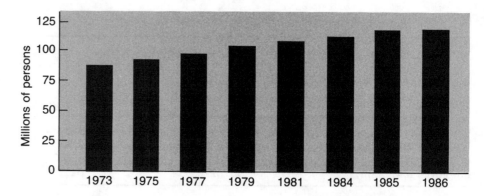

Figure 11–4   *Major medical expense protection with insurance companies in the United States.* (Source: Source Book of Health Insurance Data, 1986–1987, *Health Insurance Institute, p. 13.*)

occupations can suffer from accidents. An innocent victim might be crippled for life when some careless person runs his or her car over him. Indeed, some insurance executives believe that disability insurance is needed even more than life insurance. The probability of partial or total disability is greater than the probability of loss of life for relatively young people. Because of this likelihood, disability (often called loss of income) insurance was developed. It should be noted that most people already have some disability insurance under Social Security—this is discussed more fully in Chapter 18—but it is safe to say that Social Security disability benefits by themselves will seldom provide adequate funds.

In general, the policies are designed to cover loss of income either as the result of a temporary disability or as the result of permanent disability. The coverage will always be less than the actual earnings of the individual. If a person earns $500 per week, he or she cannot purchase a policy that would cover a loss of earnings of more than a certain percentage of that.[1]

More than a dozen varieties of limited disability insurance can be purchased to cover almost every situation imaginable. For example, an individual paying off a mortgage on a residence may purchase disability insurance to cover the mortgage payments. For a few dollars a month premium, depending on the age of the policyholder, the company will agree to pay the monthly mortgage payments.

Waiting period and length of payment

These policies are written in different ways. Most have a waiting period before benefit payments begin, and this waiting period varies. They pay

---

1. Insurance companies will not sell a person a disability policy that pays more than about 60 or 70 percent (it varies from company to company) of his or her before-tax income, in part on the theory that if the person receives that much he or she has less (perhaps not any) incentive to overcome his or her disability.

a certain percentage (which varies) of earnings for various periods. Generally they can be grouped into those which provide short-term protection or long-term protection. The short-term policies provide benefits for various time periods up to two years; the long-term policies provide for protection for more than two years; some provide benefits for up to ten years and more. A few can provide benefits until the insured is age 65 or for a lifetime.

Premium rates vary in accordance with the above conditions; the longer the waiting period before payments begin, the lower the premiums, and the longer the period over which payments are made, the higher the premiums. The rates also vary with the occupation of the individual. Professional and certain types of businesspeople find the premiums lower and the benefits more liberal than those for persons in more hazardous occupations.

This type of policy also often contains a provision stating that for dismemberment the insured is to receive a lump sum equivalent to a stated number of weeks' indemnity in the case of being disabled permanently. For example, if an individual has a policy that provides for payment of $200 a week in the event of total disablement and then loses a leg in an accident, the policy may provide that the policyholder is to receive a lump-sum payment of one hundred weeks times $200, or $20,000. Where such a lump sum is received, the individual does not receive the weekly benefits provided for in the policy.

Dismemberment

Disability generally is defined in one of two ways. Some policies define the insured as disabled if he or she no longer has the capacity to be gainfully employed in any occupation. Other policies state that disability exists if the insured cannot perform in the previous occupation. As would be expected, with the latter definition of disability, premiums are more expensive.

Definition of disability

Rehabilitation coverage may be included in a disability policy, or it may be purchased separately. This pays for the rehabilitation and retraining costs that often permit a person who otherwise might be disabled for life to become gainfully employed.

Rehabilitation

While life insurance is designed to protect the family economically in the event of the premature death of the breadwinner, much the same sort of economic catastrophe can result from a serious illness or accident. Indeed, a permanent disability may be more of a disaster than a death; not only is the income stream cut off, but expenses may rise. Consequently, along with life insurance, the individual needs protection against such contingencies as these.

HOW MUCH HEALTH INSURANCE TO BUY

Medical insurance needs

It is virtually impossible to determine precisely a person's (or family's) medical-expense insurance needs. This is because an individual cannot determine the extent of his or her potential loss due to illness or accident. Individuals cannot evaluate their health, because the cost, if they lose, it is unknown. It is strongly recommended that no breadwinner be without at least a major medical insurance policy. If one is able to obtain group insurance where one works, there is not really much choice in what kind of health insurance to buy. Usually a package is available, sometimes two or three different packages with varying benefits, so that an employee can choose from among them.

Persons who are not members of a group and hence not eligible for a group policy should consider individual policies. At the very least, everyone should have a major medical policy. The cost can be kept within reason if the person puts the deductible feature at $500. Shop around and compare the local Blue Cross-Blue Shield plan with what a private life insurance company can offer. Most insurance companies have several plans to choose from, generally referred to as Plan A, B, or C. The main differences are that the deductibles, coinsurance, and sometimes the yearly and lifetime limits vary. Naturally, the lower the deductible and the coinsurance, and the higher the limits, the higher the premiums. If one is young and healthy and on a tight budget, he or she might choose a higher deductible, but it is advised that one not skimp on annual and lifetime limitations.

Catastrophic insurance needs

Many major medical policies have relatively low limits. Moreover, even if a major medical policy has a $200,000 or $300,000 limit, that may not be enough. A person stricken with cancer or other deadly diseases can run up a bill of hundreds of thousands of dollars, and without coverage such a bill would devastate most families. Many experts believe catastrophic insurance is the most important protection of all. Many people overinsure for smaller, more normal costs by choosing a low deductible, and underinsure for catastrophe. It would be wise to take a higher deductible and invest the premiums saved in catastrophe insurance to provide for protection against the unlikely but catastrophic expenses should they occur.

Unless the client's major medial plan has at least a $1,000,000 limit, he or she should consider buying an "excess major medical" or catastrophic illness plan. Such plans are written with a deductible of $50,000, $100,000, or whatever the major medical plan limit may be, and take over when the other plans are exhausted. The good news is that such plans are amazingly cheap; premiums are about $100 per year for a young person. For older people, who perhaps need this type of insurance more, unfortunately rates are much higher.

Disability insurance needs

Disability insurance should also be high on the list of priorities. Persons who have access to a good group plan should seriously consider it. Even

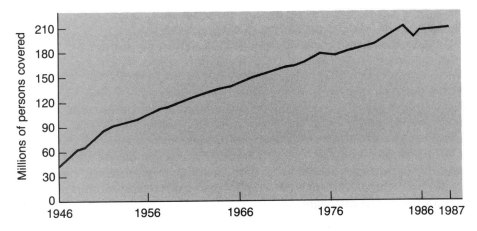

Growth of private health insurance in the United States. (Source: Source Book of Health Insurance Data, 1986–1987, *Health Insurance Institute, p. 10.*)   Figure 11–5

if it must be bought on an individual basis, it should still be high on the list of priorities, to assure a monthly income in the event that regular income is cut off due to a lengthy illness or serious accident. Often professional and other groups are able to obtain this sort of insurance at relatively low rates. Consequently, this is one of the most rapidly growing areas in the insurance industry. Figure 11–5 shows the growth of private health insurance in the United States.

To calculate the actual dollar amount of disability insurance needs, follow the same logic that was used when calculating life insurance needs. Since permanent disability terminates the income stream (just as does death), the amount of disability insurance could be calculated based on an individual's (or family) needs.[2]

To calculate disability insurance needs, follow these nine steps.

1. Gross annual living expenses.   Determine gross annual living expense requirements as shown in Chapter 10 in analyzing life insurance needs. This figure could be based on the budget or income statement, discussed in Chapters 2 and 3. Or it could be the after-tax income in some cases and the after Social Security tax income in all cases.

Disability payments are taxed in some cases, not in others. See Chapter 7, section on Disability Income Exclusion. Generally, however, disability payments are taxed if there is a group plan with the employer, who pays all or some of the premiums. They are not taxed if a person has an individual plan for which he or she pays the premiums. If the disability benefits are not taxed, subtract the tax liabilities from gross liv-

---

2. Insurance needs could, of course, be calculated based on the present value of the future income stream, or the multiple income approach could be used as in the case of life insurance. However, we concluded in Chapter 10 that the needs concept is best.

ing needs. Social Security taxes too would be eliminated in the event of disability and must be netted out.

The gross living expenses would then be further reduced by the following items.

2. Reduced living expenses stemming from disability.   Transportation costs, lunch expenses, possibly entertainment, and other costs associated with holding a job would be eliminated or reduced.

3. Insurance premium waivers.   Life insurance premiums would be eliminated if there is a disability premium waiver clause. Mortgage payments would be eliminated if there is a policy that paid off the mortgage in the event of death or disability.

4. Social Security.   Social Security disability benefit payments are not taxable in many cases (see Chapter 7) and should reduce living expenses further. Check with a local Social Security office to obtain an estimate of what one's Social Security benefits will be.

5. Spouse's income.   Spouse's current income (if working), or expected future income if spouse were to go back to work in the event of a disability.

6. Other disability benefit payments.   This would include such things as a corporate pension plan where one works.

7. Investment income.   Investment income would continue, hence it must be accounted for.

8. Total adjustment.   Add up all of the adjustments above that apply to the individual (items 2 through 7).

9. Actual disability needs.   Subtract the dollar amount in item 8 from item 1. This is a realistic figure of the actual need.

All of the items (2 through 7) may not apply in every case. One may or may not have insurance premium waivers. We have also made no allowance for

1.   paying off other debts,
2.   a college fund,
3.   an emergency fund, and
4.   savings plans for retirement or other goals.

These items could be taken care of under item 1—gross annual living expenses—in which case they would remain part of the personal family budget, although conceivably they could be taken into account by insurance; then the disability insurance needs would be greater. Table 11–5 shows the disability insurance requirements of a hypothetical Mr. and Mrs. X.

A person may also wish to adjust his or her disability insurance needs to allow for future inflation. This may be done by buying a disability policy that has an annual cost-of-living adjustment (COLA) built into it. While the premiums on such a policy are higher, it will provide for an annual escalation of benefits by 4, 5, 6, or 7 percent, or whatever is agreed upon.

One may also build inflation protection into a policy himself or herself but this would entail buying more insurance than the $4,000 shown in Table 11–5. If we assume a long-run inflation rate of 5 percent and a twenty-year disability requirement, we can get the inflationary factor. It is 33.066. It indicates that if we start with one dollar, and we add one additional dollar each year, and the entire sum is growing by 5 percent per year, it will amount to $33.066 at the end of twenty years. Multiplying that by $4,000, we find that the total disability payout over twenty years will amount to $132,264. Dividing this last figure by twenty years, we obtain $6,613, which is the average disability insurance payout per year over the entire period—that is, the disability insurance needs of Mr. and Mrs. X adjusted for inflation. Currently their needs are $4,000, but this will rise to $10,612 in the twentieth year, if inflation continues at 5 percent. If they make arrangements for $6,613.00 per year, they will have a surplus during the early years ($2,613 the first year). They should put this surplus in an interest-bearing account, and then it becomes a reserve that can be used in later years when their needs rise above $6,613. Providing for disability income of $6,613 yields slightly more than $4,000 in real terms over the years, assuming 5 percent inflation, because there will be interest on the surplus during the early years. However, this provides a hedge in the event that inflation rises above 5 percent. If the time period is increased to 25 or 30 years, the disability insurance needs rise to $7,636 and $8,859 respectively. These calculations are shown in Table 11–6.

Disability insurance needs of Mr. and Mrs. X   Table 11–5

1. Gross annual living expenses (adjusted as necessary for taxes)		$24,000
2. Reduction in living expenses	$ 800	
3. Insurance premium waivers	700	
4. Social Security benefits received	8,000	
5. Spouse's income	10,000	
6. Other disability benefits	—	
7. Investment income	1,000	
8. Total adjustments (deductions)	$20,500	
9. Actual annual disability needs		$ 4,000

Table 11—6   *Disability insurance needs of $4,000 adjusted for inflation of 5 percent*

Disability insurance need $4,000
  (in real terms)

Inflation: 5 percent
  Inflation factor 20 years = 33.066
  $4,000 × 33.066 = $132,264 ÷ 20 years = $6,613*

  Inflation factor 25 years = 47.727
  $4,000 × 47.727 = 190,908 ÷ 25 years = $7,636*

  Inflation factor 30 years = 66.439
  $4,000 × 66.439 = 265,756 ÷ 30 years = $8,859*

---

*Since in insurance, companies will not sell a policy that pays more than 60 to 70 percent of the person's income, the maximum amount of benefits our hypothetical person with income of $24,000 could purchase is $24,000 × 70% or $16,800. This is far more than he or she needs.

OTHER IMPORTANT THINGS ABOUT HEALTH INSURANCE

There are a number of other important matters about health insurance that will now be discussed.

Items not covered

Certain medical expenses are not always covered by health insurance. Some policies cover psychiatric care, some do not. Those that do often set a special limit on this item. Abortions may or may not be covered. The cost of regular checkups is usually not covered nor are the costs of eyeglasses and eye examinations, but treatment of eye disease or eye surgery is. Vasectomies may or may not be covered; the same is true of surgery to correct natural deformities—such as a clubfoot, or cosmetic surgery. The trend is toward broader coverage in these areas, however.

100 percent coverage

Since health insurance policies have a coinsurance clause that pays usually only 80 percent of the medical bills, can a person buy two policies and then receive benefits in excess of expenses? The answer is no, but one may collect more than if one had only one policy. There are, however, only a few cases where a person could get two group policies, although one could buy two individual policies; but individual policies have substantially higher premiums. Where both husband and wife work and both are eligible for group insurance, they could have two policies. Or in rare cases persons could have two group plans if they had one with their employer and another one with a professional association such as the American Accounting Association.

How would two such policies pay off if there were a claim? One policy would be classified as the primary policy; it would pay first in accordance with its terms, and the other policy would then pay part or all of the rest. In nearly all cases the primary policy is the one obtained with the employer. In the case of a husband-wife team, the primary policy would be the one from the employer of the person in the family making the claim.

Suppose a person has two policies, both with a $100 deductibility and an 80 percent coinsurance clause; assume a claim is filed for $1,100. The primary carrier would pay 80 percent of $1,000 or $800. The secondary carrier would then pay all or part of the remaining $300, depending upon what the contract said regarding secondary claims. It could be 80 percent of the $300; 80 percent of $200 ($300 less the deductibility), or 80 percent of $1,000, just as the primary carrier, with a limit of $300. In no case could a person get more than 100 percent coverage and in many cases it would be less. For this reason, it almost never pays to have two policies; a person pays double premiums and gets only marginal added protection.

Group plans: The modern way to buy health insurance

Any of the plans discussed above can be obtained on a group or individual basis. A group plan actually amounts to wholesaling insurance, and the features are the same as if an individual were to purchase his or her own policy. As a group member, however, one generally has the benefit of lower rates than if one were to purchase the policy on one's own.

There are a number of reasons why the rates are more favorable to the group, one being that there is a more favorable selection of risks. When it insures the group, the company usually insists that at least 75 percent of those eligible must join. Moreover, those who do join do not come with the idea that they will receive immediate benefits; and there are few cancellations. In some cases, the employee has no choice but to take the group insurance; it is a condition of employment. In other cases, it is voluntary, and it is in these cases that the insurance companies insist that the policy is not effective until 75 percent of the eligible employees have joined. Another reason for more favorable rates is that administrative costs are lower. As to collections, the employer customarily withholds the amount of the premiums from the employee's paycheck. The commission paid to the agent who sells the group policy is lower than if he or she were to sell the same number of policies individually.

Frequently group health policies are a part of the so-called fringe benefits in labor-management contracts. Often the employer pays all or a part of the premiums and agrees to handle much of the paperwork through the personnel office.

There is a growing trend toward the group method of meeting insurance needs, true not only of health insurance, but also of life insurance. The pattern today is to have one package negotiated on a group basis, which would then include some sort of a comprehensive health plan as described above together with some term insurance, all under one plan.

Guaranteed renewable and noncancelable policies

In some cases, the insurance company retains the right to refuse to renew the policy when it expires. Indeed, sometimes the company has the right to cancel at any time during the term of the policy. It is, however, possible to buy guaranteed renewable and noncancelable policies. A *guaranteed renewable policy* can be renewed until some predetermined age is reached, generally age sixty-five. However, each time it is renewed, premiums for a class of insureds can be increased if warranted.

A *noncancelable* policy is one that cannot be canceled during the time it was originally stated to run, and during the time, premiums cannot be raised. Therefore, if a person buys a policy that is both noncancelable and renewable, the premiums cannot be raised during the period over which the policy runs. When the period is over, the policy must be renewed if the policyholder so chooses, but premiums can be raised.

How to apply for benefits

It is easy to apply for benefits under most health insurance plans. Every person with a health insurance plan receives a wallet-sized card from the insurance company. A person in a group plan has a group number and a certificate number on the card. With a hospital bill often the hospital staff will fill out the form and send it in. With a doctor's bill or reimbursement for drugs, the insured must often fill out the form, but it is self-explanatory. Since in many cases the insurance company pays only part of the bill, instructions are sent indicating how much the patient is to pay above the insurance claim. Until a few years ago, companies often paid the doctor directly. Now more and more companies are paying the patient who in turn pays the doctor.

When retired: Supplemental plans

Most insurance companies, including Blue Cross-Blue Shield, now have supplemental plans for retired individuals who are covered by Medicare because Medicare does not pay all bills. These supplemental plans are designed to pay a portion of those costs not covered by Medicare. They work very much like regular plans in that they may have deductible features and coinsurance. That is, they treat that portion of the retired person's medical bill not covered by Medicare just as they would some other person's total bill. Because they provide less coverage, their premiums are, of course, lower.

Blue Cross-Blue Shield

In addition to being able to buy health insurance policies from profit-making life insurance companies, one can purchase health protection from the nonprofit Blue Cross-Blue Shield organization. Blue Cross-Blue Shield plans are not health insurance, technically speaking.

The policy one might buy from an insurance company is an indemnity contract and the company pays the insured what he or she is entitled to under the contract. Blue Cross-Blue Shield is a service benefit plan whereby the hospital or physician is paid directly by Blue Cross-Blue Shield. In a sense the hospital and medical expenses are prepaid.

hospital *physicians*

BC-BS

prepaid

Blue Cross is a cooperative nonprofit organization through which members prepay hospital bills. Under Blue Cross some hospitals have agreed to provide certain services for the members who prepay a monthly fee to the organization. Blue Shield is a similar nonprofit organization designed to pay physicians' expenses. The latter is sponsored by groups of physicians, and for the most part Blue Cross handles the details of selling, billing, and collecting for Blue Shield. Blue Cross-Blue Shield also provides major medical protection, the comprehensive plan discussed above, and in some areas dental insurance and even disability insurance —in fact, most of the health coverage that other insurance companies provide.

Blue Cross

The payments for a Blue Cross policy depend on area; in some states, the cost of hospitalization is more expensive than in others. More important, the rates depend on the type of contract one purchases, for some contracts provide more benefits than others. In addition, rates vary depending on whether one purchases the insurance as a member of a group or singly. The period of hospitalization covered varies from plan to plan. There is also usually a limit to how much Blue Cross will pay per day for a hospital room, but generally it is the cost of a semiprivate room.

In addition, most of the plans pay all charges for operating room, recovery room, cast room, and cystoscopic room, plus all drugs in general use.

Under most Blue Cross and Blue Shield plans anyone under the age of sixty-five may enroll on an individual basis, and no physical examination is required. The policies are noncancelable except for nonpayment of dues or the fraudulent use of the membership.

When persons retire and draw Social Security, they may keep or lose their Blue Cross-Blue Shield depending on the local plan. However, more and more plans are adopting the modified Blue Cross-Blue Shield plan for retired people who wish to retain it, a policy consisting of reduced coverage (and reduced premiums), intended to complement Medicare.

Blue Shield

While Blue Cross is designed to cover hospitalization, Blue Shield is designed to cover physicians' fees, whether surgical, surgical-medical, or general medical. Like Blue Cross, the basic rates of Blue Shield vary from state to state and from plan to plan. Most plans agree to pay the physician according to a basic schedule. The physician might charge $600 for services, and the Blue Shield payment schedule might call for a payment of $450. In such a case the subscriber would pay the balance of $150.

How much will be paid for a given operation varies from one section of the country to another. Also there are usually two or three different packages to choose from. A purchaser who is willing to pay a higher premium can obtain a higher surgical fee schedule. More and more plans, however, do not list the dollar amounts they will pay for a given operation but they state they will pay "reasonable and customary" surgical fees. That is, in effect they pay the bill the surgeon submits, unless it is deemed unreasonable.

Most Blue Cross-Blue Shield plans have a deductible clause as well as a coinsurance clause on their plan, just like the private insurance company plans. They also have a family rate and a lower rate for only a husband and wife, and a still lower rate for a single person. As noted above, Blue Cross-Blue Shield also has a major medical plan which covers major illnesses.

Health maintenance organizations (HMOs)

In recent years another type of medical expense protection has developed through **health maintenance organizations.** This method provides many of the same benefits as health insurance. It consists of group prepayment medical plans, often organized as nonprofit co-ops. These provide medical care for their members for a fixed fee per month. These groups own and operate clinics and hospitals and hire doctors, nurses, and other technicians. The professional medical personnel, including doctors, are paid an annual salary; consequently there is no set fee for each particular service. Membership may also be possible on an individual basis; but in order to join a person obviously must live in a geographical area where there is an HMO. Some of the more well-known plans are the Health Insurance Plan of Greater New York, Kaiser Foundation Health Plan, Ross-Loos Medical Group of Los Angeles, Community Health Association of Detroit, and the Group Health Cooperative of Puget Sound.

These group plans can provide most of the benefits that their members need from their own resources. If the services of a specialist are needed and none of the group's doctors qualifies, the group hires an outside specialist on a fee basis. The group cannot provide disability insurance internally, but many HMO's buy that for their members from an insurance company.

These organizations also practice preventive medicine, and have been established recently as a hopeful alternative to costly medical care. The theory behind this preventive medicine is that it is cheaper, both moneywise and in human suffering, to prevent illnesses than to cure them after they are well established. This process involves periodic medical checkups and screening programs to detect early warning signs of health breakdowns. Most of the HMOs offer more comprehensive coverage than most regular group insurance plans. Not only do they provide for regular medical checkups, but many of them have neither a deductible feature nor a coinsurance clause. That is, 100 percent of all medical expenses are taken care of.

In recent years some insurance companies have established HMOs. One of the more well known is Prucare. Some of these insurance HMOs require copayments—a small fee, usually $4 or $5 for each visit to the doctor, in addition to the fixed monthly fee. When drugs are purchased, the person may also pay up to $4 or $5 per prescription. These copayments are much smaller than the coinsurance cost that must be paid when a person has a policy with an insurance company. All other costs, including full hospitalization and surgery, are covered, including drugs administered in the hospital.

Evidence suggests that HMOs reduce medical costs because the medical dollar goes directly to the doctor; there is no (or at least there is less) expensive bureaucracy siphoning off dollars. While the salaried doctors working for an HMO generally make less money than doctors in private practice, they seem happy because they work fewer hours and they have more regular schedules.

Another advantage of HMOs is that bothersome forms to file a claim are not needed as they are when an individual has regular health insurance.

The major disadvantage, the critics of HMOs claim, is that one does not have complete control over the choice of physician. Rather, one must be chosen from the group who works for the HMO.

IPAs are a relatively new innovation which is growing very rapidly. In essence, they are a modified HMO. However, they are slightly different, and they often provided the individual with a wider choice of physicians.

Under this plan, a group of doctors get together and offer their services to members of the IPA. The association works very much like an HMO. The IPA members pay a fixed fee per month for all their health care needs, plus a small fee (usually $5 to $10) for each office visit, and a small charge for drugs. The doctors, however, while paid by the IPA, are not employees of the IPA and are not on a fixed salary. Their income is dependent on the number of patients and the type of service they provide. They are self-employed, maintain their own office, staff, nurses, and so forth, and have both IPA and non-IPA patients.

In most cases there is a much larger number of doctors to choose from by belonging to an IPA.

Individual practice associations (IPAs)

Probably the most far-reaching of the 1965 amendments to the Social Security Law was the Medicare provision. It provided for two kinds of health insurance for those over age sixty-five: hospital insurance and medical insurance. The hospital insurance has come to be known as Part A of Medicare and the medical insurance as Part B. Practically everyone sixty-five or older is eligible for the entire Medicare program.

Certain individuals get Part A (hospital insurance) automatically and need not pay for it. Moreover, these people get this insurance even if they are still working and hence not drawing Social Security; the test is to be over sixty-five and eligible for Social Security. The following people are all eligible for Part A of Medicare:

MEDICARE over 65

A = Hospital over 65, eligible for SS, Disabled <65, aged 65 > 2 yrs, get 55 who need dialysis

B = Medical

$28.60 per month.

1. Everyone over sixty-five and eligible for Social Security or railroad retirement benefits.
2. Disabled people under sixty-five who have been getting Social Security disability benefits for two years or more.
3. People insured under Social Security (but not yet getting benefits because they are under sixty-five) who need dialysis treatment or a

kidney transplant. Wives, husbands, and children of insured people under sixty-five may also be eligible if they need kidney dialysis or transplants. Moreover, these people receive all the benefits of Part A until one year after they no longer have the above-described kidney problems, e.g., a successful kidney transplant.

Those who are eligible and hence are automatically covered for Part A (hospital insurance) are not covered automatically for Part B. It is optional and may be purchased at a cost of $28.60 per month in 1990. (This cost is increased by Congress periodically. Check with the local Social Security office for the current figure.) The premiums are withheld from the retirement check of those drawing Social Security, whereas others must send them to their Social Security Field Office.

Hospital insurance (Part A)

The hospital insurance provides for the following three broad classes of benefits:

All but the first $592 of hospital costs are paid by Medicare for the first sixty days of hospitalization. The $592, then, is the deductible feature. After 60 days a copayment (coinsurance) is required. This copayment rises in two steps. From the 61st to the 90th day, the patient pays $148 per day; this rises to $296 per day from the 91st to the 150th day. After that the Medicare patient is on his or her own. Consequently, while Medicare helps, a lengthy hospital stay can be expensive. Posthospital extended care in a skilled nursing facility is available, free for 20 days, then a coinsurance payment of $74 per day up to a maximum of 80 days. Home health services and hospice care are also offered.

Medical insurance (Part B)

Medical insurance (Part B) covers treatment by physicians, as well as diagnostic tests, physical therapy, and blood transfusions. There is also a deductible, which is currently $75 per year. After that Medicare will pay 80 percent of what is referred to as the "Medicare approved" amount, which is a set amount for the various types of services. The rub is that most doctors charge more than Medicare has approved and the patient has to pay the difference.

However, there are some physicians (participating physicians) who have agreed to charge Medicare patients no more than the approved amount. Those doctors should be sought out. There is a directory of participating physicians that may be purchased from the Social Security field offices. Unfortunately, only a minority of the nation's physicians (about 20 percent currently) have agreed to participate.

Medigap policies

Supplemental policies were discussed earlier in this chapter. Many of these were designed specifically for Medicare patients. These should be investigated before retirement because some are excellent, while others are not so good.

It is also possible, if an individual is working but approaching sixty-five, that he or she may be able to convert the employer-provided health plan to an individual Medigap policy.

There are all kinds of health insurance plans; some are excellent, some good, and some only fair. However, it is generally true that the quality of the policy is closely related to the premiums paid. Nevertheless, the quality of a policy can be appraised by studying the following guidelines, and answering each question.

HOW GOOD IS
A HEALTH
INSURANCE
PLAN?

*Guidelines to
evaluate the quality
of a health
insurance plan*

1. What is the hospital room and board coverage?
     $200 to $300 per day is not too much.
     Full cost of semiprivate room is an important benefit.
     Is there an extra intensive care coverage?
2. Does it cover other hospital costs: X ray, laboratory fees, drugs, anesthesia?
     Full coverage?
     Partial coverage?
3. What is the surgical coverage?
     Set fees for various procedures? What are they?
     Reasonable and customary fees with a limit?
     Reasonable and customary fees with no limit?
4. What is the basic medical coverage?
     Is there an overall dollar limit? If so, what is it?
     What is the deductible?
     What is the coinsurance?
     Does it have a coinsurance cap?
5. What is the major medical coverage?
     What is the deductible?
     What is the coinsurance?
     What is the annual limit?
     What is the per accident or per illness limit?
     What is the lifetime limit?
6. What is the limit on the catastrophic coverage? What is its deductible?
7. What kind of disability coverage does the individual have?
     What is the waiting period before benefits are received?
     How long will benefits be paid?
     How is disability defined? A policy that defines disability as being unable to perform the regular duties of the person's *own* occupation is superior to a policy stating *any* occupation.
8. What are the premiums on the policies?
9. Is the policy noncancelable and guaranteed renewable? If so, the insurance company cannot terminate it.
10. Does the policy contain a waiver of premiums in the event of disability? Better policies do.

SUMMARY
REVIEW
QUESTIONS

These questions serve as a summary and a review of the chapter. If you are able to answer them all, you have a good understanding of the material covered by the chapter.

1. What type of protection does health insurance provide?
2. Explain various types of coverage available in health policies.
3. What is basic hospital expense insurance?
4. What is hospital confinement indemnity coverage?
5. What is major medical coverage?
6. What is meant by coinsurance and the deductible clause in health insurance?
7. Discuss comprehensive medical insurance.
8. What is disability insurance?
9. Does it pay to have two health insurance policies, both of which provide the same benefits? Why or why not?
10. What are some of the things that most health insurance policies will not cover?
11. Is it best to buy health insurance on a group or on an individual basis, assuming the person has a choice? Why?
12. What is the difference between Blue Cross and Blue Shield?
13. Discuss health maintenance organizations.
14. What are some guidelines to indicate how much health insurance to buy?

CASES

1. Bill and Jeanette Jones had the following medical bills last year:
   (a) $567 for Mark, their six-year-old son;
   (b) $650 for Suellen, their five-year-old daughter;
   (c) $740 for Jeanette; and
   (d) $210 for Bill.
   They have coverage for all medical and drug bills up to $100,000 with a $200 deductibility feature and an 80 percent coinsurance clause. How much will their policy reimburse them?

2. John Brown, aged sixty-six, recently retired and is drawing Social Security. When he left his employer, he was told his group life and health insurance would lapse. He has since purchased an individual supplement plan from Blue Cross-Blue Shield. What is a supplemental plan and how does it work? What other kind of coverage does John have?

3. Lindsay and Jim Chervenak both work for the same employer, and both are enrolled in a group plan there. Their plan is a comprehensive one that covers everything up to $100,000 per illness, with a $500 deductibility and an 80 percent coinsurance clause. Recently Jim had major surgery. The hospital bill was $200 per day for ten days. The surgical fee was $2,500, and all other expenses such as drugs and the like came to $500. How much of the total bill will his insurance pay, and how much will he pay? Will he benefit from the fact that he and his wife both have a policy? Are a primary and a secondary carrier involved? Would you recommend that the Chervenak family keep both of the policies they have?

SUGGESTED READINGS

Beam, Burton T., Jr. *Group Insurance: Basic Concepts and Alternatives.* Bryn Mawr, Pa.: The American College, 1984.

Berstein, Joan Z., and Harris, Lucy R. *Health Maintenance Organizations: Opportunities and Problems.* New York: F & S Press, 1983.

Best's Review, Life-Health Edition. Oldwick, N.J.: A. M. Best Company, Inc. Monthly publication.

Birenbaum, Arnold. *Health Care and Society.* Totowa, N.J.: Allanheld, Osmun and Co., 1983.

Black, Kenneth, and Skipper, Harold. *Life Insurance,* 11th ed. Englewood Cliffs, N.J.: Prentice-Hall, 1987.

Blue Cross-Blue Shield Fact Book. Chicago: National Association of Blue Shield Plans. Annual publication.

Blue Cross Reports. Chicago: Blue Cross Association. Quarterly publication.

A Brief Explanation of Medicare. Publication No. (SSA) 73-10043. Washington, D.C.: Department of Health, Education and Welfare.

Cockerell, Hugh. *Lloyd's of London.* Homewood, Ill.: Dow Jones-Irwin, 1984.

Davis, Karen. *National Health Insurance: Benefits, Costs, and Consequences.* Washington, D.C.: The Brookings Institution, 1985.

Dorfman, Mark S. *Introduction to Insurance,* 3rd ed. Englewood Cliffs, N.J.: Prentice-Hall, 1987.

"Duplicate Coverage." Pamphlet published by Blue Cross-Blue Shield. No date.

Eusebio, Thomas C. *Guide to Health Insurance.* Indianapolis, Ind.: Rough Notes Co., 1985.

Follmann, J. F., Jr. "Dental Care Coverage." *Best's Insurance News.*

Health Insurance for People 65 and Older. Washington, D.C.: U.S. Department of Health, Education and Welfare. You may obtain a free copy from a Social Security field office, which can be found in any large city.

"How to Shop for Health Insurance." Pueblo, Colo.: Consumer Information Center.

Inquiry, A Journal of Medical Care Organization, Provision and Financing. Chicago: Blue Cross Association.

Insurance Review. New York: The Insurance Information Institute. Monthly publication.

"The Journal of Insurance." New York: The Insurance Information Institute. Bimonthly publication.

Mehr, Robert I., and Cammack, Emerson. *Principles of Insurance.* Homewood, Ill.' Irwin, 1985.

National Underwriter. Chicago: The National Underwriter Co. Weekly publication.

Source Book of Health Insurance. New York: The Health Insurance Institute. Annual publication.

Vaughan, Emmet J. *Fundamentals of Risk and Insurance,* 5th ed. New York: John Wiley and Sons, 1988.

Your Medicare Handbook. Publication Number (HCFA) 79-10050. Baltimore, Md.: Department of Health and Human Services, 1986.

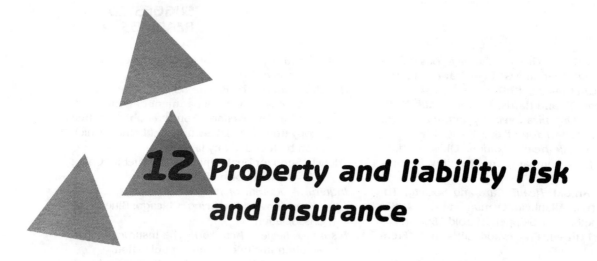

12 Property and liability risk and insurance

HIGHLIGHTS   In order to help plan an insurance program for the home and the automobile, this chapter will cover the following:

1   Liability and what it means
2   The general concepts of insurance on the home and how it works
        through the homeowner's policy
3   Liability insurance on the home
4   The deductible clause, the coinsurance clause, and how they apply
        to the home
5   The home insurance program
6   Automobile insurance—how it works, and what it covers
7   No-fault insurance
8   Other things the reader should know about auto insurance
9   An auto insurance program

INTRODUCTION: WHAT IS THE RISK?

Individuals who own a home (or even rent an apartment) are exposed to two risks. They are:

1. Loss of assets (property) due to various perils.
2. Loss of assets (savings) as a result of liability claims against a person.

An individual is exposed to the same two risks if he or she owns an automobile or a boat, or even if only driving one. These risks may be transferred to an insurance company by purchasing the following policies:

Home protection (both protected by a homeowner's policy)
    1. To protect property
    2. To protect against liability
Automobile protection (both protected by an automobile insurance policy)
    1. To protect property
    2. To protect against liability
Other protection (all provided by specialty insurance)
    1. Boat
    2. Mobile home
    3. Earthquake
    4. Flood
    5. Malpractice

Property is subject to physical destruction from a number of hazards, such as fire, flood, theft, and others. Equally likely is the possibility that a person will destroy or damage someone else's property, as in an automobile accident. Property insurance reimburses for the value of destroyed property. A policyholder should have property insurance for both personal and real property. **Personal property** includes such things as furniture, automobiles, and clothing. **Real property** includes any buildings attached to land, such as a house or garage.

Liability insurance protects the insured against claims by others. Liability can be broken down into claims by others due to bodily injury or death, and to claims due to the destruction of the property of others. People can be killed or injured on the insured's property, and the policyholder can be liable for these claims. Liability insurance is also necessary for those who drive automobiles, since automobile accidents often result in bodily injury as well as property damage.

Property and liability insurance premium payments should be regarded as payment for the protection of family material assets. The premiums paid on an insurance policy on a home are protection in the event of the destruction of the home by fire or some other disaster. A person who runs over someone with an auto exposes the family assets to loss by lawsuit.

The principle of property and liability insurance is much like the principle behind term life insurance. The risk of loss is spread over many units, and those few who actually suffer a loss are reimbursed by the insurance company—but indirectly by those policyholders who do not suffer a loss.

INSURANCE ON THE HOME

If a home burns down, it could be a financial disaster for the owner. There are other hazards the home owner faces that should be insured against, such as damage due to wind, flood, smoke, theft, or people running over lawns and shrubs with cars.

There is also the possibility that people will be injured on the client's property, resulting in a lawsuit and making him or her liable for damages. Or one could damage a neighbor's property, making him or her liable. An individual may be protected against all these hazards by means of the homeowner's policy.[1]

The homeowner's policy

The homeowner's policy provides five major kinds of insurance: (1) property insurance on the home, (2) personal property insurance, (3) liability insurance for bodily injury to others, (4) medical payment insurance, and (5) property liability insurance for damage to the property of others.

Most homeowner's policies have a Section I—which is the property section—and a Section II—which is the liability section.

---

1. There is also a special homeowner's policy for renters, which will be discussed below.

Section I covers:

1. Damage to the house due to fire, wind, hail, falling objects, smoke, motor vehicles, and a number of other perils, plus an allowance for living expenses in the event that the home owner has to live elsewhere for a time while the damaged home is being repaired.

2. Personal property insurance for loss of personal property due to fire, theft, mysterious disappearance, and so forth.

Section II provides:

1. Personal liability insurance to cover injuries occurring on the home owner's property.

2. Medical payment insurance to cover the medical bills of persons injured on the home owner's premises.

3. Property liability insurance to cover damage to the property of others.

Most insurance companies have several types of homeowner's policy packages to choose from, with names such as limited, basic, broad, all-inclusive, or all-risk. They are referred to as policies HO-1, HO-2, and so on. Generally the breadth of the extended coverage increases as one moves from policy 1 to policy 5; the premiums also increase.[2] The following seven HO policies are in general use:

1. Basic form (HO-1)

2. Broad form (HO-2)

3. All-risk (on home only) or special form (HO-3)

4. Contents broad form (HO-4) renters' insurance (HO-4)

5. Comprehensive form (all-risk on both home and personal property) (HO-5)

6. Condominium broad form (for condominium owners) (HO-6)

7. Modified coverage form (for older homes) (HO-8)[3]

Breadth of coverage

Under the homeowner's policies the breadth of the coverage will vary depending on the policy.

1. HO-1 basic coverage.   Homeowner's policy HO-1 (basic) covers the fewest items, but it covers more than just fire. It usually includes damage due to wind, hail, vehicles, and a number of other factors. With damage

---

2. The HO-1, etc. classification is generally used; however, in Texas and a few other southern states, the HO-A, HO-B, etc. classification is used.

3. There is no HO-7 policy. No one really knows why, but when the insurance industry developed the HO-8 policy, they skipped the number HO-7. Some companies have eliminated the HO-5 policy by adding its additional protection to the HO-3 policy. Some companies are also phasing out the HO-1 policy because more and more people are choosing HO-2.

to a roof due to hail, however, the basic policy will not pay for the cost of a new roof. Rather, the damaged roof will first be depreciated, and the policy will pay for a lesser amount of damages. For example, if the roof was ten years old when it was destroyed, and it is assumed it had a useful life of twenty years, the policy will pay for one-half of the cost of a new roof.

2. HO-2 broad coverage.   Under the broad coverage more perils are covered. In addition to the items under HO-1, damage from such things as falling objects, a collapsed roof due to the weight of snow or ice, and a number of other items are covered. Under the broad (HO-2) policy a hail-damaged roof is not first depreciated, and the policy pays for the entire cost of a new roof.

While nearly all homeowner's policies cover losses due to theft, in the case of the ***broad*** and ***all-risk policies,*** coverage is more generous. For example, they would pay for what is called mysterious disappearance, whereas the HO-1 would not; HO-1 requires proof of theft such as break-in or the like, whereas the broad or all-risk policy does not.

Some homeowner's policies also provide for living expenses if the home owner has to move into a hotel because the home has been so severely damaged that it is uninhabitable. If part of a home is rented, the fair rental value will be paid while the tenant vacates the home during repairs. There is a limit to the living expense allowance; usually it is a certain percentage of total dollar protection of the policy.

3. HO-3 special form, all-risk coverage.   This form covers all risks except those specifically excluded, but it applies only to the house and not personal property. Generally personal property is covered under this plan only to the extent that it is in HO-2. (However, some companies sell a rider which broadens the HO-3 coverage to include personal belongings.) Generally HO-3 covers all risks except flood, earthquake, war, nuclear radiation, volcanic eruption, and any others specified in the policy. A person should check the policy for a complete list of perils excluded.

4. HO-4 contents broad form.   This is renters' insurance. This provides no insurance on the building, which is normally the landlord's problem. It provides only personal property and liability coverage. Renters do need a personal liability policy. Even if a person is renting a house and the owner has such a personal liability policy, it generally applies only if the landlord is living in the house and it does not always protect the renter. If someone were to trip on the sidewalk and break his or her leg, the renter could be held liable.

5. HO-5 comprehensive form, all-risk coverage.   This provides for all-risk coverage except that which is specifically excluded. It is very much like HO-3, except that it covers personal property as well as the building. HO-3, you will recall, provides all-risk coverage only to the building, and covers personal property only to the extent that HO-2 does. As noted above, some companies no longer offer the HO-5 policy.

6. HO-6 condominium-owner broad form.   This provides only personal property and personal liability coverage. It does not cover the building because the condominium association has separate insurance on the building. It does, however, cover built-in appliances such as ranges, dish-washers, rugs, and the like that the condominium association's insurance would not cover.

7. HO-8 modified coverage form.   This is similar to HO-1 in that losses are paid on the basis of actual cash value rather than replacement cost. It is designed for older homes, where the replacement cost is much higher than the market value of the home. Often neither the home owner nor the insurer would be willing to insure a home valued at $75,000 for $150,000, which might be its replacement cost. Hence Form HO-8 was developed as a compromise.

Section I Coverage: Property

This section provides against the destruction of property and the coverage varies somewhat from policy to policy. Generally, coverage is superior as one moves from HO-1, to HO-2, to HO-3, and so on.

1. The house.   Section I covers the dwelling for the various hazards discussed above. Most insurance requires coverage of at least 80 percent of the replacement cost of the home, but some require as much as 100 percent. See below for a more detailed discussion of this.

2. Other structures.   Most homeowner's policies cover "other detached structures" on the property, such as tool sheds, garages, and the like. Some policies also include fences. The coverage here is limited to a percentage of the protection on the house. Other structures are generally not covered, if they are used for business purposes or are rented to someone other than a tenant.

3. Loss of use.   This item concerns additional living expenses incurred by a home owner because his or her house was destroyed or otherwise made uninhabitable. It covers increased costs for housing, transportation, and other items that must be met while the home is being repaired. The limit for this item is a certain percent of the protection on the structure.

   If part of the home is rented, the fair rental value will be paid while the tenant vacates the house during repairs.

4. Personal property coverage.   Personal property is covered under a homeowner's policy along with real property. This covers loss of furniture, clothing, cameras, rugs, drapes, furs, books, paintings, jewelry, and the like. It provides protection not only against fire but also against loss due to theft, vandalism, and in some cases mysterious disappearance. This type of policy also insures for loss of items away from the home. For example, a camera stolen from an automobile is covered by the personal property clause. This personal property coverage is written in different ways, but generally it will reimburse for losses up to 50 percent of insurance coverage carried on the home. If you have a $100,000 homeowner's policy, your personal property maximum protection would be $50,000. On certain items like jewelry, furs and collectible art, there are internal policy limits which will restrict the dollar amount recoverable for lost or damaged items.

It is wise to have a written inventory listing all personal property and its value. For expensive items such as furs, jewelry, and the like the bills of sale should be kept so that their value can be proved. Photographs are also useful. You may buy separate **policy floaters** on very valuable items such as furs, jewelry, and works of art. Insuring these items separately may reduce the value of the other personal property to about 40 percent of the value of the house and hence it will be covered by the regular homeowner's policy. Even if the total value of the personal property is under 40 percent of the value of the home, many policies limit the coverage on furs and jewelry to $2,000 unless these items are specifically listed. If they are listed they are insured for their appraised value and often without a deductible.

Section II is the liability coverage, and it includes a number of happenings.

Section II Coverage: Liability

1. Personal liability.   Personal liability coverage protects the insured against claims from bodily injury to other people. The insured is protected against lawsuits because of injuries to others caused by pets, boats, and bicycles. The policy would even cover an accident where the insured strikes another with a golf ball. It will cover any type of accident except automobile accidents and accidents related to business pursuits. If a guest slips on the sidewalk and breaks his or her leg, the home owner is covered. Or if a teenager runs over the neighbor's child with a bicycle and injures him or her, the insured is covered. It may even cover accidents away from home for which the insured or any member of the household is held responsible. If the client has a swimming pool, this must be noted in the policy to be certain that he or she has coverage, since a pool is legally considered an attractive nuisance in some states. Therefore, if a neighborhood child fell in the pool while the insured was not at home, he or she could be sued.

The basic amount of personal liability insurance coverage is $25,000 in most states, but larger amounts can be purchased. Personal

Table 12−1   *Comparison of homeowner's 76 coverages*

Coverage	HO-1 (basic form)	HO-2 (broad form)	HO-3 (special form)
Section I coverages			
A. Dwelling	$15,000 min.	$15,000 min.	$20,000 min.
B. Other Structures	10% of A	10% of A	10% of A
C. Personal Property	50% of A	50% of A	50% of A
D. Loss of Use	10% of A	20% of A	20% of A
	Fire or lightning Windstorm or hail Explosion Riot or civil commotion Aircraft Vehicles Smoke Vandalism or malicious mischief Theft Breakage of glass or safety glazing material (limit of $100) Volcanic eruption	Fire or lightning Windstorm or hail Explosion Riot or civil commotion Aircraft Vehicles Smoke Vandalism or malicious mischief Theft Breakage of glass or safety glazing material Falling objects Weight of ice, snow, or sleet Accidental discharge or overflow of water or steam Sudden and accidental tearing apart, cracking, burning, or bulging of a steam, hot water, air conditioning, or automatic fire protective sprinkler system, or appliance for heating water Freezing of a plumbing, heating, air conditioning, or automatic fire sprinkler system or from a household appliance Sudden and accidental damage from artificially generated electrical current Volcanic eruption	Dwelling and other structures covered against risks of direct physical loss to property except losses specifically excluded Personal property covered by same perils as HO-2 plus damage by glass or safety glazing material, which is part of a building, storm door, or storm window
Section II coverages			
E. Personal Liability	$100,000	$100,000	$100,000
F. Medical Payments to Others	$ 1,000 per person	$ 1,000 per person	$ 1,000 per person

HO-4 (Contents— broad form)	HO-6 (condominium unit- owners broad form)	HO-8 (modified coverage form)
Section 1 coverages		
Not Applicable	$1,000 minimum on the unit	Same as HO-1 except losses are paid on the actual amount required to repair or replace
Not Applicable	Included in Coverage A	the property using common construction materials and methods (actual cash value in
$6,000 min.	$6,000 min.	some states)
20% of C	40% of C	
Same perils as HO-2 for personal property	Same perils as HO-2 for personal property	Same perils as HO-1 except theft coverage applies only to losses on the residence premises up to a maximum of $1,000; certain other coverage restrictions also apply; glass breakage is limited to $100

Section II		
$100,000	$100,000	$1000,000
$ 1,000 per person	$ 1,000 per person	$ 1,000 per person

Note: Coverage E and Coverage F limits can be increased to higher limits.

Source: Rejda, George E. *Principles of Insurance,* Glenview, Ill.: Scott, Foresman and Company, 1989, pp. 122–123.

liability policy does not cover employees who are injured while working in the home. If a gardener, maid, or a television repairperson is injured, they are generally covered by workers' compensation, not the homeowner's policy.

2. Coverage for damage to the property of others.   This provides coverage if the insured or a member of the family damages the neighbor's property. For example, if one is burning leaves in the backyard and the fire spreads and damages the neighbor's fence (or even their house), the insured is covered. Or if the lawn mower hits a stone and flings it through the windshield of a neighbor's car, the insured is covered. This property liability coverage is generally limited to $250, $300, or $1,000, however.

3. Medical payments insurance.   Medical payments provide reasonable medical expense payments for injuries to people hurt on the premises of the insured. For example, the medical bills of a person who slips and breaks a leg on the home owner's sidewalk are paid. The coverage may apply to injuries occurring off the premises of the insured, but only if they were caused by the insured, a member of the insured's family, or their pets. Basic coverage is $500 for each person injured, but larger amounts may be purchased. Coverage is extended only to injuries of others and does not cover the home owner or members of the family.

Just as in the case of the personal liability clause in a homeowner's policy, the medical payment part does not cover employees injured while working in or around the home. In such a case, workers' compensation takes over.

Which policy is best for the client: Costs of a homeowner's policy

Generally, in most states the HO-2 (broad) policy is the best buy. It costs only slightly more than the HO-1 and provides a good deal more protection. On the other hand, when moving from the HO-2 (broad) to the HO-3 or HO-5 (all-risks) plans, premiums rise substantially while the protection rises only modestly. However, check this carefully; it may not be true in each state.

Table 12–1 summarizes the coverage provided by the various homeowner's policies. Premiums vary with the location of the property and type of construction. Certain areas are more susceptible to damage due to certain natural phenomena. Some areas are wind areas; others are in a hail belt; others, such as Florida and the Gulf Coast, are in the hurricane belt. Consequently, little can be said regarding costs regionally. Table 12–2 shows some data for a home owner's coverage in four different areas.

Within a smaller area classified as having common hazards, rates vary primarily with the type of construction. There are generally three or four classifications and three or four rates per $1,000 of insurance.

Regional premium variation on a homeowner's policy

Table 12—2

City	Premiums (annual rates)
Boston	$786
Austin, Texas	568
Los Angeles	650
Ames, Iowa	440

Note: In all cases the house is a $100,000 home exclusive of the lot. This means, of course, that there is much more house in Iowa and Texas than in Boston or Los Angeles. The premiums also include coverage on personal property, liability, and medical payments. In all cases there is an 80 percent coinsurance clause, and the deductibility is the same in all cases. The construction in all cases is the same: brick veneer. The houses are, then, the same in all respect except for size. Rates furnished by a large, well-known national company. Rates are subject to change due to rising construction costs and other factors over which the insurance industry has no control.

OTHER THINGS TO KNOW ABOUT HOME INSURANCE

A number of other important things about home ownership and homeowner's insurance with which a person should be familiar will be discussed next.

Deductible clause

Some homeowner's policies have a deductible feature, but generally it applies only to the dwelling and the personal property, not to the liability part of the policy.

The minimum deductible is $100, but many policies have more. A person may buy a $250 or a $500 deductible. The deductible may also be a percentage (usually .5 or 1 percent) of the insurance on the dwelling—and in the case of personal property, a certain percentage of that coverage. The higher the deductible, the lower the premium. For example, an insured would save about $120 per year in premiums if he or she raised the deductible from $100 to 1 percent on a $100,000 homeowner's policy.

Actual cash value versus replacement cost

Actual cash value and replacement cost are not always the same. Actual cash value is defined as replacement cost less depreciation. (Depreciation takes into account that the property is partially worn out.) In the case of personal property (furniture), most policies will reimburse for covered losses on the basis of actual cash value at the time of the loss but not to exceed the amount needed to repair or replace the property. In many cases the replacement cost is the higher, and hence the insured would have to bear some loss of his or her personal property. (A few companies offer replacement cost coverage for personal property, but at a considerably higher premium).

On the dwelling, most policies will pay losses on the basis of replacement cost with no allowance for depreciation for partially damaged homes. However, the face value is the maximum a company will pay if a house is totally destroyed, even though the replacement cost may be the higher.

Coinsurance

Most policies also have a coinsurance clause to discourage the home owner from having too little insurance on the home. This is a statement that the company shall be liable, in the event of loss, only in the proportion that the actual amount of insurance bears to the insurance theoretically required. The required or proper amount of insurance is not 100 percent of the value of the house but usually about 80 percent, although some companies may require 90 or even 100 percent. This 80 or 90 percent figure, which has been set after years of experience, reflects the fact that relatively few houses are completely destroyed by fire. The purpose of the coinsurance clause is to adjust rates equitably among the various policyholders. In the absence of a coinsurance clause, it might happen that an individual would be able to collect the full amount of the loss without paying much premium. Suppose a house is valued at $100,000 and a policy is placed on it for only $60,000. A loss occurs of $20,000, and in the absence of the coinsurance clause, the full $20,000 would be collectible. This award would be unfair to other people who had insured their property for the proper amount and who had therefore been paying higher premiums.

In an 80 percent coinsurance clause, it states, "This company shall not be liable for a greater proportion of any loss or damage to the property described herein than the sum hereby bears to 80 percent of the actual cash value of said property at the time the loss shall happen, nor for more than the proportion which this policy bears to the total insurance thereon." In other words, if the insured does not carry insurance amounting to 80 percent of the cash value of the property and if a partial loss occurs, he or she must share that loss with the company. The individual may recover only that proportion of the loss that the amount of insurance he or she actually has bears to the amount of insurance he or she should have under the coinsurance clause. This principle has long since been converted into the following formula:

$$\frac{\text{Amount carried}}{\text{Amount should carry}} \times \text{Actual loss} = \text{Recovery}$$

Suppose that the actual cash value of a home is $100,000 and that there is an 80 percent coinsurance clause in the policy. A person has insurance of only $60,000, and there is a loss of $10,000. How much of the $10,000 loss can one collect? Substituting in the formula above:

$$\frac{\text{Amount carried } (\$60,000)}{\text{Amount should carry } (\$100,000 \times .80 \text{ or } \$80,000)} \times \text{Actual loss } (\$10,000)$$

$$= \text{Recovery of } (\$7,500)$$

On the other hand, assuming the same set of facts and assuming further that the proper amount of $80,000 of insurance was carried, then:

$$\frac{\$80,000}{\$80,000} \times \$10,000 = \$10,000 = \text{(Recovery)}$$

It should be emphasized that if a house is totally destroyed by fire, the insurance company will not necessarily pay for the entire value of the house. The company will generally pay a sum equal to the face value of the policy. Therefore, if a home owner has a house with an actual cash value or replacement cost of $100,000 and because an 80 percent coinsurance clause only carries $80,000 of insurance, that is the maximum the company will pay. If the house is lost in a fire, the home owner loses $20,000. The coinsurance clause, then, protects the company against people who buy less fire insurance than they need but who still are fully protected against a fire that does not totally or almost destroy the house. For the home owner to be fully covered in case a fire totally destroys the house, he or she needs 100 percent coverage. Indeed, many mortgage lenders require the home owner to buy 100 percent coverage as a condition of making the loan.

If a home is totally destroyed: 100 percent coverage

It is wise for the home owner to reappraise the value of the house occasionally and change the insurance accordingly. The value of houses may have risen substantially because of inflation. In addition, a house may rise in value for other reasons. For example, population growth will tend to make a house rise in value in those areas of rapid growth. Also, if building costs rise (say, by more than inflation) new homes, and sometimes older homes as well, will appreciate pricewise by more than the current rate of inflation.

Keeping a policy current with inflation

Most insurance companies provide for an automatic increase yearly. However, most companies base their annual adjustment on the increase in the consumer price index (the CPI measures inflation; see Chapter 1) or on some average of the increase in overall U.S. construction costs. If the value of homes in the area is rising more rapidly than inflation, or even the national average home increase, the automatic adjustment may be inadequate. Therefore, the increased insurance needed in the area should be determined, with the aid of an insurance agent and perhaps a realtor.

OTHER INSURANCE FOR THE HOME OWNER

There are three other types of insurance that might be appropriate for the home owner. They are flood insurance, earthquake insurance, and mobile home insurance.

Flood insurance

If a person buys a homeowner's policy, he or she is covered for virtually all hazards, but an individual may need one for which he or she is not covered—flood insurance. Insurance companies will not sell flood insurance because they cannot actuarially spread the risk over large numbers —the reason being that only people living in a flood plain would buy flood insurance. Flood insurance can be purchased through an agency of the federal government, the U. S. Department of Health and Urban Development (HUD). The maximum amount of insurance which may be bought is $185,000 on a single-family home and $60,000 on its contents. Premiums will vary depending upon the area of residence. A homeowner's insurance agent can help if one needs coverage.

Earthquake insurance

Earthquake insurance, like flood insurance, is not included in the homeowner's policy. However, it may be purchased separately from many companies. If one lives in an earthquake belt like the west coast, he or she might consider it. Generally speaking, earthquake insurance has a deductible of 5 to 6 percent of total coverage provided, which means that damages caused by minor quakes would be assumed by the home owner in most cases.

Mobile home insurance

Special mobile home insurance is available from many companies and is similar to the homeowner's policies discussed above. It covers a variety of perils—fire, wind, theft, and so on. This insurance covers the mobile home, the personal property in it, and some liability coverage, just like in the case of a homeowner's policy. In some states a separate policy is required, and in others the coverage can be obtained through either a homeowner's policy or an auto policy. Generally if a "mobile home" is not truly mobile (is on blocks in a mobile-home park), a separate policy is needed, but if it is a trailer and moves about, coverage may be obtained through an auto policy by paying an extra premium.

A HOME INSURANCE PROGRAM

As noted above, either an HO-2 or an HO-3 should be purchased. Which one would depend on the budget, where one lives, and one's priorities.

Renters should consider the homeowner's policy for renters, HO-4. This would protect personal property and provide liability protection.

As noted above, there are special policies for condominium owners and owners of older homes (the HO-6 and HO-8). The pertinent one of these should be purchased.

Landlords who own a rental house might want an old-fashioned fire insurance policy with an extended coverage endorsement. Personal property coverage would not be needed if it is an unfurnished house, nor would medical payments coverage be needed. But a landlord would need liability coverage for the rental house. Both the tenant and the landlord need this since most policies cover only one or the other, and the provisions are not transferable. Someone who slipped and broke his or her neck on the sidewalk in front of the rental house could sue both the tenant and the owner. Each would need a separate policy; the policy of one would not cover the other. The landlord can buy this as a supplement to the same personal liability protection already provided by his or her homeowner's policy.

California residents should consider earthquake insurance because it is relatively inexpensive. The same can be said of flood insurance, for those who live in a flood plain.

These remains the question of how much insurance to buy. This is largely determined by the value of the house. Since most companies have an 80 or 90 percent coinsurance clause, this sets the floor on the amount of insuranace. For full protection, however, a person would need to buy a policy with a face value equal to 100 percent of the value of the house. One's own priorities will dictate whether to select 80, 90, or 100 percent coverage. The amount of liability insurance needed to be incorporated into a homeowner's policy will also vary with the home owner's priorities.

AUTOMOBILE INSURANCE

Automobile insurance is an absolute must. Anyone who owns an automobile, or even one who only drives a friend's auto, is exposed to the risk of loss. These risks include:

1. Loss of assets due to the damage or destruction of property
2. Loss of assets due to death or bodily injury
3. Loss of assets due to medical bills
4. Loss of income due to injuries that prevent a person from working

Loss of income was discussed in Chapter 11 under disability insurance. The other three risks and how to manage them will be discussed here.

The above risks can be minimized by being a careful driver, and by assuming a small portion of the risk oneself—by means of a deductible —as we shall see. However, the bulk of the risk must be transferred to an insurance company by purchasing property and liability insurance. The premiums then go into a pool and the funds are used to pay the claims of those who have accidents.

Declarations page   This page spells out the coverage and the premiums charged; it actually
consists of four separate insurance contracts as follows:

   A.   Liability coverage, which protects the insured if he or she kills or
            injures someone or destroys their property
   B.   Medical payment coverage (sometimes called *personal injury pro-
            tection—see* Table 12–3), which will pay the medical expenses of all
            passengers injured while in the insured's car
   C.   Uninsured and underinsured motorist coverage, which provides pro-
            tection if one is hit by a motorist who has no insurance, inadequate
            insurance, or is a hit-and-run driver
   D.   Coverage for damage to the auto of the insured

Table 12—3   *Declarations page*

ITEM 1:
NAMED INSURED   JOHN JONES
AND MAILING   1610 MAIN ST.
ADDRESS   AUSTIN TX.
ITEM 2: POLICY PERIOD: 12 MONTHS FROM DECEMBER 4, 1987 TO DECEMBER 4, 1988*

ITEM 3:   DESCRIPTION OF AUTO(S) OR TRAILER(S)

AUTO	MODEL YEAR	TRADE NAME	IDENTIFICATION NUMBER	TERR	CLASS	SYMBOL/FOB PRICE
1	84	HONDA	JHMAD5425EC081941	2323	1B/00	08
2	84	CHEVR	1G1AN69H4EX127634	2323	1A/00	07

ITEM 4:   Coverage is provided where a premium and a limit of liability are shown for the coverage.

"NA" means that a coverage is not afforded. When it appears in a premium column for a car,
that coverage is not afforded for that car.

COVERAGES	LIMITS OF LIABILITY	PREMIUMS AUTO 1	AUTO 2
A. Liability Coverage			
Bodily Injury Liability	$250,000 each person		
	$500,000 each accident	118	110
Property Damage Liability.	$50,000 each accident	112	104
B2. Personal Injury Protection Coverage.	$2,500 each person	29	23
C. Uninsured/Underinsured Motorists Coverage.			
Bodily Injury Liability	$20,000 each person		
	$40,000 each accident	9	8
Property Damage Liability.	$15,000 each accident		
$250 Deductible Applicablea To PD Liability.		7	7
D. Coverage for Damage To The Auto.			
Other Than Collision	actual cash value	93	76
	Less $100 Deductible		
Collision	actual cash value	157	113
	Less $500 Deductible		
	Subtotal Premium	$525	$441

Everyone definitely should have liability insurance. The case for medical payment coverage and uninsured motorist coverage is weaker, but it should be strongly considered because the premiums are relatively low. If a car is old and of little value, one may wish to forgo coverage for damage to the car and bear this risk oneself. Even if a car is quite valuable the insured may wish to bear some of this risk by choosing a fairly high deductible. This is explained in greater detail below. An example of a declarations page is shown in Table 12–3.

Policies have a section that spells out the general conditions of the insurance, such as:

Insuring agreement and general provisions

1. *Who is covered.* Generally speaking, everyone named in a policy is covered by the automobile policy. Even if they are not mentioned, all members of the insured's family may be covered, but this varies from company to company. Check the policy to make certain on this point. If an insured lends a car to a friend, he or she is covered even though the friend is not mentioned in the policy, generally speaking. College students living away from home are covered when they are home for a visit. Some companies, however, require a small extra premium for this and list them as an occasional driver.
2. *Rental cars.* This section also spells out what coverage is available for someone who rents a car while on vacation in another city. When renting a car, individuals are usually told that the rental company has full liability coverage but with a $2,000 or $3,000 deductible on their collision coverage. The renter would have to pay up to that amount in the event of an accident. Rental car companies will attempt to persuade individuals to buy a policy to provide additional protection at a rate of $10 to $13 per day; this is an astronomical rate. Before renting a car, an individual should check with his or her insurance agent. The personal policy may apply and provide the same protection for any rental car.

This paragraph spells out what is not covered. Generally, coverage is not provided in most foreign countries, although some policies do provide coverage if the claim occurs within 25 miles of the border. If the client goes into the interior of Mexico, he or she needs to buy Mexican insurance. In Canada, on the other hand, the insured has coverage.

Exclusions

Many policies exclude coverage if a car is used for business purposes. Even if only used on a part-time basis, a special rider needs to be purchased.

This provides protection against damages for (1) inflicting bodily injuries or death in an automobile accident, (2) damaging or destroying someone's property, and (3) providing legal defense if necessary.

Part A: Auto liability insurance

1. *Bodily injuries.* If an individual becomes legally liable for bodily injuries or death, the cost could ruin him or her financially. Even if it is not the insured's fault, he or she might become involved in an expensive legal battle. Proving negligence (or the lack of it) is not always easy, and courts do award high damages.
2. *Damage to the property of others.* Less property liability coverage is needed than for bodily injuries because even an expensive car, if totally wrecked, will not result in as high a damage claim as in the case of bodily injuries or death.
3. *Policy limits.* There are limits to the amount a policy will pay, both for bodily injuries and property damages. In the case of bodily injuries there is a per-person limit and a per-accident limit. Bodily injury limits might be $50,000 to $100,000, or $100,000 to $200,000 and even higher. A $50,000 to $100,000 limit means the most the insurance company will pay is $50,000 to any one victim and $100,000 for all the victims in a single accident. In the case of property liability the limits are generally $10,000, $25,000, or $50,000; the limits nearly always apply to each accident, not to each car.

It is recommended that the client choose a high limit, especially for bodily injuries, because today it is common for courts to award high damages. Moreover, premiums do not rise greatly as limits are increased. For people who have acquired wealth, a $250,000 to $500,000 limit is not unreasonable. The explanation is clear: just because one carries insurance in the amount of $100,000 does not mean that this is all he or she will be liable for; an individual may obtain a judgment against the insured for $200,000 or more. In this case, if the coverage is only $100,000 the company will pay that and the insured will be personally liable for the balance.

Since additional premiums required to finance a large liability policy are not great, it is recommended that a high priority be placed on liability coverage. Coming up with a dollar figure is difficult, but some experts feel an individual should have, at least for bodily damage, protection of an amount equal to his or her net worth. Others would add somewhat more than this to take into account future earnings. Net worth is often used because that is what is in danger if a lawsuit is filed and a person doesn't have insurance protection.

Others feel that the proper amount of liability insurance should be geared to the current pattern of jury award in the geographical area where the insured lives. According to this, one would need more insurance in New York of California, where awards are typically higher than elsewhere. On the other hand, in Mississippi, Arkansas, or North Dakota, one would need less. It is also true that sometimes there is no logical pattern to court awards, and hence it is somewhat arbitrary to determine liability insurance this way. Nevertheless, a judgment could be based on both patterns of court awards and the client's net worth.

This coverage is sometimes called *personal injury protection coverage* and provides that the company will pay within specified monetary limits, generally from $500 to $5,000, "all reasonable expenses incurred within three years from the date of the accident for necessary medical, surgical, and dental services, including prosthetic devices, and necessary ambulance, hospital, professional nursing and funeral services" to persons injured "while in or upon, or entering into or alighting from the automobile . . . of the insured."

This also covers injuries as a result of "being struck, knocked down, or run over by an automobile," or injured in a collision. If persons have this insurance, they and their family are covered while riding in another auto, as a pedestrian, on a bicycle, or in any other way. People riding in the policyholder's car are also covered. Often this insurance will pay even if the other person was at fault and his or her medical payment insurance paid for some of the client's expenses. The client's policy will pay, in such a case, that portion of the expenses that the other person's policy did not pay, up to the limits of the policy. Damages may also be recovered from the other person's auto liability coverage (Part A) if he or she was at fault. Finally, the health insurance policy (discussed in Chapter 11) may pay for any residual expenses incurred but not paid by any of the above coverage.

The rates for this coverage are relatively low, and it is highly recommended. Rates do vary with the amount of coverage. The limits on this type of insurance may be $1,000, $2,000, $3,000, and on up to $10,000. The limit applies on a per-person basis, not a per-accident basis.

Some companies break the medical insurance down into B-1 (discussed immediately above) and B-2. B-2 provides the same coverages as B-1, and in addition, some loss of income for the insured, if he or she is unable to earn income for a time. This then is short-term disability insurance and has relatively low limits.

Most states now require companies to offer policyholders the **uninsured motorist coverage** for a slight extra premium. The uninsured motorist coverage is simple and relatively inexpensive. It states that if the policyholder is injured as the result of an accident with an uninsured and negligent motorist or by a hit-and-run driver, his or her company will in effect insure that uninsured motorist for whatever amount specified in the policy. Generally the limits for bodily injury go up to $15,000 for one individual, and $30,000 for one accident. For property damage the limit may go as high as $15,000. If the policy has this coverage, the insured's own insurance company pays him or her, but generally only for bodily injuries. A few companies, however, will also pay a collision claim under this coverage if an individual has a collision policy with them.

The insurance company, after it pays the insured, has the right to sue the other motorist to recover what it paid. In practice this is often difficult because the uninsured motorist probably has no assets. Or if the driver injures someone without stopping, there is little the company can do unless the driver is subsequently apprehended.

In the case of a motorist having some insurance but less than the client's coverage under this clause, his or her company will pay that amount and the client's company will pay the difference.

Part D: Coverage for damage to the insured's own car

This provides coverage for damages to the insured's car due to collision and causes other than collision. Each is rated separately, each has a separate premium, and a separate deductible. The causes other than collision are often referred to as ***comprehensive coverage*** and this coverage protects against loss caused by a number of perils.

Collision insurance

Collision insurance coverage pays for the damages caused by a collision with another vehicle, by skidding off the road and smashing into a fixed object, or by rolling over. The insured has this protection regardless of who was at fault. If the client was at fault, the client's insurance company will pay. If the other person was at fault, his or her company will generally pay. If it's an uninsured or hit-and-run motorist, the client's company will pay in accordance with Part C, discussed above. There are several features common to all collision policies.

1. *Deductible.* Deductibles may be selected such as $100, $200, $500, or even a $1,000. The insurance covers the cost of repairs less the deductible, or the actual car value less the deductible if the car is totaled.

    The higher the deductible the lower the premiums, because the risk to the company is less. If one is a careful driver, he or she can save money by selecting a higher deductible. Table 12–4 shows how premiums decline as the deductible rises.

2. *Actual cash value.* Actual cash value is the replacement cost less depreciation; in the case of an automobile it is also usually the market value of the vehicle. On some occasions, a car can be repaired after a collision, but the cost of repairing it is greater than the value of the car before the loss. In such a case, the cost of repairs does not enter into the matter. If the car was valued at $1,000 before a loss and has a junk value of $100 after the loss, and there is a $300 deductible in the policy, the company is liable only in the amount of $700—although it might cost $1,200 to restore the car to its original condition.

3. *Cars financed on the installment plan.* If a car is financed, the lending institution usually insists that the car purchaser be insured. When a bank finances the purchase of a new car, the car itself is

Insurance premiums: collision
insurance yearly premiums

Table 12—4

Deductible	Premiums
$200	$257
250	243
500	161

These rates are for a Chevrolet Caprice. Rates will vary regionally.
Rates would be somewhat higher if
the driver were a male under 25
years of age.

used as the collateral for the loan. If the driver runs the car into a
telephone pole and wrecks it, the collateral is thereby reduced by an
amount equal to the amount of the damages. Consequently, the
bank is without collateral and, if the purchaser refused to pay the
bank, it would have no other recourse than to sue on a promissory
note that it holds; the purchaser might then have insufficient assets
with which to pay off the judgment. To protect themselves, financial
institutions demand that the auto be covered by collision and comprehensive insurance.

4. *Subrogation.* One of the concepts that should be understood in connection with collision insurance is subrogation. Under the terms of
the collision policy, the insured agrees that the company shall have
the legal right to proceed against a negligent third party causing the
loss and to provde damages in the name of the insured. The company has the right to step into the shoes of the insured, as it were,
to proceed against a person causing the loss, and the insured
agrees to cooperate fully with the company. Suppose a person is
parked in a legal manner and another person driving negligently hits
the parked car, causing damages of $1,000. If the insured has a
$200 deductible collision policy, the company will pay the insured
$800 and, under the terms of the policy, may commence a lawsuit
against the negligent party to recover the $800 plus the $200 deductible. The insured person may in this manner recover his or her
$200 out-of-pocket costs because the total amount of the suit will
be $1,000.

Comprehensive insurance covers nearly all perils other than collision.
Protection is given for any direct and accidental loss or damage to the
automobile covered, as well as damage to the equipment usually attached to the vehicle. In addition, the automobile is covered for fire and
theft. The important clause from the point of view of the insured states

*Damages to a car
by causes other
than collision:
Comprehensive
insurance*

that the company shall be liable for "breakage of glass, and other loss caused by falling objects, fire, theft, explosion, earthquake, windstorm, hail, water, flood, malicious mischief or vandalism, riot, or civil commotion." The company limits it maximum liability to the actual cash value at the time of the loss. Although it has the option of repairing or replacing the damaged property, its maximum obligation is still limited to the actual cash value. Most comprehensive policies are written with a deductible provision, generally a $50 or $100 deductible.

One coverage often put into some comprehensive policies is a clause providing for rental reimbursement for loss of use. In this case, insured persons are paid, within limitations, for a vehicle that they may rent if their car is stolen. Sometimes car rental fees are also paid by the insurance company while a car is being repaired after it has been damaged in a collision. This, however, is usually taken care of by the liability section of the other driver's insurance company if he or she was at fault.

Rates on a comprehensive policy vary with the region where one lives, based on the past experience of loss. Rates in big cities are higher than in smaller towns or in rural areas because of the greater likelihood of vandalism, accidents, and the like. In certain rural areas of Colorado and Kansas, however, the lack of vandals is more than offset by the existence of hail or a combination of wind and dust, both of which will take the paint off a car.

OTHER IMPORTANT ASPECTS OF AUTOMOBILE INSURANCE
No-fault insurance

We will now examine a number of other things about automobile insurance with which one should be familiar.

No-fault insurance was developed because it was felt that many accident victims were inadequately compensated for their losses. Due to high medical costs, legal fees, court costs, and lost wages, many victims sustained losses even after being compensated by an insurance company. On the other hand, many critics felt many victims were overcompensated for pain and suffering. No-fault was an attempt to strike a balance. A victim would be fully compensated for his or her losses, but would not be paid for pain and suffering. under no-fault insurance, the victim's insurance company will pay regardless of who is at fault. The insurance company can then sue the other driver or his or her insurance company. Often much time and money are saved by avoiding going to court, particularly if it is not clear who is at fault.

At present about twenty-four states have some variation of no-fault laws on their books, but there is no agreement regarding what is meant by no-fault insurance. Purists insist that true no-fault would bar tort lawsuits for minor injuries. The injured party would be required to accept payment for injuries and not be permitted to sue for pain and suffering.

The injured party would receive payments from his or her insurance company to compensate for these three types of losses:

1. Income lost while injured
2. Medical and hospital bills
3. Expenses incurred in hiring maids and others to perform services formerly performed by the victim.

There are presently three main types of no-fault laws on the books of the various states.

1. *Modified no-fault.* Under modified no-fault an injured person receives some benefits but is not permitted to sue the other driver unless and until the claim reaches a certain dollar amount. Above that amount the victim could sue for pain and suffering.
2. *Expanded no-fault.* These are also sometimes called add-on no-fault. Under these laws, injured parties would receive modest sums automatically. However, they would not lose the right to sue for over and above that amount, including suing for pain and suffering. The idea here is that if some benefits are paid, the injured party may be satisfied and not sue.
3. *Pure no-fault.* Under pure no-fault, and injured person could not sue under any circumstances; torts would be eliminated. A person could not collect for pain and suffering, but could collect unlimited amounts for lost wages and medical bills. No state has enacted a pure no-fault law, although Michigan has come closest. Under Michigan law torts are eliminated except in the cases of death, permanent disfigurement, or disability.

Since only about one-half of the states have no-fault insurance, there are numerous cases in which a driver from a non-no-fault (tort) state has an accident in a no-fault state with a driver covered by no-fault insurance, and vice versa. In such a case the no-fault driver is paid by his or her insurance company. Then that company and the other driver's insurance company settle the other driver's claim in the usual way. For example, if a Massachusetts driver (no-fault) has an accident in Texas (non-no-fault), the Massachusetts driver's claims are paid by his or her insurance company. This is because most no-fault policies are valid in all states. Then the Texas driver and his or her insurance company and the Massachusetts company settle the claim in the usual way, either amicably out of court or in court if necessary. If a Texas driver has an accident in Massachusetts, the same procedure is followed.

The advocates of no-fault insurance maintain that under it not only are settlements for injuries made more quickly, but they are more certain. Indeed, they are almost automatic. Under the tort (or fault) system usually lengthy legal battles must be fought. Also if the victim is partly at fault, the doctrine of contributory negligence prevents a settlement. Proponents also argue average no-fault settlements often result in the victim's getting more because there would be no court costs or attorney's fees to dilute the settlement. Under the tort system, less than one half of the liability insurance premium dollar is returned to the accident victim, according to a U.S. Department of Transportation study. Finally, proponents believe that no-fault saves time and money for the insurance companies, not only in the form of court costs and attorneys' fees, but in administrative expenses, which could reduce insurance premiums.

The opponents of no-fault say it is unfair in that it allows no settlement for pain and suffering or mental anguish. They also argue that by allowing damages automatically, many people who don't deserve them get them. (Presumably there are people who are at fault and have themselves caused or at least contributed to, their injuries.) This, opponents say, increases insurance company costs and results in higher premiums.[4]

Financial responsibility laws

A few states have compulsory insurance laws, and many others have laws concerning financial responsibility even though they have no compulsory insurance laws. In states that have financial responsibility laws, individuals must prove financial responsibility; they may do this by proving they are adequately insured. Moreover, they need only prove they have adequate liability insurance. What amount is adequate varies from states to state.

The purpose of financial responsibility laws is to protect the victims of automobile accidents. The law attempts to do this by encouraging people to have at least the minimum amount of insurance and in this way increase the probability of the victim's being able to collect to compensate for the damages.

While the purpose of financial responsibility laws is admirable, in some states these laws are ineffective because of either court rulings or poor enforcement. In others they work fairly well. In some states, the car registration of a motorist who fails to prove financial responsibility is withdrawn.

Preferred risks

Some companies issue preferred risk policies as a competitive device to increase their share of the market. They screen their policyholders carefully and then sell them a policy at a lower premium. In short, as a reward for safe driving the rate is lowered. Lowered rates are given only to se-

---

4. Both sides maintain that their system would result in lower premiums. Neither side's case can be proven. The coming of no-fault insurance has not reduced premiums; indeed they soared in recent years. However, much of this increase is attributable to inflation. A comparison of premiums in no-fault and tort states shows no discernible pattern.

lected risks, those who have had a safe record for a number of years. In addition, some companies emphasize that they specifically will sell insurance only to nondrinking drivers, and that because of this they can charge lower premiums.

Rates vary from one section of the country to another, in part because injuries typically grant larger awards in some areas. The cost of living is also higher in some sections of the country. Rates may also vary within any geographic region; generally they are higher in big cities than in small towns. Table 12–5 shows some of this regional variation for one national company.

Insurance premiums variations

Rates also vary somewhat with the age and sex of the driver. Male drivers under age 25 pay a higher premium because they have a higher accident rate. In some states those who are under 25 and married get some reduction from the general under-25 rate. The driving record may also affect the rate. In some states if a person has had several (the number varies from state to state but two to four is most common) moving traffic violations, his or her rates may be pushed above the regular rate even if there have been no accidents. If one has had an accident and got a ticket, the rate could be adjusted upward even more. On the other hand, some companies reduce rates below regular rates for those drivers between age 30 and 60 who have good driving records. The age range 30 to 60 is dependent on the theory that drivers under 30 are less cautious than those over 30, and that the reflexes of drivers over 60 have slowed down. Finally, rates on collision and comprehensive coverage vary with the type of auto as well as the factors noted above. The more expensive the auto, the more expensive the insurance.

Table 12–5   *Automobile rate comparisons*

Automobile coverage—limits	Los Angeles, California	Austin, Texas	Ames, Iowa	Boston, Massachusetts
Bodily injury-property damage 100/300/50	$ 686	$214	$122	$ 537
Medical $2,000	98	14	8	14
Collision $100 deductible	404	254	134	617
Comprehensive $100 deductible	178	81	50	293
Uninsured motorist—financial responsibility limit	84	8	6	17
Total	$1,450	$571	$320	$1,478

Note: In all cases the cars are used only for pleasure and no driver is under twenty-five. The rates are subject to change at any time due to inflation, larger court awards, rising auto repair prices, and other factors beyond the control of the insurance industry. Rates furnished by a large, well-known national company. The rates apply to a Chevrolet valued at $14,000 and are annual premiums. Includes bodily injury liability of $100,000/$300,000 and property liability of $50,000, medical insurance of $1,000, uninsured motorist coverage, and collision and comprehensive coverage—both of which have a $100 deductible.

**Box 12—2
How to lower your
client's auto
insurance
premiums**

1. *Shop around.* Not all companies charge the same premiums for the same coverage. In some states maximum rates are set by the state insurance commission, but companies may deviate their rates below these ceilings.

   The more efficiently run companies do provide insurance at a lower rate. This is true of both automobile and homeowner's insurance.

2. *Consider increasing the deductible.* Do this on both collision and comprehensive insurance.

   If one increases the collision deductible from $100 to $250 on a $10,000 car, the premiums will decline by as much as $50 per year. If one raises the deductible to $500, the premiums will drop by another $50 and sometimes more. Doing the same on comprehensive insurance will reduce premiums by similar amounts.

3. If one has an old car worth $1,000 or less, consider dropping collision entirely.

4. If there are teenagers in the family, be sure they go through an approved driver's education program when they first learn to drive. Most high schools have these programs. Many insurance companies reduce rates somewhat for people who have gone through a driver's education program.

5. Many communities have defensive driving courses, which anyone may take and which are approved and sponsored by the National Safety Council. Many insurance companies reduce rates for people who have had these courses.

6. If someone has more than one car, he or she is eligible for the multicar discount. Be sure to get it.

7. Individuals should be sure they are charged the correct rate for which the car is being used. Rates vary not only with the number of miles driven per year but also with such driving factors as:
   a. to and from work
   b. pleasure
   c. business and professional use
   d. carpool, or
   e. some combination of the above. For example, if a person stops driving to and from work and joins a carpool, this could save premium dollars.

AN INSURANCE PROGRAM: HOW MUCH AUTO INSURANCE TO BUY?

How much insurance does a person need, or how much should he or she buy? That depends. It is in part a personal value judgment based on priorities. It also depends on the income and how much the budget permits. The higher the income, the higher the insurance needs, and also the higher the amount which can be afforded. Moreover, some types of insurance deserve a higher priority than others.

*Liability insurance
needs*

Liability insurance should receive the highest priority. Indeed this is an absolute must. But how much coverage should one buy? The client's net worth is what is being protected, and that is the place to begin. Some weight might also be given to future earnings and future increase in net worth. If there is a pattern of court settlements in the area for seriously injured or killed automobile victims, consider that. One should have a fairly large liability policy even if net worth is not very great. Rates do not rise rapidly as the amount of liability insurance purchased increases.

1. *Bodily injury liability.* This should receive a higher priority than property liability because this is where the court awards are the highest. As a bare minimum we would suggest $20,000 to $40,000 bodily liability protection. However, buying a $250,000 to $500,000 limit would only cost $33 more. Table 12–6 shows how premiums rise with increased coverage.
2. *Property liability coverage.* If an individual is on a really tight budget he or she might skimp a bit here; but as Table 12–6 shows, rates too do not rise much as coverage increases.

If a person really needs a large amount of liability insurance, he or she should buy an umbrella package. Most auto insurers do not write more than $250,000/$500,000 – $100,000 of bodily injury and property liability coverage, but many have a liability umbrella policy for as high as several million dollars. An umbrella policy normally has a high deductible, so one would need that same high coverage through the regular insurance. The umbrella covers all liability claims in excess of that for both the home and the auto. For the coverages, premiums are relatively cheap; in most states a $1,000,000 umbrella policy can be purchased for about $100 per year, and a $2,000,000 policy for about $150. An umbrella policy should have a deductible equal to the auto bodily injury policy limit, and would take over when that had been exhausted.

An umbrella policy

ask Client

It should be noted that while an umbrella covers all members of the family for personal liability, it does not cover liability because of profes-

Insurance premiums for auto liability insurance—yearly rates   Table 12–6

Property liability coverage	Premiums	Bodily injury liability coverage	Premiums
$ 15,000	$103	$20,000/$40,000	$ 85
25,000	106	$25,000/$50,000	94
50,000	112	$50,000/$100,000	101
100,000	117	$100,000/$200,000	112
		$250,000/$500,000	118

These rates are for a Chevrolet Caprice. Rates will vary regionally. Also rates would be somewhat higher if the driver were a male under age 25.

sional malpractice. That is considered a commercial activity and is covered by malpractice insurance discussed below.

Collision insurance: How large a deductible should one carry?

Should one have collision insurance, and if so how large a deductible should he or she have? The answers depend upon the value of the car, how much one drives, where one drives, and the kind of driver he or she is, factors that cannot be measured mathematically.

Once a car depreciates below a given figure, collision insurance should be dropped. The more one drives the more likely he or she is to have an accident. If one drives mostly in the country or small towns, the likelihood of an accident is less than if one lives in a city and drives there, especially on freeways. Only the insured knows what kind of driver he or she is, hence only that person can judge this point. But if one drives defensively, he or she does not need insurance as much (or can live with a higher deductible) as would be the case if one drives offensively. Premiums on collision insurance vary regionally as well as with the value of the car. Calculate the annual premium plus the deductible as a percent of the car's value. Remember this percent will go up as the deductible is increased, and this is a good way to save money. This ratio may also go up as the car becomes older and loses its value. Check with an agent to see what the saving would be if the deductible were increased.

If one can reduce premiums by as much as $100 per year by increasing the deductible by $300, the insured will save money by doing so if he or she has an accident less frequently than about every three years. If a person is an average driver and has a wreck, there is about a fifty-fifty chance it will be the other person's fault, and his or her insurance company will pay. This improves the odds; now the $100 saved per year will finance the $300 additional deductible about every year and a half. Depending upon where one lives and how expensive a car is owned, he or she can save from $100 to $200 per year in premiums by choosing a $500 deductible.

When to drop collision insurance completely is a more difficult question. Once the annual premiums plus the deductible together amount to a substantial percentage of the value of the car, one should consider dropping it. Suppose a car is worth $1,000 and one has a have a $100 deductible policy with an annual premium of $100. If the car were totaled, the out-of-pocket cost would be $200 (the premium plus the deductible). The insured is paying $200 to protect $800 of property (the car's value of $1,000 less $200 out-of-pocket cost). This ratio is 25 percent, and one should consider dropping the collision insurance. The car will continue to decline in value as the years pass.

Comprehensive insurance: How large a deductible should one carry?

Comprehensive needs should be evaluated in the same manner as collision needs were evaluated. How much money can be saved by raising the deductible? Most people will want comprehensive on a new car. As the car gets older, the person will have to decide when the cost of protecting the property is costing more than it is worth, and some thought should be given as to how often a claim is filed. However, comprehensive insurance is cheaper than collision insurance and the deductible is generally lower; hence, one may want to keep comprehensive coverage for a longer time than collision coverage.

Uninsured-underinsured motorist coverage

Uninsured-underinsured motorist coverage is the cheapest insurance of all, costing only a few dollars per year, and unless one is on a very tight budget he or she should consider it. This also covers the insured in the event that he or she is the victim of a hit-and-run driver. Not only does it cover property damages, but it also reimburses one for injuries suffered at the hands of a hit-and-run driver.

OTHER MISCELLANEOUS INSURANCE

For most people automobile and home insurance will provide adequate protection. However, some individuals need additional coverage, which will be briefly discussed here. Some of these fall into the categories of property, liability, life, and specialty insurance.

Boat insurance

People who own boats will in some cases need to buy a special policy. In some states the homeowner's policy will cover a boat, but often only insofar as liability coverage is concerned. In such a case one would need a special policy for property protection. In other states the homeowner's liability coverage will not even cover a boat—or if it does, only to a limited extent. If one owns a boat, this should be investigated, and whatever additional coverage is needed should be purchased.

The boat property coverage protects aginst such hazards as fire, theft, sinking, collision, capsizing, explosion, windstorm, hail, submerged objects, vandalism, and lightning. The policies, written in much the same manner as the automobile collision policy, are generally written as either $100, $200, or $500 deductible policies.

The liability part is written to cover personal liability such as hitting a swimmer, injuring passengers as the result of a fire aboard the boat, and ramming another boat with resulting personal injury to the persons aboard that vessel. The policies are generally written with a limit of $10,000 to $25,000, but they go higher at an extra cost.

Malpractice liability insurance

Malpractice insurance primarily protect doctors and nurses against personal liability damage suits arising out of actual or alleged professional carelessness; in recent years lawyers, accountants, and other professionals have been buying it in increasing numbers. This type of insursance is sold by some fire and casualty companies.

Malpractice insurance used to be quite cheap, but this has changed in some states recently, especially with respect to doctors. Because of a changing legal philosophy, not only are large awards now being made in malpractice suits, but in addition the courts have been more liberal in making awards. In some states even hospitals have lost their immunity from lawsuit. Consequently, in malpractice suits in those states both the doctor and the hospital are sued. California and New York are two states in which more and larger awards have recently been granted. As a result, malpractice insurance rates are very high in those states. Nevertheless, most doctors feel they must have this kind of protection. In some cases, medical societies or groups of doctors have formed their own insurance pool. Each of them puts so much into a fund each month, which is then used to aid those doctors who are sued. This is really self-insurance. In the case of nurses, engineers, and certain other low-risk professionals, the cost of malpractice insurance is still low.

Trip and travel insurance

Trip and travel insurance policies are a package that includes some term life insurance and some medical insurance. The life insurance could cover a person for all accidental deaths occurring while the insured is on the trip or (at a reduced premium) just accidental deaths occurring while the insured is on the airplane, in or around the airport, or in a limousine going to or coming from the airport. Some are written so that if the insured is killed while in a common carrier his or her beneficiary(ies) get a certain amount, but get somewhat less if the insured is killed while on the trip but not in a common carrier.

Most of these policies also have a medical insurance feature that pays up to 75 percent of the principal sum for medical bills due to an accident (but not due to an illness) while on a trip. There are a few exclusions regarding the medical insurance—for example, medical bills due to a skiing or hunting accident are not covered.

Generally these single trip policies can be purchased in values from $5,000 to $300,000. A person who travels frequently may want to purchase travel insurance protection—which is available and provides the same protection described above for any trips during the year—rather than purchase it separately for each trip.

Specialty insurance: Group legal insurance

Some experts believe that before too long insurance to pay for legal fees will be available on a group basis. Even today a few people have such protection, but generally it is financed through a labor union, credit union, or other organization; insurance companies are not yet involved.

Generally, a contract is negotiated between a group and a law firm, which provides certain legal services free to the individual members of the group. The group pays the fees, and the individuals pay indirectly through higher dues or some other such method. But this uses the insurance principle by spreading actuarially over large numbers the legal fees of the few unfortunate enough to get into trouble.

Major lawsuits are not covered, but such things as divorce, drafting of wills, minor disputes with landlords or finance companies, disagreements with retail merchants, and minor traffic violations are handled. In many cases relatively small sums of money are involved, and most persons are reluctant to spend money on attorney's fees (and possible court costs). The result is they often pay any claim made or represent themselves in court and invariably lose.

SUMMARY REVIEW QUESTIONS

These questions serve as a summary and a review of the chapter. If you are able to answer them all, you have a good understanding of the material covered by the chapter.

1. What is liability coverage?
2. What is the homeowner's policy?
3. What is the nature of the coverage one receives from personal property coverage under the homeowner's policy?
4. What is medical payments coverage?
5. How should a person who rents protect himself?
6. Where may a person buy flood insurance? Why do most insurance companies not sell flood insurance?
7. What is the purpose of the apportionment clause in a policy?
8. What is meant by coinsurance? Is a 90 percent coinsurance clause superior to an 80 percent clause? Explain why or why not.
9. If someone were to say that he or she had a "twenty/forty and ten" automobile policy, what would he or she mean?
10. Explain the difference between liability insurance, collision insurance, and comprehensive insurance as it applies to a car.
11. What is no-fault auto insurance? What benefits are claimed for it? Is there general agreement regarding what is meant by no-fault insurance?
12. In general, explain the financial responsibility laws as they appear on the statute books of those states having such laws.
13. Discuss the uninsured motorist endorsement, bringing out how it works.
14. What is meant by "basic sum" of insurance?
15. What is an umbrella policy?
16. How should one determine how much collision insurance is needed?
17. Describe malpractice insurance.
18. What is specialty insurance?

CASES

1. Don and Evellen Price own a home with a replacement cost of $80,000. Recently their home was damaged by a fire, as was some of their furniture. They have a HO-2 homeowner's policy with a face amount of $64,000. It cost $20,000 to repair their home, and while the repairs are being made they live in an apartment and paid $1,000 in rent. Their lost personal property was valued at $10,000.

   (a) How much of their $20,000 home repair bill will they collect?
   (b) How much of their $10,000 personal property loss will they collect?
   (c) Will their policy cover their $1,000 rental expense?

2. Peter Green has a home valued at $80,000, and a few years ago he bought a homeowner's policy on it with an 80 percent coinsurance clause. Many of his

friends have told him 80 percent is not enough and that he should have at least 90 percent. Do you agree? Explain why or why not.

3. Tom Singer is a traveling salesman who rents an apartment that, because of the nature of his work, is often unoccupied. Tom keeps a good many valuable personal items in it, and he is afraid of fire and theft. Can you give him advice with respect to insurance coverage?

4. Jim and Jean Sargeant have two cars— a new Ford and a ten-year-old Plymouth. Jean does not think they should spend money on insurance of their old car but is willing to pay for complete coverage on the new. Jim is not so sure. Can you explain Jim's reasoning? Jean's?

5. Carolyn Roundtree has a year-old car and carries $10,000/$20,000 liability insurance, $5,000 property damage, some comprehensive, and collision with $100 deductible. Is this a wise policy? Carolyn thinks her rates are high. Can you show her how to reduce them? Carolyn's sister believes she should carry more liability insurance. Do you agree?

6. Joan Rider has just purchased a $9,000 Ford sedan. She will use it to drive to and from her job and also for pleasure. She expects to drive about twelve thousand miles per year, and she has financed the car at the local bank where she keeps her checking account. Help her work out an insurance program on her car; advise her what kind of coverage she should get and how much.

SUGGESTED READINGS

Analysis of Automobile No-Fault Statues. New York: General Adjustment Bureau, Inc.

Athearn, James L. *Risk and Insurance.* St. Paul, Minn.: West Publishing Co., 1984.

Best's Review, Property-Liability Edition. Oldwick, N.J.: A. M. Best Company, Inc. Monthly publication.

Cockerell, Hugh. *Lloyd's of London.* Homewood, Ill.: Dow Jones-Irwin, 1984.

CPCU Journal. Malvern, Pa.: The Society of Chartered Property and Casualty Underwriters (CPCU). Quarterly publication.

Dorfman, Mark S. *Introduction to Insurance,* 3rd ed. Englewood Cliffs, N.J.: Prentice-Hall, 1987.

"Family Guide to Property and Liability Insurance." New York: Insurance Information Institute.

Gordis, Philip. *Property and Casualty Insurance.* Indianapolis, Ind.: Rough Notes Company, 1984.

Greene, Mark R., and Trieschmann, James. "Risk and Insurance." Cincinnati: South-Western 1984.

Huebner, S. S., et al. *Property and Liability Insurance.* Englewood Cliffs, N.J.: Prentice-Hall, 1982.

Insurance Review. New York: The Insurance Institute. Monthly publication.

Mehr, Robert I., and Cammack, Emerson, *Principles of Insurance.* Homewood, Ill.: Dow Jones-Irwin, 1985.

National Underwriter. Chicago: The National Underwriter Co. Weekly publication.

"Property and Casualty Fact Book," New York: Insurance Information Institute. An annual publication.

Risk Management. New York: The Risk and Insurance Management Society, Inc. Monthly publication.

Vaughan, Emmet J. *Fundamentals of Risk and Insurance,* 5th ed. New York: John Wiley and Sons, 1989.

IV Managing investments

Part IV deals with investments of all kinds.

Everyone earning an income should generate some savings. These savings should then be put to work to earn an investment income.

All investors need to have some funds in a safe and liquid form for emergency purposes. These investments should be in savings institutions. There are two reasons: first; these emergency funds need to be in a very safe place; second, until the investor gains some experience with more risky investments, he or she might wish to use the savings institutions as a safe "parking lot" for funds. Because of this safety feature, generally they earn a bit less than other investments. Chapter 13 covers all of the savings institutions and also clarifies the mysteries of interest rates.

Chapter 14 introduces the reader to the fundamentals of direct investments: investing directly in corporate securities (stocks and bonds) rather than investing indirectly through savings institutions as was discussed in Chapter 13.

Chapters 15 and 16 go one step further and spell out the various types of securities. There are a number of different bonds and common and preferred stocks; all of these are discussed in Chapter 15.

Chapter 16 provides general information on securities and on the securities markets. How securities are quoted in the financial pages of the newspapers and how they are bought and sold are discussed. There is also some information on investment strategies which is intended to aid the investor in deciding *which securities* to buy and *when* to buy them.

Chapter 17, the final chapter in Part IV, covers mutual funds. Mutual funds offer professional management of funds and inherent diversification, with a variety of objectives to match various investor needs. The chapter also covers certain other investments such as rental real estate, and closes with a few comments on highly speculative investments such as gold and diamonds. While gold and diamonds are not for everyone, they might be right for a few people.

13 Savings and investing through savings institutions

HOW INTEREST RATES ARE CALCULATED
   BY MOST INSTITUTIONS
     Determining the account balance
     When interest is credited to the account

SUMMARY REVIEW QUESTIONS
CASES
SUGGESTED READINGS
APPENDIX: PRESENT AND FUTURE VALUES

HIGHLIGHTS

This chapter should provide an understanding of the role of financial institutions in the investor's savings plans, the types of savings accounts they provide, and how savings earn interest income. The following topics will be discussed:

1   Savings invested indirectly
2   Who saves and why?
3   Savings institutions and savings
4   Types of deposits
5   What to look for before deciding on a savings account
6   Penalties for early withdrawals of certificates of deposit
7   Nondepository institutions
8   U. S. savings bonds
9   The power of compounding interest
10 Nominal, real, and after-tax interest rates
11 How most institutions calculate interest

INTRODUCTION

Before seriously considering investing directly in securities (discussed in Chapters 14 through 16), the investor needs adequate cash reserves and highly liquid savings deposits for living expenses, special purchases, and emergencies. Living expense funds should be kept in a checking account, either interest bearing or noninterest bearing. These were discussed in Chapter 4; here we will discuss savings and time deposits which, generally speaking, earn a higher interest than checking accounts. Some of these deposits must be pledged for a specific period of time, and there may be a penalty for early withdrawals; others, however, may be withdrawn at any time without a penalty. This is where special purchase or emergency funds should be kept. Most people invest some of their savings in a bank, savings and loan association, credit union account, or mutual savings bank. Deregulation of these financial institutions and increasing competition have created a wide range of savings deposit options. Therefore, deposits should be managed as carefully as any investment.

All the various savings options stress safety, convenience, and interest return. The most troublesome aspect of these is the variety of accounts from which to choose. So, it's well worthwhile to examine what each type has to offer as well as things to consider before deciding on the one (or ones) best suited to achieve the client's goals.

Savings and investing indirectly

Savings come from earned income and represent that portion of income that is not spent on consumption. It is invested indirectly when money is deposited with a financial institution that, in turn, invests the money in mortgages, loans, or securities on the investor's behalf. The individual essentially is entering into a contract with an institution in which he or she is paid a stated (fixed) interest rate on the money for a fixed period of time. Thus, financial institutions serve as a channel into which many small savers' monies are deposited and from which a large dollar amount of money can then be invested in businesses, mortgages, and governments. This "flow of funds" is depicted in Figure 13–1.

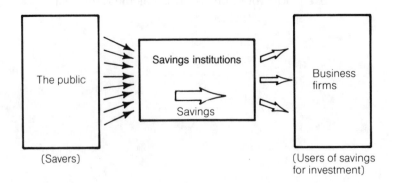

Figure 13–1   *Dollar flows through the economy*

There is an important difference between savings invested indirectly in deposits and direct investment such as stocks, bonds, and real estate. The key feature of federally insured deposits is safety. All deposits are safe because both principal and interest are insured by the full faith and credit of the U.S. government.

Direct investments, in contrast, usually involve the risk of losing principal. While there is the potential for greater rates of return compared to a savings account, there is no guarantee that this will occur. This means that direct investments should be made only with funds the client is willing to expose to more risk—that is, after he or she has invested some funds indirectly and can now afford to assume more risk. Direct investments in securities will be discussed in Chapters 14 through 16. In this chapter we will discuss the various types of deposits offered by the depository institutions, but first we will examine "who saves and why."

Most savings are generated by those whose income is high enough and who are over forty-five years of age. While many low-income groups save some money, the dollar volume is small. High savings among those over forty-five is related to the life cycle variation in the budget, discussed in Chapter 2. Up to about age forty-five or fifty are the high consumption years. After the children have left and the house is paid for and full of furniture and other consumer-durable goods, more savings are generated out of any budget.

Who saves and why?

Economists generally agree that there is a positive correlation between income and savings; that is, the higher a person's income, the higher is the dollar volume of savings. There may also be a slight correlation between interest rate and savings. If interest rates are higher, there is a greater reward and greater incentive to save. But this theory is controversial and hard to prove. Studies at the University of Michigan Survey Research Center and elsewhere have suggested that there are a number of other factors influencing savings—such as past income, direction of change in income, size of family, and age—but the effects of these variables are difficult to measure. Moreover, personal savings tend to fluctuate year-to-year. For instance, since 1980 they have fluctuated from a high of 7.5 percent to a low of 3.2 percent of after-tax income. Table 13–1 shows how personal savings have fluctuated over the years.

People save for a variety of reasons—emergencies, a down payment on a home, a vacation, a child's education, or retirement. The investor's first savings are for emergencies or a "nest egg" that should be put in a safe place where they can be obtained easily and quickly, such as a thrift institution. How large nest-egg savings should be depends on the client's age, number of dependents, stability of employment, diverse sources of income, size of insurance deductibles, disability income, and so on. It becomes a personal judgment, but a rough rule-of-thumb is an amount

Table 13—1   *Personal savings*

Year	Dollar savings in billions	Savings as % of income
1980	136.9	7.1
1981	159.4	7.5
1982	153.9	6.8
1983	130.6	5.4
1984	164.1	6.1
1985	125.4	4.4
1986	124.9	4.1
1987	101.8	3.2
1988	144.7	4.2
1989	204.4	5.4

Source: Economic Indicators, June 1990, Council of Economic Advisers, p. 6.

equal to three-to-six times the person's monthly income. Other savings may be invested differently from emergency or nest egg savings, but some of them too will be invested in savings institutions. Investments such as stocks and bonds should be considered after an adequate nest-egg savings cushion has been established. (See Chapters 14 through 17.)

SAVINGS INSTITUTIONS AND SAVINGS

Savings institutions are outlets for personal savings and are classified as **depository** and **nondepository institutions.** There are five major depository institutions in the United States:

Commercial banks
Savings and loan associations
Credit unions
Mutual savings banks
Industrial banks

They are called depository institutions because they issue a "secondary" or "indirect" security for an individual's money that is called a deposit account. The two key features of deposits are, first, they are often highly liquid (can be withdrawn at any time at the depositor's option); and second, they are safe because most deposits are insured by an agency of the U.S. government (see below.)[1] The institutions may also provide greater diversity for the client's investment.

Nondepository savings institutions are more diverse in nature; the major ones are:

Life insurance companies
Private pension funds
Money market mutual funds
Cash management accounts
U.S. savings bonds

Life insurance companies were discussed in Chapter 10, while private pension funds will be discussed in Chapter 18. In this chapter, we will focus on the role of depository institutions, money market mutual funds, cash management accounts, and nonmarketable U.S. savings bonds (not to be confused with marketable U.S. government bonds, which will be discussed in Chapter 15) in the overall savings plans.[2]

Besides providing liquidity and safety, all these institutions help the investor's money earn more money by providing investment expertise and "economies of scale" for many savers who lack the time or skill or who are too small to invest directly in securities.

THE DEPOSITORY INSTITUTIONS AND THE VARIOUS DEPOSITS

Commercial banks, savings and loan associations (also known as thrifts), and credit unions are found in all states; mutual savings banks are found in only seventeen of the fifty states, and in Puerto Rico. They are located primarily in New England, the Middle Atlantic states, and on the West Coast. While there are some technical and legal differences between mutual savings banks and savings and loan associations, for all practical purposes they are the same.

Some of these savings institutions provide the traditional checking account (discussed in Chapter 4) that does not earn interest. In addition, they all compete with each other for the public's savings dollars on which they do pay interest. Figure 13–2 shows the growth of deposits over the last few years held by commercial banks.

All depository institutions offer a variety of interest-bearing deposits, but they can be classified into four main categories—the ***passbook sav-***

---

1. Some deposits (called "certificates of deposits") are less liquid because they are pledged for a specific period of time, which may be several years. This is explained more fully below.

2. While U.S. savings bonds may not appear to be "institutions," they are direct obligations of the U.S. government and provide an outlet for individual savings. Indeed, they are one of the safest and most liquid assets available and perform the same functions as institutions. Hence, logically they may be treated as such.

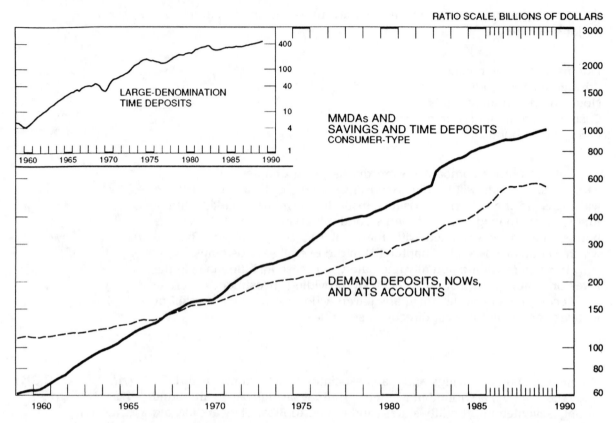

Figure 13—2   *Principal liabilities of commercial banks, seasonally adjusted, quarterly averages.*
(Source: 1989 Historical Chart Book, *Board of Governors of the Federal Reserve System, p. 79.)*

ings account, the ***interest-bearing checking account,***[3] ***money market deposit account;*** and the ***certificate of deposit (CD).***[4]

If savings are invested in a savings institution, the account is simply a contract between the investor and the savings institution. In some cases, however, funds are expected to be pledged for a specific period of

---

3. The interest-bearing checking accounts were originally called "negotiated order of withdrawal" (NOW accounts) a few years ago when only a few institutions were offering them. Now they have a number of different names, but they actually are interest-bearing checking accounts.

4. The Federal Reserve System classifies interest-bearing checking accounts and passbook accounts as savings deposits, and all of the various CDs as time deposits. The reason is that the CDs are not as liquid as the others since they cannot be withdrawn until their date of expiration without a penalty. The penalty for early withdrawal is discussed below. The Fed's terminology is unfortunate because all the various deposits earn interest and hence are savings vehicles (deposits).

time and not withdrawn before then. This is true in the case of certain CDs. If they are withdrawn early, a penalty may be imposed, as will be explained below.

Passbook savings accounts

Passbook accounts are the oldest type of savings deposits. In the olden days a depositor was given a little book into which entries showing deposits and withdrawals were made. The passbooks have largely been replaced by plastic cards and computer printouts. Some institutions such as credit unions don't even use the term "passbook" anymore, but the term "passbook savings account" is still in use.

Passbook savings deposits are very liquid because they can be withdrawn at any time without a penalty. There are usually no service charges and, in many cases, funds can be transferred to an interest-bearing checking account by telephone. Interest rates tend to be relatively low on both of these deposits (about 5 percent).

Interest-bearing checking accounts —NOW and superNOWS

Negotiable Orders of Withdrawal (NOW) accounts can be withdrawn without penalty and generally earn an interest rate comparable to passbook accounts. Their key feature, though, is that they have unlimited check-writing privileges. A monthly service fee may be charged if the balance falls below a certain level, which varies from institution to institution. In some cases these monthly service charges are assessed if the average balance falls below a certain level, and in other cases if the minimum balance does.[5] But, generally the cost is only a few dollars per month. In fact, the interest earned should more than offset the service charges unless the account is quite small.

If an individual needs a checking account, this may be the one to choose. Some institutions do not return the canceled checks. In these cases, the checkbook comes with a carbon copy for record keeping purposes, plus a regular monthly statement showing all transactions will be mailed to the customer. An individual should analyze his or her personal finances to see if collapsing the passbook and noninterest-bearing checking accounts into a new interest-bearing checking account is worthwhile. One of the factors to consider in this regard is "will service charges be eliminated?"

In summary, it may be cost effective to eliminate a noninterest-bearing checking account, unless its average balance is very small because then it will be cheaper to stay with a noninterest-bearing account. Analyze

---

5. There are significant differences between these two. When an account falls below a stated amount in a minimum balance account, the individual is charged a fee. In an average balance account, the balance can occasionally fall below the minimum but the accountholder won't be charged as long as the average balance remains above the required level.

both types of accounts to see what the service charges, if any, would be in each of them. (Most institutions waive their monthly service charge if a higher minimum balance is kept.) Remember—money left in a noninterest-bearing account is not working for the accountholder.

Institutions also have what is referred to as a SuperNOW account, although they often give it different names. Generally this account pays a higher interest rate than the NOW account, but a higher minimum or average balance is required. If the balance falls below the minimum, the individual earns the lower regular NOW account rate. Some institutions restrict the number of checks that may be written per month on a SuperNOW, others do not. Some institutions also charge so much for each check written, because they wish to restrict activity in the SuperNOW accounts.

Money market deposit accounts

Money market deposit accounts (MMDAs) came into existence in the 1970s when money market interest rates became very high. Savers began to take money out of their low-yielding passbook accounts and put them into nondepository institutions that offered the higher money market rates. (See money market funds below). To remain competitive, savings institutions began offering MMDAs whose interest rates were tied to money market rates—hence, their name. The interest rate paid on these accounts may float; that is, it is changed by the institutions periodically as money market rates change. Many institutions limit the number of checks per month that may be written on these accounts. There is a minimum balance (often as high as $5,000) on these accounts. If the balance falls below this, there may be a flat monthly fee assessed. Additional deposits may be made into a MMDA with no limit.

Certificates of deposit

Maturities of **certificates of deposit (CDs)** can extend up to ten years, and the rate of interest they pay is usually a little higher than on other deposits. Some institutions will provide a CD tailored to any number of days or months desired. Also most institutions have a minimum dollar amount below which they will not issue a CD. Generally this is $1,000 but some institutions will go as low as $500 or even $100. When money is put into a CD, expect to leave it there until maturity because of the high early withdrawal penalty. In an emergency, though, money can be borrowed at a relatively low rate of interest by using the CD as collateral for the loan. Deregulation of the banking industry has permitted some savings institutions to introduce CD's with consumer-oriented features. For example, a CD may allow withdrawals with no penalty after the first seven days or a CD that will allow additional deposits, after the intial deposit, at the same initial interest rate.

The sweep arrangement: A special account

The sweep account is an arrangement whereby surplus funds in a lower interest-yielding account are periodically (say, weekly or monthly) automatically swept into a higher-yielding account. For example, a NOW account may serve as a depository for transactions' balances, and may be balanced at, say, $2,000. Funds in excess of that amount in multiples of $100 are swept out by computer on a periodic basis into a higher-yielding account. When the NOW account falls below $2,000, multiples of $100 are swept in. The NOW account is therefore stabilized between $1,900 and $2,100.

Under deregulation, depository institutions are no longer all the same. To select one, the following factors should be considered.:

Selecting the depository institution—things to keep in mind

1. What is the quoted interest rate?
2. How is the rate compounded—quarterly, monthly, weekly, daily, or continuously—because this will affect the interest earned?
3. How is the balance on which interest is paid calculated? Is interest paid on the average monthly balance, minimum balance, day-in day-out balance, or some other method?
4. When is the interest earned credited to the account? If interest is calculated daily but only credited to the account quarterly or monthly, the investor has quarterly or monthly (not daily) compounding.
5. Is the interest rate reduced if the balance falls below a certain minimum, and how much is the reduction?
6. Is there a monthly fee if the balance falls below a certain minimum, and how much is it?
7. What is the dollar amount of any such minimum described above? Different institutions have different policies regarding minimum balances.
8. What is the penalty for early withdrawals for those deposits which have been pledged for a specific period?
9. On checking accounts, is there limited or unlimited checking privileges?
10. What are the fees, if any, for telephone transfers from one account to another?
11. What are the fees, if any, for checking the dollar balance via telephone?
12. What are the fees for stopping payment on a check?

There are other important things an individual should know about deposits. For example, don't forget about deposits; they may disappear. Also, in some cases there is a penalty for early withdrawal of deposits. In addition, the safety of deposits should be a concern.

SOME IMPORTANT NOTES ON DEPOSITS

"Use it or Lose it." Some states have five-year escheat laws. This means if the account is inactive for five years, the institution must turn it over to the state. A deposit is inactive if the depositor does not deposit into it or

Don't abandon savings deposits: The escheat laws

withdraw from it. Even if interest is paid and credited every year, the account may still be considered inactive. To protect an account, the accountholder should deposit (or withdraw) a dollar periodically. Even a CD that runs six or seven years may escheat. In some states even a one-year CD, if it is merely rolled over every year as it renews, may be considered inactive. To be sure, convert it to a CD of a different maturity periodically.

Safety of deposits:
Deposit insurance

All of the above-mentioned deposits, in most but not all of the depository institutions, are insured by an agency of the United States government up to $100,000. This is true of deposits in most commercial banks, savings and loan associations, mutual savings banks, and credit unions. There are, however, a few institutions that do not have deposit insurance, these should probably be avoided. Those institutions that are insured will display a metal sign indicating this in a prominent place, usually near the teller's windows. Remember, too, that the $100,000 of insurance applies per person per institution, not per account. Hence, if an individual has several accounts, they are commingled, and all of them together come under the $100,000 protection if they are in the name of the same person in the same institution. However, an individual and his or her spouse may each have a separate account in the same institution, and each would be insured up to $100,000, for a total insurance coverage of $200,000. A third joint account would provide total coverage of $300,000. Other members of the family could also each have $100,000 of separate coverage. If funds are in excess of that amount, they should be split between two or more insured institutions for complete coverage and safety.

Penalties for early
withdrawal of CDs

While passbook savings accounts—and any account on which checks may be written—may be withdrawn without penalty at any time, this is not usually true of the CDs. Different penalties for early withdrawal are imposed by different institutions. The most common penalty is the loss of three-months' interest if the CD was pledged for less than one year. If pledged for more than one year, six-months' loss of interest may be assessed.

To illustrate, say a saver has a two-year, 8 percent CD for $1,000, and withdraws it all after one year. A six-month penalty of $1/2 \times (0.08 \times \$1000)$ or $40 would be deducted from the CD amount. In fact, it is possible that the penalty may eat up not only any interest earned but part of the principal too. Returning to our example above, let us now assume the $1,000 CD is withdrawn a day or two after the money is deposited. In this case the saver may get only $960 back.

Obviously, penalties are imposed to discourage early withdrawals. So, as mentioned earlier, if the money is needed before maturity, investigate the possibility of using the CD as collateral for a low-interest loan. This may be less costly than paying a penalty.

There are a number of nondepository institutions, which are nevertheless considered savings institutions. One of these (life insurance companies) was discussed earlier, and one (pension funds) will be discussed in Chapter 18. Two others will be discussed here.

A *money market fund* is a mutual fund that invests the client's money in an array of very short-term, relatively safe money-market securities.[6] It issues the investor shares against a portfolio of these securities that it buys in large denominations by pooling the funds of many investors. Many are offered by brokerage houses, one of the more well known of which is Merrill Lynch's "ready assets" fund.

Money market mutual funds

Although not federally insured, only one money market fund has failed in their sixteen-year history, and those losses were minimal. Interest, net of operating expenses and management fees of 0.25% to 1.00% of the account's value, is passed through to the investor monthly. Either the interest can be reinvested into new shares or a check can be received for the interest amount. Check-writing privileges (usually $500 minimum) allow easy access to the funds.

Money market deposit accounts (provided by banks and other depository institutions) and money market funds are very similar. Interest rates on money market funds float with short-term market rates, while money market deposit accounts may or may not float depending on the institution.[7] However, MMDAs at depository institutions are government insured, whereas money market funds are usually not insured—although some do have private insurance. Despite this, the high-quality, short-term nature of their securities normally make them relatively safe. Money market funds are more impersonal than dealing with a financial institution. There is no local office for depositing and withdrawing funds. All business is done through the mail or a toll-free telephone call. Finally, money market funds generally require a smaller minimum balance, and there is no charge if the balance falls below the minimum; i.e., the depositor continues to earn the same interest rate. On the other hand, the minimum amount a check can be written for is higher.

In the early 1980s, Merrill Lynch, a major brokerage firm, introduced an innovation they called the *Cash Management Account (CMA).* The idea was to reduce the monthly paperwork for consumers by combining the

Cash management accounts

---

6. These underlying securities are almost exclusively treasury bills and commercial paper. Treasury bills are short-term debt obligation of the United States government and hence are the safest investment that may be purchased. Commercial paper is the same type of short-term debt obligation issued by large, well-known corporations with excellent credit ratings like IBM or GM. Hence they too are very safe. See Chapter 15 for more information on treasury bills.

7. A floating rate moves up (or down) automatically with changes in the market; no decision need be made by the institution's managers.

monthly statement for checking, credit card, mutual fund, and brokerage statements all into one monthly statement. Now, most brokerage houses and some banks and S and Ls offer these "all-in-one" accounts.[8]

Debit card

Using Merrill Lynch as an illustration, $20,000 is needed to open a cash management account but it can be in cash, securities, or both. The account includes a conventional securities (brokerage) account, a checking account, a credit card, and possibly a debit card. A **_debit card,_** unlike a credit card, means payments for purchases are automatically taken out of the assets in the account (see Chapter 5). There is an annual fee of $80 for this account.

Any excess cash in a cash management account, say, from dividends or interest, is swept weekly into a money market fund. In other cases, if insufficient cash is available to cover purchases of securities, Merrill loans the depositor the money up to a certain amount.[9] This is one main advantage of using a brokerage versus a bank cash management account. On the other hand, banks and S and Ls provide slight reductions in charges on certain services that brokerage firms do not offer; and as noted above, the banks' and the savings and loans' deposits are insured. The bottom line in choosing a CMA is not easy. Each one is different; and some of the features they offer may be of no value to the client, yet he or she will be paying for them. For example, some bank CMAs do not offer brokerage services but they may be more convenient to use. Bank CMAs may provide services not found in a brokerage CMA— for example safe deposits, travelers checks, copying, and notary services. Also, annual fees can vary.

UNITED STATES SAVINGS BONDS

United States government bonds can be classified into marketable and nonmarketable but redeemable.[10] The marketable bonds are sold by brokers and some banks and appeal primarily to larger investors and institutions. They will be discussed in greater detail in Chapter 15. The nonmarketable bonds will be discussed here because they are designed for the small investor and because they are classified as thrift institutions. These bonds are issued in two different series; they were formerly called

---

8. The all-in-one accounts offered by banks and S and Ls are precisely the same as a brokerage house cash management account. That is, they usually bundle *separate checking, savings,* and *credit accounts* into one statement rather than there being *one account* as with brokerage firms.

9. The amount borrowed is called a margin loan. The amount you can borrow is limited to 50 percent of the market value to your stocks on deposit and 90 percent on treasury securities. The actual interest rate you pay is based on what is called the broker loan rate, which, technically, can change day-to-day.

10. Marketable securities are those securities which are negotiable and therefore can be easily sold to third parties. Many marketable securities are listed on the New York stock exchange. Those that are not sold "over the counter." Consequently, marketable secruities may be bought or sold by making a telephone call to a broker.

Series E and series H, but in January, 1980, the Treasury made a few changes and the bonds are now called series EE and HH. The older Series E and H bonds sold prior to 1980 are, of course, still outstanding.

Series EE and HH bonds, being nonnegotiable, are also nonmarketable. They cannot be used as collateral for a loan nor can they be sold to a third party. However, they are redeemable, which means that they can be returned to the U.S. Treasury at the option of the bondholder. However, they must be held for at least six months. Because of this redeemability, their price is stabilized and they do not fluctuate inversely with changes in the interest rate.[11]

Series EE

Series EE bonds are discounted, whereas Series HH bonds are not. This merely means that Series EE bonds are sold below their face value and as time passes, their value rises to reflect accrued interest. These bonds come in denominations with face values of $50, $75, $100, $200, $500, and $1,000, $5,000, and $10,000. Since they are discounted, they are sold at a price below these figures.

Series EE bonds are sold at one-half of their face value and then appreciate as they approach maturity. On November 1, 1982, the U.S. Treasury changed the interest rate and hence the appreciation schedule of Series EE bonds. Bonds sold after that date have a floating interest rate that floats in accordance with the rate paid by the Treasury on five-year marketable securities. This variable rate works as follows. Every six months the Treasury Department compiles the average market interest rate on all Treasury marketable securities that are five years from their maturity during the previous half year. The rate on new Series EE savings bonds for the next six months is 85 percent of that market average. At the end of five years, the ten semiannual averages are added, averaged, and the average compounded on a semiannual basis to determine a bond's five-year yield. Series EE bonds held longer than five years have additional semiannual market averages computed in and compounded. This means, then, that since these bonds appreciate in value to accrue interest, their appreciation also varies; the appreciation is a function of the level of the interest rate. At maturity, the market value of these bonds may be at or above their face value. There is also a proviso in these Series EE bonds that guarantees a floor on the interest rate that the bondholder will receive if he or she holds these bonds for five years or more. This rate is 6 percent. If the interest rate were never to rise above 6 per-

---

11. The reason Congress made these bonds nonnegotiable and redeemable was to protect the small investor from the unpleasant experience that took place regarding bonds sold during World War I. Those bonds were negotiable (and hence marketable). Many people bought bonds during the war but after the war their price fell drastically as interest rates rose. If people had to liquidate them due to an emergency, they suffered a substantial capital loss. Why the price of marketable bonds fluctuates inversely with changes in the interest rate is explained in Chapter 14.

cent, these bonds' value would rise to their face value in twelve years. If interest rates on them are above 6 percent, the bonds will be redeemable at face value sooner. In this case, if the bonds are held after reaching face value, their value may rise further. The interest (appreciation) on these Series EE bonds is not taxed until realized when the bonds are cashed in (although the purchaser can elect annual taxation.). This tax deferral makes the yield a little more attractive than their rate suggests. Interest on these bonds is not subject to state and local taxes.

The new Series EE bonds with a floating interest rate tied to the market rate are a more competitive investment, which, together with their tax-deferred status, has made them a fairly popular investment.

Series HH

The interest on Series H and HH bonds, which are sold in units of $500, $1,000, $5,000, and $10,000, is payable semiannually beginning six months after issue date; it is paid on each interest date by check and mailed to the addressee of record. These bonds are always sold at their face value. They are not coupon bonds, however. They are registered bonds and the interest is automatically sent to the bondholder. Series HH (and the old H) bonds purchased before November 1982 yield 8.5 percent per year. This 8.5 percent is fixed for ten years and cannot float up as can Series EE. To receive the full 8.5 percent interest, however, the bonds must be held five years or more. If they are redeemed sooner, they will be redeemed at less than face value, so the return drops below 8.5 percent.

The Treasury stopped selling Series HH over the counter on November 1, 1982. However, Series EE may be converted to Series HH. But since November 1986, Series HH bonds pay only 6 percent.

There is a limit to how many Series EE and Series HH a person may buy each year—$30,000 (face value) in the case of Series EE and $20,000 in the case of HH. A married couple may each purchase that amount.

An investor may obtain Series EE or HH bonds (or cash them in) at any large national bank. In addition, many employers have established a means whereby employees may buy Series EE bonds through payroll withholds.

Liquidity and risk

All types of United States government securities are highly liquid. (Liquidity has to do with how quickly something can be converted to money.) The marketable bonds (all but Series EE and HH) can be sold by telephoning a broker or a bank. A highly organized market exists for these bonds. The nonmarketable Series EE and HH bonds are redeemable at the option of the bondholder. Hence they, too, are very liquid. They can be redeemed at almost any commercial bank.

While there is absolutely no risk of default involved in holding any government bonds, there is a risk of possible capital loss involved in holding all government bonds except Series EE and HH. Since their market price is permitted to fluctuate freely with the forces of supply and demand, it is possible that, if a person wishes to sell bonds before they mature, he or she will have to accept a lower price than that paid. However, since Series EE and HH are redeemable by the Treasury, their price is in effect stabilized; there is no risk whatsoever attached to these bonds.

In the case of CDs where the principal does not vary greatly, if at all, the interest calculation is relatively easy to make. The interest rate paid generally varies with the dollar amount of the CD, and the length of time for which it is pledged; that is, the larger the dollar amount and the longer it is pledged, the higher the interest rate. However, the institution merely applies the interest rate to the principal balance to obtain the dollar amount of interest.

SOME NOTES ON INTEREST RATES

There is, however, the problem of compounding. Interest can be compounded annually, semiannually, quarterly, monthly, weekly, daily, and even continuously. The way a deposit is compounded makes a great deal of difference, as we shall see below.

In the case of the passbook account and the various checking accounts, where the principal amount in the account fluctuates, a second problem arises—that is, how to determine the balance to which the agreed upon interest rate is applied. This too makes a considerable difference, as we shall see below.

First, however, we will explore the theory of interest—why it is paid, the various methods of compounding, and the effect of compounding. Then we shall examine how interest is calculated by most institutions.

Interest is mysterious to some people; it shouldn't be. Interest income is also sometimes viewed as somehow being less virtuous than other income, an erroneous view. There is nothing mysterious about interest and there should be no stigma attached to receiving it. Figure 13–3 shows how interest rates have changed over the years. Interest is the payment for the use of capital just as rent is the payment for the use of real property. Interest can be justified in several ways. Capital is productive and hence, like labor, it receives a return. Labor receives a wage; capital receives an interest payment. Liquid capital (money), however, must first be turned into real capital (plant and equipment) before it is productive.

The theory of interest

Interest is also paid because the supplier of capital (the lender) assumes a risk (large or small) that the loan will not be repaid. This is the risk of default, and lenders must be paid a fee (interest) to entice them to assume that risk. Moreover, the higher the risk of default, the higher the interest payment must be. If the risk is high enough, no one will advance the capital, and there is a fringe of unsatisfied would-be borrowers.

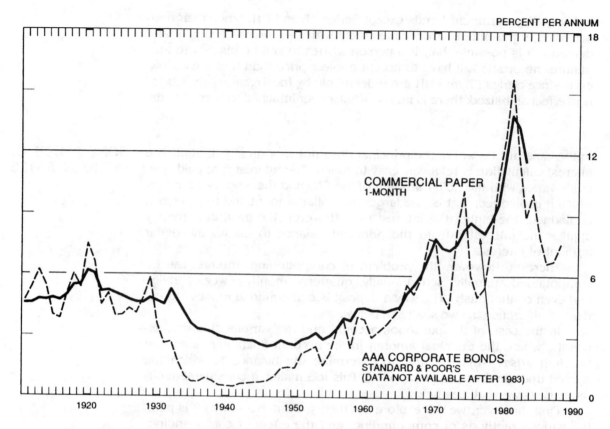

PERCENT PER ANNUM

COMMERCIAL PAPER
1-MONTH

AAA CORPORATE BONDS
STANDARD & POOR'S
(DATA NOT AVAILABLE AFTER 1983)

1920   1930   1940   1950   1960   1970   1980   1990

Figure 13–3   *Long- and short-term interest rates, annually.* (Source: 1989 Historical Chart Book, Board of Governors of the Federal Reserve System, p. 96.)

A third reason for the payment of interest is that most people prefer present dollars (or consumption) to future dollars. A lender gives up (it is hoped temporarily) present dollars, and hence present consumption, for future dollars, and hence future consumption. This is a personal sacrifice. For postponing consumption, the person must be given the reward of greater consumption in the future. Interest is a payment for abstinence, and is also called time preference. People prefer present consumption to future consumption; they have a positive time preference, and interest must be paid as a bribe to entice them to postpone consumption. Money or goods today are more valuable than the same money or goods in the future. The old saw perhaps explains interest best.: "A bird in the hand is worth two in the bush."

Simple interest

When a contract is made between a borrower and a lender, the borrower agrees to pay the lender a fixed percentage sum of the amount borrowed (called the principal) periodically. Usually the amount of interest to be paid is stated as so much per year. If the agreement calls for an 8 percent interest rate, then on a $1,000 loan the borrower must pay $80 per year. The contract could call for an $80 payment to be made every year, or it could stipulate a $40 payment every six months or $20 every three months. In each case, it would be 8 percent per year. If the interest payment is made each time it is due, the amount borrowed remains a constant ($1,000 in the case above), and the interest becomes a constant percentage of a constant principal sum. This is **simple interest.** However, this is not always what is done; and consequently, we also have compound interest.

Compound interest

If the contract calls for the interest to be retained by the borrower, the principal sum grows as time passes. If a lender makes available to a borrower $1,000 to be compounded at 8 percent for a number of years, at the end of one year the $80 interest is added to the original loan of $1,000, which now becomes $1,080. The next year the interest is 8 percent of $1,080, or $86.40. The $86.40, instead of being paid to the lender, is again added to the principal sum of $1,080, now making it $1,166.40. Now interest will be calculated on $1,166.40, and so it goes year after year. This has been called paying interest on interest; i.e., **compound interest**. Figure 13–4 shows how $10,000 will build up over the years due to compounding.

In the above case interest was compounded annually. It can also be compounded semiannually, quarterly, monthly, weekly, daily, or continuously. Compounding semiannually would call for adding $40 to the principal sum at the end of six months then figuring interest on $1,040 for the second six months and so on. Compounding results in a fixed percentage rate being calculated on an ever-increasing principal sum and becoming proportionately greater with each passing period.

The rule of 72

If a dollar is earning compound interest, it will eventually double in value. How quickly a dollar will double is determined by the interest rate and by how frequently it is compounded (annually, semiannually, quarterly, monthly, or even daily). There are tables that show how a dollar will grow over the years at various interest rates. If tables are not available, the time needed to double can be approximated by applying **the rule of 72**. Divide the interest rate into 72 to get the approximate time needed for money to double, if earnings are compounded annually; for example, at 6 percent a dollar would double in 12 years (72 ÷ 6 = 12).

Yield

Yield is similar to the interest rate, but it is not always the same. In the case where simple interest is paid, yield and interest are the same. But if interest is compounded, yield is higher than the stated interest rate. Moreover, the extent to which yield exceeds the interest rate is determined by the frequency of compounding. The more frequent the compounding, the higher the yield above the stated rate. Therefore, when

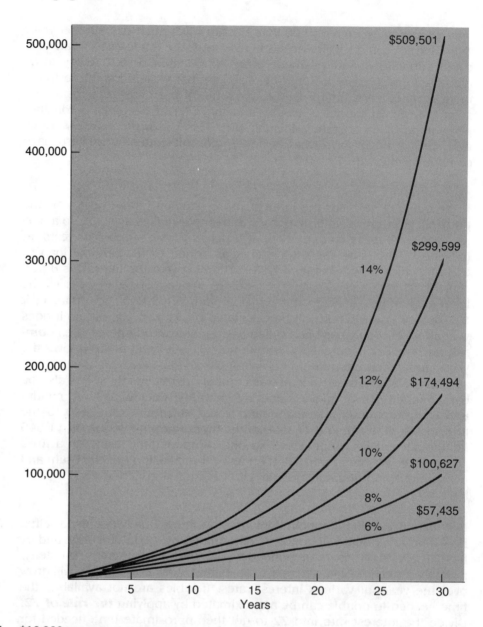

Figure 13—4   *$10,000 compounded annually*

choosing a savings institution it is important to know not only the interest rate but the frequency of compounding. Table 13—2 shows the yield that results from several different frequencies of compounding.

While the difference between interest and yield is not great when interest rates are low, at higher rates they are significant—especially if large dollar amounts are involved over a number of years. This is illustrated by Table 13—3, which shows the different rates of growth of $5,000 invested at 10 percent, but with different frequencies of com-

Real annual yield resulting from daily and continuous compounding at various interest rates Table 13—2

Stated rate (%)	Yield due to quarterly compounding	Yield due to monthly compounding	Yield due to daily compounding	Yield due to continuous compounding
5.00	5.01	5.11	5.13	5.20
5.25	5.35	5.36	5.39	5.47
5.50	5.61	5.62	5.65	5.73
5.75	5.88	5.90	5.92	6.01
6.00	6.14	6.17	6.18	6.27
6.50	6.66	6.70	6.72	6.81
7.00	7.19	7.23	7.25	7.36
7.50	7.71	7.76	7.79	7.90
8.00	8.24	8.30	8.33	8.45
8.50	8.77	8.84	8.88	9.00
9.00	9.31	9.38	9.42	9.55
9.50	9.84	9.92	9.96	10.11
10.00	10.38	10.47	10.52	10.67
10.50	10.92	11.02	11.07	11.23
11.00	11.46	11.57	11.63	11.80
11.50	12.01	12.13	12.19	12.37
12.00	12.55	12.68	12.75	12.94
12.50	13.10	13.24	13.31	13.51
13.00	13.65	13.80	13.89	14.09
13.50	14.20	14.37	14.45	14.67
14.00	14.75	14.93	15.02	15.25
14.50	15.31	15.50	15.60	15.84
15.00	15.87	16.08	16.18	16.43

pounding. In 20 years the investor will have earned an additional $3,308 with daily rather than annual compounding. This is because with daily compounding the real interest (or yield) is 10.52 percent. The extra 1/2 percent makes quite a difference.

Yield under continuous compounding

As we have seen, compounding may be frequent or infrequent. Under daily compounding, simple interest for one year is calculated; that number is then divided by 365 and added to the principal, and so on. It is even possible to compound continuously. While the mathematics of this is complex, we have tables that will approximate the result. Under continuous compounding, the year is simply broken down into a larger number of units, sometimes as many as 1,000. This, of course, can be done with modern computers.

It should be noted that the interest must be credited to the principal as soon as it is calculated or else it is not compounding. For example, some institutions calculate the interest every day, but store it in the computer and add it to the principal at the end of the quarter. In such a case this is really quarterly compounding.

Table 13–3   *Buildup of $5,000 at 10 percent with various frequencies of compounding*

Time in years	Interest compounded annually (10.00%)	Interest compounded quarterly (10.00%)	Interest compounded daily (10.00%)
1	$ 5,500	$ 5,519	$ 5,526
5	8,052	8,193	8,244
10	12,968	13,425	13,591
15	20,886	22,000	22,408
20	33,637	36,048	36,945

Table 13–2 shows the effective interest rate (or yield) that results from various methods of compounding.

Nominal and real interest rates

The **nominal interest rate** is just another name for the stated interest rate; for example, 8 percent on $1,000 is $80 per annum. The *real interest rate* is the rate that has been adjusted for inflation by subtracting the rate of inflation from the nominal rate. For instance, if inflation were 5 percent per year, then with an 8 percent nominal rate the real rate would be 3 percent (8 percent minus 5 percent) and the return in real dollars would be $30. Table 13–4 and Figure 13–5 show how real interest rates have varied over the years.

After-tax nominal interest rate

The **after-tax nominal interest rate** depends on the client's particular tax bracket. To obtain it, subtract the tax bracket from 1.00 and multiply this number by the nominal interest rate. Staying with our example, if the individual were in the 15 percent tax bracket, the after-tax nominal rate would be 6.8 percent.

$$(1.00 - 0.15) \times 0.08 = .85 \times 8 = 6.8\%$$

For someone in the 28 percent bracket, the after-tax nominal rate would be 5.76 percent.

$$(1.00 - 0.28) = .72 \times .08 = 5.76\%$$

After-tax real interest rate

The after-tax nomimal interest rate is adjusted for inflation in the same manner as the before-tax nominal rate. In our example above, the 6.80 percent after-tax nominal rate becomes 1.8 percent (after-tax nominal rate − inflation = 6.80 − 5.0 = 1.80 percent) if the individual is in the 15 percent tax bracket. Similarly, for a 28 percent bracket, the after-tax real rate would be 0.76 percent (5.76 percent − 5 percent = .76 per-

Real interest rates

Table 13–4

Year ending Dec. 31	Inflation rate	High grade corp. bonds	Real rate	3–6 month com'l. paper	Real rate
1950	5.8	2.6	−3.2	1.7	−4.1
1951	5.9	3.1	−2.8	2.3	−3.6
1952	0.9	3.0	2.1	2.3	1.4
1953	0.6	3.1	2.5	2.3	1.7
1954	−0.5	2.9	3.4	1.3	1.8
1955	0.4	3.1	2.7	3.0	2.6
1956	2.9	3.4	0.5	3.6	0.7
1957	3.0	3.7	0.7	3.8	0.8
1958	1.8	4.1	2.3	3.3	1.5
1959	1.5	4.6	3.1	4.9	3.4
1960	1.5	4.4	2.9	3.2	1.7
1961	0.7	4.4	3.7	3.2	2.5
1962	1.2	4.2	3.0	3.3	1.1
1963	1.6	4.4	2.8	4.0	2.4
1964	1.2	4.4	3.2	4.2	3.0
1965	1.9	4.7	2.8	4.7	2.8
1966	3.4	5.3	1.9	6.0	2.6
1967	3.0	6.9	3.9	5.6	2.6
1968	4.7	6.5	1.8	6.1	1.4
1969	6.1	7.8	1.7	8.8	2.7
1970	5.5	7.4	1.9	5.7	0.2
1971	3.4	7.1	3.7	6.0	2.6
1972	3.4	7.2	3.8	5.5	2.1
1973	8.8	7.7	−1.1	9.1	0.3
1974	12.2	8.6	−3.6	9.0	−3.2
1975	7.0	8.6	1.6	6.0	−1.0
1976	4.8	7.8	3.0	4.7	−0.1
1977	6.8	8.4	1.6	6.6	−0.2
1978	9.0	9.2	0.2	10.4	1.4
1979	13.3	10.6	−2.7	12.8	−0.5
1980	12.4	12.4	0.0	16.5	4.1
1981	8.9	14.5	5.6	12.1	3.2
1982	3.9	11.2	7.3	8.5	4.6
1983	3.8	12.3	8.5	9.8	6.0
1984	4.0	12.0	8.0	8.2	4.2
1985	3.8	10.1	6.3	7.6	3.8
1986	1.1	9.1	8.0	5.7	4.6
1987	4.4	9.9	5.5	7.0	2.6
1988	4.4	9.9	5.5	9.0	4.6
1989	4.6	8.8	4.2	8.3	3.7

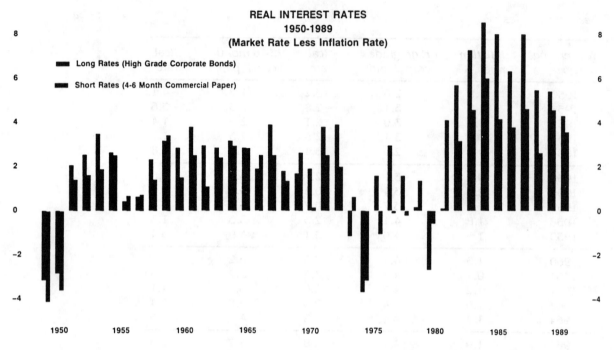

REAL INTEREST RATES
1950-1989
(Market Rate Less Inflation Rate)

■ Long Rates (High Grade Corporate Bonds)

■ Short Rates (4-6 Month Commercial Paper)

Figure 13–5 *Real interest rates, 1950–1989 (marked rate less inflation rate.)* (Source: Johnson's Investment Company Charts, 1989, *Hugh A. Johnson Co., Buffalo, N.Y., p. 27.)*

cent). This clearly demonstrates how both inflation and taxes can erode the investor's return. It is even possible for inflation rates to be greater than the nominal rate, as in the 1979 to 1981 time period, which means individuals were actually losing money in terms of purchasing power. Table 13–5 shows how taxes and inflation erode interest income and principal. Here we are earning 8 percent, but inflation is only 4 percent.

HOW INTEREST RATES ARE CALCULATED BY MOST INSTITUTIONS

We have seen above that how interest is compounded makes a difference in determining the true yield. In the case of accounts on which checks may be written, and which therefore fluctuate, two other factors are important in determining how much interest is earned. They are (1) how the institution determines the balance to which the interest rate is applied, and (2) when the interest is credited to the account.

There are three common methods used to determine the dollar amount to which the interest rate is applied.

Determining the account balance

1. Low or minimum balance. If the investor's interest period is a month, and the beginning balance was $1,000, and a deposit was made of $600 and a check was written for $500 (as shown in

Nominal interest, real interest, after-tax nominal interest, and after-tax real interest with 4 percent inflation (nominal interest 8 percent)

Table 13—5

	Percent	Dollars
1. Amount invested	%	$1,000.00
2. Nominal interest	8	80.00
3. Inflation dilution		
a. Interest—diluted by inflation ($80 × 4%)	4	3.20
b. Principal—diluted by inflation ($1,000 × 4%)	4	40.00
c. Total dilution (principal and interest)	4	43.20
4. Real interest ($80.00 − $3.20)	4	76.80
5. Tax dilution of interest		
15 percent bracket (line 2 times tax bracket)	1.2	12.00
28 percent bracket (line 2 times tax bracket)	2.24	22.40
6. After-tax nominal interest (line 2 minus line 5)		
15 percent bracket	6.8	68.00
28 percent bracket	5.76	57.60
7. After-tax real interest (line 6 adjusted for 4% inflation)		
15 percent bracket*	2.8	28.00
28 percent bracket	1.76	17.60

*If a person is in the 15 percent tax bracket, his or her investment after taxes has grown to $1,068 after one year, but after an added adjustment for inflation it is only about $1,026.87 in real terms. If, on the other hand, he or she is in the 28 percent tax bracket, the investment after one year and after taxes is $1,057.60. But after an adjustment for inflation, the investment grew only to $1,016.48. These figures do not match the figures on line 7 precisely, because of rounding. With 4 percent inflation, the after-tax nominal return is not reduced by 4 percent (the inflation rate) to get the real return, but by the reciprocal of 4 percent, which is 3.85 percent. See Chapter 1 for a discussion of how the value of money (and hence bonds) declines reciprocally with inflation. (Calculated by the author.)

the table below), the interest rate calculation would be applied to the minimum balance of $900. If the check had been written before the deposit, then only $500 (minimum balance) would have earned interest.

	Deposits	Checks	Balance
Opening Balance			$1,000
Deposit: 10th of month	$500		$1,500
Check: 20th of month		$600	$ 900

2. Average balance. In the above case the average balance of $1,133 would have earned interest.

3. Actual balance. Under this method interest is calculated every day on the actual money in the account as follows:

	Deposits	Checks	Balance
Opening balance			$1,000
Deposit: 10th of month	$5000		$1,500
Checks: 20th of month		$600	$ 900
Interest would be received on:			
$1,000 for 10 days			
$1,500 for 10 days			
$ 900 for 10 days			

In the above three examples, if the investor were earning 6 percent, he or she would receive monthly interest of $4.50 ($900 × 6% ÷ 12), $6.49, and $17 respectively, with methods one, two, and three.

This last method is the fairest and best from the depositor's viewpoint. Interest is being earned on the actual money in the account.

This latter method is sometimes called day-in day-out (DIDO) interest. The interest period is one day, and the computer calculates interest daily. Check to see what method the institution is using. The additional interest earned with a DIDO account can be substantial, especially with a fairly large account.

When interest is credited to the account

There is a difference, however, between daily interest calculation and daily interest compounding. In order to have daily compounding the interest must be calculated daily and also credited to the account daily. Many institutions calculate interest every day, but then the computer holds it and credits it to the account only at the end of the month, or sometimes not until the end of the quarter. Such a case constitutes monthly or quarterly compounding. If an account is earning 6 percent with daily compounding, the true interest or yield is really 6.18 percent, as shown in Table 13–2.

SUMMARY REVIEW QUESTIONS

These questions serve as a summary and a review of the chapter. If you are able to answer them all, you have a good understanding of the material covered by the chapter.

1. What is meant by the term "investing indirectly"?
2. Who are the savers in the United States? Is there a correlation between savings and age?
3. Discuss some of the reasons for saving.
4. What are "nest-egg" savings?
5. What are thrift institutions?
6. How do thrift institutions assist individuals in a savings program?
7. Why do many individuals place their savings in thrift institutions?
8. Distinguish between savings deposits and demand deposits.
9. What is a negotiated order of withdrawal (NOW)?

10. How do passbook savings deposits differ from a NOW account?
11. What is a certificate of deposit (CD)?
12. Discuss the money market deposit account.
13. What is the sweep arrangement?
14. Describe why most deposits in most institutions are very safe.
15. What is the penalty for early withdrawals of CDs?
16. What is the difference between Series EE and HH government bonds?
17. What are marketable bonds?
18. Why did Congress make Series EE and HH bonds nonnegotiable but redeemable?
19. What is the economic justification for the payment of interest?
20. Differentiate between compound interest and simple interest.
21. What is the rule of 72?
22. Explain briefly nominal, real, and after-tax real interest.

CASES

1. Tonia Poole invests $1,000 in three different certificates of deposit as follows:

Amount	Interest rate	Compounded
A $1,000	6%	Annually
B $1,000	5.75%	Monthly
C $1,000	5.75%	Daily

What will the $1,000 be worth after one year in each case?

2. Lyndia Christensen, aged twenty-four, is a secretary in a large city and earns $450 per week. She would like to save as much as possible for her vacation, which she hopes to spend in Miami. She would also like to earn as much interest on her savings as possible but yet keep her principal liquid. By living on a tight budget, Lyndia is able to save $40 per week. Her vacation is still almost a year off, and she requests your advice as to where to invest her savings so as to achieve her objectives. Explain why you have selected certain institutions.

3. Over the years Arthur Pedit has kept his savings in a savings deposit at the First National Bank in his town. He has accumulated almost $10,000 in his savings account, which is insured by the FDIC and on which he has been earning 5 1/4 percent interest. Can he earn more on his money by putting it in a mutual savings bank or a savings and loan association? Will his savings be as safe in these institutions? How would all of the above three compare with a credit union or Series EE bonds regarding yield and safety?

4. Bernice Wilson has saved regularly and now has $5,000 in a Los Angeles savings and loan association. Recently she received notice from the institution that they are paying 5 1/2 percent. However, her friend Dorothy Jenkins told Bernice that she is receiving 7 percent on her savings in a branch of the same savings and loan association in Santa Ana where she lives. Can you explain the apparent discrepancy to Dorothy and Bernice?

5. Bob and Virginia Waring have a $1,000, two-year, 7 percent certificate of deposit in the Essex County Savings and Loan Association, which is only one month old. Because of an automobile accident, they need the money. Can they get it? What interest in dollar amounts will they get? What interest would they have received if the CD had been one year old?

SUGGESTED READINGS

"The Arithmetic of Interest Rates." New York: The Federal Reserve Bank of New York.

The Bankers Magazine. A banking quarterly review, published by Warren, Gorham, and Lamont, Inc., Boston, Mass.

Barrons, Dow Jones and Company. Weekly publication.

"Borrowers, Lenders, and Interest Rates." Richmond, Va.: The Federal Reserve Bank of Richmond.

Carrol, Frieda. *The Joys of Saving and Economizing.* Atlanta: Bibliotheca Press, 1985.

Credit Union National Association Yearbook. Madison, Wis.: Credit Union National Association. Annual publication.

"Depository Institutions and Their Regulators." New York: The Federal Reserve Bank of New York.

Directors Digest. Chicago: United States League of Savings Associations. Monthly publication.

Federal Home Loan Bank Board Journal. Washington, D.C.: Federal Home Loan Bank Board. Monthly publication.

Finance Facts Yearbook. Washington, D.C.: National Consumer Finance Association. Annual publication.

Gup, Benton E. *Financial Intermediaries,* 2nd ed. Boston: Houghton Mifflin, 1988.

International Credit Union Yearbook. Washington, D.C.: CUNA International, Inc. Annual publication.

Mutual Savings Banks National Fact Book. New York: National Association of Mutual Savings Banks. Annual publication.

Mutual Savings Banks Annual Report. New York: National Association of Mutual Savings Banks.

Sarnat, Marshall, and Szego, Giorgio. *Saving, Investment, and Capital Markets in an Inflationary Economy.* Cambridge, Mass.: Ballinger Publishing Co., 1982.

Savings and Loan Fact Book. Chicago: United States League of Savings Associations. Annual publication.

Savings and Loan Bulletin. Chicago: United States League of Savings Associations. Monthly publication.

The Wall Street Journal. Princeton, N.J.: Dow Jones and Company. Daily publication.

14 The fundamentals of direct security investments

HIGHLIGHTS   In order to understand the fundamentals of direct investments and to set the stage for acquiring stocks and bonds, this chapter discusses the following:

1   The various forms of business organization; the investor should know about the organizational structure of the business firm in which he or she invests
2   Alternative investment objectives a person may wish to achieve
3   Short-run versus long-run investments
4   The risks inherent in any business venture
5   Techniques used in an attempt to reduce risk
6   The sources of investment data needed to make intelligent investment decisions

INTRODUCTION

In this chapter we will introduce direct investments. When we invest directly we make our savings available directly to the business that will actually use it, rather than indirectly by putting them into a depository institution. A person may invest directly by becoming part owner of a business or by directly lending it money. When investing in a business directly, securities (for example, bonds or stock) will be received to prove the investment has been made.

FORM OF BUSINESS ORGANIZATIONS

Generally business firms are organized into single proprietorships, partnerships, or corporations. While partnerships and single proprietorships outnumber corporations in the United States, they are far less important by every other test. Noncorporate businesses have fewer employees, own fewer assets, and produce and sell much less. They are primarily small businesses owned by a few people—often by a single family. There are also some family-owned corporations, but they are nearly always small. While some corporations are small, nearly all partnerships and single prioprietorships are; and all large business entities are corporations.

The single proprietorship

The **single proprietorship** is a business owned by one person. It is the simplest form of organization, and the easiest and quickest to enter. There need be no charter application or other papers to fill out to enter business. Business assets are commingled with the personal assets of the owner, as are business debt and personal debt. While there can be numerous employees, there can be only one owner. This form of business is fine for some small firms, but it cannot grow very large.

The partnership

The **partnership** can be comprised of two or more partners. It has some advantages over the single proprietorship. With several partners, usually more capital can be raised, and a number of varying talents may be brought together.

To form a partnership, a partnership agreement must be drawn up. All states have laws governing partnerships and the agreement spells out the duties, rights, and liabilities of each partner.

While a partnership has some advantages over the single proprietorship, it has some disadvantages as well. It is less flexible if several partners have to be consulted before a decision can be made. It is not permanent; the death of one partner dissolves the partnership. Perhaps the greatest single drawback of a partnership is that all partners are liable without limits for the debts of the business.[1] One partner can commit the others by the decisions he or she makes. Nevertheless, the partnership form of organization works well in many cases. If confidence exists be-

---

1. There are limited partnerships, but generally all partners are liable for all business debts.

tween partners, it may be fine for small business. But like the single proprietorship, it is virtually impossible for a partnership to grow into a truly
big business firm.

A **corporation** is a legal entity. It has been defined by Chief Justice Marshall as "an artificial being, invisible, intangible, and a device only in con-
templation of law." It has many of the rights, duties, and powers of an
individual. It can sue and be sued; it can sign contracts, borrow money,
own property, and carry out regular business affairs. A corporation raises
money by selling shares in itself called **common stock.** Because a corporation is artificial, it cannot do any of these things itself, but they are
done in its name by the corporation's board of directors, elected by its
owners.

The corporate form

The various states grant corporation charters, and a corporation
comes into existence when the certificate of incorporation is accepted by
the proper state agency, usually the secretary of state of the state in
which incorporation takes place. The people who do the incorporating are
the owners and are called the **stockholders.** They invest money by buying the corporation's stock which is then used to acquire business assets
(capital) to carry out the business activity for which the corporation was
organized.

As noted above, corporations issue and sell shares in themselves called
stock; they also issue **bonds.** If an individual buys either, he or she is
investing in a business directly.

*Corporate bonds
and stock*

Bonds are certificates of indebtedness; if an investor buys bonds he
or she is lending the business money. The investor is a creditor. All of
the terms of the loan are fixed; a certain percentage interest rate will be
received on the money for a certain period of time after which the corporation must also repay the loan.

Corporate stocks are certificates of ownership (also called **shares**);
if an investor buys stock, he or she becomes a part owner of the business
(in a sense, joining the club.) However, no return is promised on the
money. If the corporation is successful, it will earn a profit and, as an
owner, part of that will be the investor's. It will not necessarily be received
in the form of cash, because the corporation may retain it. Only if the
board of directors decides to pay out all or part of the earnings in the
form of dividends will stockholders receive cash. On the other hand, if
the corporation is unsuccessful and suffers losses, the investor will share
in those. There is no promise made that the stock will ever be redeemed.
As a stockholder, the only thing the investor is promised is that he or she
will be permitted to vote for the board of directors who will manage the
corporation.

Stockholders, then, assume more risk than bondholders. Bondholders must receive their interest before stockholders may get anything.
Stockholders are described as providing risk or venture capital.

There is also a special type of stock called **preferred stock** that stands between bonds and common stock. Preferred stockholders' claims are satisfied after bondholders' but before common stockholders'. We will discuss both bonds and stock in detail in Chapter 16.

Advantages of the corporate form of business organization

The advantages of the corporate form of organization include:

1. One's liability is limited to his or her actual investment in the corporation, and one's personal assets cannot be used to pay the debts of the corporation. In a single proprietorship or partnership, personal assets are available to pay business debts. Since the corporation is a legal entity, only corporate assets may be used to satisfy claims against the corporation. The individual stockholders can lose only what they paid for their own stock. This makes many people willing to invest in a corporation, which permits raising large aggregates of capital.

2. Shares of stock (or ownership) in a corporation are easily transferred to another person. Corporate stock is negotiable, and can be sold to any other individual, or can be inherited by survivors. This gives a corporation an indefinite life and also contributes to raising large aggregates of capital. A partnership, in contrast, is dissolved upon the death of a partner, and if a partner wishes to sell his or her share to another person, the partners must agree.

3. The small as well as the large investor may easily invest in corporations. Extremely small amounts of capital (as little as a few dollars) can be committed to the corporation by buying a single share of stock. This permits thousands of individuals collectively to be owners of businesses, which in turn also contributes to raising large amounts of capital.

4. The above advantages all contribute to the ability of the corporation to amass high sums of capital, to grow large, and to enjoy the benefits of greater efficiencies that often accompany greater size.

There may be other benefits that arise from the giant corporation. For example, if a firm is big it can hire better managerial and other specialized talent than can a small firm. On the other hand, some observers have expressed concern over the separation of ownership and control that a giant corporation makes inevitable. They state that the millions of stockholders who own (but are far removed from) the corporation cannot possibly influence the managers who control the corporation. The managers may or may not be stockholders, but in any event, they are not responsible to their constituents and this, it is alleged, is unhealthy in a democracy.

INVESTMENT OBJECTIVES

The first step in making an investment is to decide upon the investment objectives. Then those securities most likely to help to achieve them will need to be selected. Goals and objectives may be any of the following:

1. Liquidity
2. Income
3. Capital gains or growth
4. Security of principal
5. Hedging inflation

or perhaps several of all of these.

Liquidity

Liquidity has to do with how quickly and easily an asset can be turned into cash without a price concession. Money is 100 percent liquid, while other assets vary depending upon their relative "moneyness." Cash is the most liquid of all assets. The term cash equivalents is sometimes used by financial planners. It is cash or almost cash, such as savings accounts, some CDs, etc. (see Chapter 13). After cash and cash equivalents, the degree of liquidity for assets is in general followed by certain U.S. government securities, high-grade corporate bonds, preferred and common stock traded on organized exchanges, over-the-counter securities, first mortgages on a real estate, and real estate holdings. Generally, securities listed on organized exchanges are very liquid because they can be sold at the market price by making a telephone call. Selling real estate, on the other hand, takes time. Some liquidity is important for all investors—the amount desired varies.

Income

Another investment objective might be to achieve a good income. Some companies achieve higher earnings (profits) then others and they may pay out a high proportion of these earnings to the stockholder in the form of dividends. These are the income stocks. Sometimes bonds too yield a relatively high return. An investor with income as an objective would choose from among these higher-yielding securities.

Capital gains

Capital gains, or capital appreciation as it is sometimes called, is an important modern investment objective. A capital gain may be defined as "the increase in value of an asset when it is sold, over what it was when purchased." This attitude toward capital gains as an objective is something that has developed within the past thirty years. Before that, the ideas of income, liquidity, and safety were the objectives that were stressed. Many people invest in securities they believe will result in capital growth rather than income. This may involve investment in the type of firm that has growth possibilities or the purchase of a security the investor has reason to believe is depressed in value. Capital gains—if one is successful in obtaining them—often give a greater return on one's investment. This fact has made capital gains very attractive to some investors.

Security of principal

Safety or security of principal means the preservation of capital values through a conservative investment policy. It is a truism, of course, that this is the prime objective of any investor, everyone desires to preserve the original principal. This can be done by good judgment, avoidance of highly speculative risks, and attempting to preserve capital from market fluctuations. Unhappily, all this is easier said than done. Moreover, security of principal and liquidity are somewhat inconsistent with high yield. A person who wants high yield or rapid appreciation must assume more risk and accept a greater likelihood of no return or sometimes of actual loss. There are a number of different risks associated with holding securities, and they are examined in detail below.

Hedging inflation

Some investors may feel that prices will continue to rise. When prices rise, the real value of certain assets declines, whereas the value of others tends to rise with inflation. Historically, common stock and real estate were considered the best hedges against inflation. Bonds, on the other hand, since they are fixed investments, are generally eroded by inflation. If the price level doubles, the value of the dollar falls by half. If prices rise, the person with fixed dollar assets suffers a loss in value of his or her assets. If one is dependent upon fixed dollars for income—as, for example, are the retired—one's standard of living will necessarily decline. Historically speaking, however, the price of common stock has at least kept up and in many periods surpassed the rate of inflation.

The main reason why the prices of common stock should be a good hedge against inflation is that corporations often plow earnings back into the business. This means that new machinery, plants, and so forth are purchased on behalf of the stockholder. As a result, the value of one's stock should rise. If the corporation is also providing a good or service,

"Gracious, I don't want to bring him back. I'd just like his advice on some investments."
(Source: *Permission Cartoon Features Syndicate; from* The Wall Street Journal.)

the demand for which is growing rapidly, its price may be outpacing infla
tion. If so, this will reflected in corporate profits and this too should contribute to rising stock prices. Figures 14–1 and 14–2 illustrate how good
an inflationary hedge stocks have been over the long run. One chart
shows the cost of living and the Dow Jones Industrial stock average. The
other one shows the cost of living, Standard & Poor's 500 stock index,
earnings, and dividends. As you can see, stocks have more than held
their own in the long run.

How short is the short run? Any definition is, of course, arbitrary but certainly holding a security for less than a year or two is short run. Holding
a security for twenty years or even five or ten is a long-run investment.
You may draw your own chronological line. It is generally conceded that
the small investor should play largely in the long-run or in the interme-

**SHORT-RUN
VERSUS
LONG-RUN
INVESTMENTS**

Common stocks and the cost of living, 1897–1989. (Source: Johnson's Investment
Company Charts, 1989, *Hugh A. Johnson Co., Buffalo, N.Y., p. 11.*)   Figure 14–1

Figure 14—2 *Cost of living, dividends, and Standard & Poor's 500 stock index 1926—1989. (Source: Johnson's Investment Company Charts, 1989, Hugh A. Johnson Co., Buffalo, N.Y., p. 13.)*

diate-run end of the field. If an individual is a large investor, it might be worthwhile to devote the energy, time, and perhaps money needed to make a short-term gain. However, the small investor may not have the time to watch an investment constantly. Also he or she cannot hire expensive professional advice. Moreover, even if he or she does make a nice short-term gain, in absolute dollars it is likely to be small. Therefore, a small investor who gets in and out of the market frequently on a short-term basis will pay commissions that may eat heavily into any profits earned.

Therefore, most small investors probably should buy securities with an eye toward holding them for the long run. This does not mean that the investor should salt them away and forget about them. Any long-term investment can also turn sour and investors should review their portfolios periodically. Nevertheless, for most small investors the goal should be long-run investments—that is, held for at least a few years—not short-run speculation.

Our system is not a profit system as so many people like to claim. Rather it is a profit-and-loss system. Some firms prosper and show a profit while others lag behind and have losses. No firm can have losses in the long run and survive. And indeed, some firms go out of business from time to time. When they do, the stockholder absorbs the loss. Being an investor, then, is risky business. However, the reward for successfully assuming risk is financial gain, generally as profits in one form or another.

Risk refers to the possibility of future loss and how likely it is that this possibility will occur. Since there are a number of different risks involved in any investment, it is important that investors recognize those to which they may be exposed. Risks can be classified into six major types.

INVESTMENT RISKS

While some businesses prosper, others fail. In the event of business failure, a stockholder, having invested "equity" capital, may be entirely wiped out. Bondholders who have loaned money to a company may also find themselves wiped out, but not as frequently as stockholders. If the bonds are secured by certain specific corporate assets, the bondholders may sell these assets and sometimes recover all of the loan, though more often than not they recover less. If the bonds are unsecured, the holder often collects much less than the loan.

Risk of business failure

It is generally conceded that one way to lessen the likelihood of being wiped out is to diversify one's investments by types of securities and issuers and to buy only the securities of financially strong firms.

Market risk is the particular risk resulting from fluctuations in market prices of securities over time, which may or may not have anything to do with how well a business firm is doing. Stock prices may decline due to a lowering of earnings in a particular firm, such as decline stemming from poor management or even a change in the public's tastes. Or earnings may fluctuate due to the business cycle, which will cause the market price of securities to fluctuate.

Market risk

Price fluctuations in securities may also arise as a result of investor psychology. Many persons may decide simply to stay out of the market, thus reducing demand for securities and consequently lowering prices, even though firms' profit have not declined and may even have risen.

Another type of risk is that of changes in the purchasing power of money. This risk is particularly applicable to those assets whose value is stated

Price level risk

in terms of a fixed number of dollars. People who hold bonds and savings accounts are assuming this risk, as are people who hold idle cash. Indeed, those who hold idle cash are the most vulnerable to this risk.

For example, if a person holds money and the value of the dollar falls—which is another way of saying that prices rise—then in terms of real purchasing power the person who holds the money has lost. If the value of the dollar rises—which is another way of saying prices have declined—the real purchasing power of the dollar has risen and the person who holds the money gains. In a period of rising prices, the astute investor will try to move away from fixed assets into items such as common stock and real estate, which tend to appreciate with rising prices. In a period of falling prices (which we hardly see any more), the investor should move from real estate and common stock into fixed assets yielding a fixed return, such as bonds.

This brings us to the *nominal* rate of return and the *real* rate of return. The nominal rate of return is the money rate without an adjustment for inflation, and the real rate is the rate after the inflationary adjustment. If an investor holds a $1,000 bond paying 10 percent for one year during which prices rise by 8 percent, the nominal (money) rate of return is 10 percent and the real return is 2 percent. To convert the nominal rate to the real rate, subtract the rate of inflation from the nominal interest rate. In the above case, the real value of the $1,000 principal sum that was invested in the bond has also declined in real terms. The $1,000 investment grew to $1,100 in nominal terms. The real interest return was $20. The $1,000 original investment is now worth only $920 in real terms. Adding the $20 in real interest to the real value of the principal makes the total investment now worth only $940.

Interest rate risk

Interest rate risk is the risk of loss that results from changes in the price of bonds due to fluctuations in prevailing rates of interest. It is important primarily for investments in fixed obligations such as bonds and preferred stock. When interest rates rise, bond prices fall; conversely, when interest rates go down, bond prices rise. There is nothing mystical about this process; it really makes sense. We will illustrate this with an example which, while using an unrealistic low interest rate, illustrates the principle because the interest rate doubles. Suppose a corporation issues a $1,000 bond at 5 percent. This is a contractual obligation and the corporation must pay the holder $50 per year. Later, if interest rates double to 10 percent, in theory—depending upon the maturity—the old bond would drop in price to about $500. The reason is that with rates at 10 percent, any new bond issues would have to be offered with this same 10 percent yield; investors with $1,000 can now expect to get a return of $100 on their investments. Therefore, the holders of the old bonds will attempt to sell them and attain the new rate, thus forcing the price down, until its market price is such that the fixed payment of $50 becomes closer to 10 percent of the bond's market price.

Actually the price of the old bond will not go down to $500, because the company still has an obligation to repay the original $1,000 loan on the due date. If the bond becomes due the year after the new interest rate, obviously it would be foolish for the holders of the bonds to sell at $500 when all they have to do is to wait a year and then demand $1,000 from the corporation. The bonds will nevertheless decline somewhat, and if they have twenty or more years to run, they will decline considerably.

If the interest rate declines, bond prices rise. Again suppose one holds a $1,000 bond paying 10 percent or $100 per year. If the interest rate declines to 5 percent, all a new investor can now expect as a yield on an investment of $1,000 is $50. Consequently, the demand for existing bonds paying $100 will increase and *theoretically* the older bond will rise to $2,000, again depending on maturity. Competition to obtain the older bond will theoretically bid its price up to the point where the $100 interest becomes 5 percent of the price of the bond, that is, $2,000. Again for practical reasons, however, it never goes that high.[2]

Buying long-term bonds, then, is risky during periods when interest rates are volatile. An individual might think, however, that 10 percent is a fair return and is willing to hold it until maturity. Then there may be paper losses, but no actual losses; and in 20 years the investor will get back the $1,000, but then he or she will be hurt by inflation; what will $1,000 be worth in 20 years?

---

2. The longer the time to maturity, the greater the change in the price of a bond due to a given change in the interest rate. A bond would have to run to perpetuity (never become due) for a doubling of the interest rate to cut its market price in half. For example, if the interest rate rose from 12 to 15 percent, then a $1,000 bond maturing in twenty years would decline to $850, because in twenty years the bond would be redeemed at its face value of $1,000. Hence the $150 capital appreciation over this period must be prorated over twenty years and included in the $120 per year the bond pays. The bond would appreciate $7.50 per year; hence the total yield would be $127.50, which is 15 percent of $850. The formula for determining the market price (P) of a bond is

$$P = I \left| \sum_{n=1}^{M} \frac{1}{\left(1 + \dfrac{i}{2}\right)^n} \right| + F \left| \frac{1}{\left(1 + \dfrac{i}{2}\right)^M} \right|$$

where

P = current market price
I = coupon interest payment in dollars
n = payment periods per year (2 in the case of most bonds)
M = total number of payments
i = market rate of interest
F = face value of the bond

In the case of a bond maturing in ten years paying $130 per year ($65 every six months) at a time when the market rate of interest is 12 percent, we would have

$$P = \$65 \times 11.4699 + 1000 \times 0.3118$$

and the market value of the bond would be $1,057.34.

Whether long-term bonds are a good buy, then, is a function of future interest rates. This introduces an element of the unknown. If an investor thinks interest rates will go no higher, bonds might be an okay buy, especially if they are likely to come down; there would then be a nice capital gain. On the other hand, if it is believed interest rates will rise in the future, refrain from buying bonds. Wait until they do rise and then buy.

What causes changes in the interest rate? They are caused by changes in the demand for and in the supply of money. If money is thought of as any other commodity and interest as the price of the commodity, then when the demand is high and the supply constant, the price or interest rate will rise. When the demand is low, the price goes down, provided of course that the supply remains constant. The supply of money is to a degree regulated by the Federal Reserve System, and in this way so too is the interest rate. The basic reasons for this regulation of the interest rate are twofold. If the Federal Reserve had reason to fear deflation and recession, it would attempt to lower interest rates to make borrowing by businesspersons more attractive, with the idea that if interest rates are lowered and borrowing occurs, new capital will be created with a resulting upswing in the economy. On the other hand, if the Federal Reserve Board feared inflation, it would raise the interest rate, on the philosophy that if rates are high, businesspersons will be deterred from new capital formation to a certain degree and forces of inflation will be lessened.

Financial risk

Financial risk is related to the debt (bond)-equity (common stock) ratio of a company, and is related to the obligation the corporation has to bondholders, preferred stockholders, and common stockholders, respectively. A high debt-to-equity ratio means that the corporation has a large fixed obligation (interest) to pay each year. If sales and profits decline severely in any one year, this could cause a burden. It is even possible that the heavy interest payment could not be met, and there would be losses instead of profits. The higher the debt-to-equity ratio, the higher the financial risk. However, a business often has some control over this risk.

Political risk

Political risk has to do with changes in the legal environment in which the business must operate. If the government changes taxes, tariffs, subsidies, or imposes wage or price controls, these changes could affect profits. Political risk would also include the psychological response and possible overreaction on the part of the public and the business community to a statement by the president or other government leaders.

Risk and expected rate of return

There is often a trade-off between risk and rate of return. However, the future return is seldom certain; hence, we have the concept of **expected rate of return.** If the client wants a high rate of return, he or she will have to accept a high risk; or conversely, only the possibility of a high return will entice the investor to assume a high risk. Some investors are more risk adverse than others and will not commit to high-risk vehicles; they will accept a lower but more certain return.

The term expected rate of return is crucial. A high-risk investor may expect (or hope for) a high return, but he or she may not get it. If an investor makes a high-risk investment, the return will be high if it materializes, but the likelihood of it materializing is less.

The higher the risk, the higher the return if it materializes, but the probability of it materializing also declines with risk. Figure 14–3 shows the trade-off between risk and expected rate of return. To be sure, some of the rankings may be a bit arbitrary. For example, some over-the-counter stock may be less risky than some listed stock. Nevertheless, the general scale is valid.

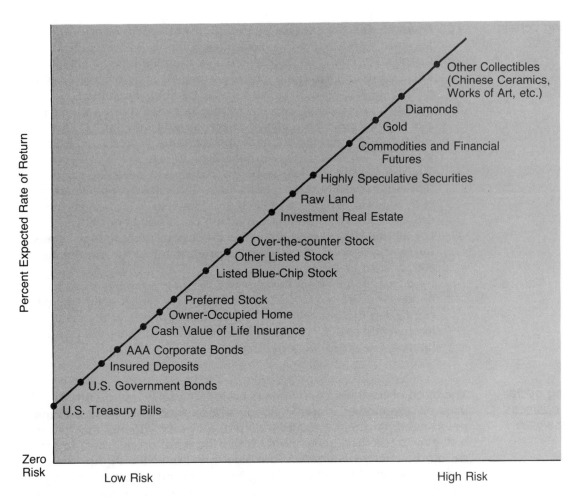

Risk and expected rate of return   Figure 14–3

REDUCING THE RISK OF INVESTMENTS

Not much can be done about political risk and one must operate within the existing political environment. Interest rate risk is difficult to diffuse. If one can forecast changes in interest rates he or she can take advantage of this, but such forecasts are extremely difficult. When buying long-term bonds, one rule might be to buy them only if the yield is attractive enough to hold them to maturity, and then do so. Any future paper losses will not be achieved. To be sure, one may possibly be prevented from taking advantage of future higher yields. If concerned about future changes in the interest rates, buy only short-term fixed obligations so the risk of capital loss is smaller. One can invest for a year or two easily and hold the securities until they mature. Then he or she will have only temporary paper losses or gains. An individual may also get a higher interest return by going short, because during periods of very high interest rates, short-term rates are often above long-term ones.

Reducing certain specific risk

1. Financial risk (excess leverage in the firm's capital structure) can be lessened by not buying the securities of highly leveraged firms. (See Chapter 15). Study balance sheets and examine the stability of earnings. A firm that has good, stable earnings is able to service a higher debt-to-equity ratio than a firm whose earnings fluctuate.
2. In reducing the price level risk, strive to invest in firms whose sales and product prices are likely to keep up with inflation. Their profits will probably keep up with inflation too, and, if profits keep up, the prices of their securities are more likely to rise.
3. The risk of business failure can be reduced by selecting companies that are financially strong, innovative, and whose products are presently in great demand and likely to remain so. With bonds, this risk can be reduced by investing only in A-rated bonds or better.
4. For market risk, some companies are less vulnerable than others—for example, companies selling a product for which the demand is stable, such as food.
5. Interest rate risk can be lessened by not investing in long-term bonds or preferred stock. Investing in short-term fixed obligation can lessen the interest rate risk, as shown above in the section on interest rate risk. By going short term, however, there will be a lower interest rate return in many cases.

Reducing overall risk by business trend analysis

The trend of business conditions is indicated weekly and monthly by figures on inventories, durable goods sales, price movements, employment, unemployment, industrial output, and GNP—figures that can give a clue as to whether the economy is moving up or down. There are cyclical movements up and down, but also broad overall long-run trends of economic expansion. By identifying broad upward or downward swings, and acting accordingly, risk can be reduced. If, for example, business conditions seem to be improving, one can buy securities with more confidence. If business conditions in general seem to be deteriorating, investors can reduce their risk by taking a more conservative stand regarding securities.

Industries are classified into groups for investment analysis—banks, food processing, rails, and the like—and a movement either upward or downward of the business cycle may affect them in varying degrees. Although generally if there is an upward movement in business conditions, all groups move upward, and if there is a downward movement, all groups have a tendency to move downward, some groups move to a lesser degree in either direction. Utility company earnings and sales are relatively stable, although there has been a secular trend upward. Auto stock tends to be more volatile, moving more rapidly upward during periods of expansion and just as rapidly downward during periods of contraction. Within each group, there are individual firms whose performance may be quite different from that of the group as a whole. Even during periods of contraction some firms earn more than others. Generally this can be attributed to good management. Within any group, one can find firms that have consistently paid good dividends to investors even during periods of severe recession, while others dealing with the same products are able to pay earnings only during relatively good times.

One can reduce risk by investing mostly in those industries that typically have done well and whose future looks more promising than that of the economy as a whole. Finally, if investors select not only industries that have done well but firms that have the best records within good industries, they can generally reduce risk even more.

Risk can be reduced by ***diversification,*** which is not putting all one's eggs in one basket. This is more difficult for a small investor than for a large one. But diversification is relative, and even a small investor should be able to obtain some. It can be achieved by firm, by industry, by type of security, and by investment objectives. If an investor decides to buy oil company stock, he or she should pick two or three or even four different companies, choosing the ones which seem best from history of the industry and firm analyses. Diversity may be achieved by buying stock of firms in different industries; or by purchasing different types of securities, say, bonds and stock. The investment objective should be diversity, that is, some investments for growth, some for income, and some for stability.[3] Diversification reduces risk by broadening the investment base, and the securities will probably include some that will fare better than average.

One excellent way of diversifying is to invest in mutual funds. These will be discussed in Chapter 17.

Reducing overall risk by diversification

---

3. From a functional point of view, common stock can be classified into income, growth, cyclical, speculative, and defensive stock, classifications discussed in Chapter 15.

SOURCES OF INVESTMENT INFORMATION

Financial information can be obtained from newspapers, magazines, books, investment services, banks, brokers, investment counselors, and other sources.

Newspapers

Greater amounts of information about business conditions are now in the financial pages of any large city newspaper, but certain newspapers are superior to others. Any serious investor should probably subscribe to *The Wall Street Journal,* a financial paper published daily in six regional editions as a morning paper. This journal publishes articles on general business and economic conditions in the United States and abroad. It also has stories and articles on specific industries and corporations and news on labor and government relations. It is a treasure house of business and financial statistics, of past, present, and future trends. It also has complete stock market quotations, including the Dow Jones averages and bond quotations. *The New York Times* also has a good financial section, containing news articles and in-depth analyses of business conditions in general and of specific businesses and industries.

Magazines and other publications

The better business and financial magazines are *Barron's Weekly, Forbes, Business Week, U.S. News and World Report,* and *Fortune Magazine.* These publications have articles on business and finance. They analyze general economic conditions, industries, and specific firms. The *Federal Reserve Bulletin* and the monthly *News Letters* published by the various district Federal Reserve Banks contain scholarly but readable articles on business and finance and many useful financial statistics. The President's Council of Economic Advisers publishes its monthly *Economics Indicators,* which contains a wealth of statistical information. All of these, and, in addition, many books and pamphlets are available in any good library.

Brokerage firms

Many large brokerage houses have libraries available to the public that contain many of the above publications. They also publish special studies and analyses made by their own research departments. Many brokerage firms have their own weekly or monthly newsletter.

Additional information may be obtained from stockbrokers regarding both industries as a whole and individual corporations. Each industry is classified in relation to the general market as "relatively favorable," "average," or "relatively unfavorable." Individual securities are listed as "long-term investment," "high income," "good quality—wider price movement," or "speculative." Such listings are in accord with the various investment objectives.

Investment services

Although there are a number of services from which one may obtain research and advisory services on whole industries and individual companies, the most popular are Standard and Poor's, Moody's Investors Service, Fitch Investors Service, the Value Line Investment Survey, and Argus Research Corporation. These services specialize in furnishing the public with the basic facts and figures on all securities publicly marketed and on the companies issuing them. From these services one may obtain information covering a period of many years on the assets, income, earnings, dividends, and stock prices of various corporations. These services also make studies of specific firms. The first page summary on one such study on American Telephone and Telegraph is shown in Figure 14—4. The cost of these services is in many hundreds of dollars, but an interested individual may examine them free in a broker's office or at most large public and university libraries. These investment services make industry studies in which they appraise the future outlook at the various firms within each industry and their common stock. Standard and Poor's publishes their listed stock report, a one- or two-page summary of every company listed on the New York Stock Exchange that provides some vital statistics and analyzes recent developments and future prospects of the firm. This summary comes out periodically with a separate sheet for each listed firm. It is called the "Yellow Sheet" in brokerage offices because it is printed on yellow paper. A reproduction of Standard and Poor's Yellow Sheet on International Business Machines is shown in Figure 14—5. Standard and Poor's also publishes a "Blue Sheet," an identical analysis for companies listed on the American Stock Exchange, and a "Green Sheet" for many over-the-counter securities, but only the better known ones.

The New York Stock Exchange has its own research department and makes available a number of publications free of charge, among them *The New York Stock Exchange Market* and the *New York Stock Exchange Fact Book*. The American Stock Exchange makes available similar booklets called *Understanding the American Stock Exchange* and *AMEX Databook*. *The stock exchanges*

Some of the smaller regional securities exchanges also have free publications. Some exchanges have libraries that contain extensive information and are open to the public. While many of the publications of the organized exchanges will not provide specific investment information, they provide good background information in the areas of business, finance, and economics.

Investment counselors will tailor an investment program for the individual investor according to the person's investment objectives. Investment counselors are professional investors and have their own skilled research departments. They, too, publish many studies, but these are available only to their customers. *Investment counselors, or advisors*

Investment counselors will first determine the investment objectives of their clients. If they are older retired persons, they may need income.

ATLANTIC RICHFIELD COMPANY

September 10, 1990
Vol. 15, No. 85

BUY

HIGHLIGHTS

Atlantic Richfield is in the unique position of producing more crude oil than its refineries consume, thus insulating it somewhat from potential crude oil shortages should fighting break out in the Middle East. The company's integrated West Coast operations stretch from substantial production facilities on Alaska's North Slope to gasoline distribution outlets in Southern California, and an expanded international exploration program is exposing the company to potentially large discoveries. But Alaska is the key to Arco's profits. The Exxon Valdez incident is taking its toll on the company in the form of higher future costs to prevent a recurrence of the disaster. On the production side, despite the hostile environment in which it operates, the company rates among the lowest in production costs. In refining and marketing, Arco is able to provide the consuming public with high volumes of "clean" gasoline because of its position as the largest producer of MTBE, a blending compound that reduces exhaust emissions. Moreover, because its two refineries use its relatively low-cost Alaskan crude, Arco is able to hold the line on gasoline prices.

Price: 139   12-Mo. Rge: 140 - 96
Symbol: ARC   Options Exch.: CBOE
DJIA: 2596.29   S&P 500: 320.46

Earnings	1989	1990E	1991E
(FY 12/31)	$11.26	$10.00	$10.70
P/E Ratio:		13.9	13.0
(vs S&P 500)		0.97	1.00
1985-89 Range: 0.67-1.11			

Earnings Growth Rates:	1985-89	1989-93
ARC	64%	11%
S&P 500	7%	6%

Div.: $5.00   Yield: 3.6%
Financial Strength: High

Expected 12-18 Month Price Behavior
    Relative to the S&P 500: Above Average
Common Shares Outstanding: 173.4 Mil.

Closing Price as of 9/6/90

RECOMMENDATION

We recommend purchasing the shares of Atlantic Richfield for above-average capital gains and secure income. At a price of $140 per share, the shares trade at a 31% discount to appraised net asset value of $204.05. Although the share price has recently exceeded the cash flow multiple of 5.7 — the highest it has been in the past 10 years — surging crude prices are expected to cause cash flow to accelerate. Furthermore, an active share repurchase program is likely to bolster per share data. The dividend, long stagnant at $1.00 per share, was boosted in the first quarter of 1989 to $1.125 and again in the first quarter of 1990 to the current $1.25. What's more, the company is unique among its peers in its ability to produce more crude than its refineries consume, placing it at a distinct advantage.

Figure 14—4   *A sample brokerage analysis. (Source: Argus Research Report. This report was reprinted courtesy of Argus Research Corporation, 17 Battery Place, N.Y.C., 10004.)*

Int'l Business Machines

1210

NYSE Symbol IBM Options on CBOE (Jan-Apr-Jul-Oct) In S&P 500

Price	Range	P-E Ratio	Dividend	Yield	S&P Ranking	Beta
Aug. 3'90	1990					
108¹/₈	123¹/₈-94¹/₂	16	4.84	4.5%	A	0.76

Summary

IBM is the world's dominant manufacturer of mainframe computers and is also a major supplier of minicomputers, computer peripheral equipment, personal computers, networking products, and system software. An earnings recovery is foreseen for 1990, reflecting the absence of restructuring costs and translation gains from a weaker dollar. In August, the company announced it would put its domestic typewriter and small printer products businesses into a new unit to be majority owned by Clayton & Dubilier.

Current Outlook

Earnings for 1990 are expected to increase to $10.00 a share from $6.47 in 1989, which included a $2.58 restructuring charge. Earnings for 1991 are projected at $11.20.

The $1.21 quarterly dividend is the minimum expectation.

Gross income should rise almost 8% in 1990 and slightly less in 1991, benefiting from healthy demand overseas and a modest resurgence in domestic demand for IBM's main hardware products, plus translation gains from a weaker dollar. Profit margins should improve, with gains from the domestic cost containment program more than offsetting pricing pressures in the mainframe and minicomputer markets.

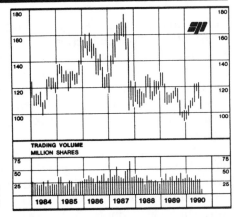

Revenues (Billion $)

Quarter:	1991	1990	1989	1988
Mar.	---	14.19	12.73	12.06
Jun.	---	16.50	15.21	13.91
Sep.	---	---	14.31	13.71
Dec.	---	---	20.46	20.00
	---	---	62.71	59.68

Revenues for the first half of 1990 advanced 10%, year to year, reflecting increased overall hardware sales and significantly higher software and leasing revenues. Profit margins benefited from the higher volume and initial benefits from the cost reduction program. After sharply higher interest expense, net income increased 6.8%, to $4.26 a share (on 1.9% fewer shares) from $3.92.

Capital Share Earnings ($)

Quarter:	1991	1990	1989	1988
Mar.	E1.85	1.81	1.61	1.57
Jun.	E2.55	2.45	2.31	1.63
Sep.	E1.80	E1.70	1.51	2.10
Dec.	E5.00	E4.04	1.04	3.97
	E11.20	E10.00	6.47	9.27

Important Developments

Aug. '90— IBM announced that it will consolidate its domestic typewriter, keyboard, intermediate and personal printers and supplies business into a new subsidiary to be majority owned by Clayton & Dubilier, Inc. IBM may also place the rest of its worldwide information products business in the subsidiary.

Feb. '90— A new line of high performance technical workstations was introduced.

Jan. '90— The company restructured its domestic operations, resulting in a $2.4 billion pretax charge in the fourth quarter of 1989, equal to $2.58 a share after taxes. Savings from expected capacity reductions and technology investment writedowns could add $1.00 to share earnings by 1991.

Nov. '89— Directors approved the repurchase of and additional $4 billion of IBM stock.

Next earnings report expected in mid-October.

Per Share Data ($)

Yr. End Dec. 31	1989	¹1988	1987	1986	1985	1984	1983	1982	1981	1980
Tangible Bk. Val.	66.33	65.78	62.81	55.40	50.60	41.79	38.02	33.13	30.66	28.18
Earnings²	6.47	9.27	8.72	7.81	10.67	10.77	9.04	7.39	5.63	6.10
Dividends	4.73	4.40	4.40	4.40	4.40	4.10	3.71	3.44	3.44	3.44
Payout Ratio	72%	47%	50%	56%	41%	38%	41%	47%	62%	56%
Prices—High	130⁷/₈	129¹/₂	175⁷/₈	161⁷/₈	158³/₄	128¹/₂	134¹/₄	98	71¹/₂	72³/₄
Low	93³/₈	104¹/₄	102	119¹/₄	117³/₈	99	92¹/₄	55⁵/₈	48³/₈	50³/₈
P/E Ratio—	20-14	14-11	20-12	21-15	15-11	12-9	15-10	13-8	13-9	12-8

Data as orig. reptd. 1. Reflects acctg. change. 2. Bef. spec. item(s) of +0.53 in 1988. E-Estimated.

Standard NYSE Stock Reports
Vol. 57/No. 156/Sec. 11

August 13, 1990
Copyright © 1990 Standard & Poor's Corp. All Rights Reserved

Standard & Poor's Corp.
25 Broadway, NY, NY 10004

Standard & Poor's "Yellow Sheet." (Source: Standard & Poor's Corporation. This report was up-to-date at the time of publication; subsequent changes are reflected in current Standard & Poor's reports.)

Figure 14—5

If they are younger persons, the objective may be growth. Once the objectives have been determined, different portfolio questions are indicated. The counselors give their clients constant surveillance of their securities. Clients may give counselors authority to buy or sell on their behalf and instruct their brokers to execute their counselor's orders. Or they may wish to retain veto power over their counselor's advice and execute their orders themselves.

Corporation reports

Before an investor buys any security, he or she may want to examine that corporation's financial reports—its balance sheet and income statement. Such reports give assets, liabilities, sales, expenses, earnings, dividends, and many more statistics, as well as top management's view concerning the future outlook of the business. Most corporations will send their balance sheet and income statement on request; brokerage houses also have many on file in their offices. (A sample balance sheet is shown in Figure 14–6).

Many laypersons are overwhelmed by these reports and feel that since they cannot understand them, there is no need to read them. However, there is nothing difficult about either the balance sheet or the income statement. The personal balance sheet and cash flow statement were studied in Chapter 3. The corporate balance sheet and income statement are similar, except that different items and larger dollar amounts are involved. We shall work through both statements below.

The balance sheet

A balance sheet contains three major parts: assets, liabilities, and owner's equity—sometimes called **net worth.** Total assets are always equal to total liabilities plus net worth. Net worth, the difference between assets and liabilities, is the stockholder's equity.

Let us examine assets first. They are split into short-term assets (current assets) and long-term assets. Short-term assets include cash, which is self-explanatory; since it is a nonearning asset, firms try to keep cash amounts low. Accounts receivable is the money owed the corporation because of sales that have been made and presumably will be collected within thirty days. Inventories, too, are self-explanatory. Fixed assets are valued at their cost less depreciation—the degree to which they are worn out. The company has total assets, with which it earns income. Assets permit the company to conduct its business.

To acquire these assets, however, the corporation has to assume some liabilities. Current liabilities are those due to be paid within a short time. Accounts payable come about because the firm buys, say, raw materials, which it will pay for within thirty days. They also include such things as accrued wages and taxes due but not yet paid. The short-term bank loans are money the company borrowed from a bank on a short-term basis. Fixed liabilities came about because when the present plant

---

I. Assets

Current Assets	
Cash	$ 200,000
Accounts receivable	14,600,000
Inventory	10,200,000
Raw materials	
Goods in process	
Finished goods	
Fixed Assets	
Land	$ 5,000,000
Building and equipment	20,000,000
Total assets	$50,000,000

II. Liabilities

Current Liabilities	
Accounts payable	$13,500,000
Short-term bank loan	15,500,000
Fixed Liabilities	
Bonds outstanding (9%)	$10,000,000
Total Liabilities	$39,000,000

III. Owner's Equity

Preferred Stock: 200,000 shares @ $10 per share	$ 2,000,000
Common Stock Outstanding: 1,000,000 of par value $1	1,000,000
Amounts in Excess of Par Value Received for Stock (paid in surplus)	7,000,000
Retained Earnings (Earned Surplus)	1,000,000
Total Owner's Equity	$11,000,000
Total Liabilities and Owner's Equity	$50,000,000

XYZ Corporation—year end income sheet, December 31, 199X.   Figure 14–6

was built, the corporation sold $10,000,000 of bonds to finance it. Total liabilities represent the total amount the corporation owes, but some of these debts need not be paid for many years, although the interest on them must be paid annually.

The final item is owner's equity, and it belongs to the stockholders. It is the residual amount—the assets with which the company operates less the liabilities the company eventually will have to pay. Net worth (or owner's equity) is split into preferred stock, common stock at par (or face) value, amount of capital paid in excess of par value, and retained earnings. Preferred stock is generally listed first because it is closer to bonds. It must be first netted out before getting the book value of the common stock. The par (or face) value of the common stock is shown and, immediately below it, the amount in excess of par received for it.[4] This third item is often referred to as paid-in surplus. The final item under net worth is retained earnings. It is also referred to as earned surplus, and it means profit the company earned in previous years but retained rather than paid out in dividends. Everything under net worth except the preferred stock belongs to the common stockholders. If that is divided by the number of shares of common stock outstanding, we obtain the book value per share of common stock (to be explained in Chapter 15).

The balance sheet shows how much capital the company has to work with as well as how much of it is represented by bonded indebtedness and how much by stock. By comparing assets and earnings (found in the income statement), the reader can ascertain the return on invested capital. By comparing earnings with net worth, the percentage return on stockholder's equity and the earning per share of common stock can be obtained.

The income statement

While the balance sheet is a presentation of the company's affairs at a given moment in time, like a photograph, the *income statement* is a presentation of what happened to the company over a period of time, usually a year, like the flow of water during a year. A hypothetical income statement is shown in Figure 14–7.

The income statement, also called a profit and loss statement or an operating statement, shows the flow of funds through the company during the year and also the company's earnings or profits. These flows or sales increase the company's (and the stockholder's) well-being; cash outflows decrease it. Cash inflows or gross receipts are the same as sales, which were $11,700,000 for our company last year. Total costs are shown at $9,400,000 and are broken down into various components. For most manufacturing firms, labor costs are by far the largest item. The other costs are self-explanatory, with the exception of depreciation. Depreciation charges are made because fixed assets such as plant and equipment eventually wear out. When they do, the company must have the money on hand to replace them. In our case, the building and equipment is valued at $20,000,000. If we assume it has a useful life of twenty years with no scrap or salvage value, we must set aside one-twentieth of its value or $1,000,000 every year so that when it wears out we will be able to replace it. Depreciation is an expense and reduces profits by $1,000,000 per year. However, it is a unique kind of cost, one that does not cause a cash outflow from the company. While the $1,000,000 depreciation expense reduces profits by that amount, the company still has the

---

4. Par value is the face value of stock. It is not as important today as it was a number of years ago. In addition, some stock is issued as no-par stock. Par value is discussed in greater detail in the next chapter.

Sales	$11,700,000
Selling costs (advertising, etc.)	350,000
Cost of raw materials	3,300,000
Labor costs	3,750,000
Interest cost (on bonds)	900,000
Other costs (utilities, telephone, etc.)	100,000
Depreciation	1,000,000
Total Cost	9,400,000
Income (before taxes)	2,300,000
Taxes	1,104,000
After-tax profits	1,196,000

XYZ Corporation—year end balance sheet, December 31, 199X.   Figure 14—7

money and will keep it invested somewhere and add to it every year until the time comes to replace the building and equipment.

After taxes, profits are $1.196 million, which is just over 10.8 percent return on total net worth. This sum of $1.196 million can be paid to the stockholders in the form of a cash dividend or it can be retained by the company, in which case it will go into the earned surplus account in the balance sheet for next year. Most companies split their after-tax profits, paying some to the stockholders and retaining some. However, in the above case there are 200,000 shares of preferred stock outstanding, and they must be paid a dividend before the common may receive anything. If we assume that they receive a 10 percent dividend on their par value of $2,000,000, this reduces profits by $200,000, which leaves a profit for the common stockholders of $996,000. This is a return of 11.07 percent on the common stockholders' equity of $9,000,000.

When analyzing balance sheets and income statements, it is often wise to read past reports to discover trends. Are sales rising and if so, how much? How have profits behaved over a number of years? Are the ratios of costs to sales rising or declining? These and many other important questions should be kept in mind when analyzing corporation reports. For example, we should also examine earnings per share. This is obtained by dividing earnings, after taxes and after making an allowance for a payment to the preferred stockholders, by the total number of shares of common stock outstanding. In our case we had after-tax earnings of $1.196 million. After the allowance shown above for preferred stockholders of 10 percent, there remains $996,000, which accrues to the common stockholder and amounts to 99.6 cents per share ($996,000 ÷ 1,000,000 shares).

Our company may or may not declare a dividend. If it does, we have a concept called **dividends per share.** By examining this over the years, we can determine if dividends per share are rising, falling, or remaining relatively constant. This may influence whether or not we wish to buy the stock.

We may also wish to compare earnings per share (99.6 cents in our case above) with the market price of the common stock. If we divide the market price of the common stock by the earnings, $.996, we get a concept called the ***price-earnings ratio.*** This ratio may be ten or twenty; it varies from stock to stock. But it is an indicator of whether the stock might be priced too high or whether it is a genuine bargain. Finally, we may want to determine the yield of the common stock. This is simply the annual dividends per share divided by the market price of the stock and expressed in percentage terms.

Security analysts do not agree whether earnings per share or dividends (yield) per share are the best indicator of a stock's value, but all of these should be taken into account in making investment decisions.

SUMMARY REVIEW QUESTIONS

These questions serve as summary and a review of the chapter. If you are able to answer them all you have a good understanding of the material covered by the chapter.

1. How does the corporate form of business organization differ from that of a partnership or single proprietorship?
2. What is the difference between corporate stock and bonds?
3. One of the advantages of a corporation is said to be its limited liability. Explain.
4. Why may a corporation survive indefinitely?
5. What are the main objectives of most investors?
6. How do common stock investments help to hedge inflation?
7. What is the difference between a short-run and a long-run investor? Should the small investor be a short-run or a long-run investor?

8. What is price level risk? What is interest rate risk?
9. Why does the price of a bond move down when the market rate of interest rises? What determines how much it comes down?
10. What is "market risk"?
11. Purchasing a number of issues of oil stock is a good example of reducing risk by diversification. Do you agree or disagree? Substantiate your position.
12. Outline the major sources of investment information.
13. The "owners equity" figure on a balance sheet is said to belong to the stockholders. Explain this in detail.
14. In examining corporate balance sheets and income statements, why is it important to examine both for several years past?

CASES

1. Dina Carroll just purchased a $1,000 bond that has a maturity of one year and yields a 9 percent return or $90 per year. Then interest rates rose to 10 percent.

(a) What is the new market price of the bond?

(b) What is the new yield on the bond?

(c) What will be the market value of the bond at maturity, one year hence?

(d) Would there be a capital gain for the new owner if Dina sold the bond? If so, how much?

2. Bob and Virginia Carels have inherited $10,000, which they would like to invest. They know that they can earn about 6 or 7 percent on their money if they put it in a savings and loan association. However, they feel that prices will rise by about 4 to 5 percent per year on the average over the next few years and would like an investment that either yields substantially more or will provide them with a hedge against inflation. What are the better methods of hedging inflation? Why is this the case?

3. Bertha Underwood is a widow whose husband left her a nice nest egg. She has a $1,000 per month annuity and an additional $50,000 that she would like to invest. She is considering two alternatives: she could buy corporate securities or she could go into partnership with her brother, who is in the trucking business. She believes the return would be about the same in either case, but one of her friends has told her that it is riskier to invest in partnerships than in corporations. Bertha cannot understand this. Can you explain?

4. Kermit and Rita Jones recently purchased $5,000 worth of high-grade corporate bonds yielding 10 percent with a maturity of twenty years. They fully expected to leave their funds invested for twenty years and then use the proceeds to help pay for their children's college education. How much interest would they earn over the twenty years if they kept their investment?

However, two years after the purchase Rita became sick and they were forced to sell the bonds to obtain emergency funds. They were surprised to find that their bonds were now worth $6,000. Can you explain this?

5. George Buck is a young Methodist minister who teaches philosophy of religion at the Southwest Theological Seminary in Dallas, Texas, and earns $26,000 per year. His wife, Marilyn, has her Ph.D. in social work from NYU, is self-employed as a consultant, and last year earned $41,600. Their combined salary provides a handsome surplus, and they would like your advice on how to invest it. They believe they have all the insurance they need; they already have $10,000 in a savings and loan association; and they own their own home. They are currently able to set aside $2,000 per month. What advice would you give them?

SUGGESTED READINGS

American Stock Exchange Annual Report. New York: American Stock Exchange.

Barron's Educational Edition. Princeton, N.J.: Dow Jones and Company.

Barron's Weekly. Princeton, N.J.: Dow Jones and Company.

"Before You Say Yes; Fifteen Questions to Ask About Investments." Pueblo, Colo.: Consumer Information Center.

Engel, Louis. *How to Buy Stocks.* New York: Bantam Books, 1983.

The Exchange. Magazine published monthly by the New York Stock Exchange, New York.

Farrell, James L., Jr., and Fuller, Russell J. *Modern Investments and Security Analysis.* New York: McGraw-Hill, 1987.

Financial Analysts Journal. New York: The Financial Analyst Federation. A bimonthly publication.

"Financial World, the Investment Magazine." New York: Financial World Partners. Monthly publication.

Fisher, Lawrence, and Lorie, James H. *Rates of Return on Investments in Common Stocks.* New York: Merrill Lynch, Pierce, Fenner, and Smith.

Fortune. A monthly magazine containing a great deal of information on business, economics, and finance.

Freund, William C., and Lee, Murray G. *Investment Fundamentals.* New York: American Bankers Association.

How to Invest in Stocks and Bonds. New York: Merrill Lynch, Pierce, Fenner, and Smith.

How Professors Use The Wall Street Journal. Princeton, N.J.: Dow Jones and Company.

How to Read a Financial Report. New York: Merrill Lynch, Pierce, Fenner, and Smith.

How to Understand Financial Statements. New York: New York Stock Exchange.

How You Get More Out of Financial News. Princeton, N.J.: Dow Jones and Company.

The Insider's Guide to the Wall Street Journal. Princeton, N.J.: Dow Jones and Company.

The Market Place. Chicago: Chicago Board of Trade.

"50 of the Most Common Financial Planning Mistakes and How to Avoid Them." New York: Dean Witter Reynolds. You may obtain this from a Dean Witter broker.

Spiro, Herbert T. *Finance For the Non-Financial Manager.* New York: John Wiley and Sons, 1982.

Time. A weekly magazine that contains a good deal of information on business and finance.

Understanding Financial Data in The Wall Street Journal. Princeton, N.J.: Dow Jones and Company.

Understanding the New York Stock Exchange. New York: New York Stock Exchange.

U. S. News & World Report. A weekly magazine that contains a good deal of information on business and finance.

The Wall Street Journal. Princeton, N.J.: Dow Jones and Company. Daily publication.

The Wall Street Journal Educational Edition. Princeton, N.J.: Dow Jones and Company.

"What Every Investor Should Know." Pueblo; Colo.: Consumer Information Center.

15 Investing in securities: Stocks and bonds

HIGHLIGHTS   Bonds and stocks should be considered for acquisition by most investors, and in order to permit the investor to make more intelligent decisions when purchasing them this chapter covers the following:

1   The various corporate bonds
2   U. S. government securities
3   State and local bonds
4   Bond ratings and bond yields
5   Common stock and some of its value concepts
6   Earnings, yield, and capital gain on common stock
7   Stock classifications in accordance with various investment objectives
8   The various types of preferred stock

INTRODUCTION

In this chapter we will examine the wide variety of securities (obligations of issuers) available to the investor. The issuers of securities are, generally, business firms and government, and they represent the demand for savings or, in other words, the supply of securities.

The buyers of securities represent the supply of savings, or the demand for securities. The demand for securities can be further broken down into institutional demand and individual demand. Institutional demands stem from life insurance companies, corporate pension funds, mutual funds, and commercial banks. We will discuss securities pertinent to the individual investor.

The securities we will be discussing are **bonds** and **stocks.** While bonds will probably not be the first investment most people will make, they are among the safest, if selected carefully. By safe here we mean safe from the risk of default. Stocks, on the other hand, are more risky. We will discuss bonds first.

THE ARRAY OF BONDS

Corporate bonds are certificates of indebtedness to the issuing corporation; they are credit instruments used in raising long-term funds. They are legal liabilities of the corporation. Bonds are long-term obligations, and the corporation is obligated to pay a fixed interest rate for so many years, then to redeem the bond at face value. This interest must be paid even if it is not earned. The interest on bonds must be paid before a payment can be made even to preferred stockholders (discussed below). In the event the corporation is liquidated, bondholders are repaid their capital before preferred stockholders. Bonds are considered senior securities: their needs must be taken care of first.

Corporate bonds in general

Corporate bonds are nearly always issued in denominations of $1,000 face value, also referred to as **par value.** When the word "bond" is used, it is assumed to be of that denomination. The interest rate shown thereon is called the coupon rate which, if 9 percent, obligates the corporation to pay $90 per year until the bond matures. Often, this would be paid as $45 every six months, or $22.50 quarterly.

Bonds may be sold at their face value, above it, or below it. If a bond is sold below par, it is said to be at a discount; if above par, it is at a premium. If a bond sells at a premium and has a coupon rate of 10 percent, the yield is less than 10 percent. A bond sold at a discount has a yield greater than its coupon rate. Yields and the coupon rate, then, are not the same. Bond prices fluctuate in the market inversely with changes in the going market interest rate, as noted in the previous chapter. Generally, when corporations offer new issues of bonds, they are issued at par or close to it.

Most corporation bonds are coupon bonds, that is, they have interest coupons attached, and generally a coupon is due and payable every six months. The bondholder clips the coupon and mails it to the trustee for the interest. Often the coupons can be redeemed at banks. These bondholders are the people Thorstein Veblen had in mind when he referred to "the coupon clippers." Noncoupon bonds do exist, the interest on which is automatically mailed to the bondholder by the trustee.

Most bonds in the United States are **registered.** They have the name of the owner on the face of the instrument, and they cannot be transferred without endorsement. The corporation issuing the bond must have a trustee (usually a bank) who keeps the records and mails interest payments.

Some bonds, however, are bearer bonds, which means that they are not registered. These are rare in the United States. Bearer bonds are always coupon bonds, whereas registered bonds can be either coupon or noncoupon bonds.

In addition to corporate bonds, there are United States government bonds and state and local bonds, called municipal bonds. Each of these can be classified into subgroups. Figure 15–1 is a picture of a corporate bond.

Debentures

A debenture bond is issued by a corporation and no specific assets are pledged. The general credit rating of the corporation is at stake, and any and all assets not otherwise pledged can be seized if these bonds are in default. For example, if certain other bonds (described below) are also outstanding for which specific assets have been pledged, then these specific assets cannot be used to satisfy the claims of debenture bondholders until the other bondholders' claims have been met. Where the debentures were issued first, they usually have a clause in them that requires they have equal rights with any future mortgage bonds. There are, however, also subordinated debentures, which are like second mortgages and stand further back. They may be subordinated to regular debentures, to mortgage bonds, or to any other kind. Since they are riskier, they usually yield a higher return.

Convertible bonds

Convertible bonds can be exchanged for a predetermined number of common stocks at the option of the bondholder. Convertible bonds are also usually debentures, but they need not be. The principle of convertible bonds is similar to that of convertible preferred stock. If the corporation does well, the convertibles take on the features of common stock, whereas if the corporation does poorly, the convertibles have the features of bonds. Convertible bonds pay a fixed interest rate like any bond and must be redeemed at maturity. However, they include a clause that permits the bondholder to convert them to common stock in the future at a rate determined when the bond is issued. If, for example, the common stock of the corporation were selling at $100 per share when the convertibles came out, the convertibility feature would permit one $1,000 bond to be converted to approximately ten shares of common stock at the op-

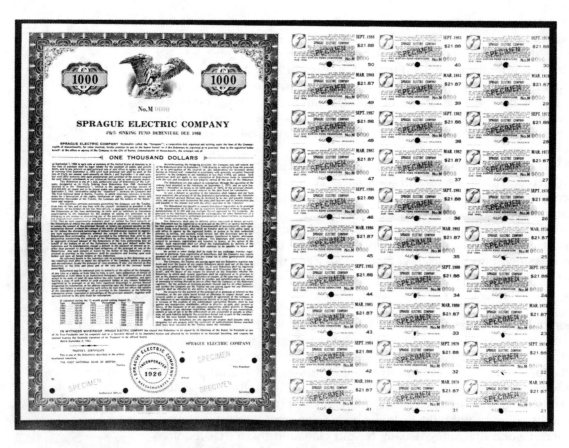

Figure 15–1   A corporate bond. (Source: Courtesy *Sprague Electric Company and the First National Bank of Boston.*)

tion of the bondholder. If two or three years later the common stock were selling at $150 per share, the $1,000 bond could be converted into securities worth about $1,500. Thus, the market price of the bond would be bid up to about $1,500. Convertible securities, then, both preferred stock and bonds, may permit the holders to have their cake and eat it too. Corporations issue them for two reasons: (1) The corporation may be weak, or it may be issuing bonds at a time when savings are in short supply, and hence it must add the convertibility feature as a sweetener to sell them; (2) It may issue convertible bonds because this reduces the interest rate, say, from 8 to 7 percent.

Callable bonds

Callable bonds might be debentures, mortgage bonds, or another kind, but in addition they can be called in and the principal repaid at the option of the corporation. The corporation will insert the call feature if it believes it can refinance later at a lower rate of interest or if it believes that it will be able in the future to operate with less bonded capital. Often they cannot be called in until a specific future time, but after that they may be redeemed at any time. The call provision usually states that if the bond is called, it will be at a premium above par. Generally, the call premium is one year's interest if the call is made a year or two from issue, and lesser amounts on later calls. There is no certainty of locking oneself in on a long-term basis at a high rate if these are purchased.

There are a number of other bonds with which you should be familiar. For example, there are **corporate mortgage bonds,** which are secured by a mortgage on a specific piece of corporate real estate. Title to the property may be transferred to a third party who acts as a trustee and can sell the property and pay the bondholders if the bonds are in default.

Other corporate bonds

There are **collateral trust bonds** secured by specific corporate assets other than real estate, such as securities of other companies.

Equipment trust bonds are secured by equipment owned by the corporation, such as machinery or rolling stock in the case of railroads. The assets behind these bonds may also be sold if necessary to satisfy bondholders' claims.

There are also **serial bonds.** These can be debentures or any other kind. Serial bonds are numbered with the different numbers maturing at different times. The corporation redeems a few each year according to a predetermined schedule.

Discount bonds are outstanding bonds that were issued some time ago. Discount bonds have a market price below their face value. Since at maturity they must be redeemed at face value, the buyer will enjoy a capital gain.

Discount bonds

There are two reasons why some bonds are sold at a discount. First, the corporation's credit rating may have worsened since the bonds were issued. Second, all bonds decline in value when the going market interest rate rises above the fixed stated interest (coupon) rate of any bond. The extent of the discount will be determined by the amount the market interest rate moves above the coupon rate and the length of time remaining until the bond matures. High discount, high quality bonds are a good buy when interest rates are at a peak and are expected to decline drastically.

These bonds, which pay no interest but are deeply discounted when sold, have become popular recently. They are much like the Series EE U.S. government savings bonds, permitting investors to lock in at a yield that can be calculated for the entire period until maturity. Ordinary positive coupon bonds yield interest, usually semiannually, and it must be reinvested at whatever the going rate may be at that time. This may be beneficial or harmful depending on what happens to interest rates after buying

Zero coupon bonds

the bonds. With zero coupon bonds, one does not have the reinvestment bother or investment cost. These bonds can be either corporate or U.S. Treasury bonds.

Unlike the other discount bonds described above, however, the annual market appreciation of these bonds is taxed as it occurs and as ordinary income, even though not yet received. For this reason, the discount bonds discussed first (Series EE) may be the better buys.

The major problem with long-term zero coupon bonds is the same as that with any long-term bond: interest rates could go even higher. There is also a second reason why an individual should think hard before buying any long-term zero coupon bonds: in 20 or 30 years the issuing corporation may not even exist. With positive coupon bonds the investor would at least have received some interest along the way.

Junk bonds

From time to time **junk bonds** become somewhat popular. Junk bonds are high-risk instruments issued by some corporations. Because the risk of default is higher, they yield a higher interest rate. Recently they have been issued by corporations to raise funds with which to take over (buy) other corporations. They are considered high risk and recently some have been in default. Nevertheless some investors buy them because of their high yield. Junk bonds, if they are rated at all, are rated as "BB" or "B" bonds or lower. See below for an explanation of bond ratings with respect to risk.

Mortgage-backed and agency bonds

Recently, **residential mortgage-backed bonds** have been developed. These are not regular corporate bonds, but rather are issued by private financial institutions and government agencies like the Government National Mortgage Association (GNMA). When an investor buy these bonds, the funds are used to finance residential housing; mortgages are the underlying securities. The home-owner's monthly mortgage payments are usually passed through, and the investor receives a monthly cash flow that represents both interest and return of principal. There are a few non-pass-through mortgage-backed bonds, however; in this case the investor receives interest every six months and then the principal in one lump sum a number of years later, just like a regular bond.

Since these bonds' yield comes from mortgages, their yield is often quite high. Those that are issued by GNMA (called agency bonds) are also riskless insofar as default is concerned, because they are guaranteed by the full faith and credit of the U.S. government; they are as safe as any U.S. government securities. Unfortunately for many small investors, the minimum purchase of such riskless bonds is $25,000. However, the small investor may buy them via a mutual fund, as we shall see in Chapter 18.

Receiving the principal back in installments over the years may present a reinvestment problem. The investor must also, of course, separate the interest received from the principal in order to calculate the yield, but there are formulas to do this. These bonds have become a popular investment outlet recently.

Three varieties of marketable securities will be discussed here. (Nonmarketable Series EE and HH savings bonds were presented in Chapter 13.)

U.S. government marketable securities

Marketable U.S. Treasury Bonds are long-term obligations generally running up to 30 years. Since they are marketable, they fluctuate in the market inversely with fluctuations in the interest rates. Financial institutions are important buyers of long-term government bonds. Insurance companies, investment companies, and private pension funds commit millions of long-term dollars in government bonds each year.

U.S. government bonds

For those bonds issued before 1986, they could be bearer bonds or registered bonds. The bearer bonds have a coupon and interest is paid every six months. To collect the interest, it is merely necessary to detach the coupon when the interest is due, take it to a bank, and deposit it. The bank will collect the interest. In the case of registered bonds, the interest, when due, is automatically deposited into the investor's bank account. Since 1986 all bonds are now sold on what is called a 'book entry'' basis, and the interest is automatically deposited in the investor's account when due.

Treasury notes are similar to Treasury bonds but generally have shorter maturities: they run from two to as high as ten years. They have a coupon (are not discounted), which provides for an interest payment every six months; they are negotiable and marketable, so they fluctuate in the market inversely with fluctuations in their interest rate. These securities are like government bonds, except their maturities are shorter. These notes are now sold only on a "book entry" basis, and the interest is automatically deposited in the investor's account.

Treasury notes

These bills are short-term bearer obligations of the United States government. Because they are discounted when issued, the interest is the difference between the price at which the Treasury sells them and their face value. The minimum amount that may be purchased is $10,000, and after the first $10,000 they can be obtained in multiples of $5000. They have a maturity of ninety days, six months, and sometimes one year. While some individuals buy them if they have funds temporarily idle while seeking long-term investments, **Treasury bills** are primarily purchased by financial institutions in order to put their funds to work immediately while they are seeking permanent long-term outlets for them. Sometimes, however, industrial corporations buy them with funds set aside for future tax or dividend payments.

Treasury bills

Relatively small investors might buy these securities during periods when interest rates are very high. This is especially true if their rates are higher than those of depository institutions.

Treasury bills can be purchased through a bank, which makes arrangements to buy them in a block and parcel them out to customers. Banks used to provide this service free, but in recent years they have begun to assess a fee. The cost varies from bank to bank, but is generally from $25 to $30 per transaction.

State and local securities

State and local government securities appeal to high-income investors because their interest income may be exempt from federal taxation. Usually bonds of a state or a political subdivision of a state are exempt from state income taxes as well. Because of this exemption, municipal bonds often yield a lower return than United States government securities. Competition on the part of wealthy investors for these securities reduces the yield below that indicated by the risk and often below that of United States Treasury obligations. The justification given for tax exemption is that it reduces the cost of financing schools and other public purposes at the local level. The opponents of tax exemption argue that it is merely a loop-hole that enables high-income groups to avoid the payment of taxes. An investor in the highest tax bracket should investigate them. A person in the 28 percent bracket would have to get an 8.3 percent return on alternative investments to be as well-off after taxes as one is with a 6 percent tax-exempt return. Table 15–1 shows the tax-equivalent yield which would have to be obtained on corporate securities to match various tax-free rates.[1]

Not only do state and local governments issue these tax exempts, but so do their political subdivisions, such as schools, sewer and water districts, toll road commissions, and others. There are different kinds of such tax-exempt securities, some of which are long-term securities (bonds) and some short-term notes. They may be classified as follows:

1. Short-term tax-exempt municipal notes
2. General obligation bonds
3. Special tax bonds
4. Revenue bonds

General obligation bonds

Many municipal bonds are general obligation bonds. They are secured by the full faith and credit of the taxing entity issuing them, that is, the full and unlimited taxing powers of the issuing government are pledged to back them up. These presumably are the least risky muncipal bonds. The risk, of course, varies from one government to another.

---

1. Prior to August 1986, all securities issued by state and local governments were tax exempt; since then some of them are not. Primarily those that are not are the industrial development bonds issued by communities to attract new businesses. Be sure to check this before purchasing them.

Table 15–1   1988 Taxable Equivalent Yield Table

Taxable Income (000)		Federal Tax	Tax-Exempt Yield Equivalents														
Single Return	Joint Return	Bracket	4.75%	5.00%	5.25%	5.50%	5.75%	6.00%	6.25%	6.50%	6.75%	7.00%	7.25%	7.50%	7.75%	8.00%	8.25%
$17.9-43.2	$29.8-71.9	28%	6.60	6.94	7.29	7.64	7.99	8.33	8.68	9.03	9.38	9.72	10.07	10.42	10.76	11.11	11.46
43.2-100.5	71.9-192.9	33	7.09	7.46	7.84	8.21	8.58	8.96	9.33	9.70	10.07	10.45	10.82	11.19	11.57	11.94	12.31
Over $100.5	Over $192.9	28	6.60	6.94	7.29	7.64	7.99	8.33	8.68	9.03	9.38	9.72	10.07	10.42	10.76	11.11	11.46

Locate the individual's tax bracket (after deductions and exemptions) and read across to see the approximate taxable yield needed to match the estimated tax-free yield of a Nuveen CIT.

For example, with joint taxable income of $29,800 to $71,900, a taxpayer would be in the 28% federal tax bracket and would need a taxable investment paying 7.64% to equal a tax-free yield of 5.50%.

Special tax bonds

Special tax bonds are secured not by the full faith and credit of the issuing government, but only by part of it. They are payable only from a specific and listed tax source. In some cases, a new specific tax is imposed to support a new bond issue when it comes out. For example, a new sewer system may be financed by such bonds which are then to be repaid by a special tax levied on the citizens. These are riskier than full faith and credit bonds of the same entity, and hence their yield is higher.

Revenue bonds

Revenue bonds are not full faith and credit bonds. These are frequently issued by certain political subdivisions such as a toll road commission or a state university, that have no taxing powers. However, the interest and principal is to be repaid by the revenue (tolls from turnpikes or rent from college dormitories) to be raised by whatever the bonds finance. Sometimes municipal water and electric departments sell such bonds, which are to be repaid solely from the water and electricity rates that are charged. Since no government's faith and credit are pledged, these revenue bonds are generally considered riskier; and their yield is higher than bonds of the same entity that have taxing power behind them.

Short-term tax-exempt municipal notes

Short-term tax-exempt municipal notes are also short-term notes generally running from six months to two years which would appeal to those investors who are uncertain about long-term interest rates and do not want to become locked in at a fixed rate for a number of years. By purchasing these, the investor will be able to reappraise the situation a year hence.

These notes may be full faith and credit or revenue obligations. The full faith and credit are sometimes tax anticipation notes, that is, taxes due in six months or a year are pledged to pay off these notes. The revenue notes are backed by revenue expected some time in the near future.

Some of these short-term notes are construction notes, sometimes called bond anticipation notes. They are used to finance the construction of something that will take a year or two. When the construction is complete, long-term bonds are sold to pay off the short-term notes.

State and local bond trusts

Recently, a number of open-end investment companies (or mutual funds)[2] have been established through which tax-exempt bonds can be purchased indirectly. They can be purchased in multiples as low as $1,000. Most of the bonds in these trusts are A-rated or better. However, some of the trusts are spiced with some lower-rated bonds in order to increase the yield. These are discussed at greater length in Chapter 17.

---

2. Open-end investment companies, which are also called mutual funds, are discussed in greater detail in Chapter 17.

Bonds and credit ratings

The amount of interest paid on corporate bonds is determined by the credit rating of the company, length of maturity of bonds, and demand for and supply of money at the time of the issuance of the bond. With U.S. government bonds, credit rating is not a factor; however, both length of maturity of bonds and demand and supply of money at the time of the issuance will determine the rate paid by the federal government. For example, if the supply of money is short, the rates of the "govenments" will be forced up just as is the interest rate with any other borrower. However, because of the relatively riskless character of the government issues, the amount paid by the government in iterest will be lower than that paid by corporations. The rate on state and local bonds, too, varies with the same factors, although, as noted above, the tax-free interest generally keeps the rate on these securities low.

Interest rates on all fixed obligations vary with the length of time the securities run to maturity. Generally when rates are relatively low, long-term bonds yield more than short-term debt obligation. However, when interest rates are relatively high, often short-term obligations yield a higher return than long-term.

With respect to credit rating, the higher the rating, the lower the interest rate on corporation bonds as well as on state and local bonds. There are services that assign a credit rating to bonds, these ratings being an attempt to measure the quality of bonds of their degree of "gilt-edgedness." Moody's, which is one of the most widely used bond rating services, has nine classifications of risk. Triple A bonds are the highest quality and C bonds the lowest. A triple A bond carries little risk of default, whereas a C bond is in default and has very little prospect of ever being paid off. If the investor buys a C bond, he or she might be buying a lawsuit.

The accompanying list gives the nine ratings assigned by Moody's. A broker can tell an investor which rating any corporate bond has. Remember any bond below Baa (which is medium grade) is a speculative bond investment.

Moody bond ratings

Aaa	
Aa	
A	
Baa	
Ba	Speculative Bonds
B	Speculative Bonds
Caa	Speculative Bonds
Ca	Speculative Bonds
C	In Default

Standard and Poor's, another service similar to Moody's, has slightly different symbols, and more classifications. Standard and Poor's ratings are shown below.

Standard and Poor's bond ratings	AAA
	AA
	A
	BBB
	BB
	B ⎫
	CCC ⎬ Speculative
	CC
	C ⎭
	DDD ⎫ In Default. The different D bonds indicate that the bondhold-
	DD ⎬ ers would get different amounts back upon liquidation,
	D ⎭ with the D rating being the lowest.

Bond yields

We have already learned that a bond has a coupon rate of interest and a market rate of interest, the latter also called the *yield.* For example, if a $1,000 bond has a coupon rate of 9 percent, this indicates that the corporation will pay a fixed dollar amount ($90) per year. But if a person purchased such a bond that matures in one year at a discount (he or she paid, say, $990.90) the actual yield is equal to the $90 interest received plus the $9.10 capital appreciation. The actual percentage yield is $99.10 ÷ 990.90 or 10 percent.

We should also recognize the following yield concepts:

1. Nominal yield and real yield
2. Average yield to maturity
3. Annual yield to maturity
4. Tax-equivalent yield of a municipal security
5. Tax-free equivalent yield of a taxable yield

Nominal yield and real yield

The nominal yield is stated in money terms and not adjusted for inflation. To convert the nominal yield to the real yield, we must subtract the rate of inflation from the money (nominal) yield. If, in the case discussed above, the price level had risen by 5 percent during the year, the real yield would, of course, be 5 percent.

Average yield to maturity

In a few cases (primarily U. S. Series EE bonds), the actual yield is not the same each year. U. S. Series EE bonds, you will recall, are discounted. In addition, the interest rate which they receive floats; it is tied to the rate of five-year U. S. government marketable securities, and varies with that market rate. Consequently, the average rate to maturity cannot be calculated until the bonds are actually cashed in. Nevertheless, it is a valid concept.

Annual yield to maturity

There is also the similar but slightly different concept of annual yield to maturity, which is important if the bond is sold at below (or above) par and has a number of years to run. This comes about because, in calculating yield to maturity, the investor must consider not only the dollar amount of interest received each year but also the annual capital gain (or loss) as the bond matures and its market price moves toward its face value. The following formula approximates the yield to maturity:

$$\frac{\left(\begin{array}{c}\text{annual interest} \\ \text{payment}\end{array}\right) + \dfrac{\text{maturity value less market price}}{\text{years to maturity}}}{\dfrac{\text{maturity value} + \text{market price}}{2}}$$

For example, a bond with a face value of $1,000 paying a coupon interest rate of 8 percent running over 10 more years, and purchased at $800, will give us:

$$\frac{\$80 + \dfrac{(\$1,000 - \$800)}{(10)}}{\dfrac{\$1,000 + \$800}{2}} = \frac{\$80 + \dfrac{200}{10}}{\$900}$$

$$\frac{80 + 20}{900} = \frac{100}{900} = 11.1 \text{ percent}$$

The tax-equivalent yield is the term used when discussing municipal bonds. Since interest on municipal bonds is not taxed, a 5 percent return there is also the after-tax yield. The tax-equivalent yield is that yield you would have to get on a corporate bond so that, after personal income tax on it, you would have the same amount left that you could have earned on a municipal bond. Consequently, the tax-equivalent yield will vary depending on the individual income tax bracket. For a person in the 28 percent tax bracket, the tax-equivalent yield to a 5 percent muncipal bond is 6.944 percent; for a person in the 15 percent tax bracket, it is 5.88 percent. The tax-equivalent yield, then, is that level to which the yield must be adjusted up to provide a sufficiently higher return so as to enable the investor to pay taxes and still be as well-off as with a tax-exempt yield.

Tax-equivalent yield of a municipal security

To obtain the tax-equivalent yield, divide the tax-free yield by 1 minus the investor's tax bracket; use the following formula:

$$\frac{\text{tax-free yield}}{1 - \text{tax bracket}} = \frac{.05}{1 - .28} = \frac{.05}{.72} = .06944$$

The tax-equivalent yield of a 5 percent tax-free yield for a person in the 28 percent tax bracket is 6.944 percent.

A table showing the various tax-equivalent yields is shown in Table 15–1.

We can also go in reverse and find the tax-free equivalent of a taxable yield. We multiply the taxable yield by 1 minus the tax bracket. Or use the formula (taxable yield) × (1 − tax bracket). In the above case:

Tax-free equivalent yield of a taxable yield

$$.06944 \times 1 - .28 = .06944 \times .72 = .049999$$

THE ARRAY OF STOCKS

Bonds, as you have seen, can be classified into several categories. Stocks have only two categories—common and preferred. Common stock represents the ultimate of risk capital; preferred stock is less so. Figure 15–2 is a picture of a common stock certificate.

Common stock in general

For all practical purposes, there is only one kind of common stock. Common stockholders are the residual recipients of a corporation's income. Because they receive what is left after all others get their prior claim, common stockholders' futures are closely tied to that of the corporation. If the corporation does well, the common stockholders do well. If the corporation does poorly, the common stockholders suffer. Common stockholders are also the last to be paid off in the event the corporation must be liquidated and sell its assets. Owning common stock then is riskier than owning other securities, and thus the market value of common stock fluctuates more than that of other securities.

Common stock ownership conveys no rights except the right to vote at stockholders meetings, where the corporation's board of directors is elected and certain other corporate decisions are made.[3]

Some value concepts of common stock

There are four general methods of valuing common stock: (1) par value, (2) book value, (3) market value, and (4) liquidation value. In most states it is now possible to issue a no-par-value common stock, and often this is done, although historically stock always had a par value. These terms can sometimes be confusing and need to be explained.

1. *Par value* is the face value of the stock printed on the certificate. A fixed and artibrary value is assigned when the stock is issued; it has little financial significance. Even when the stock is issued, it may be at or above par. Today stock is usually sold substantially above par. Historically, par value was higher and a more meaningful indicator of what the stock was worth. If a stock was sold at below par, the stockholder was often held liable for the difference between the price paid for it and par value. Today this is no longer true because stock cannot legally be sold below par when it is first issued. Stock that has no printed face value is called no-par stock. Par value has some meaning insofar as preferred stock is concerned because the dividend is often based on par value. Preferred stock is explained in greater detail below, where the importance of par value on preferred stock will become clear.

---

3. In recent years some corporations have issued non-voting common stock. If an investor buys these, he or she has no voice in corporate affairs but does share in corporate profits.

2- 1734-252 -78   LOT   1-1

Common stock certificate. (Source: Courtesy General Motors Corporation.)   Figure 15—2

2. **The book value** of common stock is an accounting concept. It is what the stock is worth today from an accounting point of view. When you examined the corporate balance sheet you were introduced to the concept of net worth (assets minus liabilities). The net worth, less a possible allowance for preferred stock, belongs to the common stockholder. It is also called the stockholder's equity. Net worth (minus preferred stock outstanding, if any) divided by the total number of shares of common stock outstanding is the book value per share.

3. **Market value** is what you have to pay for the stock if you wish to buy it—or what you will get if you sell it. It is often above book value, and, if so, it is because the expected future income has been taken into account by investors, and their demand has bid up the market price. This process is sometimes referred to as "discounting the future." Market value may also be lower than book value, if investors feel pessimistic toward that particular stock.

4. **Liquidation value** is meaningful only if the corporation is unsuccessful and goes out of business. In such a case, if there is anything left after all bills have been paid (including paying off bondholders

and preferred stockholders), it is prorated to holders of the common stock. Liquidation value may be zero or even negative. All corporate assets would have to be sold, and if they were specialized assets, no ready market for them would exist. Only some other corporation might be willing to buy them, or they might have scrap value only.

Earnings, yield, and capital gain on common stock

The earnings and yield on common stock vary greatly from firm to firm and from time to time. **Earnings** are simply the total earnings after taxes per share. The yield is less than earnings because an adjustment must be made to net out the corporation's retained earnings. **Yield** then is the actual dividends paid as a percentage of the price of the stock. An example of earnings and yield will clarify this.

$$\frac{\text{total after tax earnings}}{\text{total number of shares outstanding}} = \frac{\$7,500,000}{1,000,000 \text{ shares}} = \$7.50/\text{share}$$

In most cases part of this $7.50 is paid out in the form of dividends and part is retained and plowed back into the corporation for expansion. However, the entire $7.50 belongs to the stockholder, and that portion retained will increase the book value and hopefully the market value of the stock. Earnings per share is an important criterion in determining whether an individual might want to buy a given stock. A comparison of earnings with the market price of a given share gives us its price earnings ratio which is an important analytical tool, when comparing stock within an industry. Let's assume our stock above, earning $7.50 per share, is selling at $75. We now may calculate its price earnings ratio (PER). It is

$$\frac{\text{market price}}{\text{earnings per share}} = \frac{\$75}{\$7.50} = 10$$

Yield as noted above is simply the annual dividend payment per share divided by the market price. In our example above, assume that there is a 50 percent dividend payout rate. Then

$$\frac{\text{dividends per share}}{\text{market price per share}} = \frac{\$3.75}{\$75.00} = 5\% \text{ yield}$$

In the above case where, in addition to a $3.75 dividend, $3.75 is retained by the corporation, the market price (as well as the book value) of the stock will tend to rise. However, this is true only if the retained profits are successfully reinvested in expanding the business and its profits. In such a case the stockholders get part of their reward in the form of capital appreciation rather than in cash dividends.

Traditionally it has been felt by most investors that the total earnings on a common stock should be hgher than the yield on bonds—to compensate the investor for the greater risk associated with common stock. Generally, the dividend yield alone on common stock is lower than the yield on bonds, but the total earnings (dividends plus retained earnings) on common stock should be superior to bond yield. In many cases they are, but the retained earnings are not always reflected in common stock price appreciation, and in such a case, the yields and capital appreciation on stock combined might be below the yield on bonds. This has sometimes been the case in some years.

However, investing in common stock has traditionally been one of the better ways to participate in the future economic growth of the country because profits rise with growth, and this often shows up in the form of capital gains on stock. Economic growth is a function of population growth and of technological change. Technological change will enhance profits either by reducing costs or by bringing forth new or improved products, or by some combination of the two. New and improved products enhance profits by increasing sales.

Figure 15–3 illustrates how dividends have risen over the past eighty-six years in relation to the cost of living. If we considered the total earnings on common stock (dividends plus retained earnings), the record of common stock would look even better.

Perhaps the best measure of how good an investment a common stock has been is to take into account the total economic increment it has provided its owner. This includes cash dividends as well as capital gains, which are influenced by retained earnings but may very well be higher or lower than retained earnings indicate they should be. Suppose an investor had purchased a common stock for $50 per share. Suppose

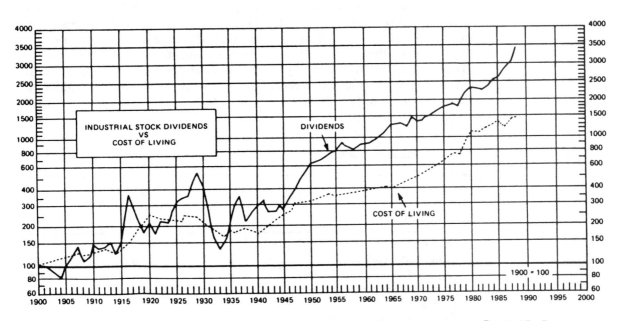

Industrial stock dividends versus cost of living. (Source: Investment Companies, Mutual Funds and Other Types, 1989, *Wiesenberger Financial Services, a division of Warren, Gorham & Lamont, Inc. p. 54.)*   Figure 15–3

too that its after-tax earnings were $5 per share and that it retained $2.50 and paid a cash dividend of $2.50. Clearly its dividend yield would be 5 percent but its total earnings 10 percent. but if the market price of the stock had increased over the year to $60 per share, the total economic increment it has provided is $12.50 (the $2.50 of retained earnings is included in the $10 capital gain, but the $2.50 dividend is not). A return of $12.50 on a $50 investment is 25 percent. To be sure, in order to realize this capital gain in the form of cash, the stockholder would have to sell the stock. Nevertheless, the capital gain cannot be ignored. The next year it may be more or less. Table 15–2 illustrates these ratios; Figure 15–4 shows how corporate dividends, profits, and taxes have fluctuated in recent years.

The capital structure of a firm: One reason why earnings vary (leverage)

Some firms have raised more capital via the sale of bonds both absolutely and relative to their total capital than other firms. This variation can be explained in part by management philosophy. However, it is also in part due to different kinds of business operation. Certain types of firms can safely raise a larger proportion of their capital by selling bonds than can others because their earnings are more stable from year to year. Such a firm may use more borrowed capital in the hope of increasing the earning (and yield) on their common stock. Raising capital via bonds imposes a fixed cost upon the corporation and introduces *leverage* into its earnings. Leverage can be positive or negative. Positive leverage comes about if a business can borrow capital at, say, 8 percent by selling bonds, and then earn 10 percent with it. The 2 percent differential accrues to the common stockholder. However, negative leverage will be generated if next year the firm earns only 6 or 7 percent on the capital it borrowed at 8 percent. Firms that have high and stabel earnings can safely build more leverage into their capital structure than can low- and fluctuating-income firms. An illustration will make leverage clear.

Table 15–2 *Possible returns on stock*

ABC stock			Percent return on investment
Purchase price		$50.00	
Earnings (per year)		5.00	10%
Dividend	$2.50		5%
Retained earnings			
Capital gains		10.00	20%
Due to retained earnings	2.50		
Due to other factors	7.50		
Economic increment		12.50	25%

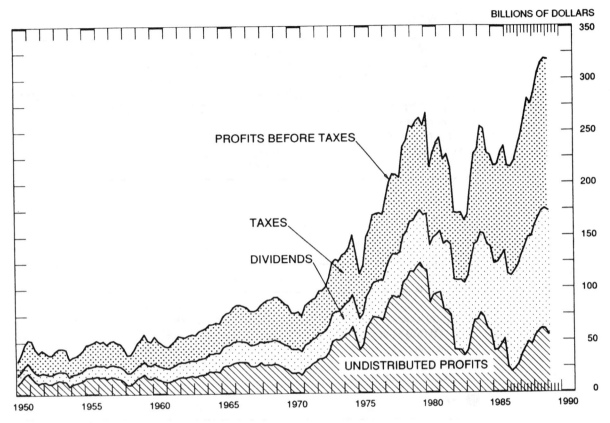

Corporate profits, taxes, and dividends, seasonally adjusted annual rates, quarterly. Figure 15—4
(Source: 1989 Historical Chart Book, *Board of Governors of the Federal Reserve System, p. 60.)*

Two hypothetical firms (see Tables 15—3 and 15—4) are identical to begin with and each earns a 10 percent return. Then they both expand, firm A by selling another million dollars of common stock and firm B by selling a million dollars of bonds. Both firms doubled in size and in sales and in profits before any interest was paid. However, the earnings return to common stock rose to 12 percent for firm B and remained unchanged for firm A. This is an illustration of positive leverage.

If, next year, both firms' incomes before interest were to fall to $120,000, then firm A would be earning 6 percent for its stockholders while firm B would earn only 4 percent. This is an illustration of negative leverage. Certain firms whose incomes are more stable, like utilities, often are able to take greater advantage of leverage. This also explains why their incomes are often higher.

While the amount of leverage a firm has built into its capital structure may influence earnings, it is by no means the only factor. The quality of management, the type of product it sells, how effectively it innovates

Table 15–3   *Capital structure of a firm*

	Before expansion		
Firm A		**Firm B**	
Capital stock	$1,000,000	Capital stock	$1,000,000
(20,000 shares at $50 per share)		(20,000 shares at $50 per share)	
After tax earnings		After tax earnings	100,000
Percentage return	100,000	Percentage net	10%
	10%		

Table 15–4   *Capital structure of a firm*

	After expansion		
Firm A		**Firm B**	
Capital stock	$2,000,000	Capital stock	$1,000,000
(40,000 shares at $50 per share)		Bonds at 8%	1,000,000
		After tax but before	
After tax earnings	200,000	interest earings	200,000
Percentage return	10%	Interest	80,000
		Earnings for shareholders	120,000
		Percentage return	12%

and creates new and better products are equally important. Nevertheless, the investor should look at a firm's capital structure before buying securities, especially if he or she is concerned that business conditions may worsen in the future and with them corporate profits. It may be a method of rejecting certain stocks if the investor is taking a defensive position.

Beta

A stock's **beta** is an indicator of its volatility relative to the market. The overall market has a beta of one. A stock's beta is the total return of that stock (both price appreciation and dividends received) relative to the return of the market—as measured by some index such as Standard and Poor's and some average of dividends for the market.

If a stock has the average beta of one, its return is proportionate to the market returns. If, on the other hand, a given stock generates a 20 percent return versus the market's 10 percent, its beta is 2. A 5 percent return versus a 10 percent return for the market indicates a beta of 0.5. Beta also measures declines. Beta is considered an indicator of risk. The higher the beta above one, the more it swings with market changes; the lower the beta is below one, the greater the stability of that stock relative to the market. To be sure, a stock's beta can change; any beta is only a reflection of what has happened in the past. Nevertheless, the past can be an indicator of what might happen in the future.

Bonds have long been rated according to their credit-worthiness, with AAA being the highest quality, as explained above. Stock ratings, or rankings, have been developed in recent years. The best known of these is Standard and Poor's. Stocks are ranked somewhat differently than bonds, however. Stocks are not ranked in degree of protection for principal and dividends. Standard and Poor's considers such things as the product produced, managerial capabilities, financial structure, and past earnings and dividends, with great emphasis placed on financial strength. An A+ rank would be a firm that is extremely strong financially, like IBM. In addition, growth and stability of earnings are assessed, and the long-run record of performance. Then a ranking is assigned, with A+ being the highest. The following eight rankings are currently used:

Rankings of common stock

A+ Highest
A   High
A− Good
B+ Median
B   Speculative
B− Highly speculative
C   Marginal
D   In reorganization

Common stock can be classified into a number of categories. It is possible to identify growth stock, income stock, cyclical stock, defensive stock, blue-chip stock, speculative stock, and others. Stocks change; so a stock that at one time may be considered a growth stock may at another time be regarded as an income stock. Also, some stock may have the characteristics of several classifications; defensive and income stocks, for instance, may in some cases be the same. Obviously some stock may have some of the attributes of all four. Income and growth stocks—indeed all stocks—have some cyclical aspects. Nevertheless, many stocks fall into patterns. You should select stock in accordance with your investment objectives, discussed in the previous chapter.

Classification of common stock

When stocks are classified as speculative or blue-chip, they are classified according to risk. These are relative terms, as there is an element of speculation in all stock and an element of investment in all. The least speculative (most blue-chip) stock over the years has probably been American Telephone and Telegraph. The most speculative (least blue-chip) stock is probably Dry Gulch Gold and Uranium, or some other stock like it. We shall examine all of these classifications.

Growth stocks are generally considered to be those that have good earnings but a very low dividend yield because the company is reinvest-

Growth stock

ing the bulk of its earnings in expansion. This investment increases both the book value and the market value of the stock, and the stockholder's goal in such a case presumably is to achieve capital gains through the appreciation of the stock. A growth company should also be doing better each year than the year before. It is not only using its earnings to expand capacity, but it is producing a product for which the demand is expected to increase in the future.

To buy a growth stock, one may have to pay a high price, as many of them have excessively high price-earnings ratios, because the stock market is said to discount the future. If the company is earning a high rate of return per dollar invested and the rate is expected to increase further because the demand for the product is going to increase in the future, the market price of the stock will be bid up. Since the future profits of the company look good, up goes the market price of its stock. This process is called *discounting future profits*. In some cases it may be too late to buy such a stock; but, if the company continues expansion at its present rate, the stock will often continue to climb.

Let us assume that a given growth stock has discounted profits five years into the future and is selling for $100 per share. Its price-earnings ratio is out of line from an investment point of view; but if it is really a growth company, then five years from now it will still have discounted profits five years into the future (or perhaps seven) and may be selling for $200 per share. The opposite possibility is that its growth may be over or slowing down and that it may not rise much above $100. The secret to success in growth stocks is to find them first. This often means buying a speculative security. The investor wants the stock of a firm that will become the IBM of the space industry. If a person buys a proven growth stock, he or she pays for it, since it has already discounted the future. Some stocks that are typically looked upon as being growth stock include those of IBM, Coca-Cola, and some of the newer, smaller minicomputer companies. Growth stocks generally appeal to people who do not need income at the present time but who want capital gains they will take later.

Income stock

Income stocks are those in companies whose earnings are good but that either are not growing much or are growing with external funds.[4] They may be mature companies producing a product for which the demand has stabilized. They are companies, moreover, that pay out a large proportion of their earnings each year in the form of dividends. Utilities, tobacco, and food are considered such income areas. Not only are dividends fairly high but they are steady because the earnings of the companies are steady. AT&T for many years has been considered an income stock par excellence; it had for a long time yielded a good, steady return. But because of divestiture of the operating companies a few years

---

4. External funds are funds obtained by selling new issues of bonds or common stock.

ago, this is no longer true. Now many of the utilities would be considered the best income stock. Income stocks in general appeal to people who may need income and who would benefit less from long-term growth. However, a good yield is one criterion that should be used by everyone in selecting stock for a well-balanced portfolio.

Cyclical stocks fluctuate widely over swings in the business cycle and have high betas. They are the stocks of those companies whose sales and earnings vary greatly. The steel, nonferrous metals, and machine tool industries are examples. Because earnings fluctuate, so too do dividends and the market price of the stock. Nearly all stock fluctuates somewhat with swings in the business cycle, but cyclical stocks do so more than others.

Cyclical stock

Investors who buy a cyclical stock are betting that economic and business conditions will improve. In this connection, a word of warning is in order. The buyer should beware of selecting a cyclical stock after there has been an unusual jump in either sales or earnings unless the outlook is relatively certain that the up-trend will continue. Once sales, earnings, or both have risen substantially, it is often already too late to buy cyclicals; now is the time to sell.

The Wall Street maxim in relation to cyclical stock is "Buy on bad news. sell on good." Investors in cyclical stock should buy when sales and earnings are down, sell when these figures are favorable. To do so one must, of course, be flexible and in a position to hold on to the stock for a considerable period of time, frequently for several years. However, this is true for any stock. No one but a professional speculator, and certainly no small investor, should go into the stock market on a short-term basis.

Defensive stock is often income stock. It would probably be more accurate to say that most defensive stock is income stock but not as many income stocks could be classified as defensive. A defensive stock is one that declines less than most on a general downturn. By the same token, it may not rise as much in a general upturn. The stocks have low betas, because the company's sales and hence its income are more stale over the business cycle since the demand for its product is more stable. Such companies include some of the food and cigarette makers, but usually utilities are considered the best defensive stocks. Some utilities have been considered growth stock recently, especially if they are in an area that is growing rapidly. Most utilities, however, pay out a considerable portion of their earnings as dividends and hence are more income and defensive than growth and defensive. Some analysts look upon defensive stock as the opposite of cyclical stock. If an individual expected the economy in general to be heading into a recession, he or she might well sell cyclical stocks and buy either bonds or defensive stock. This is known as taking a defensive position.

Defensive stock

Blue-chip stock

When classifying stock according to risk, **_blue-chip stock_** is the least risky—least risky both as to missing a dividend and declining in price, although the price does decline when the market in general declines. Generally, however, the price of blue-chip stocks will decline less in a general downturn than the average. They are the stocks of the old well-established companies that have proved they can earn profits. They cannot be classified by industries at all, because some industries have both blue-chip companies and firms that either are not tested or that for other reasons are considered highly speculative.

A list of blue-chip stock would include General Electric, American Telephone and Telegraph, Exxon, Standard Oil of California (now called Chevron), and other firms of similar financial strength.

Speculative stock

Speculative stocks are untried securities, often stocks of new, small firms whose chances for success are not great or firms that at least are untested. Some of the small mining and uranium stocks are examples, as are the small electronics companies. Investors should not put any money in these stocks unless they can afford to lose it if the worst comes. The probability of gain is small, but the amount of gain would be great if it should come. One assumes a great risk in buying them. A small investor with few funds should probably never buy highly speculative securities. A person of means may want to invest in them occasionally.

Speculation is a relative term, as pointed out before, and some people take a chance on a mildly speculative stock. Of course, all stock has at least a slight element of speculation attached to it.

Preferred stock

Many investors consider **_preferred stock_** somewhere between bonds and stock, more risky than bonds but less so than common stock. As such, it appeals to certain moderately conservative investors.

Preferred stock is a special kind of stock issued by a corporation that gives a preference to the purchaser. Generally, the preference takes the form of a fixed return or dividend and a preference as to assets. For example, a preferred stockholder may be given a 9 percent return. This 9 percent is figured on the face or par value of the stock. Thus if a stock share were issued at $100 par and it were a 9 percent preferred, the stockholder would be entitled to $9.00 per annum on each share of stock he or she holds, provided there are enough profits to pay the $9. This $9 per share, moreover, is due and payable before any distribution can be made to the common stockholders.

In addition to the preference in the form of earnings, preferred stockholders are generally entitled to share in the assets of the corporation at dissolution before the common stockholders may receive any of the money. That is, if the corporation goes out of business either voluntarily or involuntarily, preferred stockholders will divide the assets and pay themselves off at par vaue before the common stockholders may re-

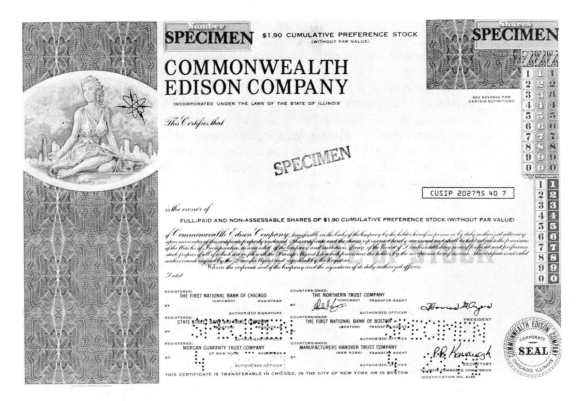

A preferred stock certificate. (Source: Courtesy of Commonwealth Edison Company and the First National Bank of Boston.)   Figure 15–5

ceive any part of the assets. Some variations of preferred stock are examined below. Figure 15–5 shows a preferred stock certificate.

Cumulative and noncumulative preferred stock

A corporation issuing 9 percent **cumulative preferred stock** is liable to the preferred stockholders for past dividends that have not been paid. Suppose a company fails to pay dividends for three years, and the stock (with a $100 par value) calls for a payment of 9 percent and is cumulative; then the company must pay the cumulative preferred stockholders $27 at the end of the three years before any money is payable to the common stockholders.

　　Notice that corporations do not have to pay dividends to preferred stockholders even if they have the profits. They must merely pay the preferred before they may pay the common; and if the preferred is cumulative, they must pay all back dividends before common can be paid. Sometimes there are limits to how far back dividends have to be paid, such as three-year or five-year cumulative. Other preferred cumulative stocks have no limits, and all back dividends have to be paid before common stockholders can receive anything. On noncumulative preferred stock the corporation need only pay the curent year's dividends before it may pay dividends on the common stock.

Participating preferred

With this type of preferred stock, if the earnings are sufficient, preferred stockholders not only are given their agreed dividends but are entitled to share equally in the dividends paid to the common stockholders. Generally where there is a ***participating preferred stock,*** the preferred stockholders are paid their agreed-upon rate, say $9 per share, then the common stockholders are paid an equal dividend, and after that the remainder of the money is distributed equally among the preferred and the common stockholders.[5]

Cumulative participating preferred

Obviously these two features can be combined, and we have then a preferred stock that must be paid past dividends before common is paid any dividends, and then will share equally with the common anything that remains.

Callable or redeemable preferred

Callable preferred stock is preferred stock issued by a corporation with a provision that the corporation has an option to buy the stock back from the preferred stockholders on terms specified at the time the stock is issued. For example, callable preferred stock may be issued at $100 per share and may be callable at $110. That is, if the corporation desires to exercise its opinion, it may buy back the stock at the call price of $110.

Corporations issue stock of this nature so that if the market is such that they could issue a new preferred at, say, 7 or 8 percent rather than at the old rate of 9, they can convert. Or they may wish to clean up their capital structure and eliminate the preferred. In the market seldom will the market price exceed the call price because of the possibility of redemption by the issuer.

Convertible preferred

This is preferred stock that can be exchanged for common stock by the stockholders at their option. The exchange ratio is determined at the time the stock is issued. Therefore, if the common stock of the corporation appreciates in the market, it will pull the preferred up with it. ***Convertible***

---

5. In this case the dividend to the common stockholder would not necessarily be $9, because the price of the common and preferred stock is not usually the same. The common stock may be selling for $50 per share, whereas the preferred in this example has a face value of $100. Moreover, the price of the common stock often fluctuates widely over time. Therefore a participating agreement must be spelled out at the time the preferred stock is issued; generally it will give the common the same percentage return that the preferred has received, after which they share equally. But this means that the common must be evaluated at the time the preferred is issued, because its price fluctuates in the market. Usually the market price (or some price near it) of the common at the time the preferred is issued is taken; the common would get 9 percent of that, and then sharing would begin.

preferred stock has all the advantages of preferred, as well as of the common, just as in the case of convertible bonds, which were discussed above.

Preferred stock may have the features of a bond or the features of common stock, or some of each. If it is participating preferred, it is a bit closer to common because it shares the good fortune of the common. However, it may not share as much of the bad. If it is noncallable and nonparticipating, it is closer to a bond. Its rate of return is fixed, and it will fluctuate in the market like a bond with variations in the interest rate. If it is convertible into common, it again shares in the good fortune of common but not necessarily in the bad because it will rise in price with the common but will not necessarily fall if the market price of the common declines.

A final note on preferred stock

SUMMARY REVIEW QUESTIONS

These questions serve as a summary and a review of the chapter. If you are able to answer them all, you have a good understanding of the material covered by the chapter.

1. How do bonds differ from common stock?
2. What is par value of a bond? What does it mean if a bond is sold at a premium?
3. What are registered bonds?
4. What is a debenture?
5. Explain convertible bonds.
6. What might lead a corporation to issue convertible bonds?
7. What are discount bonds?
8. How do U.S. government marketable securities differ from Series EE and HH bonds?
9. Discuss state and local securities.
10. What is the difference between a Treasury note and muncipal bond?
11. In the rating of bonds, how many classifications are there?
12. How does the nominal yield on a bond differ from its real yield?

13. What is meant by a stock's par value, book value, and market value?
14. What is the difference between earnings and yield, as most brokers define it, on common stock?
15. What is meant by total economic increment insofar as a common stockholder is concerned?
16. Why can some firms raise a larger percentage of their capital from the sale of bonds than can other firms?
17. What is meant by leverage?
18. What is a stock's beta?
19. Explain what is meant by a growth stock, an income stock, and a cyclical stock.
20. What are the advantages and disadvantages of preferred stock?
21. Distinguish between cumulative, noncumulative, and cumulative participating preferred stock.
22. The market price of callable preferred stock is said to have a "lid" on it. In short, there seems to be a top market price. Why is this so?

CASES

1. Kathy Nowlin, who is in the 28 percent tax bracket, purchased two sets of bonds as follows:

   Purchase A: Tax-free municipal bonds
   Purchase B: Taxable corporate bonds

	Dollar amount	Yield	Standard & Poor's rating	Maturity
A	$10,000	9.0%	BBB	20 yrs
B	5,000	8.5%	AAA	2 yrs

   (a) What is Kathy's after-tax return in both cases?
   (b) Why do the taxable bonds yield a lower before-tax return than the tax-free bonds?
   (c) Which purchase is the more liquid?
   (d) Which purchase is the more risky?

2. Sharon and John McWilliams have a portfolio of stocks consisting of the following:

Stock	No. of shares	Yield
General Motors	100	5.9%
IBM	300	3.0
Penn Power & Light	200	7.4
General Electric	400	2.8
Dry Gulch Gold & Uranium	100	0

   (a) Which stocks are growth stock?
   (b) Which stocks are cyclical stock?
   (c) Which stocks are income stock?
   (d) Which stocks are defensive stock?
   (e) Which stocks are blue-chip stock?
   (f) Which stocks are speculative stock?
   (g) Do You consider this a well-selected portfolio?
   (h) Look in the financial pages of a newspaper and calculate the value of John and Sharon's portfolio.

3. Janice Spier recently inherited some common stock. The par or face value on the stock is $10 per share, which gives Janice a total investment value of $5,000. Recently, however, she received from the corporation a report that give the book value of the stock as $25 per share, which would make her investment $12,500. Then last night at a dinner party someone mentioned the same corporation and said he had just bought 100 shares of it at $102 per share. At this point Janice is confused. Could you straighten her out? What makes the par value, the book value, and the market value differ?

4. About a year ago Dale and Genevieve MacMasters purchased one hundred shares of participating preferred common stock yielding 8 percent on their investment of $150 per share. It was a new issue at the time of purchase, and the common stock at that time was selling for $50 per share. In the first year the company had a very good year and has announced that the final dividend on the preferred stock will be paid soon. What is the dividend (for the year) on the preferred?

   The company also announced that there would be a participating dividend later after the common stockholders had received their share. What is the dividend that must be paid on the common before the common and preferred stocks share equally that which remains?

5. Thomas and Rita Andrews purchased $5,000 face value of callable convertible bonds a year ago at par, paying 9 percent coupon rate. How much money did they invest, not counting brokerage fees? What is their annual dollar income from the bonds?

    The call feature provided for a call at the option of the company at $1,025. The convertible feature permitted Thomas and Rita to convert each bond into ten shares of common stock. What was the approximate price of the common stock at the time the convertibles were issued?

    Over the past year the company has been extremely prosperous, and the price of the common stock has risen to $200. What is the price of the convertible bonds? Explain.

6. Some time ago Gordon and Lillian Rider purchased a $1,000 face value convertible bond having a coupon rate of 9 percent. They got the bond at a 5 percent discount. What is their total investment? What is their actual yield?

    The bond is convertible into twenty shares of common stock. What was the approximate price of the common stock when the bond was issued? The present market price of the common stock is $160 per share. Should Gordon and Lillian convert? It they do, what will be the value of their investment? What is the present value of their convertible bond?

7. Judy Brown is saving a few dollars a month and wants to invest them in common stock. She has heard that certain firms like utilities have more leverage built into their capital structure than some other firms. She is unclear about what leverage means. Can you explain it to her? Also Judy would like to know why utilities generally have more leverage in their capital structure than most other firms.

SUGGESTED READINGS

The ABC's of Market Forecasting. Princeton, N.J.: Dow Jones and Company.

American Stock Exchange Annual Report. New York: American Stock Exchange.

Barron's Weekly. Princeton, N.J.: Dow Jones and Company.

"Before You Say Yes: Fifteen Questions to Ask About Investments." Pueblo, Colo.: Consumer Information Center.

Blodgett, Richard. *The Merrill Lynch Guide to Financial Planning.* New York: Simon and Schuster, 1983.

"The Dow Jones Averages; A Non-Professional's Guide." Princeton, N.J.: Dow Jones and Company.

The Exchange. Magazine published monthly by the New York Stock Exchange, New York.

Farrell, James L., Jr., and Fuller, Russell J. *Modern Investments and Security Analysis.* New York: McGraw-Hill, 1987.

Financial Analysts Journal. New York: The Financial Analyst Federation. Bimonthly publication.

"Financial World, the Investment Magazine." New York: Financial World Partners.

Fischer, Donald, and Jordan, Ronald. *Security Analysis and Portfolio Management,* 4th ed. Englewood Cliffs, N.J.: Prentice-Hall, 1987.

"For Tax-Free Income, Ask About Municipal Bonds." New York: Dean Witter Reynolds. You may obtain this from your Dean Witter broker.

Hedging Highlights. Chicago: Chicago Board of Trade.

How to Invest in Stocks and Bonds. New York: Merrill, Lynch, Pierce, Fenner, and Smith.

"How to Read Stock Market Quotations." Princeton, N.J.: Dow Jones and Company.

How You Get More Out of Financial News. Princeton, N.J.: Dow Jones and Company.

The Insider's Guide to the Wall Street Journal. Princeton, N.J.: Dow Jones and Company.

Instruments of the Money Market. Richmond, Va.: Federal Reserve Bank of Richmond, 1986.

The Kiplinger Washington Letter. A weekly newsletter with a good deal of material on business and finance.

"Moody's Handbook of Common Stock." New York: Moody's Investors Services. Quarterly publication.

New York Stock Exchange Fact Book. New York: The New York Stock Exchange. Annual publication.

"Quarterly Review of the Bond Market." New York: The Federal Reserve Bank of New York.

Questions and Answers About the Stock Market. New York: Merrill, Lynch, Pierce, Fenner, and Smith.

Reilly, Frank K. *Investment Analysis and Portfolio Management.* Chicago: The Dryden Press, 1985.

Tax-Exempt Bonds and the Investor. Washington, D.C.: Investment Bankers Association of America.

Understanding Financial Data in The Wall Street Journal. Princeton, N.J.: Dow Jones and Company.

U. S. News & World Report. A weekly magazine that contains a good deal of information on business and finance.

United States Government Securities: Basic Information. Dallas: Federal Reserve Bank of Dallas.

The Wall Street Journal. Princeton, N.J.: Dow Jones and Company. Daily publication.

Well Beyond the Average: The Story of Dow Jones. Princeton, N.J.: Dow Jones and Company.

What Every Woman Investor Should Know. Washington, D.C.: Investment Bankers Association of America.

"What Every Investor Should Know." Pueblo, Col.: Consumer Information Center.

16 The investor and the securities market

HIGHLIGHTS

This chapter examines the securities market. In order to help you understand the market and to develop investment strategies, this chapter examines the following:

1 The securities exchanges, brokers, and dealers
2 The quoting of securities
3 How securities may be bought and sold
4 Dividends on common stock
5 Other things one should know about securities
6 The options market

INTRODUCTION

An investor who wishes to buy or sell securities does so in the open market. The open market for securities is "the works." It consists of all the organized exchanges on which securities are listed and also the over-the-counter market. Broadly defined, it also includes the brokers and dealers who operate in the open market and make it go. In this chapter we shall examine the open market and the buying and selling of securities therein. We will also examine earning on stock and some supplemental material on securities.

SECURITIES EXCHANGES: BROKERS AND DEALERS

In the United States there are two major organized exchanges (the New York Stock Exchange and the American Stock Exchange) whose major function is to facilitate the trading of securities. In addition, there are a number of smaller regional exchanges. While the greatest volume of business on the organized exchanges takes place in the area of common and preferred stock, they also handle the sale of some bonds and warrants. To deal directly on an exchange, one must be a member or own a seat. Many of the members are security dealers as well as brokers; they are broker-dealers. Brokers are individuals who execute orders for third parties for a commission. Dealers, on the other hand, act as principals and buy for their own accounts and also sell from them, hoping for a profit margin between the buy and sell prices. That is, they keep an inventory in securities, and in doing this they are said to make a market in the securities they buy and sell.

The New York Stock Exchange (NYSE)

The New York Stock Exchange is by far the largest of the various exchanges in the United States. About 1,500 corporations have their common stock listed thereon. In addition, about 3,000 bonds and 800 preferred stocks are also listed, which makes the total listing on the "big board" almost 5,200 securities.

In order to be listed on the New York Stock Exchange a corporation must meet certain minimum requirements. These requirements have to do with the number of shares outstanding, number of stockholders, and size of the corporation as measured by assets and earnings. In addition, listed corporations must publish their financial reports and reveal certain financial facts. The American Stock Exchange and the various regional exchanges discussed below also have minimum listing requirements, but they are less stringent than those on the NYSE.

To trade on the NYSE, one must own a seat, and obtaining a seat is not easy. The only way to do so is to buy one from a member willing to relinquish it. The exchange is a very exclusive club. Brokers who are not members must trade (buy and sell) through someone who is a member.

The members of the exchange are classified into a number of categories. About half the members are commission brokers; the rest are divided among floor brokers, specialists, registered traders, bond dealers, or a combination of the above capacities at different times.

1. *Commission brokers.* Some members act solely as commission brokers. These are the ones who are partners or officers of firms doing business with the public. They have offices where they contact the public (in the case of a large firm like Merrill Lynch they have many members and many offices throughout the country). They buy and sell securities for their customers in return for which they are paid a commission.

2. *Floor brokers.* These are the members of the exchange who assist commission brokers who are unable to handle all of the volume when trade is heavy. They ensure that orders are executed quickly. They used to be called contract brokers a few years ago, and before that "two-dollar" brokers because that was the fee they charged. Their fee is now higher and comes out of the regular fee paid to the commission broker.

3. *Specialists.* The physical area of the New York Stock Exchange being large, it is frequently impossible for a member to get around fast enough to execute customers' orders. Certain brokers therefore specialize in buying and selling certain stocks at certain posts on the exchange floor. Each security is sold at a given location, and the specialists stay at that post and execute orders for a few securities at the order of their fellow brokers. In addition, some specialists will use their inventories to fill odd lot orders (discussed below).

4. *Registered traders or floor traders.* These are members who buy and sell on their own accounts; they deal in stocks themselves with the idea of making a profit on their purchases. They are able to do so because as members of the stock exchange they do not pay a regular commission, but a greatly reduced member commission. In addition, they are also professional traders, and they get in and out of the market on a short-run basis and take advantage of short-run price movements of common stock. Sometimes they also serve either as commission brokers for a few customers or as floor brokers for other commission brokers.

People have been buying and selling securities for many years, and the market has had many ups and downs, because the market is one of the most, if not the most, sensitive of all institutions in our society. It reacts to any and all news, good or bad. Bad news will nearly always send it down; what is considered good news may send it up or down. These are the short-run fluctuations. The long-run trend has been up more often than down.

The historical record of the NYSE

While the deepest and most severe stock market decline took place with the crash in 1929, there have been other sharp declines as well. After the 1929 crash the market generally stayed depressed until the big bull market shortly after World War II. Since that time there have been a number of ups and downs, but generally the trend was up until the crash on October 19, 1987, which rivaled the crash of 1929.

At various times, different stocks have been popular. For a number of years after World War I, railroad stocks were the "in thing." While they made somewhat of a comeback after the Great Depression, they never regained their former popularity. More recently, electronics, computers, and other "hi-tech" firms have been the glamour items in the stock market. Much of the historical record of the stock market can be seen graphically in Standard and Poor's chart in Figure 16–1.

The American Stock Exchange (AMEX)

The second major stock exchange is the American Stock Exchange, called *AMEX* for short. This market was originally outside in the street, but has been inside since 1921. There are fewer securities listed on the American Stock Exchange than on the New York Exchange, and the requirements for listing are less rigorous, but the same criteria are used. About 900 securities are listed on the American Exchange. As for commission brokers, specialists, and so forth, the operation of the American Exchange is much like that of the New York Stock Exchange.

The regional exchanges

The New York and the American Stock Exchanges are national institutions. THere are also a number of smaller stock exchanges that serve only the region in which they are located. The three major regional exchanges are the Midwest Stock Exchange, the Philadelphia-Baltimore-Washington Stock Exchange, and the Pacific Coast Stock Exchange. Many of the stocks listed for the regional exchanges are also listed on either the New York or the American Stock Exchange. The existence of the Pacific Coast Exchange permits trading in those dually listed stocks three additional hours after the close of the NYSE and AMEX. In addition, the regional exchanges list some securities of regional companies that are listed nowhere else.

Brokerage commissions

There are brokerage commissions which the investor must pay when buying or selling securities. On large orders the broker will negotiate commissions in advance with the buyer or seller. On most regular orders, however, brokers have a schedule they follow, and these schedules vary somewhat from broker to broker.

The calculation of the commissions by the regular brokerage houses is complex and a table showing them is not possible. However, three variables are taken into account in setting them.

1. The dollar amount of money committed. Commissions, as a percent of the money committed, decline as the latter rises.
2. The number of shares purchased. Commissions per share decline as the number of shares purchased increases.
3. The price of shares. Commissions per share rise as the per share price of the shares selected declines. This one can offset he first two factors.

If, for example, a person buys 100 shares priced at $50 (commit $5,000), one (typical) broker will charge $101. If the person purchases 200 shares priced at $25 per share (again, commit $5,000), the same broker will charge $130; and on 500 shares at $10 the person would pay $161.

The above discussion applies to round lots of one hundred shares. If lesser amounts (odd lots) are traded, the commissions are calculated the same way, and then an additional odd-lot fee of one-eighth of one dollar ($.125) per share is added. Note that these commissions are paid when stocks are purchased as well as when sold.

Discount brokers

In recent years discount brokers (also called security discount houses) have sprung up. They charge commissions that are often substantially below those charged by regular brokerage houses. They can do this because they offer no investment advisory services and provide no research reports. They merely execute orders. On the purchases discussed above, the commissions charged by a discount broker would often be as low as one-half of those charged by regular brokers. Many of these discount brokers are affiliated with banks that have moved into the securities business; to obtain the services of one a person need merely call the bank.

Buying odd lots

On the organized exchange, transactions are usually carried out in round lots that consist of 100 shares. However, small investors would want lesser amounts. There used to be dealers who specialized in odd lots and who would maintain an inventory in stock and buy and sell in any amounts from 1 to 99, but these have passed from the scene. Odd-lot transactions are now carried out directly by some brokers who maintain an inventory of stock and stand willing to trade in any odd-lot amounts. Those (usually smaller) brokers who do not themselves maintain an inventory will fill their customer's odd-lot orders by going to members of the New York Stock Exchange (usually specialists or registered traders) who do carry an inventory and who do deal in odd lots, although this is a minor part of their business. On odd-lot purchases there is still the one-eighth of one dollar ($.125) per share odd-lot fee, which is added to the price of stock (subtracted from it when sold). This is over and above the regular commissions.

Securities dealers

Securities dealers make a market in a security and buy and sell on their own account. They are not paid a commission but earn their living on the difference between what they pay for a security and what they sell it for. For example, a share of stock may be quoted as having an asked price of $11 and a bid price of $10. This means that the dealer will pay the seller $10 for the stock share; on the other hand, the buyer must pay $11. This leaves a spread of $1, out of which the dealers pay their expenses and receive their profits. Because dealers stand ready to buy and sell at all

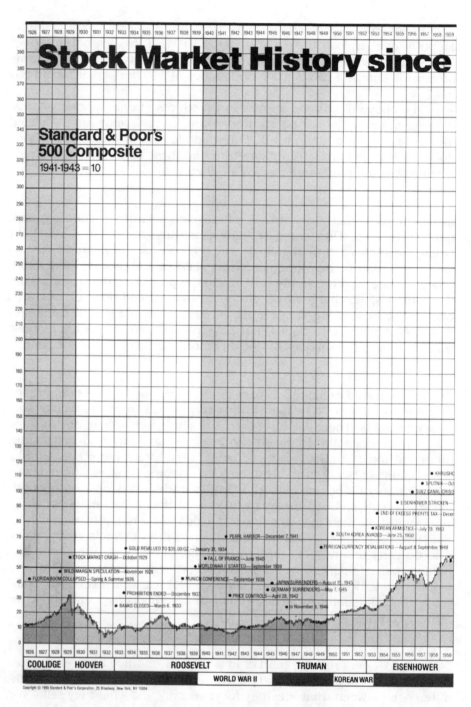

Figure 16–1   *Stock market and business history since 1926. (Source: Courtesy of Standard & Poor's Corporation. This report was up-to-date at the time of publication; subsequent changes are reflected on current Standard & Poor's reports.)*

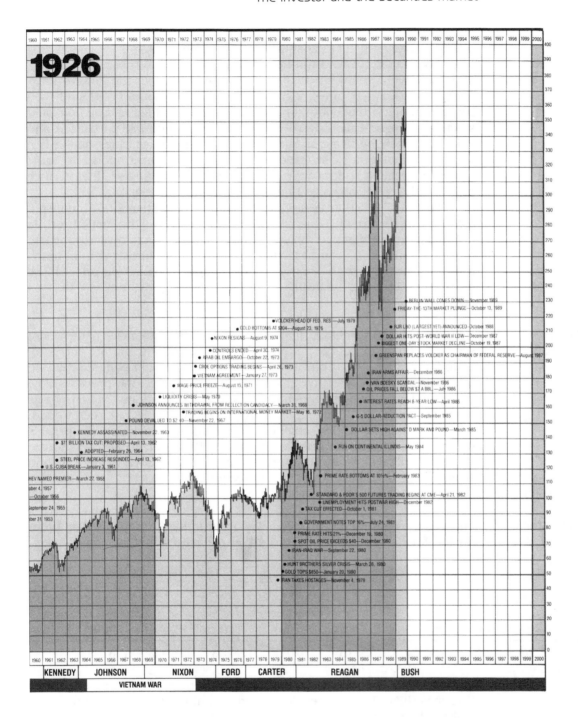

times, they are said to "make a market." Dealers' bid and asked prices are, of course, subject to change without notice.

Stocks that are sold through dealers are usually "over-the-counter" securities. While many stock issues are listed on either the New York Exchange or the American Stock Exchange and are bought and sold by a broker acting as an agent, many other issues are not listed. The nonlisted stocks are the so-called over-the-counter stocks and are purchased and sold exclusively by dealers. In the final analysis, a securities dealer is a merchant whose stock in trade consists of stocks and bonds. In most instances, dealers specialize in a few lines of merchandise, that is, they handle only a relatively small number of unlisted stocks.

When an individual desires to purchase some shares of an unlisted stock, he or she contacts a broker. The broker checks the market for the unlisted stock designated. Actually, the broker contacts dealers who are making a market for that particular issue. Then the broker gets in touch with the purchaser to inform him or her of the lowest asked price. If the purchaser still wants the issue, a sale is made.

QUOTING SECURITIES

Almost every daily metropolitan newspaper has a financial page where securities prices are quoted, some of which are more elaborate and complete than others. Most of the more complete financial pages quote the price and the activity of the stocks and bonds traded the previous day, but some late evening papers have current day quotations. The emphasis here is on the word "traded." If a particular security has not been traded, it is not listed. If ABC, Inc. has not been traded, for instance, the price is not given, obviously because no price has been set. In addition to the listed securities, the more complete financial pages carry the bid and asked prices of the over-the-counter securities.

The listed stock

Those issues traded the previous day are arranged in alphabetical order on the financial page of the more complete metropolitan newspapers, and appear as shown below.

52 weeks

High	Low	Stock	Div.	% yield	P/E ratio	Sales in 100s	High	Low	Close	Net change
129 1/2	73 1/4	IBM	3.80	3.0	16	5707	128 1/8	126 1/2	126 7/8	−1

The third column shows that the stock here is International Business Machines (IBM). Immediately to the left of that the high and low prices of that stock over the past 52 weeks are indicated. Moving now to the right, we will note all the other information the quotation conveys. Under "Div." we see 3.80 indicating that dividends of $3.80 were paid over the past year. The "% yield" column shows 3.0, the dividend yield as a percent of the market price of the stock. However, some earnings were retained by the company and hence the price-earnings ratio of 16 is shown in the next column. Then we see that sales for the day were 570,700 shares; that during the day's trade the stock of IBM fluctuated and reached a high of $128 1/8 per share, a low of $126 1/2; and that it closed at $126 7/8. On the basis of these figures, why was there a net change of −1 of a point? The net change figure is the difference between the closing price for that day and the closing price of the previous day, not the difference between the high and the low on the day in question. Obviously, yesterday's closing price can be either higher or lower than today's closing price. The preceding day's closing price in our example was 127 7/8. Note that stocks advance or decline in steps of one-eighth of one dollar.

Frequently there is a footnote in the quotations, a lower case letter. Footnotes that appear are explained at the bottom of the list of quotations under the heading of explanatory notes. A footnote under the explanatory notes may point out that the corporation is in bankruptcy or in receivership or one of a number of other valuable bits of information.

A portion of the NYSE market quotes appears in Table 16−1. Also shown (in Table 16−2) are a list of the most active stocks, a market diary indicating the number of stocks that advanced or declined, and new highs and lows on NYSE.

The Dow Jones averages

In addition to prices of individual stocks, most financial pages also publish the Dow Jones averages, which are supposed to indicate which way the market is going in general. The Dow Jones average is really four different averages: one for industrials, one for transportation, one for utilities, and one a composite of the other three. These averages date back to 1896.

The industrial average, based on the stock of thirty industrial companies, is calculated by adding the prices of these thirty stocks and then dividing to obtain an average.[1] The transportation average with twenty transportation company stocks in it (this formerly included just rails, but now it has some airlines and trucking lines as well) is calculated in the same way, as is also the utility average, which contains the stock of fifteen utilities.

There are a number of criticisms of the Dow Jones averages, especially of the industrial average. First, it is argued that thirty stocks are not a large enough sample. Second, all of the stocks in the Dow Jones averages are blue chips such as General Motors, General Electric, Exxon, and DuPont; such stocks as these, it is argued, are not representative of the market as a whole. Finally, the Dow Jones averages are only crudely adjusted for splits. Over the years many of the stocks have been split a number of times; moreover, not all of the thirty have been split the same

---

1. The divisor is not thirty, however. Rather, adjustments have been made to take into account stock splits (see the appendix for this chapter). This adjustment involves changing the divisor to account for splits.

Table 16—1   *New York Stock Exchange, consolidated trading/week ended Friday, June 5, 1988*

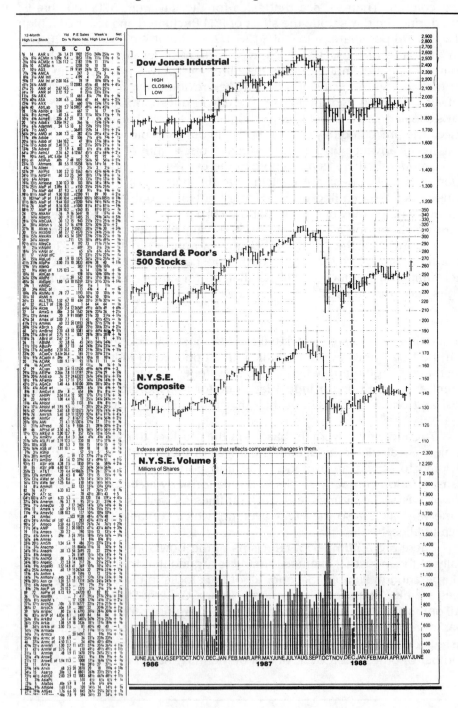

Most active stocks and market diary on NYSE   Table 16.2

Most active stocks week ended October 12, 1990 on NYSE			
Company	Volume	Close	Change
IBM	3,113,800	101	− 2 1/2
Wal-Mart Str	2,935,200	25 3/8	+ 1/4
Philip Morris	2,893,600	44 3/8	− 3/4
Fed Nat Mtg. wt	2,872,500	12 5/8	− 5/8
Fed Natl Mtg	2,757,300	26 3/4	− 7/8
Chemical Bk	2,123,000	13 1/4	− 1 3/4
Waste Mgmt	2,118,000	29 3/8	− 5/8
Ford Motor Co	2,061,800	29 7/8	− 1/8
General Elec	2,059,600	51 1/4	− 3/4
Toys R Us Inc	1,790,100	20 1/8	− 5/8
Dresser Indus	1,725,100	17 5/8	+ 7/8
Citicorp	1,706,700	13 5/8	− 1/2
Pepsico Inc	1,564,500	22 5/8	− 3/8
Marriott Corp	1,553,000	8 3/4	− 1 3/8
TJX Cos	1,481,000	9 1/8	− 1 1/2
Market Dairy	THUR	WED	WEEK AGO
Issues traded	2,007	1,990	1,976
Advances	301	356	731
Declines	1,290	1,200	780
Unchanged	401	434	465
New Highs	3	1	4
New Lows	375	278	139

amounts. Those companies that have never split their stock or have split it less have a greater weight in the averages than the others. The adjustment to correct for stock splits noted in the footnote below has only partially done so.

The Dow Jones industrial stock price averages are shown in Figure 16−2. The bar graph going back several months show the high, low, and close for the day. In this figure there is also a graph that indicates the volume or the number of issues traded.

There are a number of other indicators that attempt to show which way the market is going. These indicators, however, use index number devices (see Chapter 1). These index numbers measure movements in stock prices much like the cost of living was measured in Chapter 1. The best-known such stock indices are the Standard and Poor's and the New York Stock Exchange composite index of all common stocks that are traded on the New York Stock Exchange each day. About 2,200 stocks are listed, but a few are not traded each day. Therefore the number of stocks

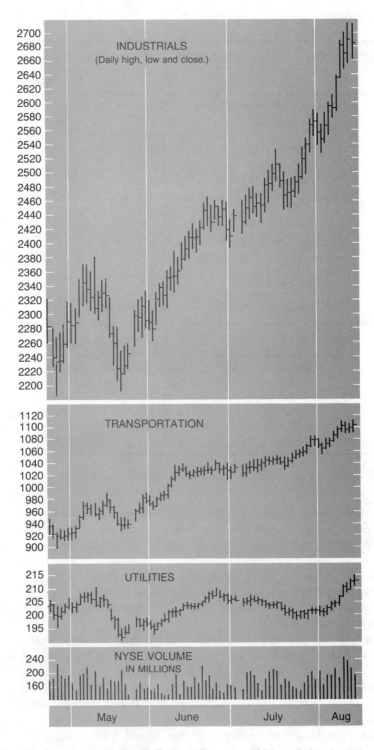

Figure 16–2   *The Dow Jones averages* (Source: Barron's, *1987, p. 71*)

in the index varies from day to day but usually is close to 2,200. The New York Stock Exchange index was started in 1966, which is the base year; the prices of all stocks traded on a given day are added up on a computer, and then the figure is compared to the base year figure. The New York Stock Exchange also has an index for industrials, consisting of 1,000 stocks; one for utilities, which includes 136 stocks; one for transportation, made up of 76 stocks' and one for the stocks of 75 financial institutions of various kinds.

The Standard and Poor's index uses the average stock prices from 1941 to 1943 as the base year and that figure has been set to 10. The current figure, then, shows the increase since then. The Standard and

STOCK MARKET
STANDARD & POOR'S PRICE INDEX
QUARTERLY AVERAGES

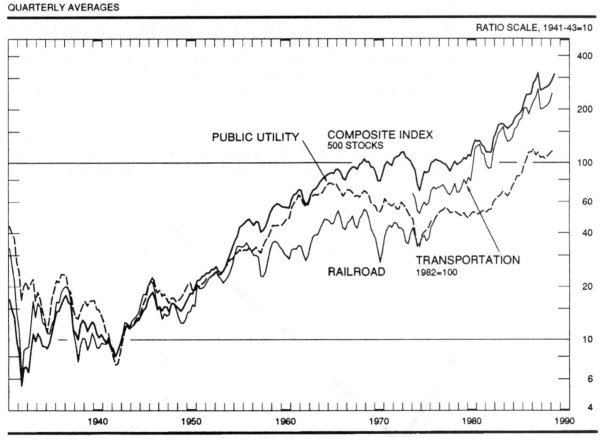

Stock price indices Standard & Poor's price index, quarterly averages. (Source: Federal Reserve Chart Book, May, 1989, *Board of Governors of the Federal Reserve System,* p. 92.)   Figure 16—3

Poor's index includes four hundred stocks in the industrial index, twenty stocks in the transportaiton industry, forty in the utility index, forty in the financial index, and a composite of all five hundred of these stocks. Both the Standard and Poor's and the New York Stock Exchange indices are considered more reliable indicators of which way the market in general is moving than the Dow Jones averages because they include more stocks. Table 16–1 shows the New York Stock Exchange, the Dow Jones averages, and the Standard & Poor's indicators for June 5, 1988. Figure 16–3 shows the movement of the Standard & Poor's indicators over the years.

Bull and **bear markets** are technical terms to indicate which way the market in general is going. If the market rises far enough and long enough, it is referred to as a bull market. If it falls far enough and long enough, it is referred to as a bear market. The stock averages discussed above are the tests used to determine whether the market is bullish or bearish. If the market just bounces around and moves up and down a bit from day to day, it is neither bearish nor bullish. To have a bull or bear market there must be a trend. The investors who buy heavily because they believe the market will rise in the future are called bulls. Those who are selling because they believe a decline is coming are called bears. And if the bulls outnumber the bears, the market will rise. If the reverse is the case, it will fall. (Figure 16–4 is a diagram of a bull and bear market.

Over-the-counter stocks

Some people have the idea that if a stock is not listed and consequently is traded over the counter, there must be something wrong with it. This is just not true. Many over-the-counter stocks are as good as and fre-

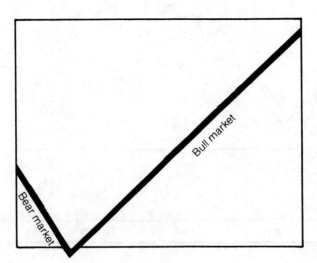

Figure 16–4   *Ups and downs of the market.*

quently better than some of the securities listed on the organized exchanges. There are, however, some securities that do not qualify for listing, and these over-the-counter stocks are riskier.[2]

There are really three **over-the-counter** markets. There is the national over-the-counter market, which is quoted in greater detail than just a few years ago. The national market is linked by the National Association of Security Dealers Automated Quotation System (NASDAQ). It is a nationwide computer system and all trades are recorded. This market has evolved to the point where it is almost like the New York Stock Exchange. A quotation would appear as follows:

365

High	Low		Sales (100s)	High	Low	Last	Net Change
20 1/2	13 3/4	Just Ind.	144	18 3/4	18 3/8	18 1/2	+ 1/4

In this case the stock is Justin industries, a manufacturer of building materials. The high and the low for the past 365 days are shown at the left. Then, as we move to the right we see that 144,000 shares changed hands; the high and the low for the day were 18 3/4 and 18 3/8 respectively, and the last sale changed hands at 18 1/2, which was 1/4 of a dollar higher than the last sale yesterday.

There are some regional over-the-counter securities that are reported less fully because they are traded less frequently. Nevertheless some dealers hold an inventory in these stocks and make a market in them; that is, they stand ready to buy and sell at all times. Their asked price is always higher than their bid price, and the difference between the two is their profit margin. These stock quotations would appear in *The Wall Street Journal* as follows:

Stock	Sales	Bid	Asked	Net Change
Amwest Ins.	47	9	9 1/2	− 1/8

The stock is American West Insurance Company. A total of 4,700 shares changed hands on that day, and dealers stood ready to buy it at 9 and sell it at 9 1/2. The net change of − 1/8 indicates that the stock dropped by 1/8 from the last bid price of the previous day.

---

2. In order to be listed, the firm must be of a certain size as measured by assets. It must also have a minimum number of common stocks outstanding and a minimum number of stockholders. And it must be willing to publish certain basic financial facts about itself. Some firms that qualify for listing prefer to remain unlisted.

The third over-the-counter market is for even smaller firms than the second market described above. It works just like the second (regional) market, but even less information is reported. Quotation appears below.

	Bid	Asked
AM Cable TV	2 1/8	2 1/4

It conveys only what the investor may buy (or sell) the stock for.

Corporate bond quotations

Corporate bonds are frequently listed on both the New York and the American exchanges. Those that are not so listed are traded over the counter. Bond quotations are not printed on the financial pages of all daily newspapers but may be found in financial papers such as *The Wall Street Journal.*

The quotations for bonds traded on the exchange are listed in alphabetical order. After the name of the company there appears the coupon rate of interest paid per $1,000, which is the face value of the corporate bonds, and the maturity date. We will use as an example ATT (American Telephone and Telegraph). They have a number of different issues outstanding but one reads as follows:

Bonds	Cur. yield	Vol.	High	Low	Close	Net change
AT&T 8 5/8 07	9.5	128	90 3/4	89 3/4	90 1/2	− 1/4

The coupon rate of 8 5/8 percent ($86.25 per $1,000 bond) will be paid until the year 2007 when the bond matures. The current yield of 9.5 percent is shown next, then the sales volume, in thousands of dollars, followed by the high and low and closing price for the day, and finally the net change in the closing price from the previous day (note that the coupon rate of 8 5/8 provides a yield of 9.5 percent because the bond is selling at $905.00).

Corporate bonds always have a face value of $1,000, but the newspaper quotations drop the last digit. A quotation of under 100 means that the bond is selling at a discount, while over 100 indicates it is at a premium.

The closing price of the bond quoted above was 90 1/2. This indicates that it was selling at $905.00, and since this is at a discount of $95.00 the actual yield is 9.5 as shown and is above the 8 5/8 coupon rate. The easy way to get the market price of a bond is to convert the stock market page quote to decimals and then multiply by 10. For example, a quote of 84 3/8 would become $84.375 × 10 = $843.75.

The person buying corporate bonds must also pay brokerage commissions. These commissions also vary from broker to broker, but generally they are a certain percentage of the money committed together with a fixed fee. This percentage declines as the amount of money involved rises. In addition to the percentage fee, there is a flat per-bond fee which is about $15. Where the fee is fixed is determined by the number of bonds purchased and the length of time to maturity, declining with the number of bonds bought and rising with the length of time to maturity. Figure 16–5 shows the growth in bond trading over the past few years.

Annual Bond Volume Growth (billions of dollars)

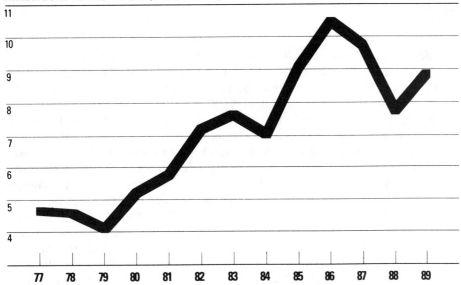

Annual bond volume growth (billions of dollars). (Source: New York Stock Exchange Fact Book, 1990, p. 44.)   Figure 16–5

Marketable United States Treasury bonds are quoted differently from corporate bonds. First, they are priced in thirty-seconds of a dollar. Second, there are bid and asked prices because they are all sold over the counter. Thus the following quotation means that this is a United States bond issue carrying a 9 1/2 percent coupon interest rate; it will mature in November, 1995. At the close of the trading day, the bid price was 114.21. Actually 114.21 means 114 and 21/32, or 114.656. Since Treasury bonds are sold in units of $1,000, 114.65 × 10 = $1,146.50, the bid price. The asked price of 114.25 means 114 and 25/32, or $114.78 × 10 = $1,147.80. The bid change of −.13 means the price has gone down by 13/32 or about .40 since the previous day. At the current price the yield or return is 7.20 percent interest.

Treasury bond quotations

Rate	Mat.	Date	Bid	Asked	Bid. Chg.	Yield
9 1/2	1995	Nov.	114.21	114.25	+ .10	7.20

BUYING AND SELLING SECURITIES

Securities can be purchased for cash or they can be purchased with borrowed funds, that is, on margin.

Cash sales

In a cash sale when the transaction is completed, a bill is sent to the purchaser, who has five business days in which to pay for the stock. When selling, the seller also has five days in which to deliver the securities. The purchaser may actually take physical possession of the stock or he or she may instruct the broker to hold the stock for him or her in the purchaser's account. This is referred to as keeping in the street name and is discussed below.

Margin purchases

Margin purchases are made with funds that are partly borrowed. The word "margin" refers to the percentage of the buyer's own funds needed to buy stock; the remainder may be borrowed from a broker. For example, if a share of stock is priced at $100 and the margin requirement is 75 percent, the purchaser must have that in cash, and may borrow no more than $25. Currently margin requirements are 50 percent; consequently, one half of the money for stock purchases may be borrowed. The Federal Reserve System sets margin requirements, and they have been as high as 100 percent in the past (no borrowed money may be used). The Federal Reserve raises margin requirements if it is believed there is excessive speculation in securities. If the market (and the economy in general) is in the doldrums, the Federal Reserve may lower margin requirements, thus making it easier for investors to enter the market with borrowed funds. This in turn, it is hoped, would increase the demand for stock and also create an environment more favorable to overall economic activity.

An investor has an incentive to buy on margin only if he or she feels the price of securities will rise by more than the interest cost of the loan. A problem could arise if the investor on margin is wrong and the market declines. Then the margin could be wiped out and the investor would have to cover. This works as follows: the rules require that the market price of the stock must be at least equal to the borrowed funds. In the case of a stock selling at $100 purchased with a 50 percent margin requirement, there would be no problem until and if the market price declined below $50. But if the price declined to $45, the borrowed funds $50) would be $5 more than the market value of the stock. The investor would be called by the broker to "cover"; that is, come up with $5 more of his or her own funds (then the market price $45 is again equal to the loan). Today with relatively high margin, the market would have to come down a good deal before an investor would have to cover. However, in former days when margins were often much lower (sometimes only 10 percent) this was sometimes a problem. For example, a $100 stock would only have to decline below $90 before a 10 percent margin was wiped out and the broker would call for the investor to cover. If he or she could not, the stock would be sold. In those days during a declining market the inability of many margin investors to cover resulted in their stock being sold. This contributed further to the decline. This is another reason why relatively high margins are required today.

Short sales

Short sales are the opposite of margin purchases. The investor has an incentive to sell short only if he or she believes the price of a stock will decline. When selling short, the stock is borrowed from a broker (stock can be borrowed just like money) and sold at its current price in the market. For example, if a stock is selling at $100 per share, an investor may borrow it from his or her broker and sell it. Then if, sometime later, its price declines to $80, it can be purchased in the open market (from the same broker it was borrowed from), and repaid, with a realized profit of $20 less brokerage fees. The short seller is also required to make up any dividend which was missed while he or she held a short position in the broker's stock. Selling short, then, is a speculative technique that enables persons to make a profit if they correctly forecast that the price of the security they purchased will decline. If those who have taken a short position are wrong and the security rises in price, they lose money.

Since both buying on margin and selling short are engaging in speculation, it is not recommended for the small investor, especially one who is a relative newcomer to security investments.

Types of orders

There are a number of types of orders either to buy or sell that an individual might place with a broker. These are the following:

1. Limit order. An order to buy or sell a certain number of shares under certain specific conditions. For example, one might order the broker to buy one hundred shares of ABC if the price declines from its present level of $50 to $45, or to sell a number of shares if the stock rises to a certain level.
2. Market order. Either a buy or a sell order of a specific number of shares of a specific security at the current market price. It is left to the broker to obtain the best price possible for the client if it is an over-the-counter security and hence subject to haggling pricewise.
3. Good-till-canceled order. A type of order continuing in force until it is either executed or canceled. This applies to conditional orders. A new order at a different price cancels the former order if made by the same customer.

4. Stop order. An order to buy or sell conditioned upon a specific price. Frequently it is used as a selling device in order to prevent losses or as an attempt to ensure a profit. For example, a person may have purchased a stock at $10 and it may have risen to $20. The purchaser may have reason to believe that it will advance even higher, but for protection in the event of a downward movement, he or she may place a stop order at $15. Thus if the stock does go down to $15 per share, the order will be executed immediately. This is sometimes called a stop loss order because it prevents the stock from falling below a certain price.

DISTRIBUTION OF EARNINGS FROM STOCKS

There are a number of reasons why people own common stock: capital gains, hedging inflation, and dividend income. Figure 16–6 illustrates how dividends, the cost of living, earnings, and stock prices have risen over the years. There are both cash dividends and stock dividends.

Cash dividends

Dividends must be paid out of corporate earnings. The percentage of earnings distributed varies from company to company, but generally runs from 40 to 80 percent. However, in some cases cash dividends are zero; the corporation retains its entire earnings. Dividends do not have to be paid, rather they are declared at the discretion of the board of directors of the company. Most states have laws providing that dividends may be paid only out of current or past earnings. They may not be given out of paid-in capital.

1. *The declaration date and the announcement date.* The day the board of directors meets and declares a dividend is the declaration date. The day this declaration is announced to the press is the announcement date. Often these two dates may be the same, but sometimes the public announcement may be delayed a few days. Firms listed n the NYSE are required to send prompt notices of dividend declarations to the Exchange.
2. *The ex-dividend data.* The **ex-dividend date** is the first day that the purchaser of a stock does not receive the dividend that has been declared on it. Thus when it is said that a stock is ex-dividend, it is being sold without the dividend. This is five business days before the record date, because the rules of the New York Stock Exchange allow five days in which to deliver stock one has sold or five days to pay for stock one has bought. The price of a stock often drops by the amount of the dividend when it goes ex-dividend.
3. *The record date.* This is the date when the corporation counts heads to determine who owns how much stock. The NYSE rules require that the record date be at least ten days later than the announcement date. Owners as of this date, according to the corporation's records, will receive the dividends.

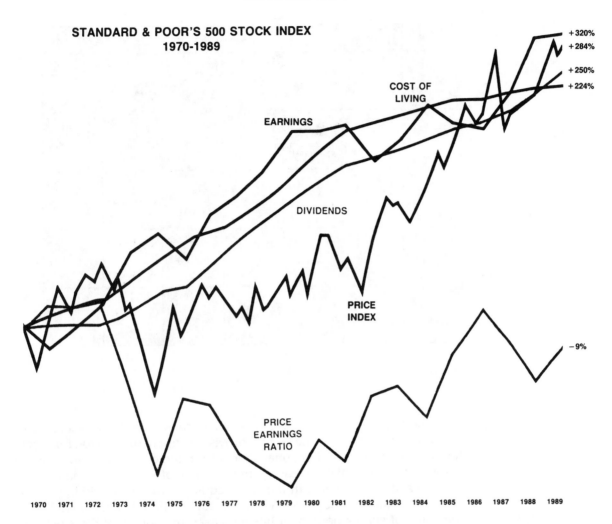

STANDARD & POOR'S 500 STOCK INDEX
1970-1989

+320%
+284%
+250%
+224%

COST OF
LIVING

EARNINGS

DIVIDENDS

PRICE
INDEX

−9%

PRICE
EARNINGS
RATIO

1970 1971 1972 1973 1974 1975 1976 1977 1978 1979 1980 1981 1982 1983 1984 1985 1986 1987 1988 1989

*Performance of the Standard & Poor's stock index 1970–1989. (Source: Johnson's   Figure 16–6
Investment Company Charts, 1989, Hugh A. Johnson Co., Buffalo, N.Y., p. 17.)*

4. *The payment date.* This is the date the dividends are actually paid. Established corporations with a good record of earning and a pattern of dividend payments usually pay dividends quarterly. The dividend checks are mailed to the stockholders of record by the trustee (usually a trust department of a bank) who keeps the stockholder records for the corporation. Figure 16–7 calendars these important dates.

Directors may avoid a cash distribution by using a stock dividend. For   *Stock dividends*
example, a 10 percent stock dividend would result in each stockholder receiving from the company one additional share of every ten shares cur-

SUNDAY	MONDAY	TUESDAY	WEDNESDAY	THURSDAY	FRIDAY	SATURDAY
			1	2	3 ABC Corp. met and declared dividend	4
5	6	7 ABC Corp. announced a dividend to be paid Sept. 30 to stockholders of record Sept. 23	8	9	10	11
12	13	14	15	16	17 Ex-dividend Date	18
19	20	21	22	23 Record Date	24	25
26	27	28	29	30 Payment Date		

Figure 16—7   *Dividend dates calendar.*

rently held. If fractional shares are issued because the stockholder's holdings are not evenly divisible by ten, provisions are usually made for stockholders to buy (or sell) fractional shares from the corporation so they can come out even. While increasing the number of ownership shares, this policy leaves the owner with the same equity as formerly held in the corporation. Although theoretically such a device should cause a decline in the value of shares because it has increased the supply of the stock, occasionally the reverse is true because it may cause more interest in that particular stock and thus create more demand for it.

SUMMARY REVIEW QUESTIONS

These questions serve as a summary and a review of the chapter. If you are able to answer them all, you have a good understanding of the material covered by the chapter.

1. How do brokers and dealers in securities differ?

2. Explain in general terms how brokerage commissions are established.

3. What is the Dow Jones average and what does it attempt to show?

4. What are some other stock market indicators besides the Dow Jones? What are the weaknesses and strengths of the stock averages?

5. Explain briefly the differences between a bear market and a bull market.
6. On over-the-counter stock, what is meant by bid, asked, and net change?
7. Who controls margin requirements, and what is the purpose of this control?
8. When a person buys stock on margin and it declines, he or she may be required to "cover." What does this mean?
9. Explain a short sale and how it differs from a conditional sale.
10. Explain what is meant by ex-dividend date and how it is determined.

CASE

1. Five years ago Leslie Christensen purchased 100 shares of XYZ stock at $60 per share. It paid quarterly dividends of $.90 ever since, and recently Leslie sold it at $90 per share.

   (a) What was Leslie's annual dividend yield?

   (b) What was her total capital gain?
   (c) What total rate of return did Leslie receive over the five years?
   (d) If inflation averaged 4 percent over the years, what was Leslie's real return?

SUGGESTED READINGS

Amex Databook. Fact book published annually by the American Stock Exchange, New York.

American Stock Exchange Annual Report. New York: American Stock Exchange.

Barron's Educational Edition. Princeton, N.J.: Dow Jones and Company.

Christy, George A., and Roden, Foster P. *Finance: Environment and Decisions.* New York: Harper & Row, 1986.

"The Dow Jones Averages; A Non-Professional's Guide." Princeton, N.J.: Dow Jones and Company.

Engel, Louis. *How to Buy Stocks.* New York: Bantam Books, 1983.

"The Exchange Market and the Public Interest." The New York Stock Exchange Annual Report. New York: New York Stock Exchange.

Farrell, James L., Jr., and Fuller, Russell J. *Modern Investments and Security Analysis.* New York: McGraw-Hill, 1987.

"Financial World, the Investment Magazine." New York: Financial World Partners. Monthly publication.

Fischer, Donald, and Jordan, Ronald. *Security Analysis and Portfolio Management,* 4th ed. Englewood Cliffs, N.J.: Prentice-Hall, 1987.

Forbes Magazine. A weekly magazine with a great deal of material about business and finance.

Francis, Jack Clark. *Investments Analysis and Management.* New York: McGraw-Hill, 1986.

Hardy, C. Colburn. *Dun and Bradstreet's Guide to Your Investments.* New York: Harper and Row, 1986.

How Over-the-Counter Securities are Traded. New York: Merrill Lynch, Pierce, Fenner, and Smith.

How Professors Use The Wall Street Journal. Princeton, N.J.: Dow Jones and Company.

"How to Read a Financial Report." New York: Merrill Lynch, Pierce, Fenner, and Smith.

"How to Read Stock Market Quotations." Princeton, N.J.: Dow Jones and Company.

"Market Statistics." Chicago: The Chicago Board of Options Exchange.

The Merrill Lynch Guide to Writing Options. New York: Merrill Lynch, Pierce, Fenner, and Smith.

"Moody's Handbook of Common Stock." This is published quarterly by Moody's Investors Services.

New York Stock Exchange Fact Book. New York: New York Stock Exchange. Annual publication.

The New York Stock Exchange Market. Princeton, N.J.: Dow Jones and Company.

"OTC Profiles." New York: Standard and Poor's. Monthly publication.

Radcliffe, Robert C. *Investments: Concepts, Analysis and Strategy.* Glenview, Ill.: Scott, Foresman, 1987.

Rates of Return on Investments in Common Stock. New York: Merrill Lynch, Pierce, Fenner, and Smith.

Standard & Poor's Stock Guide. New York: Standard & Poor's Corporation. Quarterly publication.

Reilly, Frank K. *Investment Analysis and Portfolio Management.* Chicago: The Dryden Press, 1985.

Understanding Financial Data in The Wall Street Journal. Princeton, N.J.: Dow Jones and Company.

Understanding the New York Stock Exchange. New York: New York Stock Exchange.

Well Beyond the Average: The Story of Dow Jones. Princeton, N.J.: Dow Jones and Company.

What Every Woman Investor Should Know. Washington, D.C.: Investment Bankers Association of America.

APPENDIX 16: SUPPLEMENTARY MATERIAL ON COMMON STOCK

There are a number of other points on common stock with which the investor should be familiar, among them are: what to do if one loses securities, keeping securities in the street name, stock splits, preemptive rights, stock warrants, and the options market for common stock.

What to do if a person loses securities

If a person takes physical possession of securities, they should be kept in a safe place such as a safety deposit box at a bank. Since most securities are registered, they can be replaced, but this is neither easy nor cheap. If securities are lost, notify the transfer agent immediately. If the investor does not know the name of the agent, the broker may know, although sometimes a person may have to write to the company issuing the stock. The transfer agent will want the certificate numbers of the missing shares. Consequently, the investor should have a list of these numbers available.

Upon notification, the transfer agent puts a stop on the stock to prevent its sale. The next step is to get the company to issue new replacement shares. This costs money. Nearly all companies require an indemnity bond as protection against any possible future loss. While the corporation would not suffer a loss if the old securities reappeared and were successfully sold, a brokerage house would, and the bond is used to indemnify them. Generally a bond of 100 percent of the value of the securities is required. The bond can be put up in cash or a bonding company can do it. If a bonding company is used, premiums that generally amount to about 4 percent of the stock's value will have to be paid.

Keeping securities in the street name

To eliminate the possibility of loss, some investors keep their securities in the street name. This merely means that the purchaser does not take physical possession, but rather leaves the securities with the broker, who stores them in a safe. This makes it easier to sell the securities. All that is required is a phone call; the owner need not sign them and deliver them to the broker. This also protects the individual from loss of the securities due to fire, theft, or misplacement. The reason securities held in the street name can be sold by making a phone call is that they are in the broker's name. The securities of hundreds of customers are all lumped together this way. While in theory there is some danger here, they are as safe as money in the bank. The brokers are subject to the regulations of the New York Stock Exchange and the Security and Exchange Commission. They cannot sell these securities without permission, nor may they borrow money on them. The brokers must carry a fidelity bond to cover losses due to fraud and insurance to cover theft.

Security insurance

There is some slight danger if the broker goes bankrupt, but there is protection even here. In 1970, Congress passed, and the president signed, a bill establishing the Securities Investor Protection Corporation (SIPC). It is to security buyers what the Federal Deposit Insurance Corporation (FDIC) is to bank depositors. It protects investors up to $500,000 per account against the loss of securities due to failure of broker-dealers. Many brokers have an additional $500,000 per account with private insurance companies. This does not, of course, protect the investor from losses suffered by corporations that have issued the stock. Rather, it protects investors who keep their securities in the street name and have their broker keep physical possession of them. This protection was a result of the stock market crash in 1970 that caused some broker-dealers to fail.

All broker-dealers engaged in interstate security operations must join the SIPC. They are assessed an annual fee, which varies with the size of their operations. These fees go into a fund used to reimburse security owners who suffer losses when their broker goes into bankruptcy.

Stock gifts to minors: uniform gifts to minors act

Most states have passed the Uniform Gifts to Minors Act, which makes it easier for a person to buy securities for his or her children. The security will be made out to "Jane Doe, Trustee for John Doe, Junior" under the Texas Uniform Gifts to Minors Act, or of whatever state the investor is a resident. The income is taxable only if the minor child has a high enough income to pay taxes. The gift is, and must be by law, irrevocable. However, the trustee can sell the security as long as he or she retains the principal on behalf of the child. The interest (or dividends) too must be retained for the child. The trustee may only manage the securities. No one, not even the child, can touch the fund until the child becomes twenty-one (now eighteen in many states), at which time he or she gains full control.

Many people buy small amounts of high-quality securities for their children and build a portfolio to be used later to finance specific projects such as a college education.

Stock splits and stock dividends

A stock split occurs when a corporation increases the number of shares of stock outstanding by sending additional shares of stock to existing stockholders without demanding additional payment. In so doing, the total net worth of the corporation is unaffected, and yet the book value of each individual share is reduced. Theoretically, the existing stockholders have received nothing that increases their share of the corporate assets. For purposes of illustration, assume a corporation with a net worth of $15,000,000 and one million shares, which would make the book value $15 per share. If the stock is split two for one—meaning that each shareholder is to receive two shares in exchange for each share now held—a shareholder who had one hundred shares before would now have a total of two hundred.[3] But the company, since it received no additional capital, would still have a net worth of $15,000,000. Since now twice as many shares have a claim on it, the book value of each share would drop from $15 to $7.50. If the market value had been $30 per share before the split, theoretically it would fall to $15. Often, however, the market value does not fall quite this much. The point is that the shareholders' positions would not be changed. The question then is, why do corporations split the stock?

The main reason is that lower-priced stock sometimes has a psychological attraction to investors. Then, too, lower-priced stocks are more accessible to more people. When the stock is split, more investors are attracted to the stock, and consequently there may be a tendency for market prices to be forced upward more rapidly from the lower price. Also many people, not knowing that theoretically they are no better off, think that somehow the stockholders have magically got

---

3. The stock must be exchanged because par value is cut in half. If the stock is no-par stock, a two-for-one split could be accomplished without an exchange. The company would simply mail the stockholder one additional share for each share owned.

something for nothing. Because this makes this corporation's stock more attractive to them, they buy it and bid up its price.

From a financial point of view, a stock split and a stock dividend are the same. A two-for-one split or a 100 percent stock dividend would double the number of shares a person had and would cut the book value in half. Theoretically, the market price would be cut in half, too. The two-for-one split discussed above and a 100 percent stock dividend would accomplish the same dilution per share. Generally stock dividends are used when smaller dilution is desired. (Many stock dividends are 10 to 20 percent.) Sometimes, however, stock dividends are used when a corporation cannot or does not want to pay a cash dividend but feels it must declare something to satisfy the stockholders. A stock dividend is not taxable as income. Table A16−1 and Figure A16−1 below show the stock splits and dividends over the past few years.

Preemptive rights

The capital of a firm may be reduced or increased. A capital reduction is rare, and it would necessitate returning to the stockholder part of the stockholder's capital. This could happen in a government antimonopoly action against a company which was then required to divest itself of certain assets.

It is common, however, for a corporation to increase its capital; then the question is, what are the rights of the stockholders under such a situa-

tion? It can readily be seen that the relative strength of an individual stockholder could be affected if the capital of the corporation is increased. Suppose again that there are ten stockholders, each with one share, and the total assets of the corporation consist of $1,000. Thus each of the stockholders may be said to own 10 percent of the corporation and also 10 percent of the voting rights. Suppose further that the corporation desires to issue $1,000 in additional stock so that its total asset will be $2,000. To accomplish this, it sells ten additional shares at $100 each. If an outsider buys all these shares, then his or her interest in the corporation will be 50 percent, and all old stockholders will have their interest reduced from 10 percent per share to 5 percent. Thus the old stockholders will be adversely affected by such a transaction.

To prevent this sort of imposition on the existing stockholders, "preemptive rights" have been developed. Preemptive right is the right of the existing stockholders to purchase a proportionate share in the increase of the capital stock of the corporation. This right does not always exist. In some cases it exists because the corporate charter grants it and in some cases because the state law of the state of incorporation requires it. If neither state law nor corporate charter grants preemptive rights or if they are waived, then the corporation may go to the public or outside investors if it wants to expand its capital. A **stock right,** therefore, is defined as a privilege possessed by a stockholder to purchase a **pro rata share** of a new

Table A16−1   **Stock dividends and splits, 1980-1989**

	Less than 25%	25% to 49%	50% to 99%	2-for-1 to 2½-for-1	3-for-1 to 3½-for-1	4-for-1	Over 4-for-1	Total
1989	28	9	34	66	2	2	1	142
1988	34	11	29	25	4	1	—	104
1987	36	18	59	118	10	1	2	244
1986	43	22	78	118	9	1	1	272
1985	40	17	43	60	6	—	—	166
1984	57	12	50	51	6	1	1	178
1983	54	21	80	131	12	—	2	300
1982	61	21	36	28	—	—	—	146
1981	63	23	67	98	6	2	1	260
1980	65	25	55	98	5	1	—	249

Note: Includes common and preferred issues. Data based on effective dates.

(Source: New York Stock Exchange Fact Book, 1990, p. 41)

Annual number of stock splits*

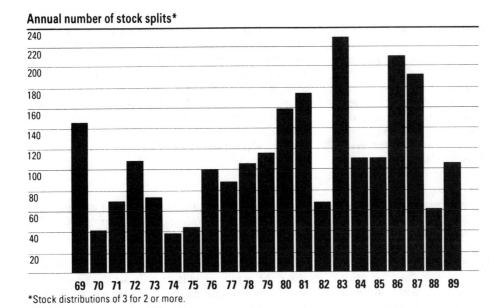

*Stock distributions of 3 for 2 or more.

Annual number of stock splits. (Stock distribution of 3 for 2 or more.) (Source: New York Stock Exchange Fact Book, 1990, p. 41.)   Figure A16—1

stock issue offered by the corporation at a specific price and for a specific time period.

Suppose a corporation desires to raise about $7,500,000. It has outstanding one hundred thousand shares of common stock valued in the market at $100 per share. If it sells one hundred thousand new shares at $75 per share, it will have its $7,500,000. In accordance with preemptive rights it will give all existing stockholders the right to buy one new share for each share they already have. In this case, the company is increasing its capital by 75 percent. I have put the example this way to simplify calculations. Usually a firm will increase its capital by only 10 to 20 percent, and a person in such a case will have the right to buy a new issue for every ten or five shares he or she owns, respectively.

The firm usually sells the new stock at a price below the market price of the outstanding shares in order to expedite the sale. Since there cannot be two prices, when the new issue comes out, the market price of the old will fall and the new will rise; and the price, in the example above, will be approximately $87.50. Mr. X, who before had one share valued at $100, purchased a new one for $75. His total investment is $175 or $87.50 per

share. If Mr. X had ignored his rights, he would now have only one share valued at $87.50. His equity would have been diluted by $12.50. The example also illustrates the value of rights; it is, in this case, $12.50.

If Mr. X could not afford to pay $75 for his new share, he could have sold his rights for $12.50 in cash and prevented a dilution of his equity in this way. That is to say, rights are valuable and if one does not have the money to exercise them, sell them. If one neither exercises nor sells them, they will expire after a time. Usually the company will offer to buy an investor's rights if he or she does not wish to exercise them. Sometimes if a large issue is coming out, an organized market develops in rights and one can both buy and sell them from a broker.

When rights are granted, the person who buys that stock in the market automatically gets the right, until the stock goes "ex-right." This is logically the same as a stock going "ex-dividend." For example, the company issuing the rights announces that stockholders of record on Wednesday, February 1, 1987, will receive the rights. The stock goes "ex-rights" in the market five days before this date because of the five day delivery rule.

When a stock goes "ex-rights" its price in the market generally declines by the amount of the value of the right.

Companies issue rights because it is an easy way to raise capital, and it is also cheaper than to come out with a general public issue. It saves the corporation investment bankers' fees; the stockholders also receive their stock more cheaply because they don't have to pay commissions.

Since persons usually get a right for every ten or twenty shares they already have, there arises the problem of fractional rights. Suppose you had fifteen shares of stock and were given rights to buy one share of new stock for every ten of the old. Obviously you cannot buy 1 1/2 new shares. Usually the company will either buy back fractional rights or offer to sell the investor enough fractions for an even number of shares.

A formula can be used to calculate the value of a right, although ordinary logic and arithmetic are all that is needed in a simple case such as the one discussed above. However, if eight or ten shares of stock are required to obtain the right to buy one new share, the formula may be helpful. It is the market price less the subscription price divided by the number of old shares plus one, which are needed to get one of the new.

Or,

$$\frac{M - S}{N + 1} = V$$

Where

M = market value of old
S = subscription price
N = number of shares needed to buy one of the new
V = value of the right

In the case above we had,

$$M = \$100$$
$$S = 75$$

and hence our formula tells us

$$\frac{\$100 - \$75}{2} = \$12.50$$

A second reason for preemptive rights—not very important in most cases—is to prevent dilution of control. For example, if an investor owned 10 percent of the stock in a given corporation, he or she would have 10 percent of the votes at the stockholders' meetings. If the person were not permitted to continue to buy the same 10 percent of any new issues, his or her relative voting strength would decline. This is not important for most stockholders because they have so few shares that they don't really have any influence at corporate elections. However, for a few large stockholders it might be a factor.

Stock warrants

A warrant is a certificate evidencing an option to purchase new securities, usually common stock, at a stated price for a stated time period. Sometimes, however, the time period is for perpetuity. The distinction between the right and the warrant is that the right is generally issued under the preemptive right privilege to existing stockholders, while a warrant may be issued aside from the preemptive rights to nonstockholders. Warrants are originally attached to other securities when they are issued and generally are attached to either bonds or preferred stock. Some warrants are not detachable, and hence they cannot be sold separately; but others are detachable, and a market exists for them.

When a corporation feels that it may have difficulty in selling a particular preferred stock or bond issue, it may offer warrants along with each security that will enable the purchaser to buy additional shares of common stock. These warrants, called "purchase warrants," are generally extended for relatively long periods of time or even perpetually. Thus the preemptive stock rights are different from warrants. The rights have a relatively short life (days or weeks). When a corporation attaches warrants to bonds or preferred stocks, it is able to sell them more easily. Since warrants permit the holder to purchase common stock at a predetermined price, they are a speculative device. They make the mother security more attractive, a fact best illustrated with an example.

Suppose the Adjax Corporation issues 9 percent bonds maturing in twenty years with detachable warrants on the bonds. Anyone who buys a bond also gets a warrant. The warrant permits the owner to purchase one share of common stock at, say, $30 per share at any time during the next three years. The common stock is presently selling for $20 per share, however, and hence the warrant has speculative value only. If it is detachable, it may sell for a dollar or $.50 or even less. But the $30 and the three-year period are fixed. If the common stock of the Adjax Corporation rises to, say, $40 before the three years have elapsed, the warrant will be worth $10; its price will have moved from $1 to $10. This is a tremendous percentage increase, but it is in the nature of warrants. They have great leverage. Once the stock rises above the warrant price, warrants have positive value and will appreciate by some multiple of the further appreciation of the common stock. Warrants also move downward with common stock but by greater magnitudes.

If you buy bonds with warrants attached, the warrant may have value in the future. If it does not, you simply remain a bond investor. Corporations attach warrants to bonds (or preferred stock) as "sweeteners"; it may reduce the interest that they have to pay. While not many corporations have issued warrants in recent years, there are still many detached ones outstanding, and they are traded almost daily. Don't take the plunge into warrants, because they are highly speculative, and are only for the brave and those who can assume great risk.

What to do with rights and warrants

Many investors have no idea what to do with either rights or warrants, some of which are destroyed physically and many of which are permitted to lapse. Three choices are open to the investor. One is to permit them to lapse; many people do just this. Another alternative is to exercise the right and the warrant if and when it has value; however, it may be that investors holding the warrants or rights are unable to do this because they lack available cash or are unwilling to because they lack any further interest in the particular stocks issued. The third alternative is to sell the rights, and the warrant if it is detachable, which can be done through any broker.

The options markets: Puts and calls

Although there are a number of other stock options[4] the major ones are puts and calls, both of which are speculative devices.

Calls

A call option is a contractual and legal privilege for buying a given number (usually one hundred) of shares of a given common stock for a given period of time at a price determined at the time the call is purchased. For example, if you buy, say for $200, a thirty-day call on United States Steel (now USX) at $25 this means that at any time during the next thirty days the seller is required to sell you one hundred shares of U.S. Steel for $25 per share if you request it. If U.S. Steel rises to $45 during this period, your $200 will have grown to $2,000. Your net return is $1,800 ($2,000 minus the $200 option price). This again is a tremendous percentage return on your money. If U.S. Steel does not move, on the other hand, you have lost $200. Options permit one to speculate in one-hundred-lot shares with only a relatively few dollars; they also hold out the possibility of a high rate of return on one's money; and the maximum amount that can be lost is the price of the option.

Puts

A put option is exactly the reverse of a call option. It is the privilege of selling 100 shares of a given stock for a given period of time at a price determined at the time the put is purchased. A person buying a put is speculating that the market price of that stock is going down.

Options may run up to nine months before they expire. A market in options is now being made on the Chicago Board of Options Exchange, the American Stock Exchange, the Philadelphia

---

4. The various stock options one can buy in the options market should not be confused with the stock-option plans many corporations make available to their key employees. In the case of corporate stock option plans, certain key executives are granted the privilege (option) of buying a certain number of shares of common stock from the corporation, usually at the market price of the stock at the time the option is granted. The option price is then, however, frozen for the executives for a period of time, usually several years or more. Then if the market price rises substantially, the option holders can execute and make a nice gain. The main justification for providing key executives stock options is to give them a vested interest in the corporation and hence a greater incentive to perform well.

Table A16—2 *Portion of the options listed on the Chicago Board of Options Exchange*

CHICAGO BOARD

Option & Strike NY Close	Price	Calls—Last Jun	Jul	Aug	Puts—Last Jun	Jul	Aug
Amdahl	40	7 7/8	r	10 7/8	r	r	r
49 1/2	45	4 1/4	r	8	5/16	3/4	2
49 1/2	50	15/16	2 1/4	3 7/8	1 1/2	2 1/2	r
A E P	30	r	r	1/4	r	r	r
AlnGrp	55	r	r	3 1/2	r	r	1 1/2
56 7/8	60	r	r	1 1/8	r	r	r
Amoco	70	6 1/8	r	r	r	r	r
75 3/4	75	r	r	r	r	r	2 1/8
75 3/4	80	r	r	l	r	r	r
75 3/4	85	r	s	1/4	r	s	r
A M P	50	r	r	1 1/2	r	r	4 1/8
Baxter	17 1/2	r	r	r	r	r	1/8
22	20	2	2 1/4	2 3/8	1/16	r	1/2
22	22 1/2	1/4	5/8	1	r	r	1 1/2
22	25	r	s	5/16	r	s	r
22	30	s	s	1/16	s	s	r
Blk Dk	20	r	2 1/4	r	r	r	r
22 1/4	22 1/2	7/16	1	1 3/8	r	1 1/4	r
22 1/4	25	s	r	3/8	s	r	r
Boeing	40	r	s	r	r	s	1/8
55 5/8	45	10 3/8	r	10 1/2	r	r	3/16
55 5/8	50	5 5/8	5 1/2	6 3/4	r	r	5/8
55 5/8	55	1 1/4	2 1/4	2 3/4	5/8	1 3/8	1 7/8
55 5/8	60	1/16	1/2	13/16	r	r	5
Bois C	35	s	s	9	s	s	r
44	40	r	r	4 1/2	r	r	r
44	45	r	r	1 3/4	r	r	r
44	50	r	s	5/8	r	s	r
Bois o	45 1/8	s	s	1 1/2	s	s	r
C B S	150	r	r	13	r	r	r
159	155	5	7 1/4	r	7/8	2 1/2	r
159	160	1 5/8	s	r	2 1/2	s	r
159	165	5/8	r	4 1/4	r	r	r
159	175	s	s	1 3/4	s	r	r
CapCit	300	9 7/8	r	r	r	r	6 3/4
309	310	r	r	r	r	r	9 1/2
309	320	7/8	r	r	r	r	r
309	330	3/4	s	r	22 1/8	r	r
309	340	1/4	s	r	r	r	r
309	350	r	s	1 1/2	r	s	r
Coke	35	2 7/8	r	3 3/4	r	r	1/2
38 1/2	40	1/8	3/8	1	1 7/8	r	r
38 1/2	45	r	r	1/8	r	s	r
Colgat	40	r	r	r	r	r	1/2
44 5/8	45	5/8	1 1/4	1 7/8	r	r	r
44 5/8	50	s	r	9/16	s	r	r
Cmw Ed	22 1/2	r	r	r	r	r	3/8
25 1/4	25	r	3/4	3/4	1/2	1	1 1/4
25 1/4	30	r	r	1/16	r	r	r
C Data	25	1 3/4	2 1/4	2 3/4	r	r	1 5/16
26 3/8	30	1/16	7/16	13/16	r	r	r
26 3/8	35	s	s	1/8	s	s	r
CornGl	45	r	r	9 3/8	r	r	5/16

CHICAGO BOARD

Option & Strike NY Close	Price	Calls—Last			Puts—Last		
		Jun	Jul	Sep	Jun	Jul	Sep
28 7/8	35	r	s	1/4	6 1/2	s	r
Whirlp	22 1/2	r	r	4 3/4	r	r	r
26 7/8	25	2	r	r	r	r	r
26 7/8	30	r	r	5/8	r	r	r
YellFr	30	r	7/8	r	r	r	r
		Jun	Jul	Oct	Jun	Jul	Oct
Alcoa	40	r	r	9 1/2	r	r	r
49 1/8	45	3 3/4	5	r	r	5/8	1 1/2
49 1/8	50	5/8	1 1/2	3 1/4	1 1/2	2 1/8	r
AT&T	25	2	2 1/8	2 3/4	1/16	1/4	3/4
26 7/8	30	r	3/16	5/8	r	3 1/4	3 1/4
26 7/8	35	s	1/16	r	s	r	r
Amrtch	85	r	7	r	r	3/8	1 3/8
91 7/8	90	r	3 1/4	r	r	r	r
91 7/8	95	r	3/4	r	r	r	r
91 7/8	100	s	r	1	s	r	r
Atl R	75	s	10 1/2	r	s	r	r
85	85	r	2 5/8	4 1/4	r	2 1/8	r
85	90	r	r	2 1/8	r	5 3/8	6 3/4
85	95	r	r	1 1/8	r	r	r
Avon	20	2 5/8	3 3/8	4	1/8	1/2	1 1/16
23 3/8	22 1/2	1 5/16	1 3/4	2	1/2	1 1/8	2 1/8
23 3/8	25	3/8	13/16	1 1/2	2 5/8	3 1/8	4 1/4
23 3/8	30	1/16	3/16	9/16	7 7/8	7 5/8	r
BankAm	7 1/2	r	3 3/8	r	r	1/16	r
11 1/8	10	1	1 3/4	1 11/16	r	1/4	7/16
11 1/8	12 1/2	1/16	1/4	3/4	r	1 7/8	2 1/8
BattlM	15	3 3/4	3 7/8	4 3/8	r	1/16	7/16
18 7/8	17 1/2	1 5/16	1 7/8	2 3/4	1/8	r	1 1/8
18 7/8	20	s	5/8	1 9/16	s	1 3/4	2 1/2
18 7/8	22 1/2	s	3/16	s	s	r	s
18 7/8	25	s	1/16	s	s	r	s
BearSt	10	r	r	r	r	r	1/2
12 5/8	12 1/2	1/2	5/8	1 3/8	r	r	r
12 5/8	15	r	3/16	7/16	r	2 3/4	r
BellAtl	65	r	r	r	r	r	1
71	70	r	2	r	7/16	r	2 3/4
71	75	s	r	1 1/2	s	r	r
Beth S	17 1/2	r	r	3 5/8	r	1/8	7/8
19 5/8	20	3/8	13/16	2	3/4	1	1 3/4
19 5/8	22 1/2	1/16	1/4	13/16	r	r	r
Burl N	60	10 1/4	10	12	r	3/8	r
69 7/8	65	4 7/8	r	7 7/8	1/4	r	r
69 7/8	70	1 1/4	2 7/8	5 1/8	1 5/8	2 3/4	r
69 7/8	75	1/8	1	3 1/2	r	r	r
C N W	22 1/2	r	3 1/8	r	r	r	r
25	25	5/8	r	r	r	r	r
ChrisC	20	s	1 7/8	r	s	s	s
ChrisC	22 1/2	r	3/4	1 7/8	r	r	r
Chryslr	17 1/2	4 1/2	4 3/8	r	r	r	r
22 1/4	20	2 5/16	2 1/2	3 1/8	1/16	1/4	7/8
22 1/4	22 1/2	3/8	7/8	1 7/8	3/4	1 3/16	2 1/16
22 1/4	25	r	1/4	1	3	3 1/8	3 7/8

Source: The Wall Street Journal, June 7, 1988, p. 54.

Stock Exchange, and the Pacific Stock Exchange. The Chicago exchange is by far the largest. It is to the options market what the New York Stock Exchange is to the stock market.

If you wish to buy (or sell) an option, your broker can make the arrangement through one of the organized options markets mentioned above. There are brokerage commissions for this that are similar to (but generally a little lower than) the stock commissions discussed above.

Table A16–2 shows some options listed on the Chicago Board of Options Exchange. An entry might appear as follows:

Option and N.Y. close	Strike price	Calls—last			Puts—last		
		Jun	Jul	Aug	Jun	Jul	Aug
IBM 114 1/8	120	1/4	1 1/4	4	5 3/4	6 7/8	8 3/4

It identifies first the corporation (IBM) on which there is an option and below it the price (114 1/8) at which IBM stock closed on the New York Stock Exchange that day. Moving to the right we see the strike price at which the shares may be purchased by the option owner. Next comes the "Jun, Jul, and Aug Calls—last", which means it is a call option and the price of the last trade is quoted just below the months shown. The months refer to when the options on IBM will expire; buyers have some choice as to how long they want their option to run. The prices 1/4, 1 1/4, and 4) are the prices per share of the last option traded for each of the three expiration dates and are called the premium. However, since options are always for 100 shares, the prices are really $25., $125., and $400. respectively. The options will expire on the third Saturday of the month shown (options always expire on the third Saturday of the month shown).[5] If an investor wants a call option for 100 shares that runs to the third Saturday of August, it will cost $400, but will permit one to buy 100 shares of IBM at $120 per share even though its current price

was 114 1/8 that day. Obviously, the buyers of this option believe the price of IBM will rise.

The next three quotations convey the same information on puts. The first quotation is for June and it is 5 3/4. This means the premium is $5.75 per share. This translates into $575. for 100 shares. The quotations also show that for $687.50 the buyer of that option has the right to sell 100 shares of IBM at $120. per share until the third Saturday (Friday) of July. Obviously, the buyers of such as option believe that the price of IBM will decline. If you examine option quotations in *The Wall Street Journal,* you will note that sometimes an "r" or an "s" appears. An "r" means that no option for that stock was traded that day; an "s" means no option going out that far exists.

Straddles and combinations

There are also options involving straddles and combinations. A "straddle" consists of both a put and a call option on the same stock, with the same strike price, and the same expiration date. A "combination" is the same as a straddle except that the put and the call have a different strike price, expiration date, or both. Straddles and combinations can become complex. However, if the investor operates in this market and the stock does not move in either direction, he or she will have earned a double premium if they are sold rather than bought.

Writing options

Instead of thinking about buying options, sophisticated investors are thinking in terms of selling them (called "writing options"). There are two ways of writing call options: covered and uncovered. If an investor writes a covered call option, this means he or she already has the stock; and uncovered call is on a stock the individual does not own and is a little riskier. Many financial advisers feel that writing covered options is a good strategy for

---

5. Since the market is closed on Saturday, the options really expire on the third Friday of the month, but this is a technicality. The option will state that it will expire on the first Saturday after the third Friday of the month in question.

conservative investors because it can increase their yield, as we shall see below.

Many option writers adhere to the following two rules of thumb. Never write a call on a stock not already owned (write only covered options). Write calls only on stock a person is thinking about selling anyway—or at least would not mind selling if the price went much higher, that is, on a stock that has risen about as much as he or she thinks it will and on which one is willing to take a capital gain or on a stock that has not done well and one is ready to sell for that reason. Some option writers, however, select what they think will be a good income stock and one that does not fluctuate much in price and then sell options on it. It is not unusual for option writers to double their yield on a stock by writing options. For example, if a person owns a stock providing a 9 percent dividend yield, writing several options per year on it could very well yield an additional 9 percent or even more. There are three ways in which an investor can benefit from owning a stock. There is, first, the dividend; second, possible capital appreciation (there is also the possibility of capital losses); and third, option income. All three should be netted to obtain the true economic improvement.

SUMMARY REVIEW QUESTIONS

These questions serve as a summary and a review of the appendix. If you are able to answer them all, you have a good understanding of the material covered by the appendix.

1. What should a person do if securities are lost?
2. What is meant by keeping securities in the street name? What are its advantages and disadvantages?

3. How does a stock split differ from a stock dividend?
4. What are preemptive rights? Discuss the differences between these rights and warrants.
5. Explain stock warrants.
6. Why do corporations use warrants?
7. What are puts and calls?
8. Would you recommend buying options or selling (calling "writing") them?

CASES

1. Alfred and Helen Walker own two different common stocks. They own one hundred shares of ABC corporation and one hundred shares of XYZ. Their ABC stock was recently split three for one, and before the split it was selling on the New York Stock Exchange for $120 per share. What, in theory, is the price now? Why may the price not fall that much? How many shares do they now own?

The Walkers' XYZ stock was selling for $140 per share on the American Stock Exchange when they received a 100 percent stock dividend. How many shares do they now own? What is the theoretical price of the XYZ stock? How big a stock dividend would they have had to receive to have the same number of shares of XYZ stock as they have of ABC? What is the difference between a stock split and a stock dividend?

2. George Kennedy owns fifty shares of common stock and the corporation has informed him he has preemptive rights on a new issue coming out. At present there are one million shares outstanding, and the new issue will consist of one hundred thousand shares. How many new shares can George buy? Why? What is the idea behind preemptive

rights? The market price of George's stock is $80 and the new issue is coming out at $75. If George decides to sell his preemptive rights rather than exercise them, what will he get for them?

3. Five years ago Bernice Edwards received 100 warrants attached to some convertible bonds she bought. These warrants entitled her to buy common stock on the same corporation at $15 per share. However, the common was selling in the market at the time for $5 per share. Yesterday, Bernice checked and found that the common is now selling at $35 per share. What are her warrants worth?

4. Bill and Betty Pasmack recently moved across country to Seattle, Washington, where Bill took a new job. After moving into their new home and unpacking, they couldn't find their securities. Betty said that since they were registered they had nothing to worry about; they would simply report it to the company and have new ones issued. Bill, however, is not sure that it is all as simple as that. Can you explain what they must do to have new securities issued? What if they do not have the serial number of their securities? What can people do to prevent or minimize the likelihood of losing securities?

5. Lisa Bolinger owns 600 shares of IBM stock. Recently she received a three-for-two stock split.
   (a) How many stocks does Lisa now own?
   (b) Is the market price per share likely to rise or decline?
   (c) If the market price was $150 per share prior to the split, what is the approximate market price after the split?
   (d) How large a stock dividend would Lisa have to receive to end up with the same number of shares?

SUGGESTED READINGS

The ABC's of Option Trading. Princeton, N.J.: Dow Jones and Company.

Barron's Weekly. A weekly financial newspaper published by Dow Jones and Company.

"Characteristics and Risks of Standardized Options." Chicago: The Options Clearing Corporation.

Fischer, Donald, and Jordan, Ronald. *Security Analysis and Portfolio Management,* 4th ed. Englewood Cliffs, N.J.: Prentice-Hall, 1987.

"How Security Investor Protection Corporation Protects You." Washington, D.C.: Security Investor Protection Corporation (SPIC).

"Interest Rate Options." Dean Witter Reynolds. You may obtain this from your Dean Witter broker.

"The Merrill Lynch Guide to Writing Options." New York: Merrill Lynch, Pierce, Fenner, and Smith.

"The Versatile Option." Chicago: The Chicago Options Exchange.

Understanding Options. Chicago: The Chicago Options Exchange.

The Wall Street Journal. A financial newspaper published daily by Dow Jones & Company.

"What Every Investor Should Know." Washington, D.C.: The Securities and Exchange Commission.

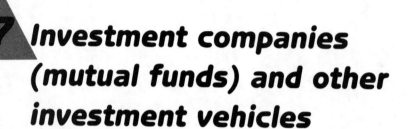

17 Investment companies (mutual funds) and other investment vehicles

HIGHLIGHTS   In order to provide the reader with an understanding of investment companies, real estate, and certain other investment vehicles and how they work, this chapter examines the following:

1   The two major types of investment companies
2   The various objectives of investment companies
3   The advantages and disadvantages of investment companies
4   Where you can obtain information on investment companies
5   The highly specialized and technical commodities market
6   The futures market in securities
7   A number of different possible real estate investments
8   A special investment company: real estate investment trusts
9   Investments in collectibles

INTRODUCTION

Some people would like to invest in corporate stocks but do not care to buy them directly, either because they feel stocks are too risky or because they lack the time needed to review their portfolio frequently—and portfolio review is required. If a client is in this category, he or she may wish to investigate investment companies, also sometimes called "mutual funds." An investment company is a financial intermediary (or financial institution) that collects, usually in small dollar amounts, the savings of many individuals. It then invests these funds in the securities of other corporations. The savings of many small savers are pooled to become one large fund to be managed collectively for the benefit of all of the participants. An investment company, therefore, is a specialized one-layer financial holding company. The persons who buy the securities of these investment companies are said to be investing indirectly. They own part of the investment company, and the investment company owns the securities of other companies. The securities the investment company owns, on behalf of its owners, are referred to as the underlying securities, and it is the value of the underlyings that gives value to the shares of the investment companies. The relationship of the investment company, its owners, and the underlying securities is shown in Figure 17–1.

CLASSIFICATION OF INVESTMENT COMPANIES, AND NET ASSET VALUE

As noted above, certain types of investment companies are also called mutual funds. The terms **mutual funds, investment company,** and **investment trust** are used to designate a variety of financial institutions that provide investors with the opportunity of investing indirectly in various corporations. In reality, however, only the open-end investment company (the open-end as opposed to the closed-end company will be explained below) is referred to as a mutual fund by the financial community. Generally, investment companies invest most funds they receive in common stock, but some companies buy substantial amounts of bonds and preferred stock. Any profits are shared among the shareholders of the mutual fund.

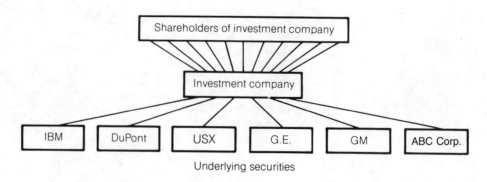

Figure 17–1   *Investment company relationships*

Investment companies can be classified as open-end and closed-end, and further classified according to their investment policies and objectives.

Closed-end investment companies have a relatively fixed amount of capital. To issue securities they need permission from the Securities and Exchange Commission (SEC), just like any corporation. They then have an authorized common stock issue, and when that is sold, they can sell no more unless another issue is approved. Once that issue is sold, therefore, an investor can no longer purchase it directly from the company but only from a broker in the open market. Moreover, closed-end investment companies do not stand ready to redeem their securities as do open-end companies. Some shares of closed-end companies are listed on the stock exchanges; some are sold over the counter. When buying and selling them, one pays the brokerage fees described in Chapter 16. The price of closed-end shares is, therefore, determined not only by the price of the underlying securities, but by all the psychological factors that affect the supply and demand of closed-end shares in the market. There have been times when the market price of closed-end shares has been below the market price of the underlying securities. This is referred to as selling at a discount. In other years some closed-end shares have been at a premium or above the value of their underlying securities.

Closed-end investment companies sometimes also acquire capital by selling bonds to the public, a practice that introduces the element of leverage into their capital structure. (See Chapter 15.) Building a lot of leverage into a firm's capital structure can in some cases result in a sudden and rapid increase in earnings and hence in the price of the common stock, and the reverse can also happen. Closed-end investment companies have various amounts of leverage built into their capital structure, the amount varying from time to time, depending on their management's appraisal of what the future holds in store.

Closed-end investment companies

There is no legally set limit to the number of shares an open-end investment company (mutual fund) may sell. The number of shares is limited only by what investors will buy. Such a company issues its shares continuously as it sells them; it is called open-end because its capitalization is not fixed.

Open-end funds also stand ready to buy back their shares from investors at any time at a price determined by the price of the underlying securities. Their price is calculated daily by dividing the total number of shares outstanding into the market values of the portfolio of the underlying securities.

Since open-end funds raise no capital by selling bonds, their entire capital is equity capital. No leverage is built into capital structure, although it might be in their underlying securities. Many open-end compa-

Open-end investment companies (mutual funds)

nies charge what is known as a loading fee when they sell their shares. These fees vary substantially from fund to fund, and some are paid when the funds are purchased and some when redeemed. Some charge both and some do not charge any loading fees at all. Loading fees are discussed in greater detail below.

It should be noted that open-end companies are much more popular than closed-end companies. Figure 17–2 shows the growth of both closed-end and open-end companies over the years.

Net asset value

The term ***net asset value*** is used to indicate the price of mutual funds. It is calculated as follows: First, the market value of all the underlying securities in the fund's portfolio are added up. Then the liabilities are totaled and subtracted from the aggregate assets. Third, the result is divided by the number of mutual fund shares outstanding. This is done daily on a computer; mutual fund shares fluctuate daily with fluctuations in the price of their underlyings. Since the price of mutual fund shares is determined directly by the price of the underlying securities, they are never sold at a premium or discount as may be the case when closed-end company shares are involved. Moreover, the funds stand ready to buy back (redeem) their shares at the net asset value whereas closed-end companies do not.

OBJECTIVES OF INVESTMENT COMPANIES

The buyer of investment company shares faces the same problem as does the direct buyer of common stock: which one to buy? There are hundreds of investment companies. Moreover, their records are not the same, and their objectives are not the same. Even among those with the same objectives, records vary. When an individual buys investment company (mutual funds) shares, he or she must first of all examine the ones with the same objectives as he or she has, and then choose what appears to be the best fund within that group.

All mutual funds state their objectives—for example, growth or income. These objectives are spelled out in the fund's prospectus. A prospectus is a document that all funds are required to make available to investors by the Securities and Exchange Commission (SEC). The SEC is a government agency that regulates the securities industry. The prospectus discloses certain information, as required by the SEC, and is useful in evaluating whether a given fund is appropriate for a given investor. To be sure, some funds may have several objectives. Nevertheless, funds may be classified as follows:

1. Growth funds
2. Income funds
3. Growth and income funds
4. Balanced funds
5. Tax-exempt funds

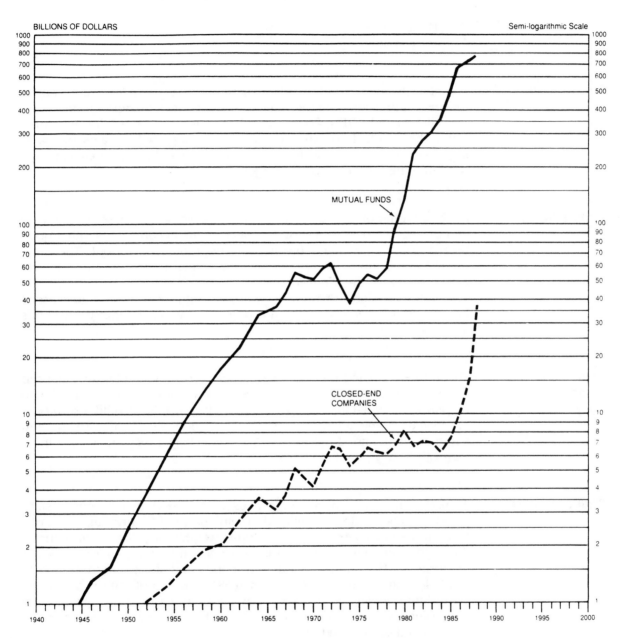

BILLIONS OF DOLLARS

Semi-logarithmic Scale

MUTUAL FUNDS

CLOSED-END
COMPANIES

Growth of investment companies. (Source: Investment Companies, 1989, Wiesenber-   Figure 17—2
ger Financial Services, a division of Warren, Gorham & Lamont, Inc., p. 12.)

6.   Money market funds
7.   Other funds

Growth funds

The objective of a growth fund's managers is to achieve long-term growth (or price appreciation) in the value of the securities in their portfolio. Certain growth industries would be selected for their portfolio and firms within those industries with a proven record of growth in sales and earnings and firms that typically plow a high percentage of their earnings back into the business are the target.

Income funds

Funds with the objective of earning income would purchase more bonds and blue-chip stocks. They would select stocks in companies with a good record of earnings and a history of a high dividend payout. There are many income funds, and they generally appeal to investors needing income, such as retired individuals.

You may wish to review growth stock and income stock (discussed in Chapter 15) because those are precisely the stocks that these funds would seek.

Growth and income funds

Those funds striving for both income and growth could be the balanced funds mentioned below or widely diversified common stock funds with an emphasis on blue-chip stocks. These funds' portfolios would also probably include some utilities, which have a good record of earnings and some of them a good record of growth, epecially if they are located in an area with heavy population growth.

Balanced funds

A fund that has balanced objectives is one that usually emphasizes growth, income, and stability or maintenance of principal. However, these three objectives are given various weights or priorities at different times. The fund has bonds, common stock, and often preferred stock in its portfolio. The relative amounts of bonds and stock vary from time to time, depending on the fund's managers' appraisal of future conditions. If the future looks gloomy, they may take a more defensive position by increasing the proportion of bonds. These balanced funds are also sometimes called diversified funds.

Tax-exempt funds

In recent years mutual funds have been established that buy only state and local bonds on which the interest is exempt from personal income tax. These appeal to investors in a high tax bracket.

In many cases, the minimum amount of state and local bonds that may be purchased directly is $5,000. Owning them indirectly through a fund makes it possible to own them in lesser amounts.

In the 1970s a number of money market funds were developed when interest rates, especially the rate for short-term notes, were very high. Money market funds specialize in buying very short-term securities in the money market. Such things as Treasury bills, commercial paper, and bankers' acceptances are selected. These are highly technical areas, and few individuals are able to buy these securities directly; it takes thousands of dollars to buy commercial paper, for example. These funds always become popular when short-term rates are high; later when rates come down, moneys are withdrawn. Money market funds feature stability of principal due to the nature of underlying securities.

Money market funds

Money market funds were developed to enable the small investor to get into this high interest area. Most of them were established and are managed by the various brokerage houses. Generally, they do not charge a commission when the small investor buys or sells. Rather they take a fraction "off the top." For example, if they earn, say, 8 percent interest, they will keep about .4 or .5 percent, leaving 7.6 for the investor. The interest on these funds fluctuates daily. Until recently thrift institutions and banks could not compete with these funds when interest rates were high, because the maximum interest they could pay was set by federal law. Today, with interest rate ceilings eliminated, the thrifts can and do compete. Indeed the thrifts have an advantage; their accounts are insured up to $100,000, whereas money market funds are not. However, money market funds still tend to pay a higher rate of interest than thrift accounts.

Some funds purchase mortgage-backed securities, such as those issued by the Government National Mortgage Association (GNMA). These are the so-called "Ginnie Mae's" and have become quite popular. These government agencies invest in residential mortgages. They are, however, very safe because the bonds are guaranteed by the U.S. government. They also often yield a bit more than most other bonds of equal risk. They appeal to the more conservative investor, who prefers income to capital appreciation. Other mortgage-backed securities are issued by the Federal National Mortgage Association (FNMA or "Fannie Mae") or the Federal Home Loan Mortgage Corporation (FHLMC or "Freddie Mac"). These securities are considered very safe but are not directly guaranteed by the U.S. government.

Mortgage-backed securities funds

There are a number of other funds. One of these is the **specialty** or **sector fund,** which invests only in a single industry, say, electronics. Needless to say, a sector fund may also be a growth or income fund. Figure 17–3 shows some of the mutual funds classified by objectives.

Other funds

At one time the so-called hedge funds were popular, but recently they have fallen from favor. They would take a very aggressive position

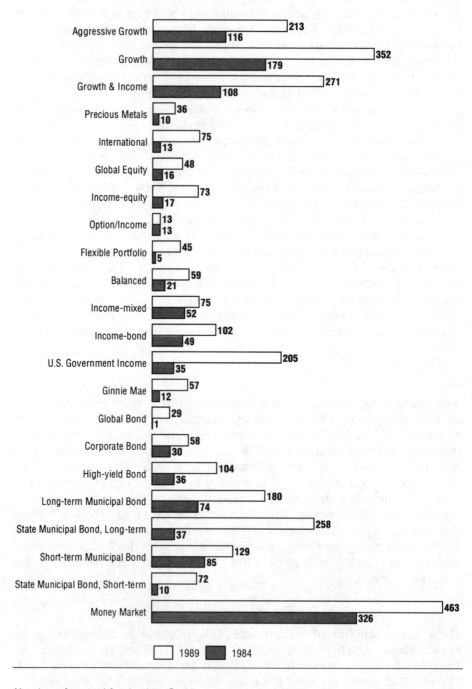

**Number of Mutual Funds
Classified by Investment Objective**

	1989	1984
Aggressive Growth	213	116
Growth	352	179
Growth & Income	271	108
Precious Metals	36	10
International	75	13
Global Equity	48	16
Income-equity	73	17
Option/Income	13	13
Flexible Portfolio	45	5
Balanced	59	21
Income-mixed	75	52
Income-bond	102	49
U.S. Government Income	205	35
Ginnie Mae	57	12
Global Bond	29	1
Corporate Bond	58	30
High-yield Bond	104	36
Long-term Municipal Bond	180	74
State Municipal Bond, Long-term	258	37
Short-term Municipal Bond	129	85
State Municipal Bond, Short-term	72	10
Money Market	463	326

Figure 17–3   *Number of mutual funds classified by investment objective.* (Source: 1990 Mutual Fund Fact Book, *Investment Company Institute, Washington, D.C., p. 29.*)

because their goal was short-term capital gains. They were highly leveraged and often purchased securities on margin.

There are also index funds, which invest only in securities that are included in the Standard and Poor's 500 industrial index or which attempt to duplicate index performance. This will ensure that they do as well as the market but no better. If a fund is willing to settle for performance equal only to the market averages, one may wonder about its "professional" management. Any investor can easily do this, if he or she has enough capital. Some funds invest only in bonds and preferred stock. These appeal to the more conservative investor.

The real estate investment trust (REIT) is another special fund that was very popular a few years ago. Technically, the real estate investment company is a trust. Nevertheless, the result is the same as that of an investment company; a number of individuals provide the capital, which is then invested in real estate. The real estate company is subjected to certain legal restrictions to prevent speculation in land. Real estate investments in general are discussed below, as well as the real estate investment company.

Finally, there is the small business investment company (SBIC) very much like the investment companies described above except that, as the name implies, it invests solely in small business. These companies have received favorable tax treatment by Congress to encourage the flow of equity capital to small firms. These investment companies work closely with the Small Business Administration, which has some federal funds available to small business.

Many mutual funds, especially the larger and more well-established ones, are set up in what are referred to as "groups" or "family of funds." One management team will handle a growth fund or income fund and perhaps several more. This amounts to several funds with different investment objectives being brought under the same roof. This union broadens the appeal of the group and, for individual investors, provides greater flexibility since they can switch from one fund to another within the group, as their investment objectives change. Making such a change may require paying a small transfer fee.

Grouping of funds

The investor should know about the advantages and disadvantages of investing in investment companies. It will also be necessary to learn where information on investment companies can be obtained to help select what will be the better ones or, more specifically, the ones most appropriate for the needs of the client. Finally, the individual should be aware of the cost of buying mutual shares. These are primarily commissions for the salespersons and are called **loading fees.** They are not uniform, and there are some no-load funds, which will be discussed below.

OTHER THINGS YOU SHOULD KNOW ABOUT INVESTMENT COMPANIES

Advantages and disadvantages of mutual funds

Three advantages may accrue to the buyer of mutual funds, as opposed to the purchase of common stock directly, especially to a small investor. They are diversification, professional management, and constant surveillance. A disadvantage of some funds is the high acquisition cost. In addition, funds charge management fees, and sometimes 12b-1 fees, which cover promotional expenses.

Diversification

The small investor, to be sure, finds it more difficult to diversify than the large investor. Diversification, as noted before, consists of investing in a number of different industries or types of investments. Small investors with only a few thousand dollars cannot buy common stock of many different industries. They either have to assume the higher risk of "putting all of their eggs in one basket," or at most a few baskets, or have to reduce the risk (and possibly the return) by investing conservatively. Mutual funds make a real contribution in aiding small investors to diversify.

Professional management

The management qualities of mutual funds vary greatly. If an investor selects a good mutual fund, the added fees paid for management are probably well worth it. On the other hand, the person might get management that is professional only in the sense that they charge a fee.

Constant surveillance

This is probably a plus. Many small investors make excellent choices regarding the common stock they buy, but then forget about them. A given stock that is a good buy today may not be so six months or a year from now. Not only should an investor try to buy good stocks at the right time, but he or she should sell them at the right time, or at least before it is too late. Small investors may not have the time (even if they have the ability) constantly to watch and analyze their portfolio.

Cost

A potential disadvantage of investing in some mutual funds is the acquisition cost. These loading fees, as they are called, vary from fund to fund, and there are some no-load funds (examined below). In addition to the loading fees that may be necessary to acquire mutual funds, management charges fees to manage the funds, generally financed out of the income that the underlying securities provide. Nevertheless, it is another cost that comes out of income the mutual fundholder otherwise would receive. However, the load may be worthwhile if the fund performs well. Although the load should be a factor in evaluating funds, it should not be the only consideration.

Management costs are a fraction of 1 percent or more of the total assets in the fund. Often this is .5 or .6 percent of the first $500,000 in the fund and is then scaled down in several steps as the size of the fund increases. It should be noted however that these managment fees are assessed annually for as long as the investor owns the shares. The acquisition cost (load) is shown in the mutual fund quotation on the financial pages of newspapers like *The Wall Street Journal.* It is the difference between the net asset value (NAV) and the offer price. It goes to the broker or other middleman from whom the investor buys the funds. Mutual fund shares are redeemable at the option of the holder and often without a redemption fee.

Some mutual funds will scale the loading fees down in a series of steps on large purchases. However, the first reduction does not usually apply until the amount purchased is about $10,000 or $15,000, depending on the fund.

Hidden costs

In recent years some mutual funds have imposed two additional hidden costs. There is, first, the so-called 12b-1 fee to cover the fund's advertising, mailing, and printing costs.[1] It can be assessed every year; it is over and above the management fees, and it can go as high as 1.25 percent of net asset value. Second, a low-load reinvestment fee has been added by a few funds. It may be as high as 3 to 4 percent of the dividends and capital gains that the fund reinvests on the client's behalf. It too can be an annual fee. The investor should investigate these hidden fees before selecting a fund. Even some of the no-load funds (discussed below) have these hidden fees.

No-load funds

A number of open-end investment companies (mutual funds) sell their shares directly to the public at the asset value and do not have a loading charge. These companies, however, do not solicit business as actively; if an individual wants to buy their shares, he or she has to take the initiative. They do not have brokers actively selling their shares; hence there are no commissions and no loading fees. Investors have a growing interest in these funds.

Because they have no sales staff, it is a little more difficult for the potential investor to obtain pertinent information on no-load funds. However, a person can write the company and get their literature and prospectuses. In addition, many of these companies have toll-free phone numbers for potential investors. Also, there is the Mutual Fund Education Alliance (MFEA) located at 1900 Erie, Suite 120, Kansas City, Mo. 64116 (telephone 816—471—1454), which is a new and additional source of information.[2]

If one writes the MFEA, they will send a list of their members. This will include the size of each of the funds, when it was organized, its investment objectives, and its address. Individuals can then select those

---

1. The term 12b-1 refers to the section of the Investment Company Act that allows this fee.

2. This alliance's members are virtually all "NO LOAD" funds, although there are a few "LOW LOAD" members. The alliance defines a low load fund as one which charges 3.5 per cent or less.

that have the same investment objectives they are seeking and contact them. Since there are no salespersons, individuals will have to contact the company itself to buy the shares.

An investor can identify the no-load funds in the financial pages easily. There is a NL in the column, "offer price." When no-load funds are purchased, they are purchased at the net asset value. Table 17–1 shows how some mutual fund listings would appear on the financial pages. "NAV" is the net asset value; the offer price is what one would have to pay. The difference between the two represents the loading fee, except where an NL appears under the offer price. "NAV chg." indicates the change in the net asset value from the previous day. Most of the early no-load funds developed out of the operations of the investment counselors; they developed their mutual fund operations to service smaller clients. Recently some no-load funds have been developed by some investment services, the incentive being the management fees they would get. The no-load funds generally charge the same management fees as the other mutual funds, and some have the hidden fees discussed above.

Liquidation or withdrawal of mutual funds

Some people invest in mutual funds for a specific purpose such as retirement income or financing a child's college education. When an investor wishes to withdraw, he or she may do so at the net asset value, and often no fees are charged. An investor may withdraw in a lump sum or in any one of a number of different installment plans, either monthly, quarterly, semiannually or annually. Further, one may withdraw only the income earned by the fund and leave the principal intact, or one may dip into the principal. If an individual withdraws from the fund for retirement purposes, he or she should consider converting the fund into an income

Table 17.1   *Sample of a mutual fund listing*

	NAV	Offer price	NAV Chg.
AAL Mutual:			
CaGr	10.29	10.80	+.21
Inco	9.45	9.92	+.03
MuBd	9.75	10.24	+.02
AARP Investment Program:			
CaGr	22.80	NL	+.51
GiniM	14.92	NL	+.01
GthInc	22.30	NL	+.22

NAV stands for net asset value per share. The offering price includes net asset value plus maximum sales charge, if any. NAV Chg. indicates the change in the net asset value from the previous day.

fund if this has not already been done. If the fund is with a family system, an investor may switch from, say, a growth fund to an income fund for only a nominal transfer fee of $5 or $10. Most of the larger funds are grouped, and have an income fund, growth fund, balanced fund, and so on. This is another reason why the mutual fund purchased must be selected with care; selecting a good group (or "family") provides greater flexibility.

If an investor switches from one fund to another within a group, in setting up a withdrawal program (or at any time), he or she may be realizing a substantial capital gain and have a tax problem. Hence taxes must be given some consideration when deciding whether to switch or not.

General information on investment companies can be obtained from the same sources that are available for any other type of investment information. The financial pages of most metropolitan newspapers carry price information and sometimes articles on certain companies. Papers like *The Wall Street Journal* and magazines like *Forbes, Business Week,* and *Barron's* are other good sources. *Forbes, Barron's,* and *Business Week* especially should be noted because they make special studies from time to time wherein they analyze and compare the past record of various investment companies. *Forbes* magazine has a special annual study of mutual funds every fall, with articles and analyses of mutual funds and statistical data on each of the major funds. There are statistics on assets, sales charges (loading fees), expenses per $100 of fund assets, dividend returns, and average annual growth rates over a number of years, as well as the performance over the most recent twelve months. Various investment services, such as Moody's, Value Line Investment Services, and Standard and Poor's, publish information on investment companies. In addition, a broker may have a wealth of useful information.

Information on investment companies

Three investment company services specialize in analyzing and publishing information on investment companies. Two of these services publish their major reports annually: *Investment Companies, Mutual Funds, and Other Types,* by Wiesenberger Financial Services, Inc., One Pennsylvania Plaza, New York 10119; and *Johnson's Investment Company Charts,* published by Hugh A. Johnson and Company, 246 Homewood Avenue, Buffalo, New York. These studies analyze most of the leading investment companies, appraise their various performances, and compare them with the performance of the stock market in general. The Wiesenberger Study and the Johnson Study can be purchased or can be perused at many brokerage houses and at any good library.

Lipper Services of New York is the third major investment company service. It publishes a wide variety of data. In addition, Lipper makes a thorough study of mutual funds quarterly, in which it analyzes past performances and presents statistics indicating the various funds' relative performance.

Which funds have done well?

When choosing what fund to buy, the investor should do so in light of the investment objectives. Even after choosing a growth fund or a balanced fund or an income fund, many choices are available. Not all funds perform the same, and differences in performance can be attributed primarily to the differences in management.

Just as stock price averages have been constructed to show how stock prices are moving, averages or indexes can also be constructed of the price of mutual funds to show how mutual funds in general are performing. There are the Lipper index, the Johnson's Charts average, and the Wiesenberger index. Figure 17—4 shows several mutual fund indexes. One is for a number of growth funds, one for growth-income funds, one for income funds, and one for a number of balanced funds. These rec-

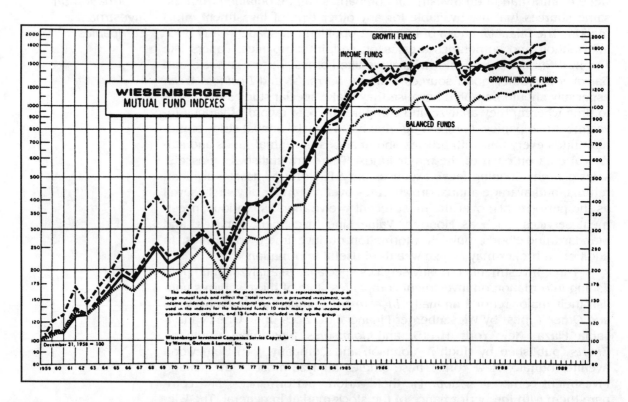

Figure 17—4   *Wiesenberger mutual fund indexes. These indexes are based on the price movements of a representative group of large mutual funds and reflect the "total return" on a presumed investment with income dividends reinvested and capital gains accepted in shares. The indexes do not, however, reflect average management performance for the various groups and should not be considered as such. Five funds are used in the indexes for the balanced funds, 10 each make up the income and growth-income categories, and 13 funds are included in the growth group. (Source: Investment Companies, 1989, Wiesenberger Financial Services, a division of Warren, Gorham & Lamont, Inc., p. 172.)*

ords can be compared with that of Standard and Poor's industrial average, or the Dow Jones averages.

We can also analyze the performance of the mutual funds with Johnson's statistics. Johnson has five mutual fund averages: (1) a growth fund average, (2) an aggressive growth fund average, (3) a growth and income fund average, (4) an income fund average, and (5) a balanced fund average. Table 17—2 shows these averages over the last few years and also the annualized rate of return. In addition, the table shows the Dow Jones Industrial Averages, the Standard and Poor's composite stock index, and other financial indicators to compare with the mutual fund average.

Lipper Services also publishes overall mutual fund performance indicators. Lipper has an index for growth funds, for growth and income funds, and for balanced funds. It is published in *The Wall Street Journal* and in *Barron's Weekly*.

SECURITIES MARKETS OF THE PAST 30 YEARS
1960 - 1989

Table 17—2

	RESULTS OF A $10,000 INVESTMENT WITH ALL INCOME REINVESTED									
	5 Years 1985-1989		10 Years 1980-1989		15 Years 1975-1989		20 Years 1970-1989		30 Years 1960-1989	
	Total	% Rate of Return	Total	% Rate of Return	Total	% Rate of Return	Total	% Rate of Return	Total	% Rate of Return
Cost of Living	11,975	3.7	16,441	5.1	24,297	6.1	33,448	6.2	42,891	5.0
Value of the Dollar	8,351	—	6,082	—	4,116	—	2,990	—	2,331	—
Dow-Jones Industrial Average	27,291	22.2	51,078	17.7	89,738	15.8	84,607	11.3	137,147	9.1
Standard & Poor's 500 Stock Index	25,055	20.2	48,907	17.2	96,584	16.3	85,661	11.3	179,682	10.1
Municipal Bonds	19,935	14.8	23,872	9.1	31,752	8.0	41,563	7.4	42,269	4.9
Long Term Corporate Bonds	20,129	15.0	33,919	13.0	44,870	10.5	62,054	9.6	73,375	6.9
Long Term Government Bonds	21,229	16.2	35,659	13.6	45,385	10.6	63,510	9.6	73,254	6.9
U.S. Treasury Bills	13,,931	6.9	23,453	8.9	32,321	8.1	43,190	7.6	63,457	6.4
Johnson Growth Fund Average	20,652	15.6	42,491	15.6	126,063	18.4	82,667	11.1	216,082	10.8
Johnson Growth & Income Fund Average	20,952	15.9	44,365	16.1	98,822	16.5	91,359	11.7	187,411	10.3
Johnson Balanced & Income Fund Average	17,828	12.3	35,045	13.4	67,297	13.6	69,948	10.2	140,437	9.2
Johnson Corporate Bond Fund Average	15,763	9.5	27,466	10.6	40,359	9.7	47,957	8.2	75,322	7.0
Johnson Gov't Securities Fund Average	15,751	9.5	26,945	10.4	32,259	8.1	47,599	8.1	—	—
Johnson Municipal Bond Fund Average	16,529	10.6	22,498	8.4	—	—	—	—	—	—

NOTE: Rate of Return is Compounded Annual Percentage Rate.

Source: Johnson's Charts, 1989, Hugh A. Johnson, Inc., Buffalo, New York. p. 18.

While mutual fund averages and indices are useful, the prospective buyer must also look at the record of individual companies. Some performed even better than the fund averages shown and some, not so well. Individuals can get literature from the fund they are interested in buying and compare its past record with both the overall fund indicators, the Standard and Poor's index, and the Dow Jones averages. This gives a clue to how well the fund is managed. A good past performance is no assurance of success in the future; however, it's probably better to bet on a past winner. In addition, the fund manager should be evaluated to ascertain past experience and to predict possible future performance.

Investors can also compare the growth of many individual funds with both the Standard and Poor's stock index and the Dow Jones averages by using Johnson's Charts, which can be found at many brokerage houses. Johnson has plotted the performance of individual funds and has included a transparent overlay of both the Dow Jones and the Standard and Poor's market indicators. By using these charts, an investor can see at a glance how funds compare with the stock market indicators.

INTRODUCTION TO OTHER OUTLETS FOR SURPLUS FUNDS

In addition to mutual funds, a person may invest in commodities, real estate, and a number of unusual (sometimes called exotic) investments. Each of these will now be examined. We hasten to add, however, that, with the exception of real estate, these are not for the typical small investor because there is a larger element of speculation involved. Nevertheless, they may be right for some people.

Traditional commodities[3]

Traditionally when one speaks of commodities, one has in mind such things as wheat, corn, sugar, sow bellies (bacon), and so on. In 1980 and early 1981 certain exotic items such as gold, diamonds, antiques, Chinese ceramics, and the like (which, with the possible exception of gold, aren't really commodities at all) gained some popularity. Then, in 1982 and 1983, they lost some of that luster, but in the future—who knows?

The price of certain commodities fluctuates widely over short periods of time for a variety of reasons. The supply can change sharply due to crop failure caused by adverse weather or loss of production due to a strike. Demand for certain commodities, too, can fluctuate due to changed public tastes or governmental policies. These sharp changes in supply and demand can create sharp price changes. Because of these fluctuations, speculators have entered the market.

There are futures prices and spot or cash prices. The spot price is the price paid for delivery today, but the futures price is the price paid

---

3. I wish to acknowledge the help I have received in developing the section on commodities from Professor Edna Villar of Pan American University.

today for commodities to be delivered at a specified time in the future. There is a one-month, two-month, three-month futures price, and so on.

If you believe the price of corn will rise and you buy corn futures, you are referred to as being "long." If you expect the price to decline and you sell, you are referred to as being "short." If your expectations come true, you make a profit. If prices turn against you, you suffer losses.

Since there are futures markets in commodities, and professional speculators that operate in them, business firms that use these commodities can hedge their operations and protect themselves from sharp price fluctuations. In the process the speculator may make a lot of money. There is the so-called "short hedge" and the "long hedge."

The short hedge works as follows: Suppose a candy manufacturer has signed a contract to supply some candy. The price has been set, and it will take a month or more to make and deliver the candy. In the meantime, the manufacturer does not want to carry a large inventory of sugar but wants to protect itself against sharp price increases. He will buy sugar futures. This will freeze the price of sugar for, say, thirty days. While the future price may be slightly higher than the present or spot prices, it is known, and presumably the candy manufacturer negotiates the contract with future prices in mind. For the small price differential, he can avoid carrying a large inventory in sugar and also protect himself (hedge) against sharp price increases in sugar, his major input cost.

The short hedge

The long hedge involves holding an inventory and selling a contract for future delivery to hedge (protect) the inventory from a sharp drop in prices. For example, a miller, storage company, or exporter may have a large inventory of wheat that he would like to hedge against a price change. If he sells a contract for future delivery and the price falls, he will suffer a loss on his inventory, but it will be offset by a profit from his futures contract. If the price rises, exactly the reverse happens.

The long hedge

There are speculators, hence a futures market, in certain foods, grains, fats and oils, textiles, and metals. Futures quotations may be found in the financial pages of large metropolitan newspapers. The Chicago Board of Trade is the largest commodities market in the nation. There are a number of others, including the Kansas City Board of Trade, the Minneapolis Board of Trade, the Chicago Mercantile Exchange, the New York Coffee, Cocoa, and Sugar Exchange, the New York Cotton Exchange, and the New York Commodity Exchange. Table 17–3 shows the futures market prices for coffee and cotton as reported in *The Wall Street Journal*.

Commodity market

There is also a futures market in Treasury bills, certain other short-term and intermediate-term and long-term U.S. government securities, and common stock. If a person believes interest rates are coming down in the

The futures market in securities

Table 17—3   *Futures prices as published in* The Wall Street Journal

—Food & Fiber—

Cocoa (CSCE)—10 metric tons; $ per ton.

July	1,585	1,598	1,576	1,583	−	2	2,160	1,534	8,155
Sept	1,612	1,618	1,602	1,609	. . .		2,204	1,555	12,780
Dec	1,642	1,646	1,631	1,641	+	2	2,197	1,587	8,092
Mr89	1,672	1,675	1,669	1,675	+	5	2,088	1,625	3,728
May	1,700	1,700	1,700	1,698	. . .		2,088	1,652	592
July	1,725	1,725	1,715	1,715	−	4	1,985	1,680	1,597
Sept	1,743	1,743	1,743	1,738	−	6	1,850	1,709	429

Est vol 3,303; vol Fri 3,955; open int 35,373, −14.

Coffee (CSCE)—37,500 lbs.; cents per lb.

July	138.00	138.10	136.15	137.47	+	2.19	146.25	110.00	9,684
Sept	138.75	138.90	137.30	138.47	+	2.30	147.75	111.01	7,986
Dec	139.50	140.00	138.40	139.90	+	2.57	150.25	114.00	3,683
Mr89	139.50	140.20	138.50	139.96	+	2.47	150.50	131.50	1,377
May	140.00	140.00	139.75	139.95	+	1.32	150.75	133.35	456

Est vol 5,775; vol Fri 6,140; open int 23,282, −324.

Cotton (CTN)—50,000 lbs.; cents per lb.

July	67.25	68.37	67.20	68.34	+	1.96	81.40	53.90	8,974
Oct	64.65	64.65	64.40	64.65	+	2.00	73.00	54.45	4,684
Dec	63.44	63.44	63.24	63.44	+	2.00	70.20	53.85	17,127
Mr89	63.00	63.89	63.00	63.89	+	2.00	67.90	54.70	2,047
May	63.50	63.98	63.13	63.98	+	2.00	65.15	56.40	456
July	63.60	64.08	63.60	64.08	+	2.00	64.08	56.50	147

Est vol 6,000; vol Fri 6,356; open int 33,435, −50.

future (government security prices are going to rise), he or she may buy security futures. If the investor is right, he or she will make money. If one's view is that interest rates will rise (security prices will fall) and the investor is right, he or she could make money by selling futures.

The trading unit for Treasury bill futures is one million dollars and for longer-term securities $100,000. However, margins are very low and only a few thousand dollars are required to take a position. It is also possible to hedge with government securities, but only very large investors or institutions such as insurance companies are in a position to do so.

With stock market futures, trading is carried out in one of the stock indexes, such as Standard and Poor's 500, the Value Line Index, or the New York Stock Exchange Composite Index. For example, if an investor buys (or sells) the Standard and Poor's index futures, he or she is speculating on the future prices of 500 different stocks. If the Standard and Poor's index is 213, but one expects it to rise to 230 and buys, he or she would make money if correct and lose if wrong. If an investor expects it to decline, he or she should do the reverse.

An individual may also buy common stock indexes on margin, generally at about 50 percent.

It is also possible to hedge via common stock indexes—just as in the case of commodities or government securities. However, this would be of interest primarily to institutional investors and wealthy individuals. While these futures markets are in securities, the actual operations are carried out not in the security exchange, but on the commodities exchange.

There are now also stock index options—that is, an investor may buy puts and calls on the indexes and not buy the index itself. (Puts and calls on stock were discussed in Chapter 16.) Several exchanges are offering options on the index futures.

It should be noted that futures are highly speculative and are not appropriate for a small investor.

REAL ESTATE INVESTMENTS

There are two major ways of investing in real estate, first, investing in mortgages, and second, owning real property outright. If an individual invests in mortgages, he or she is lending money to a home owner to help finance a home; on this loan he or she receives interest.

Mortgages

A mortgage is a legal document given by the prospective home owner (borrower) to the lender. The borrower who gives the mortgage is called the mortgagor, and the lender who receives the mortgage is called the mortgagee. The mortgage stipulates the terms of the loan such as the interest rate, the monthly payments, and the length of time over which the loan is to be repaid. In addition, the borrower agrees to pay all taxes, assessments, and other charges levied against the property, also to keep it in good repair and fully insured against fire and other hazards.

The mortgage also provides for foreclosure and repossession of the home by the mortgage lender in the event that the home owner defaults. In some states a deed of trust is used in place of a mortgage but it provides for the same arrangements.

Most mortgage loans are made by financial institutions such as savings and loan associations and mutual savings banks, but there is no reason why an individual with surplus funds cannot make such a loan to a home owner. When a person makes a mortgage loan, he or she in effect pays off the seller of the home (sometimes the builder if it is a new home) and the purchaser gives the lender a mortgage as described above.

Mortgages are negotiable just like corporate bonds, and can be sold just like corporate bonds. The interest rate on a mortgage is usually fixed for the duration of the loan, and hence if interest rates rise after a given mortgage has been agreed upon, the market price of the mortgage declines. The market price of mortgages, then, fluctuates inversely with changes in the going interest rate, and consequently mortgages may be sold at a premium or at a discount from their face value, just as in the case of corporate bonds. (See Chapter 14.)

Determination of mortgage yields

Since the price of mortgages, purchased from another mortgagee, fluctuates, the yield is not necessarily the same as the fixed interest rate specified in the mortgage itself. Also, mortgages are not as liquid as corporate bonds; it takes time to sell them to someone else. For this reason, the yield on mortgages is generally higher than that on corporate bonds. The true yield on a mortgage, of course, is determined by how much above or below face value it is sold. To determine the approximate yields, the following formula is used.[4]

$$Y = \frac{R(P) + \left(\dfrac{P - C}{N}\right)}{\left(\dfrac{P + C}{2}\right)} \times 100$$

Y = approximate yield
P = principal balance of the mortgage
C = the cost to the investor of the mortgage
N = number of years the mortgage runs until paid
R = coupon rate of interest the mortgage carries

Assume, for example, a ten-year-old mortgage with an unamortized face value of $50,000 running over ten years, bearing a fixed interest rate of 10 percent which an individual can purchase for $35,000.

$$(1) \quad Y = \frac{10(\$50,000) + \left(\dfrac{\$50,000 - \$35,000}{10}\right)}{\left(\dfrac{\$50,000 + \$35,000}{2}\right)} \times 100$$

$$(2) \quad Y = \frac{5,000 + \left(\dfrac{\$15,000}{10}\right)}{\dfrac{85,000}{2}} \times 100$$

---

4. Note the word "approximate." The reason for approximation is that the components of the problem are themselves only averages. The figures used are generally average interest earned per year. This is true where monthly payments are made (this is not the case, however, in this oversimplified problem). To be strictly accurate, yields must be figured using compound interest functions.

(3) $\quad Y = \dfrac{\$5,000 + \$1,500}{\dfrac{85,000}{2}} \times 100$

(4) $\quad Y = \dfrac{\$6,500}{\$42,500} \times 100 =$

(5) $\quad Y = 15.29$ percent approximate yield

We noted above that a mortgage is less liquid than corporate bonds, and hence the yield should be higher. Mortgages also generally are riskier than corporate bonds, which also will increase their yield above bonds. However, the degree of risk varies with the credit rating of the mortgagor. When making a mortgage loan, one must appraise the credibility of the mortgagor. A person must also consider the age and the condition of the house, and what portion of its total value he or she is financing. The general rule is that the individual should not make a mortgage loan in excess of 75 percent of the value of the house. It should also be remembered that some costs are involved if one has to foreclose and repossess the home. All this will have a bearing on the yield on mortgage loans. A person must also decide whether the yield on a given mortgage is sufficiently higher than alternative investment opportunities. If it is not, one can bargain to increase it by asking for a larger discount. Whether the above 15.29 percent yield is adequate depends on the investor's alternative investment opportunities.

Second mortgages

In the above discussion we had in mind first mortgages. There are also second mortgages, which are riskier. In the event of a foreclosure and sale of a house on which the mortgagor has defaulted, the second mortgage is not paid off until after the first mortgagee has been completely repaid. Assume a home valued at $100,000 with a $60,000 mortgage. If the home is sold, the buyer would need a $40,000 down payment to take over the existing mortgage. If he had only $25,000, he could offer a second mortgage for $15,000, and he would now have two mortgages to pay. Second mortgages are for smaller dollar amounts and run over fewer years than first, generally from five to twelve years. While riskier, second mortgages provide a higher yield; and if the mortgagor has a sufficiently high income and good enough credit rating, many mortgage lenders will assume the higher risk in order to obtain the higher yield. Second mortgages generally have a maximum amortization period of twelve years and yield as high as 20 percent. The yield on discounted second mortgages is calculated by using the above formula just as in the case of the first mortgages.

A final word of caution

When accepting a mortgage be sure that the mortgagor has a strong credit rating. This is especially true in an innovative mortgage (see Chapter 8). If a lender escalates interest on the mortgagor and it creates a hardship for him or her, it may also be unpleasant for the lender. If a mortgagor's income rises substantially over the years, the investment is probably safe; otherwise it might not be. If the mortgages in the portfolio have balloon payments, one may have to refinance them in order to avoid a default. To be sure an individual can foreclose on the loan if necessary, but that is a lengthy and expensive process.

Real estate
investment trusts

Another possible outlet for surplus funds is the real estate investment trust, which generally resembles a closed-end investment company. It is a specialized holding company that sells stock in itself to the public. However, instead of investing in stocks as the mutual fund generally does, the investment is in real estate mortgages, property, or both. The main inducement for the real estate investment is that it is exempt from paying the corporate income tax provided it distributes at least 95 percent of its income to the holders of the trust certificate of ownership.

For the trust to be exempt from the corporate income tax, it must strictly follow the law, which requires:

1. That there be more than one hundred shareholders
2. That no five persons directly or indirectly own 50 percent or more of the shares
3. That 95 percent of its taxable income must be distributed to the shareholders
4. That it derive at least 75 percent of its gain from rents, capital gains, or mortgage income
5. That it derive no more than 25 percent of its income from dividends and interest in other concerns (provided that only 75 percent of its income results from investments outlined in point 4; for example, if 85 percent of the income were from rents, then only 15 percent would have to come from dividends and interest in other concerns)
6. That it hold property for a minimum of four years
7. That it be separate from the management of the real estate it holds

The trust provides more liquidity than most real estate investments. A trust certificate may be sold like stock. If the investor wishes to become part of a trust, he or she may purchase a certificate.

Real estate investment trusts are specialized closed-end investment companies. In addition, some of them borrow money and have leverage built into their capital structure just as do some closed-end investment companies. In recent years, they have become an additional source of substantial mortgage capital, and this capital does not seem to dry up as much during periods of extremely tight credit as is the case with more traditional sources.

Real estate investment trusts (REIT) have also begun to specialize to some extent. There are now about five types: (1) equity, (2) short-term mortgage construction, (3) long-term mortgage, (4) hybrid, and (5) specialized. Most of them can be classified as those that buy securities representing real estate investments (mortgages) and receive a fixed-interest income and those that buy the real estate directly and receive a rental (and perhaps a capital gain) income.

Many individuals who invest in real estate shy away from the real estate investment trust because of the lack of individual control and the fact that the investment must be in income-producing property. For example, the trust cannot purchase a piece of raw land for development purposes or for capital gains. These two facts have prevented the trust from becoming as successful as it might have.

So far we have discussed primarily buying securities that represent real estate investments. It is also possible to own and manage real estate directly, primarily for income purposes, but also for capital gains, as a hedge against inflation, or for tax reasons.

Owning real estate directly

Income properties are generally divided into categories: residential income properties, including individual homes, duplexes, and apartment houses, and nonresidential, including commercial space, office space, and industrial or warehouse space.

When an investor buys rental property, he or she must choose whether to buy a single family dwelling, a duplex, a triplex, or an apartment. How much money one is able to invest will be a constraint that may rule out everything but a single family unit. If an individual is able to invest more and has a choice, he or she must come to grips with the following questions:

Residential

1. What type of residential unit is in the greatest demand? Indeed, what is the demand for all of the various types of units?
2. What is the supply of currently available rental units of the various types which would be in competition in providing housing? It is possible that the demand for apartments is greater than for single family units, but nevertheless apartments may be overbuilt while single family rentals are very scarce.
3. What size of family unit (small or large house) is in greatest demand relative to the available supply?
4. What part of the community is the best location for various types of residential units?
5. What is the cost of acquiring a residential unit? (Generally, the cost per square foot is less on a multifamily than on single units.)
6. What are maintenance costs and rental incomes?

All this will require an analysis of population growth in the area, residential values, monthly rents, construction rates, rental unit vacancy rates, yield on capital invested, whether the population is in large part transient or permanent, and personal income.

Until a few years ago, residential rental property has been an excellent investment. It has provided an inflationary hedge, a tax shelter, capital gains in excess of the rate of inflation, and fairly good investment return. This is less true today. However, real estate may still be a good investment in some cases, especially in certain parts of the country. In some geographical areas real estate prices have declined but then so too have rents; in those areas where rental income has remained firm, residential prices have not declined, or at least not as much. The major optimistic point in residential investing is that interest rates have declined.

Not too many years ago, investing in rental property usually resulted in at least a small positive cash flow. If a person buys rental property today, he or she will quite likely have to accept a negative cash flow, at least temporarily.[5] Nevertheless, purchasing rental property may still be a good long-run investment in certain areas, if one is very selective.

Calculating the yield on direct real estate investments

To analyze rental property as an investment, one must look at the cash flow, the tax consequences, expected future cash flow, and expected price appreciation of the property. Table 17–4 provides a starting point. An investor purchases a duplex for $150,000; makes a down payment of $40,000; and finances the remainder at 10 percent over 30 years. The net rental income amounts to $15,800, which after taxes, insurance, and mortgage payments generates a modest cash flow of $216. In earlier days, an investor could expect a larger positive yield, but this is much more difficult today.

The 1986 tax law changed the depreciation schedule on residential rental property, which must now be depreciated over 27.5 years on a straight-line basis. This means the owner may take only 3.636 percent depreciation per year ($^{100}/_{27.5} = .3636$). In our example, depreciation comes to $4,727 per year and provides that much of a tax shelter—it can offset that much of other income and shield it from taxes. Is this duplex, then, a good investment? It depends on one's tax bracket, among other things. In the 28 percent tax bracket, the depreciation on this investment will save $1,324 in taxes. In the 15 percent bracket, the tax savings will be only $709. The cost of this tax shelter is the cash-flow yield. Is it worth it? The investor should also remember that insurance, interest payments, maintenance, and property taxes (totaling $16,434) are also tax deductible. If the owner is in the 28 percent bracket, $4,322 of these payments are shifted to the government. Adding in depreciation, a total of $5,925 is shifted; at the 15 percent bracket a total of $3,174 is shifted. Table 17–5 shows this.

Also, in the future, rents will probably rise, the cash flow may become larger. Finally, the owner may have a good inflationary hedge.

---

5. A negative cash flow merely means that the mortgage payments, taxes, and insurance are in excess of rental income.

Rental property as a tax shelter   Table 17—4

Duplex:			$150,000
Down payment			40,000
Mortgage at 10 percent interest—thirty years			110,000
Rental income:			
Two units at $700 per month each	$16,800		
Maintenance, repairs, and vacancy	1,000		
Net rental income		$15,800	
Taxes and insurance		4,000	
Mortgage payment ($965.84 per month)		11,584	
Cash flow		$ 216	
Equity buildup first year (about $12.50 per month)	$150	$ 150	
Cash flow plus equity buildup		$ 366	
Depreciation over 27.5 years			
straight line ($130,000 × 3.636) per year			4,727
Interest first year (mortgage payment less equity buildup)			11,434
Taxes and insurance			4,000

Source: Calculated by author.

Potential yield and tax shelter of rental property   Table 17—5

Rental income		$16,800
Expenditures:		
Interest on mortgage	$11,434	
Insurance	1,000	
Taxes	3,000	
Maintenance and repairs	1,000	
Depreciation	4,727	
Total		21,161
Loss		4,361
Cash flow		366

Since depreciation is a noncash outflow, there is a modest $366 cash inflow.

$21,161 × 28% = $5,925 = taxes shifted to the government.
$21,161 × 15% = $3,174 = taxes shifted to the government.

Whether the above duplex is a good investment, then, depends on personal circumstances, and what the future rent increases and price appreciation will be. With respect to these latter two points, *where* the rental property is located may be crucial. If it is in a fast-growth area, the risk would be less than in a low-growth or declining area.

Real estate and leverage

We learned in Chapter 15 that borrowing money introduces leverage into the capital structure of a corporation. Leverage comes about when an individual pays less interest for borrowed money than he or she can earn with it. This is also sometimes true with real estate investments. If there is positive leverage, it is advantageous to minimize the down payment on a real estate investment, and borrow as much as possible. Keep in mind, however, that leverage can be negative as well as positive, in which case the person is paying a higher rate of interest than he or she is able to earn with the borrowed funds. Table 17–6 illustrates how leverage comes about via real estate investments.

Nonresidential real estate

Logically, investing in nonresidential property is similar to investing in residential—there is a rental cash inflow, as well as maintenance, taxes, insurance, mortgage payments, and depreciation. More money is usually needed to invest in nonresidentials.

Nonresidential property may be classified as commercial and business, office and professional, and industrial and warehouse. When investing in any of these, a person must, among other things, analyze population and business growth and their patterns, vacancy rates, parking facilities, transportation arteries, and zoning ordinances.

Older buildings

Sometimes if an individual invests in older real estate, he or she may also be able to take an investment tax credit.[6] Generally, when investing in real estate, individuals may not take this credit; but if they buy and rehabilitate older buildings, in addition to the depreciation (cost recovery) allowance described above, they may be eligible.

The investment tax credit applies only to buildings built before 1936. Expenditures incurred in rehabilitating buildings built before 1936 will qualify for a 10 percent investment tax credit. In the case of a building certified by the IRS as being a historical structure, the investment tax credit may be as much as 20 percent. The investment tax credit applies only to the rehabilitation cost, not the acquisition cost. If a person buys a building certified as a historical structure for $60,000 and spends $40,000 rehabilitating it, the rehabilitation investment tax credit could be as much as $8,000.

Undeveloped (raw) land

Some people feel undeveloped land is a superior investment to rental property. Sometimes it is, and sometimes it is not. To be sure, the owner does not have to worry about leaky roofs, broken furnaces, or poor tenants who pay the rent late and are complainers. On the other hand, it yields no income, and there are taxes to pay plus interest on the loan, which can use up money quickly. There is also no depreciation to provide

---

6. See Chapter 7 for a discussion of the investment tax credit. The 1986 tax change eliminated the ITC for most items, but retained it in a few cases, including a few real estate investments.

Leverage provided by real estate   Table 17—6

Total Investment—Duplex		$150,000
	With Leverage	Cash Transaction
Borrow	$135,000	$ 0
Owner's funds	15,000	150,000
Rental income	15,800	15,800
Interest	13,500	0
Before-tax earnings	2,300	15,800

$$\text{Before-tax return on owner's investment} = \frac{2,300}{15,000} = 15.3\% \qquad \frac{15,800}{150,000} = 10.5\%$$

To be sure, these figures are gross, or from before income taxes. In addition, property taxes and insurance have not been deducted, but they are deductible from the owner's income taxes.

The leverage after federal income (assuming a 28 percent bracket) is as follows:

$$\frac{\$1,656}{\$15,000} = 11.04\% \qquad \frac{\$11,376}{\$150,000} = 7.5\%$$

a tax shelter. The land would have to appreciate in value by substantially more than enough to offset these factors to make the investment worthwhile. If one buys land in a fast-growing area, this may happen, but such land has already been discounted into the future for a number of years, and hence is very expensive. If an investor buys land that is not in a growth area that becomes a growth area, he or she has made a shrewd investment, or was lucky and will probably have a nice capital gain.

An investor should be wary of raw land in general. It should be checked out carefully with respect to taxes, interest on the loan, expected future growth in the area, and present and possible future zoning restrictions.

For a brief period during the late 1970s and early 1980s, when inflation was at the double-digit level, gold, diamonds, and certain other items became popular as investment outlets. People thought they were inflationary hedges, but this did not prove to be the case. Speculative fever drove their prices up rapidly; then came just as rapid a price collapse.

People invested in such things as:

COLLECTIBLES: GOLD, DIAMONDS, AND OTHERS

Works of art
Chinese ceramics
Antique furniture
Antique cars
Rugs

Stamps, coins, and rare books
Gold and silver
Precious gems

It is very difficult to profit from investments in collectibles; as with other investments, the investor must maintain current and extensive knowledge of the item in order to do well. However, information on collectibles is not as readily available as for other investments. In addition, trends on collectibles are difficult to forecast.

Gold and silver

Gold and silver reached their peaks of $884 and $56 per ounce, respectively, during the speculative fever in 1980.

Gold and silver earn no interest or dividend return, and there are storage costs involved. While they are generally not inflation hedges, for psychological and historical reasons sometimes gold and silver have become a panic haven as they did in 1979 and 1980 when inflation exceeded double-digit levels.

Gold may be purchased in the form of coins—the Krugerrand, the Canadian Mapleleaf, or the Austrian Corona—rather than bullion. Each of these coins contains about one ounce of gold and fluctuates in value with the market price of bullion. Coins are easier to store than bullion, and they need not be assayed when sold.

Diamonds and other precious stones

The price of diamonds and other precious stones rose drastically in 1980, and then collapsed. Diamonds are even riskier than gold, because they are not homogeneous. It is difficult to judge the quality of the various gems or compare one with another. Gold is homogeneous; coins are stamped and bullion need only be assayed to determine its purity.

SUMMARY REVIEW QUESTIONS

These questions serve as a summary and a review of the chapter. If the reader is able to answer them all, he or she has a good understanding of the material covered by the chapter.

1. What are mutual funds and what is the underlying rationale for the existence of mutual funds?
2. Distinguish between a closed-end investment company and an open-end investment company.
3. What is net asset value?
4. What are some of the objectives of investment companies?
5. Suppose a mutual fund salesperson were selling a balanced fund. What does this mean?
6. What is an income fund?

7. How do the objectives of various mutual funds differ?
8. What are some of the advantages that one receives when one buys mutual funds? Are there any disadvantages?
9. How is the value of a share in an open-end company determined?
10. What are loading charges as related to mutual funds?
11. What is a no-load fund? How can no-load funds stay in business?
12. Where can you obtain information about mutual funds?
13. What factors should be considered before a person buys mutual funds?
14. Discuss the commodities markets.

Would you recommend investing in commodities? Why or why not?
15. Discuss the short hedge, the long hedge.
16. What is the futures market in securities?
17. What is a discounted first mortgage?
18. What factors must be taken into account when calculating the yield on a mortgage?
19. What is a second mortgage?
20. What is a real estate investment trust?
21. Discuss the advantages and disadvantages of owning real estate directly.
22. How is the yield calculated on direct real estate investments?

CASES

1. Yvonne Hagen invested $2,000 in a no-load mutual fund with a net assets value (NAV) of $10.
   (a) How many mutual fund shares did Yvonne receive?
   (b) What were her brokerage commissions?
   (c) If Yvonne had purchased a load fund what would her commission have been?
   (d) If Yvonne had purchased a closed-end fund what would her commission have been?

2. Rita Roundsetter has just inherited $25,000 and is undecided how to invest it. She has never owned common stock and is inexperienced with respect to securities. Nevertheless, she thinks she should buy equities. Is she wise? Would you recommend buying common stock directly or mutual funds? Rita is thirty-four and has no dependents. What kind of stocks (or mutual funds) would you recommend? What kind of return can Rita expect?

3. Robert Shafer works in the trust depart-

ment of the Bank of America and is earning $35,000 per year. He is twenty-eight, married, and has one child. He expects his income to be rising over the years and thinks it is time for him to acquire some equities. Since he is not going to be able to invest very much at first, he cannot get much diversification. Nevertheless, he still thinks it would be foolish for him to buy mutual shares and pay someone to handle his investments for him. Do you agree? What kind of stock (or mutual shares) would you recommend for Robert? The Shafers are also undecided between open-end and closed-end investment companies. As far as investment companies are concerned, which ones do you think they should buy?

4. Joan Rider is a twenty-four-year-old school teacher who has her own car fully paid for and $3,000 in the bank. She wants to invest in equities but is undecided whether to buy common stock directly or indirectly through a mutual fund. One of the things she dislikes

about mutual funds is the high acquisition costs. Would you advise her to invest directly or indirectly? Specifically what kind of direct or indirect investments would you advise?

5. Clem Kensington has inherited $50,000 and has savings of $20,000 in a savings and loan association that is paying 5 3/4 percent. It seems to him that he should be getting at least 8 percent, and therefore he is thinking about taking $20,000 out of the savings and loan association, putting it with $50,000 he inherited, and buying a mortgage. The other alternative is to buy a duplex, live in one unit, and rent out the other.

Clem has found out that he can get a mortgage that will yield him a 12 percent return. He has also found a duplex he can buy for $100,000 that has a net rental income of $4,800 per year. Which is the better investment? Explain fully.

6. Billie Stewart is a young lawyer with $100,000 to invest. She has decided to invest it in some real estate venture, but is uncertain what type of venture she should choose. She has investigated first mortgages and has discovered she can obtain a 10 percent yield. Now she learns that second mortgages are available. Most of these are $3,000 to $5,000 and will yield her about 14 percent return on her money. Why is the yield difference so great on first and second mortgages? Would you recommend that she buy first or second mortgages? Why? Why are the second mortgages usually only for several thousand dollars while first mortgages run up to $100,000 and more?

Ms. Stewart has also considered buying land on the edge of the city where she lives and holding it for capital gains, and buying shares in a real estate investment trust. What would you advise?

7. John and Mary Whippet, a retired couple, decided to go into a part-time business for themselves. Mary has always liked antiques and has suggested they become antique dealers. John is not so sure. They seek your advice.

SUGGESTED READINGS

The Appraisal Journal. Chicago: American Institute of Real Estate Appraisers. Quarterly publication.

Appraisal Review Journal. This journal is published three times per year by the National Association of Review Appraisers, St. Paul, Minn.

Areuea; Journal of the American Real Estate and Urban Economics Association. This journal is published quarterly.

Arnold, Alvin, Wurtzebach, Charles, and Miles, Mike. *Modern Real Estate.* New York: John Wiley and Sons, 1987.

Barrons. A weekly financial newspaper. Princeton, N.J.: Dow Jones and Company.

"Before You Speculate." Chicago: The Chicago Mercantile Exchange.

Donoghue, William E., and Tilling, Thomas. *William E. Donoghue's No-Load Mutual Fund Guide: How to Take Advantage of the Investment Opportunity of the '80s.* New York: Harper and Row, 1984.

"Forbes Mutual Fund Survey." *Forbes Magazine.* This is an annual survey that comes out every fall.

"For High Yields in Short-Term Investments Ask About Money Market Instruments." New York: Dean Witter Reynolds. You may obtain this from a Dean Witter broker.

Green, Fred T. *Thrift and Home Ownership.* Chicago: United States League of Savings Associations.

"Guide to Financial Futures." Chicago: Chicago Board of Trade, Market Planning and Support Division.

Hedging Highlights. Chicago: Chicago Board of Trade.

How to Buy and Sell Commodities. New York: Merrill Lynch, Pierce, Fenner, and Smith.

"Introduction to Hedging." Chicago: Chicago Board of Trade, Educational Services.

Investment Companies, Mutual Funds, and Other Types. Latest edition of this annual publication by Wiesenberger Financial Services, New York.

Johnson's Investment Company Charts. Latest edition of this annual publication by Hugh A. Johnson Company, Buffalo, N.Y.

Mutual Fund Fact Book. Washington, D.C.: Investment Company Institute. Annual publication.

"Profit Opportunities in a Managed Futures Account." New York: Dean Witter Reynolds. You may obtain this from any Dean Witter broker.

The Real Estate Appraiser and Analyst. This is a bimonthly publication of the Society of Real Estate Appraisers, Chicago, Ill.

Real Estate Center Journal. College Station, TX.: Texas A&M University. Quarterly publication.

Real Estate Review. Boston: Warren, Gorham & Lamont. Quarterly publication.

Rugg, Donald D., and Hale, Norman B. *The Dow Jones-Irwin Guide to Mutual Funds,* revised ed. Homewood, Ill.: Dow Jones-Irwin, 1986.

SBA, What It Is, What It Does, SBIC Financing for Small Business, SBIC Industry Review, SBIC Industry Trends. Washington, D.C.: Small Business Administration. The Small Business Administration (SBA) is a government agency and it publishes numerous pamphlets on small business management. It also publishes a *Handbook of Small Business Finance.*

Smith, Halbert, and Corgel, John. *Real Estate Prospectives.* Homewood, Ill.: Dow Jones-Irwin, 1987.

"Speculating in Futures." Chicago: Chicago Board of Trade, Educational Services.

U. S. News & World Report. A weekly magazine that contains a good deal of information on business and finance.

Well Beyond the Average: The Story of Dow Jones. Princeton, N.J.: Dow Jones and Company.

Wiedemer, John P. *Real Estate Investments.* Englewood Cliffs, N.J.: Prentice-Hall, 1987.

Wofford, Larry E. *Real Estate,* 2nd ed. New York: John Wiley and Sons, 1987.

V Retirement and estate planning

The first chapter of this section, on retirement planning, discusses three means of providing for retirement that are available for most people. There is, first of all, Social Security that most people have to build on. Also there are the client's personal investments that will yield an investment income.

The client's personal investments may, of course, be in the form of life insurance annuities, securities, rental property, and even some others.

Most people also have a pension fund with their employer. For the self-employed there are Keogh accounts, and in some cases people may have individual retirement accounts (IRAs). All of these are discussed.

The other, and last, chapter is designed to introduce the planner to techniques that may help his or her client to save estate taxes upon death and to allocate assets as desired. Wills, trusts, and gifts are discussed.

18 Retirement planning, social security, annuities, and other pension plans

HIGHLIGHTS   In order to acquaint the reader with the various techniques for achieving a decent life during the retirement years, this chapter discusses the following:

1   Social Security and what it provides
2   The Social Security tax structure, which finances Social Security benefits
3   Annuities and how they work
4   Fixed and variable annuities
5   Regular corporate pension plans and how they work
6   Two special corporate pension plans
7   Individual retirement programs available
8   The various options when funds are withdrawn

This chapter deals with retirement income. Social Security, savings and annuities, and certain pension plans are the trinity of retirement programming. Pension plans may, in turn, be broken down into corporate pension plans (or government plans for government employees) and individual pension plans. In addition, some people have other assets (for example, bonds, stocks, and rental real estate), which will also yield income during retirement. Stocks, bonds, real estate, and the like, were discussed in previous chapters; in this chapter we will discuss formal retirement plans—Social Security, annuities, and corporate and individual pension plans.

SOCIAL SECURITY

Social Security will provide the retiree with some tax-free retirement income.[1] That tax-free income is also indexed—at least currently—to protect the recipient from inflation. Social Security benefits will vary depending in part upon earned income while the person was working; but even if the individual is drawing the maximum benefits, it by itself may not provide a decent retirement standard of living, and he or she will need to supplement it. Indeed Social Security never was—and is not now—intended to provide an adequate retirement income. Rather it was intended to provide a minimum base or starting point on which to build and which, if supplemented, could provide for an adequate retirement. It was believed that with Social Security as a base most people could provide for their retirement years.

Social Security provides a total of four different benefits.

1. Old-age retirement
2. Survivors' benefits
3. Disability benefits, and
4. Medicare. (Medicare was discussed in Chapter 11; the other three will be discussed here.)

Who is covered?

Almost everyone in the labor force, including self-employed persons, is included under Social Security; this also includes members of the armed forces. Today the only exceptions are certain federal employees, some state and local employees, and ministers and other members of religious orders who file a form stating they are conscientiously opposed to receiving Social Security benefits because of religious convictions.

Prior to January 1, 1984, federal employees were not covered by Social Security. They had their own alternative pension system. In 1983,

---

1. Up to one-half of the benefits received by taxpayers whose income exceeds certain base amounts is subject to income taxation. See section entitled "Social Security and Income Taxes."

however, Congress provided for coverage for federal workers effective in 1984 and later years, but applying only to workers hired after that time. For state and local workers, coverage was voluntary prior to 1984; now it is mandatory. Moreover state and local employees could drop out before 1984. Now they may no longer terminate their participation in the Social Security system.

Everyone under Social Security must pay Social Security taxes (also called payroll taxes). In 1990 this was 7.65 percent on the first $51,300 of earnings. This is matched by the employer, and the sum is paid to the Social Security Administration. These taxes, as well as the wage base to which the taxes apply, are increased nearly every year. They are adjusted to reflect changes in wage levels.

Social Security taxes

The self-employed pay a higher tax because there is no matching contribution. In 1990 the self-employment tax was 15.30 percent on the same base of $51,300. In 1983, Congress amended the Social Security tax and raised sharply the tax that the self-employed pay. They now pay exactly double what people who work for others pay. Part of the Social Security tax is earmarked to finance Medicare, and the remainder finances retirement benefits, disability benefits, and survivors' benefits.

Both the Social Security tax and the base income to which it is applied are scheduled to rise in future years in accordance with a law already passed by Congress. The income base (taxable wage) will be adjusted upward to take into account average wage level increases throughout the U.S. Table 18–1 shows the future increases in the tax rate. Since Social Security taxes are withheld through payroll deductions, they are automatically stopped when the maximum base income is reached. However, if a worker has two or more employers, he or she may have a tax withheld in excess of the maximum because each employer is required to withhold the maximum amount. If so, the taxpayer can get it back by taking it as a credit against personal income tax when he or she files the annual return.

To build up Social Security benefits, individuals must earn what are called **quarters of coverage.** In 1990, a person receives one quarter of coverage for every $520 of earned income on which he or she pays Social Security taxes. Therefore, four quarters of coverage—the maximum that may be earned for the year—are obtained in any year during which the person paid Social Security taxes on $2,080 of earned income. (Income from dividends, interest, rent, or capital gains is not subject to Social Security taxes and hence does not count.) It does not matter when during the year a person earns this $2,080; even if earned all in one day, he or she will receive four quarters of coverage. This quarters-of-coverage base will be adjusted upward to take into account average wage-level increases in future years.

Building protection: Quarters of coverage

Table 18-1   *Social Security taxes*

		Employed		Self-employed	
Year	Taxable wage	Tax rate	Maximum tax	Tax rate	Maximum tax
1978	$17,700	6.05%	$1,070.85	8.10%	$1,433.70
1979	$22,900	6.13%	$1,403.77	8.10%	$1,854.90
1980	$25,900	6.13%	$1,587.67	8.10%	$2,097.90
1981	$29,700	6.65%	$1,975.05	9.30%	$2,762.10
1982	$32,400	6.70%	$2,170.80	9.35%	$3,029.40
1983	$35,700	6.70%	$2,391.90	9.35%	$3,337.95
1984	$37,800	7.00%	$2,646.00	14.00%	$5,292.00
1985	$39,600	7.05%	$2,791.80	14.10%	$5,583.60
1986	$42,000	7.15%	$3,003.00	14.30%	$6,006.00
1987	$43,800	7.15%	$3,131.70	14.30%	$6,263.40
1988	$45,000	7.51%	$3,379.50	15.02%	$6,759.00
1989	$48,000	7.51%	$3,604.80	15.02%	$7,209.60
1990	$51,300	7.65%	$3,924.45	15.30%	$7,848.90
1991	$53,400	7.65%	$4,085.10	15.30%	$8,170.20

Note: By law, the taxable wage will be increased automatically every year to take into account average wage-rate increases in the U.S. The tax rate too is increased frequently. Call the local Social Security Field Office for the latest figures.

Note: The 1990 tax legislation increased the base to which the Medicare part (1.45 percent) of Social Security taxes apply from $53,400 to $125,000 beginning in 1991. Hence, after the taxpayer has had $4,085.10 deducted on the first $53,400 of his salary, the tax on the remainder up to $125,000 would drop to 1.45 percent of the salary.

Source: U.S. Department of Health, Education & Welfare, Social Security Administration

Quarters of coverage are important because this determines whether a person is eligible to receive benefits. The amount of benefits is determined by the person's income while employed. That is, there is a loose and indirect connection between what a person earns (and pays in the form of Social Security taxes) and benefits received.

The number of quarters of coverage needed to qualify for Social Security benefits varies with the year in which the retiree becomes 62, in the case of retirement benefits, and with the age when a person dies or becomes disabled in the case of those benefits. These variations range from a minimum of 30 quarters to a maximum of 40 for retirement benefits, and 6 to 40 quarters in case of survivors' or disability benefits.

To calculate the quarters of coverage needed to qualify permanently for Social Security retirement benefits, work through the following three steps.

1. Take the year in which the person was born
2. Add 62 to it
3. Subtract 1951 from the result

For example

$$
\begin{array}{r}
1923 \\
+62 \\
\hline
1985 \\
-1951 \\
\hline
34
\end{array}
= \text{quarters of coverage needed.}
$$

Social Security taxes go into a special Social Security trust fund. The moneys are then invested in a special issue of U.S. government securities from which the money earns interest. Since Social Security taxes flow into the fund and Social Security benefits flow out of the trust fund, in any one year the fund may be built up or depleted. In recent years the fund has been depleted to the extent that Congress raised taxes periodically.

Social Security trust funds; What happens to money collected?

A few years ago Congress created several new trust funds; there is now a separate one for disability payments, hospital benefits, and medical benefits (see Figure 18–1). In recent years much more money has been flowing out in the form of benefits than has been flowing in in the form of taxes, and the trust funds have become dangerously depleted. Because of this in late 1983 Congress raised Social Security taxes. It should be noted that the Social Security taxes individuals pay are not earmarked to pay their benefits when they retire. Rather they are commingled and used to pay benefits to those presently retired. Later when a person retires, the members of the labor force at that time will be pay-

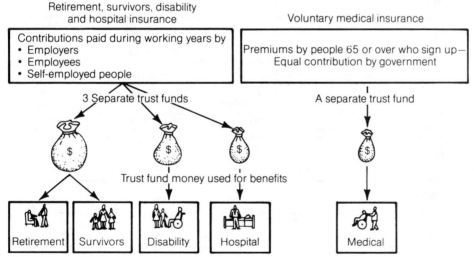

Administrative costs for each program come out of the corresponding trust fund.

Trust fund money can be used only for benefits and for the costs of administering the corresponding programs. (Source: U.S. Department of Health, Education, and Welfare.)

Figure 18–1

ing Social Security taxes that will be used to provide for his or her benefits. In this way an intergenerational transfer takes place.

The wage statement request

Once a year, anyone may check his or her records by filling out a wage statement request—as illustrated in Figure 18–2—and sending it to any district office of the Social Security Administration. This should be done at least every three years because that is the limit for correcting errors. A wage statement request card can be obtained from any Social Security

---

FOLD HERE

REQUEST FOR STATEMENT OF EARNINGS
(PLEASE PRINT IN INK OR USE TYPEWRITER)

	FOR SSA USE ONLY
AX	●
SP	●

I REQUEST A SUMMARY STATEMENT OF EARNINGS FROM MY SOCIAL SECURITY RECORD

NH | Full name you use in work or business
First | Middle Initial | Last

SN | Social Security number shown on your card | **DB** Your date of birth | Month | Day | Year | **A**

MA | Other Social Security number(s) you have used | **SX** Your Sex ☐ Male ☐ Female

AK | Other name(s) you have used (Include your maiden name)

FOLD HERE

PRIVACY STATEMENT

The Social Security Administration (SSA) is authorized to collect information asked on this form under section 205 of the Social Security Act. It is needed so SSA can quickly identify your record and prepare the earnings statement you requested. While you are not required to furnish the information, failure to do so may prevent your request from being processed. The information will be used primarily for issuing your earnings statement.

I am the individual to whom the record pertains. I understand that if I knowingly and willingly request or receive a record about an individual under false pretenses I would be guilty of a Federal crime and could be fined up to $5000.

Sign your name here: (Do not print) | TELEPHONE NO. (Area Code) | DATE

SEND THE STATEMENT TO: (to be completed in ALL cases.)

PN | Name

AD | Address (Number and Street, Apt. No., P.O. Box, or Rural Route)
City and state | **ZP** | Zip Code

Form **SSA-7004-PC-OP1** (9/85)
Destroy prior editions

Figure 18–2 *Request for statement of earnings. (Source: U.S. Department of Health, Education, and Welfare.)*

district office, and there is one in all large cities. Look in the telephone directory under United States government for the address and phone number of the nearest field office.

When a person hears from Social Security headquarters, he or she can check their figures with the amount the employer claims to have reported, shown on the W2 income tax forms. The Social Security Administration's records will not show what the tax deductions have been, but rather whether the income has been reported and its dollar amount. That is the only important item to verify because future Social Security payments will not be based directly on the taxes but rather on the income reported to the Social Security Administration. If the figures are not in agreement, the individual should contact the Social Security field office right away.

When individuals reach age 65 they may receive full benefits (and remember full benefits vary with earned income) if they have the proper quarters of coverage. One may retire any time; but if retirement occurs before age 65, he or she will receive permanently reduced benefits, as explained below.

Retirement benefits

Benefits are determined, among other things, by the income earned during the working years, but the actual dollar level is calculated by applying a complex formula. When a person is near retirement age, he or she should visit a local Social Security Field Office. While they cannot calculate the benefits precisely until retirement, they can, and will, give an approximation. When one does retire and receives benefits, they are adjusted every January to offset cost-of-living increases.

The benefits will vary with the number of dependents. A husband and wife will receive more than a single person; if there are children under 18, even larger monthly payments are made.

A married couple, both of whom work, will have a choice. Since they both pay taxes, they both earn benefits. Moreover, each will earn benefits for their spouse. When they retire, each may take his or her benefits as an individual, or one member may take his or her benefits as a worker with a spouse. They have the choice of taking the higher.

The law does, however, discriminate against some two-income married couples. In some cases there is a Social Security benefit payment reduction for any public pension (federal, state, or local) received. Affected are benefits based on a spouse's Social Security. Moreover, for the reduction to be made, a retiree must have a non-Social Security type public pension in his or her own right. This discriminates against couples of whom both work but only one has Social Security, and the one that does not has a public pension plan other than Social Security. An example will clarify this. A and B are a married couple both of whom work. A has Social Security, and B has a pension plan under a state or local government but not Social Security. When they retire, the Social Security benefits to be paid because B is a dependent of A will be reduced because B has a pension from a state or local government. The payment due B may be reduced by as much as two-thirds, depending on the size of the state benefit.

Early or late retirement

An individual may receive benefits as early as age 62, but if he or she does, those benefits are reduced. Benefits are calculated in the regular way and are then reduced by five-ninths of 1 percent for each month the retiree is under age 65 at the time of retirement. If a person retires at age 62, he or she is 36 months under age 65; hence retirement benefits are 80 percent of what they would be at age 65 ($36 \times 5/9 = 180/9 = 20$).[2] No retirement benefits are available before age 62.

Delaying retirement beyond age 65 will increase the regular benefits by 3 percent for each year up to age 70, the maximum increase being 15 percent.

Limits to earnings

The law requires that if a person is drawing Social Security benefits and is under age 70, he or she loses some benefits for any earned income above a certain level. ("Earned income" consists of wages and salaries; "unearned income" consists of interest and dividends). Unearned income is not included in the calculation. There are two different possible losses; one for people between age 65 and 70, and one for those between 62 and 65.

In 1990 the maximum amount a person 65 or over (but under 70) may earn without losing benefits is $9,360 per year. The Social Security benefits are cut by **one** dollar for every **three** dollars of earned income above this $9,360 exempt amount.

A person between the age of 62 and 65 is subject to a different rule. He or she has an exemption of only $6,800 per year. A person in this age category loses **one** dollar of benefits for every **two** dollars of earned income above the exempt amount. The exempt amount is increased yearly to offset increases in the cost of living. This provision of the law no longer applies when the recipient reaches age 70; he or she can then earn as much as desired and still receive full benefits.

Disability payments

Disability payments dollarwise are calculated exactly the same way as retirement benefits, and dollarwise they are the same amount as retirement at age 65 benefits. To qualify a person must be unable to engage in any substantial gainful activity. If the disabled person is merely unable to perform his or her regular work, that is not enough to qualify the person if

---

2. Beginning in the year 2000, early retirement benefits will be reduced by 15/18 of 1 percent for each month that a retiree under 65. At 62, then, retirement benefits would be 70 percent of what they would be at age 65 ($36 \times 15/18 = 540/18 = 30$).

other work can be performed. Moreover, the disability must be expected to last at least twelve months. Disability payments start after a five-month waiting period.

The amount of work credit (quarters of coverage) needed to qualify for disability benefits varies with the age of the person when he or she becomes disabled. Before age 24, only one and a half years (six quarters) are needed during the three-year period just before the disability started. During ages 24 through 31, the person needs credit for one-half the time between age 31 and the time the disability occurred. After age 31, the amount of credit needed varies with the age of the person from a low of five years (20 quarters) between the ages of 31 to 42, to a high of ten years' coverage for a person becoming disabled at age 62 and older.

Survivors' benefits: Family benefits

In the case of death, the survivors receive a lump-sum settlement as well as a monthly payment. The lump-sum settlement is $255.00 The monthly benefit varies with the income of the deceased as well as with the number of dependents.

Normally these dependents are unmarried children under the age of 18—up to 19 if still in high school—and a spouse. The payments are made to the mother on behalf of the children if they are under 16. From ages 16 to 18 the payments are made to the children, but they must be unmarried. If the children are in high school, the payment may continue until age 19.

A surviving spouse under 60 without dependent children does not qualify as a dependent and does not receive benefits until reaching age 60.

Social Security and income taxes

The 1983 changes in the law increased Social Security taxes for everyone, but the increase was particularly severe for the self-employed. To soothe the pain of this, Congress authorized a Social Security tax credit—but only for the self-employed—which could be used to reduce personal income taxes a bit. This tax credit was 2.3 percent in 1985, and 2 percent in 1986 through 1989. Beginning in 1990, this credit was eliminated, but it was replaced by a tax deduction equal to 50 percent of the self-employment tax.

The 1983 law also made a portion of Social Security benefits taxable, in some cases, for the first time. The law defines a base amount of income, which is $25,000 ($32,000 on a joint return). If one-half of Social Security benefits, together with adjusted gross income and interest income on tax-exempt bonds, exceeds the base amount, a tax is due. The tax would be due on the lower of the following two items:

1. One-half of Social Security benefits
2. One-half of the excess of the combined income over the base amount.

ANNUITIES

An annuity is a contract with a life insurance company in which the company agrees to pay the annuitant an income stream for a specific period of time. The income stream may be fixed in dollar amounts per month or per year, or it may be variable. The specific period of time for which the payment is to be made may be for a given number of years, or it may be for life. If it is for life, the annuitant cannot outlive his or her principal. An annuity then is a device to enable a person to retire. Annuities are sold by life insurance companies because life contingencies are involved. Life insurance protects the insured's beneficiaries from having the income stream cut off due to a premature death. An annuity can protect an annuitant from outliving his or her accumulated assets due to a lengthy retirement period.

The annuity principle

To be sure, if the assets are large enough a person can live on his or her investment income and never dip into the principal. But an annuity will enable a retiree to dip into the principal and still not outlive it. This is because, as with life insurance, the insurance company applies the law of averages to large numbers of individuals. If each individual from among a large group of people of the same age were to rely on his or her individual accumulated assets, some would outlive their principal; others would not. Insurance companies, however, can guarantee that none will outlive their principal. While the company does not know which individuals in a large group will die at what age, the company does know how many will die at each age. The insurance company can scientifically liquidate the principal sum of all the individuals. Those who live to a ripe age will be drawing on the funds of those who die earlier.

Annuities are the opposite of life insurance, but life contingencies are involved. As with life insurance, the law of averages is applied to large numbers. Annuity tables are used, which indicate how many individuals out of a large group will still be alive at the end of each year. Annuity tables go up to 110 years and are different from mortality tables.

Uses of annuities

Generally annuities are used to provide retirement income. However, they can also be used to free capital and hence increase the retirement income and sometimes to save taxes. For example, if a person had accumulated assets of $200,000 over the years, he or she could invest this conservatively at, say, 8 percent and have an annual income of $16,000 to supplement other retirement income that might be received. An annuity could increase this. A man age 65 can buy a single-premium straight-life annuity paying $10,741 per year for about $100,000. The other $100,000 could be invested to yield $8,000 or $9,000. The total income on the $200,000 is enlarged because the annuitant is scientifically liquidating part of the principal. To be sure, there may be less left for one's heirs, and hence it might not be appealing. However, in the above case, 64.7 percent of the $10,741 would not be taxable because it is a return of principal rather than interest income.

Annuity premiums can be paid monthly, quarterly, semiannually, or annually, just like life insurance. Premiums are paid over the years, and a principal sum is accumulated on behalf of the individual. Over the years the annuity builds up a cash surrender value just like permanent life insurance. In the case of annuities this is called account value. Again, as in the case of life insurance, a person can turn in an annuity at any time and take the account value. If the individual dies prior to when the payments are to begin, the beneficiaries generally receive the principal sum. However, some insurance companies pay either the account value or the sum of all premiums paid in, whichever is the greater. This method of buying an annuity is a planned savings program.

It is also possible to buy an annuity in one lump-sum payment. People of some means may do this. Also people may use the cash surrender value of their paid-up life insurance policy to buy a single premium annuity when they wish to retire. This is generally one of the settlement options of life insurance policies.

The annuitant selects when he or she wants the annuity payments to begin—monthly, quarterly, semiannually, or annually. the dollar amount of the payment an annuitant will receive is determined by several factors: first, the principal sum built up on his or her behalf. This sum is dependent on the total dollars in premiums paid, plus the interest earned over the years. Then an allowance must be made for expenses by the insurance company. Finally, the amount of the annuity is determined by the life expectancy of the annuitant, and the type of annuity selected.

The older the person is when he or she starts receiving payments, the higher the payment for any principal sum. Women, since they live longer than men, on the average, receive a slightly lower payment than men of the same age with the same principal sum, because a woman will receive the payment for a longer period of time.

Most annuities are deferred annuities; that is, premiums are paid over the years and benefits are deferred until later in life. But there are also immediate annuities, where one lump-sum premium is paid and benefits begin immediately. Whenever payments begin, there are a number of options from which to choose.

An annuitant may select a lump-sum settlement or a number of installments. There are three major installment annuities:

1. *Straight life.* This annuity provides for a periodic payment until the annuitant dies. This could be for one month or for thirty years or more, depending on how long the individual lives. If the annuitant dies after even only one monthly payment has been made, the insurance company keeps the remainder of the principal sum built up on the annuitant's behalf. There is nothing left for his or her heirs. For this reason such an annuity guarantees the annuitant the largest

possible payment. For this same reason this type of annuity is not very popular.

2. *Life annuity with period certain.* This annuity pays an income to the annuitant for life, with a minimum number of payments guaranteed. If the annuitant dies before the guaranteed number of payments have been made, they continue to be made to the beneficiary until the guaranteed minimum has been made. Quite often a 10- to 20-year (120–240 months) period is selected. The insurance company must make payments until the annuitant dies or until ten (or twenty) years have passed, whichever occurs last.

An individual of a given age with a given principal sum built up, will receive a smaller yearly payment with this guarantee than without it.

3. *Guaranteed premium refund annuity.* This annuity is also called the "installment refund annuity." It will pay an income for life with a guarantee that the total amount to be paid will be at least equal to the total premiums paid. If the person dies before collecting all the premiums he or she has paid over the years, the beneficiaries receive the difference. This difference can be taken in installments or in one lump sum.

The joint and survivorship annuity

The joint and survivorship annuity guarantees a payment for the entire life of two individuals. Since two individuals are involved, the risk to the insurance company is greater, and hence a given principal sum will provide a smaller benefit payment than will an annuity on one individual. The premiums needed to guarantee a given income are higher on a joint and survivorship annuity than on a single annuity. Often, but not always, the joint annuity is written so that when one member dies the payments, while they continue, decrease in amount. Generally this reduction is to 75 percent, 66.6 percent, or even to 50 percent of what the two individuals were receiving, which lowers the cost somewhat.

Most annuity contracts (as well as life insurance contracts with a cash surrender value) permit the option of converting to a joint annuity at the time payments are to begin.

The fixed annuity

Traditionally, annuities were nearly always fixed annuities, contracts in which everything was determined and agreed to in advance. The only thing the insurance company did not know was the dollar amount of interest the annuity would earn over the years on future premiums, but a conservative assumption was made. The premiums were invested in bonds or mortgages that yielded a known return for a known period of time. The insurance company then could calculate accurately how large a principal sum would be generated for any annuitant. When the annuitant retired, the insurance company would be able to guarantee a fixed dollar payment per month or per year for life. Actuaries have constructed tables that deplete the principal sum actuarily but also make an allowance for interest to be earned on the declining principal.

The major problem with fixed annuities is that inflation erodes the principal sum both while it is being built up and also while it is being paid out. Consequently, fixed annuities have become somewhat less popular in recent years and interest has been stimulated in the variable annuity.

The variable annuity was developed in an attempt to protect the annuitant against inflation both during the premium-paying years and during retirement. Premiums on variable annuities are invested in open-end investment companies. This is very much like investing in mutual funds, which were described in Chapter 17. Some insurance companies manage their own portfolio through a subsidiary broker-dealer and some place it with an established mutual fund. A portfolio may be designed specifically for the life insurance company involved or an existing mutual fund may be used.

The variable annuity

The investor will usually have several choices with respect to the type of portfolio into which his or her premiums are to go. For example, a growth fund, an equity income fund, a bond fund, a money market fund, or a somewhat higher risk, capital appreciation equity portfolio may be selected.

Under a variable annuity contract the premiums paid are used to buy a block of stock in the open-end investment company called an accumulation unit. For example, if premiums are $300 per month, this $300 may buy ten units in one month and fifteen units in another as the price of the unit fluctuates. The principal sum being built up on the annuitant's behalf would accumulate more and more units as time passed. These units, and hence the principal sum, would fluctuate in value. Hopefully, however, each unit would rise in the long run and this, together with the new units being purchased, would provide protection against inflation.

When the person retires, the retirement income is calculated as follows: First, the value of the accumulation units is calculated at their market value to obtain the principal sum. The first annual payment is then calculated in the same way as a fixed annuity would be. If, for example, the principal sum is $200,000, and the actuarial tables indicate that for a person of his or her age a $10,000 annual payment could be made on a fixed annuity of the type chosen, then the first payment from the variable annuity would also be $10,000. The initial payment ($10,000) is then divided by the present market value of one accumulation unit. This indicates how many accumulation units are currently required to meet the $10,000. Suppose the market value of one accumulation unit is $50; then two hundred units are needed to make the first payment, and future payments will always be equal to the fluctuating value of two hundred units. It is expected that the value of the units will rise in the long run, increasing the $10,000 annual retirement income.

Most variable annuity contracts will give an annuitant the option to convert a variable annuity into a fixed annuity at retirement. In such a case the $10,000 initial payment described above would become fixed and guaranteed. The insurance company would simply convert the $200,000 principal sum in the accumulation units into fixed obligations in order to finance this. In such a case the annuitant would have hedged against inflation during the accumulation period but not after retirement.

The cost of annuities

Several factors determine the cost of an annuity:

1. The age of the person receiving the annuity figured at the time the annuity is to begin
2. The age of the person when he or she begins paying premiums
3. The type of annuity selected
4. The monthly annuity payment desired
5. The sex of the annuitant

Since annuities are the opposite of life insurance, the older a person is when payments are to begin, the lower the cost of a given payment. This is obvious, for the older a person is, the fewer the payments will be, on the average.

Insofar as annuity premium payments are concerned, they also vary with the age of the person when he or she buys the annuity, if it is a deferred annuity. A younger person will pay premiums for more years than an older person, and hence the yearly premium will be lower.

The cost also varies with the type of annuity. The straight life annuity, where the payments continue until the death of the annuitant with no guaranteed number of payments, is the least costly.

The larger the monthly payments desired, the higher the cost.

Since women live longer than men, a fixed monthly payment for a woman will be made longer than it will for a man of the same age. Or a fixed sum of money will buy a smaller annuity income for a woman.

The taxation of annuities

Annuity premiums are after-tax dollars, but the investment incomes they earn are not taxed during the accumulation period. Rather they are deferred until the annuitant starts drawing benefits. Then the principal sum comes out tax free, but the investment income earned is taxed. Consequently, the two must be separated. There is also the problem of which comes out first. The IRS assumes they come out simultaneously, but since the dollar amounts are not necessarily the same, a calculation must be made, and this calculation also takes into account that the principal sum is earning more interest as it is being depleted. The result is that part of the benefit is taxed and part is not. The total principal sum (premiums paid plus interest and dividends earned) is annuitized to obtain the expected lifetime return. Then the following formula is used to obtain the taxable proportion:

$$\frac{\text{total premium contributions}}{\text{expected lifetime return}}$$

An example will make this clear. Suppose a person pays premiums of $2,000 per year for 20 years. At 8 percent return it would have grown to $98,845.84 in 20 years. This will buy a 65-year-old male a monthly annuity of $912.50; and a smaller amount for a younger person. The IRS has life expectancy tables; but assume for this example that the life expectancy for a 65-year-old male is 20 years. The monthly income annualized, and then annuitized ($912.50 × 12 × 20 = $219,000) is $219,000. That is the expected lifetime return. The formula mentioned above gives us the following result:

$$\frac{\text{premium contributions}}{\text{expected lifetime return}} = \frac{40,000}{219,000} = 18.26 \text{ percent.}$$

Hence 18.26 percent of the $912.50 monthly annuity payment is not taxable; the remainder is. Once the total of the nontaxable portion equals the total premium paid in (in this case $40,000), all future payments from the annuity are totally taxable.

The Internal Revenue Service imposes a penalty tax on early withdrawals from an annuity contract. A 10 percent tax is imposed on premature payments (full or partial surrender, loans or dividend payments), except under the following circumstances: (1) the contract-holder is age 59 and one-half or older; (2) the contract-holder is disabled; (3) the payment is from a qualified retirement plan; (4) the payment is made because of the death of the annuitant; or (5) the payments are made under an immediate annuity over the life of the annuitant. The life insurance company issuing the annuity contract may also impose certain back-end fees, called surrender charges, for contracts surrendered before a certain time period has elapsed, usually five to ten years after initial purchase.

PRIVATE (AND GOVERNMENT) PENSION PLANS

Most corporations of any size have developed pension plans for their employees to provide a retirement income when they retire from the labor force, usually at age 65. Such plans are designed to supplement Social Security retirement benefits. Regular money contributions are paid into the fund and are invested to earn interest. The fund then is available upon retirement. In some cases, deductions are withheld from the employee's wages, matched by the employer, and paid into the fund. In other cases, the employer makes the entire contribution.

How good a plan an individual has is determined by the retirement benefits it promises, its vesting provisions, and the extent to which it is funded. One should investigate his or her plan to determine these things.

How much the plan promises in the way of retirement benefits may be obvious, but an employee should also consider what happens to the funds built up in his or her behalf if he or she terminates employment prior to retirement, and how sound the plan is—that is, how likely it will be able to deliver what it promises.

Vesting and portability

Vesting concerns what happens to the funds built up on behalf of the employee if employment should terminate prior to retirement. If an employee is vested, employees may take the funds with them; if he or she is not vested, the funds will be lost. A few plans provide immediate and full vesting, but most plans provide for partial delayed vesting; that is, a portion of the funds are vested every so many years until eventually full vesting is achieved.

Since there is bound to be some turnover, lack of immediate vesting permits higher benefits to those who do retire, with a given cost, or reduces the cost of a pension plan with a given retirement program. Some employers also feel that delayed vesting reduces labor turnover. It is debatable whether this in itself is desirable, because it reduces the mobility of labor; mobility of both labor and resources is required, many argue, to keep our economy dynamic. In any event, those workers who leave the firm before vesting occurs subsidize those who stay and finally retire. Federal regulations that now require certain vesting provisions as well as other matters are spelled out below.

Some vested plans are also portable; if so, the funds are combined with the funds of any new employer's plan. If they are vested but not portable, the employee usually gets his or her funds in one lump sum when he or she moves. In such a case, he or she can roll them over into an IRA (see below). If this applies to your client, he or she should consider such a rollover; otherwise there can be complex tax problems.

Funding

Funding is another technical term with which a person should be familiar. A pension plan can be 100 percent funded, partially funded, or zero percent funded. If a plan is not at all funded (zero percent), it is referred to as a pay-as-you-go plan. In such a case, an employer takes whatever money is needed out of operating revenue and pays retired employees a pension; the employee contributes nothing. This, of course, reduces profits. A pay-as-you-go plan is considered actuarially unsound and there are very few of them.

At the other extreme are the fully funded plans (100 percent funded). A fully funded pension plan is one where assets are accumulated each year in an amount equal to the future pension benefits earned that year. Actuarially the future cost of a pension plan can be predicted with great accuracy. If the pension plan is then designed so that the annual buildup of future benefits (discounted to present value) is always equal to the annual buildup of assets, there is 100 percent funding. In such a case, every employee could be paid his or her pension at any and all times. One hundred percent funding can be achieved by keeping the benefits lower than in a partially funded plan, or the contributions (cost of the pension fund) higher. Most pension plans provide for substantial tax benefits (see below). To receive these tax benefits they must be approved (qualified) by the I.R.S., and to be approved they must meet certain mininum funding requirements. See below for a further discussion of this.

Funding and vesting are somewhat related. If a plan has delayed vesting, then many of the contributions made for personnel who leave the company will be left in the fund. They can be used to pay benefits to employees who actually do retire.

Employee Retirement Income Security Act (ERISA)

Prior to the passage of the Employee Retirement Income Security Act (ERISA) of 1974, there were very few federal controls over private pension funds and only loose, haphazard regulations at the state level. The act was passed in response to complaints that many workers were not obtaining their benefits upon retirement. Generally this was because either their pension funds were not adequately funded and moneys for retirement payments were not available or the plan did not provide vesting when the employee left prior to retirement.

The federal act's main purpose was to establish minimum requirements regarding vesting and funding, but it contained some other provisions as well. For example, the act provides that each fund make an annual report to the Secretary of Labor and provide all employees covered with full information regarding their benefits, including access to financial records.

The act also established the Pension Benefit Guarantee Corporation (PBGC). This is a government corporation and operates much like the FDIC. It guarantees pension rights, and if a pension fund collapses and cannot pay pension benefits the PBGC could pay eligible retirees up to $1,858 per month (1987). The PBGC is to be financed with premiums collected from the employer amounting to $16.00 per worker per year, with additional premiums due for underfunded plans.

The act established minimum vesting procedures. Employers may choose one of two alternative methods of allowing workers to obtain vesting. First, they may decide to grant full vesting after five years and provide nothing until then. Second, the employer may grant 20 percent vesting after three years, 40 percent after four years, 60 percent after five years, 80 percent after six years, and full (100 percent) after seven years.

Pension benefits

When a person retires he or she will receive pension benefit payments in accordance with the provisions of the plan. These vary. In some cases, the fund will simply buy the retiree an annuity from a life insurance company. In such a case, he or she will have to consider all types of annuities discussed above.

Some pension funds will allow a person to withdraw benefits upon retirement in one lump sum rather than in installments. Others do not give this option. If a retiree withdraws in one lump sum there could be a complex tax problem. The same is true if he or she withdraws this entire sum over, say, ten years, rather than over a longer period.

Some pension plans provide that the contributions made on the employee's behalf are earmarked for that person and are invested on his or her behalf, and then when one retires, the money built up is his or hers. If a fixed percentage of compensation is contributed by the employer each year, this is called a **money purchase plan.** If the employer can vary the annual contribution (even to zero), then the plan is known as a **profit sharing plan**. Both of these plans are known as **defined contribution plans**. The amount of benefit is determined by how much was paid in and how successful the fund managers are in investing the funds. Nothing is guaranteed while the fund is being built up. At retirement, one can usually take the benefits in one lump sum or in installments. A money purchase plan is really a fully funded plan.

There are other so-called **fixed benefit plans** (sometimes called **defined benefit plans**). Under these plans, the funds contributed on one's behalf are commingled with those of fellow employees. While each employee has a claim, there are no specific dollars designated to each person. Instead of an individual fund for each employee, there is a collectively owned group fund.

At retirement, the benefits are calculated by a formula that usually takes into account the salary range and the length of time with the company. For example, a retiree might receive 1 percent of his or her average salary over the last five years for every year with the company. If the average salary over the last five years was $30,000 and one was with the company thirty years, the pension would be $9,000 per year.

Under the fixed benefit plan the benefits then are not as directly tied to the contributions as is the case in the money purchase or profit sharing plans. Under this fixed plan, the group fund could be used to provide a monthly payment or the fund could buy an annuity with a life insurance company; the practice varies.

While most fixed benefit plans are not fully (100 percent) funded, they must meet the IRS minimum funding requirements. The law requires some funding, enough to make it actuarially sound. Also only the fixed benefit plan must pay premiums to the Pension Benefit Guarantee Corporation discussed above.

ERISA defines the minimum and maximum contributions and/or benefits to which qualified plans must adhere. If these limits are not met each year, the employer could lose the tax deduction for the plan contributions or possibly have tax penalties assessed.

Most pension plans are funded with dollars that are not taxed, and hence substantial benefits are obtained. To obtain these benefits the plan must be what is called qualified, that is, it must be approved by the Internal Revenue Service. If the plan is nondiscriminatory in that all employees participate in it on the same basis and it is in compliance with the Employee Retirement Income Security Act discussed above, it will be approved.

    The funds going into an approved plan are tax sheltered; that is, a tax is not paid on them. In addition, the interest and dividends that they earn are not taxable, nor is any capital gain that may accrue. They are taxed as income upon retirement as an individual withdraws funds. It should also be noted that any contributions made by employers are fully deductible for them on their tax return during the year in which they are made.

Tax benefits of most private pension plans: The qualified plans

There are some pension plans (known as thrift plans) into which the employee pays after-tax dollars that are then matched by the employer. The employer's contributions are not taxed to the employee until received at retirement, and neither are the fund's earnings. But since the employee's contributions were taxed before they went in, there is a special problem. When the retiree receives the benefits, his or her contributions are not taxed but the employer's contribution and the investment income it has earned are. Each benefit payment received then is partly tax free and partly taxed from the beginning. The calculation to determine what proportion is taxed is made just as in the case of an annuity discussed above.

    The total principal sum is annuitized to obtain the expected lifetime income payments just like in the case of an annuity as explained above in the section entitled "The Taxation of Annuities." Then the same formula is applied:

Employee after-tax contributions

$$\frac{\text{employee's total contribution}}{\text{expected lifetime return}}.$$

For example,

$$\frac{100,000}{500,000} = 20 \text{ percent.}$$

Therefore, 20 percent of each retirement check received is tax free and 80 percent is taxed. However, after the retiree in this example has received $100,000 tax free, the entire amount of the additional payments is taxed.

There are two special corporate pension plans. They are the Simplified Employee Pension Plan and the 401K Salary Reduction Plan.

OTHER RETIREMENT PLANS

*Two special
pension plans:
The simplified
employee pension
plan (SEP)*

Corporations that do not have a regular qualified pension plan discussed above may establish an SEP for their employees. There is less red tape involved in establishing an SEP, and fewer reports must be filed with the IRS and Department of Labor. Because of this, they appeal to smaller businesses. The employer must sponsor the plan but need not be involved in administering it; the employee may choose the custodian. Moreover, it may be a self-directed plan in which the individual has some control over the investment decisions. The employer can be the only contributor to the plan or the SEP can be set up on a salary reduction arrangement. See the next section for more detail. Under an SEP, $7,000 (as indexed) of the person's salary annually may be put away tax deferred. This figure is indexed annually to offset inflation (as measured by the CPI). (See Chapter 1). The earnings and capital gains that accrue are also tax free until the person retires and begins drawing benefits. The funds cannot be withdrawn until the year in which the individual becomes 59-1/2 years of age, and the person must start withdrawing funds when he or she reaches age 70-1/2. There is a special 10 percent penalty tax (which is over and above the regular income tax) for early withdrawal of funds. This penalty for early withdrawals is waived if a person becomes totally disabled. Or if a person dies prior to taking the funds, the dependents may withdraw them without penalty.

Finally, there is no penalty for early withdrawals if the funds are used to meet major medical expenses not covered by insurance and if the funds are distributed in the form of a life annuity, SEP contributions are fully and immediately vested.

*Cash or deferred
arrangements
(CODAs)*

These plans are defined in the section of the Internal Revenue Code known as 401(k) that permits tax-deferred salary reductions. Under this plan, a plan participant may reduce his or her salary up to a maximum of $7,000 (as indexed) annually and set the reduction aside for retirement purposes. Neither the $7,000 going into the plan nor the investment income or capital gain on it is taxed until it is withdrawn upon retirement; that is taxes are deferred. For 1990, the maximum salary reduction is $7,979, and, similar to the SEP contributions, this amount will be indexed annually to offset inflation.

As with an SEP, a person may not set up this type of a plan on his or her own. An employer must establish and sponsor a plan; employees may then tie into it. New plans may be set up or existing corporate profit-sharing plans may be amended to include 401(k) provisions. This type of plan is very complex and certain other limitations apply; but if your client's employer has one, your client should investigate it.

Employee contributions are fully and immediately vested. The penalty for early withdrawals, and its waiver noted above for the SEP, applies to this type of plan. It should be noted that the $7,000 (as indexed) annual tax-deferred limit applies only to the employee's contribution. The employer may add more, both in the case of an SEP and a cash or deferred arrangement.

All government-sponsored (administered) pension plans are exempt from the 1974 Federal Employee Retirement Income Security Act. This includes all local government plans as well as state plans. There are hundreds of government pension plans, some of which are very good and some of which are rather poor. Consequently, only certain generalizations can be made. Even though government plans are exempt from the 1974 act, they can be approved by the IRS, and if they are, the tax benefits discussed above apply.

Some government plans are managed by life insurance companies. Those are actuarially and financially very sound. Other government funds are managed by trust departments of commercial banks and are generally fairly high quality plans.

Still other government plans are managed by the governing unit itself or an agency established by the government for that purpose. In such a case, funding varies from plan to plan; it ranges from fairly high to virtually zero. Vesting provisions vary from relatively early and complete vesting to no vesting whatsoever until the employee retires. If a client is a government employee and has a pension plan, it is suggested that the plan be investigated very closely to determine just what benefits are provided.

In addition to the retirement plans discussed above, there are individual retirement accounts. The 1986 change in the tax law eliminated the deductible IRA for some people. However, many are still eligible. If a person is eligible and establishes an IRA, up to $2,000 per year of earned income may be placed into it on a tax-deferred basis. That is, the $2,000 contribution is not taxed, nor are the earnings on it until withdrawn at retirement. The contribution must be based on earned income (wages and salary); interest, dividends, rent, or other property income do not count.

An individual is eligible for a full IRA deduction if he or she is:

(1) employed but the employer does not have a pension plan.
(2) self-employed, and does not have a Keogh Plan (see the discussion of the Keogh plan below).
(3) employed and has a pension plan at work, but his or her adjusted gross income (AGI) is less than $40,000 if married, and $25,000 if single. The $40,000 ($25,000) AGI test must be met before the IRA deduction.[3]

A married individual is eligible for a reduced IRA deduction if he or she is employed, has a retirement plan at work and has an AGI of $40,000 or more (but not above $50,000). In such a case, the individual must reduce his or her deduction by 20 percent for every dollar of AGI

---

3. In calculating AGI an individual must also take into account interest and dividend income. That is, while dividend and interest income cannot be used to determine contributions to an IRA, it does count in determining eligibility.

above $40,000. For example, if AGI is $41,000, the deduction may be $1,800 (and the contribution $2,000). If AGI is $45,000, the maximum deduction is $1,000 (and the contribution $2,000). At $50,000, the deduction is completely phased out. The deduction limits for single taxpayers apply at $25,000 and $35,000, respectively.

If both spouses have earned income and are eligible as described above, each may establish a separate IRA, and hence $4,000 per year may go tax deferred into a retirement account.

There is also a spousal IRA. It is applicable to a married couple of which only one has earned income—wages and salary—and if they qualify for an IRA as described above. Then an extra $250 per year may be set aside on behalf of the non-income-earning member. The spousal IRA must also be set up as two separate accounts; they may not be commingled. Spousal accounts need not be split into $2,000 and $250, however. Varying amounts of dollars may go into them; the only rule is that the nonworking person's account must receive at least $250. But they could be split into $1,125 each.

If an individual is self-employed and the spouse has no earned income, he or she might want to consider employing the nonworking spouse at least until $2,000 is earned, so that each may establish a $2,000 IRA. In addition, the wages paid to the spouse may be deducted as a business expense. If this is done, however, be sure the spouse does bona fide work, contributes to the business, and is paid for at reasonable rates.

An IRA may then accumulate earnings and capital gains tax deferred. Regular income taxes will be due upon retirement when the money is drawn out. The individual may not touch the funds in the account until age 59-1/2 without a penalty, and withdrawals must begin at age 70-1/2, just as in the case of an SEP. The penalty for early withdrawals is also the same (10 percent extra tax) and the disability waiver applies; and dependents have the same rights in the event of the account holder's death. When funds are withdrawn, he or she may take them all in one lump-sum payment, convert them to an annuity, or choose an income stream spread over the number of years equal to the life expectancy. (If married, an individual may even spread them over the joint life expectancy of both. See the section "When Funds Are Withdrawn" below for a more detailed discussion of this.)

It should be noted that if a person has both a corporate pension plan and an IRA, and if he or she retires and takes the corporate pension in one lump sum but is not yet 70-1/2 years of age, he or she may roll the pension payment over into an IRA tax free and let it accumulate tax deferred until age 70-1/2. This should be studied very carefully, however, because if pension funds are withdrawn in one lump sum, they can, under certain circumstances, be subject to special five-year forward averaging tax provisions. On the other hand, if a retiree rolls the funds over into an IRA, he or she can postpone taxes until age 70-1/2 when they are withdrawn, but the privilege of using the five-year forward averaging for one lump-sum withdrawal will be lost.

If one (or both) spouse does not qualify for a deductible IRA, he or she may still establish nondeductible IRAs. That is, the $2,000 annual contribution is made with after-tax dollars, but it can accumulate interest, dividends, and capital gains that are tax deferred until withdrawn at retirement. Accumulating tax-deferred earnings is still very advantageous. Tables 18–2 and 18–3 and Figures 18–3 and 18–4 show the buildup of a deductible IRA, a nondeductible IRA, and a regular savings account at various interest rates and tax brackets.

The nondeductible IRA

If an individual is self-employed, he or she may establish his or her own retirement fund. These are called Keogh plans, and the only requirement for establishing one is to be self-employed. This includes people who work for a corporation and have a corporate pension plan, but they are self-employed on the side (moonlighting).

Keogh plans

The ERISA requirements for corporate plans apply equally to Keogh plans. The types of retirement plans are also the same—profit-sharing, money purchase pension or defined benefit plans. An unincorporated business must also include all employees who meet the minumum eligibility requirements. Benefits for these employees—known as common law employees—must also be comparable to the benefits provided for the owner(s).

In addition to the plan contribution, the self-employed person, or any of his or her employees, may also contribute after-tax dollars to the plan, if stated in the plan document. These funds, like the employee con-

The following table will work for most people in permitting them to calculate their deductible and nondeductible IRA.

**Box 18–1
The partially deductible IRA and the nondeductible IRA at a glance**

Single income	Married filing jointly	Allowable deductible contribution	Allowable nondeductible contribution
$25,000	$40,000	$2,000	$ 0
26,000	41,000	1,800	200
27,000	42,000	1,600	400
28,000	43,000	1,400	600
29,000	44,000	1,200	800
30,000	45,000	1,000	1,000
31,000	46,000	800	1,200
32,000	47,000	600	1,400
33,000	48,000	400	1,600
34,000	49,000	200	1,800
35,000	50,000	0	2,000

Table 18–2 Buildup of an individual retirement account—$2,000 deposited at beginning of each year—28 percent tax bracket

End of Year	Interest at 6%			Interest at 8%			Interest at 10%			Interest at 12%		
	With IRA		Without	With IRA		Without	With IRA		Without	With IRA		Without
	Deductible	Nondeductible	IRA	Deductible	Nondeductible	IRA	Deductible	Nondeductible	IRA	Deductible	Nondeductible	IRA
	1	2	3	1	2	3	1	2	3	1	2	3
5	11,951	8,604	8,189	12,672	9,124	8,544	13,431	9,670	8,913	14,230	10,246	9,296
10	27,943	20,119	18,306	31,291	22,530	19,849	35,062	25,245	21,531	39,309	28,303	23,364
15	49,345	35,528	30,805	58,649	42,227	34,807	69,899	50,328	39,394	83,507	60,125	44,654
20	77,985	56,150	46,248	98,845	71,169	54,598	125,005	90,724	64,684	161,397	116,206	76,874
25	116,313	83,745	65,327	157,709	113,694	80,785	216,364	135,782	100,485	298,668	215,041	125,625
30	167,603	120,674	88,899	244,692	176,178	115,435	361,887	260,559	151,171	540,585	389,221	199,429
35	256,242	170,094	118,023	372,204	267,787	161,281	596,254	429,303	222,927	966,926	696,187	311,109
40	328,095	236,229	154,004	559,562	402,885	221,941	973,704	701,067	324,512	1,718,285	1,237,165	480,122

Note:

Column 1 ASSUMES $2,000 ANNUAL INVESTMENT COMPOUNDED at 6%, 8%, 10% AND 12%.

Column 2 ASSUMES $1,440 ($2,000 LESS 28% TAX) ANNUAL INVESTMENT COMPOUNDED AT 6%, 8%, 10% AND 12%).

Column 3 ASSUMES $1,440 ($2,000 LESS 28% TAX) ANNUAL INVESTMENT COMPOUNDED AT 4.32% (6% LESS 28% TAX); 5.76% (8% LESS 28% TAX); 7.2% (10% LESS 28% TAX) AND 8.64% (12% LESS 28% TAX)

Value calculated as of the end of the year.

Table 18–3 Buildup of an individual retirement account—$2,000 deposited at beginning of each year—15 percent tax bracket

| End of year | Interest at 6.00 percent | | | Interest at 8.00 percent | | | Interest at 10.00 percent | | | Interest at 12.00 percent | | |
| | With IRA | | Without IRA | With IRA | | Without IRA | With IRA | | Without IRA | With IRA | | Without IRA |
	Deductible 1	Nondeductible 2	3	Deductible 1	Nondeductible 2	3	Deductible 1	Nondeductible 2	3	Deductible 1	Nondeductible 2	3
5	11,951	10,158	9,892	12,672	10,771	10,399	13,431	11,417	10,929	14,230	12,096	11,483
10	27,943	23,752	22,578	31,291	26,597	24,849	35,062	29,803	27,363	39,309	33,413	30,145
15	49,345	41,943	38,846	58,649	49,851	44,928	69,899	59,415	52,074	83,507	70,981	60,475
20	77,985	66,288	59,707	98,846	84,019	72,826	126,005	107,104	89,231	161,397	137,188	109,767
25	116,313	98,866	86,459	157,909	134,223	111,591	216,364	183,909	145,103	298,668	253,868	189,876
30	167,603	142,463	120,765	244,692	207,988	165,454	361,887	307,604	229,114	540,585	459,497	320,071
35	236,242	200,805	164,758	372,204	316,374	240,296	596,254	506,816	355,438	966,926	821,887	531,663
40	328,095	278,881	221,173	559,562	475,628	344,289	973,704	827,648	545,386	1,718,285	1,460,542	875,544

Value calculated as of the end of the year.

Column 1: $2,000 invested and compounded at 6, 8, 10, and 12 percent.

Column 2: $1,700 invested and compounded at 6,8,10, and 12 percent.

Column 3: $1,700 invested and compounded at 5.10, 6.80, 8.50, and 10.20 percent.

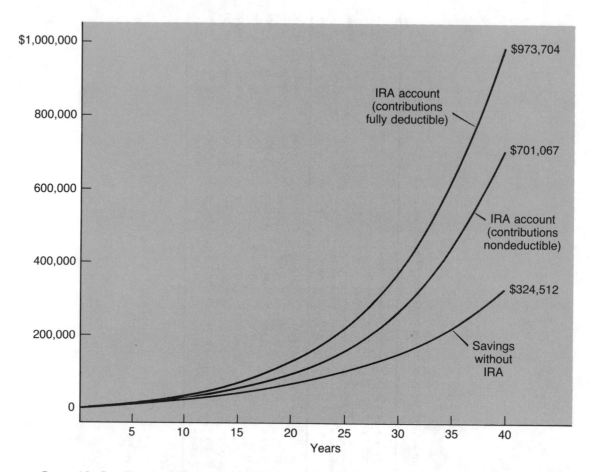

Figure 18—3   *Growth of IRA account ($2,000. per year) compared to unsheltered savings, 10 percent compounded annually, 28 percent tax bracket.*

tributions discussed under corporate plans, will accumulate tax-deferred until withdrawn.

The S corporation   In recent years many self-employed, especially service professionals—such as doctors and lawyers—have chosen the corporation rather than remaining unincorporated. If a doctor (or a group of them) incorporates, his or her fees flow into the corporation, which now pays him or her a salary. The corporation may now establish a pension fund for him or her.

A businessperson may incorporate as a traditional corporation or he or she may incorporate as what is known as an "S" corporation, which is what many professionals have done. In an S corporation all corporate income or losses is taxed a personal income or losses even if not passed through.

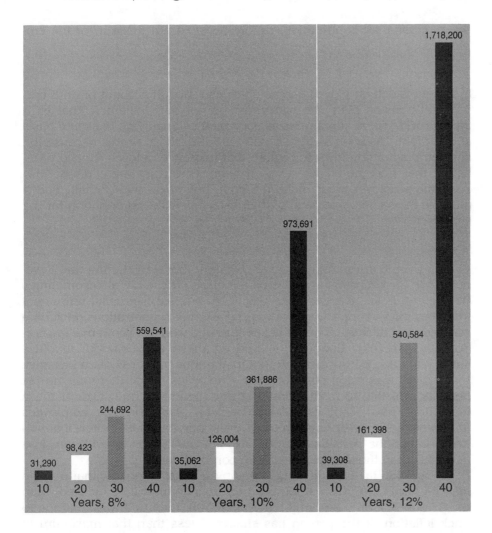

Growth of $2,000 per year in an individual retirement account for 10, 20, 30, and 40 Figure 18–4
years at 8, 10, and 12 percent (compounded annually)

If one incorporates as an S corporation, the funds which may be set aside tax-deferred are identical to those permitted under a corporate plan.

Both a Keogh Plan and an S corporation pension plan may be set up so that part of the total contribution is profit sharing and part is a mandatory (or defined) contribution; most frequently 15 percent of the total is profit sharing, and 10 percent is defined contribution. The profit-sharing contributions need not be made even if there are profits; and of course they may be made partially, or made in some years but not others. This may save money, because if the employer chooses not to make the profit-sharing contribution, he or she need not make it for the employees.

*What about
employees?*

If a client is self-employed and establishes a Keogh account or an S corporation pension plan, the plan must be nondiscriminatory. That is, it must provide for all employees as soon as they qualify on the same basis as the client. "As soon as they qualify" are the crucial words, because the law permits the employer to require that they be employed for two years before they become eligible to participate. Once they are eligible, however, the employer must make the contribution on their behalf, and it must be the same percentage of their salary as is the contribution for the employer.

*Tax-sheltered
annuities (TSA)—
403(b) plans*

Certain people are permitted under Section 403(b) of the Internal Revenue Code to purchase tax-sheltered annuities. These are also sometimes referred to as tax-deferred annuities (TDA) and supplemental retirement annuities (SRA). People who work for tax-exempt organizations, including schools and colleges, are eligible; people who work for profit-making corporations are not. Congress authorized these tax-sheltered annuities some years ago because tax-exempt institutions have less of an incentive to establish a pension plan for their employees, since there are no tax benefits available to institutions that are already exempt. Even if these institutions have since established pension plans for their employees (and most have), their employees may still purchase tax-sheltered annuities because the pensions that tax-exempt institutions provide are less generous than those of profit-making corporations.

The 1986 tax changes added a cap on the total dollars that may go into a 403(b) plan. It is $9,500 per year; this figure will be indexed when the $7,000 SEP or CODA limit reaches $9,500, then both will continue to track inflation. If the person has sheltered less than that maximum in previous years part of it may be recaptured. For example, if clients cannot afford to shelter all of the income the law allows during their thirties and forties, they may wish to recapture all or part of that during their fifties when their income does permit. There is also a recapture cap, and it is $3,000 per year, making the total sum that may be put into a 403(b) $12,500 per year.[4]

If such an annuity is purchased, neither the premium paid nor the annuity's earnings are taxed until the person retires and receives the benefits. As in the case of other plans discussed above, there is a 10 percent penalty for early withdrawal of funds prior to age 59-1/2. This penalty is waived, however, if the person becomes disabled, if the distribution is

---

4. The recapture is permitted only if the person has been with the present employer continuously for 15 years or more.

When a nondeductible IRA is withdrawn, only the income and capital gains (not the contributions) it has earned are taxable. Hence, good records are needed to separate these two items. It is advised that the nondeductible IRA be kept in a separate account to simplify this task. The retiree must prove to the satisfaction of the IRS what the total nondeductible contributions have been.

There is a new form that must be attached to the 1040. It is Form 8606 which shows the annual nondeductible contribution. When funds are withdrawn, the IRS may require the proof. Hence, all past 8606 forms must be kept. Mandatory lifetime record keeping may be upon us. However, some experts believe the IRS will eventually allow a separation of contributions and earnings to be made upon the first year of retirement, and ease the record keeping burden a bit after that. Nevertheless, this does add to the paperwork burden.

**Box 18–2
Keeping tabs on
a nondeductible
IRA**

made in the form of a life annuity, or if the funds are needed for medical payments not covered by insurance. In the event of a death, the survivors may withdraw the funds without a penalty.

Deferred compensation plans are similar to tax-sheltered annuitites, but there is a technical difference. Many college and universities, municipal and state governments and other nontaxable entities have set up these plans in addition to tax-sheltered annuities. But one or the other must be chosen, a person may not have both.

*Deferred
compensation
plans—457 plans*

Under these plans, a person may defer annually up to 25 percent of his or her salary or $7,500, whichever is less. If an individual has another tax-sheltered plan with his or her employer, the individual's contribution to it is counted within the 25 percent but the employer's contribution is not. Neither is any Keogh contribution. This deferred income and the earning or capital gains on it are not taxed until received. Unlike in the case of TSA, if a person has not deferred income in past years, he or she may not go back and pick it up.

The employer withholds this deferred income and invests it on the employee's behalf. Currently these funds may be invested in life insurance policies, annuities, mutual funds, or savings institutions. The penalty for early withdrawals described above applies. The contribution which may be made to a 457 plan is fixed and is not indexed to offset inflation.

When an individual decides to retire, there are several options available. A corporate or Keogh plan document will define what "normal retirement age" is, usually as age 65 and/or a certain number of years with the company. The corporate or Keogh plan may also define policies on early retirement, for instance, age 55 and 15 years of service, and on retirement after normal retirement age, for instance, retirement benefits frozen at

**WHEN FUNDS
ARE WITHDRAWN**

Table 18—4   *Table of joint life expectancy*

Beneficiary's age in year the retiree became 70½	Years of withdrawals
53	31.5
54	30.7
55	29.9
56	29.1
57	28.3
58	27.6
59	26.8
60	26.2
61	25.5
62	24.9
63	24.2
64	23.6
65	23.1
66	22.6
67	22.0
68	21.5
→ 69 ←	→ 21.0 ←
70	20.5
71	20.1
72	19.8
73	19.4
74	19.1
75	18.7
76	18.5
77	18.2
78	17.9
79	17.7
80	17.6
81	17.4
82	17.2

It is important to assure that these minimum distribution requirements are met because insufficient distributions after age 70½ may result in a 50% federal tax penalty on the amount by which the distribution fell short of the required minimum.

Source: Internal Revenue Service

520

If a person withdraws a retirement account in one lump sum, invests it in a withdrawable interest-earning account, and withdraws sums periodically for retirement benefits, the question arises: how long will the money last? It depends on

Box 18—3
How long will money last

1. the payout rate and
2. the earnings.

The following table illustrates this. For example, if the payout rate is 14 percent and the earnings are 9 percent, the funds will last 11.5 years.

Payout rate (Percent)	1	2	3	4	5	6	7	8	9	10	11	12	13	14	15
1															
2	69.4														
3	40.6	55.0													
4	28.8	34.7	46.3												
5	22.3	25.6	30.6	40.3											
6	18.2	20.3	23.2	27.6	35.9										
7	15.5	16.9	18.7	21.2	25.2	32.6									
8	13.4	14.4	15.7	17.4	19.7	23.2	29.8								
9	11.8	12.6	13.6	14.7	16.3	18.4	21.6	27.6							
10	10.6	11.2	11.9	12.8	13.9	15.3	17.2	20.2	25.7						
11	9.6	10.1	10.7	11.3	12.2	13.2	14.5	16.3	19.1	24.1					
12	8.7	9.2	9.7	10.2	10.8	11.6	12.6	13.8	15.5	18.0	22.7				
13	8.1	8.4	8.8	9.2	9.7	10.4	11.1	12.0	13.2	14.7	17.2	21.5			
14	7.4	7.8	8.1	8.5	8.9	9.4	10.0	10.7	11.5	12.6	14.1	16.3	20.4		
15	6.9	7.2	7.5	7.8	8.2	8.6	9.1	9.6	10.2	11.1	12.1	13.5	15.6	19.5	
16	6.5	6.7	7.0	7.2	7.6	7.9	8.2	8.7	9.2	9.9	10.7	11.7	13.2	15.0	18.7
17	6.1	6.3	6.5	6.8	7.0	7.3	7.7	8.0	8.4	8.9	9.6	10.2	11.2	12.5	14.4
18	5.7	5.9	6.2	6.3	6.6	6.8	7.1	7.4	7.7	8.2	8.7	9.2	9.9	10.8	12.1
19	5.4	5.6	5.7	6.0	6.2	6.4	6.7	6.9	7.2	7.6	7.9	8.4	8.9	9.7	10.5
20	5.2	5.3	5.5	5.7	5.8	6.0	6.2	6.4	6.7	7.0	7.3	7.7	8.2	8.7	9.3

If earnings rate is equal to or greater than payout rate money can last indefinitely

Percent earnings on investment

age 65. The method of distribution of the retirement benefits will also be defined by the plan document. Sometimes a lump-sum payment is permitted; or, the company will distribute monthly or annual payments based on the retirement formula; or, the company will purchase an annuity on behalf of the retiree.

Under no circumstances can the commencement of retirement benefits from any source (corporate, IRA, TSA, etc.) be delayed later than age 70-1/2 or else the retiree faces a severe penalty (see below). The rule is that the person must begin withdrawing funds by April 1 of the year following the year in which he or she reaches age 70-1/2.

If the person's birthday falls in the last half of any year (say, 1991) he or she does not reach age 70-1/2 until 1992. Hence, one can postpone distributions until April of the year after that—in the above case, 1993, even though he or she reached age 70-1/2 on January 1, 1992. This same rule on age 70-1/2 applies to retirement distributions from IRAs, SEPs or TSAs. "Normal retirement age" for these plans is defined as any age after 59-1/2.

When receiving retirement benefits, the retiree may elect a lump-sum withdrawal which may be eligible for five-year forward averaging, a favorable one-time tax. The retiree may not use this special tax on funds distributed from an IRA. There is a formula which permits the taxpayer to compute the special tax and hence the tax is paid all at once during the year of the distribution. However, if a retiree was age 50 or older on January 1, 1986, the tax law permits him or her to choose ten-year forward averaging as defined under the pre-1986 Internal Revenue Code.

If the retiree receives an annuity, income tax is paid on payments as received. We described that process earlier in the chapter. If the retiree receives a life expectancy distribution (directly from the plan or from a bank), the IRS has special life expectancy tables which define the minimum annual payment based on age and sex. If this method is used, each year's payment is recalculated based on the fund balance and the new year's life expectancy. For example, at age 65, John Smith's life expectancy is 17 years. He must receive 1/17 of his retirement fund as a minimum payment during this first year. The second year, John's life expectancy is 16.5 years; his minimum annual distribution must be 1/16.5 of the remaining fund balance. Until age 70-1/2, a retiree may begin payments from some sources of funds and not others; after age 70-1/2, payments from all qualified plans must begin.

If the retiree withdraws funds over the life expectancy years and he or she has a spouse, the funds may be withdrawn over the joint life expectancy.[5] This will increase the number of pull-out years, and will postpone and almost certainly reduce taxes. As a retiree pulls funds out over a single life or joint life, the balance remaining will continue to grow, tax deferred. The IRS has joint life expectancy tables that must be used. Table 18–4 is one such joint life expectancy table. It shows that a person, age 70-1/2, and his or her spouse, age 69, have a joint life expectancy of 21 years, and hence 1/21 of the sum in the retirement fund must be withdrawn that year. The next year and the one after that, the withdrawal requirements drop to 1/20.5 and 1/20.1, respectively.

If the retiree is over 70-1/2, he or she may not skip a year and then make it up by withdrawing a larger amount the following year. If the person fails to take out at least the mimimum required each year, the IRS

---

5. For actuarial reasons, and because the figures are based on averages, the joint life expectancy is somewhat longer than the longest single life expectancy of the couple. It is not, of course, the sum of the two.

will assess a 50 percent excise tax penalty on the difference between what was taken out and what the withdrawal should have been.

If IRA, SEP or CODA funds are withdrawn before age 59-1/2 for reasons other than retirement, there is a penalty in the form of a 10 percent surtax on funds withdrawn (see prior discussion under each topic in this chapter). This penalty is waived (1) if the person is totally disabled; (2) if the taxpayer has died and the beneficiary withdraws the funds; (3) if the distribution is received in the form of a life annuity; (4) if the payment is the result of a "qualified domestic relations order"—the result of a divorce settlement; or (5) in the case of a corporate plan or a TSA, the employee separates from service after age 55. This penalty is also waived for certain medical hardship distributions from plans with cash or deferred arrangements (TSAs, certain SEPs, and corporate profit-sharing plans with 401(k) provisions).

SUMMARY REVIEW QUESTIONS

These questions serve as a summary and a review of the chapter. If you are able to answer them all, you have a good understanding of the material covered by the chapter.

1. Social Security is now said to be a matter of right. How is this different from a "needs" test, which is often a necessary prerequisite for welfare payments?
2. What are the different kinds of benefits that the federal government administers under the Social Security Act?
3. Who is covered under the Social Security law?
4. What is meant by quarters of coverage?
5. How are Social Security funds invested, and how may these funds have an impact upon the economy?
6. Why should a person check his or her Social Security records every three years?
7. What happens to Social Security benefits if a person retires prior to 65, or after age 65?
8. How are Social Security benefits taxed?
9. How may it be said that the annuity is,

in the final analysis, an insurance problem?
10. Explain the three major purposes for which annuities are used.
11. Distinguish between the single-premium annuity and the annual-premium annuity.
12. Under what circumstances may it be desirable to puchase a joint and survivorship annuity?
13. Why is it that an annuity on one person is cheaper than a joint and survivorship annuity?
14. Explain briefly any three of the general types of annuity that life insurance companies sell.
15. What are the similarities and differences between the conventional or fixed annuity and the variable annuity?
16. What is portability as the term applies to pension funds?
17. What is the difference between "vesting" and "funding"?
18. Discuss the tax benefits Congress has provided for the self-employed if they establish a retirement program.

19. What is a simplified employee pension plan?

20. What is the Individual Retirement Account?

21. What provision for retirement may a self-employed person undertake?

22. What happens if funds are withdrawn from an IRA prior to age 59 1/2?

CASES

1. George Hill has a salary of $30,000 and a pension plan where he works. His wife Roberta is self-employed (part time) and earned $5,000 last year.

   (a) May Roberta establish a Keogh Plan?

   (b) May George set up an Individual Retirement Account (IRA)?

   (c) May Roberta set up an IRA?

   (d) If Roberta is eligible for an IRA, how many dollars may she contribute? deduct?

2. George Adams and Pete Gerrard are two elderly widowers drawing Social Security benefits. George is seventy-three years of age and Pete is sixty-six. Both have part-time jobs, and last year each made $12,000. Pete lost some of his Social Security benefits, but George did not. Why? Can you calculate how much Pete lost? Pete found out that his twin brother earned $15,000 last year on some investments he had as well as $7,500 because of a part-time job. Pete wonders how much Social Security ben-

efits his brother lost. Can you explain it to him?

3. Tom and Mary Brown are reaching retirement age and seek your help in converting life insurance to annuities. The only other retirement income they will have is $950 from Social Security. They are both the same age and are unclear whether they should convert their life insurance to a single or a joint and survivorship annuity. What is your advice?

4. Cynthia Jean Reed is a 39-year-old college professor and has a pension plan with her university. Recently she heard that she is eligible for a tax-sheltered annuity over and above the pension benefits she has with the university. Is this true? Currently Cynthia is contributing 7 percent of her salary to a pension plan, and this is matched by the university. Explain how a tax-sheltered annuity works and calculate how much more Cynthia could set aside for retirement purposes, tax-deferred.

SUGGESTED READINGS

Allen, Everett T., et al. *Pension Planning: Pensions, Profit Sharing and Other Deferred Compensation Plans*, 6th ed. Homewood, Ill.: Dow Jones-Irwin, 1988.

"And One Day You Retire," Hartford, Conn.: Aetna Life Insurance Co.

Brosterman, Robert, and Brosterman, Thomas. *The Complete Estate Planning Guide.* New York: A Mentor Book, 1988.

"Choosing a Retirment Plan." Dean Witter Reynolds, Inc. You may obtain this from your Dean Witter broker.

"Company Retirement Plans Eight Years After ERISA." St. Louis: Center for the Study of American Business, Washington University.

"The Economics of Retirment." St. Louis: Center for the Study of American Business, Washington University.

Esperiti, Robert A., and Peterson, Renno L. *The Handbook of Estate Planning*, 2nd edition. New York: McGraw-Hill Book Company, 1988.

"Federal Estate and Gift Taxes." Pueblo, Col: Consumer Information Center.

"Financing Your Social Security Benefits; If You Become Disabled." Washington, D.C.: U.S. Department of Health, Education and Welfare. (SSA)-79-10029. Annual Publication.

"A Guide to Individual Retirement Accounts (IRA's)." Pueblo, Col.: Consumer Information Center.

"If You Work While You Get Social Security Payments." Washington, D.C.: U.S. Department of Health, Education and Welfare, Social Security Administration. Annual Publication.

"IRA Investment Strategies." Dean Witter Reynolds, Inc. You may obtain this from a Dean Witter broker.

"IRA Rollover." Dean Witter Reynolds, Inc. You may obtain this from a Dean Witter broker.

Krass, Stephen J., and Keschner, Richard L. *The Pension Answer Book*. Greenvale, N.Y.: Panel Publishers, 1987.

Life Insurance Fact book. New York: Institute of Life Insurance. Annual publication.

"On the Way Up: A Description of Life Insurance and Annuities." Hartford, Conn.: Aetna Life Insurance Co.

"Pension Facts." Washington, D.C.: American Council of Life Insurance. Annual publication.

Questions and Answers on Retirment Plans for the Self-Employed, Retirement Plans for Self-Employed Individuals. Washington, D.C.: Internal Revenue Service.

"Social Security," and *Supplement to Social Security Handbook*, Washington, D.C.: U.S. Department of Health, Education and Welfare. You can get it free by writing or calling your local Social Security field office. Offices are located in all big cities. Annual publication.

"Social Security Information for Young Families." (SSA 10033). Washington, D.C.: U.S. Department of Health, Education and Welfare.

"Social Security in Your Financial Planning." Washington, D.C.: U.S. Department of Health, Education and Welfare. Annual publication.

Swanson, Robert E., and Swanson, Barbara M. *Tax Shelters: A Guide for Investors and Their Advisors*. Homewood Ill.: Dow Jones-Irwin, 1985.

"A Woman's Guide to Social Security." Washington, D.C.: U.S. Department of Health, Education, and Welfare. Publication No. (SSA) 79-10127.

"Your Medicare Handbook." Washington, D.C.: U.S. Government Printing Office.

"Your Social Security.' Washington, D.C.: U.S. Department of Health, Education, and Welfare. Publication No. (SSA) 05-10035.

"Your Social Security Earnings Record." U.S. Department of Health, Education and Welfare. Annual publication.

"Your Social Security Rights and Responsibilities." Washington, D.C.: U.S. Department of Health, Education, and Welfare. Publication No. 05-10077.

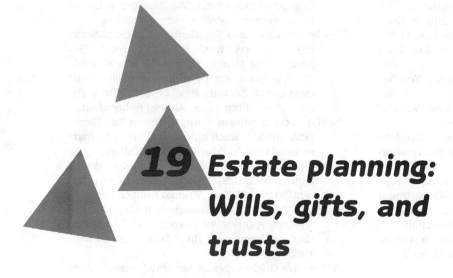

19 Estate planning: Wills, gifts, and trusts

HIGHLIGHTS   In order for a person to protect acquired assets from estate taxes and to distribute them as he or she sees fit, this chapter discusses the following:

1   Information needed to be assembled in order to engage in estate planning
2   The document known as a will and what it can do
3   What happens to property upon death in the absence of a will
4   Trusts and how they are of value in estate planning
5   Gift taxes and how gifts may reduce taxes
6   Estate taxes and how these taxes may be minimized

INTRODUCTION

No one cares to discuss his or her own death. However, it is inevitable. Consequently, everyone should think about the disposition of acquired property with some deliberate plan.

There are several reasons for this. First, if a person wishes to control the disposition of property, that person must state in writing who is to receive it. An individual may also wish to reduce taxes that would otherwise deplete the estate; there are gift and estate taxes that can be minimized by planning. Without a plan it might be necessary to dispose of a farm or business to pay estate taxes. Additionally, if there are minor children, one would want to designate the person who would act as guardian for them.

The major tools of estate planning that will be discussed in this chapter are wills, gifts, and trusts. The financial planner does not take the place of the attorney in estate planning. Nevertheless, he or she needs to be familiar with the tools of estate planning. The planner needs to appreciate the importance of a will, estate taxation, expenses involved, and the distribution of property.

WILLS

Most people should have a will for the reasons noted above; they are not just for the rich or the elderly. Moreover, as the years pass, assets do accumulate, and any individual may be worth more than he or she realizes.

Gathering the facts

Since every individual and every family is unique, each estate plan will be unique. There is, however, some basic information that is important to every estate plan, and the financial planner and the client's attorney must have the information to plan the best estate for the testator's or testatrix's needs.[1]

Residence and domicile

The residence and domicile are important to any plan. **Domicile** is the name given to a person's permanent home, and residence is the place where one lives without the intention of making a permanent home. (They may be the same place, but if not, the site of the domicile is where the person's will is to be probated.) As a general rule, marital rights that may attach to the property, such as dower or community-property rights, are determined by the domicile, as are state inheritance taxes.

Family status

The person's family status is very important. A prior marriage or a separation can have an effect on one's legal ability to make gifts of property in a will. A prior spouse may have a claim against the estate. The financial planner and the attorney will want to know whether there are plans to have more children and whether any present children are dependents.

---

1. These terms are used to describe respectively a male and a female who has a will.

528

The planner and the attorney will also want to know whether there are other living relatives from whom the person may expect an inheritance. This is important in developing an estate plan that will best conserve assets, since inheritances often constitute a large portion of the assets of an estate.

If a person has a safety deposit box, where are the box and the key? Upon a death it may be necessary for the attorney to obtain a court order to open the box, and it is simpler if the location of the box is immediately known.

Safety deposit box

The financial planner or attorney will want to know about the person's beneficiaries, their names, addresses, relationship, financial needs, and character traits. The reason for wanting to know financial needs is that the testator may wish to provide financial means to enable them to live at the same standard as at present or even better. The character traits of the proposed beneficiaries are also important. Perhaps one of the proposed beneficiaries gambles or indulges in some vice; in this case the establishment of a trust that would provide funds over time may be appropriate rather than funds in a lump sum that might be gambled away or spent in loose living.

Beneficiaries

The first step in estate planning and in making a will is to take a financial inventory. The reader was first introduced to a balance sheet in Chapter 3. At this point the balance sheet needs to be used again. All assets and liabilities are listed at their fair market value, and then the net worth is determined. The following personal balance sheet (Table 19–1) is a beginning. We have added hypothetical figures for some of the entries, and there are some blanks to fill in, also a blank to show the yield on all earning assets.

Taking a financial inventory

There are a number of things that wills can accomplish. There are also, of course, many legal technicalities one should know about wills. While this book will not make the reader an expert able to draw up wills, it should provide an appreciation for the problems involved and the importance of having the client work with an experienced and competent attorney.

Modern wills[2]

A **will** is ordinarily a writing that provides for the distribution of property on the death of the writer but confers no rights prior to that time. In short, the will is ineffective prior to the death of the writer of the will.

General definitions

---

2. If a person dies intestate (without a will) that person will be subject to the will the state of domicile has drawn up for him or her. This will be discussed further below.

Table 19—1   *Personal (or family) balance sheet*

Assets	Example	Personal entry	Percent return	Liabilities	Example	Personal entry
Cash (inc. checking accounts)	$ 750	_____	_____	Mortgage on owner-occupied home	$30,000	_____
Savings deposits (inc. certificates of dep.)	5,000	_____	_____	Other mortgages	—	_____
Life insurance (estimated cash surrender value)	15,000	_____	_____	Notes & loans payable (inc. installments)	2,000	_____
Annuities (est. cash surrender value)	5,000	_____	_____	Other unpaid bills	300	_____
				Long-term business debts	—	_____
Gov. sec. of all kinds	—	_____	_____	Short-term business liabilities (inc. accounts payable)	—	_____
Tax exempt state and local securities	—	_____	_____			
Corporation bonds	—	_____	_____		—	_____
				Loans against life insurance	—	_____
Common stock	—	_____	_____			
Mutual funds	5,000	_____	_____	Other liabilities	—	_____
Vested corp. pension benefits (exclude Soc. Sec.)	10,000	_____	_____	Total Liabilities	$32,300	_____
Individual pension benefits (inc. Personal Service Corp., Keogh, and IRA)	—	_____	_____	Net Worth	$118,450	
Stock options and profit sharing benefits	—	_____	_____			
Real estate (owner occupied)	100,000	_____	_____			
Rental property	—	_____	_____			
Other long-term business assets	—	_____	_____			
Short-term business assets (e.g., accts. receivable)	—	_____	_____			
Personal assets (furniture, car, jewelry, etc.)	10,000	_____	_____			
Other assets	—	_____	_____			
Total Assets	150,750	_____	_____			

Moreover, the writer may destroy or cancel the will at any time. The person making the will is known as the **testator,** if a man, or the **testatrix,** if a woman. If a person dies leaving a will, he or she is said to have died testate. One who dies without a will is said to have died intestate. A gift of land by way of a will is known as a devise, and the person receiving the gift, a devisee. A bequest, or legacy as it is sometimes called, is a gift of personal property, and the person to whom the personal property has been given is called a legatee. To be valid, a will must satisfy the requirements as to both the *intention* of the testator and the *formality* of expression of the intention.

There can be no will unless the testator manifests an intention in writing and in the will to make a provision that will be effective on his or her death. This is called a **testamentary intent.** There likewise can be no will unless the testator has testamentary capacity (generally the requirement that the testator be of sound mind). He or she need not possess superior or even average intelligence. He or she is only required (1) to plan conceptually the distribution of his property, (2) not to execute the will as a fraud, and (3) not to be under the undue control of some other person in the execution of the will.

Intention

Wills must be witnessed. The act of witnessing the will, known as attestation, generally includes the signing of the will by the witnesses after a clause that states that the witnesses have observed the testator sign the will. Publication is the act of the testator's informing the attesting witnesses that the document he is signing before them is his will. The person making the will need not inform the witnesses of its contents. He merely announces that the document is his will and that he requests the witnesses to attest to his signature. This constitutes the publication. In a few states, witnesses are not required but in general two or three witnesses are necessary. In those states where witnesses are required, it is generally specified that they are credible or competent and that they have no interest in the will.

Attestation

Upon the death of the testator or testatrix, the will must be probated. "Probate" means to prove. It is the job of the executor named in the will to go to court, prove that the will is valid, and carry out its terms. When specific pieces of property are to go to named persons, the executor transfers the property to those persons. Where specific property is not designated to go to named persons, it is the function of the executor to obtain a court order, sell the property, and distribute the proceeds. The first thing that the executor is bound to do is to pay off the debts of the estate and settle taxes.

Probating the will:
The executor

Executors are paid a fee for their services. If the testator or testatrix appoints an executor, the fee is generally agreed on in advance. Since probating a will is a complex and technical operation, probably an experienced attorney should be appointed. If no executor has been designated, the court will appoint one, and his or her fees will be determined in accordance with state law. Fees vary from state to state and with the size of the estate. Generally, however, executor's fees range from 4 to 5 percent of the first $5,000 or $10,000 of the estate and are then scaled down in a series of steps to about 1 to 2 percent of that portion of an estate in excess of $200,000 or $250,000.

The probating of the will is not always simple. Some states require the witnesses who attested the execution of the will to testify regarding the execution. Frequently, the witnesses are dead or for some other reason unable to testify. To forestall the possibility of preventing the probating of many wills, most states permit a will to include a self-proving clause. The will is signed and attested in the usual manner. The writer and witnesses then execute an affidavit before a notary public acknowledging their acts. The affidavit is appended to the will, which may then be admitted to probate without the testimony of these witnesses.

How to reduce assets requiring probate

Probate is time consuming and costly. Therefore, many people plan ahead to lessen the assets requiring probate. There are several methods of doing this.

1. Gifts. Obviously if a person gives away part of the estate prior to death, it will reduce the assets requiring probate. It may also reduce estate taxes, as will be explained below. To be sure, there are gift taxes, but they too can be legally avoided, as will also be explained below.
2. Joint tenancy with right of survivorship. If property is held jointly, it passes automatically to the survivor without going through probate.
3. Tenancy by the entirety. This is very similar to joint tenancy and such property also passes without going through probate. These two types of joint ownership are explained in greater detail below.
4. Trusts. If a person places property into a trust, it too passes without going through probate. The use of trusts is explained below.
5. Life insurance proceeds. The death benefits go directly to the beneficiary(ies) without going through probate.

The general contents of a will

In general, wills contain the following items:

1. A statement of the domicile of the testator or testatrix.
2. A statement revoking prior wills: "I hereby revoke all wills and codicils by me at any time heretofore made."
3. A provision for payment of debts and funeral expenses. This may read, "I direct that all my just debts and funeral expenses be paid as soon after my death as may be practicable or as they come due." The testator should communicate in the will his or her idea of the just debts that he or she intends the executor to pay or add the

clause "as they become due." A simpler "just debts" clause may be interpreted as "all debts." Consider the plight of the widow who learns that the residence she expects to live in for the rest of her life must be sold for its equity value to pay off a mortgage on it—a just debt.

4. Funeral and burial directions may sometimes be included but need not be; they may read, for instance, "I direct that my body be cremated."

5. A provision for the disposition of property. This may read, "I give and bequeath to my beloved wife Jane DeFoe all property which I shall own or be entitled to at my death." More than one person may, of course, be named as beneficiaries.

6. A secondary provision for the disposition of property to a secondary heir in the event the first-named person predeceases the testator or testatrix.

7. A statement about legacies. These are usually of two types: the general legacy and the specific legacy. The general legacy is a gift of money to an individual, paid out of the general assets of the estate. It is not a bequest of a particular thing or a particular fund designated from all others of the same kind.[3] The general legacy may read, "I give and bequeath to my dear friend Howard G. Jensen the sum of $1,000." The specific legacy is a bequest of a particular thing, which is a specified part of the estate, distinguished from all other property of the same kind.[4] If there were inadequate assets to pay all the bequests, the general legacy would be scaled down, but a specific legacy may read, "I give and bequeath to my dear friend James G. Richardson my entire stamp collection."

8. Charitable or religious bequests. Such a statement may read, "I give and bequeath the sum of $1,000 to the Lord Nelson Home for Wayward Boys."

9. A statement concerning the residual estate. This includes all of the remaining items that have not yet been disposed of by the will and is dealt with by means of a so-called residuary clause giving away or disposing of all that remains in the testator's estate. This may read, "All the rest, residue, and remainder of my estate, of whatsoever kind and nature, and wheresoever situated, of which I may be seized or possessed or to which I may be entitled at the time of my death, not hereby otherwise effectually disposed of (including any property over which I have the power of appointment), I devise and bequeath to my beloved wife, Jane DeFoe."

10. A statement naming the executor who will probate the will. Generally anyone not specifically disqualified by law will be permitted to be the executor. Often this is the surviving spouse, an adult child, or

---

3. *Armstead v. Union Trust Co.*, 61 F2d 677.
4. *Byrne v Hume*, 86 Mich. 546.

some other blood relative or close friend of the family. However, if there is a large estate and probate may be technically complex, an experienced attorney or the trust department of a bank may be named executor. Many states require that an executor furnish a bond to assure that he or she will faithfully carry out his or her duties. A will may, however, contain a statement requesting that no bond need be furnished.

11. Frequently a will appoints a guardian if there are minor children. Normally if there is a surviving spouse, no other guardian is needed; hence this provision appoints a guardian only if the spouse predeceases the testator or testatrix.

12. A statement about the witnesses and a place for them to sign their names.

13. A statement regarding the notary public who must see that the witnesses sign the will in the presence of the testator or testatrix and then notarize and sign the document. Sometimes a self-proving affidavit is added, to ease probate by vouching for the validity of the signatures.

The joint will

A joint will is defined as a single testamentary instrument that contains the wills of two or more persons. Typically, it is executed by husband and wife, and typically each leaves his or her property to the other, and only when they are both gone will the children inherit anything. These are the so-called Ma and Pa wills. Many authorities feel that the joint will should not be used because it can lay the groundwork for future litigation.

Essentially the joint will contains the same general type of clauses with regard to burial instructions and appointments of executors as does the will made by an individual. However, the residuary clause in a joint will gives the residue of the estate to each other. Another important clause in this joint or mutual will is the following:

> We do hereby declare that the mutual and reciprocal dispositive provisions [this is the clause in a will providing for the disposition of the property] herein for the benefit of the other have been made pursuant to an understanding and agreement that each has made the provisions herein in consideration of the other similarly providing, and upon condition that neither of us will during our lives alter, amend, or revoke such provisions without the written consent of the other, nor will the survivor alter, amend, or revoke the same, after the death of the first of us to die.

Such a statement is important because it expresses the intent of the parties that neither will revoke or alter the will without the consent of the other. In the absence of this clearly expressed intent, it may be held that the execution of the joint will without reference to the terms of the instrument is not sufficient evidence of an enforceable contract to devise between the testator and testatrix. In short, either of the parties may subsequently make another will that is likely to take precedence over the joint will.

All wills should have a common disaster clause. Otherwise if a husband and wife have an automobile accident and both are killed, there might be litigation to determine who died first. If the wife died first and the wife had a will leaving the property to her husband, her property, together with what he owned, would pass according to the terms of his will. However, with his wife dead, the property cannot pass to her. If there were children, the will would probably provide for them. But if there were no children and the husband's will did not specifically state who was next in line, all of the property might go to the husband's relatives and the wife's kin would receive nothing. To provide against this, a common catastrophe clause is frequently inserted in a will. This clause may read as follows: *The common disaster clause*

> Any person who shall have died at the same time as I, or in a common disaster with me, or under such circumstances that it is difficult or impossible to determine which died first, shall be deemed to have predeceased me.

Both the husband's and wife's will would then pass property as if each had died last. Each person's property would then pass according to his or her will, and if there were no children, each side's relatives would get something.

A codicil to a will is defined as an addition or change executed with the same formalities as required in the will itself. Generally it is better to draw a new will than to have a codicil. The codicil may, for instance, eliminate a person already designated as a beneficiary under the terms of the will; if so the door is left open for that beneficiary to contest the will, which is extremely costly to the estate and may end up with property not being disposed of in accordance with the intention of the testator or testatrix. *The codicil*

The codicil refers to the will and is dated. It contains a dispositive provision and is attested to by the number of witnesses required in accordance with the state statute. Above the signatures of the witnesses is the following clause:

> The foregoing instrument consists of one page and was made on the third day of July 1984, signed and sealed at the end thereof, and at the same time published and declared by James J. DeFoe, the above named Testator, as and for a Codicil to his Last Will and Testament dated the third day of June 1984, in the presence of each of us, who, this attestation clause having been read to us, did at the request of said testator, in his presence and in the presence of each other sign our names as witnesses thereto.

Holographic wills are instruments that are wholly handwritten by the testator as a will and meet only some of the formal requirements of a will. They must always be signed and dated, but witnesses are not necessary. Not all states recognize holographic wills, and those that do may recog- *Holographic wills* nize them to pass property only up to a given amount of value. Typically, a holographic will is written at the time when the testator becomes aware of impending death and decides to alter completely his or her will or suddenly realizes there is none. Holographic wills written on envelopes, napkins, and even clothing have been admitted to probate in many states.

A holographic will supersedes an existing will but often is the only will a testator has written. Why isn't every note a person would write concerning the distribution of property designated to be a holographic will? This type of will, like any other, must meet certain minimal formal requirements. More importantly, the writing must express a testamentary intention by its author.

Where a will should be kept

If a will cannot be found after the death of the testator or testatrix, it is presumed that he or she destroyed it with the intent of revoking it. This presumption can be overcome only by proving fraudulent destruction or by showing that the person was mentally incapable of possessing the intention to revoke.

There are generally four things that can be done with the will once it has been written.

1. In the majority of cases, the will is left with the attorney who drew it or a financial planner, who either puts it in an office safe or places it in a safety deposit box in a financial institution. A copy is also usually given to the testator or testatrix.
2. Where a financial institution has been named as one of the executors, the will is generally placed with that institution for safekeeping.
3. The will can be placed in the person's own safety deposit box. This is sometimes objected to on the grounds that often it takes a court order for the box to be opened after death. However, the box must be opened in any case, and the state tax department officials who are present when the box is opened will have no objection to the removal of the will after an inventory has been taken of the contents of the box.
4. The will may be kept in the home in a strongbox. This is the least recommended place, because it is too easily accessible to destruction by persons other than the testator and it may easily be lost or mislaid.

It is best to make several copies of the will and keep them in all of the above places.

A sample of a modern will is shown in Figure 19–1. Figure 19–2 is a sample of the oldest known will in existence today. It was written by the Egyptian Pharaoh, Uah, and was executed in 2548 B.C. We have also found what is believed to be the shortest will ever probated. It contained just ten words: "Being of sound mind and body, I spent it all."

KNOW ALL MEN BY THESE PRESENTS:

That I, _____ of Travis County, Texas, being of sound and disposing mind and memory, and above the age of eighteen years, do make and publish this my last will and testament, hereby revoking all wills heretofore made by me.

I.

I direct that all my just debts shall be paid.

II.

Should my beloved wife, _____, survive me, I give to her all property which I shall own or be entitled to at my death.

III.

Should my said wife not survive me, I give all property which I shall own or be entitled to at my death to my son, _____.

I hereby appoint my wife, _____, independent executrix of this my last will and testament, and I direct that no bond shall be required of her as such executrix, and I further direct that no action shall be had in the County Court or any other court in relation to the administration and settlement of my estate other than the probating and recording of this my last will and testament and filing of an inventory and list of claims in the manner provided by law.

If my said wife does not survive me, I appoint my son _____, independent executor of my will without bond under the same terms and conditions which would have obtained had my wife served as independent executrix.

IN TESTIMONY WHEREOF, I have hereunto set my hand, this the _____ day of _____, in the presence of _____ _____ and _____, who witness my signature and attest this my last will and testament at my request as attesting witnesses.

(name) _____

The above instrument was now here on the date hereinabove set forth, subscribed by _____, the testator, in our presence and in the presence of each other, and we, as attesting witnesses at his request and in his presence and in the presence of each other, sign our names hereto as attesting witnesses.

_____

_____

Before me, the undersigned authority, on this day personally appeared

_____,

_____, and

_____ known to me to be the testator and the witnesses, respectively, whose names are subscribed to the annexed or foregoing instrument in their respective capacities, and, all of said persons being by me duly sworn, the said

_____, testator, declared to me and to the said witnesses in my presence that said instrument is his last will and testament, and that he had willingly made and executed it as his free act and deed for the purposes therein expressed; and the said witnesses, each on his oath stated to me, in the presence and hearing of the said testator, that the said testator had declared to them that

Sample of a modern will.

Figure 19–1

said instrument is his last will and testament, and that he executed same as such and wanted each of them to sign it as a witness; and upon their oaths each witness stated further that they did sign the same as witnesses in the presence of the said testator and at his request; that he was at that time nineteen years of age or over and was of sound mind; and that each of said witnesses was then at least fourteen years of age.

Testator _____

Witness _____

Witness _____

Subscribed and acknowledged before me by the said _____, testator, and subscribed and sworn to before me by said _____ and _____, witnesses, this the _____ day of _____, 1984.

_____
Notary Public, Travis County, Texas

Figure 19—1 (continued)

The last letter of instructions

Every person should write a letter of last instructions and leave it in an easily accessible place as well as with every member of the family. A copy should also be given to the family lawyer, if there is one, and another copy should be placed in a safety deposit box. This letter should probably be rewritten and updated every year or two as the individual's assets and other conditions change.

It should be noted that a letter of last instructions is not a will or a substitute for a will; both are needed. A letter of last instructions is a supplementary document to a will. This letter should, among other things, include a list of all the individual's assets and liabilities and indicate where the documents are located.

As a miminum, it should include the following:

1. A statement of where the will, if any, may be found.
2. Funeral instructions, if necessary. Some people wish to be cremated, others, buried. Some wish to donate certain organs (e.g., eyes) to others after death. In any case all members of the family should have general knowledge in advance of future funeral arrangements.
3. A statement regarding a safety deposit box—where it and the key are located.
4. A list of all life insurance policies and their location.
5. An inventory of all stocks and bonds, and where they are kept.
6. A list of all other property such as real estate, mutual funds, and business property, and their location.
7. The person's Social Security number should be recorded.

AMENEMHAT IV,
Year 2, Month Paophi, Day 18

I, Uah, am giving a title to property to my wife SHEFTU, the woman of Gesab who is called Teta, the daughter of Sat Sepdu, of all things given to me by my brother Ankh-ren. She shall give it to any she desires of her children she bears me.

I am giving to her the Eastern slaves, 4 persons, that my brother Ankh-ren gave me. She shall give them to whomsoever she will of her children.

As to my tomb, let me be buried in it with my wife alone.

Moreover as to the house built for me by my brother Ankh-ren, my wife shall dwell therein without allowing her to be put forth on the ground by any person.

It is the deputy Gebu who shall act as guardian of my son.

Done in the presence of these witnesses:

KEMEN, Decorator of Columns.

APU, Doorkeeper of the Temple.

SENB, son of Senb, Doorkeeper of the Temple.

Will from 2548 B.C., translated by the American University at Cairo.

Figure 19—2

8. A statement indicating what benefits the deceased may have from his or her employer. There may be pension benefits, death benefits, profit-sharing plans, and other benefits to which the deceased's estate or survivors may have a claim.

9. A list of all deposits in banks, savings and loan associations, mutual savings banks, or credit unions.

10. A list of memberships in all unions, professional associations, lodges and fraternal organizations, and veterans groups. There may be financial benefits because of memberships in some of these organizations.

11. A list of all just debts owed to the person and accounts receivable, the interest rate they bear, the terms of payment, and where to locate the documents to prove their validity.

12. A list of all the just debts owed by the individual, the interest rate they bear, the terms of their repayment, and the location of the pertinent documents.

Living wills

In recent years, there has been some litigation over life-support systems being used to continue the life of terminally ill people who are often in great pain or in a vegetative state. Recently California passed a right-to-die-in-dignity law, and other states are likely to follow. This permits life-support systems to be withdrawn in such cases. Also some people have written living wills in which a person authorizes, permits, and requests that the life-support system be withdrawn if he or she is in a situation such as that described above. Sometimes the deceased wishes to become a donor of certain transplantable organs. If so, this should be spelled out in the living will, because eyes and certain other organs must be removed immediately upon death.

If a person dies intestate (without a will)

Everyone already has one will because the state in which the person is domiciled has drawn one up for him or her. The personal property of a person dying intestate will pass according to the intestacy laws of the state of domicile. This may not be in accordance with the wishes of the deceased. It is particularly important that individuals whose needs are not met through state intestacy laws have wills drawn to ensure appropriate distribution of property.

Intestacy laws vary from state to state. Generally, however, they distribute property in the following order of priority of claims.

1. *Spouses and children.* Surviving spouses and children are first in line and they generally receive the main share of the estate and perhaps all of it. In some states the surviving spouse will receive the bulk of the estate, but in others the children will receive a substantial amount. It is possible, then, that without a will a widow might have insufficient assets.

If a person dies intestate, it is unlikely that the deceased's property will be distributed according to his or her wishes. For example, state laws make no provision for favorite charities or special relationships to receive any funds. In the absence of a will, there may be cumbersome procedures and high legal expenses. If a person dies intestate (without a will) much higher estate taxes may be due (see the section called "Gift and estate taxes").

A problem may also arise if there are minor children. If both parents are dead they have no control over who will rear minor children. They may be sent across the country to live with a relative, while the deceased may have preferred that their children be raised by friends in the community.

If a large share of an estate passes to minor children, it may be placed in trust until they are 18. This may make the family financially strapped while the kids are growing up; then at 18 they get a large sum of money.

It is even possible in some states where the deceased was divorced and remarried that his share would go to his second wife or her children, rather than to his first wife or her children.

**Box 19—1
Make a will**

2. *Lineals.* Lineals are blood relatives of the deceased. The major portion of an estate not distributed to the surviving spouse and children is generally distributed to lineals (brothers and sisters) although sometimes parents also have a claim to part of it.
3. *Parents.* If the estate has not been exhausted by this time, the remainder is commonly distributed to the decedent's parents.
4. *Collateral heirs.* Other more distant relatives with a common ancestry are considered. Cousins, uncles, and the like are next in line. Usually there is not much left by now.

Distant relatives will exhaust any estate if it gets that far, but one more step is provided by law in most states. It takes effect in the very rare case when a person dies intestate and has no heirs—no surviving spouse, children, or parents, also no cousins or other blood relatives, and no one with a common ancestry. Where does his or her property go? It goes to his or her state tax collector.

Administration of estates is the means of distributing property of a decedent who died intestate. When no will is left, the court or an officer designated by law appoints one or more persons who are then entitled to administer the estate of the decedent. More often than not, close relatives of the deceased make application to the court for the so-called letter of administration. Such a letter gives the administrator the obligation of gathering the assets of the deceased, paying of the debts and taxes of the estate, and then distributing the assets in accordance with the statute pertaining to distribution of the estate. Generally, the letter of administra-

Administration of estates

tion is granted to the first relative or person who applies. In some cases where there are creditors of the deceased and no previous application for letter of administration has been made, the letter may be granted to a creditor. In the absence of creditor, applications, or known relatives, the letter may be issued by the court to a public administrator. In any event, once the letter has been granted to the administrator, the job becomes much the same as that of the executor of an estate.

HOW CERTAIN PROPERTY IS HELD: NONPROBATE PROPERTY

The question immediately arises: "How should major assets be held?" This is important for married couples with respect to such assets as checking accounts, savings deposits, real estate, securities, and perhaps some others. There are four legal forms of joint ownership.

1. Tenancy by the entirety
2. Joint tenancy with right of survivorship
3. Tenancy in common
4. Community property

How property is held will vary from state to state depending on the laws of that state.

Tenancy by the entirety

Only two people married to each other are able to hold real property in the form of tenancy by the entirety, and personal property cannot be held in this form. They are both equal owners. This is the one way in which a person could own his or her home in most cases in many common law states. The deed is made out to both parties, and when one dies the deed passes cleanly to the other. Both signatures must be obtained when selling the property. Some community property states do not permit property ownership in the form of tenancy by the entirety.[5]

Joint tenancy with right of survivorship

Joint tenancy can involve more than two owners. If it is between a husband and wife, it should spell out, "with rights of survivorship," under which the surviving spouse takes full title to the property on the death of the other. This type of ownership is not possible in some community property states. Hence, in states like Texas or California a husband and wife can enter into such an ownership agreement with their separate property only but not with their community property unless they first partition their community into separate property. The one exception to this is U.S. Government securities. They can be community property and still

---

5. The community property states are Arizona, California, Idaho, Louisiana, Nevada, New Mexico, Texas, and Washington. Recently Wisconsin passed legislation which provides for a similar type of arrangement.

be held in the form of a joint tenancy with right of survivorship because they are governed by federal law, which takes precedence.

This can also involve more than two owners. The ownership interest of the survivors of property held in common is not changed by the death of one owner. In community property states, only separate property of either spouse can be held in the form of tenancy in common.

Tenancy in common

Community property is a legal concept valid only in community property states. Under the law, most property acquired during a marriage is owned 50 percent by each spouse. However, each member of a married couple can have separate property. This would include property acquired prior to marriage, that acquired after marriage through a gift or inheritance, and possibly previous community property that was partitioned earlier. In a community property state, on the death of one spouse one-half of all community property passes to the deceased's estate. If there is no will spelling out who is to receive it, the property passes in accordance with the law of inheritance, and the surviving spouse and the children usually are the heirs. However, the surviving spouse may not get it all or even the main share; the children may get as much as one-half. This is true of personal as well as real property.

Community property

Real estate, securities, and bank accounts should be held jointly with rights to survivorship in most common law (based on English law) states insofar as married couples are concerned. Then, on the death of one, the survivor acquires it automatically and directly without the necessity of probating a will. In community property states, this cannot be done, and a will may be the only way to assure that the survivor will get all of the estate. In the absence of a will, the children might get some of it in certain community property states.

Gifts and trusts are useful in estate planning because both of them can reduce taxes, i.e., gift and estate taxes—not income taxes. Gift taxes are paid by the giver, not the recipient; estate taxes are taxes on the assets left by the deceased.

TRUSTS

Equally important, the use of the trust allows the creators some control over their assets even after they die. The trust can also provide financial security to those who are inexperienced or incapable of managing their financial afairs, such as minor children.

The trust is an arrangement whereby title to property is transferred by the creator or settlor to another person (trustee) for the benefit of a third party (beneficiary or *cestui que* trust). The property placed in trust is called the corpus, the trust *res*, the trust fund, or the trust property. The

Creation of the trust

title to the corpus is split, with the trustee holding the property for an ascertainable length of time, and all benefits from the corpus go to the beneficiaries. The beneficiaries who receive the income from the trust during their lifetime are known as **life tenants** (income beneficiaries); those beneficiaries who receive the corpus (principal) of the trust upon the death of the last of the life tenants are known as the **remaindermen** (principal beneficiaries).

Generally, a trust may be created for any purpose that is not against public policy. For instance, a trust created from funds obtained from the commission of a felony is void, as is a trust created to encourage divorce. There are other prerequisites that each state imposes for the creation of a valid trust. Two of the most important are intention and capacity.

There must be an intention on the part of the settlor, declared in writing, to convey property to a trust for the benefit of beneficiaries. Secret, unexpressed intentions will not effectively create a trust. There must also be a manifest intent to impose enforceable duties on the trustee to manage the property for the benefit of another.

In addition to intent, there must be capacity among all the parties involved to create a trust. The settlor must have the capacity to convey property. Thus insane persons and minors, who cannot validly convey property, lack the capacity to create a trust. The trustee must be capable of owning property and meeting the requirements of being a fiduciary. For example, no person convicted of a felony is capable of being a fiduciary. While settlors can name themselves as beneficiaries, they cannot be their own trustee. (There are exceptions to this in some states.) Finally, a definite beneficiary who is capable of owning property is required. The beneficiary must be named or, as will be discussed later, capable of being determined under a definite standard.

The inter vivos and testamentary trust

The *inter vivos* trust, or so-called living trust, is one created by the grantor during his or her lifetime. The grantor also may be the beneficiary. In general, the *inter vivos* trust may be either irrevocable or revocable. The testamentary trust is one set up through a will, and it becomes effective upon the death of the grantor.

The revocable trust

The revocable trust can be terminated by the creator at any time. It can also be set up to terminate automatically at a specific time in the future. If the beneficiary is someone other than the creator (for example, a minor child), gift taxes do not apply. It is not a gift; the creator still has full control over it. The creator can even tell the trustee how to invest the funds, and he or she can change these managerial instructions from time to time. Generally the creator will give only broad general investment instruction and leave wide discretion with the trustee. The major reason some people set up such trusts is to turn day-to-day management decisions over to someone else because they do not want to be bothered, they feel they can increase the return on their assets through a trust, or the beneficiary may be a minor or otherwise inexperienced in finance. The income earned by such a trust may be disbursed to the beneficiary or left to accumulate in the trust. In either case, it is taxable income. The trustee will report it to the creator or grantor, and he or she must then declare it on the tax return.

Irrevocable trusts

The creator can never terminate (revoke) an irrevocable trust. He also usually gives up all income earned by it, but this need not be so. The creator gives up the right not only to revoke but also to alter or amend the trust. The creator can put some loose control into the trust agreement—such as, for example, it will be invested only in bonds, or at least 50 percent in bonds—or the trustee can be given complete discretion.

The creator may set up an irrevocable (living) trust and name himself or herself as the beneficiary with the right to receive the income from it. The creator would probably name someone else to become the beneficiary after his or her death, or stipulate that the trust then be dissolved and someone receive the corpus. A reason for making the creator the beneficiary would be to achieve the peace of mind of having someone competent manage his or her financial affairs, and also to protect his or her assets from being dissipated due to possible loss of financial sophistication in the future from illness or the like. Such a trust, however, would not be protected from claims of creditors; an irrevocable trust which made someone else the beneficiary would be protected from the creator's creditors. The property of a trust in which the grantor is also the beneficiary would also be includable in the grantor's estate upon his death. Estate taxes would have to be paid at that time. Whoever received the corpus of the trust when it was dissolved (called vesting) would also be subject to estate taxes upon his or her death.

An irrevocable trust may, however, name someone other than the grantor as the beneficiary. This is looked on as a gift, and gift taxes might be due (see below) rather than estate taxes on the death of the grantor.

There are several ways in which an irrevocable trust may reduce income taxes. A person might create an irrevocable trust for the benefit of a child with the idea of creating an educational fund. In such a case the income from the corpus might not be passed through to the beneficiary until he or she had enrolled in a university. The income earned by the trust fund would be taxable to the trust, at a relatively low rate, and not to the father or mother, who might be at a high tax bracket. Thereby the grantor could accomplish two things: (1) reduce the total amount of tax paid, and (2) provide a fund for the education of his or her child. If the trust passes its earnings through to the beneficiary, he or she would pay the taxes, presumably again at a lower rate. How a trust can reduce future estate taxes is explained below.

The testamentary trust

A testamentary trust is one that is created by a provision in a will. The trust agreement would have to be written in advance, and on the death of the grantor, it would become effective. Such a trust would be subject to estate taxes, but, as we shall see below, it could reduce later estate taxes of the beneficiaries. A testamentary trust is irrevocable, and much of what was said immediately above applies. In addition to tax reduction, a reason for the creation of such a trust is to protect the beneficiary who is inexperienced. It may be undesirable, for instance, to leave a large estate consisting of investments in securities to a person lacking experience in investments. Or it may be desirable to leave property to a trustee in order to provide income for a wife for life, and at her death to provide that the corpus of the trust pass on to the children or their heirs. Often, too, property is left to trustee to hold and to invest and to pay the income to minor children, with the corpus passing to them when they become of age.

Simple and complex trusts

A trust may be simple or complex. A simple trust is one in which all of the income from the trust is given to the beneficiary; a complex trust is one that retains the income at least until some predetermined time in the future, which must be spelled out in the trust agreement, if it is an irrevocable trust. The beneficiary is liable for the taxes on the income he receives from a simple trust. With a complex trust, the trustee pays the taxes, using some of the income for this purpose, in accordance with whatever tax bracket the income of the trust indicates.

A complex trust may also be set up so that part of the income is passed through to the beneficiary and part is retained. In such a case, that portion passed through is taxed as described above under the simple trust, and that part retained is taxed as described under a complex trust.

A college trust fund and gifts to a child

If parents wish to save for their children's (or grandchildren's) college education they could establish a trust for them. This can save taxes, if they are in a higher percent bracket, by transferring income from the parent's bracket to the child's lower (usually 15 percent) rate. This must be done very carefully, however; and it must be done differently if the child is under 14 years of age than when he or she is 14 or over, as will be explained below.

Parents may set up a formal trust administered by a third party (trust department of a bank) or a custodial trust under the Uniform Gifts to Minors Act, which they themselves may administer.[6] The custodial trust may include savings deposits, stock, bonds, and so forth but all must be in the child's name.

---

6. A custodial trust is automatically established if a parent sets up a deposit (or purchases bonds or stock) in the child's name.

If a trust earns income, that income is taxed. If it is a simple trust, the beneficiary who receives the income pays that tax at his or her rate. If, however, the trust retains the income (as it does in a complex trust), then the trust must pay income tax on it. Trusts compute their income tax under a separate rate schedule that applies only to them. The table below illustrates these taxes.

Box 19—2 Income taxes paid by trusts

For tax year 1991

Taxable income		Pay +	Tax rate percent	On excess over
Over	Not over			
$ 0	$ 3,450	$ 0	15	$ 0
3,450	10,350	517.50	28	3,450
10,350	. . . .	2,449.50	31	10,350

Parents may now make gifts to the trust on the child's behalf. To avoid gift taxes, the gift must be limited to $10,000 per year ($20,000 if married); see below in the section "How Gifts Can Save Taxes" for an explanation of how the gift tax works. Parents may make periodic contributions to the trust so that when the child is ready for college the funds will be available.

If the child is 14 years of age or older, this is all that must be done; the income from the trust is taxed at the child's presumably 15 percent rate.[7]

If the child is under 14, however, it is more difficult to shift income, but it can be done. The law provides that unearned income, such as income from a trust, of a child under 14 is taxed at the parents' rate. However, this is not true of the first $1,100 of unearned income. As noted before, earned income consists of wages and salaries, and most people under age 14 have little of that. Unearned income is defined by the IRS as investment (interest and dividend) income. In the case of a child under 14, the first $550 of unearned income is not taxed, and the second $550 is taxed at the child's rate; not until income rises above $1,100 is it taxed at the parent's higher rate. As Table 19—2 shows, the tax on the first $1,100 is only $82.50. Hence, a person may still set up a college trust

---

7. A dependent child does not get the personal exemption and also does not get the standard deduction on unearned income. Hence, the entire trust income is taxed at 15 percent. Unearned income is interest or dividend income, which is what the trust income is. If the child has earned income (wages or salary), the standard deduction does apply to that income.

Table 19–2 *Tax on the first $1,000.*
of a child's trust income

Unearned income	$1,100
Standard deduction	550
Net unearned income	550
Taxed at child's rate	15%
Tax	$82.50

fund (or for any other purpose) and set aside a fairly substantial sum before its income is taxed at the parents' rate. A trust could be set up at birth and provide modest tax benefits.

The power of invasion

Unfortunately, one cannot predict the future, even in economic terms. A man may believe that he has provided sufficient cash assets to maintain his wife and child; he has established a testamentary trust and provided that the income therefrom shall go to the support of his wife and child. However, as the years pass, the cost of living may rise by far more than was anticipated. It may be then that the income from the trust fund will be insufficient to support his wife and child. In practice, therefore, a statement is frequently inserted to provide that the trust fund itself may be used to support the beneficiaries if the need arises. This dipping into the principal is called the ***power of invasion.*** It may be unlimited, with the amount to be taken from the fund left to the best judgment and discretion of either the beneficiary or the trustee; or it is sometimes limited to a certain percentage of the trust fund over the annual income per year.

Needless to say, the importance of the clause cannot be stressed too strongly if the purpose of the trust is for the support and maintenance of the beneficiaries. Although the courts can authorize the reformation of the trust agreement to allow dispersal of a portion of the corpus as long as no one beneficiary is deprived of his or her rightful share, this is undesirable for the beneficiaries since litigation is a costly and time-consuming process. If the principal is dipped into, the trust's future earnings are likely to decline, which may necessitate dipping into the principal even further. In such a case, it is possible that the beneficiary could outlive his or her principal sum.

The rule against perpetuities

This rule prevents even irrevocable trusts from going on and on. That is, while an irrevocable trust cannot be revoked by its grantor, it must eventually be liquidated. Or in legal terms, it must *vest,* that is, it must be liquidated and pass to someone. Of course, the person or persons receiving the property can immediately set up another trust. However, when a trust vests, the people receiving it must pay an estate tax when they die.

When a trust must finally be liquidated varies from state to state. Generally it must vest 21 years after the death of the "lives in being" at the time the creator dies and those who are mentioned in the trust. Unborn heirs who might be referred to in the trust do not count. A parent may set up a trust that can continue during the lives of all children, grandchildren, and great-grandchildren, if any, that were mentioned in the will and were alive on the day of his or her death, plus 21 years. Only 21 years after the death of the last survivor of the above group would the trust have to be liquidated.

In some states, this "lives in being" has been modified, and the trust must vest after the death of not more than two lives mentioned in the trust and who are living at the testator's death—the plus 21 years being removed. This is the so-called "measured lives" doctrine.

A well-drawn trust, then, must provide for a method of determining who gets what, when it is finally liquidated. If a trust spans two or more generations before liquidation, there may be grandchildren and even great-grandchildren of the creator who will finally share in the distribution of the property. A simple equal per capita distribution for all claimants would be unfair because some grandchildren might be alive and others dead, and also some grandchildren would have produced more heirs than others. Because of this, most trusts provide *per stirpes* distribution.

A *per stirpes* distribution dilutes the principal along ancestral lines. In the above case, for example, the great-grandchildren whose parents are dead should get all of their parents' share. The great-grandchildren of living parents should get nothing, or at least no more than a portion of their parents' share. (They would get their parents' share later.) Also, an only great-grandchild of one of the creator's grandchildren should get more than each of the two great-grandchildren of another one of the creator's grandchildren. Figure 19–3 illustrates a *per stirpes* distribution.

Assume those nine without crosses are alive and have a claim. In some cases the law (or proviso in the trust) would provide for nothing for the children of C and D (that is, nothing to I, J, and K, the great-grandchildren of the creator); they would get their share later through their parents when the parents die. However, the only child of D would eventually get twice what each of the two children of C would eventually get. (This assumes D has no children in the future and that both C and D neither add to nor deplete the principal.) The four offspring of A and B have claim to exactly 50 percent of the trust; if the trust were $1,000,000, they would each get $125,000. C and his offspring together would have a claim to $250,000 but the offspring might have to wait. The same is true of D and his offspring. If D were dead, his child (K, the great-grandchild of the creator) would get $250,000.

A trust that continues through two or more generations before it vests, with the heirs along the way receiving only the income, is often called a "generation-skipping" trust, and at one time it postponed taxes. There were no further estate taxes due until the death of the people into whom the trust finally vested. This has now been changed to some ex-

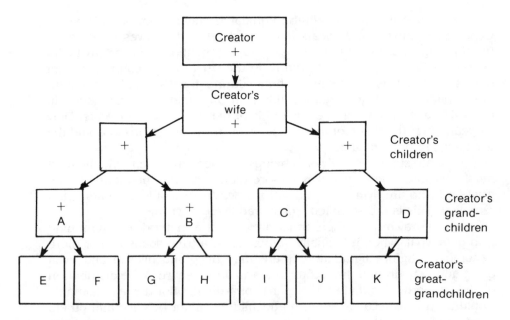

Figure 19–3   Per stirpes *distribution of property.*

tent. For example, if a trust is established in a way so that it vests, not in the children but rather in the grandchildren or even the great-grandchildren—a generation-skipping trust—estate taxes are due when the children die, in whom the trust would normally have vested.

The above, however, applies only to relatively large trusts. Taxes may still be postponed if the "generation-skipping" trust is not in excess of $1,000,000.

The power of appointment

A power of appointment is defined as a device by which the owner of property grants to another person or persons the power to designate, within whatever limits he or she wishes, how the property shall be distributed after the original beneficiary dies.

In other words, it is a device giving the beneficiary of a trust the right to alter the disposition of the trust *res* or trust fund on his or her death through his or her will. For example, *A* by will leaves property to his son, in trust, the income from the trust fund to be paid to the son for life, and the property upon the death of the son to pass to his son's children. If the son dies before his wife, it may be that his widow will have no means of support; consequently there may be included in *A*'s will a provision giving his son the power of appointment. This would mean that the son through his will could change the distribution of the property by providing that on his death the income should go to his widow for life and on her death to his children. What this does is to enable A to look into the future through the eyes of his son; what may be considered wise today may be considered absurd tomorrow. The main reason for including the power of appointment in a trust agreement, then, is to protect the fund for the several life beneficiaries.

The trustee—the role of the fiduciary

It is the prerogative of the settlor to name the trustee for the trust. Since this person is to be responsible for the corpus of the trust for a number of years, the selection of the trustee is critical. Although a private individual can be named as trustee if he or she is willing to take on the responsibilities and duties of a fiduciary for the nominal fee involved in managing the trust, the settlor generally finds it more satisfactory to name an organized trust corporation or trust department of a bank as the trustee. The settlor could expect trust companies and banks to have a larger and more experienced staff to administer the trust and a greater willingness to take on the strict liabilities of being fiduciary than could generally be found from an individual.

GIFT AND ESTATE TAXES

Gift taxes are imposed on the giver (the recipient need not pay), and estate taxes are imposed on the estate (property) of the deceased before the heirs may receive the residual. These used to be separate taxes with separate rate schedules. Recently, however, Congress combined the gift and estate tax rate in to one common schedule—the unified gift and estate tax. This tax is applicable to all taxable transfers, either through gifts while living or through an estate after death. Indeed, dying and leaving an estate are now considered as making one final gift. However, there are exclusions and exemptions before either gift or estate taxes need be paid.

State death taxes credit

Many states also have gift and estate taxes. Some even have inheritance tax, a tax on the recipient of an estate. Practices vary so much from state to state that little can be said about them except for two general comments. First, most states taxes of this sort are less severe than the federal taxes, and even the federal estate and gift taxes do not bring in vast sums. For example, in 1989, total gift and estate tax receipts at the federal level were just over $8.7 billion.[8] Second, the severity of the state taxes and exemptions varies with the closeness of the kin. Spouses are taxed less severely than children, and children less severely than other relatives. Moreover, the Federal Tax Code allows a tax credit for a *large proportion of all state inheritance and estate taxes.*

---

8. *The Federal Reserve Bulletin,* Oct. 1990, p. 29.

Foreign death taxes credit

If a person owns property in other countries, he or she may be subject to foreign death taxes. However, just like state death taxes, the U.S. tax code allows a credit against federal taxes for any foreign death taxes paid.

Annual gift tax exclusions

Every individual has an annual gift tax exclusion and a lifetime gift tax exemption. The annual exclusion is $10,000 per year per recipient. A person could give away $1 billion without paying a gift tax if he or she gave $10,000 to 100,000 people. More realistically, if a person has four children, he or she could give each $10,000 tax free annually, for a total of $40,000 per year. In addition, the law allows gifts to pay for qualified medical expenses or school tuition tax free, over and above this $10,000.

Split gifts

The split gift is sometimes referred to as a joint gift made by the husband and wife. It, too, can result in tax savings. The law provides, among other things, that a gift made by one person to any person other than his or her spouse can be considered as having been made one-half by him and one-half by her, if so elected. This is true even if only one of them has an income.

The net effect is that the annual exclusion may be doubled, and a husband and wife may make an annual gift of $20,000 times the number of donees without paying any gift tax whatsoever.

Lifetime gift or estate tax exemption

There is also an overall lifetime gift or estate tax exemption. This exemption is $600,000. Everyone has this lifetime exemption; hence a married couple together may give away (or leave an estate of) $1,200,000 tax free. This is above the $10,000 per year ($20,000 in the case of a joint gift) exclusion per recipient. It should be noted, however, that while the $10,000 exclusion applies only to gifts, the $600,000 exemption is unified and applies to the combination of the gifts and the estate.

Converting the exemption to a credit

In reality, however, the exemption is converted to a tax credit. The tax is calculated as if there were no exemption, and then the tax credit is subtracted from the tax so calculated. The tax credit on a $600,000 estate is $192,800, the same as the tax; hence no tax is due on transfers up to that amount. Table 19—3 shows how the lifetime tax exemption has risen over the years through 1987 with the tax credit equivalent.

The marital deduction

The marital deduction refers to transfers between spouses. The marital deduction applies to both gifts and estates, and it is 100 percent. All gifts to spouses and all estates left to spouses are now completely tax free.

Lifetime unified gift and estate tax exemption   Table 19–3

Year	Amount of credit	Exemption equivalent	Lowest tax bracket rate (percent)
1984	$ 96,300	$325,000	34
1985	121,800	400,000	34
1986	155,800	500,000	37
1987 and later	192,800	600,000	37

The unified gift and estate tax is progressive and varies from 18 to 55 percent. Table 19—4 shows how the tax rates have declined during the last few years. Since it often takes a few years to settle an estate, the rates in effect a few years ago are still used. Table 19—5 shows the unified federal gift and estate tax rates in effect currently; they really range from 37 to 55 percent, however, not from 18 to 55 percent as the table suggests.[9] The tax is also cumulative, and because of this, each future taxable gift is taxed at a higher and higher rate. For example, if a person makes a $100,000 taxable gift, the proper tax rate is applied; if then the next year another $100,000 taxable gift is made, the tax on it is calculated as if it were a $200,000 gift. The actual tax so obtained is then reduced by the amount of the tax paid on the previous $100,000 gift.

The estate tax is calculated just like the gift tax, by applying the proper tax rate to the sum of all previous cumulative lifetime taxable transfers plus the deceased's estate. That is, all previous taxable gifts are added to the estate before calculating the tax on it. You will recall the government now looks on leaving an estate as one final gift—and gift and estate taxes are the same. By including all previous transfers, the estate is pushed into a higher tax bracket. To be sure, a credit is given for previous gift taxes paid.

How gift and estate taxes are calculated

There are eight steps in calculating the estate tax.

The actual estate tax calculation

1. *Step 1.* Calculate the *gross estate,* which includes:
   a. Cash
   b. Real estate

---

9. Technically speaking, rates will still range from 18 to 55 percent, but the unified gift and estate tax exemption provides everyone with some relief at the lower end of the scale. That is, the exemption (which is converted to credit) exempts enough dollars so the minimum rate becomes 37 percent. The maximum estate and gift tax rate was scheduled to decline to 50 percent in 1988, but in the 1986 tax changes, Congress postponed this decline until 1993.

Table 19—4   *Reduction in top-bracket rates*

Transfers made and decedents dying in	Top-bracket rate	Top-bracket amount in excess of
1983	60%	$3,500,000
1984–1992	55	3,000,000
1993 and later	50	2,500,000

Thus when fully implemented in 1993 transfers will be taxable at progressive marginal rates ranging between 37 percent and 50 percent.

Table 19—5   *Unified federal estate and gift tax rates*

Taxable estate of gift Over (1)	But not over (2)	Tax on (1)	Rate on excess (1)
1987 and thereafter until 1993 when the maximum rate drops to 50 percent			
0	$ 10,000	$ 0	18
$ 10,000	20,000	1,800	20
20,000	40,000	3,800	22
40,000	60,000	8,200	24
60,000	80,000	13,000	26
80,000	100,000	18,200	28
100,000	150,000	23,800	30
150,000	250,000	38,800	32
250,000	500,000	70,800	34
500,000	750,000	155,800	37
750,000	1,000,000	248,300	39
1,000,000	1,250,000	345,800	41
1,250,000	1,500,000	448,300	43
1,500,000	2,000,000	555,800	45
2,000,000	$2,500,000	780,800	49
2,500,000	$3,000,000	1,025,800	53
3,000,000	—	1,290,800	55

    c. Stock and bonds
    d. Life insurance (if the ownership of the policy has been transferred to the beneficiary, generally this is not included)
    e. The home (one-half if owned jointly with spouse or if a community property state)
    f. Any other assets of value
2. *Step 2.* Subtract the deductions to obtain the *taxable estate.* The deductions include:

   a. The marital deduction
   b. Funeral expenses
   c. Administrative expenses in settling the estate
   d. Debts including mortgage debt on the home
   e. Charitable contributions—that portion of the estate, if any, which will pass to a qualified charity
   f. Taxes, if debts or administrative expenses
3. *Step 3.* Add all prior taxable gifts made since 1976.
4. *Step 4.* Calculate the tax on the amount in Step 3. This is the tentative *estate tax.*
5. *Step 5.* Subtract all taxes paid on all prior taxable gifts made since 1976.
6. *Step 6.* Subtract the unified federal gift and estate tax credit.
7. *Step 7.* Next, subtract the state death tax credit.
8. *Step 8.* Then, subtract the foreign death tax credit, if any.

The remainder is the tax due.

Table 19—6 shows the actual estate tax calculation. It should be noted that the marital deduction was not taken. This would be true in the case of a single person. However, if the deceased were married, the marital deduction could be taken where shown. This would eliminate taxes completely, because transfers between spouses (lifetime gifts or through an estate) are tax free. However, as shown below, the marital deduction does not reduce taxes; it only defers them. Setting up a trust and taking

Federal estate tax calculation Table 19—6

Gross estate		$2,000,000
Deductions:		
a. Funeral expenses	$ 5,000	
b. Administrative expenses	20,000	
c. Debts, including mortgage debts	45,000	
d. Taxes	5,000	
e. Charitable contribution	20,000	
f. Marital deduction	0	
Total deductions	$95,000	95,000
Taxable estate		$1,905,000
Taxable gifts made after 1976		800,000
Tax base (taxable gifts and estate)		$2,705,000
Tentative estate tax		1,134,450
Credit for federal gift taxes paid earlier	$ 75,000	
Unified gift and estate tax credit	192,800	
Credit for state death taxes	60,000	
Credit for foreign death taxes	0	
Total credits	$327,800	327,800
Estate tax due		$ 806,650

the marital deduction on a lesser amount will actually reduce taxes, as too will be shown below.

How gifts can save taxes

Gifts can save taxes for three reasons. First, the $10,000 ($20,000 on joint gifts) annual exclusion for a recipient, as noted above, is over and above the $600,000 unified gift and estate tax exemption.

Second, gifts prevent appreciable assets from being evaluated at a higher level later when an estate is probated, and hence reduce taxes.

Third, the $192,800 unified credit can be used earlier by making a gift. In a sense the credit is borrowed interest-free from the IRS. Table 19—7 shows how gifts are taxed. The tax on the first $700,000 taxable gift is $229,800, but the unified credit of $192,800 reduces it to $37,000. Essentially $600,000 was transferred tax free. The tax on the second taxable gift is $38,800 because the tax is progressive and cumulative, which means that previous taxable gifts must be added in when making the calculation on the second gift. Consequently, the second taxable gift of $100,000 is taxed as if it were an $800,000 gift; the tax on it of $267,800 is offset by the tax ($229,800) on the first gift, for a tax liability of $38,000. There is no unified credit for this second gift because the first gift used it all up. However, this unified credit reappears later on when the estate tax is due.

Both gifts in our example in Table 19—7 go into the estate tax base when the person dies, and hence the $600,000 exemption (converted to a credit of $192,800) reappears and can be taken again in making the final estate tax calculation. This is shown on Table 19—6. However, adding all gifts ($800,000 in our example) increases the final estate tax because the rates are progressive, but is partially offset by the unified credit.

As we shall later see, a person should also not waste that $600,000 exemption ($192,800 unified credit) when calculating the final estate tax by making excessive use of the marital deduction.

Table 19—7   *How gift taxes are calculated*

	Gift	Tax	Unified credit	Actual tax paid
First gift	$710,000			
Annual exclusion	10,000			
Taxable gift	700,000	$229,800	$192,800	$37,000
Second gift	$110,000			
Annual exclusion	10,000			
Taxable gift	100,000*	$267,800	0	$38,000

*The second gift is taxed as if it were an $800,000 gift, which makes the tax $267,800. It is then offset by $229,800, which is the tax on the previous $700,000 gift even though it was mostly nullified by the unified credit.

An irrevocable trust can also be used to reduce estate taxes, because the surviving spouse will not inherit the deceased's property. Rather the property goes into an irrevocable trust and by-passes the survivor who receives only the income from it. While the surviving spouse could inherit the entire estate tax free, there would be more taxes to pay when she died; the marital deduction could become a trap. To achieve the tax savings, $600,000 of the couple's assets (equal to the unified credit of $192,800) must bypass the surviving spouse. Then, the surviving spouse's taxable estate would be smaller, thus saving taxes. Consider the following example of a couple who have $1,200,000 of taxable assets.

How a trust can save taxes

1. The first spouse dies, and the entire estate passes tax free—due to the marital deduction there is no tax on transfers between spouses.
2. The survivor dies and leaves an estate of $1,200,000, which is taxed.
3. The tax on a $1,200,000 estate is $427,800; but after the unified credit of $192,800 is applied, the tax is $235,000.

Without a bypass trust

1. The first spouse dies and leaves nothing to the survivor. Rather, $600,000 goes into an irrevocable trust, for example, established by the deceased's will, and the survivor gets the income from it.[10]
2. There is a $192,800 tax on this $600,000 going into the trust, but after the unified credit of $192,800, it became zero. The tax is on the property of the deceased for the privilege of passing property to, in this case, the trust.
3. The survivor dies and leaves an estate of $600,000, not $1,200,000—the $600,000 in trust on her behalf is not hers.
4. The second partner's estate tax after the unified credit is also zero.
5. The total tax with trust is zero.
6. The tax savings are $235,000.

With a bypass trust

If a trust is used in the manner described above, the marital deduction will be lost. Assets placed into a regular trust—and hence not subject to the estate tax upon the death of the surviving spouse—do not qualify for the marital deduction. However, in the case above, the marital deduction is not needed; the $192,800 unified credit knocks out taxes. It should be

The exemption (unified credit) or the marital deduction?

---

10. If we are assuming a community property state, each member already owns one-half of the property and the deceased cannot put his or her spouse's property into a trust. In a noncommunity property state, the entire $1,200,000 could be put into trust, but then the tax would be on $1,200,000 just as in the case of not having a trust. The community property states are Arizona, California, Idaho, Louisiana, Nevada, New Mexico, Texas, and Washington. Property rights in these states are based on Spanish law that assumes that a man and wife are one person. In the remainder of the states—called common law states—property rights are based on English common law. Wisconsin now has a system patterned after community property.

remembered that the husband and wife each have an exemption of $600,000 (credit of $192,800), and each should use it. The deduction should not be wasted by not taking it, and relying on the marital deduction instead. For estates larger than our example, a trust of $600,000 should also be established to reduce taxes and then the marital deduction used to postpone tax on the remainder of the estate until the spouse dies.

The Q-tip trust: An alternative approach

It is possible to establish a qualified terminable interest property trust—called Q-tip Trust. This is a special trust that is subject to the estate tax when the surviving spouse dies. Because of this, the marital deduction may be taken on behalf of the deceased when the Q-tip is used. Under the Q-tip the surviving spouse would receive the income for life, and the trust's assets would then pass to the children. The advantage of the Q-tip over passing assets directly via the marital deduction is that the first partner to die does not lose control over the distribution of his or her assets after the death of the surviving spouse. This is important in the event that the surviving spouse remarries and decides to leave the assets to the new spouse, thereby freezing out the children. The Q-tip prevents this. In some cases it would be wise to set up a regular trust for $600,000 and a Q-tip trust for the remainder.

Trusts are very complex, and if one is used, it must be tailor-made to the particular situation. However, if properly used, both gifts and trusts may reduce taxes.

SUMMARY REVIEW QUESTIONS

These questions serve as a summary and a review of the chapter. If you are able to answer them all, you have a good understanding of the material covered by the chapter.

1. How may a person's domicile and residence differ, and what is the importance of this distinction from the point of view of estate planning?
2. Why is it important to draw up a personal balance sheet when planning a will?
3. What is the major purpose of a will?
4. Why is it important to have an experienced attorney draft a will or trust arrangement? Why should the executor of a will also be experienced?
5. What does probating a will entail?
6. What are the relative merits of appointing a private individual to act as trustee as opposed to a trust corporation or trust department of a bank?
7. What are the most important contents of a will?
8. What is a joint will? Should it be used?
9. What is the common disaster clause? Should each will have one? Why or why not?
10. What is a codicil to a will? Should it be used? Explain why or why not.

11. Why should a last letter of instructions be written?
12. What are the adverse possibilities of dying intestate? Would a person ever want to die intestate?
13. When is a joint tenancy a desirable form of property distribution?
14. Differentiate between the *inter vivos* trust, the irrevocable trust, the revocable trust, and the testamentary trust.
15. Differentiate between a simple and complex trust.
16. Explain the rule against perpetuities.

17. How does a *per stirpes* distribution of an estate differ from a *per capita* distribution?
18. What is the idea behind the power of invasion? Do you think it is wise? Why?
19. What are split gifts?
20. What is the annual gift tax exclusion?
21. Explain how gifts can reduce total taxes.
22. What is the marital deduction and how does it work?
23. How can a trust reduce taxes?
24. Are there any nontax reasons for making gifts?

CASES

1. John Jones and his wife Mary are beginning to plan now so as to minimize their gift and estate taxes when they are gone. They have assets of $1,000,000.
   (a) How can gifts made during their lifetime reduce taxes?
   (b) How can a trust reduce taxes?
2. Jack McCarthy and his wife Bette are in their early thirties and have two children, four and six. Jack earns $30,000 per year. He has $50,000 worth of life insurance. Bette earns $20,000 per year. They have $20,000 equity in their $100,000 house, $5,000 in cash in a savings and loan association, and $30,000 worth of personal assets including a car. Both Jack and Bette are in excellent health. A few evenings ago a lawyer friend of theirs told them everyone should have a will. Jack and Bette have always believed wills were for older people and probably for older people of means. Jack feels that because they are young and do not have many assets, they do not need a will. What do you think?
3. Peter Geldsack is a wealthy man. He is a vigorous widower in his early sixties and has the following assets.

Assets	Value
1. Farm in Connecticut	$ 450,000
2. Ski lodge in Aspen, Colorado	75,000
3. House in Bergen County, N.J.	200,000
4. Department store in Newark, N.J.	1,600,000
5. Common stock	3,452,000
6. Corporate bonds	2,500,000
7. Municipal bonds	2,000,000
Total	$10,277,000

Peter has two children to whom he would like to leave the bulk of his estate in equal parts. However, he would also like to leave approximately $100,000 to his faithful butler, and to do so in such a way that he will be well cared for during the rest of his life. The butler, moreover, knows little of investments, and Peter is afraid he might lose any outright cash grant. Peter would also like to leave his ski lodge to his dear friend and ski companion Grover Attwater of Glenwood Springs, Colorado.

What advice would a financial planner give Peter on drawing up a will that will carry out his wishes? If Peter died without a will, what would happen to his estate?

4. Bill and Sara Smith, an elderly couple, have just over $1,000,000 of tax-exempt municipal bonds yielding 8.1 percent. They also own a home free and clear and have no other substantial assets. They have three grown children to whom they will leave their estate in equal parts in their will. However, each wishes that the surviving spouse first get the entire estate and that the children receive it only when they are both gone. How can this be arranged in a will? Should they draw up a joint will? Why or why not?

   Recently they have heard they can reduce taxes by giving part of their assets away prior to death. Is this true? How does it work? What is one of the pitfalls to be avoided if they decide to give some of their assets away? How else can they reduce taxes, and increase the amount that their children will receive?

5. Don Price drafted a will in which he distributed every item of property he owned, naming each piece. Several years later, Don became wealthy and held a large number of valuable stock certificates. When he reached the age of seventy, Don realized he should provide for the distribution of his stocks. Never an inefficient man, Don reached into the wastebasket and withdrew a sheet of butcher paper that had the words "Joe's Meat Market—Baloney" stamped on one side. On the other side, Don wrote a holographic will bequeathing his stocks to the local Catholic church. Don suffered a heart attack one week later and, as the local priest was administering Don's last rites, Joe (from the meat market) entered the room. Don looked at Joe and produced a small key. "Here, Joe, you take this. This key will open up a new way of life for you." Don soon died and his executors found that the key unlocks a small strongbox in which Don kept his stock certificates. Who gets what?

SUGGESTED READINGS

Ashley, Pritcher B. *You and Your Will; The Planning and Management of Your Estate.* New York: New American Library, 1985.

Brosterman, Robert, and Brosterman, Thomas. *The Complete Estate Planning Guide.* New York: A Mentor Book, 1988.

Crumbley, D. L., and Milam, Edward E. *Estate Planning in the '80s, A Guide for Advisors and Their Clients.* Homewood, Ill.: Dow Jones-Irwin, 1986.

Englebrecht, John, and Fowler, Leslie. *Federal Taxation of Estates, Gifts, and Trusts,* 2nd ed. Englewood Cliffs, N.J.: Prentice-Hall, 1987.

Esperiti, Robert A., and Peterson, Renno L., *The Handbook of Estate Planning;* 2nd edition. New York: McGraw-Hill Book Co., 1988.

Estate Planners Quarterly. New York: Farnsworth Publishing Co.

"*Estate Tax Planning.*" Hartford, Conn.: Aetna Life Insurance Co.

Farr, James A., and Wright, Jackson. *Estate Planners Handbook.* Boston: Little, Brown, 1986.

Federal Estate and Gift Taxes. Chicago: Commerce Clearing House.

Fundamental Concepts of Estate Planning. New York: Practicing Law Institute, 1984.

Guilfoyle, A. P., Fossett, Alice W., Thomas, William W., and Scoville, Samuel S. *Tax Facts on Life Insurance.* Cincinnati, Ohio: The National Underwriter Company. Annual Publication.

"*Highlights of the Tax Reform Act of 1986.*" Chicago: Arthur Andersen & Co.

Holzman, Robert S. *Encyclopedia of Estate Planning,* revised ed. New York: Boardroom Books, 1985.

Internal Revenue Service. *A Guide to Federal Estate and Gift Taxation.* U.S. Treasury Department, Internal Revenue Service. This pamphlet can be obtained from the local IRS office.

Journal of the American Society of Chartered Life Underwriters. Bryn Mawr, Pa.: American Society of Chartered Life Underwriters. Quarterly publication.

Kahn, Arnold D. *Family Security Through Estate Planning,* 2nd ed. New York; McGraw-Hill, 1984.

"*Planning for Life and Death; Real Property, Probate and Trust Law.*" Chicago: American Bar Association Information Services.

"The Price Waterhouse Guide to the New Tax Law." New York: Bantam Books, 1986.

Sommerfield, Ray M., Anderson, Herschel M., and Brock, Horace R. *An Introduction to Taxation,* 4th ed. New York: Harcourt, Brace and World, 1988.

"*Tax Reform 1986, Analysis and Planning.*" Chicago: Arthur Andersen & Co.

Trusts and Estates, The Journal of Estate Planning and Administration. New York: Communication Channels. Monthly publication.

Use of Trusts in Estate Planning, 1986. New York: Practicing Law Institute, 1986.

"*Wills: Why You Should Have One and the Lawyer's Role In Its Preparation.*" Chicago: American Bar Association Information Services.

"*Year End Strategy for Individuals Planning for 1986 and Beyond.*" Chicago: Arthur Andersen & Co.

APPENDIX 19: TECHNICAL APPENDIX

(Glossary of Terms)

Administrator:	One who administers a decedent's estate during probate. He or she differs from the executor in that the administrator is appointed by the judge of the probate court when no executor is named by a will or when the appointed executor is unable to perform the duties.
Attestation:	The witnessing of a paper's execution and a signed statement to that effect.
Bequest:	A gift of personal property or money under a will.
Cestui que trust:	The beneficiaries of a trust. (Called cetty for short.)
Codicils:	Writings executed subsequent to a will and forming a part thereof.
Collateral heirs:	Persons who are not descendants of the decedent but who are related through a common ancestor. Generally they include cousins and aunts and uncles of the decedent.
Corpus; trust res:	The body of the trust; the assets.
Decedent:	A deceased person.
Devise:	A gift of real property by the last will and testament of the donor. In contrast, a bequest or legacy is a gift of personal property or money.
Devisee:	Person receiving a gift of land by way of will.
Domicile:	The place of the permanent home of a person. The place of domicile is largely a matter of intention, though declarations of intention contrary to the actions of a person do not always control. A person has only one domicile at one time. It is not necessarily the same place as one's residence because domicile is the home, the fixed place of habitation, whereas residence is a transient place of dwelling. The domicile is where wills are probated.

Donor:	One who makes a gift.
Escrow:	An agreement under which certain executed documents, e.g., deeds, are delivered into the hands of a third person to be held until specified conditions are fulfilled and then delivered to the person so performing or, in the case of default, returned to the person executing the document.
Estate:	The interest that anyone has in property, being used particularly in connection with the interests owned by a person in real property. Also the total property of whatever kind owned by a decedent before the property is distributed according to the terms of a will, or by the laws of inheritance if the owner died intestate.
Estate in severalty:	An estate that is held by a person in his or her own right only, without any other person being joined or connected.
Executor:	The personal representative of a testator, appointed by the testator and approved by the judge of a probate court to take charge of the testator's estate, pay the debts, and distribute the balance of the property to the beneficiaries of the will pursuant to the order of the probate court.
Fee simple:	The highest in dignity and the greatest in extent of the estates in real property.
Fiduciary:	The person or institution who manages the financial affairs of a trust.
Gift causa mortis:	An unrevoked gift of personal property made in expectation of death.
Grantee:	One to whom a conveyance is made by deed.
Grantor:	The person who creates a trust.
Holographic will:	A will written entirely by the testator with his own hand.
Inter vivos gift:	A gift among the living, in contrast to a gift by will or in anticipation of death.
Inter vivos trust:	A trust created during the lifetime of the grantor.
Intestate:	Having no will. An intestate is a decedent who left no will or a defective will. Property not included in a will is often called intestate property.
Joint tenancy:	Two or more persons owning the same land and having the same unity of interest, time, title, and possession together with the right of survivorship.
Legacy:	Specific legacy: a gift of personal property, generally a specific item of value, under a will. General legacy: a gift of a certain sum, but no specific asset cited.
Legatee:	Person receiving a legacy or bequest.
Lineals:	Blood relatives of a decedent.
Per stirpes:	The method of distribution of the assets of a grant after the death of the original beneficiary. The children (grandchildren) share in the same proportions that their parents did (or would have).
Probate:	The procedure of proving a will before a court having jurisdiction over the administration of the estate of a deceased person.
Settlor:	The creator of a trust; also called grantor, trustor, and donor.
Spendthrift trust:	A trust created to provide a fund for the maintenance of a beneficiary and at the same time to secure it against his or her improvidence or incapacity. Generally, the trust principal is beyond the reach of creditors.

Tenancy by the entirety:	Title in real property held by husband and wife together; based on the common-law concept that provides rights of survivorship. Property held by the entirety can only be disposed of by the joint action of the husband and wife.
Tenancy in common:	A type of co-ownership of property by which the owners have undivided interests in the property. The interests may be unequal in quantity, may have been created at different times, and may have been derived from different sources. The co-owners are also known as cotenants. A cotenant may sell or otherwise dispose of his or her interest without consent of the other cotenants, and the new owner takes the right of the cotenant from whom he or she took interest. There is no survivorship right between cotenants, and the undivided interest may be disposed of by will or, in the absence of a will, descends to the heirs of the deceased cotenant, as would other property of the same kind. All of the tenants, in the absence of agreement between them to the contrary, have equal rights of possession regardless of inequality in their undivided interests.
Testamentary instrument:	A legal document such as a will or trust bestowing certain rights to certain individuals after the death of the person making the instrument.
Testamentary trustee:	A trustee appointed by or acting under a will in order to carry out a trust created by a will.
Testate:	A testate is a decedent who left a will. Property included in the will is often called testate property.
Testator:	The term may be used to describe either a man who has made a will or a decedent who left a will.
Testatrix:	A female testator.
Trustee:	The person who holds the legal title to trust property for the purposes as stated by the terms of the trust.

Glossary

Accidental death benefits	A provision that may be added to a life insurance policy calling for the payment of additional benefits in the case of death by accidental means. See also *"Double Indemnity."*
Actual cash value clause	Clause in a homeowner's policy that states the insurer pays the current value of the loss, less depreciation, on the building insured, provided the loss does not exceed the face value of the policy. Thus the face value of the policy defines the maximum liability of the insurance company.
Actuary	A person professionally trained in mathematics and other technical aspects of the calculation of probabilities.
Add-on interest	Interest applied to the original balance owed even though on an installment loan the balance owed declines as the months pass and payments are made.
Adjusted gross income	The term the Internal Revenue Service (IRS) uses to describe the income after certain deductions are taken from gross, or total, incomes on page one of the tax form.
All-risk policies	The broadest of all homeowner's policies. It covers all risks except those specifically excluded, such as damage due to earthquakes.
Alternative minimum tax	A special provision in the federal income tax code that applies to high income people and corporations. Congress added it so that these taxpayers, who have found a legal way of avoiding taxes in the regular code, must pay some taxes.
American Stock Exchange (AMEX)	The second major stock exchange (after the New York Stock Exchange) in the U.S.A.
Amortization	A method of paying off a mortgage.
Annuitant	The person who has a contract with a life insurance company to receive periodic payments for a specific number of years, or perhaps for life.
Annual percentage rate (APR)	The actual, true actuarial interest rate.
Asked price	The price at which a dealer will sell a nonlisted or over-the-counter security.
Assets	Anything of value. (There are also *"Earning Assets"* and *"Non-Earning Assets."* See below.)
Assigned risk plans	Plans developed to take care of those automobile drivers who cannot obtain liability insurance because of their driving record but still wish to show financial responsibility.

564

Automated teller	A machine that will accept deposits or allow withdrawals from an account in a depository institution.
Automatic funds transfer (AFT)	Funds can be transferred automatically from one account to another account and vice versa.
Automatic premium loan (APL)	Provision in an insurance policy that grants the insured an automatic loan that is used to pay the premiums after the grace period has expired if the policy has a cash value.
Balance sheet	The method of showing all the assets and liabilities of a corporation or an individual.
Balanced fund	An investment company that holds varying proportions of bonds, preferred stocks, and common stocks in order to maintain relatively greater stability of both principal and income.
Balloon clause	A clause in an installment loan contract calling for a final payment substantially larger than the earlier payments.
Bankruptcy	The condition in which a person is legally declared unable to pay his debts.
Bear market	Technical term for a long-run downward-moving securities market.
Beneficiary	The person who receives certain benefits as spelled out in a trust or a life insurance contract.
Better business bureaus	Organizations established by the business community, whose goal is to provide better relations between businesses and the public.
Bid price	The price at which a dealer will buy nonlisted or over-the-counter securities.
Blue-chip stock	The common stock of large, well-known, financially strong corporations with good records of earnings and dividend payments over many years.
Blue Cross	An independent, nonprofit membership organization designed to cover hospitalization costs (i. e., hospital room and supplies).
Blue Shield	An independent, nonprofit membership organization designed to cover physician's fees, whether surgical, surgical-medical, or general medical.
Blue sky laws	The laws of the various states regulating the sale of securities and the activities of security salespersons, brokers, and dealers.
Bond	A certificate of indebtedness that represents a loan from the bondholder to the issuer.
Book value	The accounting concept of the value of a share of common stock. It is equal to assets minus liabilities divided by the number of shares outstanding.
Broad coverage	A type of homeowners' policy that covers substantially more risk than does a more limited basic (HO-1) policy.
Broker	A person in the business of buying and selling securities (or insurance policies) for another party for which he or she receives a commission.
Budget	A financial plan in the form of an income statement which uses current and future operations to achieve certain goals. Very often it must be an estimate of future receipts and disbursements.
Bull market	Technical term for a long-run upward-moving securities market.
Call option	A contract giving the holder the privilege of purchasing a given security at a specific price for a specific period of time.
Call price	As applied to bonds, the price at which an issuer can prematurely retire bonds.
Callable bonds	Bonds that can be called in at the option of the issuer and on which the principal will be repaid.

Callable preferred stock	Preferred stock with a provision that the corporation has an option to buy back the stock on terms specified at the time the stock is issued.
Capital	Total assets of a business.
Capital gains	The market appreciation in the value of securities or other assets.
Capital loss	The decline in the market value of securities or other assets.
Capital structure	The relative proportions of capital represented by bonds, preferred stock, and common stock.
Cash discount	When the customer receives a discount off the purchase price if cash is paid for the purchase.
Cash management account (CMA)	An stock brokerage account that includes several items such as a checking account, a mutual fund, and a brokerage statement.
Cash surrender value	The amount of cash a person may obtain by voluntarily surrendering a life insurance policy; a nonforfeiture option.
Cashier's check	A check that the bank will write on itself. Cashier's checks may be bought from a bank by a depositor or nondepositor to make payments to a designated payee.
Certificate of deposit (CD)	A deposit account into which funds are placed at a specified time, not to be withdrawn until a specified time. CDs vary in terms of their maturities and yields.
Certified check	A means of assuring the payee that the check is good in cases where the payee may lack confidence in the drawer. The sum is deducted from the drawer's account before the check is issued.
Check	A bill of exchange; a negotiable instrument. A written order drawn on a bank by a depositor, ordering the bank to pay on demand, and unconditionally, a definite amount of money to bearer or to the order of a specified person. A sight bank draft used to make payments with funds held in demand deposits.
Closed-end investment company	A company that has a definite limit to the number of shares in itself that it may sell.
Closed-end lease	A type of lease that allows the leasee to pay so much per month and to return the merchandise when the term of the lease is over and the lease itself thus terminated.
Closed-end note	A note that is for a specific period of time only.
Closing costs	Cost incurred when closing a real estate sale between two parties. Included in these costs are title insurance, attorney's fees, recording fees, and the like.
Coinsurance	Most of the medical or property and casualty insurance policies contain a feature that provides for the insurance company to pay only a part of the total expense.
Collateral trust bonds	Corporate bonds secured by collateral that consists of other corporations' stocks or bonds. Often the securities used as collateral are held in trust by a third party.
Collision insurance	Insurance that pays for major damage to your automobile in the event of an accident.
Commercial banks	Institutions that perform a wide variety of financial services, differentiating them from more specialized savings banks.
Commission brokers	Brokers who buy and sell securities for their customers, for which they receive a commission.
Common stock	Denotes equity interest in a corporation. Common stockholders are the owners of the corporation and are the last to be paid off in the event the corporation must be liquidated.

Comprehensive coverage	Coverage for damages to the insured's car due to causes other than collision, such as fire or wind damage.
Comptroller of the currency	An office of the United States Treasury that charters, supervises, and examines national banks.
Consumer credit	Credit extended to individuals for the purchase of final consumer items.
Consumer durables	Goods having a relatively long life, such as television sets, household appliances, or automobiles.
Consumer finance company	A firm specializing in loans to consumers, generally at higher interest rates than those charged by other lenders.
Consumer Leasing Act	Federal consumer credit law that requires disclosure of information that helps the consumer compare the cost and terms of one lease with another.
Consumer price index	A statistical device that measures the increase in the cost of living for consumers. Sometimes used to illustrate the extent that prices in general have risen or the amount of inflation.
Consumption expenditures	Expenditures by individuals on final goods and services.
Contract brokers	Brokers who assist the commission brokers who are unable to handle the entire volume of business by themselves. Contract brokers do not deal with the public.
Conventional mortgage	Mortgage arrangement solely between the lending institution and the buyer of the home. These are mortgages that are neither guaranteed by the VA nor insured by the FHA, but they may be insured by various private mortgage insurers.
Convertible	A bond or preferred stock that may be, under specific circumstances, exchanged for a certain number of shares of common stock.
Convertible preferred stock	Preferred stock that can be exchanged for common stock at the stockholder's option.
Corporate mortgage bonds	Bonds that are secured by a mortgage on a specific piece of corporate real estate.
Corporation	A legal entity that has many of the rights, duties, and powers of an individual. The corporation raises capital by selling shares in itself called *stock*. Corporations come into existence when the proper state agency grants the corporation its charter. The owners of the corporation are the stockholders and have liability to the extent of their investment.
Credit card	A card that permits consumers to obtain merchandise without paying at the time of purchase, receiving one bill at the end of the month for all purchases.
Credit life insurance	Special term life insurance purchased when borrowing money on an installment loan basis, which is then used to pay off the loan in the event of the borrower's death before he or she pays it off.
Credit unions	A cooperative type of depository institution designed to make loans to members for any reasonable purpose.
Cumulative preferred stock	Preferred stock that requires corporations to pay all back dividends (dividends missed in prior years) before dividends on common stock can be paid.
Dealer	A person or firm who buys or sells securities at given prices for his or her own account. Dealers differ from brokers in that they make the market in certain securities by being willing simultaneously either to buy at a given price or to sell at a different given price.
Debenture	A type of bond secured by no specific assets but by the general credit and all assets of the corporation.

Debit card	A card used to make automatic fund transfers from the account of a buyer of merchandise to that of the seller. It eliminates the need for checks or cash by initiating automatic transfer of funds via a computer.
Decreasing term policy	A type of term insurance in which the contract payout by the insurance company (or face value) decreases as time passes.
Deductible	An amount of money that the policyholder must pay, which may range anywhere from $100 to $500 or even higher, before the insurance coverage begins.
Deed of trust	A special kind of mortgage, conveying title of property to a third party (trustee) rather than to the lender.
Deflation	A continuous decrease in the overall price level (an appreciation in the value of the dollar).
Demand deposits	Deposits payable to the depositor upon demand. Funds placed in checking accounts are demand deposits.
Depository savings institution	An institution that issues secondary securities called *deposits*.
Depreciation	The expense allowance on capital goods that is allowed because capital will wear out. The depreciation expense permits the recapture of dollars invested in capital goods, so that they can be replaced after they wear out.
Disability insurance	Insurance that generally provides for payments if the policyholder's income is cut off due to disability from an accident or illness.
Discounted interest	Interest that is paid in advance.
Discounted loan	A loan on which the interest is deducted from the principal before it is made.
Diversification	Investing in the securities of a number of different firms and a number of different industries in an attempt to spread the risk and lessen the impact of losses.
Dividend	Payment made to the owners of common or preferred stock.
Double indemnity	A clause in a life insurance contract that requires a double payment in the case of an accidental death. See also "*Accidental Death Benefits.*"
Dow Jones averages	A statistical series that shows the general level and movement of 30 securities prices.
Drafts	Specialized checks written by one bank on its account in another bank. Usually utilized for payments made long distance.
Drawee	The party requested to pay the stated amount of the check, usually the bank or other savings institution.
Drawer	The person drawing the bill of exchange instrument (check). Person writing a check against his checking account, and ordering that a payment be made.
Earnest money	A deposit made by a purchaser of real estate as evidence of his good faith.
Earning assets	Those assets that yield a return, such as stocks, bonds, savings accounts, and rentable real estate. These assets may yield a return in the form of interest, dividends, or rent.
Earnings	A corporation's income after all expenses, including preferred dividend payments.
Efficient market hypothesis (EMH)	States that the prices of securities traded in the market fully reflect all available information and that the market reacts instantaneously and in an unbiased manner to all new information. The EMH may be stated in its weak, semi-strong, or strong forms. One could conclude from the EMH that, if one is big enough and diversified enough, one would do as well by picking common stock at random as by analysis.

Electronic funds transfer systems (EFTS)	Involves advanced communication systems that use electronic impulses to facilitate fund transfers among accounts. *See also* automatic funds transfer.
End products	Final goods and services.
Equal Credit Opportunity Act	Federal consumer credit law that prohibits discrimination against an applicant for credit because of age, sex, marital status, race, color, religion, national origin, or receipt of public assistance.
Equipment trust obligations	Securities (bonds) issued by corporations with specific equipment of the corporation used as security for the loan.
Estate taxes	Federal taxes that are due on the estate of the deceased.
Ex dividend	Without dividend. This means that the stock, if purchased, does not include the most recent dividend that has been declared.
Ex-dividend date	The first day that the purchaser of a stock does not receive the dividend that has been declared on it.
Expected rate of return	The annual return investors expect to receive on their investments over some future holding period.
Extended term provision	A nonforfeiture option that states that if the holder fails to pay the premiums during the grace period, the policy automatically will remain in force as a term policy for as long as the cash surrender value of the policy will permit.
Fair Credit Billing Act	Federal consumer credit law that sets up a procedure for the prompt correction of errors on a credit account and prevents damage to a credit rating while settling a dispute.
Fair Credit Reporting Act	Federal consumer credit law that sets up a procedure for the prompt correction of mistakes on the consumer's credit record and requires that the record be kept confidential.
Federal Deposit Insurance Corporation (FDIC)	A federal regulatory authority, which began operating in 1934, that provides insurance protection for small deposits (i.e., those $100,000 or less), and supervises state-chartered banks who are not members of the Federal Reserve System but insured by the FDIC.
Federal Reserve	The central bank of the United States, established by Congress in 1913. The Federal Reserve is one of the regulatory agencies that oversees and supervises certain financial institutions.
FHA mortgage	A mortgage loan made by an approved lending institution, the loan being insured by the Federal Housing Administration. Borrowers, property, and lenders must all meet FHA standards for the FHA to insure the mortgage loan.
Fiduciary	A person who has certain legal rights and powers relating to financial matters to be exercised for the benefit of another person.
Finance company	A financial institution specializing in making small loans to consumers.
Financial assets	Includes such things as stocks, bonds, bank accounts, and cash or currency.
Financial responsibility laws	Laws designed to protect the victims of automobile accidents by encouraging people to have at least the minimum amount of insurance to compensate a victim for damages.
Financial risk	Risk related to the debt-equity ratio. With a high debt-equity ratio a corporation has large fixed obligations to pay each year, and there is the possibility creditors may force the firm into bankruptcy if the firm cannot pay.
Fixed annuity	A contract with a life insurance company that provides the periodic payment of a fixed number of dollars for a specific period of time or for life.

Fixed benefit plan — A type of pension plan in which the benefits to be received are calculated by a formula. These are also called defined benefit plans.

Fixed income security — A preferred stock or a bond that has a stated or fixed percentage income return.

Floor brokers — Members of the exchange who assist commission brokers, who are unable to handle all the volume when trading is heavy.

Floor traders — Members of the New York Stock Exchange who buy and sell securities for their own account.

Funding — Technical term that refers to the buildup of assets of a pension fund.

General obligation bonds — Municipal bonds that are secured by the full faith and credit of the taxing entity issuing them.

Gift taxes — Taxes imposed on the giver; taxes on the privilege of giving something away.

Grace period — The period, usually thirty days, following the premium due date of a life insurance policy during which an overdue premium may be paid without penalty.

Graduated payment mortgage (GPM) — Under this mortgage the payments start out substantially below what they should be and then increase as time goes on.

Gross national product (GNP) — The market value of all final goods and services produced in the United States per year.

Group life insurance — Generally, insurance sold to a business firm, the firm providing each insured employee with an insurance certificate. The business firm usually withholds the premiums from the employees' salaries, and the employees are provided with an insurance package that consists of term life insurance.

Growth stock — A stock that has shown a better than average growth in earnings, hence, a better than average appreciation in its market price. Moreover, there are expectations that it should continue to do so.

Guaranteed renewable policy — A policy that can be renewed until some predetermined age is reached.

Health maintenance organizations (HMOs) — A type of medical expense protection method. HMOs provide medical care for their members, for a fixed fee per month, by owning and operating clinics and hospitals and hiring doctors, nurses, and technicians.

Hedge fund — A mutual fund (or investment company) that hedges its market commitments by holding certain securities it believes are likely to increase in value and, at the same time, sells others short because it believes they are likely to decline in value. Its main objective is capital appreciation.

Holder-in-due-course doctrine — Formerly a legal concept that if a merchant entered into a credit relationship with a consumer to finance purchased goods and then sold the installment contract to a third party (say, a finance company), a legally binding contract existed between the consumer and the third party. Previously this doctrine forced consumers to pay for goods even if they were defective. Today consumers can withhold payment for defective goods.

Home equity loans — Another name for a second mortgage. These are usually obtained when a home owner has paid off a substantial part of the mortgage and also has had the home appreciate considerably in value. It is usually used for financing some other venture.

Home Mortgage Disclosure Act — Federal consumer credit law that requires most lending institutions in metropolitan areas to let the public know where they make their mortgage and home improvement loans.

Homeowners' insurance policy	Insurance policy that provides for property insurance on the home, personal property insurance, liability insurance, and medical payment insurance.
Hospital confinement indemnity	Insurance coverage that pays so much per day to replace lost income while the insured is in the hospital.
Income bonds	Bonds on which the interest is paid only if earned.
Income statement	Depicts the financial position over a period of time, for example, a year. A flow concept. Measures dollar income inflows and dollar expenditure outflows.
Income stock	Stock of a corporation that has a historical record of above average earnings and dividends and that is likely to continue performing favorably.
Individual retirement account (IRA)	Individuals with earned income may place a portion of their earnings, sometimes tax deductible, into a special account where interest and capital gains are not taxable until the account is drawn upon.
Inflation	An overall general upward price movement of all goods and services that results in the decline in the value of a dollar.
Inheritance tax	A tax imposed on the privilege of inheriting something, imposed on the person receiving the property. There are no federal inheritance taxes, but some states impose them.
Installment credit	Consists of all credit extended to individuals that is to be repaid in two or more installments.
Insurance dividend	The payment made to owners of participating life insurance policies, as a return of unused premiums.
Interest bearing checking account	A relatively new (since 1980) type of checking account that earns interest.
Interest rate risk	The risk of loss that results from the changes in the market price of bonds due to changes in the prevailing rates of interest. A risk relevant only with regard to investments in fixed obligations such as bonds and preferred stock.
Investment company	A corporation that sells stock of itself to the public and then uses the funds to buy the securities of many other firms. There is no limit to the number of shares an open-end investment company may sell of itself whereas a closed-end investment company definitely has a limit on the number of shares it may sell.
Investment service	Service from which one may obtain research and advisory information about whole industries and individual companies that one may wish to invest in.
Investment trust	Also called an investment company. A financial institution that sells shares in itself to small investors and then uses the funds to buy stocks and bonds in other companies on behalf of its shareholders.
Irrevocable trust	A trust to which the grantor gives property without any right to or control over the income. Moreover, the grantor may never reclaim the property.
Itemized deductions	Deductions that are used to offset income if they collectively exceed the standard deduction. These include state and local taxes, charitable contributions, and the like.
Joint account	A checking account that allows two or more people to write checks against the account.
Junk bonds	Bonds that have a high risk of default.
Keogh Plan	The self-employed individual's qualified retirement plan.
Law of large numbers	A mathematical theory that probability is more accurate when a large sample is studied.

Lessee	One who holds a leasehold estate (a tenant).
Lessor	One who grants a leasehold estate (a landlord).
Level premium life insurance	Life insurance policy with fixed insurance premiums over the life of the policy. Premiums are used to build up reserves in the early years of the policy to be used in the later years. This amounts to averaging the premiums for individuals over the period of their insurance contracts.
Leverage	The use of borrowed money to increase the earnings of the common stockholder.
Liabilities	Amounts owed to others.
Liability insurance	Insurance that protects the insured in the event of losses resulting from damage to property, accidental bodily injury to another or damages awarded in the event of a claim.
Life insurance trust	A trust funded by a life insurance policy upon the death of the insured. A trustee (i.e., a bank) then administers the funds on behalf of someone else.
Life tenants	Persons who receive the income from a trust during their lifetimes.
Limit order	An order to a broker to buy a certain stock only if its price falls to a specified level or to sell a stock only if the price rises to a specified level.
Limited payment life insurance policy	A type of whole life insurance that provides for permanent protection, with the premiums paid only for a certain number of years.
Liquid	Anything easily and quickly convertible to cash without a substantial price concession.
Liquidation value	In the event a corporation is liquidated, the amount left after all debts are paid is divided by the number of shares outstanding to derive liquidation value per share.
Liquidity	Refers to how quickly assets can be converted into cash without making a price concession (or at least not a substantial price concession). Liquidity is a relative term.
Load	The fees that must be paid when buying some mutual funds or life insurance policies.
Loading fee	The fee charged by a mutual fund when it sells shares to the public or charged by a life insurance policy.
Major medical insurance	A medical insurance policy that pays large medical bills. There is a deductible feature, with the insurance company paying medical expenses beyond that.
Malpractice insurance	Primarily designed to protect professionals against personal liability damage suits arising out of actual or alleged professional carelessness.
Management fees	The fees charged by the managers of investment companies for their services in managing the portfolio.
Margin purchases	Purchases of securities with money that is partially borrowed.
Margin requirement	The percentage of the price of a security that must be paid with the buyer's own money. The remainder may be borrowed.
Market order	Either a buy or sell order of a specific number of shares of a specific security at the current market price.
Market risk	Risk resulting from fluctuations in market prices of securities over time. This applies primarily to common stock but not to bonds.
Market value	The price the individual must pay for assets if he or she wishes to buy, or the amount received if the asset is sold.

Medical insurance	Insurance that covers medical expenses, including doctors' fees, cost of drugs, hospital bills, and surgical fees.
Money market deposit account	A type of deposit account that some banks and savings and loan associations offer that pay an interest rate tied to the more competitive rate in the free (money) market.
Money market funds	Mutual funds that specialize in buying very short-term securities in the money market. These funds were developed to enable the small investor to enter the money market.
Money market instruments	Short-term credit instruments such as Treasury bills and commercial paper. Investors who buy them are lending their money on a short-term (one year or less) basis.
Money purchase plan	A pension plan that provides that the employer contributions made on the employee's behalf are earmarked for the employee and are invested on his or her behalf.
Moody's	A bond rating service that assigns credit ratings to bonds to permit investors to assess the risk associated with buying them.
Mortality tables	Tables indicating the number of deaths per thousand at various ages, which have been developed from past experience by life insurance companies.
Mortgage	Instrument used to finance real estate. Security for debt. It gives the lender the legal right to sell the property in order to repay the loan should the borrower default.
Mortgage banker	An individual or firm that primarily originates real estate loans and then sells them to institutional lenders and other investors.
Mortgage bonds	Bonds behind which specific assets of a corporation have been pledged as collateral.
Mortgagee	One to whom a mortgage is given as security for a loan (i.e., the lender).
Mortgagor	One who gives a mortgage to secure a loan (i.e., the borrower).
Municipal securities	Debt obligations of state and local governments. These securities appeal to high-income investors because their interest income is exempt from federal taxation.
Mutual fund	The more popular name for an open-end investment company. See also "Open-end Investment Company."
Mutual life insurance company	An insurance company that is owned by the policyholders.
Mutual savings banks	Financial institutions owned by depositors and similar to savings and loan associations in that they accept deposits and make primarily mortgage loans.
Net asset value	As applied to mutual funds, this is the market value of underlying securities divided by the number of mutual fund shares outstanding.
Net income	See "Taxable Income" below.
Net worth	Assets less liabilities. Net worth is the best measure of what a person or business is worth.
New York Stock Exchange (NYSE)	The largest organized stock exchange in the U.S., accounting for 78% of the total dollar volume of securities transactions on all stock exchanges.
No-load funds	Mutual funds that do not charge any commissions on the sales of their shares.
Nominal yield	Yield stated in money terms and not adjusted for inflation.
Noncancelable policy	A policy that cannot be canceled during the time it was originally stated to run. Nor can premiums be raised during this time.

Nondepository savings institution	An institution that does not issue deposits but that may hold a person's savings, such as a life insurance company.
Nonearning assets	Personal assets, such as a watch or automobile, that do not earn income.
Nonfinancial assets	Such things as clothes, automobiles, and jewelry.
Nonforfeiture options	The options available to holders of cash value life insurance policies if they discontinue the payment of premiums. Generally the policy value is taken in the form of cash, as extended term insurance, or as reduced paid-up insurance.
Noninstallment credit	Credit that consists primarily of single-payment loans and service credit.
NOW Account (Negotiated order of withdrawal)	A specialized checking account that bears interest.
Odd lot	A block of stock consisting of fewer shares than the number customarily traded at one time, which is known as a round lot of one hundred shares.
Odd-lot dealer	A dealer who buys and sells odd lots exclusively.
Open-end investment company (Also called mutual fund)	A company that has no limit as to the number of shares in itself that it may sell.
Open-end note	A note to which additional items purchased later are added.
Open order	An order to buy or sell securities at a stipulated price that remains in effect until it is executed or canceled.
Option	See *"Puts"* and *"Call Option."*
Origination fee	A finder's or lender's fee.
Overdrafts	Checks written for amounts in excess of the funds in the account. In such a case the bank will usually make the full payment for a fee later charged to the depositor.
Over-the-counter	The market for those securities not listed on any organized exchange.
Paid-up insurance	Insurance on which premiums are no longer due but which is still in force.
Par value	The face or stated value of a bond or a stock. In the case of a stock, this is meaningless. However, in the case of a bond or a preferred stock, the par value generally indicates the dollar value on which the annual interest or dividends are to be paid.
Participating preferred	Type of preferred stock in which, if the corporation's earnings are sufficient, the preferred stockholders not only are given their agreed dividends but also are entitled to share equally in the dividends paid to the common stockholders.
Partnership	Noncorporate form of business organization comprised of two or more partners. All partners are liable for the debts of the business. Partnership agreements are drawn up that spell out the duties, rights, and liabilities of each partner.
Passbook savings account	The oldest type of deposit account. Some banks and savings and loan associations still have them. They give the depositor a little book into which deposits, interest, and withdrawals are entered.
Passive income	Any income received from activity in which the taxpayer does not materially participate in the management of the enterprise.
Passive loss	Any loss from activity in which the taxpayer does not materially participate in the managment of the enterprise.

Payee	The person to whom a check is made payable.
Personal property	Includes such things as furniture, automobiles, and clothing as opposed to real property (see below).
Points	A point is one percentage point of the mortgage loan. The lender usually receives this points sum, and it is considered additional compensation to offset the fact that the regular interest rate charged to the buyer (borrower) is below the market rate.
Policy floaters	An addendum to a homeowners' policy that separately lists certain valuable items of personal property such as furs or jewelry. This is often necessary to cover these items should they be destroyed, damaged, or stolen.
Policy loan	A loan made by an insurance company to a policyholder on the cash surrender value of the policy.
Political risk	Has to do with the legal and political environment in which the business must operate.
Portfolio	The securities owned by an individual or corporation.
Power of invasion	A provision that may be inserted into a trust agreement that permits either the beneficiary or the trustee to *use* some of the principal of the trust to support the beneficiary.
Preemptive rights	The rights of existing stockholders to buy a prorated share of a new issue of common stock that a corporation may issue.
Preferred stock	Stock that receives preferential treatment over common stock with respect both to dividends and to claims on assets in the event that the corporation goes out of business.
Price-earnings ratio	The market value of a common stock divided by the company's earnings.
Price-level risk	Risk associated with inflation. This risk is particularly applicable to those assets whose value is stated in terms of a fixed number of dollars.
Private mortgage insurance (PMI)	Insurance issued by a private corporation (as opposed to the government), used to protect the lender against the borrower's default.
Prospectus	The official document that describes the shares of a security or fund being issued.
Proxy statement	The written permission that one stockholder gives to another person to vote his stock for him.
Purchase money mortgage	A mortgage that is taken by a seller from a buyer in lieu of purchase money (i.e., the seller helps finance the purchase). Usually takes the form of a second mortgage when the buyer cannot come up with a first mortgage loan to cover the purchase price.
Puts	Contracts that give a holder the right to sell a particular security at a specified price for a specific period of time.
Quarters of coverage	In earning Social Security benefits and pensions the worker receives one quarter of coverage for a certain portion of earned income per year on which Social Security taxes are paid.
Real estate investment trust (REIT)	An institution that pools capital for the purpose of investing in real estate or in mortgages.
Real Estate Settlement Procedures Act	Federal consumer credit law that requires the consumer to be given information about the services and costs involved in a settlement when real property transfers from seller to buyer.

Real income	Income derived by adjusting money income to take into account the effects of inflation.
Real property	Land and buildings attached to land such as a house or garage.
Real yield	Yield derived by adjusting the nominal yield for inflation.
Regional exchanges	A number of smaller stock exchanges that serve only the region in which they are located and not the whole nation as does the New York Stock Exchange.
Registrar	The institution that maintains a list of the common stockholders of a corporation and the number of shares that they hold.
Remaindermen	Those persons who receive the corpus (also called the principal) of a trust when the persons who receive the income from it are finally all deceased and the trust is dissolved or, in legal terminology, when the trust "vests."
Renegotiable mortgage	Sometimes called a rollover mortgage. Under this form of mortgage the interest rates are fixed but renegotiated periodically.
Reserve	The assets and their earnings that a life insurance company establishes as a liability (in reserve) to pay future claims.
Residential mortgage-backed bonds	Bonds that are sold to raise funds to buy mortgages. As the mortgages are paid off, the bonds are also paid off.
Revenue bonds	Municipal bonds that are repaid by the revenue generated from whatever the bonds finance (e.g., tollways or power plants).
Reverse mortgage	Used when one has paid off a mortgage and sells back a home to a lending institution. Monthly payments are received, and as time passes equity declines.
Risk	The probability of future loss.
Round lot	The fixed number or block of shares, usually one hundred, that is the commonly traded unit on the organized exchanges.
Safety deposit box	Steel box inside a bank vault that may be rented by bank customers in which to store valuables.
Sales credit	Credit extended by a merchant in which the customer gets the goods and promises to pay later.
Sales finance companies	Companies primarily engaged in the purchase of merchant's time-sales contracts arising out of the sale of goods to consumers.
Savings	The difference between income and expenditure.
Savings accounts	Accounts on which banks pay interest to the depositor and upon which checks cannot be written.
Savings and loan associations	Financial institutions in the business of accepting deposits and making primarily residential mortgage loans.
Second mortgage	A mortgage recorded after the first mortgage, where both mortgages are on the same property. In the event of a foreclosure and sale of a house on which the mortgager has defaulted, the second mortgage is not paid off until after the first mortgagee has been completely repaid. This usually comes into existence when the purchaser does not have sufficient funds to pay the owner his or her equity in an existing (not new) home.
Securities and Exchange Commission (SEC)	An agency of the United States government that administers the various federal security laws.

Senior securities	Securities such as bonds and preferred stock that have a higher claim than common stock on earnings as well as on assets on liquidation.
Serial bonds	Bonds that are numbered according to their issue groupings, and are retired at various times in accordance with their numbers.
Short sales	Selling securities one does not own. They are borrowed from a broker, and later (hopefully when the price falls) bought back to repay the broker.
Sight draft	A bank draft (check) payable on demand.
Simple interest	Interest that is charged only on the actual loan balance outstanding.
Small claims courts	Courts able to handle claims effectively, quickly, and at a much lower cost than by regular legal action. The amount of damages for which a person may sue is limited in a small claims court to about $500 usually.
Social Security	The nation's basic method of providing family income when earnings are reduced or stopped because of death, retirement, or disability.
Sole proprietorship	A business owned by one person where the business assets are considered commingled with the personal assets of the owner. The business has no charter and is the simplest form of organization.
Specialists	Members of the exchange who specialize in buying and selling only certain specific securities that are traded at a specific location on the exchange. The commission broker, or the contract broker, will go to whatever specialist is required to execute an order.
Specialty (sector) fund	A mutual fund or investment company that specializes and buys only the stock of companies in a given industry, the electronics industry for example.
Speculative stocks	These stocks are untried securities, often stocks of new, small firms, whose chances for success may not be great.
State and local bond trust	A closed-end investment trust established through which tax-exempt bonds can be purchased indirectly.
Stock	Certificate of ownership in a corporation. Also called "shares of ownership."
Stock dividend	A dividend paid to the shareholders in the form of additional shares of stock.
Stock exchanges	Organizations that provide their members with a place and the facilities to buy and sell securities.
Stock rights	The rights existing stockholders have to buy the same proportion of any new stock issue of a corporation as they own of the existing shares. For example, if a stockholder owns 1 percent of the existing shares, that stockholder would have the right to buy 1 percent of a new issue.
Stock split	An increase in the number of shares of a corporation brought about by division of existing shares. A two-for-one split, for example, will result in two new shares for each old share that previously existed, making a total of three.
Stock warrant	A certificate authorizing the owner to buy a specific company's stock at a specific price for a specific period of time, or perhaps in perpetuity.
Stop order	An order to buy or sell conditioned upon a specific price. This order is very often referred to as a "stop loss" order, because it prevents the stock from falling below a certain price.
Taxable income	That income that is finally subject to the federal personal income tax. Itemized deductions (or the standard deduction) and personal exemptions are subtracted from adjusted gross income to obtain table income. Taxable income is also called net income.

Tax credit A tax credit reduces the actual tax. Most of these were eliminated by the 1986 tax act, but a few still remain.

Tax preference items Income that receives more favorable treatment (preference) by the federal tax law. For example, interest on state and local bonds that is not taxed. Tax preference items may trigger alternative minimum tax.

Tax shelter In the broadest sense, any deduction from income or credit against tax. More narrowly, certain investments permit tax write-offs by generating deductible expenses such as depreciation, which can be used to offset other income. In other cases, investments will qualify for an investment tax credit (ITC). An ITC is better than depreciation expense because after the final tax liability has been calculated, the tax may be reduced dollar for dollar by the ITC.

Tenant One who rents an apartment or a house from the owner (Landlord). A tenant holds a leasehold estate.

Term insurance The simplest type of ordinary life insurance. Term insurance provides protection only over the contract period.

Testamentary intent The desire of a person to make a provision to dispose of property that will be effective on his or her death. A will is needed to do this.

Thin market A market in which there are few offers either to buy or sell. The term can be applied to a single security or to the entire market.

Time draft A bank draft (check) payable at some predetermined future time.

Treasury bills Short-term obligations of the U.S. government. Treasury bills are sold at a discount from face value with maturities of three months, six months, and one year.

Treasury bonds Marketable long-term obligations of five years or more of the U.S. government. These bonds have coupons, and itnerest is paid every six months.

Treasury notes Similar to Treasury bonds but generally with shorter maturities. They are marketable and negotiable and have coupons that provide for an interest payment every six months.

Trust An arrangement whereby title to property is transferred by the creator or settlor to another person (trustee) for the benefit of a third party (beneficiary).

Trustee service A service that looks after the financial affairs (manages assets) of someone for a fee.

Truth-in-Lending Act Federal consumer credit law that requires disclosure of the finance charge and the annual percentage rate of interest charged.

Uninsured motorist coverage This states that if an insured is injured as the result of an accident with an uninsured and negligent motorist or by a hit-and-run driver, your insurance company will in effect insure that uninsured motorist for whatever amount specified in the policy.

Universal life insurance It is a combination of term insurance and an accumulating cash value account with a varying rate of return.

United States savings bonds Generally nonmarketable U.S. government bonds designed for the small investor.

Usury Interest in excess of what the various state laws allow.

VA-guaranteed mortgage A mortgage loan on which the Veteran's Administration guarantees payment to the lending institution in the event of default by the veteran-buyer.

Variable annuity An annuity contract with a life insurance company under which the dollar payments received are not fixed but vary (or fluctuate), usually with the price of the underlying securities.

Variable costs	Those costs of any given item that are outside the fixed costs. For instance, in the case of an automobile the variable costs include costs that are incurred because of the number of miles driven.
Variable life insurance	It is whole life policy with a cash value invested in an open-end investment company.
Variable rate mortgage (VRM)	A mortgage that carries an interest rate that may move either up or down depending on market conditions.
Vesting	Concerning the legal ownership of certain benefits of a pension fund. Important if persons leave their employer prior to retirement.
Warrant	A certificate authorizing the owner to buy a specific company's stock at a specific price for a specific price for a specific period of time, or perhaps in perpetuity.
Warranty	A guarantee of the integrity of a product or service and of the maker's responsibility to repair or replace the defective product (or perform the service again if necessary).
Whole life insurance	A policy that provides protection for the entire (whole) life of the insured. The policy features an increasing cash value (guaranteed to earn a fixed percentage over the life of the contract) and fixed, level premiums.
Wrap-around mortgage	A form of mortgage financing in which the face amount of the second (wrap-around) loan is equal to the balance of the first loan plus the amount of the new financing.
Yield	Income received on investments. Usually expressed as a percentage of the market price of the security.
Zero coupon bond	A bond which has no payment coupon and, hence pays no annual interest payment. The bond is sold below its face value (discounted) and appreciates as time passes. The market price is equal to the bond's face value at maturity.

2/11 ⎤
Q-2/5 ⎦ — 1,2,3

3/3

Q-3/10

Q-3/17 — 376-384

3/24 — MIDTERM

3/31 — 364-375

Q-4/7 ⎤ 4,5,6,8 362-364
4/14 ⎦

Q-4/28 — HANDOUTS MARITAL DISSOLUTION

5/5 — 6

5/12 — FINAL